Lecture Notes in Computer Science 14216

The series Lecture Notes in Computer Science (LNCS), including its subseries Lecture Notes in Artificial Intelligence (LNAI) and Lecture Notes in Bioinformatics (LNBI), has established itself as a medium for the publication of new developments in computer science and information technology research, teaching, and education.

LNCS enjoys close cooperation with the computer science R & D community, the series counts many renowned academics among its volume editors and paper authors, and collaborates with prestigious societies. Its mission is to serve this international community by providing an invaluable service, mainly focused on the publication of conference and workshop proceedings and postproceedings. LNCS commenced publication in 1973.

Étienne André · Jun Sun
Editors

Automated Technology for Verification and Analysis

21st International Symposium, ATVA 2023
Singapore, October 24–27, 2023
Proceedings, Part II

Editors
Étienne André
Université Sorbonne Paris Nord
Villetaneuse, France

Jun Sun
Singapore Management University
Singapore, Singapore

ISSN 0302-9743 ISSN 1611-3349 (electronic)
Lecture Notes in Computer Science
ISBN 978-3-031-45331-1 ISBN 978-3-031-45332-8 (eBook)
https://doi.org/10.1007/978-3-031-45332-8

This Springer imprint is published by the registered company Springer Nature Switzerland AG
The registered company address is: Gewerbestrasse 11, 6330 Cham, Switzerland

Paper in this product is recyclable.

Preface

This volume contains the papers presented at the 21st International Symposium on Automated Technology for Verification and Analysis (ATVA 2023). ATVA intends to promote research in theoretical and practical aspects of automated analysis, verification and synthesis by providing a forum for interaction between regional and international research communities and industry in related areas.

ATVA 2023 was organized during October 24–27, 2023 in Singapore. ATVA 2023 received 115 submissions, of which 30 were accepted as regular papers and 7 as tool papers, while 65 were rejected (another 13 were withdrawn or desk-rejected). All submitted papers went through a rigorous review process with at least 3 reviews per paper, followed by an online discussion among PC members overseen by the TPC chairs. This led to a high-quality and attractive scientific program.

This edition of ATVA was blessed by the presence of three prestigious keynote speakers, who gave talks covering current hot research topics and revealing many new interesting research directions:

- David Basin (ETH Zurich, Switzerland): Correct and Efficient Policy Monitoring, a Retrospective;
- Ewen Denney (NASA Ames Research Center, USA): Dynamic Assurance Cases for Machine-Learning Based Autonomous Systems;
- Reza Shokri (NUS, Singapore): Privacy in Machine Learning.

The conference was preceded by tutorials on important topics given by three renowned experts:

- Jin Xing Lim and Palina Tolmach (Runtime Verification Inc, USA): The K Framework: A Tool Kit for Language Semantics and Verification;
- Ewen Denney (NASA Ames Research Center, USA): Developing Assurance Cases with AdvoCATE.

ATVA 2023 would not have been successful without the contribution and involvement of the Program Committee members and the external reviewers who contributed to the review process (with 311 reviews) and the selection of the best contributions. This event would not exist if authors and contributors did not submit their proposals. We address our thanks to every person, reviewer, author, program committee member and organizing committee member involved in the success of ATVA 2023. The EasyChair system was set up for the management of ATVA 2023 supporting submission, review and volume preparation processes.

The local host and sponsor School of Computing and Information Systems, Singapore Management University provided financial support and tremendous help with registration and online facilities. The other sponsor, Springer LNCS, contributed in different forms to help run the conference smoothly. Many thanks to all the local organizers and sponsors.

We wish to express our special thanks to the General Chair, Jin Song Dong, and to the steering committee members, particularly to Yu-Fang Chen, for their valuable support.

August 2023

Étienne André
Jun Sun

Organization

General Chair

Jin Song Dong	National University of Singapore

Program Co-Chairs

Jun Sun	Singapore Management University
Étienne André	Université Sorbonne Paris Nord

Local Organization Chair

Xiaofei Xie	Singapore Management University

Publicity Chair

Lei Bu	Nanjing University

Program Committee

Étienne André	Université Sorbonne Paris Nord, France
Mohamed Faouzi Atig	Uppsala University, Sweden
Kyungmin Bae	Pohang University of Science and Technology, South Korea
Saddek Bensalem	Université Grenoble Alpes, France
Udi Boker	Reichman University, Israel
Lei Bu	Nanjing University, China
Krishnendu Chatterjee	Institute of Science and Technology, Austria
Yu-Fang Chen	Academia Sinica, Taiwan
Chih-Hong Cheng	Fraunhofer IKS and TU München, Germany
Yunja Choi	Kyungpook National University, South Korea
Thao Dang	CNRS/VERIMAG, France
Susanna Donatelli	Universita' di Torino, Italy
Alexandre Duret-Lutz	EPITA, France

Bernd Finkbeiner	CISPA Helmholtz Center for Information Security, Germany
Stefan Gruner	University of Pretoria, South Africa
Osman Hasan	National University of Sciences and Technology, Pakistan
Ichiro Hasuo	National Institute of Informatics, Japan
Jie-Hong Roland Jiang	National Taiwan University, Taiwan
Ondrej Lengal	Brno University of Technology, Czech Republic
Shang-Wei Lin	Nanyang Technological University, Singapore
Doron Peled	Bar Ilan University, Israel
Jakob Piribauer	TU Dresden, Dresden
Pavithra Prabhakar	Kansas State University, USA
Sasinee Pruekprasert	National Institute of Advanced Industrial Science and Technology, Japan
Kristin Yvonne Rozier	Iowa State University, USA
Indranil Saha	Indian Institute of Technology Kanpur, India
Ocan Sankur	Univ Rennes, CNRS, France
Fu Song	ShanghaiTech University, China
Marielle Stoelinga	University of Twente, The Netherlands
Jun Sun	Singapore Management University, Singapore
Michael Tautschnig	Queen Mary University of London, UK
Tachio Terauchi	Waseda University, Japan
Bow-Yaw Wang	Academia Sinica, Taiwan
Chao Wang	University of Southern California, USA
Jingyi Wang	Zhejiang University, China
Zhilin Wu	Chinese Academy of Sciences, China
Lijun Zhang	Chinese Academy of Sciences, China

Additional Reviewers

Amparore, Elvio Gilberto
Asadian, Hooman
Ashraf, Sobia
Badings, Thom
Beutner, Raven
Bozga, Marius
Caltais, Georgiana
Cetinkaya, Ahmet
Chandshun, Wu
Chang, Yun-Sheng
Chen, Guangke
Chen, Tian-Fu
Chen, Zhenbang
Cheng, Che
Chida, Nariyoshi
Ciardo, Gianfranco
Coenen, Norine
Conrad, Esther
Correnson, Arthur
Dayekh, Hadi
Defourné, Rosalie
Dubut, Jérémy
Dziadek, Sven
Eberhart, Clovis

Fan, Yu-Wei
Fiedor, Jan
Fisman, Dana
Frenkel, Hadar
Gao, Pengfei
Graf, Susanne
Gupta, Aishwarya
Guttenberg, Roland
Hahn, Ernst Moritz
Havlena, Vojtěch
He, Fei
Henry, Léo
Ho, Kuo-Wei
Ho, Son
Holík, Lukáš
Johannsen, Chris
Jéron, Thierry
Karimov, Toghrul
Kempa, Brian
Khoussi, Siham
Ko, Yu-Hao
Kura, Satoshi
Larraz, Daniel
Lawall, Julia
Lefaucheux, Engel
Liu, Depeng
Liu, Wanwei
Lo, Fang-Yi
Luo, Yun-Rong
Mambakam, Akshay
Marinho, Dylan
Meggendorfer, Tobias
Metzger, Niklas
Monat, Raphaël
Nicoletti, Stefano
Pavela, Jiří
Perez, Mateo
Phalakarn, Kittiphon
Pommellet, Adrien
Qin, Qi
Rashid, Adnan
Requeno, Jose Ignacio
Rogalewicz, Adam
Saivasan, Prakash
Sarac, Ege
Schilling, Christian
Schlehuber-Caissier, Philipp
Schmitt, Frederik
Schumi, Richard
Siber, Julian
Soltani, Reza
Srivathsan, B.
Su, Chia-Hsuan
Svoboda, Jakub
Síč, Juraj
Takisaka, Toru
Tsai, Wei-Lun
Turrini, Andrea
van der Wal, Djurre
Waga, Masaki
Wang, Hung-En
Wang, Jiawan
Wang, Limin
Wang, Xizao
Wei, Chun-Yu
Weininger, Maximilian
Widdershoven, Cas
Wienhöft, Patrick
Winkler, Tobias
Yang, Pengfei
Yen, Di-De
Zhang, Hanwei
Zhang, Yedi
Zhao, Qingye
Zhao, Zhe
Zhu, Ziyuan
Ziemek, Robin
Žikelić, Đorđe

Contents – Part II

Tool Papers

Contents – Part I

Invited Talk

Automata

Probabilistic Systems

Synthesis

Neural Networks

Temporal Logics

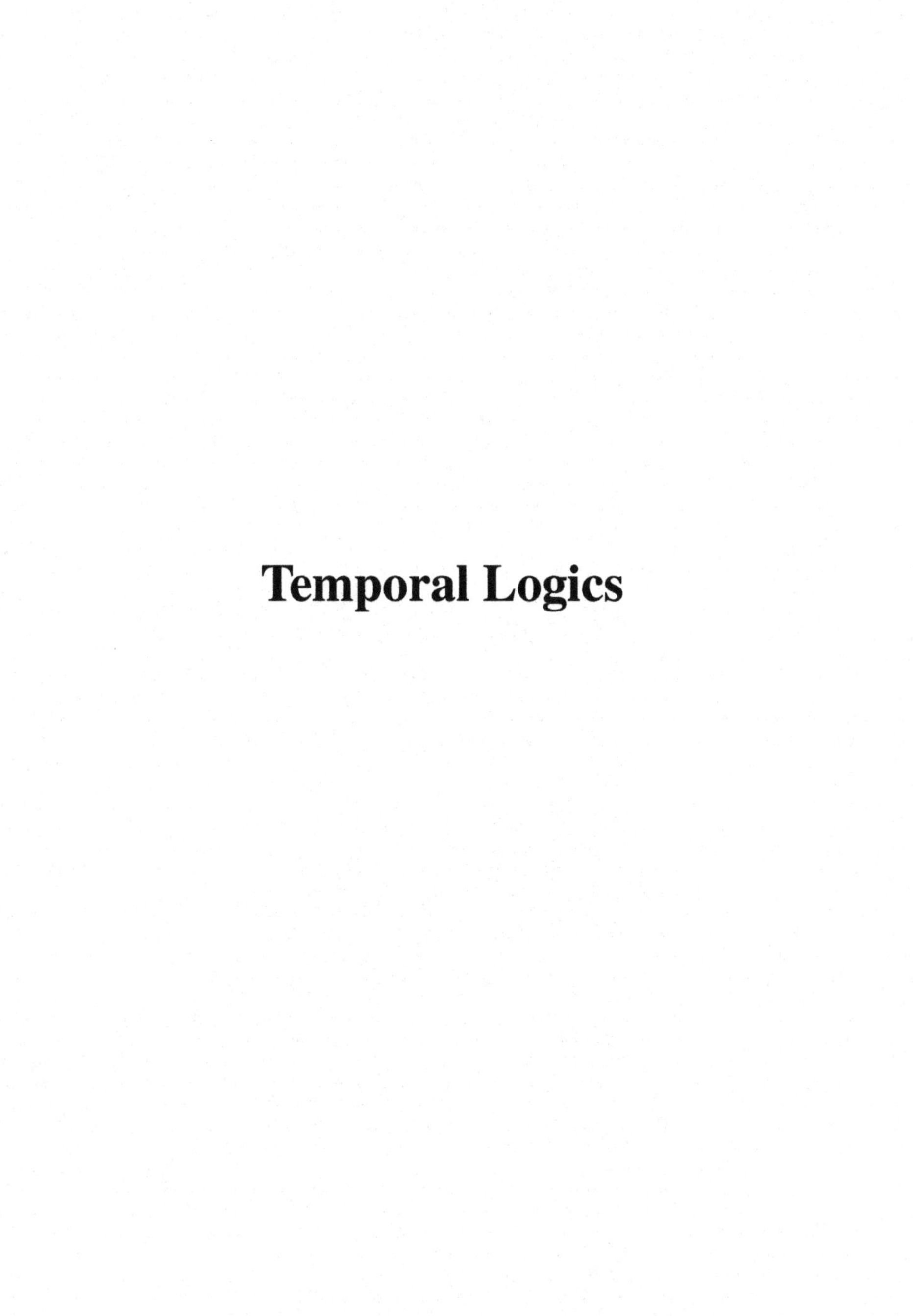

Lightweight Verification of Hyperproperties

Oyendrila Dobe[1], Stefan Schupp[2], Ezio Bartocci[2], Borzoo Bonakdarpour[1](✉), Axel Legay[3], Miroslav Pajic[4], and Yu Wang[5]

[1] Michigan State University, East Lansing, USA
borzoo@msu.edu
[2] Technische Universität Wien, Vienna, Austria
[3] UCLouvain, Ottignies-Louvain-la-Neuve, Belgium
[4] Duke University, Durham, USA
[5] University of Florida, Gainesville, USA

Abstract. Hyperproperties have been widely used to express system properties like noninterference, observational determinism, conformance, robustness, etc. However, the model checking problem for hyperproperties is challenging due to its inherent complexity of verifying properties across sets of traces and suffers from scalability issues. Previously, statistical approaches have proven effective in tackling the scalability of model checking for temporal logic. In this work, we have attempted to combine these two concepts to propose a tractable solution to model checking of hyperproperties expressed as HyperLTL on models involving nondeterminism. We have implemented our approach in PLASMA and experimented with a range of case studies to showcase its effectiveness.

Keywords: Hyperproperties · Statistical Model Checking · Nondeterminism

1 Introduction

Model checking [7] is a well-established method to verify the correctness of a system. Typically, it exhaustively checks if all possible *individual* execution traces of the system satisfy a property of interest. However, several security and privacy policies such as noninterference [36,42,49], differential privacy [26], observational determinism [57] are system-wide properties that require to reason across multiple independent system's executions simultaneously. These properties are referred to as *hyperproperties* [18].

In the last decade, researchers have proposed several adaptations of classical temporal logics to specify hyperproperties in a formal and systematic way. Examples in the non-probabilistic setting are HyperLTL [17] and its asynchronous variant A-HLTL [8]. HyperLTL extends LTL [50] with explicit quantification over

This project was partially funded by the United States NSF SaTC Awards 2245114 and 2100989, NSF Award CCF-2133160, FWF-project ZK-35, FNRS PDR - T013721, and by the Vienna Science and Technology Fund (WWTF) [10.47379/ICT19018].

É. André and J. Sun (Eds.): ATVA 2023, LNCS 14216, pp. 3–25, 2023.
https://doi.org/10.1007/978-3-031-45332-8_1

paths that allows to express relations among execution traces from independent system's runs. Recent works in [33,39,41] provide exhaustive and bounded model-checking algorithms for HyperLTL. For probabilistic hyperproperties, there are two main specification languages: HyperPCTL [2,24], which quantifies over schedulers and argues over computation trees, and Probabilistic Hyper-Logic (PHL) [22] which adds quantifiers for schedulers and reasons about traces. In both contexts, these approaches face two main challenges: scalability and the need for an explicit model. Scalability is, in particular, critical: (1) HyperLTL model checking is EXSPACE-complete [11], (2) HyperPCTL and A-HLTL model checking are in general undecidable with decidable fragments in EXSPACE [8,24], (3) PHL model checking is in general undecidable with decidable fragments (reduce to HyperCTL*) in NSPACE [22,33]. This complexity obstacle has been a major motivation for the development of alternative approaches to handle the problem. One possible approach is to provide an approximate result with certain statistical guarantees, termed statistical model checking (SMC). SMC is an approximate model checking method that is subject to a small probability of drawing a wrong conclusion [45–47]. The main idea is to simulate finitely many traces of a model and conduct *hypothesis testing* to conclude if there is enough evidence that the model satisfies or violates the property, subjecting to a small probability of drawing a wrong conclusion. Such simulation-based approaches have two main advantages: first, we can use them to approximate the probability of satisfying the desired property in a model of considerable size, which we would be otherwise unable to verify exhaustively; second, we can apply them to black-box systems for which we are unable to access the inner model. This approach is also intuitive as it can terminate early for cases where it has already found enough evidence for violation. Consider, a case where a property is required to hold for all traces. In this case, we should not be able to see a violation even if we simulate just one trace. Given these advantages, we want to study its application to verify hyperproperties. Another challenge, in terms of verification, is the handling of nondeterminism. When modeling systems, we have to take into consideration the uncertainty that can arise due to incomplete details, involvement of unknown agents, or noise, in general. From a verification perspective, we need to be able to argue that a property holds under any such possibility of nondeterministic uncertainty. Both HyperPCTL and A-HLTL model checking has the capability of reasoning over nondeterminism, however, the high complexity in their model checking solutions basically stems from the need for "scheduler" synthesis.

Our Contribution. In this work, we chose to model systems as Markov decision processes (MDPs) to effectively express nondeterminism in terms of possible actions available in a state, as well as randomization is represented as probabilistic distributions of how the system can evolve once an action is executed. PLASMA [48] is a model checker that uses a memory-efficient sampling of schedulers [20] to conduct simulation-based statistical analysis. In this work, we extend PLASMA's capability to include the verification of linear, bounded hyperproperties over systems modeled as MDPs. Our method orchestrates well-established methods from the SMC community for the analysis of an expressive model class in light of bounded HyperLTL properties. The result is a scalable, lightweight verification approach which is the first of its kind to handle this combination of model class and property. We have added and experimented with an extension that supports using recorded traces or requesting simulation of black-box components on-the-fly for hyperproperty verification. This opens the door to utilizing our approach for applications in cases where explicit modeling is not possible or error-prone. For evaluation, we present a diverse set of scaling benchmarks that raises the demand for this expressive model class and property type. We have selected systems that allow for verification of properties such as *noninterference*, *side-channel information leak*, *opacity*, and *anonymity*. The systems under inspection range from classical examples including dining cryptographers, to examples taken from robotics path planning and real code snippets. The state space of the resulting models varies in the order of magnitude from tens to hundreds of billions involving tens to thousands of nondeterministic actions. Our experimental evaluation indicates good performance on systems, unperturbed by the size of the state space. To summarize, our *main contributions* are:

1. To the best of our knowledge, we provide the first statistical model checking approach for the verification of unquantified and bounded HyperLTL properties involving nondeterminism.
2. We extend the model checker PLASMA by this class of properties. Furthermore, we add capabilities to execute black-box verification.
3. We showcase the general applicability with an extensive evaluation of our method on various scalable case studies taken from different domains.

Paper Organization: In the rest of the paper, we elaborate on the related works in Sect. 2, describe the model and specification language in Sect. 3, with the problem formulation in Sect. 4, the algorithm and implementation details in Sect. 5, and a range of case studies in Sect. 6. In Sect. 7 we describe our experimental and convergence results and in Sect. 8 we provide conclusions and future work suggestions.

2 Related Work

HyperLTL [17] was introduced to express system properties that require simultaneous quantification over multiple paths. The authors provided a model checking algorithm for a fragment of the logic based on self-composition. In [33], the authors presented the first direct automata-theoretic model checking algorithm that converts the model checking problem for HyperLTL to automaton-based problems like checking for emptiness. In recent years, there has been considerable research on HyperLTL verification [19,31,32], and monitoring [5,10,11,29,37,51]. From a tools perspective, MCHyper [19,33] has been developed for model checking, EAHyper [28] and MGHyper [27] for satisfiability checking, and RVHyper [30] for run time monitoring. A tractable bounded sublogic of HyperLTL has been proposed in [41] where the authors have suggested a QBF-based algorithm to model-check the logic. HyperQB is a model checker specifically for bounded HyperLTL [40]. However, all of the above approaches suffer from the challenges of scalability, inability to handle probabilistic systems, or lack of support for nondeterminism.

To verify hyperproperties in probabilistic systems there are two main families of approaches proposed in the literature: exact methods [2,3,23,24] and approximated ones [21,53]. Note that the specification language used in these works differs from our specification language. Exact methods exploit the underlying Markov chain structure of the probabilistic system to be verified for computing precisely (numerically) and for comparing the probabilities of satisfying temporal logic formulas of multiple and independent sequences of sets of states. HyperPCTL [2] was the first logic proposed to reason exhaustively about hyperproperties in probabilistic systems. This logic was later extended to allow reasoning over systems involving nondeterminism [3,24] and rewards [25]. A verification algorithm was implemented in the model checker HyperProb [23]. The main shortcoming of this approach is scalability. Among the approximated approaches, in [22] the authors propose an over-approximate and another under-approximate automata-based model checking algorithms for the alternation-free n-safety fragment of their logic PHL on n self-composed systems. The scheduler synthesis step is the main challenge in this work.

SMC has been explored to solve problems across different domains for analyzing dynamic software architectures [14], performing security risk assessments using attack-defense trees [34], verifying cyber-physical systems [16], validation of biochemical reaction models [58], etc. Verification of bounded LTL for MDPs has been proposed using SMC [38] and has shown promising results. Extensive tool support exists for SMC on trace properties with respect to discrete-event modeling [12], priced timed automata [13], probabilistic model checking [43,44,56], black-box systems [35]. Statistical verification of probabilistic hyperlogics has been proposed for HyperPCTL* [21,53], for continuous Markov chains [55], and for real-valued signals [6]. However, none of these works reason about models involving nondeterminism.

3 Preliminaries

We denote the set of natural and real numbers by $\mathbb{N}$ and $\mathbb{R}$, respectively. For $n \in \mathbb{N}$, let $[n] = \{1, \ldots, n\}$. The cardinality of a set is denoted by $|\cdot|$. We denote the set of all finite, non-empty finite, and infinite sequences, taken from S by S^*, S^+, and S^ω, respectively.

3.1 Model Structures

Markov Decision Process. A labeled Markov decision process (MDP) [7] is a tuple $\mathtt{M} = (\mathcal{S}, A, s_0, \mathsf{AP}, L, P)$, where (1) $\mathcal{S}$ is a finite set of states, (2) A is the finite set of actions, and $A(s)$ is the set of *enabled* actions that can be taken at state $s \in \mathcal{S}$, (3) s_0 is the initial state, (4) AP is the finite set of atomic propositions, (5) $L : \mathcal{S} \to 2^{\mathsf{AP}}$ is the state labeling function, and (6) $P : \mathcal{S} \times A \times \mathcal{S} \to [0, 1]$ is the transition probability function such that,

$$\sum_{s' \in \mathcal{S}} P(s, a, s') = \begin{cases} 1, & \text{if } a \in A(s) \\ 0, & \text{if } a \notin A(s) \end{cases} \tag{1}$$

A path of the MDP is an infinite sequence of states $\pi = s_0 s_1 s_2 \ldots$ with $s_i \in \mathcal{S}$ such that $\forall i \geq 0$, there exists $a_i \in A$ with $P(s_i, a_i, s_{i+1}) > 0$. A trace $trace\{\pi\} = L(s_0)L(s_1)L(s_2)\ldots$ is the sequence of sets of atomic propositions corresponding to a path. We use $\pi[i] = s_i$ to denote the ith state and $\pi[: i]$ and $\pi[i+1 :]$ to denote the prefix $s_0 s_1 \ldots s_i$, and the suffix $s_{i+1} s_{i+2} \ldots$, respectively.

Discrete-Time Markov Chain. A labeled discrete-time Markov chain (DTMC) [7] is a tuple $\mathcal{D} = (\mathcal{S}, s_0, \mathsf{AP}, L, P)$, where (1) $\mathcal{S}$ is the finite set of states, (2) s_0 is the initial state, (3) AP is the finite set of atomic propositions, (4) $L : \mathcal{S} \to 2^{\mathsf{AP}}$ is the state labeling function, (5) $P : \mathcal{S} \times \mathcal{S} \to [0, 1]$ is the transition probability function such that, for all $s \in \mathcal{S}$, $\sum_{s' \in \mathcal{S}} P(s, s') = 1$. A DTMC is an MDP with each state being associated with a single action.

Scheduler. A scheduler σ is a function $\sigma : \mathcal{S}^+ \to A$ that resolves the nondeterminism at each state of an MDP. It reduces an MDP to a DTMC. Different scheduler types are distinguished depending on what information is used to resolve the nondeterminism in the current state: a *history-dependent* scheduler $\sigma(s[: n]) \in A(s[n])$ would utilize the history of action and state choices to resolve which action is executed at the current state whereas a *memoryless* scheduler $\sigma(s[n]) \in A(s[n])$, bases its decision only on the current state. In this work, we consider history-dependent schedulers (which include the class of memoryless schedulers) whose memory size is bounded by the length of the paths we generate from the model. We use $\pi_{\mathtt{M}^\sigma}$ to denote a random path drawn from the DTMC that is induced by the scheduler σ on the MDP $\mathtt{M}$.

3.2 HyperLTL

HyperLTL [17] is the extension of linear-time temporal logic (LTL) [50] that allows the expression of temporal specifications involving relations between multiple paths. Each state in the path is observed as a set of atomic propositions that hold true in that state. HyperLTL involves the evaluation of specifications over these propositions. An arbitrary path variable π is used to refer to individual paths that can be generated by the model. Contrary to LTL, each proposition a^π is associated with a path variable π denoting the path on which it should be evaluated.

Syntax. We focus on unquantified and bounded HyperLTL defined by the grammar below.

$$\varphi ::= \mathsf{a}^\pi \mid \neg\varphi \mid \varphi \wedge \varphi \mid \bigcirc\varphi \mid \varphi \,\mathcal{U}^{\leq k}\, \varphi \tag{2}$$

- $\mathsf{a} \in \mathsf{AP}$ is an atomic proposition that evaluates to *true* or *false* in a state;
- π is a *random path variable* from an infinite supply of such variables Π;

- $\bigcirc$, $\Diamond^{\leq k}$, $\Box^{\leq k}$, and $\mathcal{U}^{\leq k}$ are the 'next', 'finally', 'global', and 'until' temporal operators, respectively,
- $k \in \mathbb{N}$ is the path length within which the operator has to be evaluated.

Following are the connectives defined as syntactic sugar: $\texttt{true} \equiv \mathsf{a}^\pi \vee \neg \mathsf{a}^\pi$, $\varphi \vee \varphi' \equiv \neg(\neg\varphi \wedge \neg\varphi')$, $\varphi \Rightarrow \varphi' \equiv \neg\varphi \vee \varphi'$, $\Diamond^{\leq k} \varphi \equiv \texttt{true}\, \mathcal{U}^{\leq k} \varphi$, $\Box^{\leq k} \varphi \equiv \neg \Diamond^{\leq k} \neg\varphi$. We denote $\mathcal{U}^{\leq\infty}$, $\Diamond^{\leq\infty}$, and $\Box^{\leq\infty}$ or the unbounded temporal operators by $\mathcal{U}$, $\Diamond$, and $\Box$, respectively. In our work, we consider only the bounded fragment of HyperLTL such that for all temporal operators (except $\bigcirc$), we evaluate the result on finite fragments of the simulated traces.

Semantics. The path evaluation function $V : \Pi \to \mathcal{S}^\omega$ assigns each path variable π, a concrete path of the labeled DTMC. Below we consider the semantics of HyperLTL,

$$\begin{array}{ll} V \models \mathsf{a}^\pi & \text{iff } \mathsf{a} \in L\big(V(\pi)[0]\big) \\ V \models \neg\varphi & \text{iff } V \not\models \varphi \\ V \models \varphi_1 \wedge \varphi_2 & \text{iff } V \models \varphi_1 \text{ and } V \models \varphi_2 \\ V \models \bigcirc\varphi & \text{iff } V^{(1)} \models \varphi \\ V \models \varphi_1\, \mathcal{U}^{\leq k}\, \varphi_2 & \text{iff there exists } i \in [0,k], V^{(i)} \models \varphi_2 \\ & \quad \text{and for all } j \in [0,i),\ V^{(j)} \models \varphi_1 \end{array}$$

where $V^{(i)}$ is the i-shift of path assignment V defined by $V^{(i)}(\pi) = (V(\pi))^{(i)}$. For example, the formula $V \models \mathsf{a}_1^{\pi_1}\, \mathcal{U}^k\, \mathsf{a}_2^{\pi_2}$ means that a_1 holds on the path $V(\pi_1)$ until a_2 holds on the path $V(\pi_2)$ in k steps.

3.3 Sequential Probability Ratio Test

We use Wald's sequential probability ratio test (SPRT) [52]. The idea is to continue sampling until we are either able to reach a conclusion or we have exhausted a user-provided sampling budget. Assuming we want to verify if a property φ holds on our model $\mathcal{D}$ with probability greater than and equal to θ, i.e., $\Pr_{\mathcal{D}}(\varphi) \geq \theta$. To use SPRT in this case, we add an indifference region around our bound to create two distinct and flexible hypothesis tests [4]. For a given indifference region ε, we define $p_0 = \theta + \varepsilon$ and $p_1 = \theta - \varepsilon$. Our resultant hypotheses are,

$$H_0 : \Pr_{\mathcal{D}}(\varphi) \geq p_0 \quad H_1 : \Pr_{\mathcal{D}}(\varphi) \leq p_1 \tag{3}$$

Using these newly created bounds, we define the following probability ratios,

$$ratio_t = \frac{p_1}{p_0} \quad ratio_f = \frac{1-p_1}{1-p_0} \tag{4}$$

We define an indicator function $\mathbf{1}(T \models \varphi) \in \{0,1\}$ that returns 1 if the trace T satisfies the property φ, and returns 0 otherwise. When evaluating φ on a set of sampled traces $\{T_1, \ldots, T_n\}$, we accumulate $ratio_t$ if $\mathbf{1}(T \models \varphi) = 1$ and $ratio_f$

otherwise. Assuming, we have sampled N traces, the final product of the truth value corresponds to

$$p_{ratio} = \prod_{i=1}^{N} \frac{(p_1)^{\mathbf{1}(T_i \models \varphi)}(1-p_1)^{\mathbf{1}(T_i \models \neg\varphi)}}{(p_0)^{\mathbf{1}(T_i \models \varphi)}(1-p_0)^{\mathbf{1}(T_i \models \neg\varphi)}} \tag{5}$$

We iteratively calculate this ratio until the exit condition is met. To restrict the error in the estimation of the probability θ, we specify error probabilities α as the maximum acceptable probability of incorrectly rejecting a true H_0, and β as the maximum acceptable probability of accepting a false H_0. The boundary error ratios can be defined as $A = \beta/(1-\alpha)$ and $B = (1-\beta)/\alpha$. To reach a conclusion, we accept H_0 if $p_{ratio} \leq A$, and accept H_1 if $p_{ratio} \geq B$. The case for specifications with $\Pr_{\mathcal{D}}(\varphi) \leq \theta$ is similar except we use the reciprocals of $ratio_t$ and $ratio_f$.

4 Problem Formulation

HyperLTL allows explicit quantification over traces, allowing the user to express whether they want their specification to hold across all paths associated with a path variable or in at least one of those paths. Along with the added expressiveness, this formulation distends existing challenges - (1) While checking a specification across all possible sets of paths provides a robust verification result, it is considerably expensive, making it impractical as we scale to models with larger state spaces. (2) Most real-life systems involve uncertainties in the form of randomization, nondeterminism, or partial observability. Consequently, this raises a need to express that, for instance, a fraction of the paths of the system satisfy the specification.

To handle the above challenges, we propose a practical formulation for expressing unquantified and bounded HyperLTL formulas for models that involve both probabilistic choices and nondeterminism. We quantify over the path variables by associating a probabilistic bound denoting the proportion of the set of traces that should satisfy a given specification. We can express that a specification is *almost always likely* or *highly unlikely* by adjusting the bound of the probability p to $p \geq 1$ or $p \leq 0$, respectively. Intuitively, *almost always likely* can be considered as a weaker counterpart of $\forall$ (forall) quantification, and *highly unlikely* can be considered as a weaker counterpart of $\neg\exists$ (existential) quantification over path variables. Note that these limits our expression of HyperLTL formulas with quantifier alternation in any capacity, and we leave that as an aspect worth exploring in future works.

Consider an MDP $\mathtt{M}$ and an unquantified, bounded HyperLTL formula φ that contains path variables $(\pi_1, \ldots, \pi_m)$. We consider tuples of m schedulers to simulate m traces assigned to these path variables, i.e., we have a one-to-one correspondence between schedulers and path variables. We are interested in checking if there *exists* a combination of schedulers that can satisfy the HyperLTL specification φ on our model within a given probability bound. Formally, this can be expressed as,

$$\exists\sigma_1\exists\sigma_2\ldots\exists\sigma_m \Pr_{\mathtt{M}}(V \models \varphi) \sim \theta \tag{6}$$

where $\theta \in [\varepsilon, 1-\varepsilon]$ to allow an indifference region for hypothesis testing (see Sect. 3.3), σ_i are schedulers of $\mathtt{M}$, $V(\pi_i)$ is the path drawn from the DTMC $\mathtt{M}_{\sigma_i}$ for $i \in [n]$ which is induced by σ_i on MDP $\mathtt{M}$, and $\sim \in \{\geq, \leq\}$. Note that we can involve multiple models to yield paths for each scheduler σ_i. For properties where we want to check if a given specification holds across all scheduler combinations, we negate our specification to re-formulate the problem as in Eq. 6. Since we adopt a statistical model checking algorithm, it is worth noting that we cannot directly observe if a specification holds *for all* cases, thus, we utilize this approach to check if we can satisfy its negation. We elaborate on this in Sect. 5.

5 Approach

We want to utilize the advantages of SMC to verify hyperproperties by answering our model checking problem using hypothesis testing, specifically SPRT, as described in Sect. 3.3. The overall approach involves the sampling of schedulers and traces from one (or more) given MDPs, monitoring the satisfaction of the property on these traces, and determining if we have gathered enough evidence to reach a concrete verdict for the property. In this section, we explain the concepts and parameters involved in finding the result of this test such that we can directly use it to answer our model checking question.

5.1 Scheduler Sampling

One of the main challenges when verifying MDPs is the generation of schedulers for verification. It stems from the complexity involved in the storage of history to resolve nondeterminism in the current state. We utilize the lightweight scheduler sampling feature of PLASMA [20]. This approach avoids the explicit storage of schedulers by using *uniform* pseudo-random number generators (PRNGs) to resolve non-determinism and hashes as seeds for the PRNGs. In the following, we will give an intuition of the approach inbuilt in PLASMA and how we have extended it to argue about hyperproperties.

PRNGs form the core of the smart sampling algorithm of PLASMA. Given a set of possible action choices and sufficient runs of the number generator, they allow the generation of statistically independent numbers that are uniformly distributed across a specified range. They are uniquely mapped to their seed values int_{sch}, ensuring the reproduction of the same value when the generator is provided with the same seed. Note that we can use PRNGs to identify individual schedulers but cannot identify specific schedulers. Furthermore, since the seeds only initialize the PRNGs, using problem-specific information (e.g., about the property) during the generation of the seed does not allow to relate schedulers.

Each state of the MDP is internally represented as a concatenation of the bits representing the values of the atomic propositions that are true at that state. A sequence of states can be represented by concatenating their individual bit sequences. The sum of the bits of such a sequence of numbers int_t, which is an integer, represents a trace. Concatenation of int_{sch} and int_t can be then used to uniquely identify both a scheduler and a trace. PLASMA generates a hash with this concatenated value which represents the history of both the scheduler and the trace and is used as a seed to resolve the next nondeterministic choice. PLASMA uses an efficient iterative hash using modular arithmetic that ensures efficient storage of the possible schedulers mapping the comparatively large set of schedulers to a smaller set of integers with a low probability of collision. For more details on this, we refer the reader to [20]. Once the nondeterministic choice is resolved at a state, PLASMA uses an independent PRNG to uniformly choose a successor state from the ones available under the chosen action. This is concatenated with the trace before generating the next hash for the nondeterministic resolution.

When working with hyperproperties, we would need to consider a tuple of schedulers and traces. In this aspect, we can either simulate traces from the same MDP using different schedulers, use different schedulers for each MDP, or a combination of both. We define a *scheduler tuple* $\underline{\sigma} \subseteq \Sigma^m$ as a tuple of schedulers sampled from the set of possible schedulers allowed by our MDPs and m is the number of scheduler quantifiers in our specification as shown in Eq. 6. We define a *trace tuple* as a tuple of traces sampled from our model based on the tuple of schedulers. Thus, $\omega^{\underline{\sigma}}$ represents the trace tuple ω, sampled from the DTMCs induced by the scheduler tuple $\underline{\sigma}$. For simplicity, we consider a one-to-one correspondence between our schedulers and MDPs. We define an indicator function $\mathbf{1}(\omega^{\underline{\sigma}} \models \varphi) \in \{0, 1\}$ that returns 1 if the trace tuple $\omega^{\underline{\sigma}}$ satisfies the hyperproperty φ, and returns 0 otherwise.

The aim is to verify the satisfaction of the given specification under all or some combination of nondeterministic choices in our system. Since a scheduler represents a concrete resolution of nondeterminism across the system, our problem is transformed to that of finding a scheduler tuple that satisfies our specification in the form of the described hypothesis in Eq. 6. Intuitively, SMC considers the proportion of the sampled trace tuples that individually satisfy the property to estimate the true satisfaction probability in the overall model. To bind the errors in the estimation, the algorithm uses precision and user-provided error margins.

For the case where we want to conclude all scheduler tuples satisfy the property, we negate the property and try to find a scheduler tuple that satisfies this negated property. The falsity of this property makes our original property true. For the case where we want to search if there exists a scheduler tuple, we pose the hypothesis directly. However, in this case, a false result does not necessarily guarantee the absence of a witness to the specification; it suggests that our algorithm was unable to find such a scheduler tuple within the given budget, error, and precision bound. Note that we cannot derive the exact scheduler tuple (we get the traces generated but not the reduced DTMC) due to the black-box nature of our sampling. We can only reason about its existence or absence within the given budget.

5.2 Implementation

In this section, we discuss the handling of the hypothesis testing of H_0 as shown in Eq. 3 in detail. The case for H_1 is similar except we use the reciprocals of $ratio_t$ and $ratio_f$. As shown in Algorithm 1, we begin by initializing the necessary parameters (line 1). For conducting sequential hypothesis testing on large systems, we need an additional bound to represent the maximum limit of resources we want to spend on this verification. To this end, PLASMA utilizes the concept of a user-provided *budget*. Following the idea described in [20], the algorithm automatically distributes the budget to determine the number of scheduler and trace tuples the verification should consider as described in the previous section. We generate a set of scheduler tuples $\underline{\Sigma}$ and create a mapping to store which scheduler should be used to produce which trace (deriving this information from the input specification). In lines 2-3, for each scheduler tuple, we use the internal simulator to simulate the traces as specified by the mapping. In the case of multiple initial states, we allow the choice of traces with the same or different initial states. This reduces extra subformulas on the property to decide on initial states and allows us to verify the property only on relevant trace samples. In line 4, we use a custom model checker that we have implemented in PLASMA to verify linear, bounded HyperLTL properties on sets of traces sent as input. We further allow n-ary boolean operations by extending the general idea of AND, OR, XOR, etc., to reduce the length of input property the user has to provide.

Algorithm 1. Hypothesis testing on Hyperproperties

Input: MDP model: $\mathtt{M}$, spec: φ, Hypothesis $H_0 : \Pr_{\mathtt{M}}(V \models \varphi) \geq \theta$
α, β: desired type I, type II errors,
$\mathcal{N}_{max}$: simulation budget, ε: indifference region.
Output: Success, No success, Inconclusive.

1: initialize()// Initializes $\mathcal{N}, \mathcal{M}, p_0, p_1, A, B, k, ratio_t, ratio_f$
2: $\underline{\Sigma} \leftarrow \{\mathcal{M}$ tuples of k randomly chosen seeds$\}$
3: $\forall \underline{\sigma} \in \underline{\Sigma}, \forall i \in \{1, ..., \mathcal{N}\} : \omega_i^{\underline{\sigma}} \leftarrow$ simulate($\mathtt{M}, \varphi, \underline{\sigma}$)
4: $R \leftarrow \{(\underline{\sigma}, n) | \underline{\sigma} \in \underline{\Sigma} \wedge \mathbb{N} \ni n = \sum_{i=1}^{\mathcal{N}} \mathbf{1}(\omega_i^{\underline{\sigma}} \models \varphi)\}$
5: **if** canEarlyAccept(R) **then**
6:     Accept H_0 and exit
7: $\underline{\Sigma} \leftarrow \{\underline{\sigma} \in \underline{\Sigma} | R(\underline{\sigma}) > 0\}, \mathcal{M} \leftarrow |\underline{\Sigma}| + 1$ // Remove null schedulers
8: **if** $|\underline{\Sigma}| = 0$ **then**
9:     Quit: No suitable scheduler-tuple found
10: **while** $|\underline{\Sigma}| > 1$ **do**
11:     initializeSchedulerBasedBounds() // Initializes $\alpha_M, \beta_M, A_M, B_M$
12:     **for** $\underline{\sigma} \in \underline{\Sigma}$, $i \in \{1, \ldots, |\underline{\Sigma}|\}$ **do**
13:         $ratio_i \leftarrow 1$
14:         **for** $j \in \{1, \ldots, \mathcal{N}\}$ **do**
15:             **if** simulate($\mathtt{M}, \varphi, \underline{\sigma}$) $\models \varphi$ **then**
16:                 $ratio \leftarrow ratio \cdot ratio_t$; $ratio_i \leftarrow ratio \cdot ratio_T$
17:             **else**
18:                 $ratio \leftarrow ratio \cdot ratio_f$; $ratio_i \leftarrow ratio \cdot ratio_F$
19:             **if** $ratio_i \leq A_M$ or $ratio \leq A$ **then**
20:                 Accept H_0 and quit: scheduler found
21:             **else if** $ratio_i \geq B_M$ **then**
22:                 Quit iteration for $\underline{\sigma}$: Scheduler tuple rejected
23:     **if** All schedulers were rejected **then**
24:         Quit: No scheduler found in given budget
25:     $\underline{\Sigma} \leftarrow$ filter($\underline{\Sigma}$)// Keep only the best-performing scheduler tuples
26: Inconclusive: There exists a scheduler that was neither accepted nor rejected.

In line 5 of the algorithm, we compare the ratio generated using Eq. 5 against error boundary A to check if we have already found enough witnesses to accept our null hypothesis H_0. We do not check against boundary B because the absence of a satisfying scheduler in this initial phase does not ensure that the possibility of finding such a scheduler is zero. It hints at the need for further sampling. In line 7, we filter out the null schedulers, i.e., for which none of the trace tuples satisfied the property. Since we are looking for a scheduler tuple to satisfy the property with positive probability, null schedulers cannot definitely be our best search options. For each scheduler tuple in this filtered set, we again sample $\mathcal{N}$ trace tuples. We essentially conduct multiple independent hypothesis tests, one for each scheduler tuple. Hence, similar to [20], we modify the error for each scheduler to $\alpha_M = 1 - \sqrt[\mathcal{M}]{1-\alpha}$, $\beta_M = 1 - \sqrt[\mathcal{M}]{1-\beta}$ to account for the error correction needed. In the initial phase (lines 2-9), the idea was to check if we can satisfy the boundaries A, B using the truth value of all trace tuples sampled, irrespective of its scheduler. In the rest of the algorithm, we check if we can individually accept or reject any scheduler tuple, alongside the global check for satisfaction across all sampled trace tuples. Since our trace tuples return an overall true/false for the whole tuple, the error bound for each scheduler tuple would not change when we are working with alternation-free hyperproperties instead of trace properties.

In lines 16 and 18, we re-calculate p_{ratio} (as in Eq. 5), both for each scheduler tuple and for all the sampled trace tuples. As we encounter a satisfying tuple of traces, our overall p_{ratio} decreases as $ratio_t$ is a value less than one in this case and with each non-satisfying trace tuple, it increases. If the ratio obtained over all sampled traces across all schedulers is reduced below A or its scheduler counterpart is below A_M, we either have found a scheduler tuple that satisfies the property or over all the sampled trace tuples, we have found enough evidence to reach a conclusion that our hypothesis H_0 is satisfied.

At the end of the iteration over the scheduler tuples, we can quit the test if all our scheduler tuples are rejected, or proceed to the next iteration with only the *best* scheduler tuples. We rearrange our scheduler tuples in an ascending order based on the number of trace tuples that satisfied φ. Since we are aiming to find a scheduler tuple that satisfies φ with a probability greater than θ, we only keep the first half of rearranged scheduler tuples, ensuring that we are looking only at the schedulers that have a higher chance of exceeding the bound. If our evaluation reaches line 26, the set Σ would contain one scheduler which we were neither able to accept nor reject, reaching an inconclusive decision about H_0 within the given budget and precision margins. This inconclusive result would indicate we have to retry the experiment with a higher simulation budget and/or different precision and error margins for further scrutiny.

Convergence. The algorithm will always terminate in a finite number of iterations as we eliminate half of our candidate scheduler tuples at each iteration. However, it may not have found a satisfying scheduler tuple within that boundary. For an MDP $\mathtt{M}$ and property φ, we want to find a *good* scheduler tuple, i.e., one that satisfies φ with probability $p \geq \theta - \varepsilon$. Assuming we have $|\S|$ possible scheduler tuples, and $|\S_g|$ *good* schedulers, we use $\mathbb{P}\colon \S \rightarrow [0,1]$ to denote the probability with which a scheduler tuple satisfies φ. If we sample $\mathcal{M}$ scheduler tuples and $\mathcal{N}$ trace tuples per scheduler tuple, the probability of sampling a trace tuple from a *good* scheduler tuple that satisfies φ is,

$$\underbrace{\left(1 - \left(1 - \frac{|\S_g|}{|\S|}\right)^{\mathcal{M}}\right)}_{\text{good scheduler tuple}}\underbrace{\left(1 - \left(1 - \frac{\sum_{\sigma \in \S_g} \mathbb{P}_\sigma}{|\S_g|}\right)^{\mathcal{N}}\right)}_{\text{trace satisfies } \varphi}$$

Our aim is to maximize the value of this probability by optimizing the values of $\mathcal{M}$ and $\mathcal{N}$, across which the budget $\mathcal{N}_{max}$ is the total number of sampling we want to permit. Since we need to find schedulers that satisfy the property with probability at least θ, we set $\mathcal{N} = \lceil \frac{1}{\theta} \rceil$. This ensures that we spend our sampling budget verifying scheduler tuples that have a higher probability of satisfying our property. For example, if our θ is 0.25, $\mathcal{N} = 4$. If we want to check for our specification to be $\geq \theta$, any scheduler that satisfies at least 1 of the 4 sampled traces should be a good candidate for a *good* scheduler. In case we want to check for our specification to be $\leq \theta$, finding such *good* schedulers would help us reject the hypothesis easily. We allocate the rest of the budget (such that $\mathcal{N} \cdot \mathcal{M} \sim \mathcal{N}_{max}$) to sample scheduler tuples, thus, we set $\mathcal{M} = \lceil \theta \mathcal{N}_{max} \rceil$. We have experimented with various values of budget, adjusting them based on the expected accuracy of our results.

6 Case Studies

In this section, we discuss case studies to show the applicability and scalability of our approach. One of the main advantages of statistical model checking lies in the fact that we do not necessarily need access to the underlying model to verify a system. This allowed us to utilize our approach on sets of traces generated from black-box sources. We have separated our case studies into two sections elaborating on the models of the grey-box (where we have access to the underlying model) and black-box (where we just have access to a set of traces generated by different schedulers) examples.

6.1 Grey-Box Verification

Group Anonymity in Dining Cryptographers (DC). We explored the dining cryptographers problem [15] from the perspective of how it is designed to maintain anonymity. In this model, three cryptographers go out for dinner and at the end, want to figure out who paid the bill (their manager or one of them) while respecting each other's privacy. The protocol proceeds in two stages:(1) each cryptographer flips a coin and only informs the cryptographer on their right of the outcome (head or tail), (2) the cryptographers consider both the coin tosses that they know of, to declare *agree* in case the tosses were the same, or *disagree* otherwise. However, in the case of the cryptographer that actually paid, they would declare the opposite conclusion.

Given an odd number of cryptographers, we should have an odd number of agrees if the manager pays the bill, an even number of agrees if one of the cryptographers paid, and vice versa for an even number of cryptographers. We want to verify if there is any information leakage depending on which cryptographer pays. In the model, we nondeterministically choose who pays the bill and the order in which the cryptographers toss their coin. In case one of the cryptographers pay in both traces, we expect the parity of coins at the end to be the same. As described in [9], the order of coin toss should not affect the anonymity in the protocol. This good behavior can be expressed as a hyperproperty,

$$\varphi_{DC} = \Big(\bigvee_{i \in (1,2,3)} Cpay_{i\pi_1} \wedge \bigvee_{i \in (1,2,3)} Cpay_{i\pi_2} \Big) \implies$$

$$\Diamond(done \wedge (c1 \oplus c2 \oplus c3))_{\pi_1} \bigwedge \Diamond(done \wedge (c1 \oplus c2 \oplus c3))_{\pi_2}$$

For the correctness of the model, we should not be able to find a scheduler that satisfies the bad behavior $\neg\varphi_{DC}$ with positive probability, thus, we design the hypothesis as,

$$\exists\sigma_1.\exists\sigma_2.\, \Pr_{\mathtt{M}}(V \nvDash \varphi_{DC}) > 0$$

We expect this property to be false for an odd number of cryptographers and true for even, as our model should ensure anonymity. We experimented with both unbiased and biased coins in the model to check if that affects the parity of agreement. The main challenge for this study was the size of the models as shown in Table 1. Existing exhaustive approaches would take considerable memory and execution time to verify this model. Hence, an approximate approach like SMC has its utility here.

Noninterference in Path Planning (RNI). Consider the grid in Fig. 1. We have two robots moving across a two-dimensional plane subdivided (discretized) into $n \times n$ cells. The robots can nondeterministically choose to move to their neighboring cells unrestricted (up, down, left, or right) unless it is blocked by the grid boundaries. However, with a certain error probability, the chosen target cell is not reached and instead, the robot stays in its current cell. The grid can hence, be modeled as an MDP where each state models a grid cell. Note that we do not restrict or force any specific strategy for the movement of these robots.

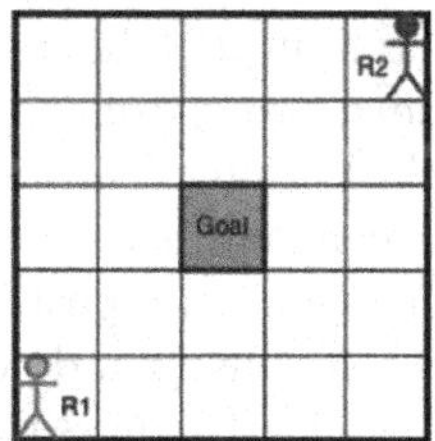

Fig. 1. Two robots attempting to reach the same goal.

Thus, each scheduler corresponds to a specific strategy that defines how the robot moves across the grid. We consider the case where two robots (R1 and R2) are placed in opposite corners of the grid and aim to reach the goal state at the center of the grid. Assume $R1$ is our robot of interest and $R2$ is an intruder. Motivated by the idea in [22], a specification of interest would be to check if the plan of $R1$ to reach the goal is affected by the plans of $R2$. We design the hypothesis as the negation of the required property. Hence, we want to determine if there exists any such scheduler tuple where the movement of $R1$ would be similar but $R1$ fails to reach the goal in one of them. The unquantified HyperLTL formula is as follows,

$$\varphi_{RNI} = \square\big(actR1_{\pi 1} = actR1_{\pi 2}\big) \bigwedge (\neg goalR1_{\pi 1}\, \mathcal{U}\, goalR2_{\pi 1}) \oplus (\neg goalR1_{\pi 2}\, \mathcal{U}\, goalR2_{\pi 2})$$

For any arbitrary probability p, we design our specification as,

$$\exists\sigma_1.\exists\sigma_2.\ \Pr_{\mathtt{M}}(V \models \varphi_{RNI}) > p$$

Current State Opacity (CSO). Consider the grid in Fig. 2 where we use only one robot on the grid, which starts from any of the starting states labeled S and aims to reach the opposite corner labeled G. The gray boxes represent obstacles. Instead of analyzing reachability, we are interested in analyzing opacity similar to [54]. Opacity requires that an unauthorized user should not be able to realize the current state of the system. In the context of a robot, opacity ensures privacy is preserved as the robot moves across the grid. An observer gets an observation corresponding to each movement of the robot. Note that we have divided the grid into three regions (blue: *near initial*, red: *between obstacles*, green: *near goal*) which would generate the same observation even when the robot is in a different position. Current state opacity specifically states that while starting from the same initial state (here: either of the lower left corners marked in blue), it is still feasible to move across the grid using different paths that can produce the same observation. By different paths, we refer to cases where the actual positions of the robot are different due to the execution of different actions (up, down, left, right). This would mean that an intruder should not be able to guess the exact location by merely gathering observations about the movement of the robot. We can express this formally as,

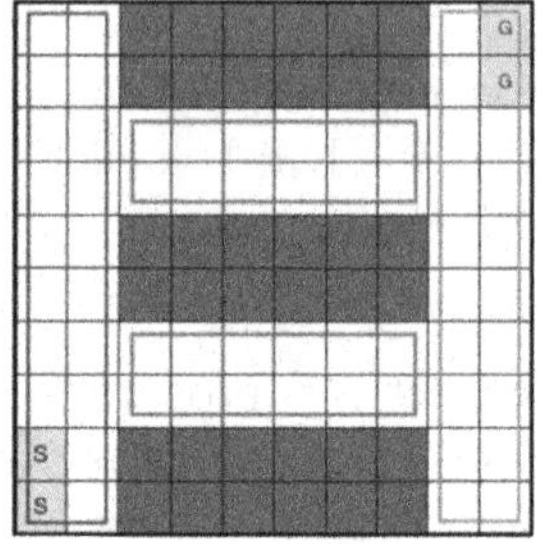

Fig. 2. Grid divided into regions to ensure opacity.

$$\varphi_{CSO} = \big(start_{\pi_1} \wedge start_{\pi_2}\big) \bigwedge \neg\square_{\leq k}(act_{\pi_1} = act_{\pi_2}) \bigwedge \square_{\leq k}(region_{\pi_1} = region_{\pi_2})$$

where *act* encodes the action taken by the robot on the grid and *region* denotes the corresponding region observed. We want to check if any such combination of schedulers exists that satisfies the current state opacity with respect to a given threshold. This is expressed as,

$$\exists\sigma_1.\exists\sigma_2.\ \Pr_{\mathtt{M}}(V \models \varphi_{CSO}) > p$$

6.2 Black-Box Verification

We use the example of a side-channel timing attack on a password checker as a black-box case study. We consider several password checkers that vary in the expected amount of information leaked by observing the execution time, resulting from different input guesses. We ran our password checkers on a microcontroller and considered numerical passwords of length 10 as input.

Following the approach described in Sect. 5.1, a scheduler is represented as a seed for a pseudo-random number generator. For a black-box model, the model checker calls a `python` script with one parameter (the scheduler seed) as an input. This seed is used by the model to resolve nondeterminism internally via a pseudo-random number generator. Internally, the script uses the scheduler seed to create a random password guess. Here, we assume the password guess and the actual password is of the same length to simplify code run on the microcontroller. The number of correct digits of the generated password guess is saved and the password is forwarded to the microcontroller via the serial interface over USB. The execution time of the microcontroller together with the number of correct bits are returned by the Python script and the out-stream is parsed and interpreted by the model checker.

We convert numerical return values (rounded to a predefined level of precision), e.g., the number of correct digits (cd) or the execution time (et) to traces whose length of consecutive symbols of a type reflects those values. For instance, the returned pair of values `execution_time=4, correct_digits=1` would be converted into the trace

$$\{et, cd\} \rightarrow \{et\} \rightarrow \{et\} \rightarrow \{et\} \rightarrow \{\} \rightarrow \dots$$

Leakage of information from an unsafe password checker can be obtained by observing the execution times for several inputs. Intuitively, if the checking of a password with more consecutive correct digits (in the front) takes longer than a password with fewer correct digits, observing the execution time for multiple guesses should allow guessing the correct password. To formalize this, we use the specification of unwanted behavior

$$\varphi_{TAM} = (\Diamond(cd_{\pi_1} \wedge \neg cd_{\pi_2}) \wedge \Diamond(et_{\pi_1} \wedge \neg et_{\pi_2})) \oplus (\Diamond(cd_{\pi_2} \wedge \neg cd_{\pi_1}) \wedge \Diamond(et_{\pi_2} \wedge \neg et_{\pi_1}))$$

Consider the example of a password checker that leaks information (BB-L) in Listing 1.1. In contrast, a simple, safe approach (BB-S) checks the whole password without the option of an early return as in Line 6 and thus always produces the same execution time regardless of the correctness of the guess g. Additionally, we can also add padding to obfuscate actual execution timing.

```
1 bool checkPassword(String g){
2   int i;
3   for(i=0; i < g.length(); ++i)
4   {
5     if(g[i]!=secret[i])
6         return false;
7   }
8   return true;
9 }
```

Listing 1.1. Possible leaky password checker (BB-L).

In our experiments, we consider a random delay (BB-*R) between 0 and 10 microseconds or a fixed delay (BB-*F) of 2 microseconds. We want to check, for an arbitrary probability p, whether a combination of schedulers exists, such that bad behavior, i.e., information leakage can be derived. This is expressed as,

$$\exists \sigma_1 . \exists \sigma_2 . \Pr_{\mathtt{M}}(V \models \varphi_{TAM}) > p$$

7 Experimentation/Evaluation

The model details of our grey-box case studies have been reported in Table 1. Experimental results for our case studies have been summarized in Table 2. The parameters in Table 2 refer to the number of schedulers (*#sch*) and traces (*#tr*) that were sampled as determined by our algorithm, and the length of the trace (k) as determined by the user based on knowledge about the model. We separately report the time required for the sampling of the scheduler (*Sim*) and trace tuples and the time required to verify (*Ver*) the hyperproperty on them. Reported timing data is the average over 10 runs. Note that in our evaluation we do not compare our results to the existing model checkers for linear hyperproperties as they cannot handle probabilistic models with non-determinism.

7.1 Black-Box Verification

Experiments were run on an Intel® Core™ i7 (6×3.30 GHz) with 32Gb RAM, the password checkers ran on an `esp32` micro-controller to alleviate variance in timing due to process scheduling. To obtain results with higher precision, we execute using multiple parameter configurations - size of the indifference region (ε), the satisfying probability (θ), and sampling budget ($\mathcal{N}_{max}$). The error probabilities α, β were kept at 0.01 for the whole experiment. Results and running times for the most accurate runs are shown in Table 2, where different variants of password checkers (see also Sect. 6) are referenced by their labels.

In total, we have run over 480 combinations of parameters to synthesize accurate results. Table 2 lists results of parameter configurations that are maximizing the probability of satisfying the property without being inconclusive to give an estimate on a worst-case scenario. In case the property could be satisfied in the majority of the 10 runs, we show results for two configurations: one leading to a large observed probability and a second one that used a higher budget and smaller indifference region which, thus, can be expected to be more precise.

From the results, we can observe that for safe password checking the tested variants with no padding (S), fixed padding (SF), and random padding (SR) do not allow information leakage about the correctness of the password guess via correlation of the observed execution time. In contrast to this, the experiments with a leaky password generator with a fixed or no padding scheme (LF, L) allow correlating execution time and correctness of passwords. Note that in most cases the created guesses had only zero to one correct digit, as we did not implement adversarial strategies to guess larger parts of the password.

7.2 Grey-Box Verification

Experiments were run on an Intel® Core™ i7 (4×2.3 GHz) with 32Gb RAM. We ran experiments on each of the described case studies by scaling them across the different parameters involved. However, due to space constraints, we report cases that are sufficient to show the scalability and robustness of our approach.

The DC component in the table corresponds to the verification of the dining cryptographers protocol described in Sect. 6.1. Our specification φ_{DC} should not hold for an odd number of cryptographers and should hold for even ones. We have scaled the model over $\#c = \{4, 7, 8, 15\}$ and witnessed the expected results. We used a constant budget of 5000 for all the cases reported. We used models directly from PRISM [1] and were able to verify them without alterations. We experimented with both biased and unbiased coins. The result produced was the same proving that the biases of the coins do not affect the outcome of the protocol. The experiment for the biased coin scenario used the exact same parameters as reported and yielded similar execution times for both scenarios.

Table 1. Model details of grey-box case studies

CS	Param.	#States	#Transitions	#Actions
DC	$c = 4$	2598	6864	5448
	$c = 7$	328760	1499472	1186040
	$c = 8$	1687113	8790480	6952248
	$c = 15$	10^{11}	10^{12}	9×10^{11}
RB	$n = 3$	1034	4888	2444
Grid	$n = 5$	12346	77152	38576
Fig. 1	$n = 10$	256926	1852972	926486
RB	$n = 10$	200	1440	720
Grid	$n = 20$	800	6080	3040
Fig. 2	$n = 30$	1800	13920	6960

The RNI section in the table corresponds to noninterference case study. We have scaled our grid for $N = \{3, 5, 10\}$. We verify the existence of scheduler tuples that fails to satisfy noninterference with probability bounds of $\{0.1, 0.2, 0.5\}$ with a budget of 2000. The trace lengths have been increased in proportion to the grid sizes. We have experimented on arbitrary trace lengths which have been adjusted as we increase the grid size. As we do not specify any smart movement strategy for the robots, these results are based on possible random walks the robots can make on the grid. The interesting observation here is the difference in execution time based on the parameters. The cases for $\theta \leq 0.1$ seem to be challenging, given the current grid and budget, resulting in an inconclusive result; for $n = 10$ our experiment ran for more than 2 d hinting at an inconclusive result within the given budget. This is expected as we are challenging the algorithm to find a scheduler with a very low probability (between 0 and 0.1) given the large search space. For $\theta \geq 0.2$, we are often able to find our target scheduler tuples in the initial sampling phase, leading to short execution time due to early exit. This is mainly because we are looking for a scheduler across a wider range of probability (between 0.2 and 1). Using $\theta \geq 0.5$ becomes challenging when scaling the model (with the same budget for comparison) due to the growing number of possible scheduler tuples, and the lack of any specific strategy that finds traces where both the robots are aiming to reach the goal. Thus, finding a scheduler with probability on the higher end (between 0.5 - 1) is not always possible in the given budget and indifference regions.

During our experiments on the opacity case study (CSO), we added a subformula to φ_{CSO} to check if the robot reaches the goal in both traces. Given that we do not enforce any smart movement strategy on the movement of the robot, it usually makes a random walk in the grid often looping in a few states for a long time. Consequently, the probability of the robot actually reaching the goal is highly unlikely. We checked the probability of satisfying our specification against $\{0.05, 0.3, 0.7\}$. We used a budget of 3000 for all versions of this experiment and increased the trace length in proportion to the increase in the grid size.

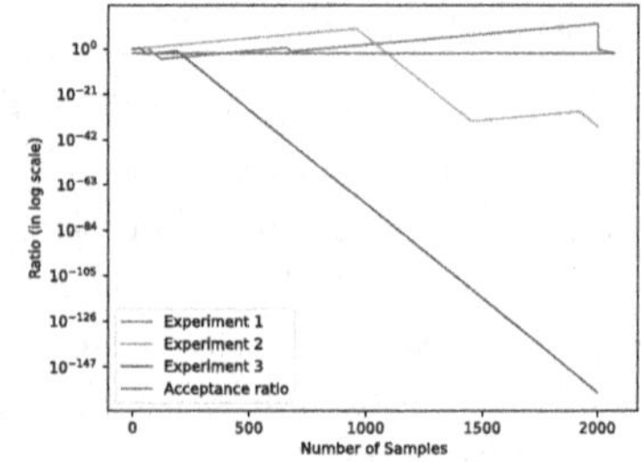

Fig. 3. DC with $n = 4$ ($\Pr \geq 0.1 \pm 0.01$)

The plots in Fig. 3,4 depict convergence results, where each line in a graph shows how the value of *ratio* changes across a single algorithm run. In each of the plots, the red line represents the ratio A in Algorithm 1 which serves as our exit condition. In Fig. 3, we use the sampling budget of 2000 to calculate the *ratio*. At the end of this phase, if the *ratio* is below A, we can declare that we have found enough evidence for a concrete result of the specification being satisfied as shown in lines labeled experiment 2 and 3. For the case of experiment 1, we could not reach a concrete conclusion in the initial round, as the line can be seen to be well above A. We were required to enter the main algorithm loop and required a few more samples (~ 75) to reach the same concrete conclusion.

The robotics case plotted in Fig. 4a shows that we were able to get a concrete result in the initial sampling for all three cases. We plotted an undecidable case in Fig. 4b. Note that in experiment 2 we were able to get a concrete result in the initial sampling round; in experiment 1, we were able to reach a concrete result in the main algorithm loop after intensive sampling within the chosen schedulers; and in experiment 3, we could neither find an accepting scheduler nor reject all schedulers, leading to an inconclusive result. This supports the

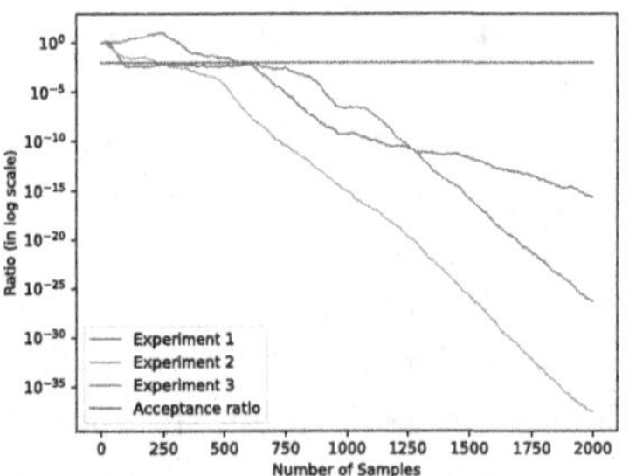

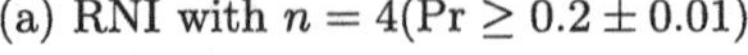

(a) RNI with $n = 4(\Pr \geq 0.2 \pm 0.01)$

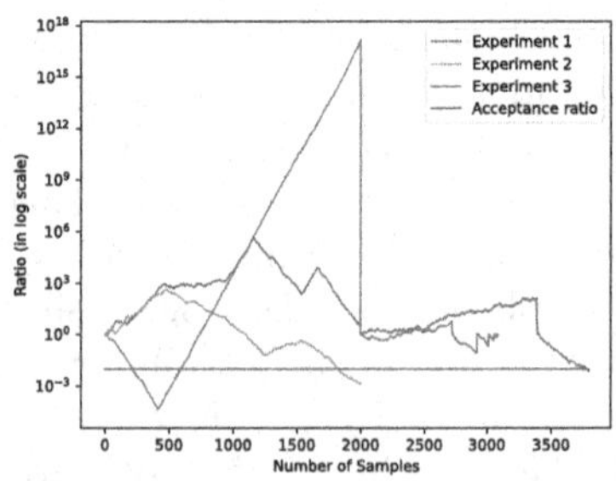

(b) RNI with $n = 4$ ($\Pr \geq 0.5 \pm 0.01$)

Fig. 4. Plots showing the change in ratio based on sampling across schedulers.

Table 2. Data from experimentation. #sch: number of scheduler-tuples sampled, #tr: number of trace tuples sampled per scheduler tuple, k: length of traces sampled. $\alpha = \beta = 0.01$.

Case Study	Specification		Result	Parameters			Time [sec]	
				#sch	*#tr*	*k*	Sim.	Ver.
BB	$\Pr(V \models \varphi_{TAM}) \geq 0.1 \pm 0.01$	# S	False	400	10	80	108	0.09
	$\Pr(V \models \varphi_{TAM}) \geq 0.1 \pm 0.01$	# SF	False	400	10	80	93.1	0.09
	$\Pr(V \models \varphi_{TAM}) \geq 0.1 \pm 0.01$	# SR	False	400	10	80	92.8	0.07
	$\Pr(V \models \varphi_{TAM}) \geq 0.3 \pm 0.1$	# L	True	1201	4	80	102	0.1
	$\Pr(V \models \varphi_{TAM}) \geq 0.25 \pm 0.01$	# L	True	1001	4	80	85.5	0.01
	$\Pr(V \models \varphi_{TAM}) \geq 0.15 \pm 0.1$	# LF	True	601	7	80	92	0.09
	$\Pr(V \models \varphi_{TAM}) \geq 0.1 \pm 0.01$	# LF	Undec	400	10	80	90	0.08
	$\Pr(V \models \varphi_{TAM}) \geq 0.1 \pm 0.01$	# LR	False	400	10	80	88.7	0.08
DC	$\Pr(V \not\models \varphi_{DC}) \geq 0.1 \pm 0.01$	$(\#c = 4)$	True	500	10	20	1.6	0.5
	$\Pr(V \not\models \varphi_{DC}) \geq 0.01 \pm 0.001$	$(\#c = 4)$	True	50	100	20	1.4	0.4
	$\Pr(V \not\models \varphi_{DC}) \geq 0.1 \pm 0.01$	$(\#c = 7)$	False	500	10	25	2.7	0.3
	$\Pr(V \not\models \varphi_{DC}) \geq 0.01 \pm 0.001$	$(\#c = 7)$	False	50	100	25	2.6	0.6
	$\Pr(V \not\models \varphi_{DC}) \geq 0.1 \pm 0.01$	$(\#c = 8)$	True	500	10	30	2.6	0.8
	$\Pr(V \not\models \varphi_{DC}) \geq 0.01 \pm 0.001$	$(\#c = 8)$	True	50	100	30	2.7	0.7
	$\Pr(V \not\models \varphi_{DC}) \geq 0.1 \pm 0.01$	$(\#c = 15)$	False	500	10	65	4.5	1.8
	$\Pr(V \not\models \varphi_{DC}) \geq 0.01 \pm 0.001$	$(\#c = 15)$	False	50	100	65	5.1	1.9
RNI	$\Pr(V \models \varphi_{RNI}) \leq 0.1 \pm 0.01$	$(n = 3)$	Undec	200	10	10	385	0.3
	$\Pr(V \models \varphi_{RNI}) \geq 0.2 \pm 0.01$	$(n = 3)$	True	400	5	10	3.8	0.2
	$\Pr(V \models \varphi_{RNI}) \geq 0.5 \pm 0.01$	$(n = 3)$	True	1000	2	10	210	0.15
	$\Pr(V \models \varphi_{RNI}) \leq 0.1 \pm 0.01$	$(n = 5)$	Undec	200	10	26	2999	0.194
	$\Pr(V \models \varphi_{RNI}) \geq 0.2 \pm 0.01$	$(n = 5)$	True	400	5	26	38.17	0.33
	$\Pr(V \models \varphi_{RNI}) \geq 0.5 \pm 0.01$	$(n = 5)$	Undec	1000	2	26	1243	0.67
	$\Pr(V \models \varphi_{RNI}) \geq 0.2 \pm 0.01$	$(n = 10)$	True	400	5	80	173.65	0.87
	$\Pr(V \models \varphi_{RNI}) \geq 0.5 \pm 0.01$	$(n = 10)$	Undec	1000	2	80	10.4k	1.38
CSO	$\Pr(V \models \varphi_{CSO}) \leq 0.05 \pm 0.001$	$(n = 10)$	Undec	150	20	30	84	0.82
	$\Pr(V \models \varphi_{CSO}) \geq 0.3 \pm 0.01$	$(n = 10)$	True	900	4	30	0.7	0.17
	$\Pr(V \models \varphi_{CSO}) \leq 0.7 \pm 0.01$	$(n = 10)$	True	2100	2	30	0.93	0.25
	$\Pr(V \models \varphi_{CSO}) \leq 0.05 \pm 0.001$	$(n = 20)$	Undec	150	20	45	376	0.41
	$\Pr(V \models \varphi_{CSO}) \geq 0.3 \pm 0.01$	$(n = 20)$	True	900	4	45	2.41	0.34
	$\Pr(V \models \varphi_{CSO}) \leq 0.7 \pm 0.01$	$(n = 20)$	True	2100	2	45	1.74	0.41
	$\Pr(V \models \varphi_{CSO}) \leq 0.05 \pm 0.001$	$(n = 30)$	True	150	20	55	511	0.35
	$\Pr(V \models \varphi_{CSO}) \geq 0.3 \pm 0.01$	$(n = 30)$	True	900	4	55	7.97	0.29
	$\Pr(V \models \varphi_{CSO}) \leq 0.7 \pm 0.01$	$(n = 30)$	True	2100	2	55	2.45	0.32

results of undecidability that the algorithm returned. The main reason can be traced back to the fact that we did not specify any strategy for the robots, thus, sampling across random walks of the robot.

8 Conclusion

We presented a probabilistic formulation of bounded, unquantified HyperLTL and provided a SMC approach to verify them over MDPs. To handle nondeterminism, our approach leverages the smart sampling algorithm presented in [20], extending it to reason about hyperproperties. We have implemented our approach as an extension of PLASMA [48] adding new capabilities to perform black-box verification and demonstrating the scalability of our approach in several case studies with large state spaces. This work aimed to showcase that SMC is a feasible solution for cases where exhaustive or bounded model checking is unable to provide us with any insight. In future directions, we would like to extend support for quantifier alternations for paths (as in HyperLTL) and scheduler tuples, as the current approach can only handle existential scheduler tuples and limits our applicability to a wider variety of security properties.

References

1. PRISM: dining cryptographers' problem. https://www.prismmodelchecker.org/casestudies/dining_crypt.php
2. Ábrahám, E., Bonakdarpour, B.: HyperPCTL: a temporal logic for probabilistic hyperproperties. In: Proceedings of the 15th International Conference on Quantitative Evaluation of Systems (QEST), pp. 20–35 (2018)
3. Ábrahám, E., Bartocci, E., Bonakdarpour, B., Dobe, O.: Probabilistic hyperproperties with nondeterminism. In: Hung, D.V., Sokolsky, O. (eds.) ATVA 2020. LNCS, vol. 12302, pp. 518–534. Springer, Cham (2020). https://doi.org/10.1007/978-3-030-59152-6_29
4. Agha, G., Palmskog, K.: A survey of statistical model checking. ACM Trans. Model. Comput. Simul. **28**(1), 1–39 (2018). https://doi.org/10.1145/3158668
5. Agrawal, S., Bonakdarpour, B.: Runtime verification of k-safety hyperproperties in HyperLTL. In: 2016 IEEE 29th Computer Security Foundations Symposium (CSF), pp. 239–252. IEEE, Lisbon (2016). https://doi.org/10.1109/CSF.2016.24
6. Arora, S., Hansen, R.R., Larsen, K.G., Legay, A., Poulsen, D.B.: Statistical model checking for probabilistic hyperproperties of real-valued signals. In: Legunsen, O., Rosu, G. (eds.) Model Checking Software, SPIN 2022. Lecture Notes in Computer Science, vol. 13255, pp. 61–78. Springer, Cham (2022). https://doi.org/10.1007/978-3-031-15077-7_4
7. Baier, C., Katoen, J.P.: Principles of Model Checking. MIT Press, Cambridge (2008)
8. Baumeister, J., Coenen, N., Bonakdarpour, B., Finkbeiner, B., Sánchez, C.: A temporal logic for asynchronous hyperproperties. In: Silva, A., Leino, K.R.M. (eds.) CAV 2021. LNCS, vol. 12759, pp. 694–717. Springer, Cham (2021). https://doi.org/10.1007/978-3-030-81685-8_33
9. Beauxis, R., Palamidessi, C.: Probabilistic and nondeterministic aspects of anonymity. Theoret. Comput. Sci. **410**(41), 4006–4025 (2009). https://doi.org/10.1016/j.tcs.2009.06.008
10. Bonakdarpour, B., Sanchez, C., Schneider, G.: Monitoring hyperproperties by combining static analysis and runtime verification. In: Margaria, T., Steffen, B. (eds.) ISoLA 2018. LNCS, vol. 11245, pp. 8–27. Springer, Cham (2018). https://doi.org/10.1007/978-3-030-03421-4_2
11. Bonakdarpour, B., Finkbeiner, B.: The complexity of monitoring hyperproperties. In: 2018 IEEE 31st Computer Security Foundations Symposium (CSF), pp. 162–174 (2018). https://doi.org/10.1109/CSF.2018.00019
12. Boyer, B., Corre, K., Legay, A., Sedwards, S.: PLASMA-lab: a flexible, distributable statistical model checking library. In: Joshi, K., Siegle, M., Stoelinga, M., D'Argenio, P.R. (eds.) QEST 2013. LNCS, vol. 8054, pp. 160–164. Springer, Heidelberg (2013). https://doi.org/10.1007/978-3-642-40196-1_12

13. Bulychev, P., et al.: UPPAAL-SMC: statistical model checking for priced timed automata. arXiv preprint arXiv:1207.1272 (2012)
14. Cavalcante, E., Quilbeuf, J., Traonouez, L.-M., Oquendo, F., Batista, T., Legay, A.: Statistical model checking of dynamic software architectures. In: Tekinerdogan, B., Zdun, U., Babar, A. (eds.) ECSA 2016. LNCS, vol. 9839, pp. 185–200. Springer, Cham (2016). https://doi.org/10.1007/978-3-319-48992-6_14
15. Chaum, D.: The dining cryptographers problem: unconditional sender and recipient untraceability. J. Cryptol. **1**(1), 65–75 (1988). https://doi.org/10.1007/BF00206326
16. Clarke, E.M., Zuliani, P.: Statistical model checking for cyber-physical systems. In: Bultan, T., Hsiung, P.-A. (eds.) ATVA 2011. LNCS, vol. 6996, pp. 1–12. Springer, Heidelberg (2011). https://doi.org/10.1007/978-3-642-24372-1_1
17. Clarkson, M.R., Finkbeiner, B., Koleini, M., Micinski, K.K., Rabe, M.N., Sánchez, C.: Temporal logics for hyperproperties. In: Abadi, M., Kremer, S. (eds.) POST 2014. LNCS, vol. 8414, pp. 265–284. Springer, Heidelberg (2014). https://doi.org/10.1007/978-3-642-54792-8_15
18. Clarkson, M.R., Schneider, F.B.: Hyperproperties. In: 2008 21st IEEE Computer Security Foundations Symposium, pp. 51–65. IEEE, Pittsburgh, PA, USA (2008). https://doi.org/10.1109/CSF.2008.7
19. Coenen, N., Finkbeiner, B., Sánchez, C., Tentrup, L.: Verifying hyperliveness. In: Dillig, I., Tasiran, S. (eds.) CAV 2019. LNCS, vol. 11561, pp. 121–139. Springer, Cham (2019). https://doi.org/10.1007/978-3-030-25540-4_7
20. D'Argenio, P., Legay, A., Sedwards, S., Traonouez, L.M.: Smart sampling for lightweight verification of Markov decision processes. Int. J. Softw. Tools Technol. Transfer **17**(4), 469–484 (2015)
21. Das, S., Prabhakar, P.: Bayesian statistical model checking for multi-agent systems using HyperPCTL* (2022)
22. Dimitrova, R., Finkbeiner, B., Torfah, H.: Probabilistic hyperproperties of Markov decision processes. In: Hung, D.V., Sokolsky, O. (eds.) ATVA 2020. LNCS, vol. 12302, pp. 484–500. Springer, Cham (2020). https://doi.org/10.1007/978-3-030-59152-6_27
23. Dobe, O., Ábrahám, E., Bartocci, E., Bonakdarpour, B.: HyperProb: a model checker for probabilistic hyperproperties. In: Huisman, M., Păsăreanu, C., Zhan, N. (eds.) FM 2021. LNCS, vol. 13047, pp. 657–666. Springer, Cham (2021). https://doi.org/10.1007/978-3-030-90870-6_35
24. Dobe, O., Ábrahám, E., Bartocci, E., Bonakdarpour, B.: Model checking hyperproperties for Markov decision processes. Inf. Comput. **289**, 104978 (2022)
25. Dobe, O., Wilke, L., Ábrahám, E., Bartocci, E., Bonakdarpour, B.: Probabilistic hyperproperties with rewards. In: Deshmukh, J.V., Havelund, K., Perez, I. (eds.) NFM 2022. Lecture Notes in Computer Science, vol. 13260, pp. 656–673. Springer, Cham (2022). https://doi.org/10.1007/978-3-031-06773-0_35
26. Dwork, C.: Differential privacy. In: Bugliesi, M., Preneel, B., Sassone, V., Wegener, I. (eds.) ICALP 2006. LNCS, vol. 4052, pp. 1–12. Springer, Heidelberg (2006). https://doi.org/10.1007/11787006_1
27. Finkbeiner, B., Hahn, C., Hans, T.: MGHyper: checking satisfiability of HyperLTL formulas beyond the $\exists^*\forall^*$ fragment. In: Lahiri, S.K., Wang, C. (eds.) ATVA 2018. LNCS, vol. 11138, pp. 521–527. Springer, Cham (2018). https://doi.org/10.1007/978-3-030-01090-4_31
28. Finkbeiner, B., Hahn, C., Stenger, M.: EAHyper: satisfiability, implication, and equivalence checking of hyperproperties. In: Majumdar, R., Kunčak, V. (eds.) CAV

2017. LNCS, vol. 10427, pp. 564–570. Springer, Cham (2017). https://doi.org/10.1007/978-3-319-63390-9_29
29. Finkbeiner, B., Hahn, C., Stenger, M., Tentrup, L.: Monitoring hyperproperties. In: Lahiri, S., Reger, G. (eds.) RV 2017. LNCS, vol. 10548, pp. 190–207. Springer, Cham (2017). https://doi.org/10.1007/978-3-319-67531-2_12
30. Finkbeiner, B., Hahn, C., Stenger, M., Tentrup, L.: RVHyper: A runtime verification tool for temporal hyperproperties. In: Beyer, D., Huisman, M. (eds.) TACAS 2018. LNCS, vol. 10806, pp. 194–200. Springer, Cham (2018). https://doi.org/10.1007/978-3-319-89963-3_11
31. Finkbeiner, B., Hahn, C., Torfah, H.: Model checking quantitative hyperproperties. In: Chockler, H., Weissenbacher, G. (eds.) CAV 2018. LNCS, vol. 10981, pp. 144–163. Springer, Cham (2018). https://doi.org/10.1007/978-3-319-96145-3_8
32. Finkbeiner, B., Müller, C., Seidl, H., Zalinescu, E.: Verifying security policies in multi-agent workflows with loops. In: Proceedings of the CCS 2017 (2017)
33. Finkbeiner, B., Rabe, M.N., Sánchez, C.: Algorithms for model checking HyperLTL and HyperCTL*. In: Kroening, D., Păsăreanu, C.S. (eds.) CAV 2015. LNCS, vol. 9206, pp. 30–48. Springer, Cham (2015). https://doi.org/10.1007/978-3-319-21690-4_3
34. Gadyatskaya, O., Hansen, R.R., Larsen, K.G., Legay, A., Olesen, M.C., Poulsen, D.B.: Modelling attack-defense trees using timed automata. In: Fränzle, M., Markey, N. (eds.) FORMATS 2016. LNCS, vol. 9884, pp. 35–50. Springer, Cham (2016). https://doi.org/10.1007/978-3-319-44878-7_3
35. Gilbert, D.R., Donaldson, R.: A monte Carlo model checker for probabilistic LTL with numerical constraints (2008)
36. Goguen, J.A., Meseguer, J.: Security policies and security models. In: IEEE Symposium on Security and Privacy, pp. 11–20 (1982)
37. Hahn, C., Stenger, M., Tentrup, L.: Constraint-based monitoring of hyperproperties. In: Vojnar, T., Zhang, L. (eds.) TACAS 2019. LNCS, vol. 11428, pp. 115–131. Springer, Cham (2019). https://doi.org/10.1007/978-3-030-17465-1_7
38. Henriques, D., Martins, J.G., Zuliani, P., Platzer, A., Clarke, E.M.: Statistical model checking for Markov decision processes. In: 2012 Ninth International Conference on Quantitative Evaluation of Systems, pp. 84–93 (2012). https://doi.org/10.1109/QEST.2012.19
39. Hsu, T., Bonakdarpour, B., Finkbeiner, B., Sánchez, C.: Bounded model checking for asynchronous hyperproperties. CoRR abs/2301.07208 (2023). https://doi.org/10.48550/arXiv.2301.07208
40. Hsu, T., Bonakdarpour, B., Sánchez, C.: HyperQube: a QBF-based bounded model checker for hyperproperties. CoRR abs/2109.12989 (2021). https://arxiv.org/abs/2109.12989
41. Hsu, T.-H., Sánchez, C., Bonakdarpour, B.: Bounded model checking for hyperproperties. In: TACAS 2021. LNCS, vol. 12651, pp. 94–112. Springer, Cham (2021). https://doi.org/10.1007/978-3-030-72016-2_6
42. Gray, J.W., III., Syverson, P.F.: A logical approach to multilevel security of probabilistic systems. Distrib. Comput. **11**(2), 73–90 (1998)
43. Katoen, J.P., Zapreev, I.S., Hahn, E.M., Hermanns, H., Jansen, D.N.: The ins and outs of the probabilistic model checker MRMC. Perform. Eval. **68**(2), 90–104 (2011)
44. Kwiatkowska, M., Norman, G., Parker, D.: PRISM 4.0: verification of probabilistic real-time systems. In: Gopalakrishnan, G., Qadeer, S. (eds.) CAV 2011. LNCS, vol. 6806, pp. 585–591. Springer, Heidelberg (2011). https://doi.org/10.1007/978-3-642-22110-1_47

45. Larsen, K.G., Legay, A.: 30 years of statistical model checking. In: Margaria, T., Steffen, B. (eds.) ISoLA 2020. LNCS, vol. 12476, pp. 325–330. Springer, Cham (2020). https://doi.org/10.1007/978-3-030-61362-4_18
46. Legay, A., Delahaye, B., Bensalem, S.: Statistical model checking: an overview. In: Barringer, H., et al. (eds.) RV 2010. LNCS, vol. 6418, pp. 122–135. Springer, Heidelberg (2010). https://doi.org/10.1007/978-3-642-16612-9_11
47. Legay, A., Lukina, A., Traonouez, L.M., Yang, J., Smolka, S.A., Grosu, R.: Statistical model checking. In: Steffen, B., Woeginger, G. (eds.) Computing and Software Science. LNCS, vol. 10000, pp. 478–504. Springer, Cham (2019). https://doi.org/10.1007/978-3-319-91908-9_23
48. Legay, A., Sedwards, S.: On statistical model checking with PLASMA. In: The 8th International Symposium on Theoretical Aspects of Software Engineering (2014)
49. O'Neill, K.R., Clarkson, M.R., Chong, S.: Information-flow security for interactive programs. In: CSFW, pp. 190–201. IEEE Computer Society (2006)
50. Pnueli, A.: The temporal logic of programs. In: 18th Annual Symposium on Foundations of Computer Science (SFCS 1977), pp. 46–57. IEEE (1977)
51. Stucki, S., Sánchez, C., Schneider, G., Bonakdarpour, B.: Gray-box monitoring of hyperproperties. In: ter Beek, M.H., McIver, A., Oliveira, J.N. (eds.) FM 2019. LNCS, vol. 11800, pp. 406–424. Springer, Cham (2019). https://doi.org/10.1007/978-3-030-30942-8_25
52. Wald, A.: Sequential tests of statistical hypotheses. Ann. Math. Stat. **16**(2), 117–186 (1945). https://doi.org/10.1214/aoms/1177731118
53. Wang, Y., Nalluri, S., Bonakdarpour, B., Pajic, M.: Statistical model checking for hyperproperties. In: IEEE Computer Security Foundations Symposium, pp. 1–16. Dubrovnik, Croatia (2021)
54. Wang, Y., Nalluri, S., Pajic, M.: Hyperproperties for robotics: planning via HyperLTL. In: 2020 IEEE International Conference on Robotics and Automation (ICRA), pp. 8462–8468 (2020). https://doi.org/10.1109/ICRA40945.2020.9196874
55. Wang, Y., Zarei, M., Bonakdarpour, B., Pajic, M.: Statistical verification of hyperproperties for cyber-physical systems. ACM Trans. Embed. Comput. Syst. **18**(5), 92 (2019). https://doi.org/10.1145/3358232
56. Younes, H.L.S.: Ymer: a statistical model checker. In: Etessami, K., Rajamani, S.K. (eds.) CAV 2005. LNCS, vol. 3576, pp. 429–433. Springer, Heidelberg (2005). https://doi.org/10.1007/11513988_43
57. Zdancewic, S., Myers, A.C.: Observational determinism for concurrent program security. In: 16th IEEE Computer Security Foundations Workshop (CSFW-16 2003), 30 June–2 July 2003, Pacific Grove, CA, USA, p. 29. IEEE Computer Society (2003). https://doi.org/10.1109/CSFW.2003.1212703
58. Zuliani, P.: Statistical model checking for biological applications. Int. J. Softw. Tools Technol. Transfer **17**, 527–536 (2015)

Specification Sketching for Linear Temporal Logic

Simon Lutz[1,2(✉)], Daniel Neider[1,2], and Rajarshi Roy[3]

[1] TU Dortmund University, Dortmund, Germany
simon.lutz@tu-dortmund.de
[2] Center for Trustworthy Data Science and Security, UA Ruhr, Dortmund, Germany
[3] Max Planck Institute for Software Systems, Kaiserslautern, Germany

Abstract. Virtually all verification and synthesis techniques assume that formal specifications are readily available, functionally correct, and fully match the engineer's understanding of the given system. However, this assumption is often unrealistic in practice: formalizing system requirements is notoriously difficult, error-prone, and requires substantial training. To alleviate this hurdle, we propose a novel approach of assisting engineers in writing specifications based on their high-level understanding of the system. We formalize the high-level understanding as an LTL *sketch* that is a partial LTL formula, where parts that are hard to formalize can be left out. Given an LTL sketch and a set of examples of system behavior that the specification should or should not allow, the task of a so-called *sketching algorithm* is then to complete the sketch such that the resulting LTL formula is consistent with the examples. We show that deciding whether a sketch can be completed falls into the complexity class NP and present two SAT-based sketching algorithms. Finally, we implement a prototype with our algorithms and compare it against two prominent LTL miners to demonstrate the benefits of using LTL sketches.

1 Introduction

Due to its unique ability to prove the absence of errors mathematically, formal verification is a time-tested method of ensuring the safe and reliable operation of safety-critical systems. Success stories of formal methods include application domains such as communication system [21,34], railway transportation [3,4], aerospace [16,24], and operating systems [30,50] to name but a few.

However, there is an essential and often overlooked catch with formal verification: virtually all techniques assume that the specification required for the design or verification of a system is available in a suitable format, is functionally correct, and expresses precisely the properties the engineers had in mind. These assumptions are often unrealistic in practice. Formalizing system requirements is notoriously difficult and error-prone [9,38,44,45]. Even worse, the training effort required to reach proficiency with specification languages can be disproportionate to the expected benefits [17], and the use of formalisms such as temporal logics require a level of sophistication that many users might never develop [25,28].

É. André and J. Sun (Eds.): ATVA 2023, LNCS 14216, pp. 26–48, 2023.
https://doi.org/10.1007/978-3-031-45332-8_2

To aid the process of formalizing specifications, we introduce a fundamentally novel approach to writing formal specifications, named *specification sketching*. Inspired by recent advances in automated program synthesis [47,48], our new paradigm allows engineers to express their high-level insights about a system in terms of a partial specification, named *specification sketch*, where parts that are difficult or error-prone to formalize can be left out. To single out their desired specification, our paradigm additionally allows the engineers to provide positive (i.e., desirable) and negative (i.e., undesirable) examples of system execution. Based on this additional data, a so-called *sketching algorithm* fills in the missing low-level details to obtain a complete specification.

To demonstrate how our paradigm works, let us consider a simple scenario. Imagine that an engineer wishes to formalize the following request-response property P: every request p has to be answered eventually by a response q. This property can be expressed in Linear Temporal Logic (LTL)—a popular specification language in software verification—as $\mathsf{G}(p \rightarrow \mathsf{X}\,\mathsf{F}\,q)$ using standard temporal modalities F ("Finally"), G ("Globally"), and X ("neXt"). However, for the sake of this example, assume that the engineer is unsure of how exactly to formalize P. In such a situation, our sketching paradigm allows them to express their high-level insights in the form of a sketch, say $\mathsf{G}(p \rightarrow ?)$, where the question mark indicates the missing part of the specification. Additionally, they can provide example executions. Assume that they provide the following infinite executions of the system: (i) a positive execution $\{p\}\{q\}\{p\}\{q\}\{p\}\{q\}\cdots$, in which every request is answered by a response in the next time point, and (ii) a negative execution $\{p\}\{q\}\{p\}\{p\}\{p\}\cdots$, in which there are infinitely many requests that are not answered by a response. Our sketching algorithm then computes a substitution for the question mark such that the completed LTL formula is consistent with the examples (e.g., $? := \mathsf{X}\,\mathsf{F}\,q$). In this example, the engineer left out an entire temporal formula in the sketch. However, our paradigm also allows one to leave out Boolean and temporal operators. For instance, one could also provide $?(p \rightarrow \mathsf{X}\,\mathsf{F}\,p)$ as a sketch, where the question mark now indicates a missing unary operator (G in our example).

While the concept of specification sketching can be conceived for a wide range of specification languages, in this work, we focus on Linear Temporal Logic (LTL) [39]. Our rationale behind choosing LTL is threefold. First, LTL is popular in academia and widely used in industry [23,24,27,49], making it the de facto standard for expressing (temporal) properties in verification and synthesis. Second, LTL is well-understood and enjoys good algorithmic properties [15,39]. Third, its intuitive and variable-free syntax have recently prompted several efforts to adopt LTL (over finite words) also in artificial intelligence (e.g., as explainable models [13,43], as reward functions in reinforcement learning [12], etc.). We introduce LTL and other necessary definitions in Sect. 2.

In Sect. 3, we then formally state the problem of specification sketching for LTL (or LTL sketching for short). It turns out that the LTL sketching problem might not always have a solution: there are sketches for which no substitutions exist that makes them consistent with the given examples (see the example at the end of Sect. 3). However, we show in Sect. 4 that the problem of deciding whether such a substitution exists is in the complexity class NP. Moreover, we develop an effective decision procedure that reduces the original question to a satisfiability problem in propositional logic. This reduction permits us to apply highly-optimized, off-the-shelf SAT solvers to check whether a consistent substitution exists.

In Sect. 5, we develop two sketching algorithms for LTL. Following Occam's razor principle, both algorithms are biased towards finding "small" (concise) substitutions for the question marks in a sketch. The rationale behind this choice is that small formulas are arguably easier for engineers to understand and, thus, can be safely deployed in practice.

By exploiting the decision procedure of Sect. 4 as a sub-routine, our first algorithm transforms the sketching problem into several "classical" LTL learning tasks (i.e., learning of LTL formulas from positive and negative data). This transformation allows us to apply a diverse array of LTL learning algorithms, which have been proposed during the last five years [13,37,41]. In addition, our algorithm immediately benefits from any advances in this field of research.

While the first algorithm builds on top of existing work and, hence, is easy to use, we observed that it tends to produce non-optimal substitutions for the unspecified parts of a sketch. Our second algorithm tackles this by searching for substitutions of increasing size using a SAT-based approach that is inspired by Neider and Gavran [37]. We formally prove that this algorithm can, in fact, produce small substitutions (if they exist).

In Sect. 6, we present an experimental evaluation of our algorithms using a prototype implementation `LTL-Sketcher`. We demonstrate that our algorithms are effective in completing sketches with different types of missing information. Further, we compare `LTL-Sketcher` against two state-of-the-art specification mining tools for LTL. From the comparison, we demonstrate that `LTL-Sketcher`'s ability to complete missing temporal formulas and temporal operators enables it to complete more specifications. Moreover, we observe that providing high-level insights as a sketch reduces the number of examples required to derive the correct specification. Finally, we conclude in Sect. 7 with a discussion on future work. All the proofs and additional experimental results can be found in the extended version of this paper [35].

Related Work. Specification sketching can be seen as a form of specification mining [1]. In this area, the general idea of allowing partial specifications is not entirely new, but it has not yet been investigated as generally as in this work. For instance, a closely related setting is the one in which so-called templates are used to mine temporal specifications from system executions. In this context, a template is a partial formula similar to a sketch. Unlike a sketch, however, a template is typically completed with a single atomic proposition or a simple, usually Boolean formula (e.g., a restricted Boolean combination of atomic propositions). A prime example of this approach is Texada [31,32], a specification miner for LTL_f formulas (i.e., LTL over a finite horizon). Texada takes a template (property type in their terminology) and a set of system executions as input and completes the template with atomic propositions such that the resulting LTL formula satisfies all system executions. In contrast to Texada, our paradigm assists engineers in completing more complex temporal formulas in their specifications, thus alleviating an even larger burden off an engineer. Another example in this setting is the concept of temporal logic queries, introduced by Chan [14] for CTL, and later developed by Bruns and Godefroid [10] for a wide range of temporal logics. However, unlike our paradigm, temporal logic queries allow only a single placeholder in their template that can be filled with only atomic propositions.

Various other techniques operate in settings where the templates are even more restricted. For example, Li et al. [33] mine LTL specification based on templates from the GR(1)-fragment of LTL (e.g., $\mathsf{G}\,\mathsf{F}?$, $\mathsf{G}(?_1 \rightarrow \mathsf{X}?_2)$, etc.), while Shah et al. [46] mine LTL formulas that are conjunctions of the set of common temporal properties identified by Dwyer et al. [19]. In addition, Kim et al. [29] consider a set of interpretable LTL templates, widely used in the development of software systems, to obtain LTL formulas robust to noise in the input data. In the context of CTL, on the other hand, Wasylkowski and Zeller [51] mine specifications using templates of the form $\mathsf{A}\,\mathsf{F}?$, $\mathsf{A}\,\mathsf{G}(?_1 \rightarrow \mathsf{F}?_2)$, etc. However, all of the approaches above complete the templates only with atomic propositions (and their negations in some cases).

Another setting is where general (and complex) temporal specifications are learned from system executions without any information about the structure of the specification. The most notable work in this setting is by Neider and Gavran [37], who learn LTL formulas from system executions using a SAT solver. Similar to their work is the work by Camacho et al. [13], which proposes a SAT-based learning algorithm for LTL_f formulas via Alternating Finite Automata as an intermediate representation. Raha et al. [40] present a scalable approach for learning formulas in a fragment of LTL_f without the U-operator, while Roy, Fisman, and Neider [42] consider the Property Specification Language (PSL). However, all of these works are "unguided" in that none of them exploit insights about the structure of the specification to aid the learning/mining process.

Finally, it is worth mentioning that LTL sketching can also be seen as a particular case of syntax-guided synthesis (SyGuS), where syntactic constraints on the resulting formulas are expressed in terms of a context-free grammar. An example of a syntax-guided approach is SySLite [2], a CVC4-based tool for learning Past-time LTL over finite executions. However, to the best of our knowledge, we are unaware of any SyGuS engine that can infer specifications in LTL over infinite (i.e., ultimately-periodic) system executions.

2 Preliminaries

We first set up the notation and definitions that are used throughout the paper.

To model trajectories of a system, we exploit the notion of *words* defined over an alphabet consisting of relevant system events. Formally, an *alphabet* Σ is a nonempty, finite set whose elements are called *symbols*. A *finite word* over an alphabet Σ is a sequence $u = a_0 \ldots a_n$ of symbols $a_i \in \Sigma$ for $i \in \{0, \ldots, n\}$. The empty sequence, referred to as *empty word*, is denoted by ε. The length of a finite word u is denoted by $|u|$, where $|\varepsilon| = 0$. Moreover, Σ^* denotes the set of all finite words over Σ, while $\Sigma^+ = \Sigma^* \setminus \varepsilon$ denotes the set of all non-empty words.

An *infinite word* over Σ is an infinite sequence $\alpha = a_0 a_1 \ldots$ of symbols $a_i \in \Sigma$ for $i \in \mathbb{N}$. We denote the i-th symbol of an infinite word α by $\alpha[i]$ and the finite infix of α from position i up to (and excluding) position j with $\alpha[i, j) = a_i a_{i+1} \cdots a_{j-1}$. We use the convention that $\alpha[i, j) = \varepsilon$ for any $i \geq j$. Further, we denote the infinite suffix starting at position $j \in \mathbb{N}$ by $\alpha[j, \infty) = a_j a_{j+1} \cdots$. Given $u \in \Sigma^+$, the infinite repetition of u is the infinite word $u^\omega = uu \cdots \in \Sigma^\omega$. An infinite word α is called *ultimately periodic* if it is of the form $\alpha = uv^\omega$ for a $u \in \Sigma^*$ and $v \in \Sigma^+$. Finally, Σ^ω denotes the set of all infinite words over Σ.

Since our algorithms rely on the Satisfiability (SAT) problem, as a prerequisite, we introduce *Propositional Logic*. Let *Var* be a set of propositional variables, which take Boolean values from $\mathbb{B} = \{0, 1\}$ (0 representing *false* and 1 representing *true*). Formulas in propositional (Boolean) logic, denoted by capital Greek letters, are inductively constructed as follows:

- each $x \in Var$ is a propositional formula; and
- if Ψ and Φ are propositional formulas, so are $\neg\Psi$ and $\Psi \vee \Phi$.

Moreover, as syntactic sugar, we allow the formulas *true*, *false*, $\Psi \wedge \Phi, \Psi \Rightarrow \Phi$, and $\Psi \Leftrightarrow \Phi$, which are defined as usual. A propositional valuation is a mapping $v : Var \to \mathbb{B}$ that assigns Boolean values to propositional variables. The semantics of propositional logic is given by a satisfaction relation $\models$ that is inductively defined as follows: $v \models x$ if and only if $v(x) = 1, v \models \neg\Phi$ if and only if $v \not\models \Phi$, and $v \models \Psi \vee \Phi$ if and only if $v \models \Psi$ or $v \models \Phi$. In the case that $v \models \Phi$, we say that v satisfies Φ and call it a *model* of Φ. A propositional formula Φ is *satisfiable* if there exists a model v of Φ. The *size* of a formula is the number of its subformulas (defined in the usual way). The satisfiability (SAT) problem is the well-known NP-complete problem of deciding whether a given propositional formula is satisfiable. In the recent past, numerous optimized decision procedures have been designed to handle the SAT problem effectively [6].

Linear Temporal Logic is a logic to reason about sequences of relevant statements about a system by using temporal modalities. Formally, given a set $\mathcal{P}$ of propositions that represent relevant statements about a system, an LTL formula, denoted by small Greek letters, is defined inductively as follows:

- each proposition $p \in \mathcal{P}$ is an LTL formula; and
- if ψ and φ are LTL formulas, so are $\neg\psi$, $\psi \vee \varphi$, $\mathsf{X}\,\psi$ ("neXt"), and $\psi\,\mathsf{U}\,\varphi$ ("Until").

As syntactic sugar, we allow standard Boolean formulas such as *true*, *false*, $\psi \wedge \varphi$, and $\psi \to \varphi$ and temporal formulas such as $\mathsf{F}\,\psi := \mathit{true}\,\mathsf{U}\,\psi$ ("Finally") and $\mathsf{G}\,\psi := \neg\,\mathsf{F}\,\neg\psi$ ("Globally"). While we restrict to these formulas, our paradigm extends naturally to all temporal operators (e.g., "Release", "Weak until", etc.).

LTL formulas are interpreted over infinite words $\alpha \in (2^{\mathcal{P}})^\omega$. To define how an LTL formula is interpreted on a word, we use a valuation function

V. This function maps an LTL formula and a word to a Boolean value and is defined inductively as: $V(p, \alpha) = 1$ if and only if $p \in \alpha[0]$, $V(\neg\varphi, \alpha) = 1 - V(\varphi, \alpha)$, $V(\varphi \vee \psi, \alpha) = \max\{V(\varphi, \alpha), V(\psi, \alpha)\}$, $V(\mathsf{X}\,\varphi, \alpha) = V(\varphi, \alpha[1, \infty))$, and $V(\varphi \,\mathsf{U}\, \psi, \alpha) = \max_{i \geq 0}\{\min\{V(\psi, \alpha[i, \infty)), \min_{0 \leq j < i}\{V(\varphi, \alpha[j, \infty))\}\}\}$. We call $V(\varphi, \alpha)$ the *valuation of* φ *on* α and say that α *satisfies* φ if $V(\varphi, \alpha) = 1$.

For a graphical representation of LTL formulas, we rely on *syntax DAGs*. A syntax DAG is a directed acyclic graph (DAG) obtained from the syntax tree of a formula by merging the common subformulas, resulting in a canonical representation. Figure 1 illustrates the syntax DAG of the formula $(p \,\mathsf{U}\, \mathsf{G}\, q) \vee \mathsf{F}\,\mathsf{G}\, q$.

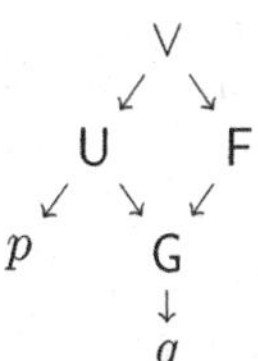

Fig. 1. Syntax DAG of $(p \,\mathsf{U}\, \mathsf{G}\, q) \vee (\mathsf{F}(\mathsf{G}\, q))$

The size of an LTL formula $|\varphi|$ is defined as the number of unique subformulas, which also corresponds to the number of nodes in the syntax DAG of φ. For instance, the size of the formula in Fig. 1 is six.

We denote the set of all LTL operators as $\Lambda = \mathcal{P} \cup \Lambda_U \cup \Lambda_B$. Here, the propositions are the nullary operators, $\Lambda_U = \{\neg, \mathsf{X}, \mathsf{F}, \mathsf{G}\}$ are the unary operators and $\Lambda_B = \{\vee, \wedge, \mathsf{U}\}$ are the binary operators of LTL. Further, let $\mathcal{F}_{\mathrm{LTL}}$ denote the set of all LTL formulas.

3 Problem Formulation

Since the problem of *LTL sketching* relies heavily on LTL sketches, we begin with formalizing them first.

LTL Sketch. An *LTL sketch* is an incomplete LTL formula in which parts that are difficult to formalize can be left out. The left-out parts are represented using placeholders, denoted by ?'s. An example of an LTL sketch can be seen in Fig. 2. We comment on the superscripts on the placeholders in the figure shortly.

Formally, an LTL sketch $\varphi^?$ is simply an LTL formula whose syntax is augmented with placeholders. The placeholders we allow can be of three types: placeholders of arity zero referred to as Type-0 placeholders, that replace missing LTL formulas; placeholders of arity one referred to as Type-1 placeholders, that replace missing unary operators; and placeholders of arity two referred to as Type-2 placeholders, that replace missing binary operators. In Fig. 2 (and throughout the paper), Type-i placeholders are represented using $?^i$.

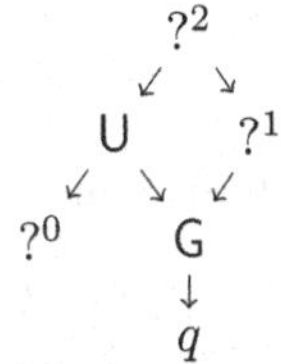

Fig. 2. An LTL sketch

Given (possibly empty) sets Π^0, Π^1 and Π^2 consisting of Type-0, Type-1 and Type-2 placeholders, respectively, we define LTL sketches inductively as follows:

- each element of $\mathcal{P} \cup \Pi^0$ is an LTL sketch; and
- if $\varphi_1^?$ and $\varphi_2^?$ are LTL sketches, $\circ\,\varphi_1^?$ is an LTL sketch for $\circ \in \Lambda_U \cup \Pi^1$ and so is $\varphi_1^? \circ \varphi_2^?$ for $\circ \in \Lambda_B \cup \Pi^2$.

Note that an LTL sketch in which $\Pi^0 = \Pi^1 = \Pi^2 = \emptyset$ is simply an LTL formula. Further, let $\Pi_{\varphi^?} = \Pi^0 \cup \Pi^1 \cup \Pi^2$ denote the set of all placeholders in an sketch $\varphi^?$. For the sketch in Fig. 2, $\Pi_{\varphi^?} = \{?^0, ?^1, ?^2\}$. For brevity, in the rest of the paper, we refer to an LTL sketch as a sketch.

The placeholders are abstract symbols that apriori do not have meaning. To assign meaning to a sketch, we need to substitute all Type-0 placeholders with LTL formulas, all Type-1 placeholders with unary operators, and all Type-2 placeholders with binary operators. We do this using a so-called substitution function (or substitution for short).

Formally, a *substitution* function s maps placeholders and operators present in a sketch to LTL operators and LTL formulas in such a way that: $s(?) \in \mathcal{F}_{\text{LTL}}$ if $? \in \Pi^0$; $s(?) \in \Lambda_U$ if $? \in \Pi^1$; $s(?) \in \Lambda_B$ if $? \in \Pi^2$; and $s(\lambda) = \lambda$ for any LTL operator $\lambda \in \Lambda$. Moreover, a substitution s is said to be *complete* for a sketch $\varphi^?$ if s is defined for every element in $\Lambda \cup \Pi_{\varphi^?}$ in $\varphi^?$. For example, a possible complete substitution s for the sketch $\varphi^?$ in Fig. 2 can be $s(?^0) = p$, $s(?^1) = \mathsf{F}$, $s(?^2) = \vee$, and $s(\lambda) = \lambda$ for $\lambda \in \Lambda$.

A complete substitution s can be applied to a sketch $\varphi^?$ to obtain an LTL formula. To make this precise, we define a function f_s, which is defined recursively on the structure of $\varphi^?$ as: $f_s(\varphi_1^? \; ?^2 \; \varphi_2^?) = f_s(\varphi_1^?) \circ f_s(\varphi_2^?)$, where $\circ = s(?^2)$; $f_s(?^1\varphi^?)) = \circ f_s(\varphi^?)$, where $\circ = s(?^1)$; $f_s(?^0) = s(?^0)$; and $f_s(\varphi^?) = \varphi^?$ if $\Pi_{\varphi^?} = \emptyset$. For the complete substitution s for $\varphi^?$ defined in the last paragraph we get $f_s(\varphi^?) = (p \,\mathsf{U}\, \mathsf{G}\, q) \vee (\mathsf{F}(\mathsf{G}\, q))$.

Input Sample. While there can be many ways to complete a sketch, we direct our search based on two finite, disjoint sets: a set P of positive executions and a set N of negative executions. We consider the executions to be ultimately periodic words, i.e., words of the form uv^ω, where $u \in (2^{\mathcal{P}})^*$ and $v \in (2^{\mathcal{P}})^+$, since they are sufficient to uniquely characterize ω-regular languages [11] (and thus, LTL formulas). We accumulate all the executions in what we call a *sample* $\mathcal{S} = (P, N)$ where $P \cap N = \emptyset$. We define its size to be $|\mathcal{S}| = \sum_{uv^\omega \in P \cup N} |uv|$.

We say that an LTL formula φ is *consistent* with a sample $\mathcal{S} = (P, N)$ if $V(\varphi, uv^\omega) = 1$ for each $uv^\omega \in P$ (i.e., all positive words satisfy φ) and $V(\varphi, uv^\omega) = 0$ for each $uv^\omega \in N$ (i.e., all negative words do not satisfy φ).

The LTL Sketching Problem. We now state the central problem of the paper.

Problem 1 (LTL sketching). Given an LTL sketch $\varphi^?$ and a sample $\mathcal{S} = (P, N)$, find a complete substitution s for $\varphi^?$ such that $f_s(\varphi^?)$ is consistent with $\mathcal{S}$.

Unlike the classical *LTL learning* problem [37], a solution to the *LTL sketching* problem does not always exist. This can be illustrated using the following simple example. Consider the sketch $\mathsf{G}(?^0)$ and a sample consisting of a single positive word $\alpha = \{p\}\{q\}^\omega$ and a single negative word $\beta = \{q\}^\omega$. For this sketch and sample, there does not exist any substitution that leads to an LTL formula consistent with the sample. Towards contradiction, let us assume that there exists an LTL formula $\mathsf{G}(\varphi)$ such that $V(\mathsf{G}(\varphi), \alpha) = 1$ and $V(\mathsf{G}(\varphi), \beta) = 0$.

Based on the semantics of the G-operator, $V(\mathsf{G}(\varphi), \alpha) = V(\mathsf{G}(\varphi), \alpha[1, \infty)) = 1$. On the other hand, $V(\mathsf{G}(\varphi), \beta) = V(\mathsf{G}(\varphi), \alpha[1, \infty)) = 0$ since $\beta = \alpha[1, \infty)$.

Since, for a given LTL sketch and a sample, there might not exist any complete substitution, a naive enumeration-like algorithm to search over all substitutions may not terminate. To show that one can indeed design a terminating sketching algorithm, in the next section, we prove the decidability of *LTL sketching*.

4 Existence of a Complete Sketch

To devise a terminating algorithm for the *LTL sketching* problem, we first introduce the related decision problem, which is the following:

Problem 2 (LTL sketch existence). Given an LTL sketch $\varphi^?$ and a sample $\mathcal{S} = (P, N)$, does there exist a complete substitution s for $\varphi^?$ such that $f_s(\varphi^?)$ is consistent with $\mathcal{S}$.

In what follows, we prove that this problem is indeed decidable and belongs to the complexity class NP. Thereafter, we devise a decision procedure for the problem by exploiting the satisfiability (SAT) problem.

4.1 The Decidability Result

For the decidability result, we begin by introducing some concepts as a preparation. Let us first observe the following key property of ultimately periodic words.

Observation 1. *Let* $uv^\omega \in (2^{\mathcal{P}})^\omega$ *and* φ *be an LTL formula. Then,* $uv^\omega[|u|+i] = uv^\omega[|u|+j]$ *for* $j \equiv i \mod |v|$. *Thus,* $V(\varphi, uv^\omega[|u|+i, \infty)) = V(\varphi, uv^\omega[|u|+j, \infty))$.

This observation indicates that, for a word uv^ω, there exists only a finite number of distinct suffixes of uv^ω, all of which originate in the initial uv portion of uv^ω. Let us then define $\mathit{suf}(uv^\omega) = \{uv^\omega[i, \infty) \mid 0 \leq i < |uv|\}$ as the set of all (possibly) distinct suffixes of a word uv^ω. Moreover, let $\mathit{suf}(\mathcal{S}) = \bigcup_{uv^\omega \in (P \cup N)} \mathit{suf}(uv^\omega)$ to be the set of suffixes of all words in $\mathcal{S}$. Now, Observation 1 also indicates that, to determine the evaluation of an LTL formula φ on an ultimately periodic word uv^ω, it is sufficient to determine its evaluation on the initial $|uv|$ suffixes of uv^ω.

Thus, for a compact representation of the evaluation of φ on uv^ω, we introduce a table notation $T^\varphi_{uv^\omega}$. Mathematically speaking, a table $T^\varphi_{uv^\omega}$ is a $|\varphi| \times |uv|$ matrix that consists of the satisfaction of all the subformulas φ' of φ on the suffixes of uv^ω. We define the entries of this matrix as: $T^\varphi_{uv^\omega}[\varphi', t] = V(\varphi', uv^\omega[t, \infty))$ for all subformulas φ' of φ and $0 \leq t < |uv|$.

Based on the above definition of the table $T^\varphi_{uv^\omega}$, we identify three properties of these tables, which form the main building blocks of the decidability proof (i.e., proof of Theorem 1), as we see later.

The first property, or as we call it, the *Semantic* property, is that various rows of the table are related to each other in a way that reflects the semantics of LTL. To explain this further, we use $T^\varphi_{uv^\omega}[\varphi', \cdot]$ to represent the row of $T^\varphi_{uv^\omega}$ corresponding to the subformula φ'.

We first demonstrate the Semantic property on an example. Consider the formula $\psi = p \vee \mathsf{X}\, q$ and the word $\alpha = \{p,q\}\{p\}\{q\}^\omega$. The table T^ψ_α is illustrated in Fig. 3. From the figure, one can see that the row $T^\psi_\alpha[p \vee \mathsf{X}\, q, \cdot]$ corresponds to the bitwise-OR of the rows $T^\psi_\alpha[p,\cdot]$ and $T^\psi_\alpha[\mathsf{X}\, q, \cdot]$, reflecting the semantics of the $\vee$-operator that combines formulas p and $\mathsf{X}\, q$.

	0	1	2
p	1	1	0
q	1	0	1
$\mathsf{X}\, q$	0	1	1
$p \vee \mathsf{X}\, q$	1	1	1

Fig. 3. Table T^ψ_α for $\psi = p \vee \mathsf{X}\, q$ and $\alpha = \{p,q\}\{p\}\{q\}^\omega$

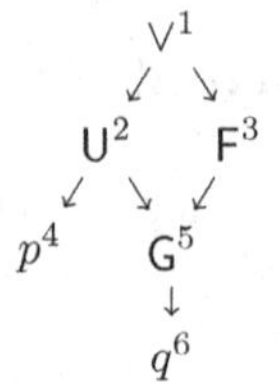

$$
\begin{array}{ccccc}
 & & \vee^1 & & \\
 & \swarrow & & \searrow & \\
 & \mathsf{U}^2 & & & \mathsf{F}^3 \\
\swarrow & & \searrow & \swarrow & \\
p^4 & & \mathsf{G}^5 & & \\
 & & \downarrow & & \\
 & & q^6 & &
\end{array}
$$

Fig. 4. Syntax DAG of $(p \,\mathsf{U}\, \mathsf{G}\, q) \vee \mathsf{F}(\mathsf{G}\, q)$ with identifiers (in superscripts)

To define these semantic relations between the rows, we must uniquely identify the subformula that corresponds to each row. As a result, we assign unique identifiers $i \in \{1,\dots,n\}$ to each node of the syntax DAG of φ enabling us to denote the subformula rooted at Node i using $\varphi[i]$. For assigning identifiers, we follow the strategy that: (i) we assign the root node with 1; and (ii) we assign each node with an identifier smaller than its children (i.e., if it has any). Note that one can analogously assign identifiers to syntax DAGs of sketches. Figure 4 demonstrates identifiers for the formula $(p \,\mathsf{U}\, \mathsf{G}\, q) \vee \mathsf{F}(\mathsf{G}\, q)$. We further define a function $\ell\colon \{1,\dots,n\} \mapsto \Lambda$ that maps the identifiers to the corresponding operators in the syntax DAG.

We now describe the set of equations that formalize the relation between the rows. How a row $T^\varphi_{uv^\omega}[\varphi[i],\cdot]$ relates to the others depends on the operator $\ell(i)$ in the root node of $\varphi[i]$. For instance, if $\ell(i) = p$ for some proposition p, then we have the following relation:

$$T^\varphi_{uv^\omega}[\varphi[i],t] = \begin{cases} 1 \text{ if } p \in uv^\omega[t] \\ 0 \text{ otherwise} \end{cases} \tag{1}$$

If, on the other hand, $\ell(i)$ is a X-operator and Node j is the left child of Node i, we have the following relation:

$$T^\varphi_{uv^\omega}[\varphi[i],t] = \begin{cases} T^\varphi_{uv^\omega}[\varphi[j],t+1] & \text{for } 0 \le t < |uv|-1 \\ T^\varphi_{uv^\omega}[\varphi[j],|u|] & \text{for } t = |uv|-1 \end{cases} \tag{2}$$

The above equation exploits the semantics of the X-operator. Further, it exploits Observation 1 and determines the entry $T^\varphi_{uv^\omega}[\varphi[i],|uv|-1]$ using the evaluation of $\varphi[j]$ at $uv^\omega[|u|,\infty)$, i.e., the start of the periodic part.

If $\ell(i)$ is a $\vee$-operator, and Node j and Node j' are the left and right children of Node i, respectively, then we have the following relation:

$$T^{\varphi}_{uv^\omega}[\varphi[i],t] = T^{\varphi}_{uv^\omega}[\varphi[j],t] \vee T^{\varphi}_{uv^\omega}[\varphi[j'],t] \text{ for } 0 \leq t < |uv| \tag{3}$$

Again, one can see that the above equation follows from the semantics of the $\vee$-operator. For other LTL operators, the relation between rows follows the semantics of the corresponding LTL operator in a similar fashion (see extended version [35] for details). Whenever necessary, we use Observation 1 to determine the semantics of the operator by "looping" around in the period part of uv^ω.

Next, we describe the second property, the *Consistency* property. This property ensures that $T^{\varphi}_{uv^\omega}[\varphi,0] = 1$ if and only if uv^ω satisfies φ. Thus, for an LTL formula φ consistent with $\mathcal{S}$, we have the following relation:

$$T^{\varphi}_{uv^\omega}[\varphi,0] = 1 \text{ for all } uv^\omega \in P, \text{ and } T^{\varphi}_{uv^\omega}[\varphi,0] = 0 \text{ for all } uv^\omega \in N \tag{4}$$

The final property we observe is called the *Suffix* property. This property originates from the fact that LTL, being a future-time logic, has the same evaluation on equal suffixes, i.e., $V(\varphi, u_1v_1^\omega[t,\infty)) = V(\varphi, u_2v_2^\omega[t',\infty))$ for $u_1v_1^\omega[t,\infty) = u_2v_2^\omega[t',\infty)$. Formally, we state the property as follows:

$$T^{\varphi}_{u_1v_1^\omega}[\varphi,t] = T^{\varphi}_{u_2v_2^\omega}[\varphi,t'] \text{ for all } u_1v_1^\omega[t,\infty) = u_2v_2^\omega[t',\infty) \tag{5}$$

This property becomes significant later, especially for constructing LTL formulas to substitute Type-0 placeholders.

With the prerequisites set up, we now proceed to describe an NP algorithm for deciding the *LTL sketch existence* problem. For an easy presentation of the algorithm, we consider the simple (but crucial) case where the only missing information in $\varphi^?$ is a single Type-0 placeholder. While one might assume that non-deterministically guessing a substitution for the placeholder should suffice; it does not. This is because, apriori, the size of the LTL formula required to substitute the Type-0 placeholder is not known.

Thus, in our NP algorithm, instead of guessing substitutions, we guess the entries of the table $T^{\varphi^?}_{uv^\omega}$ for each uv^ω in $\mathcal{S}$. Note that the tables have a finite dimension, precisely $|\varphi^?| \times |uv|$, for each word uv^ω. Thus, the overall process of simply guessing the table entries can be done in time $\mathcal{O}(\mathsf{poly}(|\varphi^?|, |\mathcal{S}|))$.

After guessing the table entries, we must verify that the guessed tables satisfy the three properties, Semantic, Consistency, and Suffix, discussed earlier in this section. It is easy to verify that checking the first two properties for the tables requires time $\mathcal{O}(\mathsf{poly}(|\varphi^?|, |uv|))$ (i.e., polynomial in $|\varphi^?|$ and $|uv|$) for each uv^ω in $\mathcal{S}$. For checking the Suffix property, one must identify the equal suffixes in $\mathit{suf}(\mathcal{S})$. This can be also done in time $\mathcal{O}(\mathsf{poly}(|\mathcal{S}|))$, simply by unrolling the periodic part of the suffixes to a fixed length (see extended version [35] for the details).

This algorithm naturally also extends to multiple Type-0 placeholder. The following lemma now asserts that if the guessed tables satisfy the three properties, then one can find a suitable complete LTL formula. We present a proof sketch of the lemma here (for the full proof, see the extended version [35]).

Lemma 1. *Let $\mathcal{S} = (P, N)$ be a sample and $\varphi^?$ be a sketch with only Type-0 placeholders. Then, the following holds: there exists tables $T^{\varphi^?}_{uv^\omega}$ (i.e., $|\varphi^?| \times |uv|$*

matrices with $\{0,1\}$ *entries) for each* $uv^\omega \in P \cup N$ *that satisfy the Semantic, Consistency, and Suffix properties if and only if there exists a substitution* s *such that LTL formula* $f_s(\varphi^?)$ *is consistent with* $\mathcal{S}$.

Proof sketch: For simplicity, we consider $\varphi^?$ to consist of only one Type-0 placeholder $?^0$. For the forward direction, we explicitly construct an LTL formula for $?^0$, based on tables $T^{\varphi^?}_{uv^\omega}$. Towards this, we first construct a sample $\mathcal{S}' = (P', N')$ as: $P' = \{uv^\omega[t,\infty) \in \mathit{suf}(\mathcal{S}) \mid T^{\varphi^?}_{uv^\omega}[?^0, t] = 1\}$, $N' = \{uv^\omega[t,\infty) \in \mathit{suf}(\mathcal{S}) \mid T^{\varphi^?}_{uv^\omega}[?^0, t] = 0\}$. Since the tables satisfy the Suffix property, $P' \cap N' = \emptyset$. We can now construct a generic LTL formula ψ consistent with $\mathcal{S}'$ using *LTL learning* [37]. For the other direction, we construct $T^{\varphi^?}_{uv^\omega}$ based on $T^{f_s(\varphi^?)}_{uv^\omega}$ as: $T^{\varphi^?}_{uv^\omega}[\varphi^?[i], \cdot] = T^{f_s(\varphi^?)}_{uv^\omega}[f_s(\varphi^?)[i], \cdot]$ for each $uv^\omega \in P \cup N$ and $0 \leq i < |\varphi^?|$. □

With this, we conclude the NP algorithm for the case where $\varphi^?$ only has Type-0 placeholders. We can easily extend the algorithm to the case where $\varphi^?$ consists of Type-1 and Type-2 placeholders. In particular, we first guess the operators to be substituted for the Type-1 and Type-2 placeholders and substitute them. We then obtain a sketch consisting of only Type-0 placeholders. We now apply our algorithm that relies on guessing tables, as described above.

Theorem 1. *The LTL sketch existence problem is in* NP.

We conjecture that the complexity lower-bound of *LTL sketch existence* is NP-hard based on the NP-hardness of *LTL learning* for certain fragments of LTL [22]. However, we have to leave the exact lower-bound of the problem for future work.

4.2 The Decision Procedure

Based on the NP algorithm described above, we now devise a decision procedure to decide the *LTL sketch existence* problem. The decision procedure relies upon reducing the existence of tables $T^{\varphi}_{uv^\omega}$ satisfying the three properties discussed in Sect. 4.1 to a satisfiability (SAT) problem.

This reduction relies on a symbolic encoding of the entries of the tables. To this end, we introduce propositional variables $y^{u,v}_{i,t}$ for each $i \in \{1,\ldots,n\}$, $t \in \{0,\ldots,|uv|-1\}$, and $uv^\omega \in P \cup N$. A variable $y^{u,v}_{i,t}$ encodes the entry $T^{\varphi}_{uv^\omega}[\varphi[i], t]$. Further, we encode the operators to be substituted for the Type-1 and Type-2 placeholders in $\varphi^?$ using the following variables: (i) $x_{i,\lambda}$ for each Node i where $\ell(i)$ is a Type-1 placeholder and each $\lambda \in \Lambda_U$; and (ii) $x_{i,\lambda}$ for each Node i where $\ell(i)$ is a Type-2 placeholder and each $\lambda \in \Lambda_B$.

We now impose constraints on the introduced variables to ensure that the prospective tables satisfy the three properties necessary for inferring a consistent LTL formula. We achieve this by constructing a propositional formula $\Phi^{\varphi^?,\mathcal{S}}$. This formula ensures that variables $y^{u,v}_{i,t}$ encode appropriate tables and using Lemma 1, its satisfiability ensures the existence of a suitable substitution for $\varphi^?$.

Internally, $\Phi^{\varphi^?,\mathcal{S}} := \Phi^{1,2}_? \wedge \Phi_{sem} \wedge \Phi_{con} \wedge \Phi_{suf}$ is a conjunction of four formulas. The first conjunct $\Phi^{1,2}_?$ ensures that the Type-1 and Type-2 placeholders are substituted by appropriate operators. The conjuncts Φ_{sem}, Φ_{con} and Φ_{suf} ensure that the variables $y_{i,t}^{u,v}$ encode entries of tables that satisfy the Semantic property (e.g., Eqs. 1, 2, etc.), the Consistency property (Eq. 4) and the Suffix property (Eq. 5), respectively. In the remainder of the section, we describe the construction of each of the four formulas.

We begin by introducing the constraints required for $\Phi_{?}^{1,2}$. For each Node i labeled with a Type-1 placeholder (i.e., $\ell(i) \in \Pi^1$), we design the following constraint:

$$\Big[\bigvee_{\lambda \in \Lambda_U} x_{i,\lambda}\Big] \wedge \Big[\bigwedge_{\lambda \neq \lambda' \in \Lambda_U} \neg x_{i,\lambda} \vee \neg x_{i,\lambda'}\Big], \tag{6}$$

which ensures that the Type-1 placeholders are substituted with a unique unary operator. For Type-2 placeholders, we have the exact same constraint except that the operators range from the set of binary operators Λ_B. We now construct $\Phi_{?}^{1,2}$ simply by taking a conjunction of all such constraints for the nodes labeled with Type-1 and Type-2 placeholders.

Next, we define Φ_{sem} as the conjunction $\bigwedge_{uv^\omega \in P \cup N} \Phi^{u,v}$, where $\Phi^{u,v}$ denotes a formula that ensures that the variables $y_{i,t}^{u,v}$ satisfy the semantic relations for the word uv^ω. In the formula $\Phi^{u,v}$, for each Node i labeled with the X-operator (i.e., $\ell(i) = \mathsf{X}$) and having Node j as its left child, we have the following constraint:

$$\Big[\bigwedge_{0 \leq t < |uv|-1} \Big[y_{i,t}^{u,v} \leftrightarrow y_{j,t+1}^{u,v}\Big]\Big] \wedge \Big[y_{i,|uv|-1}^{u,v} \leftrightarrow y_{j,|u|}^{u,v}\Big] \tag{7}$$

This constraint ensures that the variables $y_{i,t}^{u,v}$ satisfy Eq. 2 for the word uv^ω. For nodes labeled with other operators, we construct similar constraints based on their corresponding semantic relations. If the nodes are labeled with Type-1 or Type-2 placeholders, we additionally rely on variables $x_{i,\lambda}$ to determine the operator λ to be substituted in Node i. Based on the operator label λ, we devise appropriate semantic constraints. Finally, we construct $\Phi^{u,v}$ as the conjunction of all such semantic constraints.

We construct the following constraint to ensure Eq. 4 is satisfied for the prospective tables:

$$\Phi_{con} := [\bigwedge_{uv^\omega \in P} y_{1,0}^{u,v}] \wedge [\bigwedge_{uv^\omega \in N} \neg y_{1,0}^{u,v}] \tag{8}$$

Finally, for Φ_{suf}, we have the following constraint for each Node i labeled with a Type-0 placeholder (i.e., $\ell(i) \in \Pi^0$):

$$\bigwedge_{u_1 v_1^\omega[t,\infty) = u_2 v_2^\omega[t',\infty) \in suf(\mathcal{S})} \Big[y_{i,t}^{u_1,v_1} \leftrightarrow y_{i,t'}^{u_2,v_2}\Big], \tag{9}$$

which ensures that Eq. 5 is satisfied for the prospective tables.

Overall, we construct a formula $\Phi^{\varphi^?,\mathcal{S}}$ that ranges over $\mathcal{O}(n + nm)$ variables and is of size $\mathcal{O}(n + nm^3 + m^2)$, where $n = |\varphi^?|$ and $m = |\mathcal{S}|$. We conclude this section by stating the correctness of $\Phi^{\varphi^?,\mathcal{S}}$.

Theorem 2. *Let $\varphi^?$ be a sketch, $\mathcal{S}$ a sample, and $\Phi^{\varphi^?,\mathcal{S}}$ the formula as defined above. Then, $\Phi^{\varphi^?,\mathcal{S}}$ is satisfiable if and only if there exists a complete substitution s such that $f_s(\varphi^?)$ is consistent with $\mathcal{S}$.*

Proof sketch: For the forward direction, based on a model v of $\Phi^{\varphi^?,\mathcal{S}}$, we construct a complete substitution s such that $f_s(\varphi^?)$ is consistent with $\mathcal{S}$. First, due to constraints like Constraint 6, we can substitute any Type-1 or Type-2 placeholder, say at Node i, with the unique operator λ for which $v(x_{i,\lambda}) = 1$. Second, we construct substitutions for Type-0 placeholders by relying on tables $T^{\varphi^?}_{uv^\omega}$ that we construct from v as follows: $T^{\varphi^?}_{uv^\omega}[\varphi^?[i], uv^w[t,\infty)] = v(y^{u,v}_{i,t})$ for each $uv^\omega \in P \cup N$ and $i \in \{1, \ldots, n\}$. Due to Constraints 7, 8, and 9, the constructed tables $T^{\varphi^?}_{uv^\omega}$ satisfy the Semantic, Consistency, and Suffix properties. As a result, one can explicitly construct substitutions for Type-0 placeholders based on tables $T^{\varphi^?}_{uv^\omega}$, exploiting Lemma 1. For the other direction, based on the substitution s, we simply construct a unique assignment v that satisfies $\Phi^{\varphi^?,\mathcal{S}}$. □

5 Algorithms to Complete an LTL Sketch

We now describe two novel algorithms for solving the *LTL sketching* problem, which aim at searching for concise LTL formulas from sketches, as alluded to in the introduction. Thus, our first algorithm relies on existing techniques to learn *minimal* LTL formulas. Our second algorithm, alternatively, searches for formulas of increasing size based on constraint solving.

5.1 Algorithm Based on LTL Learning

This algorithm, which we refer to as `Algo1`, builds upon the decision procedure for checking the existence of a complete substitution presented in Sect. 4.2. In particular, it relies on $\Phi^{\varphi^?,\mathcal{S}}$ from the decision procedure to construct substitutions for placeholders of a sketch. While it is straightforward to substitute Type-1 and Type-2 placeholders, the algorithm relies on the classic LTL learning problem to substitute Type-0 placeholders.

The first step of the algorithm is to construct $\Phi^{\varphi^?,\mathcal{S}}$ from the given sample and sketch, as described in Sect. 4.2. If $\Phi^{\varphi^?,\mathcal{S}}$ is unsatisfiable, the algorithm straightaway returns that no solution exists, as established by Theorem 2. If satisfiable, we use a model, say v, of $\Phi^{\varphi^?,\mathcal{S}}$ (obtained from any off-the-shelf SAT solver) to complete $\varphi^?$, the details of which we describe next.

Given a model v of $\Phi^{\varphi^?,\mathcal{S}}$, one can substitute the Type-1 and Type-2 placeholders in $\varphi^?$ as follows: for each Node i where $\ell(i)$ is a Type-1 and Type-2 placeholders, assign $s(\ell(i)) = \lambda$, where λ is the unique operator for which $v(x_{i,\lambda}) = 1$.

The Type-0 placeholders, however, are more challenging to substitute. This is because they represent entire LTL formulas. Towards substituting Type-0 placeholders, for every Node i for which $\ell(i)$ is a Type-0 placeholder (i.e., $\ell(i) \in \Pi^0$), we first construct a sample $\mathcal{S}_i = (P_i, N_i)$ as $P_i = \{uv^\omega[t,\infty) \in \mathit{suf}(\mathcal{S}) \mid v(y^{u,v}_{i,t}) = 1\}$, and $N_i = \{uv^\omega[t,\infty) \in \mathit{suf}(\mathcal{S}) \mid v(y^{u,v}_{i,t}) = 0\}$. We now learn a minimal

LTL formula φ_i consistent with the sample $\mathcal{S}_i$ (using some *LTL learning* algorithm [37,40,41]) for substituting $\ell(i)$. Intuitively, such formulas φ_i ensure that the tables $T^{\varphi}_{uv^\omega}$ of φ obtained by completing $\varphi^?$ satisfy the Semantic, Consistency and Suffix properties described in Sect. 4.1.

We now establish the correctness of the algorithm using the following theorem:

Theorem 3. *Given sketch $\varphi^?$ and sample $\mathcal{S}$,* `Algo1` *completes $\varphi^?$ to output an LTL formula that is consistent with $\mathcal{S}$ if such a formula exists, otherwise returns that no such formula exists.*

Observe that this algorithm constructs new samples for each Type-0 placeholder, each of which have size $\mathcal{O}(|suf(\mathcal{S})|) = \mathcal{O}(|\mathcal{S}|^2)$. This poses a challenge to the scalability of this algorithm. Furthermore, the new samples are not optimized to produce the minimal possible substitutions. Our next algorithm improves both the runtime and the size of the inferred specification.

5.2 Algorithm Based on Incremental SAT Solving

We now describe an algorithm, abbreviated as `Algo2`, that reduces *LTL sketching* to a series of SAT solving problems, inspired by the SAT-based algorithm of Neider and Gavran [37]. Given a sample $\mathcal{S}$ and a number $n \in \mathbb{N}\backslash\{0\}$, we construct a propositional formula $\Psi_n^{\varphi^?,\mathcal{S}}$, of size $\mathsf{poly}(|\varphi^?|, |\mathcal{S}|)$, that has the properties that: (i) $\Psi_n^{\varphi^?,\mathcal{S}}$ is satisfiable if and only if one can complete $\varphi^?$ to obtain an LTL formula of size at most n that is consistent with $\mathcal{S}$; and (ii) using a model v of $\Psi_n^{\varphi^?,\mathcal{S}}$, one can complete $\varphi^?$ to construct a consistent LTL formula of size at most n.

However, in contrast to the algorithms by Neider and Gavran, we first solve $\Phi^{\varphi^?,\mathcal{S}}$ (discussed in Sect. 4.2) to determine the existence of a complete substitution. If and only if $\Phi^{\varphi^?,\mathcal{S}}$ is satisfiable, our algorithm checks the satisfiability of $\Psi_n^{\varphi^?,\mathcal{S}}$ for increasing values of n (starting from $|\varphi^?| - 1$) to search for an LTL formula of size at most n that has the same syntactic structure as $\varphi^?$. We construct the resulting LTL formula by substituting the placeholders in $\varphi^?$ based on a model v of the formula $\Psi_n^{\varphi^?,\mathcal{S}}$, similar to what we do in `Algo1`. The termination of this algorithm is guaranteed by the decision procedure encoded by $\Phi^{\varphi^?,\mathcal{S}}$. The procedure ensures that we search for a solution only if there exists a complete and consistent LTL formula, to begin with. Moreover, the properties of $\Psi_n^{\varphi^?,\mathcal{S}}$ ensure that we find the suitable LTL formula if there exists one.

On a technical level, the formula $\Psi_n^{\varphi^?,\mathcal{S}}$ is obtained by modifying certain parts of the formula $\Phi^{\varphi^?,\mathcal{S}}$. Precisely, $\Psi_n^{\varphi^?,\mathcal{S}} := \Phi_?^{1,2} \wedge \Phi'_{sem} \wedge \Phi_{con} \wedge \Phi^0_{?,n}$ and it introduces two modifications in $\Phi^{\varphi^?,\mathcal{S}}$: a new formula $\Phi^0_{?,n}$ replaces Φ_{suf}; and Φ'_{sem} adds more constraints to Φ_{sem}. The formula $\Phi^0_{?,n}$ encodes the structure of LTL formulas that substitute the Type-0 placeholders. Φ'_{sem}, again as in Φ_{sem}, ensures that the variables $y^{u,v}_{i,t}$ encode table entries $T^{\varphi}_{uv^\omega}[\varphi[i], t]$ that satisfy equations (e.g., Eqs. 1, 2, etc.) describing the Semantic property. We now briefly describe the constraints for the newly introduced formulas.

The formula $\Phi^0_{?,n}$ relies on an additional set of variables: (i) $x_{i,\lambda}$ for each Node i where $\ell(i)$ is a Type-0 placeholder or $i \in \{|\varphi^?|+1,\ldots,n\}$, and each $\lambda \in \Lambda$; and (ii) $l_{i,j}$ and $r_{i,j}$ for each Node i where $\ell(i)$ is a Type-0 placeholder or $i \in \{|\varphi^?|+1,\ldots,n\}$, and each $j \in \{\max(i,|\varphi^?|+1),\ldots,n\}$. The variable $x_{i,\lambda}$, again, encodes that Node i is labeled with λ. The variables $l_{i,j}$ (and $r_{i,j}$) encode that the left child (and the right child) of Node i is Node j. Together the new variables encode the structure of the prospective LTL formulas for Type-0 placeholders.

We now impose constraints, similar to Constraint 6, on the variables $x_{i,\lambda}$ to ensure each node is labeled by a unique LTL operator from Λ. Further, we impose constraints to ensure that each Node i has a unique left and right child. Finally, we construct $\Phi^0_{?,n}$ as the conjunction of all such structural constraints.

The formula Φ'_{sem} also relies on new variables $y^{u,v}_{i,t}$ for each Node i labeled with a Type-0 variables or $i \in \{|\varphi^?|+1,\ldots,n\}$, each $t \in \{0,\ldots,|uv|-1\}$ and each uv^ω in $\mathcal{S}$. Now, we construct semantic constraints such as:

$$\Big[x_{i,\mathsf{X}} \wedge l_{i,j}\Big] \rightarrow \bigwedge_{0\leq t<|uv|-1} \Big[y^{u,v}_{i,t} \leftrightarrow y^{u,v}_{j,t+1}\Big] \wedge \Big[y^{u,v}_{i,|uv|-1} \leftrightarrow y^{u,v}_{j,|u|}\Big], \tag{10}$$

that ensures that the $y^{u,v}_{i,t}$ variables encode entries of table that satisfy Eq. 2. We construct Φ'_{sem} as the conjunction of Φ_{sem} and the new semantic constraints.

We establish the correctness guarantees using the following theorem:

Theorem 4. *Given sketch $\varphi^?$ and sample $\mathcal{S}$,* `Algo2` *completes $\varphi^?$ to output an LTL formula that is consistent with $\mathcal{S}$ if such a formula exists, otherwise returns no such formula exists.*

`Algo2` searches for substitutions of Type-0 placeholders of increasing size and, thus, is able to find small substitutions for the sketch. However, it may not always find a minimal consistent LTL formula because a minimal formula may require the parts of the substitution to share subformulas from the existing sketch.

To demonstrate this, consider the sketch $\mathsf{F}(?_0) \vee \mathsf{F}\,\mathsf{G}\,p$ and the sample consisting of one positive word $\{\}\{p\}^\omega$ and one negative word $\{\}^\omega$. For this input, a possible output by `Algo2` is the formula $\mathsf{F}\,p \vee \mathsf{F}\,\mathsf{G}\,p$, which is of size 5. However, the minimal consistent formula $\mathsf{F}\,\mathsf{G}\,p \vee \mathsf{F}\,\mathsf{G}\,p$ is of size 4. In this example, substituting $?_0$ with $\mathsf{G}\,p$ produces a smaller formula than substituting it with p, since $\mathsf{G}\,p$ allows more sharing of subformulas.

While `Algo2` may not always return a minimal formula, we can provide an upper bound on its size, thus ensuring its conciseness. To compute this bound, we define the syntax size $|\varphi|_s$ of a formula φ to be the number of operators and propositions appearing in φ. Typically, the syntax size $|\varphi|_s$ is larger than the (DAG) size $|\varphi|$, since it counts all the operators and propositions, including the repeating ones. For instance, for $\varphi = \mathsf{F}\,\mathsf{G}\,q \vee \mathsf{F}\,\mathsf{G}\,q$, $|\varphi|_s = 7$, while $|\varphi| = 4$.

We now state the guarantee on the size of the formula returned by `Algo2` in the following theorem. Intuitively, the theorem states the size $|\varphi|$ of the formula that `Algo2` returns is bounded by the syntax size $|\varphi^*|_s$ of the minimal (DAG size) solution φ^*.

Theorem 5. *Given sketch $\varphi^?$ and sample $\mathcal{S}$, let φ^* be a minimal formula that is consistent with $\mathcal{S}$ and can be obtained by completing $\varphi^?$. Then,* `Algo2` *returns a formula φ that is consistent with $\mathcal{S}$, can be obtained by completing $\varphi^?$ and has size $|\varphi| \leq |\varphi^*|_s$.*

Proof sketch: Towards contradiction, we assume that the LTL formula φ returned by `Algo2` has size $|\varphi| > |\varphi^*|_s$. Now, based on the property of $\Psi_n^{\varphi^?,\mathcal{S}}$ (see first paragraph of Sect. 5.2), $\Psi_n^{\varphi^?,\mathcal{S}}$ is satisfiable for $n = |\varphi^*|_s$. This is because there exists a consistent LTL formula of size at most $n = |\varphi^*|_s$, φ^* itself. Thus, `Algo2`, due to its incremental search, should have returned φ^*, contradicting our assumption. □

6 Experimental Evaluation

In this section, we design experiments to answer the following research questions:

RQ1: Which of the two presented sketching algorithms is more effective?
RQ2: How do our algorithms compare against other specification mining tools for LTL?

To answer these questions, we have implemented a prototype of our algorithms in `Python3`, named `LTL-Sketcher`[1]. In `LTL-Sketcher`, we additionally implement two heuristics to improve the runtime of our algorithms, both of which are directed toward optimizing the SAT encoding used in the algorithms. We briefly mention the idea behind the heuristics.

The first heuristic is inspired by the SAT encoding used in Bounded Model Checking [8]. The encoding exploits a succinct description of the semantics of LTL using expansion laws [5]. Exemplarily, the expansion law for the U-operator is $\varphi \mathbin{\mathsf{U}} \psi = \psi \vee (\varphi \wedge \mathsf{X}(\varphi \mathbin{\mathsf{U}} \psi))$, which relies on checking satisfaction in the next position using X-operator. Using the LTL expansion laws reduces the number of variables required in Φ_{sem}. In the second heuristic, we create variables $y_{i,t}^{u,v}$ only for the distinct suffixes uv^ω in $\mathcal{S}$. This is sufficient because LTL formulas have the same evaluation on equal suffixes (which is also the basis for Eq. 5). Hence, if two words share a suffix, we can create the variables encoding the semantics only once, reducing the total number of variables. Also, in this heuristic, the constraint Φ_{suf} imposing the Suffix property becomes unnecessary. We refer interested readers to the extended version [35] for the details of the heuristics.

Benchmarks. For evaluating our algorithms, following the literature in *LTL learning*, we rely on benchmarks generated synthetically using common LTL formulas used in practice [19]. We choose the same nine formulas also chosen by

[1] The code can be found in https://github.com/rajarshi008/LTLSketcher.

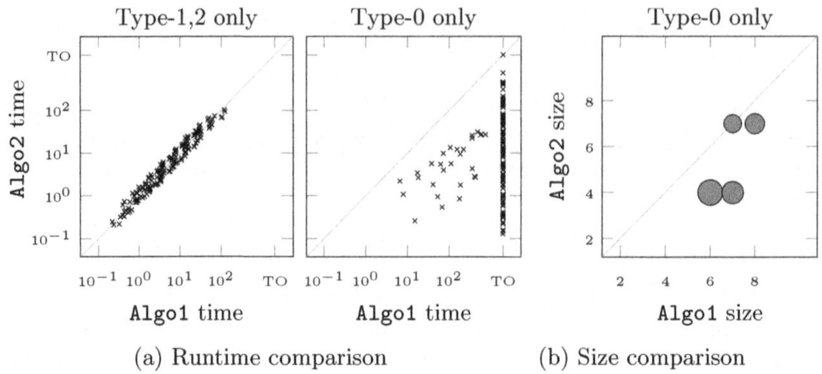

(a) Runtime comparison (b) Size comparison

Fig. 5. Comparison of `Algo1` and `Algo2` with respect to runtime (in seconds) and the size of inferred formulas. The points below the diagonal are where `Algo2` performs better. In Fig. 5a, "TO" denotes timeouts. In Fig. 5b, the size of a bubble is proportional to the number of cases.

Neider and Gavran [37] for generating their benchmarks. We, however, deviate from their method of generating benchmarks. This is because, as observed by Raha et al. [40], their method, being fairly naive, consumes more time and often does not generate adequately different trajectories from a chosen LTL formula. We, in contrast, design a novel method of generating samples based on random sampling of words from Büchi automata [7] constructed from the LTL formulas (using `Spot` [18]). Overall, we generate 18 samples for each of the nine formulas (i.e., 162 samples in total), with the number of examples varying from 20 to 800 and the length of words varying from 4 to 16. We conduct all the experiments on a single core of an Intel Xeon E7-8857 CPU (at 3 GHz) using upto 6 GB of RAM.

RQ1: Comparison of Sketching Algorithms. To answer RQ1, we compare `Algo1` (from Sect. 5.1) and `Algo2` (from Sect. 5.2) based on their running times and the size of formula inferred. For this comparison, as sketches, we remove parts (upto 50% in size) of each formula to construct two kinds of sketches: one with only Type-1 or Type-2 placeholders and one with only Type-0 placeholders (see extended version [35] for the entire list). Exemplarily, for $\mathsf{G}(q \rightarrow \mathsf{G}(\neg p))$, we construct two sketches: $?^1_1(q \rightarrow ?^1_2(\neg p))$ and $\mathsf{G}(q \rightarrow ?^0)$; for $\mathsf{F}(q) \rightarrow (p \,\mathsf{U}\, q)$, we construct two sketches $?^0 \rightarrow (p \,\mathsf{U}\, q)$ and $?^1(q) \rightarrow (p ?^2 q)$, etc. We now run the algorithms on the 18 samples and two sketches generated from each of the nine formulas with a timeout of 900 secs.

We depict the runtime comparisons in Fig. 5a. We observe that while both the algorithms have comparable runtime on sketches with only Type-1 or Type-2 placeholders, `Algo1` performs significantly worse on sketches with only Type-0 placeholders with 134 timeouts. We also depict the comparison of formula size in Fig. 5b. We notice that `Algo2` returns smaller formulas than `Algo1` in many cases. The reason `Algo1` performs slow and returns large formulas is that it solves *LTL learning* on potentially large intermediate samples for sketches with Type-0 placeholders. Thus, we answer RQ1 in favor of `Algo2`.

RQ2: Comparison Against LTL Mining Tools. To address RQ2, we compared `LTL-Sketcher` against two prominent approaches for mining specifications in LTL. The first approach completes user-defined templates with (Boolean combinations of) atomic propositions. For this approach, we select the popular LTL miner `Texada` [31]. The second approach learns LTL formulas of minimal size without syntactic constraints. For this approach, we choose `Flie` [37] as a prototypical example of this class of algorithms.

The setting of `Texada` differs from ours in that it permits positive examples only, and these examples have to be finite words. Thus, in order to have a fair comparison, we make minor modifications to our SAT encoding (specifically to the X-operator) to handle finite words. Furthermore, our tool does not require one to provide negative examples and, hence, can immediately be applied.

Table 1. Number of successes for completing sketches

Sketch	Tool	$\mathsf{F}(q) \rightarrow (\neg p \,\mathsf{U}\, q)$	$\mathsf{F}(q) \rightarrow (p \,\mathsf{U}\, q)$	$\mathsf{G}(q \rightarrow \mathsf{G}(\neg p))$
full	`LTL-Sketcher`	10	10	10
	`Texada`	6	9	10
medium	`LTL-Sketcher`	10	10	10
	`Texada`	0	1	10
small	`LTL-Sketcher`	10	10	10
	`Texada`	0	1	0

To compare `Texada` and `LTL-Sketcher`, we considered six of the nine formulas used in RQ1, dropping the smallest three. For each formula, we created ten samples with only positive, finite words by truncating ultimately periodic and ensuring consistency with the formula. Also, we created three sketches for each formula, retaining different amounts of information: in a *full sketch*, we only replaced each atomic proposition with a different Type-0 placeholder; in a *medium sketch*, we replaced a larger subformula containing at least one temporal operator; and in a *small sketch*, we replaced the formula with a single Type-0 placeholder. As an example, from formula $\mathsf{F}(q) \rightarrow (\neg p \,\mathsf{U}\, q)$, we constructed the full sketch $\mathsf{F}(?^0_1) \rightarrow (\neg ?^0_2 \,\mathsf{U}\, ?^0_3)$, the medium sketch $\mathsf{F}(?^0_1) \rightarrow ?^0_2$ and the small sketch $?^0_1$.

We ran `Texada` and `LTL-Sketcher` on each of these sketches and all corresponding samples and counted the cases in which the tools could provide a substitution. A selection of the results on three prototypical formulas is shown in Table 1. The remaining results follow the same trend and can be found in the extended version [35]. We notice that `Texada` found substitutions for the

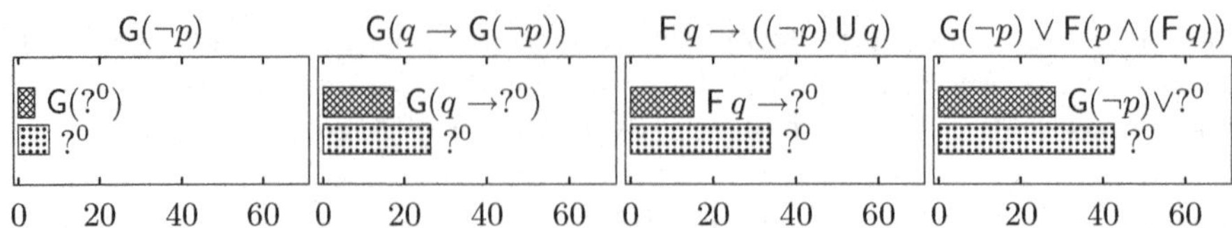

Fig. 6. The average sample sizes required to recover the original formula (mentioned in the chart titles). In each chart, the trivial sketch $?^0$ indicates the run for `Flie`, while the other one indicates the run for `LTL-Sketcher`.

full sketches in most cases. However, when we removed more structural information from the specifications (i.e., medium and small sketches), `Texada` was rarely able to complete a sketch. By contrast, `LTL-Sketcher` provided a substitution in every benchmark. The reason is that `Texada`'s strategy of exclusively searching for atomic propositions is only feasible if the user can provide a detailed template where all temporal operators are specified. Our tool, in contrast, alleviates the burden of writing complex temporal operators and, thus, is more flexible.

To compare `Flie` and `LTL-Sketcher`, we estimated how many examples are required to infer the desired specification. For this experiment, we used the same set of nine LTL formulas and sketches with varying amounts of missing information, some of which can be seen in Fig. 6. To calculate the number of examples required, we designed a counterexample-guided strategy to compute a *minimal* sample required for both tools to obtain the desired formula from a sketch of it. In this strategy, if a tool does not return the desired formula with the current sample, we add one of the shortest counterexamples to the sample that helps eliminate the current solution formula. We continue this process and end up with a minimal sample of both tools for each sketch.

Figure 6 presents the average size of minimal samples (over ten runs) required to recover the desired formulas from their sketches. While we present the result for some formulas here, the remaining results follow the same pattern (see extended version [35]). We observed that `Flie` required more examples than `LTL-Sketcher` to single out the correct specifications in all the cases. This asserted the fact that providing high-level insights as a sketch reduces the number of examples required to derive the desired specification. Thus, to answer RQ2, the ability to handle sketches provides `LTL-Sketcher` an edge over existing LTL mining tools.

7 Conclusion and Future Work

In this work, we introduce LTL sketching—a novel way of writing formal specifications in LTL. The key idea is that a user can write a partial specification, i.e., a sketch, which is then completed based on given examples of desired and undesired system behavior. We have shown that the sketching problem is in NP, presented two SAT-based sketching algorithms and some heuristics to improve their performance. Our experimental evaluation has shown that our algorithms can effectively complete sketches consisting of different types of missing information. Further, the ability to handle sketches provides our algorithms an edge over existing LTL mining approaches.

A natural direction for future work is to lift the idea of specification sketching to other specification languages, such as Signal Temporal Logic (STL) [36], the Property Specification Language (PSL) [20], or even visual specifications, such as UML (high-level) message sequence charts [26]. Moreover, we intend to extend the notion of sketching beyond the use of examples (e.g., by allowing the engineer to constrain placeholders using simple logical formulas or regular expressions).

Acknowledgements. This work has been financially supported by Deutsche Forschungsgemeinschaft, DFG Project numbers 434592664 and 459419731, and the Research Center Trustworthy Data Science and Security (https://rc-trust.ai), one of the Research Alliance centers within the UA Ruhr (https://uaruhr.de).

References

1. Ammons, G., Bodík, R., Larus, J.R.: Mining specifications. In: Launchbury, J., Mitchell, J.C. (eds.) Conference Record of POPL 2002: The 29th SIGPLAN-SIGACT Symposium on Principles of Programming Languages, Portland, OR, USA, 16–18 January 2002, pp. 4–16. ACM (2002). https://doi.org/10.1145/503272.503275
2. Arif, M.F., Larraz, D., Echeverria, M., Reynolds, A., Chowdhury, O., Tinelli, C.: SYSLITE: syntax-guided synthesis of PLTL formulas from finite traces. In: FMCAD, pp. 93–103. IEEE (2020)
3. Bacherini, S., Fantechi, A., Tempestini, M., Zingoni, N.: A story about formal methods adoption by a railway signaling manufacturer. In: Misra, J., Nipkow, T., Sekerinski, E. (eds.) FM 2006. LNCS, vol. 4085, pp. 179–189. Springer, Heidelberg (2006). https://doi.org/10.1007/11813040_13
4. Badeau, F., Amelot, A.: Using B as a high level programming language in an industrial project: roissy VAL. In: Treharne, H., King, S., Henson, M., Schneider, S. (eds.) ZB 2005. LNCS, vol. 3455, pp. 334–354. Springer, Heidelberg (2005). https://doi.org/10.1007/11415787_20
5. Baier, C., Katoen, J.P.: Principles of Model Checking. MIT Press, Cambridge (2008)
6. Balyo, T., Heule, M.J.H., Järvisalo, M.: SAT competition 2016: recent developments. In: 31st AAAI Conference on Artificial Intelligence, AAAI '17, pp. 5061–5063. AAAI Press (2017)
7. Bernardi, O., Giménez, O.: A linear algorithm for the random sampling from regular languages. Algorithmica **62**(1–2), 130–145 (2012)
8. Biere, A., Cimatti, A., Clarke, E.M., Strichman, O., Zhu, Y.: Bounded model checking. Advances in Computers, vol. 58, pp. 117–148. Elsevier (2003). https://doi.org/10.1016/S0065-2458(03)58003-2, https://www.sciencedirect.com/science/article/pii/S0065245803580032
9. Bowen, J.P.: Gerard o'regan: concise guide to formal methods: theory, fundamentals and industry applications. Form. Aspects Comput. **32**(1), 147–148 (2020)
10. Bruns, G., Godefroid, P.: Temporal logic query checking. In: 16th Annual IEEE Symposium on Logic in Computer Science, Boston, Massachusetts, USA, 16–19

June 2001, Proceedings, pp. 409–417. IEEE Computer Society (2001). https://doi.org/10.1109/LICS.2001.932516

11. Calbrix, H., Nivat, M., Podelski, A.: Ultimately periodic words of rational ω-languages. In: Brookes, S., Main, M., Melton, A., Mislove, M., Schmidt, D. (eds.) MFPS 1993. LNCS, vol. 802, pp. 554–566. Springer, Heidelberg (1994). https://doi.org/10.1007/3-540-58027-1_27
12. Camacho, A., Icarte, R.T., Klassen, T.Q., Valenzano, R.A., McIlraith, S.A.: LTL and beyond: formal languages for reward function specification in reinforcement learning. In: Kraus, S. (ed.) Proceedings of the Twenty-Eighth International Joint Conference on Artificial Intelligence, IJCAI 2019, Macao, China, 10–16 August 2019, pp. 6065–6073. ijcai.org (2019). https://doi.org/10.24963/ijcai.2019/840
13. Camacho, A., McIlraith, S.A.: Learning interpretable models expressed in linear temporal logic. In: ICAPS, pp. 621–630. AAAI Press (2019)
14. Chan, W.: Temporal-logic queries. In: Emerson, E.A., Sistla, A.P. (eds.) CAV 2000. LNCS, vol. 1855, pp. 450–463. Springer, Heidelberg (2000). https://doi.org/10.1007/10722167_34
15. Clarke, E.M., Emerson, E.A.: Design and synthesis of synchronization skeletons using branching time temporal logic. In: Kozen, D. (ed.) Logic of Programs 1981. LNCS, vol. 131, pp. 52–71. Springer, Heidelberg (1982). https://doi.org/10.1007/BFb0025774
16. Cofer, D., Miller, S.: DO-333 certification case studies. In: Badger, J.M., Rozier, K.Y. (eds.) NFM 2014. LNCS, vol. 8430, pp. 1–15. Springer, Cham (2014). https://doi.org/10.1007/978-3-319-06200-6_1
17. Courtois, P.J., Seidel, F., Gallardo, F., Bowell, M.: Licensing of safety critical software for nuclear reactors. Common position of international nuclear regulators and authorised technical support organisations, December 2015. https://doi.org/10.13140/RG.2.1.2789.8968
18. Duret-Lutz, A., Lewkowicz, A., Fauchille, A., Michaud, T., Renault, É., Xu, L.: Spot 2.0 — a framework for LTL and ω-automata manipulation. In: Artho, C., Legay, A., Peled, D. (eds.) ATVA 2016. LNCS, vol. 9938, pp. 122–129. Springer, Cham (2016). https://doi.org/10.1007/978-3-319-46520-3_8
19. Dwyer, M.B., Avrunin, G.S., Corbett, J.C.: Property specification patterns for finite-state verification. In: FMSP, pp. 7–15. ACM (1998)
20. Eisner, C., Fisman, D.: A Practical Introduction to PSL. Series on Integrated Circuits and Systems, Springer, New York (2006). https://doi.org/10.1007/978-0-387-36123-9
21. Fecko, M.A., et al.: A success story of formal description techniques: Estelle specification and test generation for MIL-STD 188–220. Comput. Commun. **23**(12), 1196–1213 (2000)
22. Fijalkow, N., Lagarde, G.: The complexity of learning linear temporal formulas from examples. In: ICGI. Proceedings of Machine Learning Research, vol. 153, pp. 237–250. PMLR (2021)
23. Fix, L.: Fifteen years of formal property verification in intel. In: Grumberg, O., Veith, H. (eds.) 25 Years of Model Checking. LNCS, vol. 5000, pp. 139–144. Springer, Heidelberg (2008). https://doi.org/10.1007/978-3-540-69850-0_8
24. Gario, M., Cimatti, A., Mattarei, C., Tonetta, S., Rozier, K.Y.: Model checking at scale: automated air traffic control design space exploration. In: Chaudhuri, S., Farzan, A. (eds.) CAV 2016. LNCS, vol. 9780, pp. 3–22. Springer, Cham (2016). https://doi.org/10.1007/978-3-319-41540-6_1

25. Greenman, B., Saarinen, S., Nelson, T., Krishnamurthi, S.: Little tricky logic: misconceptions in the understanding of LTL. Art Sci. Eng. Program. **7**(2), 7:1–7:37 (2023)
26. Harel, D., Thiagarajan, P.S.: Message sequence charts. In: UML for Real - Design of Embedded Real-Time Systems, pp. 77–105. Kluwer (2003). https://doi.org/10.1007/0-306-48738-1_4
27. Holzmann, G.J.: The model checker SPIN. IEEE Trans. Softw. Eng. **23**(5), 279–295 (1997)
28. Holzmann, G.J.: The logic of bugs. In: SIGSOFT FSE, pp. 81–87. ACM (2002)
29. Kim, J., Muise, C., Shah, A., Agarwal, S., Shah, J.: Bayesian inference of linear temporal logic specifications for contrastive explanations. In: IJCAI, pp. 5591–5598. ijcai.org (2019)
30. Klein, G., et al.: SeL4: formal verification of an operating-system kernel. Commun. ACM **53**(6), 107–115 (2010)
31. Lemieux, C., Beschastnikh, I.: Investigating program behavior using the texada LTL specifications miner. In: ASE, pp. 870–875. IEEE Computer Society (2015)
32. Lemieux, C., Park, D., Beschastnikh, I.: General LTL specification mining (T). In: ASE, pp. 81–92. IEEE Computer Society (2015)
33. Li, W., Dworkin, L., Seshia, S.A.: Mining assumptions for synthesis. In: MEMOCODE, pp. 43–50. IEEE (2011)
34. Lowe, G.: Breaking and fixing the needham-schroeder public-key protocol using FDR. Softw. Concepts Tools **17**(3), 93–102 (1996)
35. Lutz, S., Neider, D., Roy, R.: Specification sketching for linear temporal logic. arXiv preprint arXiv:2206.06722 (2022)
36. Maler, O., Nickovic, D.: Monitoring temporal properties of continuous signals. In: Lakhnech, Y., Yovine, S. (eds.) FORMATS/FTRTFT -2004. LNCS, vol. 3253, pp. 152–166. Springer, Heidelberg (2004). https://doi.org/10.1007/978-3-540-30206-3_12
37. Neider, D., Gavran, I.: Learning linear temporal properties. In: FMCAD, pp. 1–10. IEEE (2018)
38. Pakonen, A., Pang, C., Buzhinsky, I., Vyatkin, V.: User-friendly formal specification languages - conclusions drawn from industrial experience on model checking. In: ETFA, pp. 1–8. IEEE (2016)
39. Pnueli, A.: The temporal logic of programs. In: FOCS, pp. 46–57. IEEE Computer Society (1977)
40. Raha, R., Roy, R., Fijalkow, N., Neider, D.: Scalable anytime algorithms for learning fragments of linear temporal logic. In: TACAS 2022. LNCS, vol. 13243, pp. 263–280. Springer, Cham (2022). https://doi.org/10.1007/978-3-030-99524-9_14
41. Riener, H.: Exact synthesis of LTL properties from traces. In: FDL, pp. 1–6. IEEE (2019)
42. Roy, R., Fisman, D., Neider, D.: Learning interpretable models in the property specification language. In: IJCAI, pp. 2213–2219. ijcai.org (2020)
43. Roy, R., Gaglione, J.R., Baharisangari, N., Neider, D., Xu, Z., Topcu, U.: Learning interpretable temporal properties from positive examples only. In: Proceedings of the AAAI Conference on Artificial Intelligence, vol. 37, no. 5, pp. 6507–6515, June 2023. https://doi.org/10.1609/aaai.v37i5.25800, https://ojs.aaai.org/index.php/AAAI/article/view/25800
44. Rozier, K.Y.: Specification: the biggest bottleneck in formal methods and autonomy. In: Blazy, S., Chechik, M. (eds.) VSTTE 2016. LNCS, vol. 9971, pp. 8–26. Springer, Cham (2016). https://doi.org/10.1007/978-3-319-48869-1_2

45. Schlör, R., Josko, B., Werth, D.: Using a visual formalism for design verification in industrial environments. In: Margaria, T., Steffen, B., Rückert, R., Posegga, J. (eds.) Services and Visualization Towards User-Friendly Design. LNCS, vol. 1385, pp. 208–221. Springer, Heidelberg (1998). https://doi.org/10.1007/BFb0053507
46. Shah, A., Kamath, P., Shah, J.A., Li, S.: Bayesian inference of temporal task specifications from demonstrations. In: NeurIPS, pp. 3808–3817 (2018)
47. Solar-Lezama, A.: Program sketching. Int. J. Softw. Tools Technol. Transf. **15**(5–6), 475–495 (2013)
48. Solar-Lezama, A., Rabbah, R.M., Bodík, R., Ebcioglu, K.: Programming by sketching for bit-streaming programs. In: PLDI, pp. 281–294. ACM (2005)
49. Vardi, M.Y.: Branching vs. linear time: final showdown. In: Margaria, T., Yi, W. (eds.) TACAS 2001. LNCS, vol. 2031, pp. 1–22. Springer, Heidelberg (2001). https://doi.org/10.1007/3-540-45319-9_1
50. Verhulst, E., de Jong, G.: OpenComRTOS: an ultra-small network centric embedded RTOS designed using formal modeling. In: Gaudin, E., Najm, E., Reed, R. (eds.) SDL 2007. LNCS, vol. 4745, pp. 258–271. Springer, Heidelberg (2007). https://doi.org/10.1007/978-3-540-74984-4_16
51. Wasylkowski, A., Zeller, A.: Mining temporal specifications from object usage. Autom. Softw. Eng. **18**(3–4), 263–292 (2011)

Data Structures and Heuristics

On the Difficulty of Intersection Checking with Polynomial Zonotopes

Yushen Huang(✉), Ertai Luo, Stanley Bak, and Yifan Sun

Stony Brook University, Stony Brook, NY 11790, USA
{yushen.huang,ertai.luo,stanley.bak,yifan.sun}@stonybrook.edu

Abstract. Polynomial zonotopes, a non-convex set representation, have a wide range of applications from real-time motion planning and control in robotics, to reachability analysis of nonlinear systems and safety shielding in reinforcement learning. Despite this widespread use, a frequently overlooked difficulty associated with polynomial zonotopes is intersection checking. Determining whether the reachable set, represented as a polynomial zonotope, intersects an unsafe set is not straightforward. In fact, we show that this fundamental operation is NP-hard, even for a simple class of polynomial zonotopes.

The standard method for intersection checking with polynomial zonotopes is a two-part algorithm that overapproximates a polynomial zonotope with a regular zonotope and then, if the overapproximation error is deemed too large, splits the set and recursively tries again. Beyond the possible need for a large number of splits, we identify two sources of concern related to this algorithm: (1) overapproximating a polynomial zonotope with a zonotope has unbounded error, and (2) after splitting a polynomial zonotope, the overapproximation error can actually increase. Taken together, this implies there may be a possibility that the algorithm does not always terminate. We perform a rigorous analysis of the method and detail sufficient conditions for the union of overapproximations to provably converge to the original polynomial zonotope.

1 Introduction

Set-based analysis is the foundation of many formal analysis approaches including abstract interpretation methods for software [8] and reachability analysis methods for cyber-physical and hybrid systems [3]. The usefulness of a set representation is determined by what operations can be efficiently supported.

For safety verification, one fundamental operation is intersection checking; does the set of possible states intersect the set of unsafe states? In this context, one common way to represent sets is using zonotopes [10,12], which are affine transformations of a unit box. Zonotopes offer a compact representation, efficiently encode linear transformations, and support linear-time optimization. However, zonotopes cannot represent non-convex sets and so are less useful when a nonlinear operation is applied to a set. In contrast, polynomial zonotopes [1] are closed under polynomial maps and can therefore exactly represent more complex

É. André and J. Sun (Eds.): ATVA 2023, LNCS 14216, pp. 51–71, 2023.
https://doi.org/10.1007/978-3-031-45332-8_3

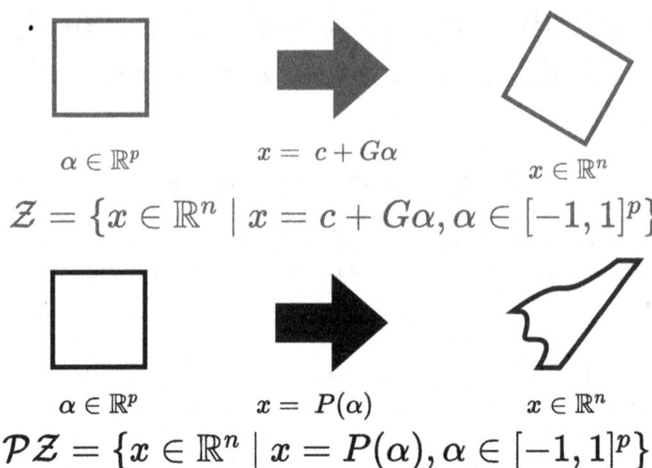

Fig. 1. A zonotope (blue, top) is a convex n-dimensional set represented as an affine transformation of a unit box in p dimensions. A polynomial zonotope (black, bottom) is a possibly non-convex n-dimensional set represented as a polynomial transformation of a unit box in p dimensions ($P(\cdot)$ is a polynomial). (Color figure online)

sets. Polynomial zonotopes can be considered as polynomial transformations of a unit box. The two representations are illustrated in Fig. 1.

One drawback of polynomial zonotopes is that intersection checking is significantly more complex than zonotopes. Although it is known that the characterization of solutions of general nonlinear equations with box-constrained domains is NP-hard [14, Sec. 4.1], is the problem easier for polynomial zonotopes, since the transformation is always a polynomial? Would the problem become easier if we only check for halfspace intersections or if we only consider simple polynomials? In this work we prove that intersection checking is NP-hard for polynomial zonotopes, regardless of such attempts at simplification.

Setting aside the worst-case time complexity, the existing algorithm proposed to check for intersections, as well as perform plotting, is based on a combination of overapproximation using zonotopes and refinement using splitting [4,15]. Is this algorithm guaranteed to converge to the true set, even given infinite runtime? We identify two sources of concern: (i) the overapproximation of a polynomial zonotope with a zonotope can have unbounded error, and (ii) the error of polynomial zonotope overapproximation can actually *increase* after splitting is performed. This work analyses the proposed algorithm in detail, and derives fairness conditions that are sufficient to prove the algorithm provably converges.

Practical Example. While the contributions of this work are theoretical in nature, they are grounded in practical issues the authors observed while working with polynomial zonotopes. Figure 2 shows a plot of a 2-d projection of a polynomial zonotope, obtained when computing the reachable set of an uncertain time-varying system [24] using the overapproximate and split algorithm

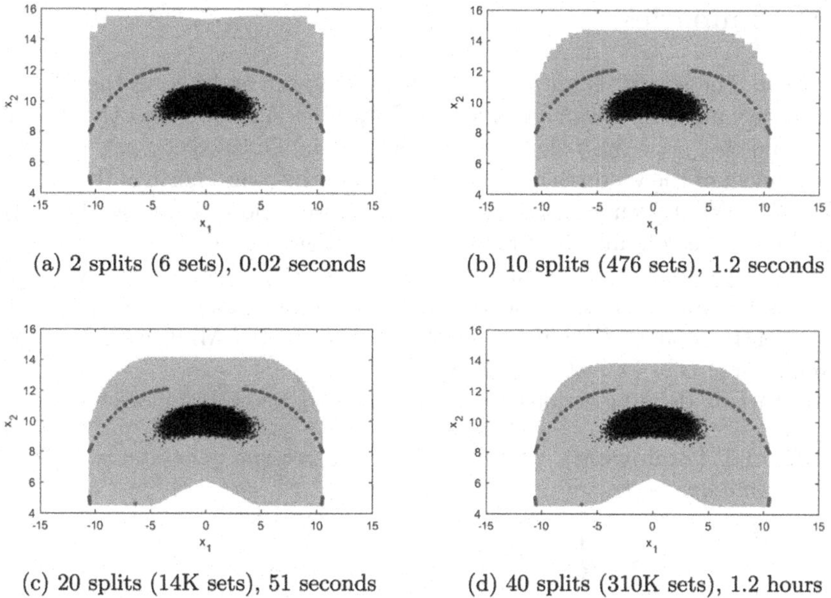

(a) 2 splits (6 sets), 0.02 seconds

(b) 10 splits (476 sets), 1.2 seconds

(c) 20 splits (14K sets), 51 seconds

(d) 40 splits (310K sets), 1.2 hours

Fig. 2. Plotting a polynomial zonotope using the overapproximate and split algorithm (light gray) does not converge to the true set even after an hour of computation time. The red dots are the true boundary points and the black dots are random samples. (Color figure online)

from the CORA tool [2]. Splitting seems to have diminishing returns, as the light gray overapproximation of the polynomial zonotope remains far from the true boundary (red points), even when the algorithm runs for over an hour.

Contributions. The key contributions of this paper are:

- We prove that polynomial zonotope intersection checking is NP-hard, even for simple halfspace constraints and bilinear polynomials (Sect. 3).
- We review the standard intersection-checking algorithm, and demonstrate two sources of concern, that overapproximation error is unbounded and that overapproximation error can increase after splitting (Sect. 4).
- We provide conditions where the polynomial zonotope refinement algorithm provably converges to the original polynomial zonotope (Sect. 5).

First, we review preliminaries and formally define zonotopes and polynomial zonotopes in Sect. 2.

2 Preliminaries

Notation. The set $\mathbb{R}^n$ is an n-dimensional real space and $\mathbb{Z}_{\geq 0}$ is the set of all non-negative integers. Given a matrix $A \in \mathbb{R}^{n \times m}$, let $A(i, \cdot)$ be the i-th row of the matrix and $A(\cdot, j)$ be the j-th column of the matrix. Given vector $\mathbf{x} \in \mathbb{R}^n$, the i-th component of the vector is referred to as x_i and the (one-) norm of the vector is $\|\mathbf{x}\| = \sum_{i=1}^{n} |x_i|$. Given a set $S \subseteq \{1, 2, \cdots, m\}$, we denote $A(\cdot, S)$ as the matrix consisting of the column index belonging to S. For example if $S = \{1, 3\}$, then $A(\cdot, S) = \big[A(\cdot, 1)\ A(\cdot, 3)\big]$. Similarly, given a set $S \subseteq \{1, 2, \cdots, n\}$, we denote $A(S, \cdot)$ as the matrix that consists of the row index belong to S. We call the $n \times n$ identity matrix I_n. Given two sets A and B, the Minkowsiki sum of is written as $A \oplus B = \big\{\mathbf{z} \bigm| \mathbf{z} = \mathbf{x} + \mathbf{y},\ \mathbf{x} \in A,\ \mathbf{y} \in B\big\}$.

We start by defining zonotopes and polynomial zonotopes more formally.

Definition 1 (Zonotope). *Given a center* $\mathbf{c} \in \mathbb{R}^n$ *and generator matrix* $G \in \mathbb{R}^{n \times p}$, *a zonotope is the set*

$$\mathcal{Z} = \left\{ \mathbf{c} + \sum_{j=1}^{p} \alpha_j G(\cdot, i) \;\middle|\; \alpha_j \in [-1, 1] \right\}.$$

We refer to a zonotope using the shorthand notation $\mathcal{Z} = \langle \mathbf{c}, G \rangle_{\mathcal{Z}}$. Note in the illustration in Fig. 1, α was a p-dimensional point, whereas in the definition we refer to each element as a scalar α_j, which we call a *factor.*

As mentioned in the introduction, a polynomial zonotope is a polynomial transformation of a p-dimensional unit hypercube. Following the sparse formulation of polynomial zonotopes [17], we explicitly split the factors from the p-dimensional point into two sets $\alpha \in \mathbb{R}^r$ and $\beta \in \mathbb{R}^q$, with $p = r + q$. The β factors are called *independent* and only occur in terms by themselves and with an exponent of one, whereas the α factors are called *dependent* and are allowed to multiply other (dependent) factors within the same term or have higher powers.

Definition 2 (Polynomial Zonotope). *Given center* $c \in \mathbb{R}^n$, *dependent factor generator matrix* $G_D \in \mathbb{R}^{n \times h}$, *independent factor generator matrix* $G_I \in \mathbb{R}^{n \times q}$, *and exponent matrix* $E \in \mathbb{Z}_{\geq 0}^{r \times h}$, *a polynomial zonotope is the set:*

$$\mathcal{PZ} = \left\{ c + \sum_{i=1}^{h} \left(\prod_{k=1}^{r} \alpha_k^{E(k,i)} \right) G_{D(\cdot,i)} + \sum_{j=1}^{q} \beta_j \, G_{I(\cdot,j)} \;\middle|\; \alpha_k, \beta_j \in [-1, 1] \right\}.$$

The intuition why we separate the dependent factors from the independent factors is that in this way the polynomial zonotope can always be written as a Minkowski sum of two sets:

$$\mathcal{PZ} = \mathcal{Z}_I \oplus \mathcal{PZ}_D$$

where

$$\mathcal{Z}_I = \Big\{ c + \sum_{j=1}^{q} \beta_j G_{I(\cdot,j)} \;\Big|\; \beta_j \in [-1,1] \Big\},$$

$$\mathcal{PZ}_D = \Big\{ \sum_{i=1}^{h} \Big(\prod_{k=1}^{r} \alpha_k^{E(k,i)} \Big) G_{D(\cdot,i)} \;\Big|\; \alpha_k \in [-1,1] \Big\}.$$

This splits the general polynomial zonotope into the independent part $\mathcal{Z}_I$ which is a zonotope, and the polynomial zonotope $\mathcal{PZ}_D$ which contains only terms where factors multiply each other or have higher powers. For intersection checking, the complexity arises from the dependent part and so we will often use a form with only dependent terms like $\mathcal{PZ}_D$. In this paper, such a polynomial zonotope, with only dependent terms, will be written using the shorthand notation $\langle G_D, E \rangle_{\mathcal{PZ}}$.

Example 1. (Fig. 1, bottom) Consider a polynomial zonotope defined as:

$$\mathcal{PZ} = \Big\{ \begin{bmatrix} 4 \\ 4 \end{bmatrix} + \beta_1 \begin{bmatrix} 1 \\ 0 \end{bmatrix} + \alpha_1 \begin{bmatrix} 2 \\ 0 \end{bmatrix} + \alpha_2 \begin{bmatrix} 1 \\ 2 \end{bmatrix} + \alpha_1^3 \alpha_2 \begin{bmatrix} 2 \\ 2 \end{bmatrix} \;\Big|\; \alpha_i, \beta_i \in [-1,1] \Big\}.$$

In this example, $q = 1, r = 2$ and $h = 3$. We can split $\mathcal{PZ}$ into the Minkowski sum of two sets $\mathcal{PZ} = \mathcal{Z}_I \oplus \mathcal{PZ}_D$, with

$$\mathcal{Z}_I = \Big\langle \begin{bmatrix} 4 \\ 4 \end{bmatrix}, \begin{bmatrix} 1 \\ 0 \end{bmatrix} \Big\rangle_{\mathcal{Z}} \quad \mathcal{PZ}_D = \Big\langle \begin{bmatrix} 2 & 1 & 2 \\ 0 & 2 & 2 \end{bmatrix}, \begin{bmatrix} 1 & 0 & 3 \\ 0 & 1 & 1 \end{bmatrix} \Big\rangle_{\mathcal{PZ}}.$$

3 Intersection Checking is NP-Hard

Given a polynomial zonotope $\mathcal{PZ} = \mathcal{Z}_I \oplus \mathcal{PZ}_D$ and a linear objective direction $\mathbf{d}$ the *polynomial zonotope optimization problem* computes the value:

$$\min_{\mathbf{x} \in \mathcal{PZ}} \mathbf{x}^T \mathbf{d} = \min_{\mathbf{x}_1 \in \mathcal{Z}_I} \mathbf{x}_1^T \mathbf{d} + \min_{\mathbf{x}_2 \in \mathcal{PZ}_D} \mathbf{x}_2^T \mathbf{d}. \tag{1}$$

If we want to check whether a polynomial zonotope $\mathcal{PZ}$ has intersection with a halfspace $\mathcal{H} = \{\mathbf{x} \mid \mathbf{x}^T \mathbf{d} \leq c\}$, we only need to check if the solution of (1) is larger than c. Since linear optimization of zonotopes is efficient, the main challenge lies in computing the optimal value in the polynomial zonotope of dependent terms $\mathcal{PZ}_D$. This is illustrated in the following example:

Example 2. Consider checking if the polynomial zonotope $\mathcal{PZ}$ from Example 1 has an intersection with the halfspace

$$\mathcal{H} = \Big\{ \mathbf{x} \in \mathbb{R}^2 \;\Big|\; \mathbf{x}^T \begin{bmatrix} 1 \\ 1 \end{bmatrix} \leq 0 \Big\}.$$

In order to check this, we only need to check whether the solution of the problem below is larger or equal to 0:

$$\begin{aligned}\min_{\mathbf{x}\in\mathcal{PZ}} \mathbf{x}^T \begin{bmatrix}1\\1\end{bmatrix} &= \min_{\alpha_k,\beta_k\in[-1,1]} \left(\begin{bmatrix}4\\4\end{bmatrix} + \beta_1\begin{bmatrix}1\\0\end{bmatrix} + \alpha_1\begin{bmatrix}2\\0\end{bmatrix} + \alpha_2\begin{bmatrix}1\\2\end{bmatrix} + \alpha_1^3\alpha_2\begin{bmatrix}2\\2\end{bmatrix}\right)^T \begin{bmatrix}1\\1\end{bmatrix}\\
&= \min_{\alpha_k,\beta_k\in[-1,1]} 8 + \beta_1 + 2\alpha_1 + 3\alpha_2 + 4\alpha_1^3\alpha_2\\
&= \min_{\beta_k\in[-1,1]} 8 + \beta_1 + \min_{\alpha_k\in[-1,1]} 2\alpha_1 + 3\alpha_2 + 4\alpha_1^3\alpha_2\\
&= 7 + (-5) = 2\end{aligned}$$

The minimum value is larger than 0 so there is no intersection with the halfspace.

As we saw in the above example, solving the optimization problem in (1) can be used to check whether a polynomial zonotope has an intersection with a halfspace. Furthermore, the generators of the polynomial zonotope can be projected onto the optimization direction resulting in a 1-D optimization problem. How difficult is this problem? As mentioned in the introduction, the full characterization of solutions of nonlinear equations given box domains is NP-hard [14, Sec. 4.1]. In fact, even if we restrict ourselves to optimization and only consider *bilinear polynomial zonotopes*—the simplest class of polynomial zonotopes with two variables per term each with an exponent of one—the problem is still NP-hard, which we show next.

First we introduce the 1-D *multi-affine polynomial optimization problem.*

Definition 3. *Consider the polynomial defined as:*

$$p(x_1, x_2, \cdots, x_n) = \sum_{I\subseteq\{1,2,\cdots,n\}} a_I \prod_{i\in I} x_i, \tag{2}$$

where $a_I \in \mathbb{R}$. The 1-D multi-affine polynomial optimization problem is:

$$\min_{\substack{x_1,\ldots,x_n\\ x_i\in[-1,1]}} p(x_1, x_2, \cdots, x_n).$$

Since all variables in a multi-affine optimization problem have an exponent of one, the partial derivative along each variable cannot change sign. This means that the optimal value must occur on one of the corners of the n-dimensional box of the domain and it is sufficient to consider this finite set when optimizing.

$$\min_{\substack{x_1,\ldots,x_n\\ x_i\in[-1,1]}} p(x_1, x_2, \cdots, x_n) = \min_{\substack{x_1,\ldots,x_n\\ x_i\in\{-1\}\cup\{1\}}} p(x_1, x_2, \cdots, x_n)$$

Note that the polynomial zonotope motivating our work in Fig. 2 was a multi-affine polynomial zonotope; we obtained the true boundary points shown in red using a version of this corner enumeration strategy.

The simplest type of non-trivial multi-affine optimization problem has two variables per term, since any terms with a single variable could be optimized by simply looking at the sign of a_I similar to optimization methods for zonotopes. We call this a *bilinear optimization problem*, which corresponds to optimization of a linear objective function over the dependent factors part of a bilinear polynomial zonotope, which has the corresponding restrictions on its terms

$$\min_{\substack{x_1,\ldots,x_n \\ x_i \in \{-1\} \cup \{1\}}} \sum_{i=1}^{n} \sum_{j=i+1}^{n} a_{i,j} x_i x_j. \tag{3}$$

Theorem 1. *Optimization over bilinear polynomial zonotopes is NP-complete.*

Proof. We show that if we could solve the bilinear optimzation problem from (3), then we could also solve the *minimum edge-deletion graph bipartization* problem, which is NP-complete [11,34]. The minimum edge-deletion graph bipartization problem is the problem of computing the minimum number of edges that must be deleted so that an undirected graph G becomes a bipartite graph[1]. Let $G = (V, E)$ be an arbitrary undirected graph with vertices $V = \{1, 2, \ldots, n\}$ and edges E, where an edge $e \in E$ connecting vertices i and j is represented as $e = (i, j)$, with convention $i < j$. Let δ_G be the least number of edges we need to remove to make graph G bipartite. In (3), we assign $a_{i,j} = \begin{cases} \frac{1}{2} & (i,j) \in E \\ 0 & (i,j) \notin E \end{cases}$.

Now define the assignment of the variables corresponding to the optimal solution of (3) as

$$x_1^*, \cdots, x_n^* = \underset{x_i \in \{-1\} \cup \{1\}}{\arg\min} \sum_{i=1}^{n} \sum_{j=i+1}^{n} a_{i,j} x_i x_j$$

and define the value δ as

$$\delta = \frac{|E|}{2} + \sum_{i=1}^{n} \sum_{j=i+1}^{n} a_{i,j} x_i^* x_j^* \tag{4}$$

Now consider a bipartie partitioning $V = V_1 \cup V_2$, where $V_1 = \{i \in V \mid x_i^* = -1\}$ and $V_2 = \{i \in V \mid x_i^* = 1\}$. Let $\tilde{E}$ be the set of edges $= (i, j)$ where either $i, j \in V_1$ or $i, j \in V_2$; these are the edges to be removed such that G becomes a bipartite graph. By the definition of δ_G, we must have $|\tilde{E}| \geq \delta_G$. Now since $x_i^* x_j^* = 1$ when $(i, j) \in \tilde{E}$, and $x_i^* x_j^* = -1$ when $(i, j) \in E/\tilde{E}$ we have

[1] In a bipartite graph, there are two groups of vertices, and edges are only allowed between the groups, not within each group.

$$
\begin{aligned}
|\tilde{E}| &= \sum_{(i,j)\in\tilde{E}} x_i^* x_j^* \\
&= \underbrace{\frac{1}{2}\left(\sum_{(i,j)\in\tilde{E}} x_i^* x_j^* - \sum_{(i,j)\in E/\tilde{E}} x_i^* x_j^*\right)}_{\frac{|E|}{2}} + \underbrace{\frac{1}{2}\left(\sum_{(i,j)\in\tilde{E}} x_i^* x_j^* + \sum_{(i,j)\in E/\tilde{E}} x_i^* x_j^*\right)}_{\sum_{i=1}^{n}\sum_{j=i+1}^{n} a_{i,j} x_i^* x_j^*} \\
&= \frac{|E|}{2} + \sum_{i=1}^{n}\sum_{j=i+1}^{n} a_{i,j} x_i^* x_j^* \\
&= \delta
\end{aligned}
$$

Hence $\delta \geq \delta_G$.

Next, define E_G to be the smallest set of edges that need to removed to make G bipartite, so that $|E_G| = \delta_G$. The graph $\tilde{G} = (V, E/E_G)$ is bipartite, so we can partition the graph $\tilde{G}$ into the two bipartite sets V_1^* and V_2^* such that there are only edges are between V_1^* and V_2^*. Now define:

$$
x_i' = \begin{cases} -1, \; i \in V_1^*, \\ 1, \;\; i \in V_2^*. \end{cases}
$$

Then, since δ comes from the solution of the minimization problem in (4):

$$
\begin{aligned}
\delta \leq \frac{|E|}{2} + \sum_{i=1}^{n}\sum_{j=i+1}^{n} a_{i,j} x_i' x_j' &= \frac{|E|}{2} + \frac{1}{2}\underbrace{\sum_{(i,j)\in E/E_G} x_i' x_j'}_{(|E|-|E_G|)(-1)} + \frac{1}{2}\underbrace{\sum_{(i,j)\in E_G} x_i' x_j'}_{|E_G|} \\
&= \frac{|E|}{2} - \left(\frac{|E| - |E_G|}{2}\right) + \frac{|E_G|}{2} \\
&= |E_G| = \delta_G
\end{aligned}
$$

Therefore $\delta \leq \delta_G$ and combining both parts $\delta = \delta_G$. Hence finding the solution of *minimum edge-deletion graph bipartization* problem reduces to solving (3). □

Corollary 1. *Polynomial zonotope intersection checking is NP-hard.*

Proof. Since optimization of bilinear polynomial zonotopes is NP-complete, intersection checking of bilinear polynomial zonotopes is also NP-complete. As these are a type of polynomial zonotope, halfspace intersection checking of general polynomial zonotopes is also at least as difficult, and so is NP-hard. □

4 The Overapproximate and Split Algorithm

While Corollary 1 showed that checking the intersection between a polynomial zonotope and another set can be a difficult problem, what algorithm is used in practice? The existing method [4,15] consists of two steps. In step one, the

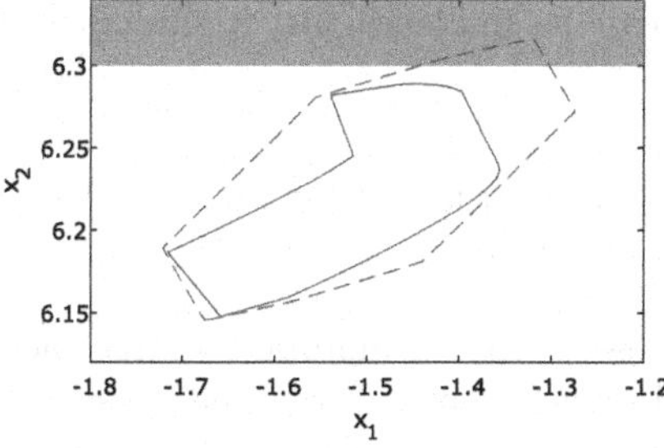

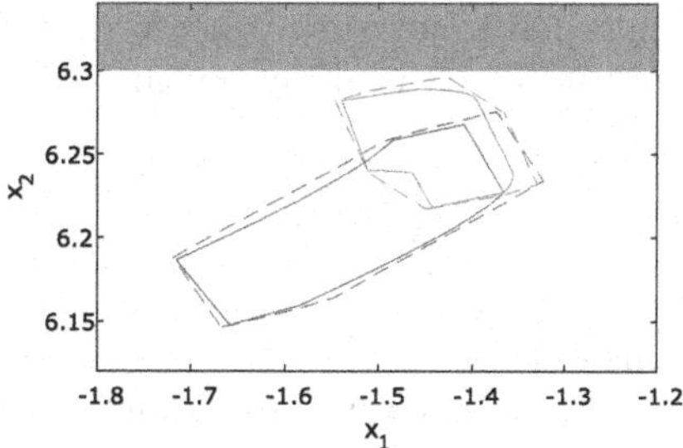

Fig. 3. An illustration of the overapproximate and split intersection algorithm, where the zonotope over-approximation (dashed line) of the original polynomial zonotope is too conservative (left) while after splitting the zonotope over-approximation of the two split polynomial zonotopes is accurate enough to show there is no intersection with the red shaded region (image from [4]). (Color figure online)

polynomial zonotope is overapproximated using a zonotope. If this zonotope overapproximation does not intersect the other set, then the smaller polynomial zonotope does not intersect the other set either and the algorithm terminates. Otherwise, a point is sampled from inside the polynomial zonotope and tested if it is inside the other set[2]. If so, a witness point for the intersection has been found and the algorithm terminates. If neither of these are applicable, in step two, the algorithm divides the polynomial zonotope into two smaller polynomial zonotopes and repeats from step one recursively.

The algorithm used to plot a polynomial zonotope is similar, using a recursive depth bound and then plotting the zonotope overapproximations at the tree leaves. For this method to obtain high precision, we may need to split the polynomial zonotope into a large number of smaller pieces, compute the zonotope approximation for each piece, and then take the union of those zonotopes to serve as the overapproximation of the original polynomial zonotope. Figure 3 shows a visualization of the overapproximate and split intersection algorithm.

4.1 Algorithm Definition

The algorithm consists of two steps: (i) overapproximate and (ii) split.

Overapproximation Step. The key observation motivating the overapproximation step is that since each factor $\alpha_k \in [-1, 1]$, the product of factors in each term in outer sum is also in $[-1, 1]$:

$$\prod_{k=1}^{r} \alpha_k^{E(k,i)} \in [-1, 1]$$

Therefore, we can replace this product with a new variable $\beta_i \in [-1, 1]$. This results in an overapproximation because it drops dependencies that the factors

[2] The specific sample point is not important for convergence, although it is typically heuristically derived from the zonotope overapproximation.

α_k may have had with other terms. This can be made slightly tighter if the exponent $E(k,i)$ is always even:

$$\prod_{k=1}^{r} \alpha_k^{E(k,i)} \in [0,1] \qquad (E(k,i) \text{ is even for all } k).$$

In this case, we replace the product with $\frac{\beta_i+1}{2}$, since a zonotope requires each $\beta_i \in [-1,1]$. Now we give the formal definition of the overapproximation step:

Definition 4. *Let $\mathcal{PZ} = \mathcal{Z}_I \oplus \mathcal{PZ}_D$ be a polynomial zonotope with $\mathcal{PZ}_D = \langle G_D, E \rangle$. The zonotope overapproximation of $\mathcal{PZ}$ is defined as:*

$$\mathcal{Z} = \mathcal{Z}_I \oplus \mathcal{Z}_D \tag{5}$$

with

$$\mathcal{Z}_D = \left\{ \sum_{i\in K} \beta_i G_D(\cdot,i) + \sum_{i\in H} \left(\frac{\beta_i+1}{2}\right) G_D(\cdot,i) \;\middle|\; \beta_i \in [-1,1] \right\}$$

where H is the set of indices of terms with all even powers,

$$H = \{ i \mid \forall k \; E(k,i) \equiv 0 (\text{mod } 2) \}$$

and K the set of remaining indices

$$K = \{1, \cdots, h\}/H$$

Split Step. When the overapproximation of a polynomial zonotope is too large, step two of the algorithm splits the polynomial zonotope into two smaller pieces. This is done by choosing some factor α_s to split and then noting:

$$[-1,1] = \underbrace{\left\{ \frac{1+\alpha_s}{2} \;\middle|\; \alpha_s \in [-1,1] \right\}}_{[0,1]} \cup \underbrace{\left\{ -\frac{1+\alpha_s}{2} \;\middle|\; \alpha_s \in [-1,1] \right\}}_{[-1,0]}. \tag{6}$$

We split the dependent part of a polynomial zonotope $\mathcal{PZ}_D = \langle G_D, E \rangle_{\mathcal{PZ}}$ into:

$$\mathcal{PZ}_{D_{1,s}} = \left\{ \sum_{i=1}^{h} A_{s,i} \left(\frac{1+\alpha_s}{2}\right)^{E(s,i)} G_D(\cdot,i) \;\middle|\; \alpha_k \in [-1,1] \right\}$$

and

$$\mathcal{PZ}_{D_{2,s}} = \left\{ \sum_{i=1}^{h} A_{s,i} \left(-\frac{1+\alpha_s}{2}\right)^{E(s,i)} G_D(\cdot,i) \;\middle|\; \alpha_k \in [-1,1] \right\}$$

where $A_{s,i}$ is the product of all the factors in the ith term excluding α_s:

$$A_{s,i} = \prod_{k=1,k\neq s}^{r} \alpha_k^{E(k,i)}. \tag{7}$$

Proposition 1. *If* $\mathcal{PZ} = \mathcal{Z}_I \oplus \mathcal{PZ}_D$*, where* $\mathcal{PZ}_{1,s} = \mathcal{Z}_I \oplus \mathcal{PZ}_{D_{1,s}}$ *and* $\mathcal{PZ}_{2,s} = \mathcal{Z}_I \oplus \mathcal{PZ}_{D_{2,s}}$*, then* $\mathcal{PZ}_{1,s}$ *and* $\mathcal{PZ}_{2,s}$ *are polynomial zonotopes and*

$$\mathcal{PZ} = \mathcal{PZ}_{1,s} \bigcup \mathcal{PZ}_{2,s}.$$

Proof. This follows from the definitions of $\mathcal{PZ}_{1,s}$ and $\mathcal{PZ}_{2,s}$ using (6).

4.2 Convergence Concerns

While the overapproximate and split algorithm for polynomial zonotopes has been simply stated in prior work [4,15], we now identify two non-obvious concerns with the approach, given in Propositions 2 and 3.

Convergence Concern 1: As the sizes of the polynomial zonotopes get smaller in the algorithm due to splitting, we may expect the corresponding zonotope overapproximation is also getting smaller. However, this is not true in general.

Proposition 2. *Overapproximation error can increase during the overapproximate and split algorithm.*

Proof. Consider the following polynomial zonotope:

$$\mathcal{PZ} = \{\alpha_1^2 \mid \alpha_1 \in [-1,1]\} = [0,1]$$

The overapproximation of $\mathcal{PZ}$ is the zonotope

$$\mathcal{Z} = \left\{ \frac{1+\beta_1}{2} \;\middle|\; \beta_1 \in [-1,1] \right\} = [0,1]$$

However, if we split $\mathcal{PZ}$ into two parts using (6):

$$\mathcal{PZ}_1 = \mathcal{PZ}_2 = \left\{ \frac{1}{4}\left(1 + \alpha_1^2 + 2\alpha_1\right) \;\middle|\; \alpha_1 \in [-1,1] \right\}$$

The overapproximation of $\mathcal{PZ}_1$ and $\mathcal{PZ}_2$ is

$$\mathcal{Z}_1 = \mathcal{Z}_2 = \left\{ \frac{1}{4}\left(\frac{3}{2} + \frac{1}{2}\beta_1 + 2\beta_2\right) \;\middle|\; \beta_1, \beta_2 \in [-1,1] \right\} = \left[-\frac{1}{4}, 1\right]$$

Consequently, the original overapproximation $\mathcal{Z} \subset \mathcal{Z}_1 \bigcup \mathcal{Z}_2$. After performing splitting, the union of the zonotope overapproximations became larger than the overapproximation before splitting—the overapproximation error has grown. □

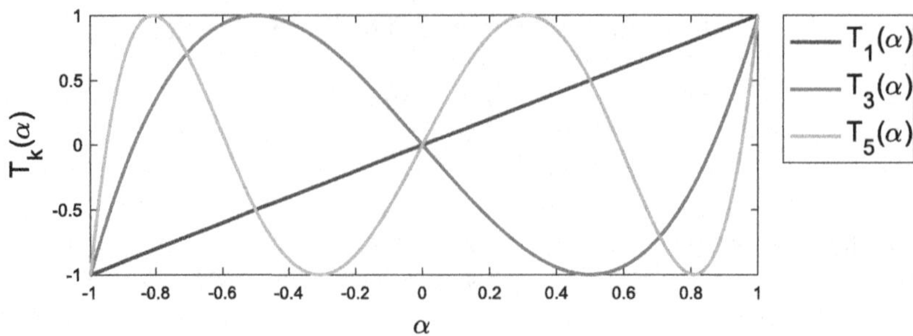

Fig. 4. When $\alpha \in [-1, 1]$, the odd Chebyshev polynomials are between $[-1, 1]$, but the zonotope overapproximation using Definition 4 grows unbounded.

Convergence Concern 2: As shown above, overapproximation error can increase during the algorithm, although the individual split polynomial zonotopes are getting smaller. Is there a bound between the error of a polynomial zonotope and its overapproximation? No.

Proposition 3. *The error between a polynomial zonotope and its zonotope overapproximation is unbounded.*

Proof. Consider the odd Chebyshev polynomials of first kind:

$$\begin{aligned} T_1(\alpha) &= \alpha \\ T_3(\alpha) &= 4\alpha^3 - 3\alpha \\ T_5(\alpha) &= 16\alpha^5 - 20\alpha^3 + 5\alpha \\ &\dots \end{aligned}$$

For Chebyshev polynomials, when $\alpha \in [-1, 1]$ it is known that $T_k(\alpha) \in [-1, 1]$ (see Fig. 4). However, the number of terms in the odd Chebyshev polynomials grows unbounded as k increases. As a result, if we construct a polynomial zonotope from T_k and overapproximate it with a zonotope using Definition 4, the overapproximation also grows without bound as k increases. □

Given Propositions 2 and 3, there is a real concern that overapproximate and split algorithm may not always converge. In the next section, we identify sufficient conditions where convergence can be guaranteed.

5 Guaranteeing Convergence

While the overapproximate and split algorithm has been presented in prior work, as discussed in the previous section there is a real concern it may not always terminate. In this section, we discuss conditions needed to ensure overapproximation error converges. First, we define the Hausdorff distance between two sets to serve as a criterion to evaluate the error of the zonotope overapproximation.

Definition 5 (Hausdorff distance). *Given sets S_1 and S_2, the Hausdorff distance is:*

$$d(S_1, S_2) = \max\left\{ \sup_{x \in S_1} \inf_{y \in S_2} \|x - y\|, \sup_{y \in S_2} \inf_{x \in S_1} \|x - y\| \right\}.$$

Note that in the case of nested sets $S_1 \subset S_2$, the first term is always 0, and the distance simplifies to

$$d(S_1, S_2) = \sup_{y \in S_2} \inf_{x \in S_1} \|x - y\|.$$

We now show that the Hausdorff distance between a polynomial zonotope and its zonotope overapproximation can be bounded using the norm of the generator matrix. We will use the entry-wise matrix one-norm: $\|A\| = \sum_{j=1}^{m} \|A(\cdot, j)\|$.

Lemma 1. *Let $\mathcal{PZ} = \mathcal{Z}_I \oplus \mathcal{PZ}_D$ with dependent part $\mathcal{PZ}_D = \langle G_D, E \rangle_{PZ_D}$ and zonotope overapproximation $\mathcal{Z} = \mathcal{Z}_I \oplus \mathcal{Z}_D$ from Definition 4,*

$$d(\mathcal{PZ}, \mathcal{Z}) \leq \|G_D\|.$$

Proof. Since $\mathcal{PZ} \subset \mathcal{Z}$, then

$$d(\mathcal{PZ}, \mathcal{Z}) = \sup_{y \in \mathcal{Z}} \inf_{x \in \mathcal{PZ}} \|x - y\|.$$

Now for any point y in the zonotope overapproximation we can write it as:

$$y = y_I + y_D$$

where $y_I \in Z_I$ and

$$y_D = \left(\sum_{i \in K} \beta_i G_D(\cdot, i) + \sum_{i \in H} \frac{\beta_i + 1}{2} G_D(\cdot, i) \right) \in Z_D.$$

Since $y_I \in \mathcal{PZ}$, we have:

$$d(\mathcal{PZ}, \mathcal{Z}) = \sup_{y \in \mathcal{Z}} \inf_{x \in \mathcal{PZ}} \|x - y\| \leq \sup_{y \in \mathcal{Z}} \|y_I - y\| = \sup_{y \in \mathcal{Z}} \|y_D\|.$$

Using the triangle inequality,

$$\|y_D\| = \left\| \sum_{i \in K} \beta_i G_D(\cdot, i) + \sum_{i \in H} \frac{\beta_i + 1}{2} G_D(\cdot, i) \right\| \leq \sum_{i \in H \bigcup K} \|G_D(\cdot, i)\| = \|G_D\|$$

thus completing the proof. □

Since the union of the split polynomial zonotopes forms the original polynomial zonotope (Proposition 1), to demonstrate that the union of zonotope approximations converges to the original polynomial zonotope, we first establish that each zonotope overapproximation converges to its respective polynomial zonotope. Using Lemma 1, we only need to show that the norm of the dependent matrix decreases after splitting.

In order to show this, we need additional constraints on how this splitting variable s is chosen. Various heuristics for choosing s can be found in the literature, but to ensure convergence we require a *fairness* assumption, in that each factor needs to be selected an infinite number of times. We assume s is chosen cyclically to satisfy this requirement. Let us first consider a simple example which tells us why the norm of the dependent matrix decreases after splitting cyclically.

Example 3. Let us first consider a polynomial zonotope $\mathcal{PZ} = \{\alpha_1^E \mid \alpha_1 \in [-1,1]\}$ which only has a single factor α_1, the dependent matrix $G_D = 1$ and exponent E In this case, when split,

$$\left(\pm\frac{1+\alpha}{2}\right)^E = \frac{\pm 1}{2^E} + \frac{1}{2^E}\sum_{j=1}^{E}\binom{E}{j}(\pm 1)^j \alpha_k^j \tag{8}$$

and since the constant will belong to independent part, dependent generator becomes

$$G_D^{1,1} = \frac{1}{2^E}\left[\binom{E}{1}, \binom{E}{2}, \cdots, \binom{E}{E}\right], \qquad G_D^{2,1} = \frac{1}{2^E}\left[-\binom{E}{1}, \binom{E}{2}, \cdots, (-1)^E\binom{E}{E}\right]$$

and thus the generator norm has shrunk

$$\|G_D^{j,1}\| = 1 - \frac{1}{2^E}.$$

Next we present the more general result.

Lemma 2. *Let $\mathcal{PZ}$ be a given polynomial zonotope with dependent part $\mathcal{PZ}_D = \langle G_D, E\rangle$, with r factors and h generators. Assuming cyclical splitting, after splitting s times, we have 2^s polynomial zonotopes $\mathcal{PZ}_1^s, \mathcal{PZ}_2^s, \cdots, \mathcal{PZ}_{2^s}^s$. When $s < r$, the norm cannot increase*

$$\|G_D^{j,s}\| \leq \|G_D\|$$

When $s = r$, the norm decreases by a factor $\rho < 1$,

$$\|G_D^{j,s}\| \leq \rho\|G_D\|$$

where $\rho = \max_{i\in\{1,2\cdots,h\}}\left(1 - (\frac{1}{2})^{\|E(\cdot,i)\|}\right)$, $j \in \{1, 2, \cdots, 2^s\}$ and $G_D^{j,s}$ is the dependent factor generator of $\mathcal{PZ}_j^s$

Importantly, the factor ρ does not depend on the number of splits, it only depends on the original $\mathcal{PZ}$.

Proof. When $s < r$, let us consider the dependent part of $\mathcal{PZ}_j^s$, it will have the following form:

$$(\mathcal{PZ}_j^s)_D = \left\{ \sum_{i=1}^{h} A_{s,i}^j \zeta_j^i \prod_{k=1}^{s} \left(\frac{1+\alpha_k}{2}\right)^{E(k,i)} G_D(\cdot,i) \;\middle|\; \alpha_k \in [-1,1] \right\} \tag{9}$$

where $\zeta_j^i \in \{-1,1\}$ distinguishes between the 2^s polynomial zonotopes based on which side of each factor was chosen while splitting, and $A_{s,i}^j$ is the product of factors that have not yet been split:

$$A_{s,i}^j = \prod_{k=s+1}^{r} \alpha_k^{E(k,i)}$$

Now because $|a_k| \leq 1$, we have both $|A_{s,i}^j| \leq 1$ and

$$\left| \prod_{k=1}^{s} \left(\frac{1+\alpha_k}{2}\right)^{E(k,i)} \right| \leq 1$$

As a result the absolute value of their product, the value that multiplies $G_D(\cdot,i)$ in Eq. 9 is also less than 1. Therefore, when $s < r$ for any $j \in \{1,2,\cdots,2^s\}$, we have:

$$\|G_D^{j,s}\| \leq \sum_{i=1}^{h} \|G_D(\cdot,i)\| = \|G_D\|$$

Next, in the other case when $s = r$ we can expand the exponent:

$$\prod_{k=1}^{r} \left(\frac{1+\alpha_k}{2}\right)^{E(k,i)} = \sum_{\xi_1,\xi_2,\cdots,\xi_r} c_{\xi_1,\cdots,\xi_k} \prod_{k=1}^{r} \alpha_k^{\xi_r}$$

where all the coefficients are positive and the first one $c_{0,\cdots,0}^i = \left(\frac{1}{2}\right)^{\|E(\cdot,i)\|}$. By taking $\alpha_k = 1$ for all α_k, we obtain:

$$\sum_{\xi_1,\cdots,\xi_k} c_{\xi_1,\cdots,\xi_r}^i = 1$$

As a result, we have

$$\sum_{i=1}^{h} A_{s,i}^j \zeta_j^i \prod_{k=1}^{s} \left(\frac{1+\alpha_k}{2}\right)^{E(k,i)} G_D(\cdot,i) = \sum_{i=1}^{h} \zeta_j^i \prod_{k=1}^{r} \left(\frac{1+\alpha_k}{2}\right)^{E(k,i)} G_D(\cdot,i)$$

$$= \underbrace{\left(\sum_{i=1}^{h} \zeta_j^i \left(c_{0,\cdots,0}^i G_D(\cdot,i)\right)\right)}_{\text{(constant)}} + \left(\sum_{i=1}^{h} \zeta_j^i \sum_{\xi_1,\cdots,\xi_r}^{(\sum_{k=1}^{r}\xi_k)\geq 1} c_{\xi_1,\cdots,\xi_r}^i \prod_{k=1}^{r} (\alpha_k)^{\xi_k} G_D(\cdot,i)\right)$$

In this case, the constant part will not be in the dependent part of $\mathcal{PZ}_j^r$ but will be moved to the independent part, so that:

$$(\mathcal{PZ}_j^r)_D = \left\{ \sum_{i=1}^{h} \zeta_j^i \sum_{\xi_1,\cdots,\xi_r}^{(\sum_{k=1}^{r}\xi_k)\geq 1} c^i_{\xi_1,\cdots,\xi_r} \prod_{k=1}^{r} (\alpha_k)^{\xi_k} G_D(\cdot,i) \middle| \alpha_k \in [-1,1] \right\}$$

For any $j \in \{1,2,\cdots,2^s\}$, we will have:

$$\begin{aligned}
\|G_D^{j,r}\| &= \left\| \sum_{i=1}^{h} \zeta_j^i \sum_{\xi_1,\cdots,\xi_r}^{(\sum_{k=1}^{r}\xi_k)\geq 1} c^i_{\xi_1,\cdots,\xi_r} G_D(\cdot,i) \right\| \\
&\leq \sum_{i=1}^{h} \underbrace{\sum_{\xi_1,\cdots,\xi_r}^{(\sum_{k=1}^{r}\xi_k)\geq 1} c^i_{\xi_1,\cdots,\xi_r}}_{1-(\frac{1}{2})^{\|E(\cdot,i)\|}} \|G_D(\cdot,i)\| \\
&= \sum_{i=1}^{h} \left(1 - \left(\frac{1}{2}\right)^{\|E(\cdot,i)\|}\right) \|G_D(\cdot,i)\| \\
&\leq \rho \sum_{i=1}^{h} \|G_D(\cdot,i)\| = \rho \|G_D\|
\end{aligned}$$

□

Corollary 2. *Let $\mathcal{PZ}$ be a given polynomial zonotope with dependent part $\mathcal{PZ}_D = \langle G_D, E\rangle$. Using cyclical splitting, after splitting s times, the factor with index $1 + ((s-1)(mod\ r))$ will be split. Let $\mathcal{PZ}_1^s, \mathcal{PZ}_2^s, \cdots, \mathcal{PZ}_{2^s}^s$ be the split polynomial zonotope after s iterations. Then for any $0 < j \leq 2^s$*

$$\|G_D^{j,s}\| \leq \rho^{\lfloor s/r \rfloor} \|G_D\|$$

where $G_D^{j,s}$ is the dependent factor generator matrix of $\mathcal{PZ}_j^s$.

With this, we can now show that the union of the zonotope overapproximations converges to the original polynomial zonotope.

Theorem 2. *Let $\mathcal{PZ}$ be a given polynomial zonotope with dependent part $\mathcal{PZ}_D = \langle G_D, E\rangle$. Using cyclical splitting, after splitting s times, the factor with index $1+((s-1)(mod\ r))$ will be split. The corresponding split polynomial zonotopes are $\mathcal{PZ}_1^s, \mathcal{PZ}_2^s, \cdots, \mathcal{PZ}_{2^s}^s$ and zonotope overapproximation for $\mathcal{PZ}_j^s$ is $\mathcal{Z}_j^s$. As we split more often, the overapproximation error converges to zero:*

$$\lim_{s\to\infty} d\left(\mathcal{PZ}, \bigcup_{j=1}^{2^s} \mathcal{Z}_j^s\right) = 0$$

Proof. Since $\mathcal{PZ} \subseteq \bigcup_{j=1}^{2^s} \mathcal{Z}_j^s$,

$$\begin{aligned} d(\mathcal{PZ}, \bigcup_{j=1}^{2^s} \mathcal{Z}_j^s) &= \sup_{y \in \bigcup_{j=1}^{2^s} \mathcal{Z}_j^s} \inf_{x \in \mathcal{PZ}} \|x - y\| \\ &= \max_j \sup_{y \in \mathcal{Z}_j^s} \inf_{x \in \mathcal{PZ}} \|x - y\| \\ &\leq \max_j d(\mathcal{Z}_j^s, \mathcal{PZ}_j^s) \\ &\leq \rho^{\lfloor s/r \rfloor} \|G_D\| \quad \text{(by Corollary 2 and Lemma 1).} \end{aligned}$$

Since $0 < \rho < 1$, the value of limit of $\rho^{\lfloor s/r \rfloor}$ converges to zero. □

Although we have been assuming cyclical variables splitting, the above theorem could be adapted to more general splitting schemes by noting that the generator matrix norm must reduce after every factor has been selected at least once. As long as the spitting approach is fair, in the sense that it does not ignore any factors forever, the dependent generator matrix norm will decrease by a factor of ρ after each full round. Applied repeatedly, the norm of the dependent matrix will therefore decrease log-linearly to 0, in terms of the number of rounds.

Lastly, in Fig. 2, we motivated our work with a practical example where the overapproximate and split algorithm did not appear to converge to the true polynomial zonotope. Based on our results in Theorem 2, we know that convergence is guaranteed, but you may need to split along each dependent factor. In the polynomial zonotope in the figure, the number of dependent factors was around 50, so even after 40 splits the overapproximation error can remain large.

6 Related Work

Polynomial zonotopes were originally designed to represent non-convex sets to tightly enclose the reachable sets for a nonlinear system [1]. A sparse version of the representation was proposed in follow up work [15,17] to support a more compact representation while still being closed under key nonlinear operations. Recent extensions add nonlinear constraints to the domain which are called constrained polynomial zonotopes [16]. Although this was not the focus of the current paper, the intersection and plotting algorithms for constrained polynomial zonotopes is basically the same as for polynomial zonotopes, except the overapproximation step results in constrained zonotopes [32] (also called star sets [9] or $\mathcal{AH}$-Polytopes [31]) rather than zonotopes. Therefore, we expect the analysis results from this paper to also be transferable to constrained zonotopes.

Besides reachability analysis of nonlinear systems, polynomial zonotopes have been used for reachability of linear systems with uncertain parameters [24] which resulted in more accurate reachable sets comparing to zonotope methods. The representation has also been used for set-based propagation through neural networks [19], real-time planning and control scenarios [26] and safety shielding for reinforcement learning systems [18].

In cases where the model of the dynamical system is not given, polynomial zonotopes can also be used for reachability with Koopman linearized surrogate models obtained from trajectory data [4]. Since Koopman linearization requires lifting the state through a nonlinear transformation, convex initial sets in the original space can become complex non-convex sets. Polynomial zonotopes can provide tight enclosures of these lifted initial sets.

Taylor models [25] are a related set representation sometimes used for reachability analysis [7] that are similar to polynomial zonotopes with interval remainders added to each variable. Taylor model arithmetic allows one to approximate arbitrary smooth functions, although the intersection and plotting algorithms are essentially grid pavings over the domain of the set.

As mentioned in the introduction, polynomial zonotope intersection checking is equivalent to the box-constrained polynomial optimization problem. There are several methods to solve such problems, for example augmented Lagrangian methods or sum of squares programming [20,27,28,33]. Augmented Lagrangian methods consider box constrained polynomial constraint problems as a general nonlinear programming problem. General nonlinear programming with convex constraints can usually be solved by considering the KKT conditions [5,6,30]. The KKT points can be found by augmented Lagrangian methods [13,29]. The exact augmented Lagrangian methods must solve a subproblem in each update. Hence the inexact augmented Lagrangian methods(iALM) are used in practice. Although there are many works on iALM [22,23], such methods guarantee local convergence with local optimal solutions. Therefore, they are not commonly used for polynomial optimization problems. Sum-of-squares polynomials are polynomials that can be formulated as the sum of the square of several polynomials. If the polynomial can be formulated in this way, or reformulated after a series of liftings [21], then the optimization problem can be formulated as semidefinite programming and solved using convex optimization (although the resulting problem may be very large).

7 Conclusions

In this work we discussed the difficulty of the fundamental intersection checking operation for the polynomial zonotope set representation. This difficulty is rarely directly addressed in papers that use polynomial zonotopes, although it can be a practical limitation of any algorithm that builds upon the set representation. The complexity is both theoretical and practically relevant, as we have shown cases, specifically Fig. 2, where accurate approximation using the overapproximate and split approach is intractable. While polynomial zonotopes are a powerful tool for formal verification, they are not a panacea, as much of the problem complexity can be often hidden within the representation itself, manifesting when performing set intersections.

Acknowledgements. Thanks for Professor Steven Skiena for the initial discussion around Theorem 1. This material is based upon work supported by the Air Force Office of Scientific Research and the Office of Naval Research under award numbers FA9550-19-1-0288, FA9550-21-1-0121, FA9550-23-1-0066 and N00014-22-1-2156. Any opinions, findings, and conclusions or recommendations expressed in this material are those of the author(s) and do not necessarily reflect the views of the United States Air Force or the United States Navy.

References

1. Althoff, M.: Reachability analysis of nonlinear systems using conservative polynomialization and non-convex sets. In: Proceedings of the 16th International Conference on Hybrid Systems: Computation and Control, pp. 173–182 (2013). https://doi.org/10.1145/2461328.2461358
2. Althoff, M.: An introduction to cora 2015. ARCH@ CPSWeek **34**, 120–151 (2015). https://doi.org/10.29007/zbkv
3. Althoff, M., Frehse, G., Girard, A.: Set propagation techniques for reachability analysis. Annu. Rev. Control Robot. Auton. Syst. **4**, 369–395 (2021). https://doi.org/10.1146/annurev-control-071420-081941
4. Bak, S., Bogomolov, S., Hencey, B., Kochdumper, N., Lew, E., Potomkin, K.: Reachability of Koopman linearized systems using random Fourier feature observables and polynomial zonotope refinement. In: Shoham, S., Vizel, Y. (eds.) Computer Aided Verification. CAV 2022. LNCS, vol. 13371, pp. 490–510. Springer, Cham (2022). https://doi.org/10.1007/978-3-031-13185-1_24
5. Bazaraa, M.S., Sherali, H.D., Shetty, C.M.: Nonlinear Programming: Theory and Algorithms. John Wiley & Sons, Hoboken (2013)
6. Boyd, S., Boyd, S.P., Vandenberghe, L.: Convex Optimization. Cambridge University Press, Cambridge (2004)
7. Chen, X., Ábrahám, E., Sankaranarayanan, S.: Flow*: an analyzer for non-linear hybrid systems. In: Sharygina, N., Veith, H. (eds.) CAV 2013. LNCS, vol. 8044, pp. 258–263. Springer, Heidelberg (2013). https://doi.org/10.1007/978-3-642-39799-8_18
8. Cousot, P., Cousot, R.: Abstract interpretation: a unified lattice model for static analysis of programs by construction or approximation of fixpoints. In: Proceedings of the 4th ACM SIGACT-SIGPLAN Symposium on Principles of Programming Languages, pp. 238–252 (1977). https://doi.org/10.1145/512950.512973
9. Duggirala, P.S., Viswanathan, M.: Parsimonious, simulation based verification of linear systems. In: Chaudhuri, S., Farzan, A. (eds.) CAV 2016. LNCS, vol. 9779, pp. 477–494. Springer, Cham (2016). https://doi.org/10.1007/978-3-319-41528-4_26
10. Eppstein, D.: Zonohedra and zonotopes. Technical report 95–53, UC Irvine, Information and Computer Science (1995)
11. Garey, M.R., Johnson, D.S., Stockmeyer, L.: Some simplified np-complete problems. In: Proceedings of the Sixth Annual ACM Symposium on Theory of Computing, pp. 47–63 (1974). https://doi.org/10.1145/800119.803884
12. Girard, A.: Reachability of uncertain linear systems using zonotopes. In: Morari, M., Thiele, L. (eds.) Hybrid Systems: Computation and Control. HSCC 2005. LNCS, vol. 3414, pp. 291–305. Springer, Berlin, Heidelberg (2005). https://doi.org/10.1007/978-3-540-31954-2_19
13. Hestenes, M.R.: Multiplier and gradient methods. J. Optim. Theory Appl. **4**(5), 303–320 (1969). https://doi.org/10.1007/BF00927673

14. Jaulin, L., et al.: Interval Analysis. Springer, London (2001). https://doi.org/10.1007/978-1-4471-0249-6_2
15. Kochdumper, N.: Extensions of Polynomial Zonotopes and their Application to Verification of Cyber-Physical Systems. Ph.D. thesis, Technische Universität München (2022)
16. Kochdumper, N., Althoff, M.: Constrained polynomial zonotopes. arXiv preprint arXiv:2005.08849 (2020). https://doi.org/10.48550/arXiv.2005.08849
17. Kochdumper, N., Althoff, M.: Sparse polynomial zonotopes: a novel set representation for reachability analysis. IEEE Trans. Autom. Control **66**(9), 4043–4058 (2020). https://doi.org/10.1109/TAC.2020.3024348
18. Kochdumper, N., Krasowski, H., Wang, X., Bak, S., Althoff, M.: Provably safe reinforcement learning via action projection using reachability analysis and polynomial zonotopes. IEEE Open J. Control Syst. **2**, 79–92 (2023). https://doi.org/10.1109/OJCSYS.2023.3256305
19. Kochdumper, N., Schilling, C., Althoff, M., Bak, S.: Open-and closed-loop neural network verification using polynomial zonotopes. In: NASA Formal Methods Symposium (2023). https://doi.org/10.1007/978-3-031-33170-1_2
20. Lasserre, J.B.: Global optimization with polynomials and the problem of moments. SIAM J. Optim. **11**(3), 796–817 (2001). https://doi.org/10.1137/S1052623400366802
21. Lasserre, J.B.: A sum of squares approximation of nonnegative polynomials. SIAM Rev. **49**(4), 651–669 (2007). https://doi.org/10.1137/04061413X
22. Li, Z., Chen, P.Y., Liu, S., Lu, S., Xu, Y.: Rate-improved inexact augmented lagrangian method for constrained nonconvex optimization. In: International Conference on Artificial Intelligence and Statistics, pp. 2170–2178. PMLR (2021)
23. Li, Z., Xu, Y.: Augmented lagrangian-based first-order methods for convex-constrained programs with weakly convex objective. INFORMS J. Optim. **3**(4), 373–397 (2021). https://doi.org/10.1287/ijoo.2021.0052
24. Luo, E., Kochdumper, N., Bak, S.: Reachability analysis for linear systems with uncertain parameters using polynomial zonotopes. In: Proceedings of the 26th ACM International Conference on Hybrid Systems: Computation and Control. HSCC '23, Association for Computing Machinery, New York, NY, USA (2023). https://doi.org/10.1145/3575870.3587130
25. Makino, K., Berz, M.: Taylor models and other validated functional inclusion methods. Int. J. Pure Appl. Math. **6**, 239–316 (2003)
26. Michaux, J., et al.: Can't touch this: real-time, safe motion planning and control for manipulators under uncertainty. arXiv preprint arXiv:2301.13308 (2023). https://doi.org/10.48550/arXiv.2301.13308
27. Parrilo, P.A.: Structured semidefinite programs and semialgebraic geometry methods in robustness and optimization. California Institute of Technology (2000)
28. Parrilo, P.A.: Semidefinite programming relaxations for semialgebraic problems. Math. Program. **96**, 293–320 (2003). https://doi.org/10.1007/s10107-003-0387-5
29. Powell, M.J.: A method for nonlinear constraints in minimization problems. Optimization, pp. 283–298 (1969)
30. Rockafellar, R.T.: Convex Analysis, vol. 11. Princeton University Press, Princeton (1997). https://doi.org/10.1515/9781400873173
31. Sadraddini, S., Tedrake, R.: Linear encodings for polytope containment problems. In: 2019 IEEE 58th Conference on Decision and Control (CDC), pp. 4367–4372. IEEE (2019). https://doi.org/10.1109/CDC40024.2019.9029363

32. Scott, J.K., Raimondo, D.M., Marseglia, G.R., Braatz, R.D.: Constrained zonotopes: a new tool for set-based estimation and fault detection. Automatica **69**, 126–136 (2016). https://doi.org/10.1016/j.automatica.2016.02.036
33. Shor, N.Z.: Class of global minimum bounds of polynomial functions. Cybernetics **23**(6), 731–734 (1987). https://doi.org/10.1007/BF01070233
34. Yannakakis, M.: Node-and edge-deletion NP-complete problems. In: Proceedings of the Tenth Annual ACM Symposium on Theory of Computing, pp. 253–264 (1978). https://doi.org/10.1145/800133.804355

Predicting Memory Demands of BDD Operations Using Maximum Graph Cuts

Steffan Christ Sølvsten(✉) and Jaco van de Pol

Aarhus University, Aarhus, Denmark
{soelvsten,jaco}@cs.au.dk

Abstract. The BDD package Adiar manipulates Binary Decision Diagrams (BDDs) in external memory. This enables handling big BDDs, but the performance suffers when dealing with moderate-sized BDDs. This is mostly due to initializing expensive external memory data structures, even if their contents can fit entirely inside internal memory.

The contents of these auxiliary data structures always correspond to a graph cut in an input or output BDD. Specifically, these cuts respect the levels of the BDD. We formalise the shape of these cuts and prove sound upper bounds on their maximum size for each BDD operation.

We have implemented these upper bounds within Adiar. With these bounds, it can predict whether a faster internal memory variant of the auxiliary data structures can be used. In practice, this improves Adiar's running time across the board. Specifically for the moderate-sized BDDs, this results in an average reduction of the computation time by 86.1% (median of 89.7%). In some cases, the difference is even 99.9%. When checking equivalence of hardware circuits from the EPFL Benchmark Suite, for one of the instances the time was decreased by 52 h.

Keywords: Binary Decision Diagrams · Directed Acyclic Graphs · Maximum Graph Cuts · External Memory Algorithms

1 Introduction

A Binary Decision Diagrams (BDD) [8] is a data structure that has found great use within the field of combinatorial logic and verification. Its ability to concisely represent and manipulate Boolean formulae is the key to many symbolic model checkers, e.g. [3,14,15,17,18,20,23]. Bryant and Heule recently found a use for BDDs to create SAT and QBF solvers with certification capabilities [9–11] that are better at proof generation than conventional SAT solvers.

Adiar [38] is a redesign of the classical BDD algorithms such that they are optimal in the I/O model of Aggarwal and Vitter [1], based on ideas from Lars Arge [4]. As shown in Fig. 1, this enables Adiar to handle BDDs beyond the limits of main memory with only a minor slowdown in performance, unlike conventional BDD implementations. Adiar is implemented on top of the TPIE library [28,41], which provides external memory sorting algorithms, file access, and priority

É. André and J. Sun (Eds.): ATVA 2023, LNCS 14216, pp. 72–92, 2023.
https://doi.org/10.1007/978-3-031-45332-8_4

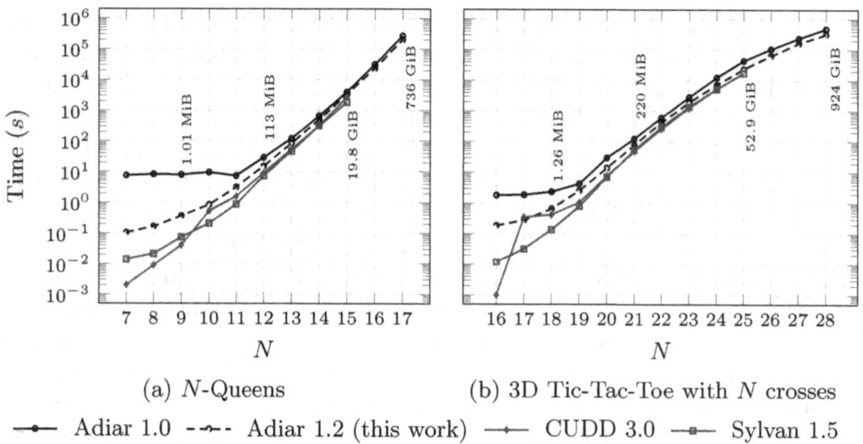

Fig. 1. Running time solving combinatorial BDD benchmarks. Some instances are labelled with the size of the largest BDD constructed to solve them.

queues. These external memory data structures work by loading one or more blocks from files on disk into internal memory and manipulating the elements within these blocks before storing them again on disk. Their I/O-efficiency stems from a carefully designed order in which these blocks are retrieved, manipulated, and stored. Yet, initializing the internal memory in preparation to do so is itself costly. This is evident in Fig. 1 (cf. Sect. 4.3 for more details) where Adiar's performance is several orders of magnitude worse than conventional BDD packages for smaller instance sizes. In fact, Adiar's performance decreases when the amount of internal memory increases.

This shortcoming is not desirable for a BDD package: while our research focuses on enabling large-scale BDD manipulation, end users should not have to consider whether their BDDs will be large enough to benefit from Adiar. Solving this also paves the way for Adiar to include complex BDD operations where conventional implementations recurse on intermediate results, e.g. *Multi-variable Quantification*, *Relational Product*, and *Variable Reordering*. To implement the same, Adiar has to run multiple sweeps. Yet, each of these sweeps suffer when they unecessarily use external memory data structures. Hence, it is vital to overcome this shortcomming, to ensure that an I/O-efficient implementations of these complex BDD operations will also be usable in practice.

The linearithmic I/O- and time-complexity of Adiar's algorithms also applies to the lower levels of the memory hierarchy, i.e. between the cache and RAM. Hence, there is no reason to believe that the bad performance for smaller instances is inherently due to the algorithms themselves; if they used an internal memory variant of all auxiliary data structures, then Adiar ought to perform well for much smaller instances.

We argue that simple solutions are unsatisfactory: A first idea would be to start running classical, depth-first BDD algorithms until main memory is exhausted. In that case, the computation is aborted and restarted with external memory algorithms. But, this strategy doubles the running time. While it would work well for small instances, the slowdown for large instances would be unacceptable. Alternatively, both variants could be run in parallel. But, this would halve the amount of available memory and again slow down large instances.

A second idea would be to start running Adiar's I/O-efficient algorithms with an implementation of all auxiliary data structures in internal memory. In this case, if memory is exhausted, the data could be copied to disk, and the computation could be resumed with external memory. This could be implemented neatly with the *state pattern*: a wrapper switches transparently to the external memory variant when needed. Yet, moving elements from one sorted data structure to another requires at least linear time. Even worse, such a wrapper adds an expensive level of indirection and hinders the compiler in inlining and optimising, since the actual data structure is unknown at compile-time.

Instead, we propose to use the faster, internal-memory version of Adiar's algorithms only when it is guaranteed to succeed. This avoids re-computations, duplicate storage, as well as the costs of indirection. The main research question is how to predict a sound upper bound on the memory required for a BDD operation, and what information to store to compute these bounds efficiently.

1.1 Contributions

In Sect. 3, we introduce the notion of an i-level cut for Directed Acyclic Graphs (DAGs). Essentially, the shape of these cuts is constricted to span at most i levels of the given DAG. Previous results in [22] show that for $i \geq 4$ the problem of computing the maximum i-level cut is NP-complete. We show that for $i \in \{1,2\}$ this problem is still computable in polynomial time. These polynomial-time algorithms can be implemented using a linearithmic amount of time and I/Os. But instead, we use over-approximations of these cuts. As described in Sect. 3.4, their computation can be piggybacked on existing BDD algorithms, which is considerably cheaper: for 1-level cuts, this only adds a 1% linear-time overhead and does not increase the number of I/O operations.

Investigating the structure of BDDs from the perspective of i-level cuts for $i \in \{1,2\}$ in Sect. 3.1 and 3.2, we obtain sound upper bounds on the maximum i-level cuts of a BDD operation's output, purely based on the maximum i-level cut of its inputs. Using these upper bounds, Adiar can decide in constant time whether to run the next algorithm with internal or external memory data structures. Here, only one variant is run, all memory is dedicated to it, and the exact type of the auxiliary data structures are available to the compiler.

Our experiments in Sect. 4 show that it is a good strategy to compute the 1-level cuts, and to use them to infer an upper bound on the 2-level cuts. This strategy is sufficient to address Adiar's performance issues for the moderate-sized instances while also requiring the least computational overhead. As Fig. 1 shows, adding these cuts to Adiar with version 1.2 removes the overhead introduced by initializing TPIE's external memory data structures and so greatly improves Adiar's performance. For example, to verify the correctness of the small and moderate instances of the EPFL combinational benchmark circuits [2], the use of i-level cuts decreases the running time from 56.5 h down to 4.0 h.

2 Preliminaries

2.1 Graph and Cuts

A directed graph is a tuple (V, A) where V is a finite set of vertices and $A \subseteq V \times V$ a set of arcs between vertices. The set of incoming arcs to a vertex $v \in V$ is $in(v) = A \cap (V \times \{v\})$, its outgoing arcs are $out(v) = A \cap (\{v\} \times V)$, and v is a *source* if its indegree $|in(v)| = 0$ and a *sink* if its outdegree $|out(v)| = 0$.

A cut of a directed graph (V, A) is a partitioning (S, T) of V such that $S \cup T = V$ and $S \cap T = \emptyset$. Given a weight function $w : A \to \mathbb{R}$ the weighted maximum cut problem is to find a cut (S, T) such that $\sum_{a \in S \times T \cap A} w(a)$ is maximal, i.e. where the total weight of arcs crossing from some vertex in S to one in T is maximised. Without decreasing the weight of a cut, one may assume that all sources in V are part of the partition S and all sinks are part of T. The maximum cut problem is NP-complete for directed graphs [30] and restricting the problem to directed acyclic graphs (DAGs) does not decrease the problem's complexity [22].

If the weight function w merely counts the number of arcs that cross a cut, i.e. $\forall a \in A : w(a) = 1$, the problem above reduces to the *unweighted* maximum cut problem where a cut's weight and size are interchangeable.

2.2 Binary Decision Diagrams

A Binary Decision Diagram (BDD) [8], as depicted in Fig. 2, is a DAG (V, A) that represents an n-ary Boolean function. It has a single source vertex $r \in V$, usually referred to as the *root*, and up to two sinks for the Boolean values $\mathbb{B} = \{\bot, \top\}$, usually referred to as *terminals* or *leaves*. Each non-sink vertex $v \in V \backslash \mathbb{B}$ is referred to as a BDD *node* and is associated with an input variable $x_i \in \{x_0, x_1, \ldots, x_{n-1}\}$ where $label(v) = i$. Each arc is associated with a Boolean value, i.e. $A \subseteq V \times \mathbb{B} \times V$ (written as $v \xrightarrow{b} v'$ for a $(v, b, v') \in A$), such that each BDD node v represents a binary choice on its input variable. That is, $out(v) = \{v \xrightarrow{\bot} v', v \xrightarrow{\top} v''\}$, reflecting x_i being assigned the value $\bot$, resp. $\top$. Here, v' is said to be v's *low* child while v'' is its *high* child.

An Ordered Binary Decision Diagram (OBDD) restricts the DAG such that all paths follow some total variable ordering π: for every arc $v_1 \to v_2$ between two distinct nodes v_1 and v_2, $label(v_1)$ must precede $label(v_2)$ according to the order π. A Reduced Ordered Binary Decision Diagram (ROBDD) further adds the restriction that for each node v where $out(v) = \{v \xrightarrow{\bot} v', v \xrightarrow{\top} v''\}$, (1) $v' \neq v''$ and (2) there exists no other node $u \in V$ such that $label(v) = label(u)$ and $out(u) = \{u \xrightarrow{\bot} v', u \xrightarrow{\top} v''\}$. The first requirement removes *don't care* nodes while the second removes *duplicates*. Assuming a fixed variable ordering π, an ROBDD is a canonical representation of the Boolean function it represents [8]. Without loss of generality, we will assume π is the identity.

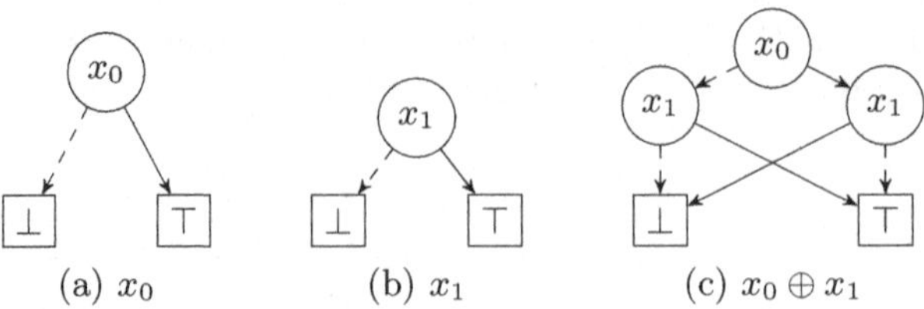

Fig. 2. Examples of Reduced Ordered Binary Decision Diagrams. Terminals are drawn as boxes with the Boolean value and BDD nodes as circles with the decision variable. *Low* edges are drawn dashed while *high* edges are solid.

This graph-based representation allows one to indirectly manipulate Boolean formulae by instead manipulating the corresponding DAGs. For simplicity, we will focus on the Apply operation in this paper, but our results can be generalised to other operations. Apply computes the ROBDD for $f \odot g$ given ROBDDs for f and g and a binary operator $\odot : \mathbb{B} \times \mathbb{B} \rightarrow \mathbb{B}$. This is done with a product construction of the two DAGs, starting from the pair (r_f, r_g) of the roots of f and g. If terminals b_f from f and b_g from g are paired then the resulting terminal is $b_f \odot b_g$. Otherwise, when nodes v_f from f and v_g from g are paired, a new BDD node is created with label $\ell = \min(\mathit{label}(v_f), \mathit{label}(v_g))$, and its low and high child are computed recursively from pairs (v'_f, v'_g). For the low child, v'_f is $v_f.\mathit{low}$ if $\mathit{label}(v_f) = \ell$ and v_f otherwise; v'_g is defined symmetrically. The recursive tuple for the high child is defined similarly.

Zero-Suppressed Decision Diagrams. A Zero-suppressed Decision Diagram (ZDD) [26] is a variation of BDDs where the first reduction rule is changed: a node v for the variable $\mathit{label}(v)$ with $\mathit{out}(v) = \{v \xrightarrow{\bot} v', v \xrightarrow{\top} v''\}$ is not suppressed if v is a *don't care* node, i.e. if $v' = v''$, but rather if it assigns the variable $\mathit{label}(v)$ to $\bot$, i.e. if $v'' = \bot$. This makes ZDDs a better choice in practice than BDDs to represent functions f where its on-set, $\{\boldsymbol{x} \mid f(\boldsymbol{x}) = \top\}$, is sparse.

The basic notions behind the BDD algorithms persist when translated to ZDDs, but it is important for correctness that the ZDD operations account for the shape of the suppressed nodes. For example, the *union* operation needs to replace recursion requests for (v_f, v_g) with $(v_f, \bot)$ if $\mathit{label}(v_f) < \mathit{label}(v_g)$ and with $(\bot, v_g)$ if $\mathit{label}(v_f) > \mathit{label}(v_g)$.

Levelised Algorithms in Adiar. BDDs and ZDDs are usually manipulated with recursive algorithms that use two hash tables: one for memoisation and another to enforce the two reduction rules [7,27]. Lars Arge noted in [4,5] that this approach is not efficient in the I/O-model of Aggarwal and Vitter [1]. He proposed to address this issue by processing all BDDs iteratively level by level with the time-forward processing technique [13,24]: recursive calls are not executed at the time of issuing the request but are instead deferred with one or more priority queues until the necessary elements are encountered in the inputs.

2a: [$((0,0),\bot,\top)$]
2b: [$((1,0),\bot,\top)$]
2c: [$((0,0),(1,0),(1,1))$, $((1,0),\bot,\top)$, $((1,1),\top,\bot)$]

Fig. 3. In-order representation of BDDs of Fig. 2

In [38], we implemented this approach in the BDD package Adiar. Furthermore, with version 1.1 we have extended this approach to ZDDs [34].

In Adiar, each decision diagram is represented as a sequence of its BDD nodes. Each BDD node is uniquely identifiable by the pair (ℓ, i) of its level ℓ, i.e. its variable label, and its level-index i. And so, each BDD node can be represented as a triple of its own and its two children's unique identifiers (uids). The entire sequence of BDD nodes follows a level by level ordering of nodes which is equivalent to a lexicographical sorting on their uid. For example, the three BDDs in Fig. 2 are stored on disk as the lists in Fig. 3.

The conventional recursive algorithms traverse the input (and the output) with random-access as dictated by the call stack. Adiar replaces this stack with a priority queue that is sorted such that it is synchronised with a sequential traversal through the input(s). Specifically, the recursion requests $s \to t$ from a BDD node s to t is sorted on the target t – this way the requests for t are at the top of the priority queue when t is reached in the input. For example, after processing the root $(0,0)$ of the BDD in Fig. 2c, the priority queue includes the arcs $(0,0) \xrightarrow{\bot} (1,0)$ and $(0,0) \xrightarrow{\top} (1,1)$, in that order. Notice, this is exactly in the same order as the sequence of nodes in Fig. 3. Essentially, this priority queue maintains the yet unresolved parts of the recursion tree (V', A') throughout a level by level top-down sweep. Yet, since the ordering of the priority queue groups together requests for the same t, the graph (V', A') is not a tree but a DAG.

For BDD algorithms that produce an output BDD, e.g. the Apply algorithm, Adiar first constructs (V', A') level by level. When the output BDD node $t \in V'$ is created from nodes $v_f \in V_f$ and $v_g \in V_g$, the top of the priority queues provides all ingoing arcs, which are placed in the output. Outgoing arcs to a terminal, $out(t) \cap (V' \times \mathbb{B} \times \mathbb{B})$, are also immediately placed in a separate output. On the other hand, recursion requests from t to its yet unresolved non-terminal children, $out(t) \backslash (V' \times \mathbb{B} \times \mathbb{B})$, have to be processed later. To do so, these unresolved arcs are put back into the priority queue as arcs $(t \xrightarrow{b} (v'_f, v'_g)) \in V' \times \mathbb{B} \times (V_f \times V_g)$ where the arc's target is the tuple of input nodes $v'_f \in V_f$ and $v'_g \in V_g$. This essentially makes the priority queue contain all the yet unresolved arcs of the output. For example, when using Apply to produce Fig. 2c from Fig. 2a and 2b, the root node of the output is resolved to have uid $(0,0)$ and the priority queue contains arcs $(0,0) \xrightarrow{\bot} (\bot,(1,0))$ and $(0,0) \xrightarrow{\top} (\top,(1,0))$. Both of these arcs are then later resolved, creating the nodes $(1,0)$ and $(1,1)$, respectively.

Yet, these *top-down sweeps* of Adiar produce sequences of arcs rather than nodes. Furthermore, the DAG (V', A') is not necessarily a reduced OBDD. Hence, as shown in Fig. 4, Adiar follows up on the above top-down sweep with

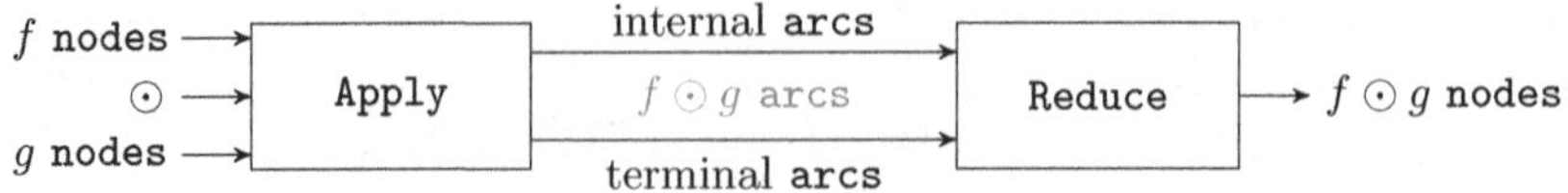

Fig. 4. The Apply–Reduce pipeline in Adiar

a *bottom-up sweep* that I/O-efficiently recreates Bryant's original Reduce algorithm in [8]. Here, a priority queue forwards the uid of t' that is the result from applying the reduction rules to a BDD node t in (V', A') to the to-be reduced parents s of t. These parents are immediately available by a sequential reading of (V', A') since $in(t)$ was output together within the prior top-down sweep. Both reduction rules are applied by accumulating all nodes at level j from the arcs in the priority queue, filtering out *don't care* nodes, sorting the remaining nodes such that duplicates come in succession and can be eliminated efficiently, and finally passing the necessary information to their parents via the priority queue.

3 Levelised Cuts of a Directed Acyclic Graph

Any DAG can be divided in one or more ways into several *levels*, where all vertices at a given level only have outgoing arcs to vertices at later levels.

Definition 1. *Given a DAG (V, A) a levelisation of vertices in V is a function $\mathcal{L} : V \to \mathbb{N} \cup \{\infty\}$ such that for any two vertices $v, v' \in V$, if there exists an arc $v \to v'$ in A then $\mathcal{L}(v) < \mathcal{L}(v')$.*

Intuitively, $\mathcal{L}$ is a labeling of vertices $v \in V$ that respects a topological ordering of V. Since (V, A) is a DAG, such a topological ordering always exists and hence such an $\mathcal{L}$ must also always exist. Specifically, let π_V in be the longest path in (V, A) and π_v be the longest path of any given $v \in V$ to any sink $t \in V$, then $\mathcal{L}(v)$ can be defined to be the difference of their lengths, i.e. $|\pi_V| - |\pi_v|$.

Given a DAG and a levelisation $\mathcal{L}$, we can restrict the freedom of a cut to be constricted within a small window with respect to $\mathcal{L}$. Figure 5a provides a visual depiction of the following definition.

Definition 2. *An* i-level cut *for $i \geq 1$ is a cut (S, T) of a DAG (V, A) with levelisation $\mathcal{L}$ for which there exists a $j \in \mathbb{N}$ such that $\mathcal{L}(s) < j + i$ for all $s \in S$ and $\mathcal{L}(t) > j$ for all $t \in T$.*

As will become apparent later, deriving the i-level cut with maximum weight for $i \in \{1, 2\}$ will be of special interest. Figure 5b shows two 1-level cuts and three 2-level cuts in the BDD for the exclusive-or of the two variables x_0 and x_1. A 1-level cut is by definition a cut between two adjacent levels whereas a 2-level cut allows nodes on level $j + 1$ to be either in S or in T. In Fig. 5b, both the maximum 1-level and 2-level cuts have size 4.

Proposition 1. *The maximum 1-level cut in a DAG (V, A) with levelisation $\mathcal{L}$ is computable in polynomial time.*

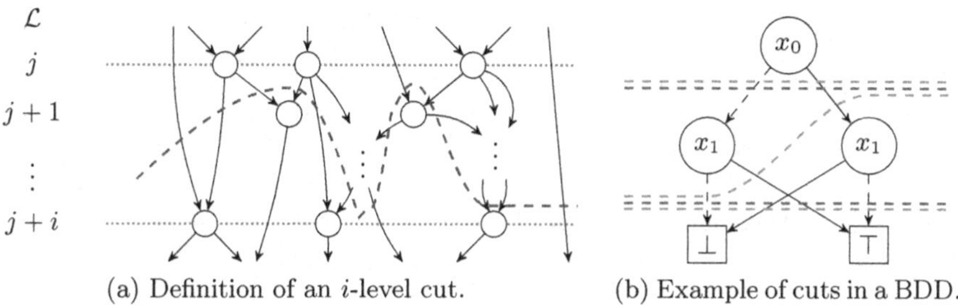

(a) Definition of an i-level cut. (b) Example of cuts in a BDD.

Fig. 5. Visualization of i-level (purple), 1-level (cyan) and 2-level (orange) cuts. (Color figure online)

Proof. For a specific $j \in \mathcal{L}(V)$ we can compute the size of the 1-level cut at j in $O(A)$ time by computing the sum of $w((s,t))$ over all arcs $(s,t) \in A$ where $\mathcal{L}(s) \leq j$ and $\mathcal{L}(t) > j$. This cut is by definition unique for j and hence maximal. Repeating this for each $j \in \mathcal{L}(V)$ we obtain the maximum 1-level cut of the entire DAG in $O(|\mathcal{L}(V)| \cdot |A|) = O(|V| \cdot |A|)$ time. □

Proposition 2. *The maximum* 2*-level cut in a DAG* (V, A) *with levelisation* $\mathcal{L}$ *is computable in polynomial time.*

Proof. Given a level $j \in \mathcal{L}(V)$, any 2-level cut for $j-1$ has all vertices $v \in V$ with $\mathcal{L}(v) \neq j$ fixed to be in S or in T. That is, only vertices v where $\mathcal{L}(v) = j$ may be part of either S or of T. A vertex v at level j can greedily be placed in S if $\sum_{a \in out(v)} w(a) < \sum_{a \in in(v)} w(a)$ and in T otherwise. This greedy decision procedure runs in $O(|A|)$ time for each level, resulting in an $O(|\mathcal{L}(V)| \cdot |A|) = O(|V| \cdot |A|)$ total running time. □

Lampis, Kaouri, and Mitsou [22] prove NP-completeness for computing the maximum cut of a DAG by a reduction from the *not-all-equal SAT problem* (NAE3SAT) to a DAG with 5 levels. That is, they prove NP-completeness for computing the size of the maximum i-level cut for $i \geq 4$. This still leaves the complexity of the maximum i-level cut for $i = 3$ as an open problem.

3.1 Maximum Levelised Cuts in BDD Manipulation

For an OBDD, represented by the DAG (V, A), we will consider the levelisation function $\mathcal{L}_{OBDD}$ where all nodes with the same label are on the same level.

$$\mathcal{L}_{OBDD}(v) \triangleq \begin{cases} label(v) & \text{if } v \notin \mathbb{B} \\ \infty & \text{if } v \in \mathbb{B} \end{cases}$$

For a BDD f with the DAG (V, A), let $N_f \triangleq |V \setminus \mathbb{B}|$ be the number of internal nodes in V. Let $C_{i:f}$ denote the size of the unweighted maximum i-level cut in (V, A); in Sect. 3.2 we will consider weighted maximum cuts, where one or more terminals are ignored. Finally, we introduce the arc $(-\infty) \rightarrow r_f$ to the root. This simplifies the results that follow since $in(v) \neq \emptyset$ for all $v \in V$.

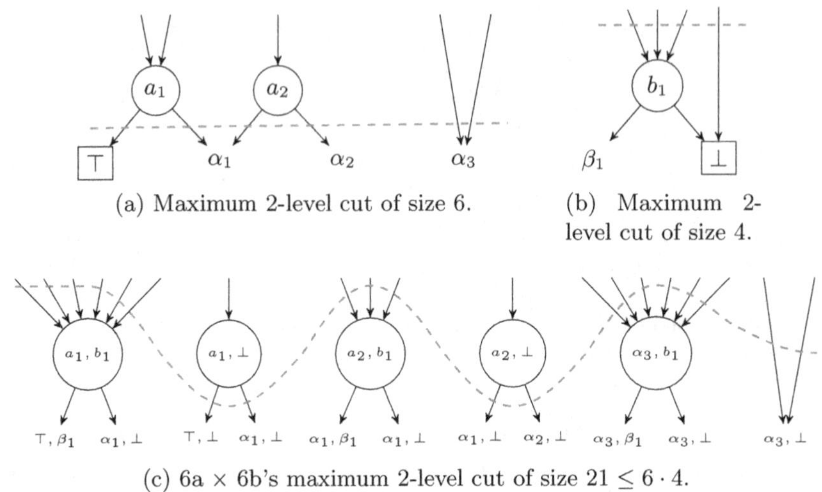

(a) Maximum 2-level cut of size 6.

(b) Maximum 2-level cut of size 4.

(c) 6a × 6b's maximum 2-level cut of size $21 \leq 6 \cdot 4$.

Fig. 6. Relation between the maximal 2-level cut of two BDDs' internal arcs and the maximum 2-level cut of their product.

Theorem 1. *The maximum cut of the BDD f has a size of at most $N_f + 1$.*

Proof. This is proven via the stronger statement that the maximum cut of a multi-rooted decision diagram is less than or equal to $N + r$ where N is the number of internal nodes and $r \geq 1$ is the number of roots. This, in turn, is done by induction on the number of internal nodes N (See the full paper [37]). □

This bound is tight for i-level cuts, as is evident from Fig. 5b where the size of the maximum (i-level) cut is 4. Yet, in general, one can obtain a better upper bound on the maximum i-level cut of the (unreduced) output of each BDD operation when the maximum i-level cut of the input is known.

Theorem 2. *For $i \in \{1, 2\}$, the maximum i-level cut of the (unreduced) output of Apply of f and g is at most $C_{i:f} \cdot C_{i:g}$.*

Proof. Let us only consider the more complex case of $i = 2$; the proof for $i = 1$ follows from the same line of thought.

Every node of the output represents a tuple (v_f, v_g) where v_f, resp. v_g, is an internal node of f, resp. g, or is one of the terminals $\mathbb{B} = \{\bot, \top\}$. An example of this situation is shown in Fig. 6. The node (v_f, v_g) contributes with $\max(|in((v_f, v_g))|, |out((v_f, v_g))|)$ to the maximum 2-level cut at that level. Since it is a BDD node, $|out((v_f, v_g))| = 2$. We have that $|in((v_f, v_g))| \leq |in(v_f)| \cdot |in(v_g)|$ since all combinations of in-going arcs may potentially exist and lead to this product of v_f and v_g. Expanding on this, we obtain

$$
\begin{aligned}
|in((v_f, v_g))| &\leq |in(v_f)| \cdot |in(v_g)| \\
&\leq \max(|in(v_f)|, |out(v_f)|) \cdot \max(|in(v_g)|, |out(v_g)|).
\end{aligned}
$$

That is, the maximum 2-level cut for a level is less than or equal to the product of the maximum 2-level cuts of the input at the same level. Taking the maximum 2-level cut across all levels we obtain the final product of $C_{2:f}$ and $C_{2:g}$. □

The bounds in Theorem 2 are better than what can be derived from Theorem 1 since $C_{i:f}$ and $C_{i:g}$ are themselves cuts and hence their product must be at most the bound based on the possible number of nodes. They are also tight: the maximum i-level cut for $i \in \{1, 2\}$ of the BDDs for the variables x_0 and x_1 in Fig. 2a and 2b both have size 2 while the BDD for the exclusive-or of them in Fig. 2c has, as shown in Fig. 5b, a maximum i-level cut of size 4.

Theorem 2 is of course only an over-approximation. The gap between the upper bound and the actual maximum i-level cut arises because Theorem 2 does not account for pairs (v_f, v_g), where node v_f sits above f's maximum 2-level cut and v_g sits below g's maximum 2-level cut, and vice versa. In this case, outgoing arcs of v_f are paired with ingoing arcs of v_g, even though this would be strictly larger than the arcs of their product. Furthermore, similar to Theorem 1, this bound does not account for arcs that cannot be paired as they reflect conflicting assignments to one or more input variables. For example, in the case where the out-degree is greater for both nodes, the above bound mistakenly pairs the low arcs with the high arcs and vice versa.

3.2 Improving Bounds by Accounting for Terminal Arcs

Some of the imprecision in the over-approximation of Theorem 2 highlighted above can partially be addressed by explicitly accounting for the arcs to each terminal. For $B \subseteq \mathbb{B}$, let w_B be the weight function that only cares for arcs to internal BDD nodes and to the terminals in B.

$$w_B(s \xrightarrow{b} t) = \begin{cases} 1 & \text{if } t \in V \backslash \mathbb{B} \text{ or } t \in B \\ 0 & \text{otherwise} \end{cases} .$$

Let $C_{i:f}^{B}$ be the maximum i-level cut of f with respect to $\mathcal{L}_{OBDD}$ and w_B.

The constant hidden within the $O(|V| \cdot |A|)$ running time of the algorithm in the proof of Proposition 1 is smaller than the one in the proof of Proposition 2. Hence, the following slight over-approximation of $C_{2:f}^{B}$ given $C_{1:f}^{B}$ may be useful (proved in the full paper [37]).

Lemma 1. *For $B \subseteq \mathbb{B}$, $C_{2:f}$ is at most $\frac{1}{2} \cdot C_{1:f}^{\emptyset} + C_{1:f}^{B}$.*

Finally, we can tighten the bound in Theorem 2 by making sure (1) not to unnecessarily pair terminals in f with terminals in g and (2) not to pair terminals from f and g with nodes of the other when said terminal shortcuts the operator.

Lemma 2. *The maximum 2-level cut of the (unreduced) output $f \odot g$ of Apply excluding arcs to terminals, $C_{2:f \odot g}^{\emptyset}$, is at most*

$$C_{2:f}^{B_{left(\odot)}} \cdot C_{2:g}^{\emptyset} + C_{2:f}^{\emptyset} \cdot C_{2:g}^{B_{right(\odot)}} - C_{2:f}^{\emptyset} \cdot C_{2:g}^{\emptyset},$$

where $B_{left(\odot)}, B_{right(\odot)} \subseteq \mathbb{B}$ are the terminals that do not shortcut $\odot$.

3.3 Maximum Levelised Cuts in ZDD Manipulation

The results in Sect. 3.1 and 3.2 are loosely yet subtly coupled to the reduction rules of BDDs. Specifically, Theorem 1 is applicable to ZDDs as-is but Theorem 2 and its derivatives provide unsound bounds for ZDDs. This is due to the fact that, unlike for BDDs, a suppressed ZDD node may re-emerge during a ZDD product construction algorithm. For example in the case of the *union* operation, when processing a pair of nodes with two different levels, its high child becomes the product of a node v in one ZDD and the $\bot$ terminal in the other – even if there was no arc to $\bot$ in the original two cuts for f and g.

The solution is to introduce another special arc similar to $(-\infty) \to r_f$ which accounts for this specific case: if there are no arcs to $\bot$ to pair with, then the arc $(-\infty) \to \bot$ is counted as part of the input's cut. That is, all prior results for BDDs apply to ZDDs, assuming $C^B_{i:f}$ is replaced with $ZC^B_{i:f}$ defined to be

$$ZC^B_{i:f} = \begin{cases} C^B_{i:f} + 1 & \text{if } \bot \in B \text{ and } C^B_{i:f} = C^{B\setminus\{\bot\}}_{i:f} \\ C^B_{i:f} & \text{otherwise} \end{cases} .$$

3.4 Adding Levelised Cuts to Adiar's Algorithms

The description of Adiar in Sect. 2.2 leads to the following observations.

- The contents of the priority queues in the top-down Apply algorithms are always a 1-level or a 2-level cut of the input or of the output – possibly excluding arcs to one or both terminals.
- The contents of the priority queue in the bottom-up Reduce algorithm are always a 1-level cut of the input, excluding any arcs to terminals.

Specifically, the priority queues always contain an i-level cut (S, T), where S is the set of processed diagram nodes and T is the set of yet unresolved diagram nodes. For example, the 2-level cuts depicted in Fig. 5b reflect the states of the top-down priority queue within the Apply to compute the exclusive-or of Fig. 2a and 2b to create Fig. 2c. In turn, the 1-level cuts in Fig. 5b are also the states of the bottom-up priority queue of the Reduce sweep that follows.

Hence, the upper bounds on the 1 and 2-level cuts in Sect. 3.1, 3.2, and 3.3 are also upper bounds on the size of all auxiliary data structures. That is, upper bounds on the i-level cuts of the input can be used to derive a sound guarantee of whether the much faster internal memory variants can fit into memory. To only add a minimal overhead to the performance, computing these i-level cuts should

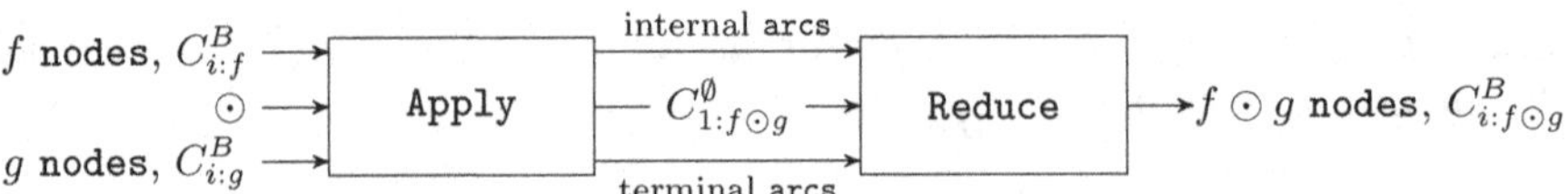

Fig. 7. The Apply–Reduce pipeline in Adiar with i-level cuts.

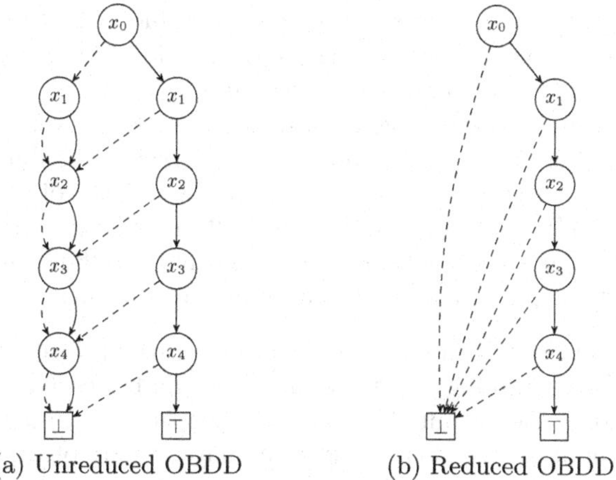

(a) Unreduced OBDD (b) Reduced OBDD

Fig. 8. Example of reduction increasing the 1 and 2-level maximum cut.

be done as part of the preceding algorithm that created the very input. This extends the tandem in Fig. 4 as depicted in Fig. 7 with the i-level cuts necessary for the next algorithm.

What is left is to compute within each sweep an upper bound on these cuts.

1-Level Cut within Top-Down Sweeps. The priority queues of a top-down sweep only contain arcs between non-terminal nodes of its output. While their contents in general form a 2-level cut, the sweep also enumerates all 1-level cuts when it has finished processing one level, and is about to start processing the next. That is, the top-down algorithm that constructs the unreduced decision diagram (V', A') for f' can compute $C^{\emptyset}_{1:f'}$ in $O(|\mathcal{L}_{OBDD}(V')|)$ time by accumulating the maximum size of its own priority queue when switching from one level to another. The number of I/O operations is not affected at all.

***i*-Level Cuts Within the Bottom-Up Reduce.** To compute the 1-level and 2-level cuts of the output during the Reduce algorithm, the algorithms in the proofs of Proposition 1 and 2 need to be incorporated. Since the Reduce algorithm works bottom-up, it cannot compute these cuts exactly: the bottom-up nature only allows information to flow from lower levels upwards while an exact result also requires information to be passed downwards. Specifically, Fig. 8 shows an unreduced BDD whose maximum 1 and 2-level cut is increased due to the reduction removing nodes above the cut. Both over-approximation algorithms below are tight since for the input in Fig. 8 they compute the exact result.

Over-Approximating the 1*-Level Cut.* Starting from the bottom, when processing a level $k \in \mathcal{L}_{OBDD}(V)$ we may over-approximate the 1-level cut $C^{B}_{1:f}$ for $B \subseteq \{\bot, \top\}$ at $j = k$ by summing the following four disjoint contributions.

1. After having obtained all outgoing arcs for unreduced nodes for level k, the priority queue only contains outgoing arcs from a level $\ell < k$ to a level $\ell' > k$. All of these arcs (may) contribute to the cut.
2. After having obtained all outgoing arcs for level k, all yet unread arcs to terminals $b \in B$ are from some level $\ell < k$ and (may) contribute to the cut.
3. BDD nodes v removed by the first reduction rule in favor of its reduced child v' and $w_B(\_ \rightarrow v') = 1$ (may) contribute up to $|in(v')|$ arcs to the cut.
4. BDD nodes v' that are output on level k after merging duplicates (definitely) contribute with $w_B(v'.low) + w_B(v'.high)$ arcs to the cut.

1 and 2 can be obtained with some bookkeeping on the priority queue and the contents of the file containing arcs to terminals. 4 can be resolved when reduced nodes are pushed to the output. Yet, 3 cannot just use the immediate indegree of the removed node v since, as in Fig. 8, it may be part of a longer chain of redundant nodes. Here, the actual contribution to the cut at level $j = k$ is the indegree to the entire chain ending in v. Due to the single bottom-up sweep style of the Reduce algorithm, the best we can do is to assume the worst and always count reduced arcs $s' \rightarrow t'$ where a node v has been removed between s' and t' as part of the maximum cut.

Over-Approximating the 2*-Level Cut.* The above over-approximation of the 1-level cut can be extended to recreate the greedy algorithm from the proof of Proposition 2. Notice, the 1-level (S, T) cut mentioned before places all nodes of level j in S, whereas these nodes are free to be moved to T in the 2-level cut for $j-1$. Specifically, Part 4 should be changed such that v' contributes with

$$\max(w_B(v'.low) + w_B(v'.high), |in(v')|) \ .$$

This requires knowing $|in(v')|$. The Reduce algorithm in [38] reads from a file containing the parents of an unreduced node v, so information about the reduced result v' can be forwarded to its unreduced parents. Hence, one can accumulate the number of parents, $|in(v)|$. If $|in(v')|$ is not affected by the first reduction rule then this is an upper bound of $|in(v')|$. Otherwise, it still is sound in combination with the above over-counting to solve the 3rd type of contribution.

4 Experimental Evaluation

We have extended Adiar to incorporate the ideas presented in Sect. 3. Each algorithm has been extended to compute sound upper bounds for the next phase. Based on these, each algorithm chooses during initialisation between running with TPIE's internal or external memory data structures. This choice is encapsulated within C++ templates, which avoids introducing any costly indirection when using the auxiliary data structures.

Section 3.4 motivates the following three levels of granularity:

- **#nodes:** Theorem 1 is used based on knowing the number of internal nodes in the input and deriving the trivial worst-case size of the output.

- **1-level:** Extends #nodes with Theorem 2. The i-level cuts are given by computing the 1-level cut with the proof of Proposition 1 as described in Sect. 3.4 and then applying Lemma 1 to obtain a bound on the 2-level cut.
- **2-level:** Extends the 1-level variant by computing 2-level cuts directly with the algorithm based on the proof of Proposition 2 in Sect. 3.4.

All three variants include the computation of 1-level cuts – even the #nodes one. This reduces the number of variables in our measurements. We have separately measured the slowdown introduced by computing 1-level cuts to be 1.0%.

4.1 Benchmarks

We have evaluated the quality of our modifications on the four benchmarks below that are publicly available at [32]. These were also used to measure the performance of Adiar 1.0 (BDDs) and 1.1 (ZDDs) in [34,38]. The first benchmark is a circuit verification problem and the others are combinatorial problems.

- ***EPFL* Combinational Benchmark Suite** [2]. The task is to check equivalence between an original hardware circuit (specification) and an optimised circuit (implementation). We construct BDDs for all output gates in both circuits, and check if they are equivalent. We focus on the 23 out of the 46 optimised circuits that Adiar could verify in [38]. Input gates are encoded as a single variable, x_i, with a maximum 2-level cut of size 2.
- **Knight's Tour.** On an $N_r \times N_c$ chessboard, the set of all paths of a Knight is created by intersecting the valid transitions for each of the $N_r N_c$ time steps. The cut of each such ZDD constraint is $\sim 8N_r N_c$. Then, each Hamiltonian constraint with cut size 4 is imposed onto this set [34].
- **N-Queens.** On an $N \times N$ chessboard, the constraints on placing queens are combined per row, based on a base case for each cell. Each row constraint is finally accumulated into the complete solution [21]. For BDDs, each basic cell constraint has a cut size of $\sim 3N$, while for ZDDs it is only 3.
- **Tic-Tac-Toe.** Initially, a BDD or ZDD with cut size $\sim N$ is created to represent that N crosses have been set within a $4 \times 4 \times 4$ cube. Then for each of the 76 lines, a constraint is added to exclude any *non-draw* states [21]. Each such line constraint has a cut size of 4 with BDDs and 6 with ZDDs.

4.2 Tradeoff Between Precision and Running Time

We have run all benchmarks on a consumer-grade laptop with one 2.6 GHz Intel i7-4720HQ processor, 8 GiB of RAM, 230 GiB of available SSD disk, running Fedora 36, and compiling code with GCC 12.2.1. For each of these 71 benchmark instances, Adiar has been given 128 MiB or 4 GiB of internal memory.

All combinatorial benchmarks use a unary operation at the end to count the number of solutions. Table 1 shows the average ratio between the predicted and actual maximum size of this operation's priority queue. As instances grow larger, the quality of the #nodes heuristic deteriorates for BDDs. On the other

Table 1. Geometric mean of the ratio between the predicted and the actual maximum size of the unary Count operation's priority queue. This average is also weighed by the input size to gauge the predictions' quality for larger BDDs.

	BDD			ZDD		
	#nodes	1-level	2-level	#nodes	1-level	2-level
Unweighted Avg.	2.1%	69.2%	86.3%	15.2%	47.8%	67.0%
Weighted Avg.	0.1%	76.5%	77.4%	25.0%	50.7%	61.8%

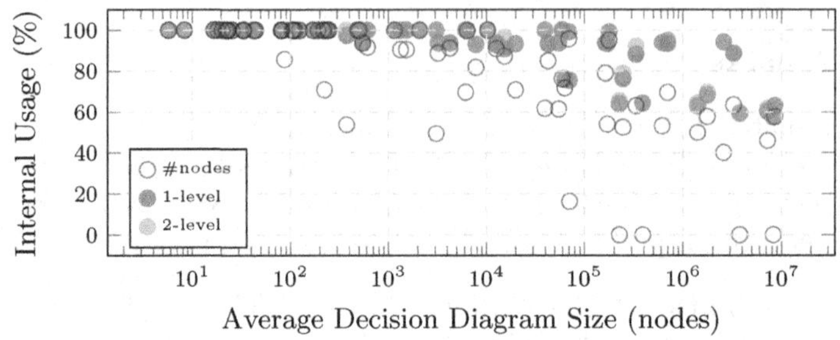

Fig. 9. *Internal* vs. *external* memory usage for product constructions (128 MiB).

hand, the 1 and 2-level cut heuristics are at most off by a factor of 2. Hence, since the priority queue's maximum size is some 2-level cut, the algorithms in Sect. 3.4 are only over-approximating the actual maximum 2-level cut by a factor of 2. The result of this is that i-level cuts can safely identify that a BDD with $5.2 \cdot 10^7$ nodes (1.1 GiB) can be processed purely within 128 MiB of internal memory available. The precision of i-level cuts are worse for ZDDs, but still allow processing a ZDD with $4.3 \cdot 10^7$ nodes (978 MiB) with 128 MiB of memory.

This difference in precision affects the product construction algorithms, e.g. the Apply operation. Figure 9 shows the amount of product constructions that each heuristic enables to run with internal memory data structures. Even when the average BDD was 10^7 nodes (229 MiB) or larger, with i-level cuts at least 59.5% of all algorithms were run purely in 128 MiB of memory, whereas with #nodes sometimes none of them were. Yet, while there is a major difference between #nodes and 1-level cuts, going further to 2-level cuts only has a minor effect.

How often internal memory could be used is also reflected in Adiar's performance. Figure 10 shows the difference in the running time between using i-level cuts and only using #nodes. All benchmarks runs were interleaved and repeated at least 8 times. The minimum measured running time is reported as it minimises any noise due to hardware and the operating system [12]. Since the #nodes version also includes the computation for the 1-level cuts but does not use them, any performance decrease in Fig. 10 for 1-level cuts is due to noise.

Using the geometric mean, 1-level cuts provide a 4.9% improvement over #nodes. Considering the 1.0% overhead for computing the 1-level cuts, this

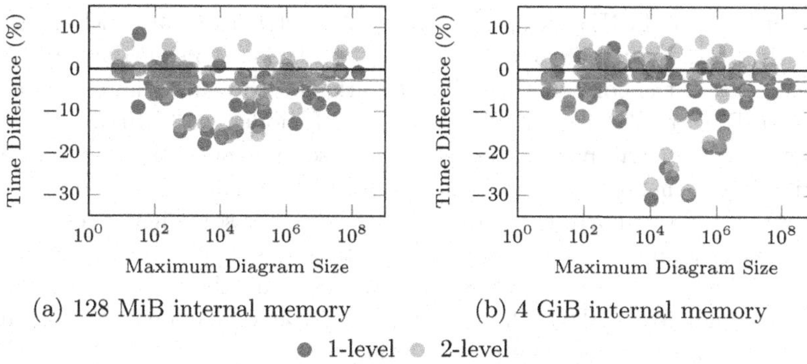

Fig. 10. Adiar with i-level cuts compared to #nodes (lower is better). Horizontal lines show the average difference in performance.

is a net improvement of 3.9%. More importantly, in a considerable amount of benchmarks, using i-level cuts improves the performance by more than 10%, sometimes by 30%. These are the benchmark instances where only i-level cuts can guarantee that all auxiliary data structures can fit within internal memory, yet the instances are still so small that there is a major overhead in initialising TPIE's external memory data structures.

The improvement in precision obtained by using 2-level cuts does not pay off in comparison to using 1-level cuts. On average, using 2-level cuts only improves the performance of using #nodes with 2.6%. That is, the additional cost of computing 2-level cuts outweighs the benefits of its added precision.

Adiar with i-level cuts did not slow down as internal memory was increased from 128 MiB to 4 GiB. That is, the precision of both these bounds – unlike #nodes – ensures that external memory data structures are only used when their initialisation cost is negligible. Hence, Adiar with 1-level cuts covers all our needs at the minimal computational cost and so is included in Adiar 1.2.

4.3 Impact of Introducing Cuts on Adiar's Running Time

In [34,38] we measured the performance of Adiar 1.0 and 1.1 against the conventional BDD packages CUDD 3.0 [39] and Sylvan 1.5 [16]. In those experiments [33,35], Sylvan was not using multi-threading and all experiments were run on machines with 384 GiB of RAM of which 300 GiB was given to the BDD package. To gauge the impact of using cuts, we now compare our previous measurements without cuts to new ones with cuts on the exact same hardware and settings. The results of our new measurements are available at [36].

With 300 GiB internal memory available, all three modified versions of Adiar essentially behave the same. Hence, in Fig. 1 (cf. Sect. 1) we show the best performance for all three versions on top of the data reported in [38]. Even on the largest benchmarks we see a performance increase by exploiting cuts. Most important is the increase in performance for the moderate-size instances where the initialisation of TPIE's external memory data structures are costly, e.g. N-Queens with $N < 11$ and Tic-Tac-Toe with $N < 19$. Based on the data in [34,38] these instances of the combinatorial benchmarks are the ones where the largest constructed BDD or ZDD is smaller than $4.9 \cdot 10^6$ nodes (113 MiB).

Using the geometric mean, the time spent solving both the combinatorial and verification benchmarks decreased with Adiar 1.2 on average by 86.1% (with median 89.7%) in comparison to previous versions. For some instances this difference is even 99.9%. In fact, Adiar 1.2 is in some specific instances of the Tic-Tac-Toe benchmarks faster than CUDD. These are the very instances that are large enough for CUDD's first – and comparatively expensive – garbage collection to kick in and dominate its running time.

Verifying the EPFL benchmarks involves constructing a few BDDs that are larger than the 113 MiB bound mentioned above, but most BDDs are much smaller. For the 15 EPFL circuits that only generate BDDs smaller than 113 MiB, using cuts decreases the computation time on average by 92% (with median 92%). While Adiar v1.0 still took 56.5 h to verify these 15 circuits, now with Adiar 1.2 it only takes 4.0 h to do the same. These 52.5 h are primarily saved within one of the 15 circuits. Specifically, using cuts has decreased the time to verify the `sin` circuit optimised for depth by 52.1 h. Here, the average BDD size is 2.9 KiB, the largest BDD constructed is 25.5 MiB in size, and up to 42,462 BDDs are in use concurrently.

Despite this massive performance improvement with Adiar 1.2 due to our new technique, there is still a significant gap of 3.7 h with CUDD and Sylvan on these 15 circuits. We attribute this to the fact that these benchmarks also include many computations on really tiny BDDs. Although we keep the auxiliary data structures in internal memory, the resulting BDDs are still stored on disk, even when they consist of only a few nodes.

5 Conclusion

We introduce the idea of a maximum i-level cut for DAGs that restricts the cut to be within a certain window. For $i \in \{1, 2\}$ the problem of computing the maximum i-level cut is polynomial-time computable. But, we have been able to piggyback a slight over-approximation with only a 1% linear overhead onto Adiar's I/O-efficient bottom-up Reduce operation.

An i-level cut captures the shape of Adiar's auxiliary data structures during the execution of its I/O-efficient time-forward processing algorithms. Hence, similar to how conventional recursive BDD algorithms have the size of their call stack linearly dependent on the depth of the input, the maximum 2-level cuts provide a sound upper bound on the memory used during Adiar's computation. Using this, Adiar 1.2 can deduce soundly whether using exclusively internal memory is possible, increasing its performance in those cases. Doing so decreases computation time for moderate-size instances up to 99.9% and on average by 86.1% (with median 89.7%).

5.1 Related and Future Work

Many approaches tried to achieve large-scale BDD manipulation with distributed memory algorithms, some based on breadth-first algorithms, e.g. [21,25,40,42]. Yet, none of these approaches obtained a satisfactory performance. The speedup obtained by a multicore implementation [16] relies on parallel depth-first algorithms using concurrent hash tables, which doesn't scale to external memory.

CAL [31] (based on a breadth-first approach [6,29]) is to the best of our knowledge the only other BDD package designed to process large BDDs on a single machine. CAL is I/O efficient, assuming that a single BDD level fits into main memory; the I/O efficiency of Adiar does not depend on this assumption. Similar to Adiar, CAL suffers from bad performance for small instances. To deal with this, CAL switches to the classical recursive depth-first algorithms when all the given input BDDs contain fewer than 2^{19} nodes (15 MiB). As far as we can tell, CAL's threshold is purely based on experimental results of performance and without any guarantees of soundness. That is, the output may potentially exceed main memory despite all inputs being smaller than 2^{19} nodes, which would slow it down significantly due to random-access. For BDDs smaller than CAL's threshold of 2^{19} nodes, Adiar 1.2 with i-level cuts could run almost all of our experiments with auxiliary data structures purely in internal memory.

Yet, as is evident in Fig. 1, when dealing with decision diagrams smaller than 44.000 nodes (1 MiB), there is still a considerable gap between Adiar's performance and conventional depth-first based BDD packages (see also end of Sect. 4.3). Apparently, we have reached a lower bound on the BDD size for which time-forward processing on external memory is efficient. Solving this would require an entirely different approach: one that can efficiently and seamlessly combine BDDs stored in internal memory with BDDs stored in external memory.

5.2 Applicability Beyond Decision Diagrams

Our idea is generalisable to all time-forward processing algorithms: the contents of the priority queues are at any point in time a 2-level cut with respect to the input and/or output DAG. Hence, one can bound the algorithm's memory usage if one can compute a levelisation function and the 1-level cuts of the inputs.

A levelisation function is derivable with the preprocessing step in [19] and the cut sizes can be computed with an I/O-efficient version of the greedy algorithm presented in this paper. Yet for our approach to be useful in practice, one has to identify a levelisation function that best captures the structure of the DAG in relation to the succeeding algorithms and where both the computation of the levelisation and the 1-level cut can be computed with only a negligible overhead.

Acknowledgements. We want to thank Anna Blume Jakobsen for her help implementing the use of i-level cuts in Adiar and Kristoffer Arnsfelt Hansen for his input on the computational complexity of these cuts. Finally, thanks to the Centre for Scientific Computing, Aarhus, (phys.au.dk/forskning/cscaa/) for running our benchmarks.

References

1. Aggarwal, A., Vitter, J.S.: The input/output complexity of sorting and related problems. Commun. ACM **31**(9), 1116–1127 (1988). https://doi.org/10.1145/48529.48535
2. Amarú, L., Gaillardon, P.E., De Micheli, G.: The EPFL combinational benchmark suite. In: 24th International Workshop on Logic & Synthesis (2015)
3. Amparore, E.G., Donatelli, S., Gallà, F.: starMC: an automata based CTL* model checker. PeerJ Comput. Sci. **8**, e823 (2022)
4. Arge, L.: The I/O-complexity of ordered binary-decision diagram manipulation. In: Staples, J., Eades, P., Katoh, N., Moffat, A. (eds.) ISAAC 1995. LNCS, vol. 1004, pp. 82–91. Springer, Heidelberg (1995). https://doi.org/10.1007/BFb0015411
5. Arge, L.: The I/O-complexity of ordered binary-decision diagram. In: BRICS RS preprint series, vol. 29. Department of Computer Science, University of Aarhus (1996). https://doi.org/10.7146/brics.v3i29.20010
6. Ashar, P., Cheong, M.: Efficient breadth-first manipulation of binary decision diagrams. In: IEEE/ACM International Conference on Computer-Aided Design (ICCAD), pp. 622–627. IEEE Computer Society Press (1994). https://doi.org/10.1109/ICCAD.1994.629886
7. Brace, K.S., Rudell, R.L., Bryant, R.E.: Efficient implementation of a BDD package. In: 27th Design Automation Conference (DAC), pp. 40–45. Association for Computing Machinery (1990). https://doi.org/10.1109/DAC.1990.114826
8. Bryant, R.E.: Graph-based algorithms for Boolean function manipulation. IEEE Trans. Comput. **C-35**(8), 677–691 (1986). https://doi.org/10.1109/TC.1986.1676819
9. Bryant, R.E., Biere, A., Heule, M.J.H.: Clausal proofs for pseudo-Boolean reasoning. In: TACAS 2022. LNCS, vol. 13243, pp. 443–461. Springer, Cham (2022). https://doi.org/10.1007/978-3-030-99524-9_25
10. Bryant, R.E., Heule, M.J.H.: Dual proof generation for quantified Boolean formulas with a BDD-based solver. In: Platzer, A., Sutcliffe, G. (eds.) CADE 2021. LNCS (LNAI), vol. 12699, pp. 433–449. Springer, Cham (2021). https://doi.org/10.1007/978-3-030-79876-5_25
11. Bryant, R.E., Heule, M.J.H.: Generating extended resolution proofs with a BDD-based SAT solver. In: TACAS 2021. LNCS, vol. 12651, pp. 76–93. Springer, Cham (2021). https://doi.org/10.1007/978-3-030-72016-2_5
12. Chen, J., Revels, J.: Robust benchmarking in noisy environments. arXiv (2016). https://arxiv.org/abs/1608.04295
13. Chiang, Y.J., Goodrich, M.T., Grove, E.F., Tamassia, R., Vengroff, D.E., Vitter, J.S.: External-memory graph algorithms. In: Proceedings of the Sixth Annual ACM-SIAM Symposium on Discrete Algorithms, pp. 139–149. SODA 1995, Society for Industrial and Applied Mathematics (1995)
14. Ciardo, G., Miner, A.S., Wan, M.: Advanced features in SMART: the stochastic model checking analyzer for reliability and timing. SIGMETRICS Perform. Evaluation Rev. **36**(4), 58–63 (2009)
15. Cimatti, A., Clarke, E., Giunchiglia, F., Roveri, M.: NuSMV: a new symbolic model checker. Int. J. Softw. Tools Technol. Transfer **2**, 410–425 (2000). https://doi.org/10.1007/s100090050046
16. Van Dijk, T., Van de Pol, J.: Sylvan: multi-core framework for decision diagrams. Int. J. Softw. Tools Technol. Transfer **19**, 675–696 (2016). https://doi.org/10.1007/s10009-016-0433-2

17. Gammie, P., van der Meyden, R.: MCK: model checking the logic of knowledge. In: Alur, R., Peled, D.A. (eds.) CAV 2004. LNCS, vol. 3114, pp. 479–483. Springer, Heidelberg (2004). https://doi.org/10.1007/978-3-540-27813-9_41
18. He, L., Liu, G.: Petri net based symbolic model checking for computation tree logic of knowledge. arXiv (2020). https://arxiv.org/abs/2012.10126
19. Hellings, J., Fletcher, G.H., Haverkort, H.: Efficient external-memory bisimulation on DAGs. In: Proceedings of the 2012 ACM SIGMOD International Conference on Management of Data, pp. 553–564. SIGMOD 2012, Association for Computing Machinery (2012). https://doi.org/10.1145/2213836.2213899, https://doi.org/10.1145/2213836.2213899
20. Kant, G., Laarman, A., Meijer, J., van de Pol, J., Blom, S., van Dijk, T.: LTSmin: high-performance language-independent model checking. In: Baier, C., Tinelli, C. (eds.) TACAS 2015. LNCS, vol. 9035, pp. 692–707. Springer, Heidelberg (2015). https://doi.org/10.1007/978-3-662-46681-0_61
21. Kunkle, D., Slavici, V., Cooperman, G.: Parallel disk-based computation for large, monolithic binary decision diagrams. In: 4th International Workshop on Parallel Symbolic Computation (PASCO), pp. 63–72 (2010). https://doi.org/10.1145/1837210.1837222
22. Lampis, M., Kaouri, G., Mitsou, V.: On the algorithmic effectiveness of digraph decompositions and complexity measures. Discrete Optim. **8**(1), 129–138 (2011). https://doi.org/10.1016/j.disopt.2010.03.010. parameterized Complexity of Discrete Optimization
23. Lomuscio, A., Qu, H., Raimondi, F.: MCMAS: an open-source model checker for the verification of multi-agent systems. Int. J. Softw. Tools Technol. Transfer **19**(1), 9–30 (2015). https://doi.org/10.1007/s10009-015-0378-x
24. Meyer, U., Sanders, P., Sibeyn, J.: Algorithms for Memory Hierarchies: Advanced Lectures. Springer, Heidelberg (2003). https://doi.org/10.1007/3-540-36574-5
25. Milvang-Jensen, K., Hu, A.J.: BDDNOW: a parallel BDD package. In: Gopalakrishnan, G., Windley, P. (eds.) FMCAD 1998. LNCS, vol. 1522, pp. 501–507. Springer, Heidelberg (1998). https://doi.org/10.1007/3-540-49519-3_32
26. Minato, S.I.: Zero-suppressed BDDs for set manipulation in combinatorial problems. In: 30th Design Automation Conference (DAC), pp. 272–277. Association for Computing Machinery (1993). https://doi.org/10.1145/157485.164890
27. Minato, S.I., Ishiura, N., Yajima, S.: Shared binary decision diagram with attributed edges for efficient Boolean function manipulation. In: 27th Design Automation Conference (DAC), pp. 52–57. Association for Computing Machinery (1990). https://doi.org/10.1145/123186.123225
28. Mølhave, T.: Using TPIE for processing massive data sets in C++. Duke University, Durham, NC, Technical report (2012)
29. Ochi, H., Yasuoka, K., Yajima, S.: Breadth-first manipulation of very large binary-decision diagrams. In: International Conference on Computer Aided Design (ICCAD), pp. 48–55. IEEE Computer Society Press (1993). https://doi.org/10.1109/ICCAD.1993.580030
30. Papadimitriou, C.H., Yannakakis, M.: Optimization, approximation, and complexity classes. J. Comput. Syst. Sci. **43**(3), 425–440 (1991). https://doi.org/10.1016/0022-0000(91)90023-X
31. Sanghavi, J.V., Ranjan, R.K., Brayton, R.K., Sangiovanni-Vincentelli, A.: High performance BDD package by exploiting memory hierarchy. In: 33rd Design Automation Conference (DAC), pp. 635–640. Association for Computing Machinery (1996). https://doi.org/10.1145/240518.240638

32. Sølvsten, S.C.: BDD Benchmark. Zenodo (2023). https://doi.org/10.5281/zenodo.7040263
33. Sølvsten, S.C., van de Pol, J.: Adiar 1.0.1 : Experiment data (11 2021). https://doi.org/10.5281/zenodo.5638551
34. Sølvsten, S.C., van de Pol, J.: Adiar 1.1: zero-suppressed decision diagrams in external memory. In: Rozier, K.Y., Chaudhuri, S. (eds.) NFM 2023. LNCS, vol. 13903, pp. 464–471. Springer, Heidelberg (2023). https://doi.org/10.1007/978-3-031-33170-1_28
35. Sølvsten, S.C., van de Pol, J.: Adiar 1.1.0 : experiment data (2023). https://doi.org/10.5281/zenodo.7709134
36. Sølvsten, S.C., van de Pol, J.: Adiar 1.2.0 : experiment data (2023). https://doi.org/10.5281/zenodo.8124120
37. Sølvsten, S.C., van de Pol, J.: Predicting memory demands of BDD operations using maximum graph cuts (extended paper) (2023)
38. Sølvsten, S.C., de Pol, J., Jakobsen, A.B., Thomasen, M.W.B.: Adiar binary decision diagrams in external memory. In: TACAS 2022. LNCS, vol. 13244, pp. 295–313. Springer, Cham (2022). https://doi.org/10.1007/978-3-030-99527-0_16
39. Somenzi, F.: CUDD: CU decision diagram package, 3.0. Technical report, University of Colorado at Boulder (2015)
40. Stornetta, T., Brewer, F.: Implementation of an efficient parallel BDD package. In: Design Automation Conference Proceedings, vol. 33, pp. 641–644 (1996). https://doi.org/10.1109/DAC.1996.545653
41. Vengroff, D.E.: A transparent parallel I/O environment. In: In Proceedings of 1994 DAGS Symposium on Parallel Computation, pp. 117–134 (1994)
42. Yang, B., O'Hallaron, D.R.: Parallel breadth-first BDD construction. SIGPLAN Not. **32**(7), 145–156 (1997). https://doi.org/10.1145/263767.263784

Better Predicates and Heuristics for Improved Commutativity Synthesis

Adam Chen[1(✉)], Parisa Fathololumi[1], Mihai Nicola[1], Jared Pincus[2], Tegan Brennan[1], and Eric Koskinen[1]

[1] Stevens Institute of Technology, Hoboken, NJ, USA
{achen19,pfathol1,lnicola,tbrenna5,ekoskine}@stevens.edu
[2] Boston University, Boston, MA, USA
pincus@bu.edu

Abstract. Code commutativity has increasingly many applications including proof methodologies for concurrency, reductions, automated parallelization, distributed systems and blockchain smart contracts. While there has been some work on automatically generating commutativity conditions through abstraction refinement, the performance of such refinement algorithms critically depends on (i) the universe of predicates and (ii) the choice of the next predicate during search, and thus far this has not been examined in detail.

In this paper, we improve commutativity synthesis by addressing these under-explored requirements. We prune the universe of predicates through a combination of better predicate generation, new *a priori* syntactic filtering, and through dynamic reduction of the search space. We also present new predicate selection heuristics: one based on look-ahead, and one that utilizes model counting to greedily cover the search space.

Our work is embodied in the new commutativity synthesis tool SERVOIS2, a generational improvement over the state-of-the-art tool SERVOIS. SERVOIS2 is implemented in a faster language and has support for CVC5 and Z3. We contribute new, non-trivial commutativity benchmarks. All of the new features in SERVOIS2 are shown to either increase performance (geomean 3.58× speedup) or simplify the conditions generated, when compared against SERVOIS. We also show that our look-ahead heuristic leads to better scaling with respect to the number of predicates.

1 Introduction

Commutativity of data structure methods and program code applies to a wide variety of contexts, ranging from proof methodologies for concurrency (*e.g.* SIEVER [1], CIVL [2], Anchor [3]) to exploiting multicore (*e.g.* parallelizing compilers [4], transactional memory [5] declarative programming [6,7], scalable systems [8]) to distributed systems (*e.g.* CRDTs [9] and blockchain [10,11]).

Accordingly, there have been a variety of techniques and tools for reasoning about commutativity, including program analysis [4], sampling [12], random interpretation [13], and abstract interpretation [11]. A recent workshop[1] exemplifies the rising interest in commutativity.

[1] https://pldi22.sigplan.org/home/cora-2022.

É. André and J. Sun (Eds.): ATVA 2023, LNCS 14216, pp. 93–113, 2023.
https://doi.org/10.1007/978-3-031-45332-8_5

In many contexts program code does not always commute, and it is therefore helpful to specify the *conditions* under which code commutes. In a hashtable, for example, inserting key k commutes with removing key k' only when $k \neq k'$. Bansal *et al.* [14,15] introduced an abstraction-refinement method for automatically synthesizing such commutativity conditions. The idea is to recursively test the logical space using an SMT solver, accumulating conditions that imply commutativity or non-commutativity in disjunctive normal form. While the authors provided a proof-of-concept abstraction-refinement algorithm, they did not explore deeper performance considerations including more aggressive search heuristics, semantic predicate treatment, model counting optimizations, scalability, etc.

This paper focuses on how commutativity condition refinement can be improved by addressing the key search parameters. By addressing these performance considerations, we improve speed and scalability, as well as quality of outputted conditions. We encapsulate our results in a new tool that is a generation improvement in synthesizing commutativity conditions.

Contributions. Our work improves the state-of-the-art in the following ways:

1. *Predicate semantics* (Sect. 3). In the state of the art, predicates must be built by manually writing terms, and are then mildly filtered and used without any information as to how one predicate relates to another. Refinement is exponential in the number of predicates so it is important to focus on important predicates. To that end, we improve the treatment of predicates by both syntactically and then semantically filtering redundant predicates. We next show how the information from filtering can be used to construct a lattice of predicates, ordered by implication, and use this lattice to better filter predicates and prune the state space during search. We also automatically extract terms from the input problem's pre/post relations.
2. *Search heuristics* (Sect. 4). A key step in the algorithm is choosing the next predicate to divide the search space. We implement two new heuristics:
   - `poke2`: A new predicate selection heuristic which avoids redundant SMT work, while also using the information obtained more directly. Consequently, it performs at most half as many SMT queries, if not fewer, than SERVOIS's original implementation.
   - `mcMax`: A heuristic that employs model counting to more quickly cover the search space. Model counting is the problem of computing the number of models (*i.e.* distinct assignments to variables) that satisfy a given predicate [16]. As many predicates have infinitely many solutions, model-counting constraint solvers return the number of solutions for a given predicate within a given bound [17,18]. The `mcMax` heuristic takes a quantitative approach to predicate selection by leveraging model-counting to greedily pick predicates based on the largest covering of the state space, making choices based on approximate finite-domain information, yet maintaining soundness of the overall infinite-domain algorithm.
3. *New implementation and pragmatic concerns* (Sect. 5). We implemented SERVOIS2 in OCaml, exploiting the expected performance benefits of OCaml

over Python. Our implementation is parametric on SMT solver, now supporting CVC4, CVC5 and Z3. We therefore inherit the expanded theory support, expanding the domains in which commute conditions can be synthesized. SERVOIS2 can now, for example, synthesize commute conditions for Strings operations like `hasChar` and `concat`. We also support interruption, emitting a sound but incomplete condition, allowing SERVOIS2 to be used in a larger variety of new settings. Finally, SERVOIS2 has a more well-defined API (as an OCaml type), allowing one to use it as a library. SERVOIS2 is publicly available at: `github.com/veracity-lang/servois2`. The artifact, which contains a copy of the code, is available at: https://www.doi.org/10.5281/zenodo.7935263.

4. Evaluation (Sect. 6). In order to show that our approaches improve performance in practice, we introduced new, non-trivial benchmarks that Bansal *et al.* [14]'s tool SERVOIS struggles to solve. We evaluated all of SERVOIS2's new approaches, including the `poke2` and `mcMax` heuristics, in comparison to a faithful re-implementation of the `poke` heuristic in our new OCaml implementation on both the original benchmarks and our new ones. We also compared the performance improvements between heuristics with additional options for tuning the synthesis (see Sect. 6). Our experiments demonstrate that our approaches do give a substantial speedup—3.58× (geometric mean) faster. In cases that involve theories where model counting can be done efficiently (strings, linear integer arithmetic, integer arrays), `mcMax` is often able to offer better performance. Furthermore, `poke2` scales approximately linearly with the number of state variables, while the other heuristics (including all those in the prior work) diverge after only a few variables. Finally, given this wide variety of options, we used a portfolio approach, running each case with all options (solvers, heuristics, approaches to terms, etc.) and reporting back the first one to finish.

2 Background: Commutativity Synthesis

We begin with a brief review of abstraction-refinement commutativity condition synthesis, emphasizing key steps.

Suppose we have an abstract data type (ADT) method call $m(\bar{a})/r_m$, with method name m, taking argument vector $\bar{a}$ and returning value r_m. Similarly, consider a second method call $n(\bar{b})/r_n$. We say these method calls *commute* from an initial ADT state σ, provided that when methods are applied in either order, they lead to the same final ADT state, and will have observed the same return values along the way. We notate this $m \bowtie_{\sigma,\bar{a},\bar{b},r_m,r_n} n$, with subscripts omitted when the context is clear. A commutativity *condition* is a logical formula $\varphi_m^n(\sigma, \bar{a}, \bar{b})$ describing the conditions on the initial ADT state σ (and parameters $\bar{a}$ and $\bar{b}$) under which m and n always commute. (A non-commutativity condition $\tilde{\varphi}$ describes conditions when they always do not commute.) As an example, a Set ADT with methods `insert`(x) and `remove`(y), a sufficient commutativity condition would be $\varphi_{\texttt{insert}}^{\texttt{remove}} \equiv x \neq y$.

```
REFINE_n^m(H, P){                                  main (spec, terms){
  if valid(H ⇒ m ⋈̂ n) then                           φ := false;  φ̃ := false;
    φ := φ ∨ H;                                      let P = BUILD(terms) in
  else if valid(H ⇒ m ⋈̸̂ n) then                     try {REFINE_n^m(true, P); }
    φ̃ := φ̃ ∨ H;                                     catch (Interrupt e) {skip;}
  else                                               return(φ, φ̃); }
    let χ_c = counterexs. to ⋈̂
        χ_nc = counterexs. to ⋈̸̂ in
    let p = CHOOSE(H, P, χ_c, χ_nc) in
    REFINE_n^m(H ∧ p, P \ {p});
    REFINE_n^m(H ∧ ¬p, P \ {p});
}
```

Fig. 1. The commutativity condition REFINE algorithm [14].

We synthesize a commutativity condition φ via the REFINE algorithm [14], which takes as input, an ADT specification, with methods' pre/post conditions written in SMTLIB. The algorithm uses the binary operator $\hat{\bowtie}$, which is defined as $\bowtie$ on a lifted (total) version of the ADT; we omit the full details as they are not relevant to our improvements on the work. When run on a given pair of methods m and n, the output of the algorithm is a pair $(\varphi_m^n, \tilde{\varphi}_m^n)$ of commutativity/non-commutativity conditions. Consider as an example input, an ADT for a hashtable that has three variables representing the state: a size integer, a Set over sort E of keys, and a finite array H mapping elements of sort E to sort F. Then, for each method, *e.g.*, put(k, v), the input ADT specification includes a pre-condition (in this case true) and a post-condition relating the pre-state with input vector (size, keys, H, k, v) to a tuple of new values with return value (in this case, true or false representing success) (size_new, keys_new, H_new, r). The REFINE algorithm as output synthesizes commutativity conditions for the input method pair. In the case of the hashtable example, the solution for the commutativity synthesis of two calls of the same method put(k_1, v_1) and put(k_2, v_2) generated by the algorithm is $\varphi \equiv (v_1 = v_2 \wedge \mathsf{H}[k_1] = v_2 \wedge k_1 \in \mathsf{H}) \vee \ldots$ (truncated). Other cases (disjuncts) omitted for brevity.

The REFINE algorithm is presented in Fig. 1. The algorithm recursively partitions the logical space along conjunctions of predicates, which are selected from a set of predicates $\mathcal{P}$. When the algorithm finds a region of the state space H that is a sufficient condition for commutativity (or *mutatis mutandis* non-commutativity), it adds it to an accumulated DNF logical commutativity condition. Otherwise, the recursive calls use counterexamples to select a predicate p that differentiates the two counterexamples χ_c and χ_{nc}. This predicate is conjunctively added to H and used in the children recursive calls, and similarly for its negation. Figure 2 illustrates this process of partitioning the logical space through the use of differentiating counterexamples.

This process continues until a necessary and sufficient commutativity condition is found, or all combinations of predicates are exhausted. Typically, exhaustion of predicates is unlikely as there are exponentially many combinations of them. Furthermore, the algorithm can theoretically be interrupted (*e.g.* after a timeout) to yield a sound commutativity condition.

While the REFINE algorithm is a somewhat straightforward form of abstraction-refinement, the effectiveness of the technique and implementation thereof critically depends on how predicates are handled, selected, pruned, etc. We now discuss these details and how SERVOIS2 improves on each of them.

3 Semantic Treatment of Predicates

REFINE has worst-case exponential runtime in the number of predicates. While a CHOOSE function that picks good predicates helps, it is still important to generate a small set $\mathcal{P}$ of relevant predicates and be selective during each recursive call. At the very least, reducing the number of predicates gives linear improvements on runtime, as SMT solvers, as well as CHOOSE, must handle every predicate in $\mathcal{P}$. In this section, we describe better methods of reducing the size of this set $\mathcal{P}$.

(a) Improved predicate filtering. In SERVOIS, after the initial list of predicates was built from manually provided terms, the SMT solver was queried twice for each predicate, and any predicate that was tautologically true or false was discarded. We retain this functionality, but first perform an additional syntactic layer of filtering by dropping any predicate that is:

1. A reflexive operation on two identical terms,
2. An operation between two constants, or
3. A symmetric case of another predicate already included.

Since all of these filters are done purely syntactically, we save SMT work.

(b) Pruning by exploiting implication. We next determine which predicates imply other predicates. This can be done via syntactic implication rules such as $x > y \Rightarrow x+n > y+n$. As a benefit, we are able to compute the closure of the logical implication relation, and are able to sort predicates into equivalence classes. Thus by removing redundant predicates, the size of the set of predicates can be reduced.

Given logical implication relations, we can build a lattice out of the partially ordered set of predicates, ordered by the $\Rightarrow$ relation. This lattice information can

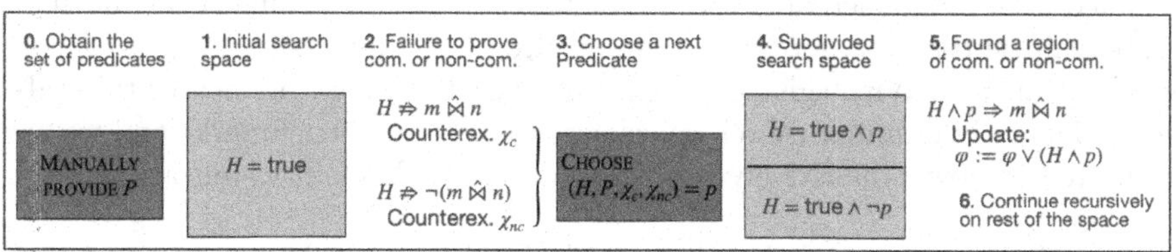

Fig. 2. REFINE recursively divides the logical search space using $\mathcal{P}$.

be used to dynamically prune predicates that become redundant during runtime due to selection of other, related predicates. For example, consider the following LIA benchmark `multiVarA` $\bowtie$ `multiVarB`. (Technically Servois/Servois2 inputs are given as ADT pre/post specifications, but we write this example as code illustration purposes).

```
int x, y;
bool multiVarA() {if(x>0) { x = 2*x + y; }; return true}
bool multiVarB() {if(x>y) { x = x - 2*y; } else { x = x - y; }; return true}
```

Here, the lattice identifies implication chains such as $0 > (2x + y) \Rightarrow (2x + y) \leq 0 \Rightarrow 2 > (2x + y) \Rightarrow (2x + y) \leq 2$, or $0 > (2x + y) \Rightarrow 0 \neq (2x + y)$. During search, we are able to use these chains to efficiently pruning the predicate lattice, effectively reducing the height of the lattice and thus width of the search tree.

Figure 3 illustrates our modifications to the original algorithm in Fig. 1. Starting from `main`, we perform automated predicate generation PredGen, which we will discuss below. From this set $\mathcal{P}$, we construct the lattice $\mathcal{L}$ with MkLat. Within Refine, we parameterize Choose by $\mathcal{L}$, allowing the Choose heuristics discussed in Sect. 4 to make choices based on $\mathcal{L}$. Finally, we prune the search space by using RmUpper to remove all predicates that are weaker, *i.e.* higher in the lattice, than the selected predicate pair $(p, \neg p)$. We may do similarly with the predicates stronger than the negation (RmLower). As a result, recursive calls will not have to consider any predicates that are already entailed by H.

Constructing the lattice can be costly as the size of the relation is quadratic in the number of predicates. Furthermore, syntactic rules cannot discover all implications, so an SMT solver must be invoked if more precision is desired. As we will see, it is not always worth this overhead. We have thus kept our lattice treatment as an optional feature. When disabled, the lattice simply behaves as a set of predicates (*i.e.* any predicate is only related to itself), à la Fig. 1, and assume that the set of predicates is closed under negation[2].

(c) Automatic predicate generation via term extraction. Servois requires the programmer to manually provide *terms* with each method in the ADT specification, which can be error-prone and tedious. These terms are then used to build predicates by using boolean relations such as $=, >$, etc. We are able to automatically generate the terms for synthesizing the predicates by traversing the method specification (state variables, method arguments, pre/post-condition), and extracting basic expressions (categorized by type). The expressions are then combined with predefined operations for each type (*e.g.* in-/equality for Integers, membership/subset/etc. for Sets, contains/prefix/etc. for Strings, ...) to generate the predicates. With this approach, we generate enough predicates to establish a sufficiently granular search space across all of our benchmarks and we are not limited in how exhaustively terms are provided. Manual-vs-automatic term

[2] To satisfy closure, we include negations of all predicates. This comes at no performance loss, as such additions can be skipped over by Choose. This is valid because Refine recurses upon the negation of the chosen predicate.

```
Refine^m_n(H, 𝓛){
  if valid(H ⇒ m ⋈̂ n) then
    φ := φ ∨ H;
  else if valid(H ⇒ m ⋈̸̂ n) then
    φ̃ := φ̃ ∨ H;
  else
    let χc = counterexs. to ⋈̂
        χnc = counterexs. to ⋈̸̂ in
    let p = Choose(H, 𝒫, χc, χnc) in
    let 𝓛' = 𝓛 \ {p, ¬p} in
    Refine^m_n(H ∧ p, RmLower(
                RmUpper(𝓛', p), ¬p));
    Refine^m_n(H ∧ ¬p, RmLower(
                RmUpper(𝓛', ¬p), p));
}

main (spec){
  φ := false;  φ̃ := false;
  let 𝒫 = PredGen(spec) in
  try {Refine^m_n(true, MkLat(𝒫)); }
  catch (Interrupt e) {skip;}
  return (φ, φ̃);
}
RmUpper(𝓛, p){
  return 𝓛 \ {p' | p ⇒ p' ∧ p ≠ p'};
}
RmLower(𝓛, p){
  return 𝓛 \ {p' | p' ⇒ p ∧ p ≠ p'};
}
```

Fig. 3. Our modified algorithm. Figure 1 is recovered when taking $\mathcal{L}$ to be the trivial lattice over negation completion.

extraction leads to different sets and quantities of predicates, which may affect how conditions are expressed. In Sect. 6 we discuss the performance impact.

(d) Syntax-based generation of predicates. Once predicates are automatically generated, it is natural to consider whether more complex predicates can be generated. While the original tool only considered predicates on two given terms, we found that often, compound terms that may not be provided or directly in the specification's syntax would be present in commutativity conditions. We added the expansion of terms with known and provided functions to allow for the automated generation of compound terms and predicates. Thus more complex commutativity conditions could be expressed, and the user does not have to already have specific predicates in mind when listing terms. Due to the exponential nature of syntax expansion, we get a greatly increased number of predicates. We found that this increase was too detrimental to performance to be practical—two or more iterations often times out. However there were still some test cases that benefited from performing one or two iterations, and the approach would likely be beneficial with improved pruning.

4 Search Heuristics

At each step, the Refine algorithm must Choose a predicate that differentiates the commutative and non-commutative examples. While any implementation of Choose maintains the soundness of Refine, due to the exponential nature of the number of subsets of predicates, choosing a "good" predicate is important both to efficiency and quality of the form of the emitted condition. We refer to a Choose strategy as a "heuristic". Bansal *et al.* [14] describe a heuristic—referred to as poke—which performs a greedy one-step look-ahead.

```
(1)  CHOOSE_poke2(H, 𝒫, χ_c, χ_nc){
(2)    let 𝒫′ = DiffingPreds(𝒫, χ_c, χ_nc) in
(3)    let weight(p) =
(4)      let p′ = if(⟦p⟧_χc) then p else !p in
(5)      if valid(H ∧ p′ ⇒ m ⋈̂ n) then
(6)        return 0;
(7)      else if valid(H∧ !p′ ⇒ m ⋈̸̂ n) then
(8)        return 0;
(9)      else
(10)       letχ′_c = counterexs. to ⋈̂ in
(11)       let χ′_nc = counterexs. to ⋈̸̂ in
(12)       return Length(
(13)             DiffingPreds(𝒫′, χ′_c, χ′_nc))
(14)   in list_min(weight, 𝒫′)
(15) }
(16) DiffingPreds(𝒫, χ_c, χ_nc){
(17)   return filter((fun p → ⟦p⟧_χc ≠ ⟦p⟧_χnc), 𝒫);
(18) }
```

Fig. 4. Pseudocode for our poke2 heuristic for choosing which predicate to recurse upon. Here, $\mathcal{P}$ may be obtained from $\mathcal{L}$ by taking the underlying set of predicates. list_min($f, \mathcal{P}$) returns the element of $\mathcal{P}$ that minimizes f.

In this section we introduce two new predicate selection heuristics called CHOOSE$_{\text{poke2}}$ and CHOOSE$_{\text{mcMax}}$ (or simply, poke2 and mcMax) that, as we show in Sect. 6, perform better than the CHOOSE$_{\text{poke}}$ of Bansal *et al.* [14], with trade-offs to consider between the two of them.

4.1 The poke2 Heuristic

We begin by formalizing the poke2 heuristic, and compare it to the previous poke heuristic. When the SMT solver is invoked with the "valid()" queries in REFINE, we obtain two satisfying counterexamples: χ_c for commutativity and χ_{nc} for non-commutativity. poke and poke2 share the common behavior to then proceed with two steps: (1) Test each predicate to see which hold in which counterexample (if either); this can be done in the same SMT query that was used for valid. This testing lets one find predicates that differ between the commutative counterexample and the non-commutative counterexample. This is summarized in *DiffingPreds*; the pseudocode for this subroutine is given at the bottom of Fig. 4. (2) Next, perform a partial look-ahead on each of these predicates—however, the way this is done differs between the heuristics.

- **The poke2 heuristic.** The full pseudocode for poke2 is given in Fig. 4. The partial look-ahead is encapsulated in the *weight* function. If a predicate was true in the commutative case then we can tentatively conjoin it with the commutativity condition and its inverse with the non-commutativity condition (*mutatis mutandis* for false—keeping track of which case is done on Line 4), then query the solver (Lines 5 and 7) to see how many predicates still

```
(1) CHOOSE_mcMax(H, P, χc, χnc){
(2)   let P′ = DiffingPreds(P, χc, χnc) in
(3)   let cover(p) = #(⟦p⟧) / #(Σ)
(4)       cover(¬p) = 1 − cover(p) in
(5)   let P″ =  list_max(cover, P′) in
(6)   return first(P″)
(7) }
```

(a) mcMax

```
(1) CHOOSE_mcMax-poke2(H, P, χc, χnc)
(2)   let P′ = DiffingPreds(P, χc, χnc) in
(3)   let cover(p) = #(⟦p⟧) / #(Σ)
(4)       cover(¬p) = 1 − cover(p) in
(5)   let P″ =  list_max(cover, P′) in
(6)   return list_min(weight, P″)
(7) }
```

(b) mcMax-poke2

Fig. 5. Pseudocode for mcMax heuristics. As before, $\mathcal{P}$ is obtained by taking the underlying set of $\mathcal{L}$.

differentiate the two cases. We define the number of remaining differentiating predicates to be the weight of the predicate (Lines 9–11). Finally we pick the differentiating predicate that results in the fewest remaining differentiating predicates in the look-ahead (Line 12). In the case that two predicates have the same number of new differentiating predicates, we prefer the simpler (measured in number of atoms) one (not shown).

- **The poke heuristic.** By contrast, in poke the predicate and its inverse were tested with both the commutative case and the non-commutative case, irrespective of whether it was true or false in the commutative case. This resulted in many degenerate return values, which not only increased SMT time, but also could pick less beneficial predicates.

There is no need to prove correctness of poke2, as the REFINE algorithm is correct for any implementation of CHOOSE that picks a differentiating predicate. Our evaluation of poke2 is thus based on runtime (more detail in Sect. 6.1).

4.2 The mcMax Heuristic

For theories where model counting is efficiently supported by existing tools, we introduce an additional heuristic called mcMax. mcMax uses model counting to determine the number of satisfying solutions for each constraint on the state space. It then uses this count to quantify how well each predicate covers the state space and picks the predicate with the best coverage.

Model counting requires a finite domain, so we treat state variables as finite on a bounded domain, *e.g.*, treating integers as fixed-length bit vectors. Recall that any implementation of CHOOSE is sound, so bounding the domain (temporarily as a heuristic hint) does not threaten soundness. For such fixed-length bit representations, we ideally require a bit width bound that is large enough to properly differentiate between coverage ratios. Experimentally, we found that a bound as low as 4-bit representation of integers was sufficient for LIA constraints with relatively small coefficients and a length of 4 was sufficient for string constraints.

We now describe how mcMax proceeds using the pseudocode given in Fig. 5. The mcMax heuristic starts off on Line 2 in a similar manner as poke heuristic by constructing the subset of differentiating predicates $\mathcal{P}'$ from the two satisfying counterexamples. In the next step (Lines 3–4), we calculate the coverage ratio for both p and its complement $\neg p$ as the fraction of their corresponding models' count. Finally, the predicate found to represent the largest state region is chosen (Line 5). Recall that REFINE traverses both the given predicate *and* its negation (shown in the recursive calls in Fig. 1). In the case that execution is interrupted, we observe the first recursive call may be explored, while the second is not. In these cases `mcMax` often leads to a better (higher coverage ratio) predicate compared to a non-model-counting heuristic, since we greedily pick the larger conjuncts.

To overcome the arbitrary first choice among equally covering predicates at line 6 in Fig. 5a, the variant `mcMax-poke2` equips `mcMax` with the weight-based ranking of predicates from `poke2`. Whenever the list of maximal coverage predicates returned by `mcMax` has at least two candidates, the predicate selection is turned over to `poke2` applied to the candidate list.

5 Implementation

SERVOIS2 is implemented in OCaml and is publicly released under the MIT License[3]. The tool has an underlying representation for SMT expressions, and parses input YAML files and the SMTLIB2 expressions within them. Examples of the SERVOIS/SERVOIS2 input format are available in the repository. The output commutativity condition is also an SMTLIB2 expression, but may be further constrained: since it is always in disjunctive normal form, and we add one conjunct at a time, we may model disjunctive normal form as a list of conjuncts, which are in turn lists of atoms. The lattice is implemented as a module parameterized by any module exposing an ordering relation, and is encoded as a graph with vertices stored in a map and two edge sets: that of covering elements and that of elements covered by it.

Model Counting. For counting the solutions satisfied by each predicate, we use the state-of-the-art model-counting constraint solver ABC [18] that, among other strengths, allows for passing the specific domain bound along with the model-counting query. ABC supports precise solving of model-counting queries over strings, booleans, and linear integer arithmetic. We memorize the counting results in an association list to reuse them in subsequent calls of $\text{CHOOSE}_{\texttt{mcMax}}$.

Model Counting for Integer Arrays. We expand the applicability of `mcMax` heuristics to predicates over array terms by adopting a method similar to the state-of-the-art model counter for bounded array constraints MCBAT [19]. This approach involves applying a sequence of model-count preserving reductions from the theory of arrays to the theory of uninterpreted functions and linear integer arithmetic before dispatching the query to ABC. While MCBAT focuses on formulas that are universally quantified over index variables, our procedure below

[3] https://github.com/veracity-lang/servois2.

addresses quantifier-free array constraints with terms $a[i]$ representing the value stored in the array a at index i.

Consider for example, the problem of counting the solutions $\langle x, i, j\rangle$ satisfying the predicate $(x[i] \geq x[j] - 1)$, where i, j are integer variables and x represents arrays of size 4. We accomplish the task in three stages. First, we translate the predicate into a list of linear integer arithmetic constraints that are conjoined into a formula. Then we count the number of satisfying solutions $\langle x_i, x_j, i, j\rangle$ by running ABC on this query:

$$(i \geq 0) \wedge (i < 4) \wedge (j \geq 0) \wedge (j < 4) \wedge (i = j \Rightarrow x_i = x_j) \wedge (x_i \geq x_j - 1)$$

Finally, we obtain the total model count by multiplying the translated query result with the value domain size twice, once for each of the unaccounted and implicitly unconstrained array values.

The reductions below summarize the steps of our model counting procedure for formulas with integer array constraints:

1. Replace all compound array index expressions e with fresh variables i and add corresponding constraints of the form $e = i$. Perform the replacement from the outermost expression inwardly. Consider, for example, the term $x[k+j-2] > 3$ occuring in the query. We first replace the access term $k + j - 2$ by a fresh variable i, and then introduce an additional constraint $i = k + j - 2$ which captures this replacement.
2. Add array bounds constraints for each array index variable i.
3. Perform Ackermann's reduction:
   - Replace all occurrences of array index terms $a[i]$ with fresh variables a_i, keeping track of the replaced mappings for each array variable a.
   - Add functional consistency constraints for each array variable and each pair of array index terms occurring in the query, i.e. $(i = j) \Rightarrow (a_i = a_j)$.
4. Dispatch the set of constraints to ABC and obtain the model-count $\#mc_{tr}$. Thus far, there are only minimal differences to the approach in [19].
5. Identify the unaccounted mappings for each array variable and compute the partial model-count by considering their summation and the unconstrained value domain: $\#mc_{unacc} = |\mathbb{Z}|^{unacc}$.
6. Obtain final model count as $\#mc = (\#mc_{tr} \ * \ \#mc_{unacc})$.

Additional Solvers & Theories. Servois was hardcoded to work with CVC4 [20]. We have parameterized Servois2 by SMT solver via OCaml modules and extended support for CVC5 [21] and for Z3 [22]. While mostly an implementation detail, this does allow us to leverage the additional strength of the other solvers. For example, CVC4 (as of version 1.8) did not have good support for modulus and division. Both CVC5 and Z3 are able to support such operations, and Servois2 is able to generate commutativity/non-commutativity conditions for modular arithmetic examples.

With expanded solver support, Servois2 can tackle more theories, including ones for which specialized solvers are useful. Neither *bit-vectors* nor *strings* were supported in the original release of SERVOIS, but SERVOIS2 can synthesize commutativity conditions for both theories. As an example, we showed that SERVOIS2 is capable of inferring that bit-vector negation always commutes with itself. We also benchmarked a few string examples, such as substr $\bowtie$ hasChar, as they also demonstrate the usefulness of model counting.

Early Termination. The following theorem is presented in Bansal *et al.* [14]:

Theorem 1. *For each* REFINE_n^m *iteration:* $\varphi \Rightarrow m \mathrel{\hat{\bowtie}} n$*, and* $\tilde{\varphi} \Rightarrow m \mathrel{\hat{\not\bowtie}} n$*.*

Thus, if updates to φ and $\tilde{\varphi}$ are atomic, then terminating the algorithm at any point will yield valid conditions. We take advantage of this in SERVOIS2 by allowing timeouts: the algorithm gracefully terminates after a designated time by outputting the incomplete (yet valid) conditions $\varphi, \tilde{\varphi}$.

This proves useful in practice, as not all commutativity conditions may be expressible in terms of the predicates available; a necessary and sufficient condition for synthesis of a complete commutativity condition via the REFINE algorithm is given in Bansal *et al.* [14]. In such cases, the algorithm must finish its exponential run-time, only to determine that no complete commutativity condition is expressible. Even if the algorithm does terminate, after a certain point, the commutativity condition may be more complex than is useful. Thus it is usually more useful to cut the execution short and report only the most important few disjuncts of the commutativity conditions. In Sect. 6.2 we describe an instance of both a case where the algorithm does not terminate and a case where the algorithm terminates, but we still may obtain a reasonable condition by limiting the execution time.

6 Evaluation

We evaluated whether SERVOIS2 improved over the state-of-the-art SERVOIS in terms of performance (speed) and expressivity. All experiments below were run on a machine with an AMD EPYC 7452 32-Core CPU, 128 GB RAM, Ubuntu 20.04, and OCaml 4.14.0.

Benchmarks. Our suite of 68 benchmarks begins with those used to evaluate SERVOIS in the prior work [14]. Since the core goal of our work is to improve performance, we have pruned down this set, removing those benchmarks for which all tested heuristics can synthesize a condition after zero or one iteration(s). For example, we omitted the counter and accumulator examples because the conditions generated were either true/false or a single atom. We also removed all similar method pairs with simple commutativity conditions from the remaining data structures: sets, hashtables (HT), and stacks (Sta).

In addition to these benchmarks, we contribute new benchmarks for strings (Str) and linear integer arithmetic calculations (LIA), and a benchmark based on rigid motions on hexagons (DiH, for "dihedral"). These serve to show the application of model counting, which works best on these domains. The model counter is not applicable to the other data sets due to presence of custom data declarations. It could also be run on the counter and accumulator benchmarks, but we do not expect that to be illustrative due to triviality.

Moreover, we used Veracity[4] project [6] benchmarks as additional nontrivial benchmarks. There are 26 reported benchmarks in Veracity that use commutativity synthesis. We have also implemented some new benchmarks, *e.g.* Solidity examples translated to Veracity, to demonstrate various aspects of our improvements in addition to more speedup. We elaborate on the usage of Veracity benchmarks in Sect. 6.2.

6.1 Performance Results

We would ideally compare the performance of SERVOIS2 versus SERVOIS, but since SERVOIS2 is written in OCaml, and SERVOIS is written in Python, there is an obvious speedup from compilation, and indeed we found SERVOIS2 to be at least twice as fast even using the same heuristics and on the same inputs. (As an example: the Hashtable put/put example was the slowest running benchmark—it took 5.31 s with SERVOIS using `poke`, and 2.61 s with SERVOIS2 using the same heuristic.)

However, our work is not aimed at comparing Python vs OCaml, so we instead benchmark across our new heuristics (`poke2` and `mcMax`) and features in comparison to a faithful re-implementation of SERVOIS's `poke` in OCaml. The re-implementation was created by manually translating the source code of SERVOIS.

Comparison to `poke` Baseline. To test the variety of features we have added, we ran each benchmark with all combinations of features:

- The heuristics `poke`, `poke2`, and `mcMax`/`mcMax-poke2` (when applicable).
- With each of the CVC4, CVC5, and Z3 solvers.
- With and without automatic term extraction (Sect. 3).

We report the configuration with the best performance in Table 1[5], using `poke` with CVC4 and no lattice, no term extraction as a reference point for comparison. The heuristic and solver is given, then whether term extraction was performed (notated TG). The geometric mean of the speedup ratio of the best configuration over `poke` was 3.58×. Note that this speedup is conservative, as the several benchmarks that timed out with `poke` (and did not with SERVOIS2) are excluded. We also report the change in the complexity of the synthesized commutativity condition in ΔA, indicating the change in the number of atoms in the synthesized condition. The full generated conditions are omitted; note that if synthesis terminates with a complete condition, the generated conditions will be logically equivalent, but sometimes the order of the terms changed. (†) indicates the cases where the tool terminated with an incomplete condition. We terminated the benchmarks at 120 s, and indicate the ones that still did not finish

[4] http://www.veracity-lang.org.

[5] mVarA and mVarB are short for multiVarA and multiVarB.

Table 1. Total number of benchmarks: 68 (33 trivial ones omitted)
Benchmarks that previously timed out: 3
Benchmarks that previously crashed: 2
† means condition generated was incomplete. $\boldsymbol{\Delta A}$ is change in atom count.
T indicates time out (set at 120 s). ☢ indicates cannot be run.

Benchmark	poke (s)	SRV2 (s)	**Spdup**	Δ**A**	Best Configuration		
DiH: motion ⋈ motion	☢	4.71	n/a	n/a	mcmax,	Z3,	
HT: put ⋈ put	2.22	1.28	1.73×	0	poke2,	CVC4,	
LIA: mVarA ⋈ mVarB	16.23	3.48	4.66×	0	poke2,	CVC5,	
LIA: sum ⋈ multiVarSum	$8.45^{\dagger}$	$8.36^{\dagger}$	1.01×	0	poke,	CVC4,	
LIA: sum ⋈ posSum	4.38	0.71	6.21×	0	poke2,	CVC4,	
Str2: set ⋈ concat	$9.89^{\dagger}$	$6.66^{\dagger}$	1.48×	−1	poke2,	Z3,	TG
Str3: read ⋈ write	$5.31^{\dagger}$	$0.86^{\dagger}$	6.21×	43	poke,	CVC5,	
Str: hasChar ⋈ concat	2.93	0.57	5.14×	0	mcmax,	CVC5,	TG
Str: substr ⋈ hasChar	1.75	0.74	2.35×	0	mcmaxpoke2,	CVC4,	
Vcy: array-disjoint	1.16	0.46	2.52×	0	poke2,	CVC4,	TG
Vcy: array1	1.51	0.51	2.96×	−2	mcmax,	CVC4,	
Vcy: array2	2.91	0.98	2.97×	0	poke2,	CVC4,	
Vcy: array3	1.92	0.53	3.62×	0	poke2,	Z3,	
Vcy: auction3	76.66	23.17	3.31×	8	poke2,	CVC4,	
Vcy: auction4	1.79	0.34	5.26×	0	poke2,	Z3,	TG
Vcy: dict	13.37	2.82	4.74×	0	poke2,	CVC5,	
Vcy: even-odd	☢	$1.02^{\dagger}$	n/a	n/a	poke2,	CVC5,	
Vcy: ht-add-put	7.63	3.37	2.26×	0	poke2,	CVC4,	
Vcy: ht-cond-mem-get	$1.28^{\dagger}$	$1.19^{\dagger}$	1.08×	−2	poke2,	CVC5,	
Vcy: ht-cond-size-get	1.66	0.71	2.34×	0	poke2,	CVC4,	
Vcy: ht-simple	38.84	18.78	2.07×	4	poke2,	CVC4,	
Vcy: linear-bool	3.15	0.90	3.50×	−2	mcmax,	CVC4,	
Vcy: linear-cond	2.09	1.30	1.61×	−1	poke2,	Z3,	
Vcy: loop-amt	$11.35^{\dagger}$	$0.30^{\dagger}$	37.83×	10	mcmax,	Z3,	
Vcy: loop-inter	7.83	2.40	3.26×	−21	mcmax,	CVC5,	
Vcy: matrix	3.17	0.24	13.21×	0	poke2,	Z3,	
Vcy: nested-counter_1	1.12	0.51	2.20×	0	poke2,	CVC4,	
Vcy: nested-counter_2	$4.74^{\dagger}$	$1.42^{\dagger}$	3.34×	−19	mcmax,	CVC5,	
Vcy: nonlinear	7.44	0.59	12.61×	0	poke2,	Z3,	
Vcy: pullPayment	7.69	1.59	4.84×	0	poke2,	Z3,	
Vcy: simple	$7.69^{\dagger}$	$2.29^{\dagger}$	3.36×	26	poke2,	CVC4,	
Vcy: standardToken2	**T**	11.31	n/a	n/a	poke2,	Z3,	TG
Vcy: standardToken3	**T**	1.45	n/a	n/a	poke2,	Z3,	TG
Vcy: standardToken4	2.34	0.35	6.69×	0	poke2,	Z3,	
Vcy: standardToken5	**T**	13.25	n/a	n/a	poke2,	Z3,	

within this time with **T**. A few benchmarks could not be run under CVC4, and those are marked with ☢. All benchmarks whose poke baseline took less than 1 s to execute were omitted from the table due to triviality.

Table 2. Comparison of runtimes for cases where lattice construction and model counting is applicable. Note that in many cases, lattice construction always times out or errors. Lattice timeout was defined at 300 s for Veracity benches and 30 s for other benches. Those rows are marked with n/a. `mVarA` is short for `multiVarA`.

Benchmark	Best Non-Latt.	Best Latt.	Spdup	ΔA	Best Config.	Latt Cnstr.
DiH: motion ⋈ motion	4.71	n/a	n/a	n/a	n/a	**T**
HT: put ⋈ put	1.28	1.16	1.11×	0	poke2, CVC4	0.31
LIA: mVarA ⋈ mVarB	3.48	1.14	3.07×	0	poke2, CVC4	10.39
LIA: sum ⋈ multiVarSum	8.36†	3.69†	2.27×	-53	mcmax, CVC4	1.87
Str2: set ⋈ concat	6.66†	n/a	n/a	n/a	n/a	**T**
Vcy: auction3	23.17	n/a	n/a	n/a	n/a	**T**
Vcy: dict	2.82	2.59	1.09×	0	poke2, CVC5	34.09
Vcy: even-odd	1.02†	0.98†	1.04×	0	poke2, CVC5	1.46
Vcy: ht-add-put	3.37	3.14	1.07×	0	poke2, CVC4	7.50
Vcy: ht-cond-mem-get	1.19†	n/a	n/a	n/a	n/a	**T**
Vcy: ht-simple	18.78	18.06	1.04×	0	poke2, CVC4	100.86
Vcy: linear-cond	1.30	1.06	1.23×	0	poke2, Z3	1.44
Vcy: loop-inter	2.40	n/a	n/a	n/a	n/a	**T**
Vcy: nested-counter_2	1.42†	n/a	n/a	n/a	n/a	**T**
Vcy: pullPayment	1.59	n/a	n/a	n/a	n/a	**T**
Vcy: simple	2.29†	2.11†	1.09×	0	poke2, CVC4	5.51
Vcy: standardToken2	11.31	10.31	1.10×	0	poke2, Z3, TG	113.51
Vcy: standardToken3	1.45	n/a	n/a	n/a	n/a	**T**
Vcy: standardToken5	13.25	n/a	n/a	n/a	n/a	**T**

The `mcMax` heuristic only applies to ADTs with theories supported by the model counter ABC [23] extended with our procedure in Sect. 5, hence our results using that heuristic are limited to the String, LIA, and Dihedral ADTs, as well as the Veracity benchmarks. Our extension for integer arrays allowed for the use of `mcMax` on the majority of the Veracity benchmarks. In some cases, `mcMax` provides a significant speedup over `poke` and even `poke2`. For example, in the hasChar ⋈ concat benchmark, `mcMax` is 2.89× as fast as `poke2` (not shown) and over 5.41× as fast as `poke`, with the same configuration aside from heuristic. In other cases, such as in the sum ⋈ multiVarSum analysis, `mcMax` underperforms compared to `poke2` and `poke`.

The performance of `mcMax` seems to depend on the methods considered, but there are cases where it can significantly improve run time. In future work, we hope to explore additional model-counting heuristics such as bisecting the search space rather than greedily covering it.

Extraction of Terms. The original SERVOIS tool required users to provide *terms*, sacrificing some degree of automation which is inconvenient and error-prone. As described in Sect. 3, SERVOIS2 now can automatically extract terms from the method specifications. As shown in Table 1, denoted by TG, the automated term extraction can even outperform manually provided terms.

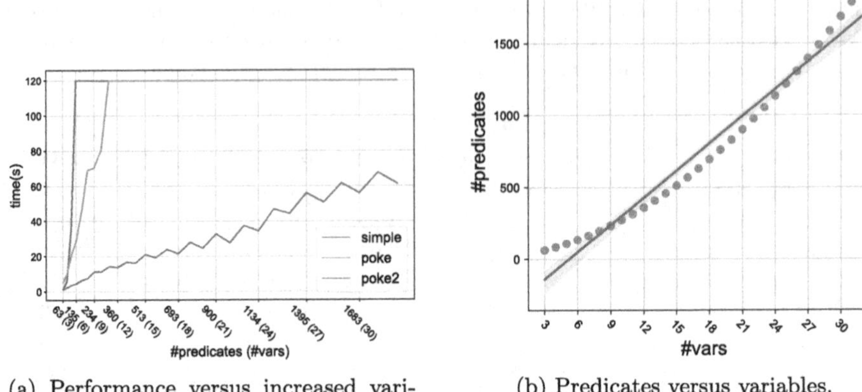

(a) Performance versus increased variables/predicates.

(b) Predicates versus variables.

Fig. 6. Experimental results on the scalability of general-purpose heuristics

In addition, by automatically extracting terms, our approach is another step closer to a fully automated commutativity synthesizer—the user does not have to do the manual work of providing terms. We believe that in conjunction with comparable performance, this makes automated term extraction preferable.

Predicate Lattice. We also evaluated the performance using the predicate lattice approach outlined in Sect. 3. In practice, we found that the overhead of lattice construction using SMT queries was typically too high, and it did not substantially improve synthesis time in most cases. When using syntactic rules (using a preliminary set of inference rules and axioms), we did not discover enough implications to be useful in any cases, with still substantial, albeit greatly reduced overhead. However, we did find that some LIA examples were improved by using the SMT implication lattice. `sum`$\bowtie$`multiVarSum` in particular saw a 2.27× speedup from 8.36 s to 3.69 s, which is a substantial speedup even accounting for the lattice construction time of 1.87 s. In `multiVarA`$\bowtie$`multiVarB`, the discovery of logically equivalent predicates filtered more than half of the initial list of predicates—from 280 (including negations of predicates) to 106. For the complete results, see Table 2. While it remains unclear whether the predicate lattice can be used for performance gains in most cases, the preliminary results suggest that further work may yield larger gains in difficult cases.

Scalability. Consider the toy example below, where we have a possibly ordered set described by x variables and we want to compute another element a that can potentially be added to the set after applying a marginal decrement. In this (somewhat artificial) example, the number of predicates increases (Fig. 6b) with the number of variables, while the commutativity problem has a straightforward solution: $(b = 0) \vee ((b \neq 0) \wedge (a \geq 0) \wedge (a - b \geq 0) \bigwedge_{i=1}^{n-1}(x_i < x_{i+1}))$.

```
int a, b, x1, x2, ..., xn;
bool sum(){
    a := (a - b); return true; }
bool multiVarSum(){
    if (a>0 && x1<x2 && x2<x3 &&  ... && xn-1<xn){
       a := (xn + a); return true;
    } else {
       a := (xn - a); return true; }}
```

Although mcMax shows promising results, due to reduced applicability to cases where efficient model counting is supported, we did not consider it for this particular experiment. Our focus here is on general-purpose heuristics. Figure 6a reports the results of our experiments running the heuristics simple (presented in [14]), poke, and poke2 on the above example, with increasingly many variables (up to 30) and, consequently, increasingly many predicates. For the precise ADT specification, refer to the "lia_scale_var_template" file in the artifact or Github provided in Sect. 1. We observe an impressive performance benefit from the poke2 heuristic. Firstly, observe that starting from only a small number of predicates, poke2 proved to be one order of magnitude faster than poke which timed out early in our experiment. Secondly, the increase in the number of state variables x is roughly linear with the increase of poke2 synthesis time. And lastly, the poke2 heuristic led to synthesizing the utmost simple condition, namely the one humanly inferred.

6.2 Case Study: commute Blocks in Veracity

To show SERVOIS2's applicability, we present the case study of its use in the Veracity[6] project [6], recalled below. The original SERVOIS lacked features (*e.g.* solvers, theories, early termination) and performance to be used in such a setting. Despite the use of SERVOIS2 in Veracity, the improvements described in the current paper are orthogonal.

Veracity is a parallelizing compiler for a language in which programmers directly express conditions under which sequential blocks of code commute [6]. Expanding programs with such commutativity annotations enables parallelization of sequential code that has dataflow dependencies, which previously could not be parallelized. We omit the finer details as it is outside the scope of commutativity synthesis. Consider for example, the following Veracity benchmark even-odd includes a commute statement, with a blank commutativity condition to be synthesized (or provided by the user):

```
commute (_) { { if(x%2==0) x:=x+y;}         (1)
              { x:=x+y; }             }     (2)
```

Veracity needs SERVOIS2 in order to synthesize the following commutativity condition for these program fragments labeled (1) and (2): $y = 0 \vee (y \neq 0 \wedge x\%2 =$

[6] http://www.veracity-lang.org.

Table 3. A selected subset of Veracity benchmarks. (Times are in seconds.)

Program	Time	Inferred Conditions
dict	3.82	`i != r && c + x != y || c + x == y`
ht-simple	30.64	`x + a != z && 3 == tbl[z] && y != z`
loop-amt	> 120	`0 == i && amt == i_pre && ctr - 1 > i_pre && i_pre <= amt && 0 != i_pre && i_pre <= ctr && amt != amt_pre && ctr - 1 > amt_pre && amt_pre <= amt && 0 != amt_pre && amt_pre <= ctr && ctr - 1 != 1 && 1 != ctr && 1 != amt && 1 == ctr + amt || ... || amt == i && 1 == ctr && 1 != amt && 1 == ctr + amt`

$x + y$). In more detail, SERVOIS2 is used by first having the Veracity compiler translate the program code into methods, say $block_1()$ and $block_2()$ on an ADT whose state are the program variables `x` and `y`. Then, the synthesized commutativity conditions are translated back and inserted in place of the "_" in the Veracity `commute` block. Unfortunately the original SERVOIS's limited support for solvers/theories (as well as limited performance) prevents it from synthesizing a commutativity condition for this benchmark. The divergent behavior of SERVOIS on some benchmarks was a further impediment to its use in Veracity.

A few selected benchmarks are shown in Table 3. These benchmarks are illustrative of the different kinds of typical output from SERVOIS2. Most cases were similar to the `dict` example, terminating in a few seconds with a sensible result. The `ht-simple` case takes more time. The condition is complete, but due to the longer time, it may be worth terminating the algorithm early and only receiving one or two of the disjuncts, especially if they cover the most common cases. Finally, `loop-amt` is a case that is not amenable to commutativity inference and it would be better to terminate sooner and allow the user to attempt a different approach.

Unlike direct ADT benchmarks, those derived from Veracity programs involve the composition of numerous effects and thus involve complex commutativity conditions. Consequently, most of the Veracity benchmarks make substantially more complex queries to SERVOIS2 than the handwritten ADT specifications. We thus used all of the Veracity benchmarks to test the different configurations, as mentioned before and shown in Table 1.

New non-trivial benchmarks were manually translated into the Veracity programming language. These were various combinations of functions from the SmartContract/Auction, Solidity/StandardToken, and Solidity/PullPayment source codes. Most of these new benchmarks perform better on the new heuristic `poke2` compared to the previously presented approach `poke`. Also, for several of them, `poke` did not terminate, so we had to use the early termination feature to synthesize the commutativity condition within a specific time frame. For StandardToken, for example, after executing `TransferForm` $\bowtie$ `Approve` with using `poke` and 120 s timeout, we get an incomplete condition; however, with `poke2`, we can get a complete condition in about 10 s with a reasonable number of atoms.

7 Conclusion and Future Work

We have shown a more mature and performant method of automatically synthesizing commutativity conditions in the SERVOIS2 synthesizer. Our results confirm what one might expect: that more advanced heuristics and better treatment of predicates leads to overall performance improvement. Furthermore, we have released a far more usable tool that has already been used in recent work [6] and is ready to be integrated into other commutativity settings such as proof methodologies [1–3] or distributed systems [9,11]. There are several directions for future work in this space, discussed below.

Algorithmic Improvements. We saw great improvements in the performance of the heuristic in keeping track of which predicates aligned with the commutative (resp. non-commutative) case. The algorithm is currently agnostic to which condition is being pursued, and it may be possible to tag such information in the recursive calls, leading to similar improvements in performance. Furthermore, the disjunctive nature of the algorithm may be amenable to parallelization. However, it is unclear whether the actual reasoning is amenable to parallelization or if it is not worth the overhead.

Extended Use of Model Counting. `mcMax` uses the model-counting solver ABC [23], which targets string, LIA, and boolean constraints, but we could also use other model counters with support for other theories. Approximate model counters [24] are a promising avenue for handling model-counting queries across additional theories, and the integration of such a model counter might lead to further applicability of `mcMax`.

The `mcMax` heuristic provides one model counting heuristic to inform predicate selection, but we hypothesize that additional heuristics might provide advantages on different benchmarks, for example, by maximizing partitioning rather than covering. Given the promising results of `mcMax`, we plan to pursue a more extensive evaluation of model-counting heuristics.

Model counting might find an additional use in cases where our commutativity analysis terminates early. Using model counting, we can determine what portion of the input domain is covered by the resulting commutativity and non-commutativity conditions, augmenting our analysis with additional reliability information in cases of early termination. It also may be possible to use this information to determine when to terminate.

Improving the Use of the Predicate Lattice. Our experiments indicate that the overhead of lattice construction is significant. Thus for the lattice to be practical, one would need to both increase its performance benefit and decrease the overhead from construction. Although REFINE prunes predicates based on the lattice, none of the current heuristics use information about implication chains, and there may be even more gains to be had by using lattices. There are also more sophisticated approaches to building the lattice data structure of logical implications, such as by using the framework GreenTrie [25]. The number of queries can be greatly reduced through semantic reasoning and caching of subformulas. This could greatly reduce the overhead of lattice construction, thus making their use more appealing.

Acknowledgements. This work is supported in part by NSF Award #2008633 and #2107169.

References

1. Farzan, A., Vandikas, A.: Reductions for safety proofs. In: Proceedings of the ACM on Programming Languages, vol. 4, no. POPL, pp. 1–28 (2019)
2. Kragl, B., Qadeer, S.: The civl verifier. In: 2021 Formal Methods in Computer Aided Design (FMCAD), pp. 143–152. IEEE (2021)
3. Flanagan, C., Freund, S.N.: The anchor verifier for blocking and non-blocking concurrent software. In: Proceedings of the ACM on Programming Languages, vol. 4, no. OOPSLA, pp. 1–29 (2020)
4. Rinard, M.C., Diniz, P.C.: Commutativity analysis: a new analysis technique for parallelizing compilers. ACM Trans. Program. Lang. Syst. (TOPLAS) **19**(6), 942–991 (1997). https://citeseer.ist.psu.edu/rinard97commutativity.html
5. Spiegelman, A., Golan-Gueta, G., Keidar, I.: Transactional data structure libraries. ACM SIGPLAN Not. **51**(6), 682–696 (2016)
6. Chen, A., Fathololumi, P., Koskinen, E., Pincus, J.: Veracity: declarative multicore programming with commutativity). In: Proceedings of the ACM Programming Language, vol. 6, no. OOPSLA2, pp. 186:1–186:31 (2022). https://doi.org/10.1145/3563349
7. Prabhu, P., Ghosh, S., Zhang, Y., Johnson, N.P., August, D.I.: Commutative set: a language extension for implicit parallel programming. In: Proceedings of the 32nd ACM SIGPLAN Conference on Programming Language Design and Implementation, pp. 1–11 (2011)
8. Clements, A.T., Kaashoek, M.F., Zeldovich, N., Morris, R.T., Kohler, E.: The scalable commutativity rule: designing scalable software for multicore processors. ACM Trans. Comput. Syst. (TOCS) **32**(4), 1–47 (2015)
9. Shapiro, M., Preguiça, N., Baquero, C., Zawirski, M.: A comprehensive study of convergent and commutative replicated data types. Ph.D. dissertation, Inria-Centre Paris-Rocquencourt; INRIA (2011)
10. Dickerson, T., Gazzillo, P., Herlihy, M., Koskinen, E.: Adding concurrency to smart contracts. In: Proceedings of the ACM Symposium on Principles of Distributed Computing, Series PODC 2017, pp. 303–312. ACM, New York (2017). https://doi.acm.org/10.1145/3087801.3087835
11. Pîrlea, G., Kumar, A., Sergey, I.: Practical smart contract sharding with ownership and commutativity analysis. In: Freund, S.N., Yahav, E. (eds.) PLDI 2021: 42nd ACM SIGPLAN International Conference on Programming Language Design and Implementation, Virtual Event, Canada, 20–25 June 2021, pp. 1327–1341. ACM (2021). https://doi.org/10.1145/3453483.3454112
12. Gehr, T., Dimitrov, D., Vechev, M.: Learning commutativity specifications. In: Kroening, D., Păsăreanu, C.S. (eds.) CAV 2015, Part I. LNCS, vol. 9206, pp. 307–323. Springer, Cham (2015). https://doi.org/10.1007/978-3-319-21690-4_18
13. Aleen, F., Clark, N.: Commutativity analysis for software parallelization: letting program transformations see the big picture. In: Soffa, M.L., Irwin, M.J. (eds.) Proceedings of the 14th International Conference on Architectural Support for Programming Languages and Operating Systems (ASPLOS-XII), pp. 241–252. ACM (2009)

14. Bansal, K., Koskinen, E., Tripp, O.: Automatic generation of precise and useful commutativity conditions. In: Beyer, D., Huisman, M. (eds.) TACAS 2018. LNCS, vol. 10805, pp. 115–132. Springer, Cham (2018). https://doi.org/10.1007/978-3-319-89960-2_7
15. Bansal, K., Koskinen, E., Tripp, O.: Synthesizing precise and useful commutativity conditions. J. Autom. Reason. **64**(7), 1333–1359 (2020)
16. Gomes, C.P., Sabharwal, A., Selman, B.: Model counting. In: Handbook of Satisfiability, pp. 993–1014. IOS Press (2021)
17. De Loera, J.A., Hemmecke, R., Tauzer, J., Yoshida, R.: Effective lattice point counting in rational convex polytopes. J. Symb. Comput. **38**(4), 1273–1302 (2004)
18. Aydin, A., Bang, L., Bultan, T.: Automata-based model counting for string constraints. In: Kroening, D., Păsăreanu, C.S. (eds.) CAV 2015. LNCS, vol. 9206, pp. 255–272. Springer, Cham (2015). https://doi.org/10.1007/978-3-319-21690-4_15
19. Molavi, A., Schneider, T., Downing, M., Bang, L.: MCBAT: model counting for constraints over bounded integer arrays. In: Christakis, M., Polikarpova, N., Duggirala, P.S., Schrammel, P. (eds.) NSV/VSTTE -2020. LNCS, vol. 12549, pp. 124–143. Springer, Cham (2020). https://doi.org/10.1007/978-3-030-63618-0_8
20. Barrett, C., et al.: CVC4. In: Gopalakrishnan, G., Qadeer, S. (eds.) CAV 2011. LNCS, vol. 6806, pp. 171–177. Springer, Heidelberg (2011). https://doi.org/10.1007/978-3-642-22110-1_14
21. Barbosa, H., et al.: cvc5: a versatile and industrial-strength SMT solver. In: Fisman, D., Rosu, G. (eds.) TACAS 2022, Part I. LNCS, vol. 13243, pp. 415–442. Springer, Cham (2022). https://doi.org/10.1007/978-3-030-99524-9_24
22. de Moura, L., Bjørner, N.: Z3: an efficient SMT solver. In: Ramakrishnan, C.R., Rehof, J. (eds.) TACAS 2008. LNCS, vol. 4963, pp. 337–340. Springer, Heidelberg (2008). https://doi.org/10.1007/978-3-540-78800-3_24
23. Aydin, A., Bang, L., Bultan, T.: Automata-based model counting for string constraints. In: Kroening, D., Păsăreanu, C.S. (eds.) CAV 2015. LNCS, vol. 9206, pp. 255–272. Springer, Cham (2015). https://doi.org/10.1007/978-3-319-21690-4_15
24. Chakraborty, S., Meel, K.S., Vardi, M.Y.: Approximate model counting. In: Handbook of Satisfiability, pp. 1015–1045. IOS Press (2021)
25. Jia, X., Ghezzi, C., Ying, S.: Enhancing reuse of constraint solutions to improve symbolic execution. In: Proceedings of the 2015 International Symposium on Software Testing and Analysis, ISSTA 2015, pp. 177–187. Association for Computing Machinery, New York (2015). https://doi.org/10.1145/2771783.2771806

Verification of Programs and Hardware

Structure-Guided Solution of Constrained Horn Clauses

Omer Rappoport(✉), Orna Grumberg, and Yakir Vizel

Technion - Israel Institute of Technology, Haifa, Israel
{omer.r,orna,yvizel}@cs.technion.ac.il

Abstract. We present StHorn, a novel technique for solving the satisfiability problem of CHCs, which works lazily and incrementally and is guided by the structure of the set of CHCs. Our technique is driven by the idea that a set of CHCs can be solved in parts, making it an easier problem for the CHC-solver. Furthermore, solving a set of CHCs can benefit from an interpretation revealed by the solver for its subsets. Our technique is *lazy* in that it gradually extends the set of checked CHCs, as needed. It is *incremental* in the way it constructs a solution by using satisfying interpretations obtained for previously checked subsets. In order to capture the structure of the problem, we define an *induced CHC hypergraph* that precisely corresponds to the set of CHCs. The paths in this graph are explored and used to select the clauses to be solved.

We implemented StHorn on top of two CHC-solvers, SPACER and ELDARICA. Our evaluation shows that StHorn complements both tools and can solve instances that cannot be solved by the other tools. We conclude that StHorn can improve upon the state-of-the-art in CHC solving.

Keywords: Constrained Horn Clauses · CHC-SAT · Verification

1 Introduction

Constrained Horn Clauses (CHCs) is a fragment of First Order Logic (FOL) that has gained much attention in recent years. One main reason for the rising interest in CHCs is the ability to reduce many verification problems to satisfiability of CHCs [5,7,11,17,18,20,25,33]. For example, program verification can naturally be described as the satisfiability of CHCs modulo a background theory such as Linear Integer Arithmetic [7]. CHC-solvers can be used as the back-end for a variety of verification tools [15,19,27,30], separating the generation of verification conditions from the decision procedure that determines their correctness.

In this paper we present StHorn, a novel, structure-guided, lazy and incremental technique for solving the satisfiability problem of CHCs modulo a background theory. Our technique is driven by the idea that a set of CHCs can be solved in parts, making each sub-problem easier to solve. Furthermore, solving a set

This research is partially funded by the Israel Science Foundation (ISF), grant no. 2875/21.

É. André and J. Sun (Eds.): ATVA 2023, LNCS 14216, pp. 117–138, 2023.
https://doi.org/10.1007/978-3-031-45332-8_6

of CHCs can benefit from satisfying interpretations, which are revealed when handling its subsets.

StHorn uses an existing CHC-solver [12,14,23,24,28,34] as a "black-box". Given a set of CHCs Π, it chooses a subset of CHCs and tries to solve it using the existing CHC-solver. If it finds that the subset is unsatisfiable, then it concludes the entire set of CHCs is unsatisfiable. Otherwise, if a satisfying interpretation is found, StHorn extends the subset of CHCs, adapts the satisfying interpreation to be consistent with the new extended subset, and reinvokes the CHC-solver on the extended subset of CHCs. This process continues iteratively until either a subset is found to be unsatisfiable, or a satisfying interpretation is found for the entire set of CHCs Π.

There are three pillars to StHorn: (i) the *structure-guided* selection of CHC subsets to be processed; (ii) the *incremental* usage of satisfying interpretations when solving the different subsets of CHCs; and lastly (iii) the *lazy* processing of CHCs only when needed (when none of the processed subsets is unsatisfiable).

In order to capture the structure of the problem, we define an *induced CHC hypergraph* that precisely corresponds to the set of CHCs and depicts the dependencies between them. We present an algorithm for finding the shortest nontrivial hyperpath in the graph. This algorithm is used for selecting the CHC subsets to be solved, resulting in minimal clause addition at each iteration. Our selection strategy is based on the understanding that solving small subsets is often easier and can be advantageous to the overall solution.

To be incremental, StHorn maintains an interpretation that is injected into the CHC-solver as a starting point at each iteration, enabling the solver to search in a reduced state space. When a subset of CHCs is extended, it must be ensured that the existing satisfying interpretation is consistent with the extended subset. To this end, StHorn implements an amending procedure, which receives a set of CHCs and an interpretation, which might not satisfy all of them, and amends the interpretation such that it becomes consistent with the extended subset.

The combination of the choice of the examined subsets and the way in which the interpretation is amended defines how StHorn guides the search for a satisfying interpretation. Intuitively, StHorn guides the search based on the structure of the CHCs as reflected by the induced CHC hypergraph.

We implemented StHorn on top of two CHC-solvers: Spacer [28] and Eldarica [24]. For evaluation, we used the CHC-COMP'22 [13] benchmarks, and compared StHorn against Spacer and Eldarica. Our evaluation shows that StHorn complements both tools and can solve instances that cannot be solved by the other tools. We conclude that StHorn can improve upon the state-of-the-art in CHC solving.

The main contributions of this work are as follows:

- We develop an efficient technique for solving CHCs, which considers the structure of the CHCs during the search for a solution.
- The search for a solution is done incrementally, based on interpretations learned in previous iterations.

- We implemented a generic framework that can be used with any existing CHC-solver. In addition, we implemented two instances of StHorn: one using SPACER and the other that uses ELDARICA and evaluated their performance. Our implementation is open-source and publicly available.

2 Preliminaries

We consider first-order logic (FOL) modulo a background theory $\mathcal{T}$ and denote it by FOL($\mathcal{T}$). We adopt the standard notation and terminology, where FOL($\mathcal{T}$) is defined over a signature Σ that consists of constant, predicate and function symbols, some of which may be interpreted by $\mathcal{T}$. The set of uninterpreted predicate symbols in Σ is denoted by $\mathcal{P}$. From now on, we fix the background theory $\mathcal{T}$.

A *p-formula* is an application of the form $p(t_1, \ldots, t_n)$ for some predicate symbol $p \in \mathcal{P}$ and first-order terms t_i. Given a set $\mathcal{S}$ of symbols, a formula φ is $\mathcal{S}$*-free* if no $\mathcal{S}$ symbols occur in φ. We write $\varphi[X]$ for a formula φ with free variables X. We use $\top$ and $\bot$ to represent the constant symbols TRUE and FALSE, respectively.

2.1 Constrained Horn Clauses

Definition 1. *A* Constrained Horn Clause *(*CHC *or* clause*) is a FOL formula* π *of the form* $\forall X.(B[X] \rightarrow H[X])$, *where*

- $H[X]$, *denoted* head(π), *is either a p-formula for some* $p \in \mathcal{P}$, *or is* $\mathcal{P}$*-free.*
- $B[X]$, *denoted* body(π), *is a formula either of the form* $\psi_1 \wedge \cdots \wedge \psi_k \wedge \varphi$ *or* φ, *where each* ψ_i *is a p-formula for some* $p \in \mathcal{P}$, *and* φ *is a* $\mathcal{P}$*-free constraint.*

A clause is called a *query* if its head is $\mathcal{P}$-free; otherwise, it is called a *rule*. A rule with $\mathcal{P}$-free body is called a *fact*. A clause is *linear* if its body contains at most one predicate symbol from $\mathcal{P}$; otherwise, it is *non-linear*. We refrain from explicitly adding the universal quantifier when the set of variables is clear from the context.

A set of CHCs Π is *satisfiable* if there exists an interpretation of the uninterpreted predicate symbols in $\mathcal{P}$ such that each CHC π in Π is valid under the interpretation (modulo $\mathcal{T}$). CHC-solvers attempt to determine the satisfiability of a set of CHCs by searching for a satisfying interpretation that is definable in $\mathcal{T}$. Such an interpretation is called a $\mathcal{T}$-interpretation. Formally, a $\mathcal{T}$*-interpretation* $\mathcal{I}$ associates every $p \in \mathcal{P}$ with a $\mathcal{P}$-free formula $\mathcal{I}(p)$ over the signature Σ of FOL($\mathcal{T}$). Given a CHC π and a $\mathcal{T}$-interpretation $\mathcal{I}$, we denote by $\mathcal{I}(\pi)$ the formula obtained after substituting every p-formula that occurs in π with $\mathcal{I}(p)$. A $\mathcal{T}$-interpretation $\mathcal{I}$ *satisfies* a CHC π, denoted $\mathcal{I} \models \pi$, if $\mathcal{I}(\pi)$ is valid (modulo $\mathcal{T}$). A $\mathcal{T}$-interpretation $\mathcal{I}$ satisfies a set of CHCs Π, denoted $\mathcal{I} \models \Pi$, if $\mathcal{I} \models \pi$ for every $\pi \in \Pi$. Note that, if there exists a satisfying $\mathcal{T}$-interpretation for Π, then Π is satisfiable. The converse, however, may not hold due to the limited expressiveness of FOL($\mathcal{T}$). Henceforth, we will only consider $\mathcal{T}$-interpretations and refer to them simply as interpretations.

Definition 2 (The CHC-SAT Problem). *Given a set of CHCs Π, determine whether Π is satisfiable.*

Note that, if Π is *unsatisfiable*, then there exists a refutation (a proof of unsatisfiability) in the form of a ground derivation of $\bot$ [8]. Along with determining whether Π is satisfiable, we are often interested in finding a solution to it. A *solution* for a set of CHCs Π is either a satisfying interpretation, when Π is satisfiable, or a ground refutation, when Π is unsatisfiable.

Finally, for a FOL formula ψ, we denote by $\mathcal{P}^{\psi}$ the set of all uninterpreted predicate symbols that occur in ψ. Given a set of FOL formulas Ψ, $\mathcal{P}^{\Psi}$ denotes the set $\bigcup_{\psi \in \Psi} \mathcal{P}^{\psi}$. Note that an interpretation for Π is defined over $\mathcal{P}^{\Pi}$.

Example 1. As an example, consider the following schematic set of CHCs over the set $\{p_1, p_2, p_3, p_4\}$ of uninterpreted predicate symbols:

$$\top \rightarrow p_1(x) \tag{1}$$

$$p_1(x) \wedge \varphi_2(x, y) \rightarrow p_2(x, y) \tag{2}$$

$$p_1(x) \wedge \varphi_3(x, z) \rightarrow p_3(z) \tag{3}$$

$$p_1(x) \wedge p_1(y) \wedge p_3(z) \wedge \varphi_4(x, y, z) \rightarrow p_4(x, y) \tag{4}$$

$$p_4(x, y) \wedge \varphi_5(x, y, z) \rightarrow p_2(x, z) \tag{5}$$

$$p_2(x, z) \wedge \varphi_6(x, z) \rightarrow \bot \tag{6}$$

It consists of 5 rules (Clauses 1–5) and a query (Clause 6). Clause 1 is a fact and Clause 4 is nonlinear, since it includes more than one predicate symbol in its body. Note that, the predicate symbol p_1 occurs twice in the body of Clause 4. However, $\mathcal{P}^{body(4)}$ is the set $\{p_1, p_3\}$ (rather than a multiset), where repetitions are ignored.

2.2 Hypergraphs and Hyperpaths

The definitions in this subsection resemble [1]. A *directed hypergraph* $G = (V, E)$ consists of a nonempty set of nodes V and a set of hyperedges E. A *hyperedge* connects several source nodes to a single target node. It is represented by a pair $e = (S, t)$, where $S \subseteq V$ is the (nonempty) set of source nodes of e, denoted $source(e)$ and $t \in V$ is the target node of e, denoted $target(e)$.

Definition 3 (Nontrivial Hyperpath). *A* nontrivial hyperpath *in $G = (V, E)$ from a set of sources $S \subseteq V$ to a target $t \in V$ is a nonempty set of hyperedges $E_{S,t} \subseteq E$ with the following property: the hyperedges in $E_{S,t}$ can be ordered as a vector $(e_1, \ldots, e_k)$ where,*

1. *$source(e_i) \subseteq (S \cup \{target(e_1), \ldots, target(e_{i-1})\})$ for every e_i in $E_{S,t}$.*
2. *$target(e_k) = t$.*
3. *There is no nonempty $E' \subset E_{S,t}$ that satisfies 1 and 2.*

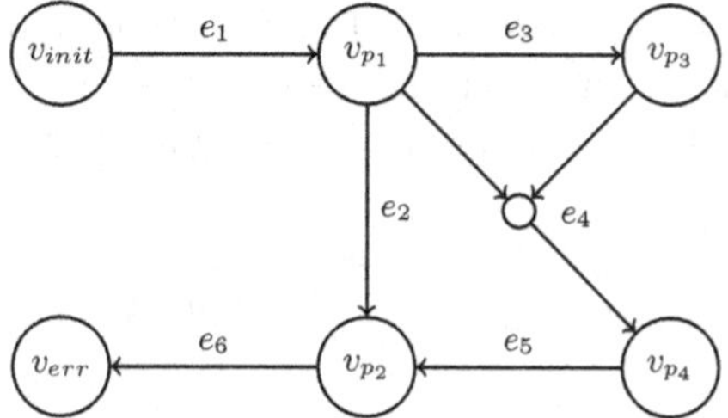

Fig. 1. A hypergraph example.

According to the above definition, a hyperpath must include at least one hyperedge. We therefore refer to such hyperpaths as nontrivial. Note that a hyperpath with an empty set of hyperedges (*trivial hyperpath*) is possible in [1], however, in our context we do not consider such hyperpaths. In the sequel, hyperpaths are always nontrivial.

Let $E_{S,t}$ be a hyperpath form S to t. Due to the minimality of a hyperpath (condition 3 above), it holds that for every two different hyperedges $e_i, e_j \in E_{S,t}$, $target(e_i) \neq target(e_j)$. This and Definition 3 imply the following property.

Property 1. Let $E_{S,t}$ be a hyperpath form S to t and let (X, t) be the unique hyperedge in $E_{S,t}$ leading to t. Then, $E_{S,t}$ can be written as follows:

$$E_{S,t} = \{(X,t)\} \cup (\bigcup_{x \in (X \setminus S)} E_{S,x}),$$

where for every $x \in (X \setminus S)$, $E_{S,x}$ is the hyperpath from S to x included in $E_{S,t}$.

Next, we add weights to the hyperedges of a hypergraph $G = (V, E)$. This is done with a *weight function* $w : E \to \mathbb{N}$, which associates a non-negative integer with each hyperedge. A weight function w for hyperedges can be lifted to a weight function $\hat{w}$ for hyperpaths, as follows.

Definition 4 (Weight Function for Hyperpaths). *Let $E_{S,t}$ be a hyperpath from S to t and let (X, t) be the unique hyperedge in $E_{S,t}$ leading to t. According to Property 1, $E_{S,t} = \{(X,t)\} \cup (\bigcup_{x \in (X \setminus S)} E_{S,x})$. The* weight function $\hat{w}$ *for $E_{S,t}$ is defined inductively in the following way:*

$$\hat{w}(E_{S,t}) = w((X,t)) + \sum_{x \in (X \setminus S)} \hat{w}(E_{S,x})$$

That is, the weight of a hyperpath is defined as the sum of the weight of its last hyperedge with the weights of the hyperpaths leading to each of its sources.[1]

[1] This weight function is called the traversal cost in [1]. For this weight function, computing the shortest nontrivial hyperpath (see Sect. 4) is polynomial.

Example 2. Consider the hypergraph in Fig. 1 and the hyperpath $E_{\{v_{init}\},v_{P4}} = \{e_1, e_3, e_4\}$. Assume the weight function for each edge is the number of its sources: $w(e_i) = 1$ for each $i \neq 4$ and $w(e_4) = 2$. The weight of this hyperpath is

$$\begin{aligned}\hat{w}(E_{\{v_{init}\},v_{P4}}) &= w(e_4) + \hat{w}(E_{\{v_{init}\},v_{P1}}) + \hat{w}(E_{\{v_{init}\},v_{P3}})\\ &= w(e_4) + \hat{w}(E_{\{v_{init}\},v_{P1}}) + (w(e_3) + \hat{w}(E_{\{v_{init}\},v_{P1}}))\\ &= w(e_4) + w(e_1) + (w(e_3) + w(e_1)) = 2 + 1 + (1 + 1) = 5.\end{aligned}$$

Notice that the weight of e_1 is considered twice in the weight of $E_{\{v_{init}\},v_{P4}}$ since e_1 belongs to both $E_{\{v_{init}\},v_{P1}} = \{e_1\}$ and $E_{\{v_{init}\},v_{P3}} = \{e_1, e_3\}$.

3 Structure-Guided, Lazy and Incremental CHC Solving

In this section, we present StHorn - a structure-guided, lazy and incremental technique for CHC-solving. Given a set Π of CHCs, StHorn constructs a solution for Π by iteratively examining a monotone sequence of its subsets. It starts by choosing a subset of clauses $\Delta \subseteq \Pi$, and iteratively adds clauses to it, as needed. If at any point, the subset becomes unsatisfiable, StHorn halts and returns UNSAT. Otherwise, if a subset of clauses is satisfiable, StHorn tries to extend the satisfying interpretation for the subset into an interpretation for Π in an incremental fashion. To this end, StHorn maintains an interpretation $\mathcal{I}$ that is injected into the CHC-solver as a starting point at each iteration, enabling the solver to search for a solution within a reduced state space. In order for the solver to return a sound solution when it is invoked to solve the current Δ, $\mathcal{I}$ must satisfy all rules in Δ. The following definition captures this requirement.

Definition 5 (Rule-Satisfiability). *Let Δ be a set of CHCs, and $\mathcal{I}$ be an interpretation. $\mathcal{I}$* rule-satisfies *Δ, denoted $\mathcal{I} \models_r \Delta$, if $\mathcal{I} \models \pi$ for every rule $\pi \in \Delta$. Note that in this case, $\mathcal{I}$ may not satisfy some of the queries in Δ.*

In what follows, we assume that the underlying used CHC-solver can receive a set Δ of CHCs and an initial interpretation $\mathcal{I}$ for the predicates in $\mathcal{P}^{\Delta}$. Further, we assume that the solver returns a sound solution whenever $\mathcal{I} \models_r \Delta$. We leave the discussion on this assumption to the end of the section.

In Sect. 6.1 we show that, in fact, the StHorn technique can be implemented on top of any existing CHC-solver. This includes solvers that cannot receive initial interpretations for the predicates.

We start with a simple, high-level description of the technique. In the following sections, we go into the fine-grained details of the implementation. The pseudo-code of StHorn appears in Algorithm 1. The specifications of the algorithm and of its internal procedures are summarized in Fig. 2.

StHorn receives a set Π of CHCs. As mentioned, it maintains a subset of clauses $\Delta \subseteq \Pi$ and an interpretation $\mathcal{I}$ that rule-satisfies Δ. StHorn starts by calling `Select` (line 1) and initializing Δ to be some subset of Π (i.e., $\Delta \subseteq \Pi$). Next, it initializes the interpretation $\mathcal{I}$ of every uninterpreted predicate that

Algorithm 1. StHorn(Π)

Input: A set Π of CHCs
Output: A solution to Π

```
1  Δ ← Select(Π, ∅)
2  I(p) ← ⊤, ∀p ∈ P^Δ
3  while ⊤ do
4      (res, I′, R) ← Solve(Δ, I)
5      if res = UNSAT then
6          return (UNSAT, −, R)
7      else                                  ▷ i.e., res = SAT
8          if Δ = Π then
9              return (SAT, I′, −)
10         else                              ▷ i.e., Δ ⊂ Π
11             δ ← Select(Π, Δ)
12             Δ ← Δ ∪ δ
13             I ← Amend(I′, Δ, δ)
14         end if
15     end if
16 end while
```

occurs in Δ to $\top$ (line 2). Note that after initialization, $\mathcal{I} \models_r \Delta$ (see the proof of Theorem 1).

StHorn then moves to the main loop (line 3). Every iteration begins by checking the satisfiability of Δ by invoking the underlying CHC-solver with a call to `Solve` (line 4). Consider the case in which `Solve` returns UNSAT and a ground refutation $\mathcal{R}$ for Δ. Since Δ consists entirely of clauses from Π, $\mathcal{R}$ is also a refutation for Π. Thus, StHorn returns UNSAT and $\mathcal{R}$ (line 6). Now, consider the case in which `Solve` returns SAT and a satisfying interpretation $\mathcal{I}'$ for Δ. If Δ is equal to Π, StHorn returns SAT and $\mathcal{I}'$ as the satisfying interpretation of Π (line 9). Otherwise, Δ is a strict subset of Π. As a preparation for the next iteration, Δ is extended and the interpretation is amended accordingly. First, the method `Select` selects a set of fresh clauses δ from $\Pi \setminus \Delta$ (line 11) that are added to Δ (line 12). We require that at least one clause is selected (i.e., $\delta \neq \emptyset$) to guarantee progress. At this stage, $\mathcal{I}'$ may no longer be a rule-satisfying interpretation with respect to the extended Δ. As a remedy, StHorn invokes `Amend` (line 13), which modifies $\mathcal{I}'$ in order to make it rule-satisfying for Δ before the subsequent call to `Solve`.[2]

Remark 1 (Termination of StHorn). In general, the CHC-SAT problem is undecidable, so termination is not guaranteed. However, if every call to `Solve` made by StHorn terminates, then StHorn terminates as well. The reason for this is the requirement that `Select` must always return at least one fresh clause from Π.

[2] The underlying CHC-solver may also return UNKNOWN. This case can be handled similarly to the case where SAT is returned and is omitted for simplicity of presentation.

$(res, \mathcal{I}', \mathcal{R}) \leftarrow \mathsf{StHorn}(\Pi)$
Requires: $\top$
Ensures: $(res = \text{SAT} \Rightarrow \mathcal{I}' \models \Pi)$ **and**
$(res = \text{UNSAT} \Rightarrow \mathcal{R}$ is a ground refutation of $\Pi)$

$(res, \mathcal{I}', \mathcal{R}) \leftarrow \texttt{Solve}(\Delta, \mathcal{I})$
Requires: $\mathcal{I} \models_r \Delta$
Ensures: $(res = \text{SAT} \Rightarrow \mathcal{I}' \models \Delta)$ **and**
$(res = \text{UNSAT} \Rightarrow \mathcal{R}$ is a ground refutation of $\Delta)$

$\delta \leftarrow \texttt{Select}(\Pi, \Delta)$
Requires: $\Delta \subseteq \Pi$
Ensures: $\delta \subseteq \Pi \setminus \Delta$ **and** $(\Delta \subset \Pi \Rightarrow \delta \neq \emptyset)$

$\mathcal{I} \leftarrow \texttt{Amend}(\mathcal{I}', \Delta, \delta)$
Requires: $\delta \subseteq \Delta$ **and** $\mathcal{I}' \models \Delta \setminus \delta$
Ensures: $\mathcal{I} \models_r \Delta$

Fig. 2. Specifications for the StHorn Algorithm and its Procedures

Theorem 1 (Correctness of StHorn). *Let Π be a set of CHCs given to StHorn. If StHorn returns SAT (UNSAT), then Π is satisfiable (unsatisfiable).*

Proof. First, we show that at every call to `Solve`, $\mathcal{I} \models_r \Delta$. When `Solve` is called for the first time, following the initialization of $\mathcal{I}$, it holds that $\mathcal{I}(p) = \top$ for all $p \in \mathcal{P}^{\Delta}$. Let $\pi := p_1 \wedge \cdots \wedge p_k \wedge \varphi \rightarrow q$ be a rule in Δ. The formula $\mathcal{I}(q)$, which is $\top$, is implied by any other formula, and in particular, it is implied by $\mathcal{I}(p_1) \wedge \cdots \wedge \mathcal{I}(p_k) \wedge \varphi$. Therefore, $\mathcal{I}(\pi)$ is valid, i.e., $\mathcal{I} \models \pi$. Accordingly, $\mathcal{I} \models_r \Delta$. In later iterations, `Solve` is called after `Amend`, which ensures $\mathcal{I} \models_r \Delta$ as well. Therefore, the requirement in the specifications of `Solve` holds in every invocation.

Assume StHorn returns SAT. From the definition of the algorithm, it follows that `Solve` was invoked at the last iteration with Π, and that it returned SAT and $\mathcal{I}'$. By the specifications of `Solve`, it is guaranteed that Π is indeed satisfiable and that $\mathcal{I}'$, which is returned by StHorn, satisfies Π. Finally, assume StHorn returns UNSAT. From the definition of StHorn, it follows that `Solve` was invoked at the last iteration with a subset $\Delta \subseteq \Pi$, and that it returned UNSAT and $\mathcal{R}$. By the specifications of `Solve`, it is guaranteed that Δ is indeed unsatisfiable and that $\mathcal{R}$, which is returned by StHorn, is a ground refutation for Δ. Since Δ consists entirely of clauses from Π, $\mathcal{R}$ is also a ground refutation for Π. □

Requiring Rule-Satisfiablity. We require the CHC-solver to return a sound solution, given a set of CHCs and a rule-satisfying interpretation. This is essential, since if there exists a rule that is not satisfied by the injected interpretation, the solver may return an incorrect result. As an example, consider the following unsatisfiable set Π of CHCs: $\{x = 0 \rightarrow p(x),\ p(x) \wedge x = 0 \rightarrow \bot\}$. When given an interpretation that is not rule-satisfying, such as the one that maps $p(x)$ to $\bot$, the CHC-solver might conclude that Π is satisfiable after examining the query and observing that it is satisfied by the injected interpretation.

Rule-satisfiablity is also important in that, whenever a set of CHCs is satisfiable, any rule-satisfying interpretation for it can be strengthened into a satisfying one.[3] For example, consider the following satisfiable set Π' of CHCs: $\{x = 0 \rightarrow p(x),\ p(x) \wedge x \neq 0 \rightarrow \bot\}$. Π' is clearly satisfied by the interpretation that maps $p(x)$ to the formula $x = 0$. Now, consider the interpretation that maps $p(x)$ to $x \geq 0$. While this rule-satisfying interpretation does not satisfy Π', as it does not satisfy its query, it can be strengthened by the solver into the above satisfying interpretation. Note also, that supplying the solver with this initial interpretation narrows its search space, as otherwise it would have began with the interpretation that maps $p(x)$ to $\top$.

4 Structure-Guided Selection of CHCs

Recall that a CHC is of the form $p_1 \wedge \cdots \wedge p_k \wedge \varphi \rightarrow q$ (the variable vectors are omitted for readability). For brevity, we denote such a clause by the triple $\langle\{p_1, \ldots, p_k\}, \varphi, q\rangle$. Similarly, a fact and a query are denoted by $\langle\emptyset, \varphi, q\rangle$ and $\langle\{p_1, \ldots, p_k\}, \varphi, \bot\rangle$, respectively.[4] It should be noted that a clause may contain several occurrences of the same predicate symbol in its body (see, for example, rule 4 of Example 1). For the purpose of guiding the CHC selection, it is sufficient to refer to the predicates appearing in the clause body as a set rather than a multiset. That is, repetitions of predicate symbols in the same body are ignored. In what follows, Π is the given set of CHCs.

There are two key ingredients that affect the efficiency of StHorn: (1) the choice of clauses to be examined at each iteration; and (2) the incremental construction of the interpretation. The first task is performed by the procedure `Select`, which we describe in this section. The second task is performed by the underlying CHC-solver and the procedure `Amend`, which we describe in Sect. 5.

For capturing the structure of the problem, it is useful to model Π as a directed hypergraph with parallel edges, whose vertices and hyperedges represent the predicate symbols and clauses, respectively.

Definition 6 (Induced CHC Hypergraph). *Let Π be a set of CHCs. The* induced CHC hypergraph *of Π is a directed hypergraph $G_\Pi = (V_\Pi, E_\Pi)$, where*

$$\begin{aligned} V_\Pi &= \{v_p \mid p \in \mathcal{P}^\Pi\} \cup \{v_{init}, v_{err}\} \\ E_\Pi &= \{(\{v_{init}\}, v_q) \mid \langle\emptyset, \varphi, q\rangle \in \Pi\} \cup \\ &\quad \{(\{v_{p_1}, \ldots, v_{p_k}\}, v_q) \mid \langle\{p_1, \ldots, p_k\}, \varphi, q\rangle \in \Pi\} \cup \\ &\quad \{(\{v_{p_1}, \ldots, v_{p_k}\}, v_{err}) \mid \langle\{p_1, \ldots, p_k\}, \varphi, \bot\rangle \in \Pi\} \end{aligned}$$

[3] Strengthening can be achieved as follows: if $\mathcal{I} \models_r \Pi$ and $\mathcal{I}' \models \Pi$ then the interpretation that maps every $p \in \mathcal{P}^\Pi$ to $\mathcal{I}(p) \wedge \mathcal{I}'(p)$ satisfies Π.

[4] We assume, w.l.o.g., that the head of a query is $\bot$.

There is a correspondence between the hypergraph (vertices and hyperedges) and the set of CHCs (predicates and clauses). More precisely, a vertex $v_p \in V_\Pi$ corresponds to the predicate $p \in \mathcal{P}^\Pi$, and the vertices v_{init} and v_{err} correspond to $\top$ and $\bot$, respectively. Also, an edge $e_\pi \in E_\Pi$ corresponds to the clause $\pi \in \Pi$.[5] We assume that all the edges of the CHC hypergraph are on a hyperpath from v_{init} to v_{err} (see Definition 3). Otherwise, such edges can be removed from the graph without changing the solution of Π.

Example 3. The hypergraph depicted in Fig. 1 is exactly the induced CHC hypergraph for the set of clauses of Example 1. Note that, Clause 4 is represented by the hyperedge e_4, whose set of sources is $\{v_{p_1}, v_{p_3}\}$. As mentioned above, for our algorithms, there is no need to remember the repetitions of the predicate symbol p_1 in the body of Clause 4.

The procedure `Select` is iteratively called by StHorn in order to select the subsets $\Delta \subseteq \Pi$ to be examined. For this purpose, it explores paths in the induced CHC hypergraph. Our approach is aimed at finding a solution to Π lazily and incrementally, so `Select` chooses small subsets of clauses that correspond to shortest nontrivial hyperpaths in the graph. The proposed selection strategy is based on the understanding that solving small subsets is often easier and can be advantageous to the overall solution.

Recall that there is no restriction on the selected subsets, except that they must include at least one fresh clause from Π to guarantee progress. Nevertheless, we further require `Select` to produce only subsets in which all clauses are on a hyperpath from v_{init} to v_{err}. Otherwise, if there exists a node v_p which is not reachable from v_{init}, then there exists a trivial interpretation that assigns $\bot$ to p. Similarly, if v_{err} is not reachable from v_p, then there exists a trivial interpretation that assigns $\top$ to p.

We start by presenting the algorithm `ShortNt` for finding the shortest nontrivial hyperpath from a set of sources U to each node in the graph. This algorithm is a modification of the algorithm presented in [3,4], for finding the shortest hyperpath in a directed, weighted hypergraph, from a given node to each of the nodes in the graph. Our algorithm is different from the above in two ways. First, the shortest path starts at a given *set of source nodes* U. Second, we search for only *nontrivial hyperpaths.* That is, hyperpaths that consist of at least one hyperedge.

Algorithm `ShortNt`, depicted in Algorithm 2, gets as input a hypergraph $G = (V, E)$, a weight function $w : E \rightarrow \mathbb{N}$ and a source set $U \subseteq V$. It returns a map $Dist : V \rightarrow \mathbb{N} \cup \{\infty\}$, which associates with each node v the weight of the shortest, nontrivial hyperpath $E_{U,v}$ from U to v (i.e., $\hat{w}(E_{U,v})$). It also returns a map $Last : V \rightarrow E \cup \{\texttt{null}\}$, which associates with each node v, the hyperedge e on $E_{U,v}$ for which $target(e) = v$. If v is not reachable from U along a nontrivial

[5] In fact, the induced CHC hypergraph may include parallel hyperedges originating from two CHCs that differ only in their constraints. While we support such a case, we omit it here for simplicity of presentation.

Algorithm 2. ShortNt(G, w, U)

Input: A hypergraph $G = (V, E)$, a hyperedge weight function $w : E \to \mathbb{N}$ and a source set $U \subseteq V$

Output: A map $Dist : V \to \mathbb{N} \cup \{\infty\}$ and a map $Last : V \to E \cup \{\texttt{null}\}$

```
1  Count(e) ← |S|, ∀e = (S, t) ∈ E
2  Dist(v) ← ∞, ∀v ∈ V
3  Last(v) ← null, ∀v ∈ V
4  Q ← ∅
5  for all v ∈ U do
6      Visit(v)
7  end for
8  while Q ≠ ∅ do
9      v ← arg min_{u∈Q} Dist(u)
10     Q ← Q \ {v}
11     Visit(v)
12 end while
13 return (Dist, Last)

Visit(v)
14 for all e = (S, t) ∈ E s.t. v ∈ S do
15     Count(e) ← Count(e) − 1
16     if Count(e) = 0 then
17         D ← w(e) + Σ_{v∈(S\U)} Dist(v)
18         if D < Dist(t) then
19             Dist(t) ← D
20             Last(t) ← e
21             Q ← Q ∪ {t}
22         end if
23     end if
24 end for
```

hyperpath, then the values $Dist(v) = \infty$ and $Last(v) = \texttt{null}$ are returned. Initially, $Dist(v) = \infty$ and $Last(v) = \texttt{null}$, for every $v \in V$ (lines 2, 3).

In addition to *Dist* and *Last*, `ShortNt` maintains a map $Count : E \to \mathbb{N}$, such that for each hyperedge e, $Count(e)$ is the number of sources of e that have not been visited so far. $Count(e)$ is initialized to $|source(e)|$ (line 1). It is decremented by 1 whenever a source node of e is visited (line 15). Only when it is set to 0, the hyperedge e is processed (lines 16–21). `ShortNT` also maintains a set $\mathcal{Q}$, which contains the nodes in V that are yet to be processed.

`ShortNT` first processes all source nodes $v \in U$ (lines 5–7). It goes over all edges e for which v is a source (line 14) and decrements $Count(e)$. If $Count(e)$ is now 0, meaning that all its sources have already been visited, then $Dist(target(e))$ and $Last(target(e))$ are updated. This is done when a shorter hyperpath to $target(e)$, containing e, is found. In this case, $target(e)$ is added to $\mathcal{Q}$ (lines 16–21). As long as $\mathcal{Q}$ is not empty, a node v with minimal $Dist(v)$ is removed from $\mathcal{Q}$ and is processed (lines 8–11).

Remark 2 (Complexity of `ShortNt`*).* By a similar argument to the correctness proof of Dijkstra's shortest path algorithm, we can show that `ShortNt` inserts every node to $\mathcal{Q}$ and processes it at most once. Consequently, the algorithm is polynomial in the size of the hypergraph.

Lemma 1 (Correctness of *ShortNT*). *Given a graph $G = (V, E)$, a weight function w and a source set U, then for every node $v \in V$ reachable from U, ShortNT returns $Dist(v)$ and $Last(v)$ so that $Dist(v)$ is the weight of the shortest, nontrivial hyperpath $E_{U,v}$ from U to v, and $Last(v)$ is the edge e in $E_{U,v}$ such that $target(e) = v$.*

Algorithm 3. `Select`(Π, Δ)

Input: A set Π of CHCs and a subset $\Delta \subseteq \Pi$
Output: A subset $\delta \subseteq \Pi \setminus \Delta$ such that $\delta \neq \emptyset$ if $\Delta \subset \Pi$
1 let $G_{\Pi\setminus\Delta} = (V_{\Pi\setminus\Delta}, E_{\Pi\setminus\Delta})$
2 $\mathit{Reach} \leftarrow \{v_p \in V_{\Pi\setminus\Delta} \mid p \in \mathcal{P}^{\Delta}\}$
3 $w(e) \leftarrow |S|, \forall e = (S,t) \in E_{\Pi\setminus\Delta}$
4 $(\mathit{Dist}, \mathit{Last}) \leftarrow$ `ShortNt`$(G_{\Pi\setminus\Delta}, w, \{v_{init}\} \cup \mathit{Reach})$
5 $v \leftarrow \arg\min_{u \in \mathit{Reach} \cup \{v_{err}\}} \mathit{Dist}(u)$
6 $\mathit{Opt} \leftarrow \{v\}$
7 $\delta \leftarrow \emptyset$
8 **while** $\mathit{Opt} \neq \emptyset$ **do**
9   let $u \in \mathit{Opt}$
10     $\mathit{Opt} \leftarrow \mathit{Opt} \setminus \{u\}$
11   **if** $u \notin (\{v_{init}\} \cup \mathit{Reach})$ **then**
12         $e \leftarrow \mathit{Last}(u)$
13         $\delta \leftarrow \delta \cup \{\pi(e)\}$
14         $\mathit{Opt} \leftarrow \mathit{Opt} \cup \mathit{source}(e)$
15   **end if**
16 **end while**
17 **return** δ

Next, we describe the procedure `Select`, given in Algorithm 3. It gets as input a subset of clauses $\Delta \subseteq \Pi$ and explores the graph $G_{\Pi\setminus\Delta}$. It returns a set $\delta \subseteq \Pi\setminus\Delta$, which is nonempty if Δ is a strict subset of Π. `Select` starts by initializing a set of nodes *Reach*, which consists of all nodes in $G_{\Pi\setminus\Delta}$, corresponding to predicate symbols that appear in Δ (line 2). Next, it sets the weight of each hyperedge to the number of its sources (line 3). It now computes *Dist* and *Last* by calling `ShortNt` on the graph $G_{\Pi\setminus\Delta}$, with weights w as defined above, and the set of sources $\{v_{init}\} \cup \mathit{Reach}$ (line 4). Note that, any node in the graph originating from the previously processed set Δ is now a source for `ShortNt`.

From all shortest paths computed by `ShortNt`, `Select` chooses the shortest among those whose final target is a node v in either *Reach* or $\{v_{err}\}$ (line 5). Thus, the chosen path $E_{H,v}$ starts at $H = \{v_{init}\} \cup \mathit{Reach}$ and ends in $v \in (\{v_{err}\} \cup \mathit{Reach})$. In lines 6–16, the chosen path is traversed backwards from v, producing the set of hyperedges on it and accumulating their corresponding clauses in δ (line 13). Note that, $\pi(e)$ in line 13 returns the clause corresponding to the hyperedge e.

Lemma 2 (Correctness of `Select`). *Given a set Π of CHCs and a subset $\Delta \subseteq \Pi$,* `Select` *returns a subset $\delta \subseteq \Pi\setminus\Delta$, which is nonempty if $\Delta \subset \Pi$.*

5 Ensuring Rule-Satisfiability

In this section, we describe the procedure `Amend`. First, we describe a simplified version of the procedure, and then present two modifications that can enhance its performance (Sects. 5.1 and 5.2).

Algorithm 4. $\texttt{Amend}(\mathcal{I}', \Delta, \delta)$

Input: A set Δ of CHCs, a subset $\delta \subseteq \Delta$ and an interpretation $\mathcal{I}'$ that satisfies $\Delta \setminus \delta$
Output: An interpretation $\mathcal{I}$ that rule-satisfies Δ

1 $\mathcal{I}(p) \leftarrow \mathcal{I}'(p), \forall p \in \mathcal{P}^{\Delta \setminus \delta}$
2 $\mathcal{I}(p) \leftarrow \top, \forall p \in (\mathcal{P}^{\delta} \setminus (\mathcal{P}^{\Delta \setminus \delta}))$
3 $\mathcal{Q} \leftarrow \{\pi \in \delta \mid head(\pi) \neq \bot\}$
4 **while** $\mathcal{Q} \neq \emptyset$ **do**
5   let $\pi = \langle X, \varphi, q \rangle \in \mathcal{Q}$
6     $\mathcal{Q} \leftarrow \mathcal{Q} \setminus \{\pi\}$
7     $(res, -, -) \leftarrow \texttt{Solve}(\{\mathcal{I}(\pi)\}, -)$
8   **if** $res =$ UNSAT **then**
9         $\mathcal{I}(q) \leftarrow \top$
10         $\mathcal{Q} \leftarrow \mathcal{Q} \cup \{\pi' \in \Delta \mid q \in \mathcal{P}^{body(\pi')} \wedge head(\pi') \neq \bot\}$
11   **end if**
12 **end while**

Consider the StHorn algorithm again. At line 12, a subset δ of new clauses from Π is added to Δ. At this point, it is no longer guaranteed that the current interpretation $\mathcal{I}'$ rule-satisfies Δ. In order to maintain the correctness of StHorn, $\mathcal{I}'$ must be modified before the next call to Solve. The modification of $\mathcal{I}'$ is performed by the procedure Amend. The goal of Amend is to construct an interpretation $\mathcal{I}$ such that $\mathcal{I} \models_r \Delta$, while preserving as many parts as possible from the existing interpretation $\mathcal{I}'$. This makes StHorn incremental when invoking Solve, as it allows the CHC-solver to use previously learned information that narrows the state space. In the worst case, predicates in $\mathcal{I}$ are reset back to $\top$.

The pseudo-code of the procedure appears in Algorithm 4. Amend is given a set Δ of CHCs, a subset $\delta \subseteq \Delta$, and an interpretation $\mathcal{I}'$ that satisfies all clauses in Δ, except possibly the clauses in δ. The procedure constructs and returns an interpretation $\mathcal{I}$ that rule-satisfies Δ. First, the interpretation of all predicates that occur in the previous examined subset $(\Delta \setminus \delta)$ is initialized to the current interpretation $\mathcal{I}'$ (line 1) and the interpretation of all *fresh* predicates (i.e., predicates that occur in δ but not in $\Delta \setminus \delta$) is initialized to $\top$ (line 2). The procedure maintains a set of clauses $\mathcal{Q}$, consisting of all rules in Δ that might not be satisfied by $\mathcal{I}$. According to the specifications of the procedure, those clauses are initially the rules in δ, so $\mathcal{Q}$ is initialized accordingly (line 3).

Amend then proceeds to its main loop (line 4). At each iteration, a clause $\pi = \langle X, \varphi, q \rangle$ is removed from $\mathcal{Q}$ (lines 5–6). Then, in order to check whether $\mathcal{I} \models \pi$, a new CHC-SAT problem consisting of a single clause $\mathcal{I}(\pi)$ is constructed and sent to Solve (line 7). As $\mathcal{I}(\pi)$ does not contain any uninterpreted predicate symbol, no initial interpretation is injected into the solver. If $\mathcal{I} \models \pi$, then nothing has to be done and a new iteration begins. Otherwise, the interpretation of the head predicate q is reset to $\top$ (line 9). After weakening the interpretation of q, $\mathcal{I}$ may no longer satisfy all rules in Δ where q is one of the body predicates. Therefore, any such rule is added to $\mathcal{Q}$ (line 10), and the forward amendment process continues.

Remark 3 (**Termination of** `Amend`**).** During the execution of `Amend`, a rule in Δ is added to $\mathcal{Q}$ only if the interpretation of one of its body predicates is reset to $\top$ (lines 9–10). For every predicate $q \in \mathcal{P}^{\Delta}$, such a reset can occur at most once, since afterward every rule with q as the head predicate is satisfied trivially. Due to the above, and since every rule has a finite number of body predicates, a rule is inserted into $\mathcal{Q}$ finitely many times. Therefore, if every call to `Solve` during the execution of `Amend` terminates, then `Amend` terminates as well.

Lemma 3 (Correctness of `Amend`**).** *Let Δ be a subset of CHCs, δ be a subset of Δ, and $\mathcal{I}'$ an interpretation that satisfies $\Delta \setminus \delta$. Then, if* `Amend` *terminates on Δ, δ and $\mathcal{I}'$, it returns an interpretation $\mathcal{I}$ that rule-satisfies Δ.*

Proof. Let $\pi = p_1 \wedge \cdots \wedge p_k \wedge \varphi \rightarrow q$ be a rule in Δ. Let n be the number of iterations that the main loop of `Amend` was executed and ℓ be the last iteration in which π was removed from $\mathcal{Q}$. We denote by $\mathcal{I}_j$ the interpretation after the j-th iteration of the loop. We will show that $\mathcal{I}_n \models \pi$, i.e., that $\mathcal{I}_n(p_1) \wedge \cdots \wedge \mathcal{I}_n(p_k) \wedge \varphi \Rightarrow \mathcal{I}_n(q)$.

Consider the case in which $\ell = 0$. In this case, π was never added to $\mathcal{Q}$ during the execution of `Amend`. First, we claim that $\mathcal{I}_n(p_i) = \mathcal{I}_0(p_i)$ for $1 \leq i \leq k$. This holds, because, if there existed an iteration in which the interpretation of some p_i was changed (line 9), then π would have been added to $\mathcal{Q}$ (line 10). Moreover, by the initialization of $\mathcal{I}$ and $\mathcal{Q}$ (lines 1 and 3), we have that $\mathcal{I}_0$ agrees with $\mathcal{I}'$ on all predicates in $\mathcal{P}^{\Delta \setminus \delta}$ and that $\pi \in \Delta \setminus \delta$. Therefore, since it is required that $\mathcal{I}' \models \Delta \setminus \delta$, it holds that $\mathcal{I}_0 \models \pi$. Finally, because the interpretation of every predicate may only be weakened in `Amend`, for every $j_1 < j_2$ and $r \in \mathcal{P}^{\Delta}$ it holds that $\mathcal{I}_{j_1}(r) \Rightarrow \mathcal{I}_{j_2}(r)$. Therefore, $\mathcal{I}_0(q)$ implies $\mathcal{I}_n(q)$. To summarize, we have:

$$\mathcal{I}_n(p_1) \wedge \cdots \wedge \mathcal{I}_n(p_k) \wedge \varphi \equiv \mathcal{I}_0(p_1) \wedge \cdots \wedge \mathcal{I}_0(p_k) \wedge \varphi \Rightarrow \mathcal{I}_0(q) \Rightarrow \mathcal{I}_n(q)$$

Now, consider the case in which $\ell > 0$. Similarly, we establish the following:

$$\mathcal{I}_n(p_1) \wedge \cdots \wedge \mathcal{I}_n(p_k) \wedge \varphi \equiv \mathcal{I}_\ell(p_1) \wedge \cdots \wedge \mathcal{I}_\ell(p_k) \wedge \varphi \Rightarrow \mathcal{I}_\ell(q) \Rightarrow \mathcal{I}_n(q)$$

Here, the first implication holds since when a CHC is removed from $\mathcal{Q}$, it is either satisfied by the current interpretation, or the interpretation of its head predicate is set to true. Thus, $\mathcal{I}_n \models \pi$ as needed. □

In the remainder of the section, we describe two modifications to `Amend` aimed at extracting and preserving more information from the amended interpretation.

5.1 Exploiting Conjunctive Interpretations

The first modification to `Amend` exploits the shape of the interpretation formulas. Many solvers operate on formulas in the form $c_1 \wedge \cdots \wedge c_n$ (e.g. Conjunctive Normal Form). Recall that `Amend` checks whether $\mathcal{I} \models_r \Delta$ after the addition of new clauses from Π. For every checked rule $\pi = p_1 \wedge \cdots \wedge p_k \wedge \varphi \rightarrow q$, it is checked whether $\mathcal{I}(p_1) \wedge \cdots \wedge \mathcal{I}(p_k) \wedge \varphi \rightarrow \mathcal{I}(q)$ is valid. If $\mathcal{I}(q)$ is not implied by

$\mathcal{I}(p_1) \wedge \cdots \wedge \mathcal{I}(p_k) \wedge \varphi$, then $\mathcal{I}(q)$ is reset to $\top$. After this update to $\mathcal{I}$, it holds that $\mathcal{I} \models \pi$. However, all the information previously learnt regarding q is lost. When $\mathcal{I}(q)$ is a conjunction formula $c_1 \wedge \cdots \wedge c_n$, we can check each conjunct separately, i.e., for every $1 \leq i \leq n$ we check whether $\mathcal{I}(p_1) \wedge \cdots \wedge \mathcal{I}(p_k) \wedge \varphi \rightarrow c_i$ is valid. Then, we remove from $\mathcal{I}(q)$ only the conjuncts c_i that are not implied. In the worst case, no conjuncts are implied, and $\mathcal{I}(q)$ is reset to $\top$. In practice, we can often retain significant parts of the interpretation using this approach. After applying this optimization, rules in Δ might be inserted into $\mathcal{Q}$ additional times. Nevertheless, since every conjunctive interpretation has a finite number of conjuncts, each rule is still inserted into $\mathcal{Q}$ a finite number of times.

5.2 Extending Existing Interpretations

In this subsection, we introduce a preliminary step that, if successful, will eliminate the need to run `Amend`. Before amending the interpretation, one can try to extend $\mathcal{I}'$ for the fresh predicates (i.e., predicates in $\mathcal{P}^{\delta} \setminus (\mathcal{P}^{\Delta \setminus \delta})$). For this, we construct a new CHC-SAT problem with the following set of CHCs: $\delta' = \{\mathcal{I}'(\pi) \mid \pi \in \delta \wedge \mathit{head}(\pi) \neq \bot\}$. δ' is created by substituting every non-fresh predicate (i.e., every predicate in $\mathcal{P}^{\Delta \setminus \delta}$) with its $\mathcal{I}'$ interpretation in every rule in δ. All fresh predicates remain uninterpreted.

When `Amend` is invoked, it first constructs δ' and calls `Solve`. If δ' is satisfiable, $\mathcal{I}'$ is extended for the fresh predicates according to the satisfying interpretation returned by `Solve`. In this case, `Amend` halts and returns the new interpretation without further checks. Otherwise, if δ' is unsatisfiable, `Amend` is executed as before.

6 Implementation Details and Experimental Evaluation

6.1 Implementation Details

We implemented StHorn as an open-source generic framework in C++. In addition, we implemented two instances of StHorn: one using Spacer [28] through the C++ API of Z3's [32]. The other uses Eldarica [24] as a CHC-solver. For the Eldarica instance we implemented a JAVA API for Eldarica (which is implemented in Scala). Then, we used JNI in order to invoke Eldarica (through the JAVA API we implemented) from our C++ framework. Our implementation is available in https://github.com/omerap/StructuralHorn.

StHorn with Spacer*:* We denote this instance of StHorn as StHorn$_S$. Spacer is based on IC3/PDR [9,23,28]. Satisfying interpretations are given in Conjunctive Normal Form (CNF), and the Z3 API allows to pre-load interpretations for the predicates appearing in the CHCs. This is done by adding conjuncts to a given predicate. Adding "partial" interpretations to the predicates allowed us to use Spacer incrementally seamlessly, without modifying the set of CHCs.

StHorn with ELDARICA*:* We denote this instance of StHorn as StHorn_E. In contrast to SPACER, ELDARICA is based on Predicate Abstraction, Counterexample-Guided Abstraction Refinement (CEGAR) and Interpolation. In addition, ELDARICA's API does not enable to load an interpretation for a predicate. Instead, it supports an incremental usage where solving can be invoked with a substitution map such that predicates are completely substituted with a given formula.

For using ELDARICA in StHorn, we implemented a satisfiability-preserving transformation for CHCs. Let Π be the set of CHCs. The transformation uses additional predicates that are added in the following way. First, we add the set $\mathcal{P}_g^{\Pi} := \{p_g \mid p \in \mathcal{P}^{\Pi}\}$ that consists of a *ghost* predicate for every predicate in Π. Then, we add the set $\mathcal{P}_{en}^{\Pi} := \{p_\pi \mid \pi \in \Pi\}$ that consists of an *enable* predicate for every clause in Π. While ghost predicates have the same arity as their original counterparts, enable predicates have 0-arity (i.e., they are uninterpreted Boolean constants). The new set of uninterpreted predicates is $\mathcal{P}^{\Pi} \cup \mathcal{P}_g^{\Pi} \cup \mathcal{P}_{en}^{\Pi}$.

Next, the clauses are modified such that the enable predicate p_π is added (as a conjunct) to the body of every clause π. Then, if the body of a clause contains a p-formula $p(t_1, \ldots, t_n)$, where $p \in \mathcal{P}^{\Pi}$, the p_g-formula $p_g(t_1, \ldots, t_n)$ is added (as a conjunct) to the body as well. In this way, StHorn can use ELDARICA's incremental API by supplying every call to the solver with a substitution map that substitutes every ghost predicate with its current rule-satisfying interpretation, and using the enable predicates to control what subset of clauses is being considered (in a similar manner to enable literals in SAT).

Remark 4. Importantly, while this transformation is satisfiability-preserving and allows StHorn to use any CHC-solver (even one that is not incremental), it is more limiting than what the Z3 API is allowing. The main reason is that using this method can only result in strengthening of the rule-satisfying interpretation, since the given substitutions are not modified by the solver. Both SPACER and ELDARICA employ various optimizations that can help convergence. The above transformation may interfere with such optimizations. As an example, by employing "global guidance" [29], SPACER can generalize a set of lemmas that are already present in an interpretation of a predicate (during its execution). If we would have used the above transformation with SPACER, we would have most likely interfere with this optimization.

6.2 Experimental Evaluation

In this section, we present our experimental results. We used the CHC-COMP'22 benchmarks [13], and compared StHorn against SPACER and ELDARICA. The comparison is done with respect to the corresponding instance. Namely, StHorn_S against SPACER and StHorn_E against ELDARICA. For the comparison we used two categories: (1) linear clauses over the theory of Linear Integer Arithmetic (LIA), and (2) non-linear clauses over the theory of LIA. Overall, there are 499 CHC instances for the linear CHCs, and 456 non-linear CHCs instances. All experiments were executed on a workstation with AMD EPYC 74F3, a 24-Core CPU. Every instance was given 900 s and 8 GB of memory.

Table 1. Comparison of StHorn and SPACER

Benchmarks	Tool	Total		SAT		UNSAT		Hard	
		Solved	Time [s]	Solved	Time [s]	Solved	Time [s]	Solved	Time [s]
Linear CHCs	SPACER	320 (7)	76.5	234	67.2	86	101.2	43	468.8
	StHorn_S	**322 (9)**	**67.4**	234	**63.4**	**88**	**78.2**	**45**	**411.2**
	portfolio	329	53.5	239	48.7	90	66.5	52	326.9
Non-Linear CHCs	SPACER	386 (2)	60.4	276	**48.8**	110	88.1	68	265.4
	StHorn_S	**406 (22)**	**48.9**	**286**	56.7	**120**	**30.2**	**88**	**198.4**
	portfolio	408	23.8	287	30.6	121	7.7	90	100.3

In the case of Z3, to increase the reliability of the evaluation and demonstrate that the results were not determined by random decisions made by Z3, all experiments were executed with three different random seeds (a Z3 parameter), and the results presented are an average of these runs.[6]

Table 1 and Table 2 summarize the experiments comparing StHorn with SPACER and ELDARICA, respectively. The tables present both the total number of solved instances and the average run-time, as well as a distinction between satisfiable and unsatisfiable instances. The reported average runtimes only consider the instances that were solved by at least one of the tools (if both tools report "unknown", the instance is not counted). The numbers in brackets represent uniquely solved instances. In addition, both tables present results for *hard* instances, which are instances where at least one of the tools required at least 60 s to solve. Lastly, the tables also present the results of a portfolio solver. Namely, a solver that runs both variants simultaneously (StHorn_S and SPACER for Table 1; StHorn_E and ELDARICA for Table 2) and halts when one of them terminates with a definitive result. In the following we analyze the results of both tables, divided by linear and non-linear CHCs instances.

StHorn_S vs Spacer

Linear CHCs: In this category, StHorn_S solves two more instances than SPACER and also performs better w.r.t. runtime (though the difference is not big). The set of instances they solve are also different as StHorn_S solves 9 instances not solved by SPACER, while SPACER solves 7 instances not solved by StHorn_S.

Non-Linear CHCs: On these instances, StHorn_S solves 20 more instances than SPACER. As can be seen from the table, the average runtime is in favor of StHorn_S. When further analyzing the results we discover that if one considers only unsatisfiable instances, not only StHorn_S solves more instances, it also performs almost 3 times faster.

Portfolio: We also present the results for a portfolio solver that runs both StHorn_S and SPACER simultaneously. From these results we see that the portfo-

[6] We were not able to find such a parameter for ELDARICA.

Table 2. Comparison of StHorn and ELDARICA

Benchmarks	Tool	Total		SAT		UNSAT		Hard	
		Solved	Time [s]	Solved	Time [s]	Solved	Time [s]	Solved	Time [s]
Linear CHCs	ELDARICA	226 (18)	140.2	**156**	98.9	70	220	40	532.7
	StHorn_E	**231 (23)**	**108.7**	151	**97.5**	**80**	**130.2**	**45**	**403.3**
	portfolio	249	65.6	164	50	85	95.6	63	239.5
Non-Linear CHCs	ELDARICA	**325 (40)**	**74.5**	**198**	**81.5**	**127**	**63.2**	**134**	**156.4**
	StHorn_E	302 (17)	168.3	194	129.1	108	231.5	111	366.7
	portfolio	342	27.3	211	19.1	131	40.5	151	53

lio solver shows a great improvement in runtime over each of the solvers alone, in both categories. This shows that StHorn_S can complement SPACER.

StHorn_E vs Eldarica

Linear CHCs: StHorn_E performs better than ELDARICA on the set of linear CHCs as it solves more instances and performs better w.r.t. runtime. In addition, the set of instances solved by each tool is different: StHorn_E solves 23 instances not solved by ELDARICA, while ELDARICA solves 18 instances not solved by StHorn_E. Analyzing the instances based on their satisfiability shows that the biggest improvement is achieved on unsatisfiable instances (1.7 times faster).

Non-Linear CHCs: On these instances, however, ELDARICA performs better than StHorn_E, on both number of solved instances and average runtime. A more detailed analysis of the results reveal that for StHorn_E, the time spent in the `Amend` procedure is significant. This has a few reasons. First, the interpretations returned by ELDARICA are not necessarily a set of conjuncts, which limits StHorn_E's ability to retain parts of the satisfying interpretations returned when analyzing a subset of clauses. Second, since ELDARICA does not have an API that allows "pre-loading" a rule-satisfying interpretation for a predicate, we used a satisfiability-preserving transformation. However, this transformation limits StHorn_E (see Remark 4) such that it can only "strengthen" the given rule-satisfying interpretation when invoking `Solve`. Lastly, since StHorn_E makes many calls to ELDARICA through JNI, this imposes an overhead.

Portfolio: Despite all of the above, when considering a portfolio solver that invokes both StHorn_E and ELDARICA, performance improve quite significantly both in the number of solved instances and runtime. This again shows that StHorn_E can complement ELDARICA and improve its performance.

Summary. Overall, StHorn solved more instances and had a faster runtime than SPACER and ELDARICA. One exception is the Non-linear category, where ELDARICA outperforms StHorn. StHorn, however, demonstrated substantial improvements in the portfolio solver, both in the latter category and the rest, indicating that it complements both tools by allowing them to solve new instances more efficiently. In addition, our evaluation indicates a greater improvement for UNSAT instances, but also a promising improvement for SAT instances. It is therefore evident that StHorn can improve upon the state-of-the-art in CHC solving.

7 Related Work

There is a large body of work on solving the CHC-SAT problem, with a plethora of algorithms and tools that are based on different methods such as IC3/PDR, interpolation, Counterexample-Guided Abstraction Refinement (CEGAR), Predicate Abstraction, and Machine Learning [7,8,12,14,16,23,24, 28,34]. The technique presented in this paper, StHorn, is orthogonal to these algorithms as it uses a CHC-solver as a "black-box".

CHCs gained popularity in recent years since many program, and recently hardware, verification problems can be reduced to the satisfiability of CHCs [7, 17,20,26,33]. Many program verification algorithms work by analyzing different paths in the program separately, when trying to establish the correctness of the whole program [10,21,22,31]. In this sense, StHorn draws its intuition from path-sensitive verification algorithms. However, most program verification algorithms that operate on paths consider bounded execution paths in the control flow graph, while StHorn considers complete paths in the graph, that may include loops. Intuitively, this is similar to analyzing complete fragments of a program that include loops, without unrolling them explicitly. The closest work to ours in this regard is [6] where complete fragments of a program (i.e., "path programs") are considered. The usage, however, is quite different as they use "path invariants" to eliminate spurious counterexamples in the context of CEGAR, whereas we construct satisfying interpretations for CHC sets incrementally based on interpretations of satisfiable subsets.

Hypergraphs have been suggested before in [2] for solving propositional Horn formulas, in which the uninterpreted predicate symbols are Boolean. That is, they can be assigned either $\top$ or $\bot$. Given a propositional Horn formula, they show how to maintain on-line information about its satisfiability during the insertion of new clauses. Clearly, this is a different problem.

Lastly, StHorn uses a structure-guided heuristic for selecting the subsets to be solved and tries to re-use information when analyzing different subsets. We are unaware of a similar heuristic for prioritizing clauses during the search for a satisfying interpretation.

8 Conclusion

In this work, we present StHorn, a technique for deciding the satisfiability of a set Π of CHCs. StHorn handles monotonically larger subsets of Π, which are selected based on its structure. The technique exploits a satisfying interpretation obtained for one subset as a basis for solving subsequent subsets. We use a CHC-solver as a "black-box". Our evaluation shows that StHorn, when added on top of Spacer, improves upon state-of-the-art. Moreover, it complements both Spacer and Eldarica, allowing them to solve new instances more efficiently.

Future research plans include: (i) designing domain-oriented selection strategies; (ii) enhancing current (syntactic) strategies with semantic hints; and (iii) integrating the technique natively into a CHC-solver, reducing the overhead imposed by its API and further improving performance.

References

1. Ausiello, G., Franciosa, P.G., Frigioni, D.: Directed hypergraphs: problems, algorithmic results, and a novel decremental approach. In: ICTCS 2001. LNCS, vol. 2202, pp. 312–328. Springer, Heidelberg (2001). https://doi.org/10.1007/3-540-45446-2_20
2. Ausiello, G., Italiano, G.F.: On-line algorithms for polynomially solvable satisfiability problems. J. Log. Program. **10**(1), 69–90 (1991). https://doi.org/10.1016/0743-1066(91)90006-B
3. Ausiello, G., Italiano, G.F., Nanni, U.: Optimal traversal of directed hypergraphs. Technical report, TR-92-073 (1992)
4. Ausiello, G., Italiano, G.F., Nanni, U.: Hypergraph traversal revisited: cost measures and dynamic algorithms. In: Brim, L., Gruska, J., Zlatuška, J. (eds.) MFCS 1998. LNCS, vol. 1450, pp. 1–16. Springer, Heidelberg (1998). https://doi.org/10.1007/BFb0055754
5. Beyene, T.A., Popeea, C., Rybalchenko, A.: Efficient CTL verification via horn constraints solving. In: Gallagher, J.P., Rümmer, P. (eds.) Proceedings 3rd Workshop on Horn Clauses for Verification and Synthesis, HCVS@ETAPS 2016, Eindhoven, The Netherlands, 3 April 2016. EPTCS, vol. 219, pp. 1–14 (2016). https://doi.org/10.4204/EPTCS.219.1
6. Beyer, D., Henzinger, T.A., Majumdar, R., Rybalchenko, A.: Path invariants. In: Ferrante, J., McKinley, K.S. (eds.) Proceedings of the ACM SIGPLAN 2007 Conference on Programming Language Design and Implementation, San Diego, California, USA, 10–13 June 2007, pp. 300–309. ACM (2007). https://doi.org/10.1145/1250734.1250769
7. Bjørner, N., Gurfinkel, A., McMillan, K., Rybalchenko, A.: Horn clause solvers for program verification. In: Beklemishev, L.D., Blass, A., Dershowitz, N., Finkbeiner, B., Schulte, W. (eds.) Fields of Logic and Computation II. LNCS, vol. 9300, pp. 24–51. Springer, Cham (2015). https://doi.org/10.1007/978-3-319-23534-9_2
8. Bjørner, N., McMillan, K., Rybalchenko, A.: On solving universally quantified horn clauses. In: Logozzo, F., Fähndrich, M. (eds.) SAS 2013. LNCS, vol. 7935, pp. 105–125. Springer, Heidelberg (2013). https://doi.org/10.1007/978-3-642-38856-9_8
9. Bradley, A.R.: SAT-based model checking without unrolling. In: Jhala, R., Schmidt, D. (eds.) VMCAI 2011. LNCS, vol. 6538, pp. 70–87. Springer, Heidelberg (2011). https://doi.org/10.1007/978-3-642-18275-4_7
10. Das, M., Lerner, S., Seigle, M.: ESP: path-sensitive program verification in polynomial time. In: Knoop, J., Hendren, L.J. (eds.) Proceedings of the 2002 ACM SIGPLAN Conference on Programming Language Design and Implementation (PLDI), Berlin, Germany, 17–19 June 2002, pp. 57–68. ACM (2002). https://doi.org/10.1145/512529.512538
11. De Angelis, E., Fioravanti, F., Gallagher, J.P., Hermenegildo, M.V., Pettorossi, A., Proietti, M.: Analysis and transformation of constrained horn clauses for program verification. Theory Pract. Logic Program. **22**(6), 974–1042 (2022). https://doi.org/10.1017/S1471068421000211

12. De Angelis, E., Fioravanti, F., Pettorossi, A., Proietti, M.: VeriMAP: a tool for verifying programs through transformations. In: Ábrahám, E., Havelund, K. (eds.) TACAS 2014. LNCS, vol. 8413, pp. 568–574. Springer, Heidelberg (2014). https://doi.org/10.1007/978-3-642-54862-8_47
13. De Angelis, E., Govind, V.K.H.: CHC-COMP 2022: competition report. In: Hamilton, G.W., Kahsai, T., Proietti, M. (eds.) Proceedings 9th Workshop on Horn Clauses for Verification and Synthesis and 10th International Workshop on Verification and Program Transformation, HCVS/VPT@ETAPS 2022, and 10th International Workshop on Verification and Program TransformationMunich, Germany, 3rd April 2022. EPTCS, vol. 373, pp. 44–62 (2022). https://doi.org/10.4204/EPTCS.373.5
14. Fedyukovich, G., Kaufman, S.J., Bodík, R.: Sampling invariants from frequency distributions. In: Stewart, D., Weissenbacher, G. (eds.) 2017 Formal Methods in Computer Aided Design, FMCAD 2017, Vienna, Austria, 2–6 October 2017, pp. 100–107. IEEE (2017). https://doi.org/10.23919/FMCAD.2017.8102247
15. Grebenshchikov, S., Gupta, A., Lopes, N.P., Popeea, C., Rybalchenko, A.: HSF(C): a software verifier based on horn clauses. In: Flanagan, C., König, B. (eds.) TACAS 2012. LNCS, vol. 7214, pp. 549–551. Springer, Heidelberg (2012). https://doi.org/10.1007/978-3-642-28756-5_46
16. Grebenshchikov, S., Lopes, N.P., Popeea, C., Rybalchenko, A.: Synthesizing software verifiers from proof rules. In: Vitek, J., Lin, H., Tip, F. (eds.) ACM SIGPLAN Conference on Programming Language Design and Implementation, PLDI 2012, Beijing, China, 11–16 June 2012, pp. 405–416. ACM (2012). https://doi.org/10.1145/2254064.2254112
17. Gupta, A., Popeea, C., Rybalchenko, A.: Threader: a constraint-based verifier for multi-threaded programs. In: Gopalakrishnan, G., Qadeer, S. (eds.) CAV 2011. LNCS, vol. 6806, pp. 412–417. Springer, Heidelberg (2011). https://doi.org/10.1007/978-3-642-22110-1_32
18. Gurfinkel, A.: Program verification with constrained horn clauses (invited paper). In: Shoham, S., Vizel, Y. (eds.) CAV 2022. LNCS, vol. 13371, pp. 19–29. Springer, Cham (2022). https://doi.org/10.1007/978-3-031-13185-1_2
19. Gurfinkel, A., Kahsai, T., Komuravelli, A., Navas, J.A.: The SeaHorn verification framework. In: Kroening, D., Păsăreanu, C.S. (eds.) CAV 2015, Part I. LNCS, vol. 9206, pp. 343–361. Springer, Cham (2015). https://doi.org/10.1007/978-3-319-21690-4_20
20. Gurfinkel, A., Shoham, S., Meshman, Y.: SMT-based verification of parameterized systems. In: Zimmermann, T., Cleland-Huang, J., Su, Z. (eds.) Proceedings of the 24th ACM SIGSOFT International Symposium on Foundations of Software Engineering, FSE 2016, Seattle, WA, USA, 13–18 November 2016, pp. 338–348. ACM (2016). https://doi.org/10.1145/2950290.2950330
21. Harris, W.R., Sankaranarayanan, S., Ivancic, F., Gupta, A.: Program analysis via satisfiability modulo path programs. In: Hermenegildo, M.V., Palsberg, J. (eds.) Proceedings of the 37th ACM SIGPLAN-SIGACT Symposium on Principles of Programming Languages, POPL 2010, Madrid, Spain, 17–23 January 2010, pp. 71–82. ACM (2010). https://doi.org/10.1145/1706299.1706309
22. Henzinger, T.A., Jhala, R., Majumdar, R., McMillan, K.L.: Abstractions from proofs. In: Jones, N.D., Leroy, X. (eds.) Proceedings of the 31st ACM SIGPLAN-SIGACT Symposium on Principles of Programming Languages, POPL 2004, Venice, Italy, 14–16 January 2004, pp. 232–244. ACM (2004). https://doi.org/10.1145/964001.964021

23. Hoder, K., Bjørner, N.: Generalized property directed reachability. In: Cimatti, A., Sebastiani, R. (eds.) SAT 2012. LNCS, vol. 7317, pp. 157–171. Springer, Heidelberg (2012). https://doi.org/10.1007/978-3-642-31612-8_13
24. Hojjat, H., Rümmer, P.: The ELDARICA horn solver. In: Bjørner, N., Gurfinkel, A. (eds.) 2018 Formal Methods in Computer Aided Design, FMCAD 2018, Austin, TX, USA, 30 October–2 November 2018, pp. 1–7. IEEE (2018). https://doi.org/10.23919/FMCAD.2018.8603013
25. Hojjat, H., Rümmer, P., McClurg, J., Cerný, P., Foster, N.: Optimizing horn solvers for network repair. In: Piskac, R., Talupur, M. (eds.) 2016 Formal Methods in Computer-Aided Design, FMCAD 2016, Mountain View, CA, USA, 3–6 October 2016, pp. 73–80. IEEE (2016). https://doi.org/10.1109/FMCAD.2016.7886663
26. Govind, H.V.K., Fedyukovich, G., Gurfinkel, A.: Word level property directed reachability. In: IEEE/ACM International Conference On Computer Aided Design, ICCAD 2020, San Diego, CA, USA, 2–5 November 2020, pp. 107:1–107:9. IEEE (2020). https://doi.org/10.1145/3400302.3415708
27. Kahsai, T., Rümmer, P., Sanchez, H., Schäf, M.: JayHorn: a framework for verifying java programs. In: Chaudhuri, S., Farzan, A. (eds.) CAV 2016. LNCS, vol. 9779, pp. 352–358. Springer, Cham (2016). https://doi.org/10.1007/978-3-319-41528-4_19
28. Komuravelli, A., Gurfinkel, A., Chaki, S.: SMT-based model checking for recursive programs. Formal Methods Syst. Des. **48**(3), 175–205 (2016). https://doi.org/10.1007/s10703-016-0249-4
29. Vediramana Krishnan, H.G., Chen, Y.T., Shoham, S., Gurfinkel, A.: Global guidance for local generalization in model checking. In: Lahiri, S.K., Wang, C. (eds.) CAV 2020. LNCS, vol. 12225, pp. 101–125. Springer, Cham (2020). https://doi.org/10.1007/978-3-030-53291-8_7
30. Matsushita, Y., Tsukada, T., Kobayashi, N.: RustHorn: CHC-based verification for rust programs. ACM Trans. Program. Lang. Syst. **43**(4), 15:1–15:54 (2021). https://doi.org/10.1145/3462205
31. McMillan, K.L.: Lazy abstraction with interpolants. In: Ball, T., Jones, R.B. (eds.) CAV 2006. LNCS, vol. 4144, pp. 123–136. Springer, Heidelberg (2006). https://doi.org/10.1007/11817963_14
32. de Moura, L., Bjørner, N.: Z3: an efficient SMT solver. In: Ramakrishnan, C.R., Rehof, J. (eds.) TACAS 2008. LNCS, vol. 4963, pp. 337–340. Springer, Heidelberg (2008). https://doi.org/10.1007/978-3-540-78800-3_24
33. Zhang, H., Gupta, A., Malik, S.: Syntax-guided synthesis for lemma generation in hardware model checking. In: Henglein, F., Shoham, S., Vizel, Y. (eds.) VMCAI 2021. LNCS, vol. 12597, pp. 325–349. Springer, Cham (2021). https://doi.org/10.1007/978-3-030-67067-2_15
34. Zhu, H., Magill, S., Jagannathan, S.: A data-driven CHC solver. In: Foster, J.S., Grossman, D. (eds.) Proceedings of the 39th ACM SIGPLAN Conference on Programming Language Design and Implementation, PLDI 2018, Philadelphia, PA, USA, 18–22 June 2018, pp. 707–721. ACM (2018). https://doi.org/10.1145/3192366.3192416

Automated Property Directed Self Composition

Akshatha Shenoy[1(✉)], Sumanth Prabhu[1], Kumar Madhukar[2], Ron Shemer[3], and Mandayam Srivas[4]

[1] TCS Research, Pune, India
{shenoy.akshatha,sumanth.prabhu}@tcs.com
[2] Indian Institute of Technology Delhi, New Delhi, India
madhukar@cse.iitd.ac.in
[3] Mend.io, Tel Aviv, Israel
[4] Chennai Mathematical Institute, Chennai, India

Abstract. We consider the problem of hypersafety verification, i.e. of verifying k-safety properties of a program. While this can, in principle, be addressed by self composition, which reduces the k-safety verification task into a standard (1−)safety verification exercise, verifying self-composed programs is not easy. The proofs often require that the functionality of every component program be captured fully, making invariant inference a challenge. Recently, a technique for property directed self composition (or, PDSC) was proposed to tackle this problem. PDSC tries to come up with a semantic self-composition function, together with the inductive invariant that is needed to verify the safety of the self-composed program. One of its crucial limitations, however, is that it relies on users to supply a set of predicates in which the composition and the invariant may be expressed. It is quite challenging even for a user to supply such a set of predicates – the set needs to be sufficiently expressive, so that the invariant can be expressed using those predicates (and their boolean combinations), but not overly expressive to increase the search-space unnecessarily. This paper proposes a technique to automate PDSC fully, by discovering new predicates whenever the given set is found to be insufficient. We present three different approaches for obtaining predicates – relying on syntax-guided synthesis, quantifier elimination, and interpolation – and discuss the strengths and limitations of these.

1 Introduction

A hypersafety or a k-safety property is a program safety property whose violation needs at least k program runs to be demonstrated. Determinism and non-interference are common examples of such properties. A straightforward way to transform a k-safety property into a usual (1-)safety property is *self-composition* [7], in which k memory-disjoint copies of the program are composed with each other. Since the copies are memory-disjoint, the composition may be thought of as an asynchronous parallel composition in which all interleavings

É. André and J. Sun (Eds.): ATVA 2023, LNCS 14216, pp. 139–158, 2023.
https://doi.org/10.1007/978-3-031-45332-8_7

have the same behavior. Thus, a hypersafety property that holds in some interleaving holds for all interleavings. A trace of such a composed program naturally corresponds to an interleaving of k traces of the original program, and that is how self-composition reduces a k-safety property to a safety property.

As a technique, self-composition is both sound and complete for k-safety [37]. It also allows us to use the rich literature that exists for verifying (1-)safety properties. However, verifying self-composed programs is not an easy exercise. For instance, if the programs are composed sequentially, proving properties may often require that the functionality of every component be captured fully, and the required invariants can be difficult to obtain even for very simple programs and properties. Since all interleavings (or compositions) behave similarly, it helps to shift the focus of the problem on finding one which is easy to prove correct [16,37].

A recent technique of property directed self composition [37] addresses this problem by appealing to this very insight – that the way the copies are composed determines how complicated it is to verify the composed program. Note that since the copies are memory-disjoint, all compositions are safe if any one of them is proved safe. Informally speaking, PDSC attempts to find an *easy-to-prove* composition and prove that it is safe. It comes up with a semantic self-composition function, together with the inductive invariant that is needed to verify the safety of the program composed according to that function. Since this problem is undecidable in general, it is made tractable by fixing a language of proofs, described by a given set of predicates and their boolean combinations, and navigating the space of all possible compositions to see if one of them can be proved safe by finding an inductive invariant in this language. The algorithm relies on the property that a transition system has an inductive invariant in a language of predicates (and boolean combinations) if and only if its abstraction using those predicates is safe. Thus, by using predicate abstraction, PDSC either obtains an inductive invariant or is able to prove that none exists in the given language.

Interestingly, 2-safety verification is closely related to the task of checking equivalence of two programs. Program equivalence is an important problem owing to its diverse applications, that include translation validation and compiler correctness [22,27,29], code refactoring [33], program synthesis [4], hypersafety verification [3,16,37], superoptimization [10,35], and programming and software engineering education [24] amongst many others. Naturally, self-composition offers a solution for this too, but verifying the composed programs can be quite challenging. Consider, for example, two programs that sum all the numbers in the range $[1, n]$ – even if both the programs are iterating over the digits from 1 to n and adding it to the sum, a sequential composition of these two programs requires non-linear inductive invariants to establish equivalence. An ideal composition in this case would be one where the program statements (or loop iterations) are composed statement by statement, i.e. in *lock-step*. The property itself, that the two sums are equal, becomes an inductive invariant of the lock-step composition. Thus, PDSC becomes a useful technique for addressing the problem of program equivalence as well.

An important caveat of PDSC, however, is that it relies on users to supply a set of predicates in which the composition and the invariant may be expressed. It is quite challenging even for a user to supply such a set of predicates – the set needs to be sufficiently expressive, so that the invariant can be expressed using those predicates (and their boolean combinations), but not overly expressive to increase the search-space unnecessarily. Therefore, it is crucial for the usefulness of PDSC that an automatic way of obtaining these predicates be devised and developed. While there are techniques that can mine predicates (to construct invariants) from program source [18–20,30], and PDSC itself proposes to do this in order to lessen the user-dependence, the necessary predicates may very often be absent from the source code (our motivating example, for instance, in Sect. 2). Another limitation of the PDSC algorithm is that it only tries to find an invariant that can establish the given k-safety property. If it fails in doing so, it does not look for a counterexample (a refutation witness).

This paper proposes an algorithm that works on top of PDSC, to *i)* automatically enrich the set of predicates, when it realizes that the current set is insufficient, till a proof is derived, and *ii)* look for a counterexample when it cannot obtain a proof with a given set of predicates, so that new predicates are added only if a refutation witness can also not be derived so far. Though explained later (in Sect. 3.4), the insufficiency of a given set of predicates emerges as an abstract counterexample trace. This trace must be spurious if the property holds, and if the property does not hold then it may correspond to an actual concrete counterexample. Therefore, the purpose of new predicates is to capture the reason for spuriousness. We have designed two different approaches to synthesize new predicates, one that uses a counterexample-guided method of predicate refinement, and another one that obtains them as interpolants from the infeasibility-proof of the counterexample trace. For the first approach, we encode the task as an abduction query, and solve it either using a Syntax-Guided Synthesis (SyGuS) solver (with CVC4-1.8 [6]) or an SMT Solver (Z3 [13]). For the second one, we compute interpolants using MathSAT5 [11]. An experimental comparison of these techniques have been presented in Sect. 6.

The core contributions of this paper are:

1. An improvement of the PDSC algorithm that not only makes it capable to look for proofs as well as refutations, but also removes its user-dependence and enables it to strengthen its proof language iteratively, on demand, in a counterexample-guided way.
2. An implementation on top of PDSC, with three different methods for deriving new predicates – using a SyGuS solver, or an SMT solver, or an interpolating prover. And an experimental comparison of these on several hypersafety verification and program equivalence benchmarks from the literature.

Outline of the paper. The rest of the paper is organized as follows. We start with a motivating example in Sect. 2, and then move to the necessary background in Sect. 3, which includes a description of the PDSC algorithm that we build upon. Section 4 talks about the challenges and the key contributions that we have made.

We describe our algorithm in Sect. 5, and the details of our implementation and experiments in Sect. 6. Section 7 discusses the related work, and Sect. 8 contains our concluding remarks.

2 Motivating Example

Consider the example shown in Fig. 1(a) and (b). This is a benchmark from [37]; for ease of understanding, we have presented it as two separate programs, and refer to the underlying 2-safety property simply as an equivalence check. The task is prove that these programs compute the same output value, given the same input. This is indeed true; both the programs take an integer x as input and compute $2 * x^2$, although differently. The first program (`v1`) goes through the while loop $2x$ times, adding x to y each time. The second program (`v2`) goes through the loop only x times, incrementing y by x each time, but doubles the value of y before it returns.

A self-composition approach that does a sequential composition in this case would require that both the programs be completely analyzed individually before the outputs can be compared. For example, one needs to synthesize invariants for loops in both programs separately, which in this case are non-linear expressions: $(0 \leq z \leq 2x) \wedge y = x * (2x - z)$ and $(0 \leq z \leq x) \wedge y = x * (x - z)$, for the versions `v1` and `v2` respectively.

```
dblSqr-v1(x){

  y = 0;
  z = 2 * x;

  while (z > 0) {
    z = z - 1;
    y = y + x;
  }

  return y;
}
```

(a)

```
dblSqr-v2(x){

  y = 0;
  z = x;

  while (z > 0){
    z = z - 1;
    y = y + x;
  }

  y = 2 * y;
  return y;
}
```

(b)

Fig. 1. doubleSquare example, from [37]

An alternative approach could be to analyze their runs in an interleaved fashion, up to selected "checkpoints" in each program. An advantage of using such an interleaved composition for analysis is that the required invariants are likely to be simpler because of the choice of the checkpoints as synchronization points for interleaving. The checkpoints can be chosen where the outputs are expected to be behaviorally equivalent, or if not, then at least there is a linear relation between them. For instance, for the programs shown in Fig. 1, the checkpoints can be added such that the components synchronized after every two iterations of the loop in `v1` and one iteration of the loop in `v2`. If this happens, then at each synchronization point the value of y in `v1` will be double that of y in `v2`. After the loop exit, before the programs return, since `v1` does not run any instruction, while `v2` multiplies its copy of y by 2, it becomes evident – by only tracking linear relation in the variables – that the programs are doing the same thing.

The technical challenge in this approach lies in finding good synchronization points, or equivalently, a suitable composition, that has an *easy-to-find* safe inductive invariant. An additional challenge lies in that the expressiveness of the proof language (i.e., the one in which invariants have to be searched) is dependent on the choice of the composition candidate. In the next section, we will understand how the PDSC technique addresses these concerns, and discuss the limitations and challenges that lie ahead.

3 Background

3.1 Programs, Safety Properties, and Invariants

Similar to [37], we model a program as a transition system that defines its behavior. A transition system is a tuple $T = (S, R, F)$, where S is a set of states, $R \subseteq S \times S$ is a transition relation that specifies an arbitrary step in an execution of the program, and $F \subseteq S$ is a set of terminal states such that every terminal state $s \in F$ has an outgoing transition to itself and no additional outgoing transitions (terminal states allow us to reason about *pre-post* specifications of programs).

An execution (or trace) of the program is given by a sequence of states $\pi = s_0, s_1, ...$ such that for every $i \geq 0, (s_i, s_{i+1}) \in R$. An execution is called *terminating* if its corresponding sequence has the suffix $s_i, s_i, ..$ for some $s_i \in F$, and the terminating execution is said to *end at* s_i.

We denote the set of variables by V, and the transition relation by a formula over $V \cup V'$ where post-states of transitions are over V'. We use sets of states and their symbolic representation via formulas interchangeably.

We consider safety properties defined via a $(pre, post)$ pair, where *pre* and *post* are formulas over V , representing sets of states. T satisfies $(pre, post)$ if every terminating execution of T that starts in a state that satisfies *pre*, ends at a state that satisfies *post*.

An inductive invariant, for a transition system T and a safety property given as $(pre, post)$, is a formula *Inv* such that the following conditions hold.

$$(1)\ pre \Rightarrow Inv,\ (2)\ Inv \wedge R \Rightarrow Inv',\ (3)\ Inv \Rightarrow (F \Rightarrow post)$$

Inv' denotes the formula *Inv* with every variable replaced by its corresponding primed version.

It is noteworthy that any inductive invariant satisfies the first two conditions, while the last condition holds only for an invariant that is sufficiently strong to discharge the given safety property. We sometimes refer to such an inductive invariant, one that satisfies all the three conditions above, as a *safe* inductive invariant, and even as a safety *proof.*

A k-safety property refers to k interacting executions of T, and is also given by a $(pre, post)$ pair, except that *pre* and *post* are defined over $V_1 \uplus \ldots \uplus V_k$ where V_i denotes the ith copy of program variables. Naturally, *pre* and *post* represent sets of k-tuples of program states, and a specific k-tuple of states $(s_1, \ldots, s_k)$ in the k-cartesian product of S can be represented as a conjunction of formulas over $V_1 \uplus \ldots \uplus V_k$. A terminal k-tuple of states is one in which all individual states are terminal, and a k execution is terminating if it ends at a terminal k-tuple of states. T is said to satisfy a k-safety property $(pre, post)$ if for every k terminating executions that start in states $s_1, \ldots, s_k$ such that $(s_1, \ldots, s_k) \models pre$, it holds that they end at states $t_1, \ldots, t_k$ such that $(t_1, \ldots, t_k) \models post$.

3.2 Abduction

Abductive inference [14] is a form of backward logical reasoning, to infer likely hypothesis from a given conclusion. Formally, given an invalid implication $\Gamma \Rightarrow \phi$, abductive inference finds a formula ψ such that $\Gamma \wedge \psi \Rightarrow \phi$ is valid, and $\Gamma \wedge \psi$ is satisfiable.

Note that ϕ is a trivial solution but it is not useful because it completely disregards our existing knowledge (of Γ). In this paper (as discussed later, Sect. 5.2), we rely on SyGuS and SMT solvers for doing abductive inference.

3.3 Interpolation

Consider an unsatisfiable set of clauses which have been partitioned into two sets, A and B. An interpolant [12] I for the pair (A, B) is a formula for which the following hold:

- $A \Rightarrow I$
- $I \wedge B$ is unsatisfiable
- I refers only to the common variables of A and B.

Such an interpolant, for first-order theories can be generated in linear time [31] from the resolution proof of unsatisfiability (of A and B).

3.4 Property Directed Self Composition

Property directed self composition, or PDSC, is a recent technique that combines the search of invariants with that of a composition. It does this by fixing a language of proofs, $\mathcal{L}_{\mathcal{P}}$, described by a given set of predicates, $\mathcal{P}$, and their boolean combinations, and navigating the space of all possible compositions to see if one of them has a proof in this language. Fixing the language not only makes the search tractable, it also allows PDSC to rely on the property that a transition system has an inductive invariant in $\mathcal{L}_{\mathcal{P}}$ if and only if its abstraction using $\mathcal{P}$ is safe. Therefore, by using predicate abstraction, it is possible with PDSC to either obtain an inductive invariant in $\mathcal{L}_{\mathcal{P}}$, or prove that none exists.

The way PDSC navigates through the composition space is by defining a composition function $f : S^k \rightarrow \mathbb{P}(\{1..k\})$, mapping each k-state to a non-empty set of copies that are to participate in the next step of the self composed program. This composition function is *semantic*, in that it does not necessarily depend on what are the syntactic constructs used in the next step of the component programs. This allows PDSC to explore beyond syntactic compositions, which may not always be possible or useful.

Given a composition function f, PDSC creates a composed transition relation $T^f = (S^k, R^f, F^k)$, where the set of states consists of all k-states, the terminal states are those in which all individual states are terminal, and R^f includes a transition from $(s_1, ..., s_k)$ to $(s'_1, ..., s'_k)$ *if and only if* $f(s_1, ..., s_k) = M$, and $(\forall i \in M.\ (s_i, s'_i) \in R) \wedge (\forall i \notin M.\ s_i = s'_i)$.

Intuitively, the composition function tells, for any state, what are the copies that are scheduled to move next, and the composed transition relation ensures that the components move as per their individual transition relation in the copies that are scheduled to move, and not move at all in any other copy.

Algorithm 1. Property Directed Self Composition

```
𝓕_block ← ∅                                   ▷ block compositions that cannot be proved safe
f ← lockstep
while true do
    𝒯^f = compose(f, T_1, ..., T_k)
    𝒜_𝒫^{𝒯^f} = abstract(𝒯^f, 𝒫)
    (res, inv, cex) = isBadReachable(𝒜_𝒫^{𝒯^f}, pre, post)   ▷ where bad is negated post
    if (res = safe) then
        return (f, inv)
    else
        𝓕_block ← 𝓕_block ∪ {f}                ▷ block f to get rid of cex
        if (not all compositions are blocked) then
            f ← pickUnblockedComposition(𝓕_block)   ▷ try a different, unblocked, composition
        else
            return (no proof in the language of 𝒫)
```

Algorithm 1 presents an overview of how PDSC works. The composition is set to lockstep in the beginning, and the composed transition relation is obtained and abstracted with the given set of predicates. If the abstraction is found to be safe, at any stage, the algorithm returns a composition-invariant pair; otherwise, the composition is modified and the process is repeated. If none of the compositions succeed, the algorithm concludes that no invariant, which is a boolean combination of these given predicates, is inductive and safe. In other words, either the language is not rich enough to capture a safety proof for any of the compositions, or the program is not safe.

We have presented only a brief overview of the PDSC algorithm, with the aim of making this paper self-contained. We refer the interested readers to [37] for a detailed discussion.

3.5 Revisiting Our Motivating Example

Let us recall the example shown in Fig. 1. We argued earlier that the loops in the two programs may be synchronized such that for every two iterations of the loop in the first one, we run only one iteration of that in the second one. This way of composing the loops of the two programs gives us a simpler loop invariant: $y_1 = 2*y_2$. The way PDSC arrives at this composition automatically is by fixing a proof language, and then by searching among the possible compositions allowed by the language.

Figure 2 shows the composition and the proof obtained automatically by PDSC, for our motivating example. Intuitively, PDSC takes the input set of predicates (defining the proof language), and uses it to construct abstract states for every (consistent) combination of predicates and their negation. And then it explores transitions, labelled by the program copies whose next statement/block has to be executed, between these states to find a path to a final state where the property holds (e.g. the rightmost state in Fig. 2). Clearly, the search depends on the input set of predicates. For this example, PDSC expects four predicates from the user (without which it would not have been able to construct the three states shown in Fig. 2 and discharge the proof): z_1==2*z_2, y_1==2*y_2, z_1==2*z_2-1, and y_1==2*y_2+x_2. Note that the predicates y_1==y_2 and x_1==x_2 are available as the postcondition and precondition respectively, and thus need not be supplied externally.

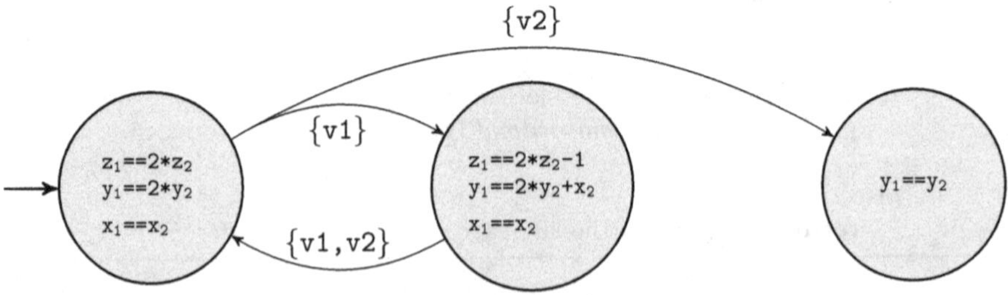

Fig. 2. Composition and proof obtained by PDSC, for the example in Fig. 1

4 Challenges and Contributions

We look at the important caveats of PDSC– *i*) it works for finding proofs but cannot detect real counterexamples, *ii*) it requires a set of predicates supplied externally, and *iii*) it cannot make progress if the supplied predicates are found to be insufficient to express a safe inductive invariant. The following key components of our algorithm helps us overcome these limitations.

1. *spuriousness checker*, to obtain a real counterexample trace if the programs do not satisfy the desired k-safety property (or, in our case, behave differently for the same input)
2. *predicate synthesizer*, to eliminate spurious counterexample traces and to enrich the language for finding safe invariants.

It is noteworthy that since PDSC works by checking safety of an abstraction of the composed transition relation, it may be possible to do the above by interfacing PDSC with a predicate-abstraction engine that can supply the predicates for refinement. However, interfacing with a black-box engine is not very useful because these predicates define the language of proofs, which in turn, decides the complexity of the composition-invariant search, and therefore it is important to have control on their quality and quantity to get a scalable solution.

We describe our algorithm formally in the next section, along with the details of the two components that we have added, and a proof that our algorithm works.

5 Algorithm

Algorithm 2 presents a pseudo-code of our approach, which enhances the original PDSC algorithm (shown in Algorithm 1) with the ability to synthesize predicates, to strengthen the language of proofs whenever necessary. In particular, the proposed enhancement is captured in lines 14-20, that *i*) returns the counterexample (*cex*) generated in line 7 if it is indeed a feasible trace by using a *spuriousness* check (lines 14 and 15), *ii*) adds a predicate to refine the counterexample if spurious (lines 18 and 18), and *iii*) resets the composition space and restarts the search from the lockstep composition (lines 19 and 20).

The next two subsections describe the two procedures – *isSpurious* and *synthesizePredicates* – mentioned in the algorithm.

5.1 Spuriousness Check

The counterexample obtained in line 7 of Algorithm 2 is essentially a sequence of abstract states that end in a bad state, i.e., a state that violates the *post*. Each abstract state is defined by a valuation of all the predicates in $\mathcal{P}$. Let us denote this sequence of abstract states as: $A_0, A_1, \ldots, A_{bad}$. These states, in the counterexample trace, are connected by a transition relation which is defined by the transition relations of the component programs, and the *current* composition

Algorithm 2. PDSC with Predicate Synthesis

```
𝓕_block ← ∅                                        ▷ block compositions that cannot be proved safe
f ← lockstep
while true do
    𝓣^f = compose(f, T_1, ..., T_k)
    A_𝓟^{𝓣^f} = abstract(𝓣^f, 𝓟)
    (res, inv, cex) = isBadReachable(A_𝓟^{𝓣^f}, pre, post)
                                                    ▷ where bad is negated post
    if (res = safe) then
        return (f, inv)
    else
        𝓕_block ← 𝓕_block ∪ {f}                     ▷ block f to get rid of cex
        if (not all compositions are blocked) then
            f ← pickUnblockedComposition(𝓕_block)
                                                    ▷ try a different, unblocked, composition
        else
            if (isSpurious(cex) is false) then
                return (unsafe, cex)
            else                                    ▷ cex is spurious
                𝓟' ← synthesizePredicates(cex)
                                                    ▷ new predicates that eliminate cex
                𝓟 = 𝓟 ∪ 𝓟'                          ▷ strengthen the language of proofs
                𝓕_block ← ∅                         ▷ unblock the blocked compositions
                f ← lockstep                        ▷ restart, with lockstep composition
```

function. We start by taking a concrete initial state c_0, a model of A_0, and then applying the transitions of the trace on c_0 step by step. After taking the ith step, it is checked that the concrete target state arrived at, let us call it c_i, is actually a model of the corresponding abstract state A_i. If this indeed holds all the way up to A_{bad}, then we have an actual counterexample trace. Otherwise, there must be a transition $\langle A_i, \mathcal{T}^f, A_{i+1}\rangle$ in the abstract trace that could not be taken by the concrete state c_i (i.e., $c_{i+1} \wedge A_{i+1}$ was unsat), where c_{i+1} is the concrete state reached after taking $\mathcal{T}^f$ from c_i, and $\mathcal{T}^f$ is the composed transition relation as per the current composition function f.

Intuitively, this means that it is not possible to go from a part of A_i (that part exists, because we know that c_i belongs to it) to A_{i+1} along the composed transition relation. Therefore, in order to refine this spuriousness, it is necessary to add a predicate that identifies the part. The goal of the *synthesizePredicates* procedure is to find such a predicate.

5.2 Synthesizing Predicates from Counterexamples

We illustrate how a spurious transition of the form $\langle A_{src}, \mathcal{T}^f, A_{tgt}\rangle$, where $\mathcal{T}^f$ is the composed transition relation and A_{src} and A_{tgt} are the source and target states, is blocked by doing a counterexample-guided abstraction refinement. The problem of blocking a spurious transition is essentially a problem of logical abduction [15], which works towards finding an explanatory hypothesis for a desired outcome. The desired outcome here is that A_{tgt} should not be reachable along $\mathcal{T}^f$ from A_{src}, but currently it is. In other words,

$$A_{src}(V) \wedge \mathcal{T}^f(V, V') \not\Rightarrow \neg A_{tgt}(V')$$

Therefore, we need to find a hypothesis, $p(X)$, possibly over a subset of variables, i.e. $X \subseteq V$, such that

$$p(X \subseteq V) \wedge A_{src}(V) \wedge \mathcal{T}^f(V, V') \Rightarrow \neg A_{tgt}(V')$$

But, at the same time, it is important to discard *trivial* solutions – one that uses the consequent itself as p, and another that makes the antecedent *false*. Therefore, the abducer looks for a minimal (logically weakest) solution under the condition that

$$p(X \subseteq V) \wedge A_{src}(V) \wedge \mathcal{T}^f(V, V') \not\Rightarrow \bot$$

We use the following two ways to solve for p.

Using a SyGuS Solver. We encode these constraints directly into the SyGuS input language [32], and use CVC4 [6] (version 1.8) to obtain a solution. SyGuS allows an enumerative search strategy that leads to smaller predicates.

Quantifier Elimination Using Z3. A solution to the abductive inference problem is given by

$$\forall\ ((V \cup V') \setminus X).\ A_{src}(V) \wedge \mathcal{T}^f(V, V') \Rightarrow \neg A_{tgt}(V')$$

or, equivalently, by the negation of

$$\exists\ ((V \cup V') \setminus X).\ A_{src}(V) \wedge \mathcal{T}^f(V, V') \wedge A_{tgt}(V')$$

We obtain a solution by quantifier elimination using Z3 [13]. Since we are looking at the problem of predicate refinement, it is not necessary to negate the solution (negating a predicate does not affect the expressiveness of our proof language in any way).

Given an input program and a safety property specified as $(pre, post)$, and an initial proof language – defined by predicates that are needed to specify *pre* and *post* and their boolean combinations – Algorithm 2 either terminates with a proof, or a counterexample, or goes on enriching the language of proofs, in each iteration making it provably more expressive than the earlier one. The algorithm is not guaranteed to terminate, since the problem of finding the composition-invariant pair is undecidable in general [37]. It can, in principle, terminate for finite state systems, although with exponential complexity, since the set of possible composition-invariant pairs is itself finite for finite state systems. Note the number of predicates is also finite in a finite-state systems.

Theorem 1. *The proposed refinement ensures progress, i.e., the predicate added in every step, which is the solution of the abduction query, gets rid of the spurious counterexample, and strictly strengthens the proof language.*

Proof. It is easy to see that the refinement indeed removes the spurious counterexample, because the queries given to SyGuS solver and to Z3 exactly encode this constraint that the target should not be reachable from the source. We also know that a solution certainly exists, because the concrete state corresponding to the A_{src} is itself a non-trivial solution.

To argue that the newly added predicate p_n (say) strictly enriches the proof language given by $\mathcal{P} = \{p_1, \ldots, p_{n-1}\}$, let us assume, on the contrary, that it does not. In that case, p_n can be written as a boolean combination of the predicates in $\mathcal{P}$. Since A_{src} is also a boolean combination of predicates in $\mathcal{P}$, they (A_{src} and p_n) must either agree on all predicates in $\mathcal{P}$ or disagree on at least one of them. The latter is not possible since this disagreement would mean that abduction problem was solved trivially by falsifying the antecedent, however we know that it is not true because trivial solutions are avoided. On the other hand, if they agree on all the predicates $\{p_1, \ldots, p_{n-1}\}$ then $A_{src} \wedge p_n$ is simply A_{src} and the spuriousness could not have been removed. Hence, a contradiction.

The soundness of our algorithm follows directly from the soundness of PDSC.

5.3 Obtaining Predicates from Infeasibility Proofs

As described in Sect. 5.1, an abstract counterexample trace is a sequence of transitions that begin at the initial abstract state and end at a bad state. Note that the transitions in such a trace are labelled by program statements from the two (or more) program copies/components. To check whether an abstract trace is feasible, we can collect the program statements from the transitions of the entire trace, and give it to a solver to check for satisfiability. This gives us an alternate, more general way to check if the abstract counterexample was spurious, independent of any concrete initial state.

If the solver returns *sat*, we get an actual counterexample trace as a model, which demonstrates that the desired property fails to hold. However, if the solver returns *unsat*, then the sequence interpolants [26] obtained from the infeasibility proof (of the concrete trace) may be used as additional predicates to strengthen the proof language. Although at this point it would be sound to add all the interpolants as predicates to strengthen the proof language, it must be noted that the search of a proof gets more and more difficult as the proof language gets richer (because the number of abstract states is exponential in the number of predicates, and PDSC searches through the states to find a composition-invariant pair). Therefore, there is a downside to making the proof language needlessly expressive – the search of a composition-invariant pair will become considerably harder in every iteration. A practical solution, naturally, is to add only a few interpolants or even sub-expressions from what the prover gives us. In particular, our implementation:

- is parametrized to add at most p predicates each time (in our experiments, we use $p = 2$)
- prioritizes expressions that relate variables that have not been related so far in the existing set of predicates
- prioritizes adding shorter and logically stronger expressions.

Note that this approach is still sound, though we cannot guarantee now that the newly added predicates necessarily remove the spurious counterexample. Adding all the interpolants obtained from the infeasibility proof would certainly eliminate the counterexample, but it will make the algorithm quite inefficient. Our experiments support that the compromise of adding only a few interpolants, or sub-expressions derived from them, is indeed very useful in practice.

6 Implementation and Experiments

6.1 Implementation

We have implemented our approach in a tool[1], PDSCSYNTH, which is built on the PDSC tool[2]. Like PDSC, our input is a transition system encoded by Constrained Horn Clauses (CHC) in SMT2 format, a correctness (k-safety) property, and a set of predicates that specify the *pre* and *post* conditions. While PDSC expects an additional set of predicates (that may be mined automatically from the program syntax, or supplied manually), PDSCSYNTH gets them automatically, lazily on demand, by doing:

1. Syntax-Guided Synthesis, using CVC4 [6], version 1.8
2. Quantifier Elimination, using Z3 [13], version 4.8.9, *and*
3. Craig Interpolation, using MathSAT5 [11], version 5.6.6.

In CVC4, we use restrict ourselves to Linear Integer Arithmetic (which is what our benchmarks are also restricted to), and use the default grammar that CVC provides for LIA. The variables and the constants for the grammar come from the program. Quantifier elimination is performed using the recursive QSAT technique [8], available in Z3 tool.

6.2 Benchmarks

An interesting use-case of 2-safety verification is automated evaluation of programming assignments which may be done by checking equivalence between a submitted program and a reference solution. With this in mind, we have used 9 programming assignments samples in our experiments, derived from [24]. In addition, our benchmarks consists of 7 examples derived from [37], and 3 crafted examples. Each benchmark consists of two component programs (that may be copies, or syntactically/semantically different programs), and the correctness

---

[1] Artifacts available at: https://github.com/Akshatha-Shenoy/PdscSynth.

[2] https://bitbucket.org/sharonsh/pdsc/src/master/.

property is stated as a set of pre- and post-conditions. Intuitively, we check the equivalence property for all the benchmarks, except in case of `squareSum` where the components compute the sum of squares of integers in a given interval, and the property is that a bigger interval leads to a bigger sum.

We call a benchmark *safe* if the composed programs in the benchmark satisfy the given correctness property, and *unsafe* otherwise. Since the sample programming assignment solutions include correct as well as incorrect solutions, we have 6 unsafe benchmarks and 3 safe ones. The benchmarks derived from the PDSC paper are all safe, and we got them by deleting *all* the manually supplied predicates (excluding those predicates that are necessary to specify the pre- and post-condition). For the `doubleSquare` benchmark, we also created instances of varying difficulty by retaining some of the manually supplied predicates. The crafted benchmarks were obtained from two different programs: one that sums all numbers from 1 to n (a safe and an unsafe version), and another one that increments two equal numbers by different values and then decrements them by the same value to get equal numbers in the end again (safe version).

6.3 Results

We ran PDSCSYNTH on all the 19 benchmarks described above. Table 1 shows the results of our experiments. The columns SyGuS, QE, and Interpolation contain, except in case of timeouts, two comma-separated entries – the number of predicates synthesized on the left, and the time taken to produce a proof (or a counterexample) on the right. The letters 'm' and 's' denote minutes and seconds, respectively. The experiments were run on an Intel i5 machine running at 1.70 GHz, with 16 GB of RAM. The 'timeout' indicates that the technique could not decide the benchmark within 10 min.

It is noteworthy that interpolation was able to produce the desired predicates in *every* case. The time taken and the predicates added by the interpolation technique confirm that the technique was effective (in its selection of predicates to add, so that the proof language becomes richer but not needlessly expressive). In several unsafe benchmarks (`fig4_1`, `fig4_2`, `subsume_1`, `subsume_2` and `puzzle_1`), interpolation needed fewer predicates in comparison to QE and SyGuS. This is because with SyGuS and QE, we check the spuriousness of one concretization of the abstract trace at a time, unlike in case of interpolation where all possible concretizations are checked at once. Thus, interpolation adds a predicate only when none of the concretizations of an abstract trace is feasible. Whereas, QE and SyGuS may add a predicate needlessly even though the current abstract trace has a feasible concretization (which hasn't been looked at yet).

The quantifier elimination with Z3 was also able to get the necessary and sufficient predicates in a larger number of cases (in particular, where SyGuS could not scale). For the examples where SyGuS also worked, it almost always got smaller predicates than QE, though not necessarily fewer in numbers (for `sum_pc`, SyGuS had to synthesize four more predicates as compared to quantifier elimination, whereas for `inc_dec` SyGuS managed with two predicates lesser). The quantifier elimination with Z3 performed quite well in comparison to interpolation as well, solving all the benchmarks except `halfSquare` and most of `doubleSquare` variants. However, the proofs generated with QE were often quite big, as the technique obtained predicates that were much bigger in size compared to SyGuS and Interpolation.

Table 1. No. of predicates synthesized, and the time taken by SyGuS (Syntax-Guided Synthesis, using CVC4-1.8), QE (Quantifier Elimination, using Z3 4.8.9), and Interpolation (using MathSAT5 5.6.6), and a comparison with LLRÊVE on our benchmarks

S. No.	Benchmark	Source	Safe/Unsafe	SyGuS(#pred, time)	QE (#preds, time)	Interpolation (#preds, time)	LLRÊVE
1.	sum_to_n	crafted	safe	timeout	8, 1 m 32 s	3, 17.36 s	0.056 s
2.	sum_to_n_err	crafted	unsafe	0, 0.34 s	0, 0.77 s	0, 1.43 s	0.069 s
3.	inc_dec	crafted	safe	2, 9.15 s	4, 20.95 s	3, 13.95 s	unknown
4.	squareSum	cav19	safe	0, 0.66 s	0, 1.14 s	0, 1.67 s	–
5.	sum_pc	cav19	safe	5, 1 m 32 s	1, 13.58 s	4, 1m28s	unknown
6.	fig4_1	icse16	unsafe	1, 3.65 s	2, 7.16 s	0, 2.26 s	0.038 s
7.	fig4_2	icse16	unsafe	1, 3.86 s	2, 7.24 s	0, 2.27 s	0.067 s
8.	fig4_ref_ref	icse16	safe	0, 0.11 s	0, 0.58 s	0, 0.96 s	0.044 s
9.	subsume_1	icse16	unsafe	timeout	3, 7.88 s	0, 2.20 s	0.041 s
10.	subsume_2	icse16	unsafe	timeout	2, 5.22 s	0, 2.24 s	0.061 s
11.	subsume_ref_ref	icse16	safe	timeout	1, 3.9 s	8, 24.48 s	0.051 s
12.	puzzle_1	derived from icse16	unsafe	timeout	4, 26.8 s	2, 9.04 s	0.040 s
13.	puzzle_2	derived from icse16	unsafe	timeout	8, 2 m 31 s	8, 4 m 7 s	0.029 s
14.	puzzle_ref_ref	derived from icse16	safe	timeout	2, 10.33 s	1, 5.73 s	0.061 s
15.	halfSquare	cav19	safe	timeout	timeout	3, 6 m 9 s	unknown
16.	doubleSquare_1	derived from cav19	safe	timeout	timeout	11, 3 m 42 s	timeout
17.	doubleSquare_2	derived from cav19	safe	timeout	timeout	10, 3 m 14 s	timeout
18.	doubleSquare_3	derived from cav19	safe	timeout	timeout	7, 1 m 50 s	timeout
19.	doubleSquare_4	derived from cav19	safe	4, 1 m 19 s	9, 3 m 26 s	1, 17.12 s	timeout

6.4 Performance on Our Motivating Example

Let us recall our motivating example once again. As described in Sect. 3.5, PDSC was able to construct a proof with the help of four user-supplied predicates: z_1==2*z_2, y_1==2*y_2, z_1==2*z_2-1, and y_1==2*y_2+x_2. We created four variants of this benchmark: `doubleSquare_1` (where none of these four were supplied), `doubleSquare_2` (where only z_1==2*z_2 was supplied), `doubleSquare_3` (where z_1==2*z_2 and y_1==2*y_2 were supplied), and `doubleSquare_4` (where y_1==2*y_2 was removed, the other three were supplied). As shown in the results table, PDSC-SYNTH was able to solve all the four benchmarks using Interpolation, whereas none of the other techniques could work even for the simpler variants (except `doubleSquare_4` which could be solved but needed more predicates and a lot more time with SyGuS and QE).

6.5 Comparison with LLRÊVE

We also compared PDSCSYNTH with LLRÊVE[3], an automated regression verification tool, as it can automatically check programs for equivalence [21]. Table 1

[3] https://formal.kastel.kit.edu/projects/improve/reve/.

shows the results of this comparison; we used both Z3 v4.8.9 and Eldarica v2.0.8 as the backend solver, and have reported the better of the two results. While LLRÊVE could solve all the unsafe benchmarks fairly quickly, the only safe benchmarks that it could solve were the ones for which the components were exactly the same. There were four such benchmarks in our experiments: `sum_to_n`, and the `*_ref_ref` benchmarks where reference implementations for programming assignments were compared to themselves. For all other safe benchmarks, LLRÊVE could not decide that they were indeed safe, even though we let it run beyond the timeout for about 30 min. Also, note that we could not run LLRÊVE on the `squareSum` benchmark because the safety property there is not an equivalence check.

6.6 Reducing Predicate Size for Quantifier Elimination

In order to discover smaller predicates as solutions, we implemented a strategy for Z3 to eliminate as many variables as possible, and return a solution in the smallest set of variables possible, under the broad assumption that predicates in fewer variables would also be smaller. This is not always true; in fact, we realized that it is better to eliminate all but two variables to begin with, and come to eliminating all but one variable only in the end. In general, while this strategy helps in reducing the size of predicates, such strategies can impact the performance adversely. Striking a good balance between scalability and usefulness of the predicates, therefore, is crucial, and makes for an important direction of future work.

7 Related Work

The novelty of our work lies in giving a completely automatic approach for doing property directed self composition [37] to address the problem of k-safety verification. While the user-dependence has been described here as a problem only for PDSC, related techniques like [9] are also dependent on predicates that may be used to align the component programs. In particular, [9] uses an alignment predicate to construct a program alignment automaton that semantically aligns the programs between which equivalence is to be checked, quite like how PDSC composes the component programs. The predicates play an important role in these techniques, and therefore it is crucial to have techniques that can generate useful predicates completely automatically.

Since self-composition poses the same challenges for proving equivalence of programs as it does for 2-safety verification, an automated property directed self composition technique can be helpful in a number of applications of program equivalence. This includes evaluation of programming assignment w.r.t. a given correct implementation [3], semantic alignment [9], translation validation [23,38], design and verification of compiler optimizations [28,39], and program synthesis and superoptimization [5,36], among several others. We reiterate that it is the combined strength of PDSC and the automation that makes this approach usable and effective in practice.

Our method relies on different techniques for synthesizing predicates: SyGuS [2], Abductive inference [14], and Interpolation [25]. These techniques are certainly related in the way they can address a common problem, which in our case is the strengthening of the proof language. They have also been used together, sometimes in conjunction with other techniques, to address related problems like inferring inductive invariants [17,20] and maximal specifications [1,34]. The commonality of the techniques, which makes them suitable for these problems, is their ability to generalize (from examples or counterexamples). Whereas, they differ in how they perform the generalization, and thus have different strengths as confirmed by our experiments.

8 Conclusion and Future Work

This paper proposes an algorithm that builds on top of a property directed self composition technique for hypersafety verification, and overcomes some of its important caveats. PDSC expects users to supply a *proof language* in which it searches for an easy-to-prove composition. Our algorithm gets rid of the user-dependence that PDSC has, and makes it capable to do refutations as well. We have implemented, and experimented with three different techniques relying on SyGuS, Quantifier Elimination, and Interpolation, that can construct and enrich the proof language as and when required for a given program and a property. Our experiments demonstrate that the proposed techniques are effective as well as efficient.

Looking ahead, we see several interesting directions of future work. For one, since the space of compositions is navigated repeatedly, it may be useful to identify good and bad regions of the composition space each time, and use it in subsequent iterations to scale better. However, this is challenging as the composition space changes every time the proof language is strengthened. For certain applications, e.g. while proving equivalence of programs, it may be desirable to obtain proofs that are shorter and thus easier to understand. Therefore, the task of finding smaller, and few but useful predicates is an important one, and makes for an interesting future work. It would also be worthwhile to enhance our technique to handle programs with arrays and other data-structures so that we can look at a wider set of benchmarks.

References

1. Albarghouthi, A., Dillig, I., Gurfinkel, A.: Maximal specification synthesis. In Proceedings of the 43rd Annual ACM SIGPLAN-SIGACT Symposium on Principles of Programming Languages, POPL 2016, pp. 789–801. Association for Computing Machinery, New York, NY, USA (2016)
2. Alur, R., et al.: Syntax-guided synthesis. In: Formal Methods in Computer-Aided Design, FMCAD 2013, Portland, OR, USA, 20–23 October 2013, pp. 1–8 (2013)

3. Anil, J.K., Prabhu, S., Madhukar, K., Venkatesh, R.: Using hypersafety verification for proving correctness of programming assignments. In: Rothermel, G., Bae, D., (eds.) ICSE-NIER 2020: 42nd International Conference on Software Engineering, New Ideas and Emerging Results, Seoul, South Korea, 27 June - 19 July, 2020, pp. 81–84. ACM (2020)
4. Bansal, S., Aiken, A.: Automatic generation of peephole superoptimizers. In: Proceedings of the 12th International Conference on Architectural Support for Programming Languages and Operating Systems, ASPLOS XII, pp. 394–403. Association for Computing Machinery, New York, NY, USA (2006)
5. Bansal, S., Aiken, A.: Automatic generation of peephole superoptimizers. SIGARCH Comput. Archit. News **34**(5), 394–403 (2006)
6. Barrett, C., et al.: CVC4. In: Gopalakrishnan, G., Qadeer, S. (eds.) CAV 2011. LNCS, vol. 6806, pp. 171–177. Springer, Heidelberg (2011). https://doi.org/10.1007/978-3-642-22110-1_14
7. Barthe, G., D'argenio, P.R., Rezk, T.: Secure information flow by self-composition. In: Proceedings of the 17th IEEE Workshop on Computer Security Foundations, CSFW 2004, p. 100. IEEE Computer Society, USA (2004)
8. Bjørner, N., Janota, M.: Playing with quantified satisfaction. LPAR (Short Papers) **35**, 15–27 (2015)
9. Churchill, B., Padon, O., Sharma, R., Aiken, A.: Semantic program alignment for equivalence checking. In: Proceedings of the 40th ACM SIGPLAN Conference on Programming Language Design and Implementation, PLDI 2019, pp. 1027–1040. Association for Computing Machinery, New York, NY, USA (2019)
10. Churchill, B., Sharma, R., Bastien, J.F., Aiken, A.: Sound loop superoptimization for google native client. In: Proceedings of the Twenty-Second International Conference on Architectural Support for Programming Languages and Operating Systems, ASPLOS 2017, pp. 313–326. Association for Computing Machinery, New York, NY, USA (2017)
11. Cimatti, A., Griggio, A., Schaafsma, B.J., Sebastiani, R.: The MathSAT5 SMT solver. In: Piterman, N., Smolka, S.A. (eds.) TACAS 2013. LNCS, vol. 7795, pp. 93–107. Springer, Heidelberg (2013). https://doi.org/10.1007/978-3-642-36742-7_7
12. Craig, W.: Linear reasoning. A new form of the Herbrand-Gentzen theorem. J. Symbolic Logic **22**(3), 250–268 (1957)
13. de Moura, L., Bjørner, N.: Z3: an efficient SMT solver. In: Ramakrishnan, C.R., Rehof, J. (eds.) TACAS 2008. LNCS, vol. 4963, pp. 337–340. Springer, Heidelberg (2008). https://doi.org/10.1007/978-3-540-78800-3_24
14. Dillig, I.: Abductive inference and its applications in program analysis, verification, and synthesis. In: Kaivola, R., Wahl, T., (eds.) Formal Methods in Computer-Aided Design, FMCAD 2015, Austin, Texas, USA, 27–30 September 2015, p. 4. IEEE (2015)
15. Dillig, I., Dillig, T., Aiken, A.: Automated error diagnosis using abductive inference. In: Proceedings of the 33rd ACM SIGPLAN Conference on Programming Language Design and Implementation, PLDI 2012, pp. 181–192. Association for Computing Machinery, New York, NY, USA (2012)
16. Farzan, A., Vandikas, A.: Automated hypersafety verification. In: Dillig, I., Tasiran, S. (eds.) CAV 2019. LNCS, vol. 11561, pp. 200–218. Springer, Cham (2019). https://doi.org/10.1007/978-3-030-25540-4_11
17. Fedyukovich, G., Bodík, R.: Accelerating syntax-guided invariant synthesis. In: Beyer, D., Huisman, M. (eds.) TACAS 2018. LNCS, vol. 10805, pp. 251–269. Springer, Cham (2018). https://doi.org/10.1007/978-3-319-89960-2_14

18. Fedyukovich, G., Kaufman, S.J., Bodík, R.: Sampling invariants from frequency distributions. In: 2017 Formal Methods in Computer Aided Design, FMCAD 2017, Vienna, Austria, 2–6 October 2017, pp. 100–107 (2017)
19. Fedyukovich, G., Prabhu, S., Madhukar, K., Gupta, A.: Solving constrained horn clauses using syntax and data. In: 2018 Formal Methods in Computer Aided Design, FMCAD 2018, Austin, TX, USA, October 30 - November 2, 2018, pp. 1–9 (2018)
20. Fedyukovich, G., Prabhu, S., Madhukar, K., Gupta, A.: Quantified invariants via syntax-guided synthesis. In: Dillig, I., Tasiran, S. (eds.) CAV 2019. LNCS, vol. 11561, pp. 259–277. Springer, Cham (2019). https://doi.org/10.1007/978-3-030-25540-4_14
21. Felsing, D., Grebing, S., Klebanov, V., Rümmer, P., Ulbrich, M.: Automating regression verification. In: *29th IEEE/ACM International Conference on Automated Software Engineering (ASE 2014)*, ASE 2014, pp. 349–360. ACM (2014)
22. Goldberg, B., Zuck, L., Barrett, C.: Into the loops: practical issues in translation validation for optimizing compilers. Electron. Notes Theor. Comput. Sci. **132**(1), 53–71 (2005). Proceedings of the 3rd International Workshop on Compiler Optimization Meets Compiler Verification (COCV 2004)
23. Kundu, S., Tatlock, Z., Lerner, S.: Proving optimizations correct using parameterized program equivalence. SIGPLAN Not. **44**(6), 327–337 (2009)
24. Li, S., Xiao, X., Bassett, B., Xie, T., Tillmann, N.: Measuring code behavioral similarity for programming and software engineering education. In: Proceedings of the 38th International Conference on Software Engineering Companion, ICSE 2016, pp. 501–510. ACM, New York, NY, USA (2016)
25. McMillan, K.L.: Interpolation and SAT-based model checking. In: Hunt, W.A., Somenzi, F. (eds.) CAV 2003. LNCS, vol. 2725, pp. 1–13. Springer, Heidelberg (2003). https://doi.org/10.1007/978-3-540-45069-6_1
26. McMillan, K.L.: Lazy abstraction with interpolants. In: Ball, T., Jones, R.B. (eds.) CAV 2006. LNCS, vol. 4144, pp. 123–136. Springer, Heidelberg (2006). https://doi.org/10.1007/11817963_14
27. Necula, G.C.: Translation validation for an optimizing compiler. In: Proceedings of the ACM SIGPLAN 2000 Conference on Programming Language Design and Implementation, PLDI 2000, pp. 83–94. Association for Computing Machinery, New York, NY, USA (2000)
28. Necula, G.C.: Translation validation for an optimizing compiler. SIGPLAN Not. **35**(5), 83–94 (2000)
29. Pnueli, A., Siegel, M., Singerman, E.: Translation validation. In: Steffen, B. (ed.) TACAS 1998. LNCS, vol. 1384, pp. 151–166. Springer, Heidelberg (1998). https://doi.org/10.1007/BFb0054170
30. Prabhu, S., Madhukar, K., Venkatesh, R.: Efficiently learning safety proofs from appearance as well as behaviours. In: Podelski, A. (ed.) SAS 2018. LNCS, vol. 11002, pp. 326–343. Springer, Cham (2018). https://doi.org/10.1007/978-3-319-99725-4_20
31. Pudlák, P.: Lower bounds for resolution and cutting plane proofs and monotone computations. J. Symb. Log. **62**(3), 981–998 (1997)
32. Raghothaman, M., Udupa, A.: Language to specify syntax-guided synthesis problems. CoRR, abs/1405.5590 (2014)
33. Ramos, D.A., Engler, D.R.: Practical, low-effort equivalence verification of real code. In: Gopalakrishnan, G., Qadeer, S. (eds.) CAV 2011. LNCS, vol. 6806, pp. 669–685. Springer, Heidelberg (2011). https://doi.org/10.1007/978-3-642-22110-1_55

34. Prabhu, S., Fedyukovich, G., Madhukar, K.,D'Souza, D.: Specification synthesis with constrained horn clauses. In: Freund, S.N., Yahav, E., (eds.) PLDI 2021: 42nd ACM SIGPLAN International Conference on Programming Language Design and Implementation, Virtual Event, Canada, 20–25 June 2021, pp. 1203–1217. ACM (2021)
35. Schkufza, E., Sharma, R., Aiken, A.: Stochastic superoptimization. In: Proceedings of the Eighteenth International Conference on Architectural Support for Programming Languages and Operating Systems, ASPLOS 2013, pp. 305–316. Association for Computing Machinery, New York, NY, USA (2013)
36. Schkufza, E., Sharma, R., Aiken, A.: Stochastic superoptimization. SIGARCH Comput. Archit. News **41**(1), 305–316 (2013)
37. Shemer, R., Gurfinkel, A., Shoham, S., Vizel, Y.: Property directed self composition. In: Dillig, I., Tasiran, S. (eds.) CAV 2019. LNCS, vol. 11561, pp. 161–179. Springer, Cham (2019). https://doi.org/10.1007/978-3-030-25540-4_9
38. Tate, R., Stepp, M., Tatlock, Z., Lerner, S.: Equality saturation: a new approach to optimization. In: POPL 2009: Proceedings of the 36th annual ACM SIGPLAN-SIGACT Symposium on Principles of Programming Languages, pp. 264–276. ACM, New York, NY, USA (2009)
39. Tristan, J.-B., Govereau, P., Morrisett, G.: Evaluating value-graph translation validation for LLVM. SIGPLAN Not. **46**(6), 295–305 (2011)

Minimally Comparing Relational Abstract Domains

Kenny Ballou(✉) and Elena Sherman

Boise State University, Boise, USA
kennyballou@u.boisestate.edu, elenasherman@boisestate.edu

Abstract. Value-based static analysis techniques express computed program invariants as logical formula over program variables. Researchers and practitioners use these invariants to aid in software engineering and verification tasks. When selecting abstract domains, practitioners weigh the cost of a domain against its expressiveness. However, an abstract domain's expressiveness tends to be stated in absolute terms; either mathematically via the sub-polyhedra the domain is capable of describing, empirically using a set of known properties to verify, or empirically via logical entailment using the entire invariant of the domain at each program point. Due to *carry-over* effects, however, the last technique can be problematic because it tends to provide simplistic and imprecise comparisons.

We address these limitations of comparing, in general, abstract domains via logical entailment in this work. We provide a fixed-point algorithm for including the minimally necessary variables from each domain into the compared formula. Furthermore, we empirically evaluate our algorithm, comparing different techniques of widening over the Zones domain and comparing Zones to an incomparable Relational Predicates domain. Our empirical evaluation of our technique shows an improved granularity of comparison. It lowered the number of more precise invariants when comparing analysis techniques, thus, limiting the prevalent *carry-over* effects. Moreover, it removed undecidable invariants and lowered the number of incomparable invariants when comparing two incomparable relational abstract domain.

Keywords: Static Analysis · Abstract Domain Comparison · Data-Flow Analysis · Abstract Interpretation

1 Introduction

Various value-based static analysis techniques express computed program invariants as a logical formula over program variables. For example, abstract interpretation [7] uses abstract domains such as Zones [16] and Octagons [18] to describe an invariant as a set of linear integer inequalities in a restricted format. Other techniques such as symbolic execution [12] and predicate analysis combined with a symbolic component [21] do the same, only using a general

É. André and J. Sun (Eds.): ATVA 2023, LNCS 14216, pp. 159–175, 2023.
https://doi.org/10.1007/978-3-031-45332-8_8

linear integer arithmetic format. These invariants are then used for program verification [4,24], program optimization [1,11], and for software development tasks.

Static analysis developers rarely use a computed invariant by itself, but rather compare them to determine effects of new algorithms or abstract domain choices on the invariant precision. For example, to evaluate tuning analyzer parameters, static analysis researchers compare invariant values $\mathcal{I}$ and $\widetilde{\mathcal{I}}$ from the original and tuned analyzer runs, respectively. If an invariant becomes more precise, we conclude that the new technique or a different domain choice results in a more precise analysis. For relational domains, one can use queries to an SMT solver, such as Z3 [19], to determine which invariant is more precise by checking their implication relations.

However, to objectively measure such effects in a computed invariant after statement s, $\mathcal{I}_s$, we need to compare only the part of $\mathcal{I}_s$ affected by the transfer function of s, τ_s. This way, if $\widetilde{\mathcal{I}}$ has already been more precise than $\mathcal{I}$ before s and τ_s has not changed the relevant facts, then the comparison should disregard the *carry-over* precision improvement in $\widetilde{\mathcal{I}}_s$.

The comparison of two relational invariants $\mathcal{I}$ and $\widetilde{\mathcal{I}}$ involves two steps: (1) identifying a changed component of each invariant at a given statement and (2) performing minimal comparison between the changed components of $\mathcal{I}$ and $\widetilde{\mathcal{I}}$. In our previous work [3] we addressed step (1) for the Zones domain where using data-flow analysis (DFA) information, we developed efficient algorithms that find a minimally changed set of inequalities in a Zone invariant.

In this work we target step (2), assuming that an abstract domain has some means to perform step (1) using either elementary or sophisticated algorithms. Thus, the contributions of this paper include: **(a)** development and analysis of a minimal comparison algorithm for relational abstract domains and **(b)** investigating its effect on comparisons between different widening techniques for Zones domain as well as comparison between Zones and incomparable Predicate domains with a relational component.

The rest of the paper is organized as follows. In Sect. 2, we provide the background, context, and motivation for our work. In Sect. 3, we describe our fixed-point algorithm. In Sect. 4, we explain our experimental setup and evaluation, and in Sect. 5, we examine the results of our experiments. We connect this work with previous research in Sect. 6. Finally, we conclude and discuss future work in Sect. 7.

2 Background and Motivation

We refer to an invariant and the corresponding abstract domain as relational if it is expressed as a conjunction of formulas over program variables, e.g., a set of linear integer inequalities. We first explain the concept of the minimal/dependent change for an invariant and then explain challenges of comparing two relational domains, and sketch how our proposed approach works.

2.1 Minimal Changes in Relational Abstract Domains

Consider the relational invariants computed by a data-flow analysis framework using the Zones abstract domain as shown in Fig. 1a. Let us assume the analyzed code has four program variables: w, x, y, and z. Here, the incoming flow to the conditional statement has the following invariant: $\mathcal{I}_{in} = z \leq x \wedge w \rightarrow \top \wedge y \rightarrow \top$. That is, variables w and y are unbounded while x and z are bounded by a $\leq$ relation. The transfer function of the true branch adds the $y \leq x$ inequality, thus, making y bounded. This results in the $\mathcal{I}_t = z \leq x \wedge y \leq x \wedge w \rightarrow \top$ invariant. Similarly, the invariant for the false branch becomes $\mathcal{I}_f = z \leq x \wedge x \leq y - 1 \wedge w \rightarrow \top$.

Even though $\mathcal{I}_f$ and $\mathcal{I}_t$ are new invariants, they inherit two unchanged inequalities $z \leq x$ and $w \rightarrow \top$ from $\mathcal{I}_{in}$. This suggests that some part of a previously computed invariants have not changed by the transfer function of the conditional statement. Thus, if for some program, $\mathcal{I}_{in}$ is more precise because of $z \leq x$ and remains more precise in $\mathcal{I}_t$ because of the same inequality, such *carry-over* precision results should be disregarded.

Previous work determining minimal changes in a relational abstract domain approach [3] addresses this problem by identifying the dependent portion of the invariant affected by the statement's transfer function. For example, the minimal change algorithm for Zones [3] can compute the minimal sub-formula given the potentially changed variables x and y. Specifically, the algorithm identifies only the $y \leq x$ part of $\mathcal{I}_t$ having changed from $\mathcal{I}_{in}$. Likewise for $\mathcal{I}_f$, the algorithm identifies two inequalities: $z \leq x$ and $x \leq y - 1$ as the changed portion of the invariant[1].

The minimal change algorithm can be sophisticated and accurately compute the changed part of the invariants, or can be over-approximating, and in the worst case return the entire invariant. In our previous work we developed an efficient collection of such algorithms for the Zones abstract domain. In this work, we assume that a relational domain has an invariant change method Δ implemented, which takes as input an invariant and a set of updated variables and returns a portion of $\mathcal{I}$, e.g., in this example $\Delta(\mathcal{I}_t, \{x, y\}) = y \leq x$. The shaded regions of the invariants in the Figs. 1a and 1b indicate the changed parts of the out state for each branch.

2.2 Comparing Relational Domains

Now consider invariants in Fig. 1b computed for the same code fragment, but using an improved algorithm. This algorithm is able to compute additional information for $\widetilde{\mathcal{I}}_{in} = z \leq x \wedge w \leq y$, which is more precise than $\mathcal{I}_{in}$ since $\widetilde{\mathcal{I}}_{in}$ constrains the values of w and y. The checkmark symbol, ✓, by $\widetilde{\mathcal{I}}$ in Fig. 1b indicates an increased precision comparing to the corresponding invariants $\mathcal{I}$ in Fig. 1a.

[1] $z \leq x$ is included due to transitive effects through x.

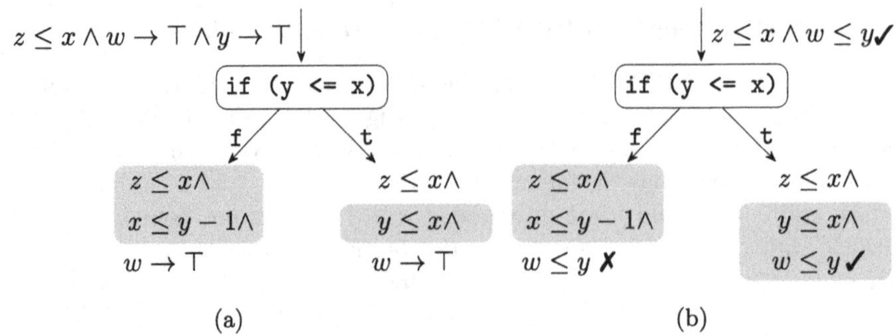

Fig. 1. Original Static Analysis (a) and Improved Static Analysis (b)

When we compare using the entirety of the invariants instead of simply the changed portion of the invariants for the false branch, the result would be that $\widetilde{\mathcal{I}_t}$ is more precise than $\mathcal{I}_t$. Thus, simply applying Δ for both invariants can filter out erroneous, *carry-over* improvements, which we annotate with the ✗ symbol.

In the case of the false branch, the set of variables in their respective changed portions of the invariants are the same. However, this is not always the case, which we can see on the true branch. There, $\Delta(\mathcal{I}_t, \{x, y\}) = y \leq x$, but $\Delta(\widetilde{\mathcal{I}_t}, \{x, y\}) = y \leq x \wedge w \leq y$ has an extra variable w. To make a sound comparison, we need to conjoin $w \rightarrow \top$ with the result of $\Delta(\mathcal{I}_t, \{x, y\})$. The challenge here is to identify the smallest necessary additions to the changed portions of the invariants to perform a sound comparison.

In the next section we present our proposed approach that addressees this problem by developing a fixed-point algorithm that, in each iteration, discovers a minimal set of inequalities (modulo Δ) in one invariant that is adequate for comparison with the changed part of the other invariant.

3 Approach

In this section, we explain the theoretical basis for our approach to minimally compare relational invariants via logical entailment. We start by defining the problem, and then we present our algorithm that solves it. At the end, we perform an analysis of the proposed algorithm.

3.1 Problem Definition

We define the problem in a context of a DFA framework, where the framework provides a set of updated variables, dv, that resulted in a new invariant $\mathcal{I}$. An abstract domain for $\mathcal{I}$ has a function Δ implemented, which returns a portion of $\mathcal{I}$ that have been updated or are dependent on the variables in the set dv. In the worst case, $\Delta(\mathcal{I}, dv) = \mathcal{I}$, i.e., a transfer function affects the entire invariant. In the best case $\Delta(\mathcal{I}, dv) = \emptyset$, i.e., nothing has changed. We also introduce a

Algorithm 1. Common minimal changed variable set

Require: $V(\mathcal{I}_1) = V(\mathcal{I}_2) \wedge V(\Delta(\mathcal{I}_1, dv_1)) \subseteq V(\mathcal{I}_1) \wedge V(\Delta(\mathcal{I}_2, dv_2)) \subseteq V(\mathcal{I}_2)$
Ensure: $S_1 = S_2 \subseteq V(\mathcal{I}_1)$

```
function CommonVarSet(dv1, dv2, I1, I2)
    S1 ← V(Δ(I1, dv1))
    S2 ← V(Δ(I2, dv2))
    while S1 ≠ S2 do
        if S1 ⊃ S2 then
            dv2 ← S1 \ S2
            S2 ← S2 ∪ V(Δ(I2, dv2)))
        else if S2 ⊃ S1 then
            dv1 ← S2 \ S1
            S1 ← S1 ∪ V(Δ(I1, dv1)))
        else if S1 ⊃⊂ S2 then
            dv1 ← S2 \ S1
            dv2 ← S1 \ S2
            S1 ← S1 ∪ V(Δ(I1, dv1)))
            S2 ← S2 ∪ V(Δ(I2, dv2)))
        end if
    end while
    return S1
end function
```

function V that returns the set of variables used in $\mathcal{I}$. For example, we use it to define the following property: $V(\Delta(\mathcal{I}, dv)) \subseteq V(\mathcal{I})$.

Let $\mathcal{I}_1$ and $\mathcal{I}_2$ be two relational invariants, and let dv_1 and dv_2 be their corresponding sets of updated variables. Then the problem of finding a minimal changed part of two invariants reduces to finding a common minimal updated set of variables S such that

$$S = V(\Delta(\mathcal{I}_1, S)) = V(\Delta(\mathcal{I}_2, S)) \quad (1)$$

A minimal solution for such recursive definitions is commonly obtained by a fixed-point iteration algorithm with initial values S_0 set to the smallest set, which in our case is $S_0 = dv_1 \cup dv_2$. If $S_0 = \emptyset$, then $dv_1 = dv_2 = \emptyset$, $\Delta(\mathcal{I}_1, dv_1) = \emptyset$, $\Delta(\mathcal{I}_2, dv_2) = \emptyset$, and, ultimately, $S = \emptyset$. That is, nothing has changed between the two invariants. However, if $S_0 \neq \emptyset$, then we need to iteratively solve for S in Eq. 1.

3.2 Finding a Common Changed Variable Set

Algorithm 1 shows the pseudocode of the optimized fixed-point computation algorithm to solve Eq. 1. The algorithm takes as arguments, the updated variables for each domain, dv_1 and dv_2, two invariants to compare, $\mathcal{I}_1$ and $\mathcal{I}_2$. It requires basic conditions for its correctness: each set of invariants are described over the same set of variables and Δ does not introduce any new variables. The output is the solution for Eq. 1.

The algorithm first computes the initial changed variable sets, S_1 and S_2 for each invariant, lines 2 and 3, affected by the updated variables dv_1 and dv_2, respectively.

At line 4, the algorithm compares the two sets and if they are not equal, i.e., the fixed-point has not been reached, the algorithm enters the main iteration loop. Inside the body of the loop, the algorithm first tests whether one set of variables is a proper superset of the other, lines 5 and 8.

As a simple optimization, if one of the sets is a proper superset, it only augments the smaller set as done on lines 6–7 and lines 9–10, respectively. For example, if $S_1 \supset S_2$, S_2 is augmented by the variables which are not already in S_2. Afterwards, a new updated variable set is computed from the set difference of S_1 and S_2, line 6. Then, the algorithm computes the changed variable set as the union between the existing set S_2 and the newly computed minimum variables, line 7. Similar computations are done for the case when $S_2 \supset S_1$, lines 9–10.

Finally, when the changed variable sets are incomparable— line 11— then both changed variable sets are recomputed in a similar fashion as described in lines 12–15. Upon the loop's termination, i.e., when $S_1 = S_2$, the algorithm returns one of the dependent sets, line 18.

To demonstrate how Algorithm 1 compares two invariants, consider the invariants on the true branch from our example in Fig. 1b. There, $\mathcal{I}_1 = z \leq x \wedge y \leq x \wedge w \rightarrow \top$ and $\mathcal{I}_2 = z \leq x \wedge y \leq x \wedge w \leq y$. The updated variables are $dv_1 = \{x, y\}$ and $dv_2 = \{x, y\}$.

The algorithm computes $\{x, y\}$ for S_1 and $\{w, x, y\}$ for S_2. Since S_2 is a proper superset of S_1, we recompute S_1, lines 9 and 10. Specifically, dv_1 becomes $\{w\}$. S_1 is then recomputed: $S_1 = S_1 \cup V(\Delta(\mathcal{I}_1, dv_1))$, which results in $S_1 = \{x, y\} \cup \{w\} = \{w, x, y\}$. At this point, $S_1 = S_2$, terminating the loop, and the algorithm returns the set $S_1 = \{w, x, y\}$. Then, an SMT solver can be used to compare logical relations of $\Delta(\mathcal{I}_1, S_1)$ and $\Delta(\mathcal{I}_2, S_1)$, for example, using implication relations. Or, in case of comparisons between Zones, one can use its custom equivalence and inclusion operations [16].

As mentioned, under worst-case conditions, Algorithm 1 returns the entire set of variables. In other words, it devolves into a full invariant comparison. This can happen if the variables within the invariant are tightly coupled with all other variables. Another situation which can cause a worst-case comparison is when an abstract domain has an ineffective Δ function, which performs a basic dependency analysis such as slicing [3,23].

Below we present termination and complexity analysis for Algorithm 1. We start with a proof sketch of termination.

Proof. First, we begin with the following assumptions: the variable projections for both domains are equivalent, i.e., $V(\mathcal{I}_1) = V(\mathcal{I}_2)$; and we assume the invariant minimization functions for each domain yield a subset of the variable projections, that is, $\Delta(\mathcal{I}_1, dv_1) \subseteq V(\mathcal{I}_1)$, and similarly for $\mathcal{I}_2$.

At each iteration, the union of variables over the minimization function is always increasing by at least one variable in either S_1 or S_2. Therefore, within a finite number of iterations S_1 and S_2 reach fixed-point, which is bounded by $V(\mathcal{I}_1) = V(\mathcal{I}_2)$ condition. Thus, Algorithm 1 terminates. □

The time-complexity of Algorithm 1 depends on the number of variables and the complexity of the Δ functions of the abstract domains. That is, the complexity of Algorithm 1 is $O(N) \cdot (C_{\Delta_1} + C_{\Delta_2})$, where N is the number of variables in the program under analysis and C_{Δ_i} is the complexity of the invariant minimization function for the corresponding domain. In the worst-case, at each iteration the sets S_1 and S_2 augmented by a single variable from Δ computations.

4 Methodology

To determine the effectiveness of the proposed algorithm, we use it to compare invariants produced by different techniques and by different relational abstract domains on the same program. For each subject program, each analysis outputs invariants after each statement. Over the corpus of programs, we compute 6564 total invariants. We store the invariants as logical formulas in SMT-LIB format. We run analyses on two relational domains, Zones and Relational Predicates [21], and compare the results of a standard Zones analysis to advanced Zones analyses, and Zones analysis to Relational Predicates analysis.

The goal of the empirical evaluation is to answer the following research questions:

RQ1 Does our technique affect the invariant comparison between different analysis techniques for the same abstract domain?
RQ2 Does our technique affect the invariant comparison between two different relational domains?
RQ3 How effective and efficient is Algorithm 1 on real-world invariant comparisons?

We consider different analysis techniques over the Zones domain to measure the precision gained by various advanced techniques. We consider the iteration parameter before widening. We also consider the widening method employed, which ensures termination for Zones analysis.

We then compare the most precise Zones technique to Relational Predicates [21], two incomparable domains. Our previous work [3] has shown the benefit of minimally comparing incomparable domains to demonstrate realized precision. However, in this case, we extend the invariants of the Predicates domain with a symbolic relational component.

For Relational Predicates, the minimization function is a selection based solely on notions of variable reachability, e.g., variable dependence, but it might not be minimal because of the generality of inequalities used in the relational part. We also computed minimization over Relational Predicates using a purely

```
(push)
(forall ((w Int) (x Int) (y Int) (z Int))
        (assert (=> (and (<= z y) (<= y x))
                    (and (<= z y) (<= y x) (<= w x)))))
(check-sat)
(pop)
(push)
(forall ((w Int) (x Int) (y Int) (z Int))
        (assert (=> (and (<= z y) (<= y x) (<= w x))
                    (and (<= z y) (<= y x)))))
(check-sat)
(pop)
```

Fig. 2. Logical implication between two example abstract states in SMT-LIB.

connected component concept, similar to the technique by Visser et al. [23], however, the reachable variant performed marginally better.

We use the Minimal Neighbors (MN) minimization function from our previous work [3] for Zones which provides the smallest invariant partition given a set of changed variables. This minimization algorithm considers the semantics of the formulas under the changed variables. Using these semantics, it selects the minimal dependent substate from the logical formula representing the invariant.

Subject Programs. Our subject programs consist of 192 Java methods from previous research on the Predicates domain [21]. These methods were extracted from a wide range of real-world, open-source projects and have a high number of integer operations. The subject programs range from 1 to 1993 Jimple instructions, a three address intermediate representation. The average branch count for the methods is 6 ($\sigma = 11$), with one method containing a maximal 56 branches. A plurality of our subject methods, 81 methods, contain at least one loop, with one method containing 12 loops.

Experimental Platform. We execute each of the analyses on a cluster of CentOS 7 GNU/Linux compute nodes, running Linux version `3.10.0-1160.76.1`, each equipped with an Intel® Xeon® Gold 6252 and 192 GB of system memory. We use an existing DFA static analysis tool [2,21] implemented in the Java programming language. The analysis framework uses Soot [20,22] version `4.2.1`. Similarly, we use Z3 [19], version `4.8.17` with Java bindings to compare SMT expressions for the abstract domain states. Finally, we use Java version 11 to execute the analyses, providing the following JVM options: `-Xms4g`, `-XX:+UseG1GC`, `-XX:+UseStringDeduplication`, and `-XX:+UseNUMA`.

Implementation. We modified an existing DFA framework such that the Zones analysis outputs its entire invariant for each program point. Each invariant is further reduced using a redundant inequality reduction technique proposed by

Larsen et al. [13]. For all domains, unbounded variables are set to top, $\top$, and excluded from the output expression. This further simplifies the formulas. Using the formulas from each analysis, in the usual way, we entail them into implication SMT formulas. For example, if an analysis produces $\mathcal{I}_1 = z \leq x \wedge y \leq x$ and another produces $\mathcal{I}_2 = z \leq x \wedge y \leq x \wedge w \leq y$. We entail these two expressions into the logical implication SMT query as shown in Fig. 2.

After entailment, we use Z3, using the linear integer arithmetic (LIA) theory for Zones to Zones comparisons and the non-linear integer arithmetic (NIA) theory for Zones to Relational Predicates comparisons, to decide model behavior of each domain. While Zones, and numerical abstract domains in general, have understood equality mechanisms such as double inclusion based deciders, entailment allows us to determine the pre-order between the two domain instances.

Evaluations. In total, we perform *three* different invariant comparisons, summarized in the following list:

$Z \preceq Z_{k=5}$—Zones using standard widening after two iterations and Zones widening after five iterations.
$Z \preceq Z_{ths}$—Zones with standard widening and Zones with threshold widening.
$Z_{ths} \prec\succ P$—Zones with threshold widening and Relational Predicates.

In all instances of Zones sans $Z_{k=5}$, widening happens after *two* iterations over widening nodes. We use a generic set of thresholds for Zones based on powers of 10: $\{0, 1, 10, 100, 1000\}$. Using a tuned set of thresholds for each program would yield better individual results, but overall does not affect our conclusions.

We use a generic disjoint domain for the basis of the Relational Predicates, based on Collberg et al.'s [6] study of numerical constants in Java Programs. Specifically, the predicate domain used in this study consists of the following set of disjoint elements: $\{(-\infty, -5],\ (-5, -2],\ -1,\ 0,\ 1,\ [2, 5),\ [5, +\infty)\}$. The relational component of the Predicates domain consists of symbolic information gathered through the process of analysis [21].

5 Evaluation Results and Discussions

In this section, we present the results of our experiments and discuss their implications to the research questions posed in the previous section.

5.1 Technique Comparisons

To answer **RQ1**, we consider the comparisons of different techniques using the Zones abstract domain. Since different techniques using the same domain create a partial ordering of their respective precision, we need only consider equivalent and less precise outcomes. To verify correctness of our implementation, however, we ensured that no other precision outcomes occurred.

Table 1. Zones $k = 2$ widening compared to Zones $k = 5$ widening

Comparison	$Z \equiv Z_{k=5}$	$Z \prec Z_{k=5}$
Full	6555	9
Minimal	6562	2

Table 2. Zones compared to Zones with Threshold Widening

Comparison	$Z \equiv Z_{ths}$	$Z \prec Z_{ths}$
Full	6519	45
Minimal	6545	19

Table 3. Zones with Threshold Widening compared to Relational Predicates

Comparison	$Z_{ths} \equiv P$	$Z_{ths} \prec P$	$Z_{ths} \succ P$	$Z_{ths} \prec\succ P$	$Z_{ths} ? P$
Full	1227	3173	196	1947	21
Minimal	3675	2353	248	288	0

Table 1 shows the breakdown of invariants computed by standard widening after *two* iterations and standard widening after *five* iterations. Comparing invariants using the entire invariant, deferred widening produces *nine* more precise invariants. However, when using our minimized comparison technique, the slim advantage reduces to *two* invariants.

Table 2 shows the breakdown of invariants between standard widening after two iterations and threshold widening after two iterations. Here, we see the largest gain in precision. Using the entire invariant to compare, threshold widening computes 45 more precise invariants. Again, however, the precision gain is cut by more than 50% when using minimal comparisons. The choice of thresholds could improve the precision, but for best results, the set of thresholds needs to be tailored specifically to each program.

As we can see between $Z \preceq Z_{k=5}$ and $Z \preceq Z_{ths}$, our comparison technique lowers the number of more precise invariants, thus eliminating the *carry-over* precision instances. That is, our technique lowers the number of more precise invariants advanced techniques compute. However, in doing so, our technique presents a more nuanced image of the realized precision gain advanced techniques offer.

5.2 Zones Versus Relational Predicates

Table 3 shows the precision breakdown of Zones with threshold widening compared to Relational Predicates, **RQ2**. Given that Zones and Predicates are inherently incomparable domains, we must consider all precision comparison categories. With the full invariant compairsions, Relational Predicates are more precise than Zones in about 50% of the invariants. The next largest category of invariants is incomparable, $\prec\succ$, which accounts for 30% of invariants. Here, Zones and Predicates are complementary, neither more nor less precise than the other. Zones and Predicates are equivalent in 19% of all invariants, and Zones are more precise in about 3% of all invariants. Finally, using the full invariant, 21 of the program points, the relation between two invariants could not be established by Z3 since it returned `UNKNOWN`.

Our technique eliminates the undecidable results. Moreover, it dramatically reduces the number of incomparable invariants– only 4% of invariants remain incomparable. Similar to *carry-over* precision, incomparable invariants arise when one domain computes a more precise invariant for one variable, and the other domain computes a more precise invariant for another, unrelated variable at a later program point. Considering the entire invariant results in incomparable precision. However, by comparing only the relevant, changed variables, our technique largely disentangles the imprecision in the comparison.

The equivalent invariant category is the next largest affected category, where more than half, 56%, of computed invariants between Zones and Relational Predicates become equivalent. Relational Predicates lose 13% of more precise invariants, and Zones gains about 1% of invariants which it computes more precisely than Relational Predicates.

By comparing only the necessary variables at each program point, our technique allows general, relational abstract domains to be compared without undecidable results. The reduction in incomparable invariants between two otherwise difficult to compare domains provides a clearer precision performance picture between the two domains.

Effect on Efficiency of Comparison. To demonstrate the effect on efficiency of comparing our minimal comparison to the full state comparison with respect to the logical entailment and solver queries, we collected five (5) executions of the Z3 solver processing the logical entailment queries. Figure 3 shows the averaged runtime comparisons between Z3 comparing states using the entire state and our proposed minimal technique. In Fig. 3 (a), we compare the runtimes for Zones versus Zones with Threshold Widening. We see the two runtimes appear similar. Indeed, a statistical t-test confirms the two distributions fail to be rejected as similar. However, in the range above the average, 0.04, the majority of the points are below the diagonal line, indicating that the minimum comparison is faster than the full comparison. This runtime behavior is expected for these two abstract domains since the two domains are similar and as shown in Table 2, the number of states where the two domains are equal is significant. In Fig. 3 (b), we compare the runtimes of Zones with Threshold Widening against Relational Predicates. The average runtime for the full comparisons is about 2.7 s. The minimum comparison has an average of about 0.8 s. We see a significant difference between the two visually as the majority of points are below the diagonal line. As before, these results seem intuitive since the resulting queries for the proposed technique result in fewer invariants per abstract state. Overall, we see our technique improves the efficiency of relational domain comparison.

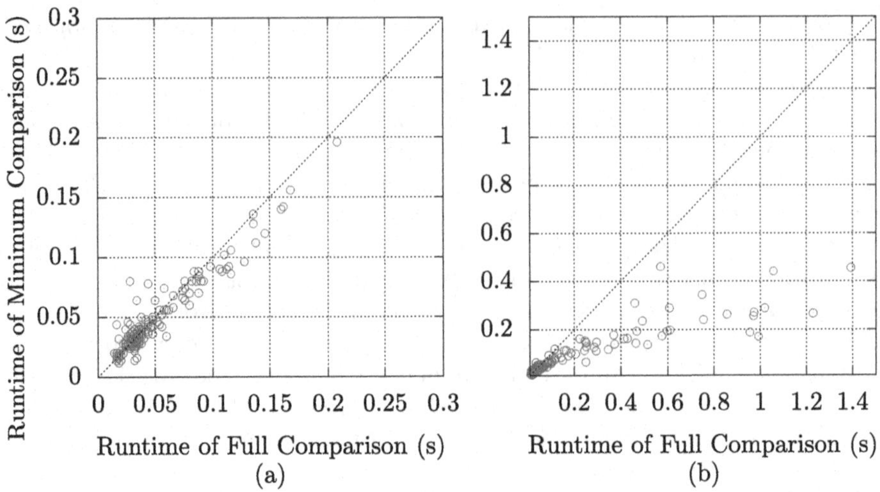

Fig. 3. Runtime (in seconds) comparisons between full and minimum invariant sets using Z3 to compute logical entailment. In (a) compares Zones to Zones with Threshold Widening. In (b) compares Zones with Threshold Widening to Relational Predicates.

5.3 Iterations and Variable Reductions

To determine if Algorithm 1 is efficient, **RQ3**, we use the iteration depth count to determine how many times the algorithm iterates before it reaches a stable set of variables for comparison. Over all instances of Zones comparisons, the iteration count was either *zero* or *one*, with no outliers. That is, either Zones computed the same set of changed variables and the dependent set between two techniques was immediately equivalent. Or, the set of dependent variables is captured with only a single extension, mostly to the Zones using standard widening, Z.

Comparing Zones to Relational Predicates, we see similar results. The average number of iterations is between *zero* and *one* iteration. However, we have several outliers at two iterations. Instrumentation found 12 instances of extreme outliers, 11 for *three* iterations, and one instance of *four* iterations. Furthermore, more variety exists in the branches for Zones versus Relational Predicates. Unlike comparing techniques between Zones invariants, comparing Zones to a more general, relational formula required more augmentation by each domain.

To evaluate effectiveness of Algorithm 1, **RQ3**, we consider the proportion of variables necessary for comparison. We instrumented our algorithm to compute the proportion of variables it returns after reaching a stable set, compared to the variable projection of the incoming invariants. We plot the frequency of proportions of variables returned by Algorithm 1 in Fig. 4. In Fig. 4a, we plot variable reductions across all comparisons of Zones: standard widening after two iterations versus standard widening after five iterations and standard widening versus threshold widening. Figure 4b shows the variable reductions for Zones with threshold widening versus Relational Predicates. Considering a single bin in

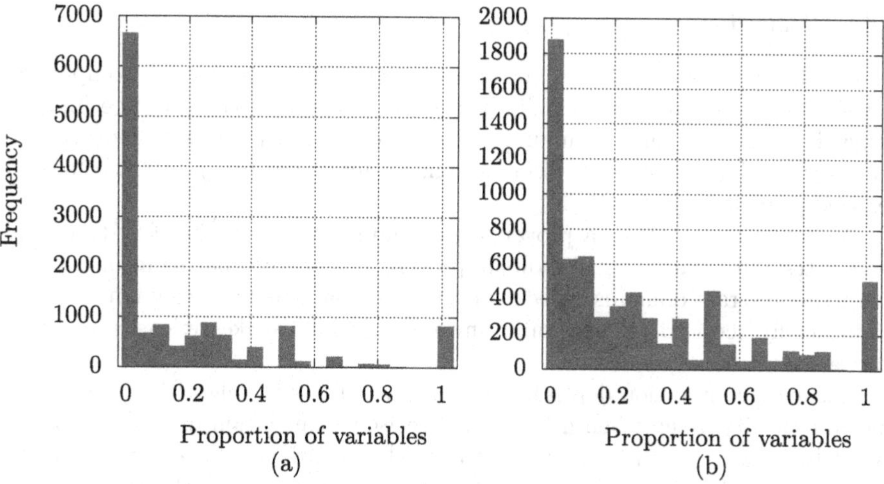

Fig. 4. Frequency plot of proportion of variables selected by Algorithm 1 which are necessary for comparing two invariants. (a) represents the frequencies of proportions when comparing techniques using Zones. (b) represents the frequencies of proportions when comparing Zones to Relational Predicates.

Fig. 4, for example, 0.1, represents the frequency where Algorithm 1 needed only 10% of the variables occurring in the original invariants to adequately compare the two.

Shown in Fig. 4, the large frequencies in the 0 bin shows our technique was able to remove all variables from the invariants from comparison, eliminating the need to compare the two invariants. Comparing advanced techniques utilizing Zones shows more than 6500 instances, and about 1850 in Zones versus Relational Predicates.

Our technique reduces the number of variables necessary for comparison by 50% or more in 90% of comparisons between techniques of Zones, and at least by 25% in 93% of comparisons. For Zones and Relational Predicates, our technique reduces the necessary, relevant variables by 50% or more in 80% of comparisons and by 12% in 93% of comparisons. That is, in the majority of comparisons, our technique reduces the number of variables necessary for comparing two relational domains or techniques. The quality of a domain's Δ function affects the performance and effectiveness of Algorithm 1. We see only a few iterations in the algorithm when comparing analysis techniques utilizing Zones since we used a minimal Δ function for Zones. However, we see an increase in iterations when comparing with a non-optimal Δ, as in Zones and Relational Predicates. That is, the quality of Δ can have an outsized impact on the practicality of our technique. However, given the preponderance of variable reductions and low iteration counts over the corpus of methods and comparisons, we conclude that the proposed algorithm is practical and effective.

5.4 Discussion

The evaluation results show our technique enables more precise comparison between relational abstract domain invariants. When comparing two techniques using the same domain, our minimal comparison strategy precisely captures the techniques' relative precision, disentangling accumulated *carry-over* effects from realized precision gains.

While we do not have a proven state minimization function for Relational Predicates, our technique still shows improvement when comparing incomparable relational abstract domains. Specifically, our comparison removes unknowns and dramatically reduced incomparable invariants, which makes it easier to make software engineering decisions.

The average iteration depth for Algorithm 1 shows the algorithm's efficiency and practicality. Even when using an imprecise minimization function for Relational Predicates, our technique only needed a maximum of *four* iterations to arrive at a stable set of common variables for comparison. Moreover, in the majority of comparisons, Algorithm 1 returned a significantly smaller proportion of variables than the entirety of the variables in each invariant, demonstrating the efficacy of the technique.

6 Related Work

Our previous work [3] found a set of algorithms for efficiently computing Δ for the Zones domain. Using the algorithms, it compared Zones to other non-relational domains, which in the context of data-flow analysis (DFA) and this work, have trivial Δ functions. We extend the previous work by considering comparisons between relational abstract domains, abstracting the Δ function for each domain.

Comparing the precision gain of new analysis techniques or comparing the precision of newly proposed abstract domains is a common problem in the literature. Previous work in this area generally compare precision in one of two ways. One, the comparison is based on known *a priori* program properties over benchmark programs [8–10,14,15]. Two, the comparison is based on logical entailment of computed invariants [10,17,21].

Close to our work, Casso et al. [5] propose several metrics for computing the *distance* between different abstract domain elements and, consequently, the distance between different analyses over those abstract domains. Thus, using distance metrics as a proxy, they are able to compute a categorization of precision over different abstract domains. However, the work and proposed metrics are constrained to non-numerical abstract domains within (Constraint) Logic Programming. We believe a combination of approaches toward (a set of) metrics that measures across different weakly-relational numerical abstract domains to be an interesting line of future work.

To the best of our knowledge, this work represents one of the first studies improving the granularity of precision characteristics for categorization of relational abstract precision comparisons. We believe this work would benefit existing work which compares relational abstract domains or new analysis techniques using relational abstract domains.

7 Conclusion and Future Work

In this study, we defined the problem of minimally comparing relational invariants, proposed an algorithm which solves the problem, and experimentally evaluated whether the algorithm indeed solves the problem using real-world programs. Using our algorithm, we can remove the precision *carry-over* effects advanced analysis techniques introduce, providing clear precision benefits for advanced techniques. For example, the benefits of deferred widening and threshold widening are smaller than anticipated. Moreover, our technique enables the comparison of relational abstract domains which are otherwise difficult to compare directly. Specifically, we see our technique removed the `UNKNOWN` invariants and dramatically reduced the incomparable invariants when comparing Zones to Relational Predicates. Finally, Algorithm 1's average iteration depth and variable reduction demonstrate the algorithm's overall practicality and usefulness when comparing analysis techniques and relational abstract domains.

Future Work. Developing a minimization function, Δ for Relational Predicates would enable a comprehensive, empirical study of the relative precision of weakly-relational numerical abstract domains to Predicates. Furthermore, we believe the proposed technique of comparison can benefit adaptive analysis techniques which selectively choose the appropriate abstract domain during analysis. Similarly, an interesting, additional empirical comparison to consider is one where strictly the exit invariants are considered between domains and strategies. Octagons [18] are not included in this study because a minimization strategy for Octagons has not been developed. However, this is an interesting avenue to pursue and we intend to use the technique of this work to compare Zones to Octagons, which will empirically quantify the precision gain of Octagons over Zones.

Acknowledgments. The work reported here was supported by the U.S. National Science Foundation under award CCF-19-42044.

References

1. Abate, C., et al.: An extended account of trace-relating compiler correctness and secure compilation. ACM Trans. Program. Lang. Syst. **43**(4), 1–48 (2021). https://doi.org/10.1145/3460860
2. Ballou, K., Sherman, E.: Incremental transitive closure for zonal abstract domain. In: Deshmukh, J.V., Havelund, K., Perez, I. (eds.) NASA Formal Methods. NFM 2022. LNCS, vol. 13260, pp. 800–808. Springer, Cham (2022). https://doi.org/10.1007/978-3-031-06773-0_43, http://dx.doi.org/10.1007/978-3-031-06773-0_43

3. Ballou, K., Sherman, E.: Identifying minimal changes in the zone abstract domain. In: David, C., Sun, M. (eds.) Theoretical Aspects of Software Engineering, vol. 13931, pp. 221–239. Springer, Cham (2023). https://doi.org/10.1007/978-3-031-35257-7_13, http://dx.doi.org/10.1007/978-3-031-35257-7_13
4. Blanchet, B., et al.: A static analyzer for large safety-critical software. In: Proceedings of the ACM SIGPLAN 2003 Conference on Programming Language Design and Implementation - PLDI '03 (2003). https://doi.org/10.1145/781131.781153
5. Casso, I., Morales, J.F., López-García, P., Giacobazzi, R., Hermenegildo, M.V.: Computing abstract distances in logic programs. In: Gabbrielli, M. (ed.) LOPSTR 2019. LNCS, vol. 12042, pp. 57–72. Springer, Cham (2020). https://doi.org/10.1007/978-3-030-45260-5_4
6. Collberg, C., Myles, G., Stepp, M.: An empirical study of java bytecode programs. Softw. Pract. Exp. **37**(6), 581–641 (2007). https://doi.org/10.1002/spe.776
7. Cousot, P., Cousot, R.: Abstract interpretation: a unified lattice model for static analysis of programs by construction or approximation of fixpoints. In: Proceedings of the 4th ACM SIGACT-SIGPLAN Symposium on Principles of Programming Languages, pp. 238–252. POPL '77, Association for Computing Machinery, New York, NY, USA, January 1977. https://doi.org/10.1145/512950.512973
8. Gange, G., Ma, Z., Navas, J.A., Schachte, P., Søndergaard, H., Stuckey, P.J.: A fresh look at zones and octagons. ACM Trans. Program. Lang. Syst. **43**(3), 1–51 (2021). https://doi.org/10.1145/3457885
9. Gurfinkel, A., Chaki, S.: Boxes: a symbolic abstract domain of boxes. In: Cousot, R., Martel, M. (eds.) SAS 2010. LNCS, vol. 6337, pp. 287–303. Springer, Heidelberg (2010). https://doi.org/10.1007/978-3-642-15769-1_18
10. Howe, J.M., King, A.: Logahedra: a new weakly relational domain. In: Liu, Z., Ravn, A.P. (eds.) ATVA 2009. LNCS, vol. 5799, pp. 306–320. Springer, Heidelberg (2009). https://doi.org/10.1007/978-3-642-04761-9_23
11. Katz, S.: Program optimization using invariants. IEEE Trans. Softw. Eng. **SE-4**(5), 378–389 (1978). https://doi.org/10.1109/tse.1978.233858
12. King, J.C.: Symbolic execution and program testing. Commun. ACM **19**(7), 385–394 (1976). https://doi.org/10.1145/360248.360252, http://dx.doi.org/10.1145/360248.360252
13. Larsen, K., Larsson, F., Pettersson, P., Yi, W.: Efficient verification of real-time systems: compact data structure and state-space reduction. In: Proceedings Real-Time Systems Symposium, pp. 14–24. IEEE Computer Society (1997). https://doi.org/10.1109/real.1997.641265
14. Laviron, V., Logozzo, F.: SubPolyhedra: a (more) scalable approach to infer linear inequalities. In: Jones, N.D., Müller-Olm, M. (eds.) VMCAI 2009. LNCS, vol. 5403, pp. 229–244. Springer, Heidelberg (2008). https://doi.org/10.1007/978-3-540-93900-9_20
15. Logozzo, F., Fähndrich, M.: Pentagons: a weakly relational abstract domain for the efficient validation of array accesses. Sci. Comput. Program. **75**(9), 796–807 (2010). https://doi.org/10.1016/j.scico.2009.04.004
16. Miné, A.: A new numerical abstract domain based on difference-bound matrices. In: Danvy, O., Filinski, A. (eds.) PADO 2001. LNCS, vol. 2053, pp. 155–172. Springer, Heidelberg (2001). https://doi.org/10.1007/3-540-44978-7_10
17. Miné, A.: Weakly Relational Numerical Abstract Domains, December 2004. https://pastel.archives-ouvertes.fr/tel-00136630
18. Miné, A.: The octagon abstract domain. High.-Order Symb. Comput. **19**(1), 31–100 (2006). https://doi.org/10.1007/s10990-006-8609-1, http://dx.doi.org/10.1007/s10990-006-8609-1

19. de Moura, L., Bjørner, N.: Z3: an efficient SMT solver. In: Ramakrishnan, C.R., Rehof, J. (eds.) TACAS 2008. LNCS, vol. 4963, pp. 337–340. Springer, Heidelberg (2008). https://doi.org/10.1007/978-3-540-78800-3_24
20. OSS, S.: Soot (2020). https://soot-oss.github.io/soot/
21. Sherman, E., Dwyer, M.B.: Exploiting domain and program structure to synthesize efficient and precise data flow analyses (t). In: 2015 30th IEEE/ACM International Conference on Automated Software Engineering (ASE), November 2015. https://doi.org/10.1109/ase.2015.41
22. Vallée-Rai, R. Co, P., Gagnon, E., Hendren, L., Lam, P., Sundaresan, V.: Soot - a java bytecode optimization framework. In: Proceedings of the 1999 Conference of the Centre for Advanced Studies on Collaborative Research, p. 13. CASCON '99, IBM Press (1999)
23. Visser, W., Geldenhuys, J., Dwyer, M.B.: Green: reducing, reusing and recycling constraints in program analysis. In; Proceedings of the ACM SIGSOFT 20th International Symposium on the Foundations of Software Engineering, November 2012. https://doi.org/10.1145/2393596.2393665, http://dx.doi.org/10.1145/2393596.2393665
24. Zhu, H., Magill, S., Jagannathan, S.: A data-driven CHC solver. In: Proceedings of the 39th ACM SIGPLAN Conference on Programming Language Design and Implementation, June 2018. https://doi.org/10.1145/3192366.3192416

Tailoring Stateless Model Checking for Event-Driven Multi-threaded Programs

Parosh Aziz Abdulla[1], Mohamed Faouzi Atig[1], Frederik Meyer Bønneland[2], Sarbojit Das[1(✉)], Bengt Jonsson[1], Magnus Lång[1], and Konstantinos Sagonas[1,3]

[1] Uppsala University, Uppsala, Sweden
sarbojit.das@it.uu.se
[2] Aalborg University, Aalborg, Denmark
[3] National Technical University of Athens, Athens, Greece

Abstract. Event-driven multi-threaded programming is an important idiom for structuring concurrent computations. Stateless Model Checking (SMC) is an effective verification technique for multi-threaded programs, especially when coupled with Dynamic Partial Order Reduction (DPOR). Existing SMC techniques are often ineffective in handling event-driven programs, since they will typically explore all possible orderings of event processing, even when events do not conflict. We present Event-DPOR, a DPOR algorithm tailored to event-driven multi-threaded programs. It is based on Optimal-DPOR, an optimal DPOR algorithm for multi-threaded programs; we show how it can be extended for event-driven programs. We prove correctness of Event-DPOR for all programs, and optimality for a large subclass. One complication is that an operation in Event-DPOR, which checks for redundancy of new executions, is NP-hard, as we show in this paper; we address this by a sequence of inexpensive (but incomplete) tests which check for redundancy efficiently. Our implementation and experimental evaluation show that, in comparison with other tools in which handler threads are simulated using locks, Event-DPOR can be exponentially faster than other state-of-the-art DPOR algorithms on a variety of programs and manages to completely avoid unnecessary exploration of executions.

1 Introduction

Event-driven multi-threaded programming is an important idiom for structuring concurrent computations in distributed message-passing applications, file systems [31], high-performance servers [11], systems programming [12], smartphone applications [33], and many other domains. In this idiom, multiple threads execute concurrently and can communicate through shared objects. In addition, some threads, called *handler threads*, have an associated event pool to which all threads can post events. Each handler thread executes an event processing loop in which events from its pool are processed sequentially, one after the other,

É. André and J. Sun (Eds.): ATVA 2023, LNCS 14216, pp. 176–198, 2023.
https://doi.org/10.1007/978-3-031-45332-8_9

interleaved with the execution of other threads. An event is processed by invoking an appropriate handler, which can be, e.g., a callback function.

Testing and verification of event-driven multi-threaded programming faces all the usual challenges of testing and verification for multi-threaded programs, and furthermore suffers from additional complexity, since the order of event execution is determined dynamically and non-deterministically. A successful and fully automatic technique for finding concurrency bugs in multithreaded programs (i.e., defects that arise only under some thread schedulings) and for verifying their absence is *stateless model checking* (SMC) [15]. Given a terminating program and fixed input data, SMC systematically explores the set of all thread schedulings that are possible during program runs. A special runtime scheduler drives the SMC exploration by making decisions on scheduling whenever such choices may affect the interaction between threads. SMC has been implemented in many tools (e.g., VeriSoft [16], CHESS [34], Concuerror [10], NIDHUGG [2], rInspect [42], CDSCHECKER [35], RCMC [22], and GENMC [26]), and successfully applied to realistic programs (e.g., [17] and [25]). To reduce the number of explored executions, SMC tools typically employ *dynamic partial order reduction* (DPOR) [1,13]. DPOR defines an equivalence relation on executions, which preserves relevant correctness properties, such as reachability of local states and assertion violations, and explores at least one execution in each equivalence class.

Existing DPOR techniques for multi-threaded programs lack effectiveness in handling the complications brought by event-driven programming, as has been observed by e.g., Jensen et al. [20] and Maiya et al. [28]. A naïve way to handle such a program is to consider all pairs of events as conflicting, implying that different orderings of event executions by a handler thread will be considered inequivalent. A major drawback is then that a DPOR algorithm cannot exploit the fact that different orderings of event executions by a single handler thread can be considered equivalent in the case that events are non-conflicting. In this way, a program in which n non-conflicting events are posted to a handler thread by n concurrent threads can give rise to $n!$ explorations by a standard DPOR algorithm, whereas all of them are in fact equivalent. On the other hand, some events may be conflicting, so a DPOR algorithm for event-driven programs should explore only the necessary inequivalent orderings between conflicting events. This can be achieved by defining an equivalence on executions, which respects only the ordering of conflicting accesses to shared variables, irrespective of the order in which events are executed. For plain multi-threaded programs, this equivalence is the basis for several effective DPOR algorithms [1,13]. The challenge is to develop an effective DPOR algorithm also for event-driven programs.

In this paper, we present Event-DPOR, a DPOR algorithm for event-driven multi-threaded programs where handlers can execute events from their event pool in arbitrary order (i.e., the event pool is viewed as a multiset). The multiset semantics is used in many works [20,21,37], often with the significant restriction that there is only one handler thread; we consider the more general case with an arbitrary number of handler threads. Event-DPOR is based on Optimal-DPOR [1,3], a DPOR algorithm for multi-threaded programs. The basic working mode of Optimal-DPOR is similar to several other DPOR algorithms: Given a terminating program, one of its executions is explored and then analyzed to construct initial fragments of new executions; each fragment that is not redundant (i.e., which can be extended to an execution that is not equivalent to a previously explored execution), is subsequently extended to a maximal execution, which is analyzed to construct initial fragments of new executions, and so on. Event-DPOR employs the same basic mode of operation as Optimal-DPOR, but must be extended to cope with the event-driven execution model. One complication is that the constructed initial fragments must satisfy the constraints imposed by the fact that event executions on a handler are serialized; this may necessitate reordering of several events when constructing new executions from an already explored one. Another complication is that the check whether a new fragment is redundant is NP-hard in the event-driven setting, as we prove in this paper. We alleviate this by defining a sequence of inexpensive but incomplete rendundancy checks, using a complete decision procedure only as a last resort.

We prove that the Event-DPOR algorithm is *correct* (explores at least one execution in each equivalence class) for event-driven programs. We also prove that it is *optimal* (explores exactly one execution in each equivalence class) for the class of so-called *non-branching* programs, in which the possible sequences of shared variable accesses that can be performed during execution of an event, whose handler also executes other events, does not depend on how its execution is interleaved with other threads.

We have implemented Event-DPOR in an extension of the NIDHUGG tool [2]. Our experimental evaluation shows that, when compared with other SMC tools in which event handlers are simulated using locks, Event-DPOR incurs only a moderate constant overhead, but can be exponentially faster than other state-of-the-art DPOR algorithms. The same evaluation also shows that, unlike other algorithms that can achieve analogous reduction, Event-DPOR manages to completely avoid unnecessary exploration of executions that cannot be serialized. Moreover, in all the programs we tried, also those that are not non-branching, Event-DPOR explored the optimal number of traces, suggesting that Event-DPOR is optimal not only for non-branching programs but also for a good number of branching ones. Also, our sequence of inexpensive checks for redundancy was sufficient in all tried programs, i.e., we never had to invoke the decision procedure for this NP-hard problem.

2 Related Work

Stateless model checking has been implemented in many tools for analysis of multithreaded programs (e.g., [2,10,16,22,26,34,35,42]). It often employs DPOR, introduced by Flanagan and Godefroid [13] to reduce the number of schedulings that must be explored. Further developments of DPOR reduce this number further, by being optimal (i.e., exploring only one scheduling in each equivalence class) [1,3,7,23] or by weakening the equivalence [5–7,9].

DPOR has been adapted to event-driven multi-threaded programs. Jensen et al. [20] consider an execution model in which events are processed in arbitrary order (multiset semantics) and apply it to JavaScript programs. Maiya et al. [28] consider a model where events are processed in the order they are received (FIFO semantics), and develop a tool, EM-Explorer, for analyzing Android applications which, given a particular sequence of event executions, produces a set of reorderings of its events which reverses its conflicts. The above works are based on the algorithm of Flanagan and Godefroid [13], implying that they do not take advantage of subsequent improvements in DPOR algorithms [1,3,23], nor do they employ techniques such as sleep sets for avoiding redundant explorations. It is known [3] that even with sleep sets, the algorithm of Flanagan and Godefroid can explore an exponential number of redundant executions compared to more recently proposed DPOR algorithms which are optimal [1,3,23]. Without sleep sets, the amount of redundant exploration will increase further. Recently, Trimananda et al. [39] have proposed an adaptation of stateful DPOR [40,41] to non-terminating event-driven programs, which has been implemented in Java PathFinder. For analogous reason as for prior DPOR algorithms for event-driven programs [20,28], also this approach does not avoid performing redundant explorations.

For actor-based programs, in which processes communicate by message-passing, Aronis et al. [7] have presented an improvement of Optimal-DPOR in which two postings of messages to a mailbox are considered as conflicting only if their order affects the subsequent behavior of the receiver. Better reduction can then be achieved if the receiver selects messages from its mailbox based on some criterion, such as by pattern matching on the structure of the message. However, this execution model differs from the one we consider in this paper.

Event-driven programs where handlers select messages in arbitrary order from their mailbox can be analyzed by modeling messages as (mini-)threads that compete for handler threads by taking locks, and applying any SMC algorithm for shared-variable programs with locks. Since typical SMC algorithms always consider different lock-protected code sections as conflicting, this approach has the drawback of exploring all possible orderings of events on a handler. There exists a technique to avoid exploring of all these orderings in programs with locks, in which lock sections can be considered non-conflicting if they do not perform conflicting accesses to shared variables. This LAPOR technique [24] is based on optimistically executing lock-protected code regions in parallel, and aborting executions in which lock-protected regions cannot be serialized. This can led to significant useless exploration, as also shown in our evaluation in Sect. 8.

The problem of detecting potentially harmful data races in single executions of event-driven programs has been addressed by several works. The main challenge for data race detection is to capture the often hidden dependencies for applications on Android [8,18,19,30] or on other platforms [29,36–38]. Detecting data races is a different problem than exploring all possible executions of a program, in that it considers only one (possibly long) execution, but tries to detect whether it (or some other similar execution) exhibits data races.

3 Main Concepts and Challenges

In this section, we informally present core concepts of our approach by examples[1]

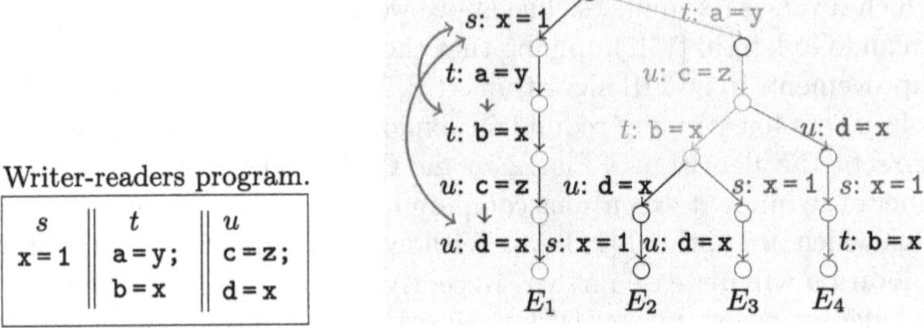

Fig. 1. A program and its execution tree with the four executions that Optimal-DPOR will explore. In E_1, the red arcs show the conflict order; the blue arrows the program order. The first wakeup sequence is shown in green; the remaining two continue with blue. (Color figure online)

3.1 Review of Optimal-DPOR

Our DPOR algorithm for event-driven programs is an extension of Optimal-DPOR [1]. Let us illustrate Optimal-DPOR on the program snippet shown in Fig. 1. In this code, three threads s, t, and u access three shared variables x, y, and z,[2] whereas a, b, c, and d are thread-local registers. Optimal-DPOR first explores a maximal execution, which it inspects to detect races. From each race, it constructs an initial fragment of an alternative execution which reverses the race and branches off from the explored execution just before the race. Let us illustrate with the program in Fig. 1. Assume that the first execution is E_1 (cf. the tree in Fig. 1). The DPOR algorithm first computes its happens-before order, denoted $\xrightarrow{\text{hb}}_{E_1}$, which is the transitive closure of the union of: (i) the *program order*, which totally orders the events in each thread (small blue arrows to the left of E_1), and (ii) the *conflict order* which orders conflicting events: two events are conflicting if they access a common shared variable and at least one is a write (red arcs left of E_1). A *race* consists of two conflicting events in different threads that are adjacent in the $\xrightarrow{\text{hb}}_{E_1}$-order. The execution E_1 contains two races (red arcs in Fig. 1). Let us consider the first race, in which the first event is s: x=1 and the second event is t: b=x. The alternative execution is generated by concatenating the sequence of events in E_1 that do not succeed

[1] Note that in the remainder of the paper, we will use the term *message* to refer to what was called *event* in Sects. 1 and 2, for the reason that the literature on DPOR has reserved the term *event* to denote an execution of a program statement. We will also use *mailbox* instead of *event pool*.

[2] Throughout this paper, we assume that threads are spawned by a main thread, and that all shared variables get initialized to 0, also by the main thread.

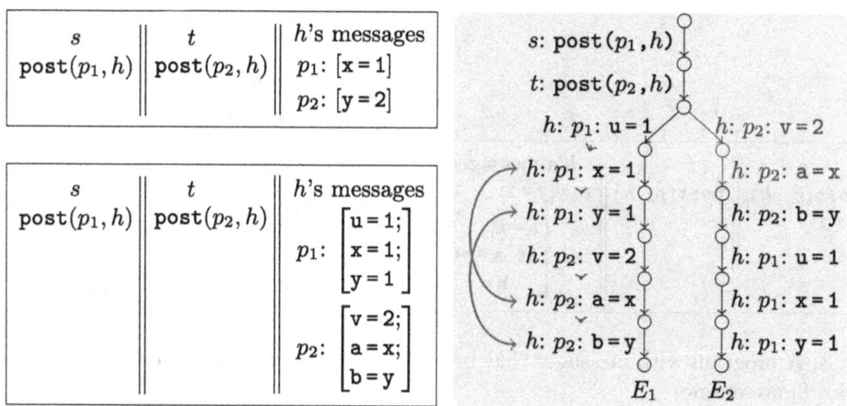

Fig. 2. An event-driven program with non-conflicting messages (top left). A program with non-atomic conflicting messages (bottom left) and its tree of executions (right).

the first event in the $\xrightarrow{\text{hb}}_{E_1}$ order (i.e., t: a = y; u: c = z) with the second event of the race t: b=x. This forms a *wakeup sequence*, which branches off from E_1 just before the race, i.e., at the beginning of the exploration (green in Fig. 1). The second race, between s: x=1 and u: d=x induces the wakeup sequence $t.u.u$ formed from the sequence t: a = y; u: c = z and the second event u: d = x, also branching off at the beginning (note that $t.u.u$ does not contain the second event t: b=x of t since it succeeds s: x=1 in the $\xrightarrow{\text{hb}}_{E_1}$-ordering). When attempting to insert $t.u.u$, the algorithm will discover that this sequence is *redundant*, since its events are consistently contained in a continuation ($t.u.t.u$) of the already inserted wakeup sequence $t.u.t$, and it will therefore not insert $t.u.u$. After this, the algorithm will reclaim the space for E_1, extend $t.u.t$ into a maximal execution E_2, in which races are detected that generate two new wakeup sequences (which start in green and continue in blue), which are extended to two additional executions (cf. Fig. 1).

3.2 Challenges for Event-Driven Programs

A naïve way in which existing DPOR algorithms can handle event-driven programs is to consider all pairs of messages as conflicting. However, such an approach is *not* effective, since it will lead to exploration of all different serialization orders of the messages, even if they are non-conflicting, as is the case for the top left program of Fig. 2 in which two threads s and t post two messages p_1 and p_2 to a handler thread h. (We show messages labeled by the message identifier and wrapped in brackets.) Since the events of p_1 and p_2 are non-conflicting, exploring only one execution suffices. In general, some messages of a program may be conflicting and some may not be, so a DPOR algorithm for event-driven programs should explore only the necessary inequivalent orderings between conflicting messages. Event-DPOR achieves this by extending Optimal-DPOR's technique for reversing races between events in different threads to a mechanism for reversing races between events in different messages.

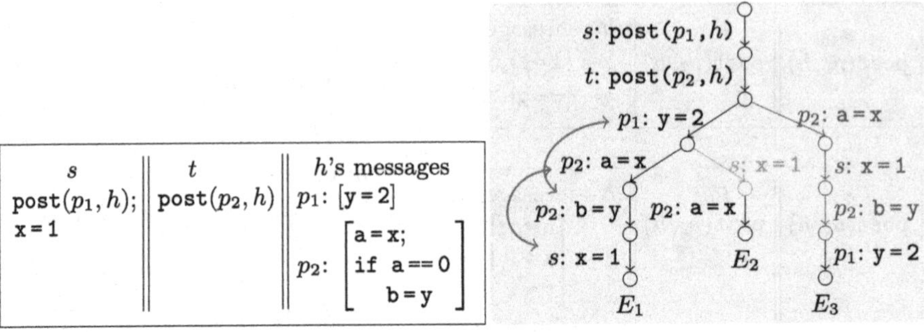

Fig. 3. A program with messages that branch on read values and its exploration tree. (Color figure online)

We illustrate this mechanism on the program at the bottom left of Fig. 2. Assume that the first explored execution is E_1. It contains two races between events in the two messages, one on x and one on y. According to Optimal-DPOR's principle for race reversal, the race on x should induce an alternative execution composed of the sequence of events that do not happen-after the first event (i.e., h: p_1: u = 1 h: p_2: v = 2) and the second event h: p_2: a = x (for brevity, we do not show the two post events). However, since message execution is serialized, these events cannot form an execution. Therefore, Event-DPOR forms the alternative execution (shown in blue) by appending the second event h: p_2: a = x to a maximal subset of the events of E_1 which is closed under $\xrightarrow{\text{hb}}_{E_1}$-predecessors (i.e., if it contains an event e then it also contains all its $\xrightarrow{\text{hb}}_{E_1}$-predecessors), and which can form an execution that does not contain the first event. Later, this wakeup sequence is extended to execution E_2. Let us then consider the race on y. The constructed wakeup sequence should append the second event h: p_2: b = y to a maximal subset of events that do not happen-after the first event h: p_1: y = 1. However, there is no execution that satisfies these constraints, since it would have to include h: p_2: a = x before its $\xrightarrow{\text{hb}}_{E_1}$-predecessor h: p_1: x = 1. The conclusion is that the race on y cannot (and should not) be considered for reversal, whereas that on x should be reversed. More generally, if two messages executing on the same handler thread are in conflict, then a wakeup sequence is constructed consisting of only the second message up until and including its first conflicting event.

When messages can branch on values read from shared variables, reversing the order of two messages may change the control flow of each involved message. Also in this case, Event-DPOR's principles for reversing races work fine. We illustrate this on the program in Fig. 3, consisting of two threads s and t and a handler thread h. Thread s posts a message p_1 to h and thereafter writes to x. Thread t posts message p_2 to h that reads from x and *may* then read from y.

Assume that the first execution is E_1, where s's access to x goes last. The execution has two races: one on y between p_1: y = 2 and p_2: b = y, and one on x between p_2: a = x and s: x = 1. The race on x can be handled in the same way as in Optimal-DPOR: the wakeup sequence is s: x = 1, which branches off after the prefix $s.t.p_1$ (green in Fig. 3), and will subsequently be extended to execution E_2.

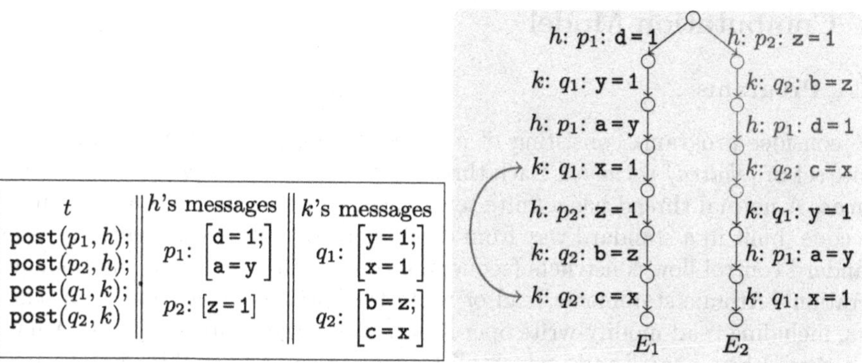

Fig. 4. A program in which a reversal of the race on x will reorder messages on the handler k, and two executions that will be explored.

The race on y is a race between events in two messages on the same handler thread. As in the previous example, the wakeup sequence will include the second message up until and including the first racing event, which is p_2: b = y. Included in the events that do not happen-after the first event is also s: x = 1, which must be placed after its predecessor p_2: a = x, yielding the wakeup sequence p_2: a = x; s: x = 1; p_2: b = y, which branches off after s: post(p_1,h), t: post(p_2,h). This is the blue rightmost branch of the tree in Fig. 3, and is later extended into the execution E_3. Execution E_3 has a race on x. Its reversal produces the wakeup sequence s: x = 1, which is a tentative branch next to p_2: a = x. However, this wakeup sequence is not in conflict with the left branch labeled p_1: b = y, which means that it will not be inserted for the reason that it is equivalent to a subsequence of an execution starting with p_1: b = y, namely E_2.

Reordering Messages when Reversing Races. Event-DPOR's principles for reversing races may necessitate reordering of messages on handlers that are not involved in the race. Consider the program in Fig. 4. Assume that the first explored execution is E_1, where we have omitted the initial sequence of post events of thread t for succinctness. In E_1, message p_1 is processed before p_2, and q_1 is processed before q_2. There are three races in E_1, one on each of the shared variables x, y, z. Let us consider the race on x, shown by the red arrow. A wakeup sequence which reverses this race must include all events of q_2, since these are the $\xrightarrow{\text{hb}}_{E_1}$-predecessors of q_2: c = x. It must also include the write to z by p_2 since it is a $\xrightarrow{\text{hb}}_{E_1}$-predecessor of events in q_2. On the other hand, it cannot include any part of the message q_1, since q_1 must now occur after q_2, and therefore it also cannot include the read of y by p_1 since its predecessor in q_1 is missing. In summary, the wakeup sequence contains two fully processed messages p_2 and q_2, the event h: p_1: d = 1 of p_1, but no events from q_1. Such a wakeup sequence must branch off after the post events of t, i.e., from the root of the tree to the right in Fig. 4. Later, this wakeup sequence is extended to a full execution E_2. In total, the program of Fig. 4 has eight inequivalent executions (the other six are not shown).

4 Computation Model

4.1 Programs

We consider programs consisting of a finite set of *threads* that interact via a finite set of *(shared) variables*. Each thread is either a *normal thread* or a *handler thread*. A normal thread has a finite set of local registers and runs a deterministic code, built in a standard way from expressions and atomic statements, using standard control flow constructs (sequential composition, selection and bounded iteration). Atomic statements read or write to shared variables and local registers, including read-modify-write operations, such as compare-and-swap. A handler thread has a *mailbox* to which all threads (also handler threads) can post messages. A mailbox has unbounded capacity, implying that the posting of a message to a mailbox can never block. A message consists of a deterministic code, built in the same way as the code of a thread. We let $\texttt{post}(p, h)$ denote the statement which posts the message p into the mailbox of handler thread h. A handler thread repeatedly extracts a message from its mailbox, executes the code of the message to completion, then extracts a next message and executes its code, and so on. Messages are extracted from the mailbox in arbitrary order. The execution of a message is interleaved with the statements of other threads.

The local state of a thread is a valuation of its local registers together with the contents of its mailbox. A global state of a program consists of a local state of each thread together with a valuation of the shared variables. The program has a unique initial state, in which mailboxes are empty.

Recall that we use *message* to denote what is called *event* in Sect. 1.

4.2 Events, Executions, Happens-Before Ordering, and Equivalence

We use $s, t, \ldots$ for threads, $p, q, \ldots$ for messages and non-handler threads, x, y, z for shared variables, and a, b, c, d for local registers. We assume, wlog, that the first event of a message does not access a shared variable, but only performs a local action, e.g., related to initialization of message execution. In order to simplify the presentation, we henceforth extend the term *message* to refer not only to a message but also to a non-handler thread.

The execution of a program statement is an *event*, which affects the global state of the program. An event is denoted by a pair $\langle p, i \rangle$, where p denotes the message containing the event and i is a positive integer, denoting that the event results from the i-th execution step in message p. An *execution sequence* E is a finite sequence of events, starting from the initial state of the program. Since thread and message codes are deterministic, an execution sequence E can be uniquely characterized by the sequence of messages (including non-handler threads) that perform execution steps in E, where we use dot(.) as concatenation operator. Thus $p.p.q$ denotes the execution sequence consisting first of two events of p, followed by an event of q.

We let *enabled*(E) denote the set of messages that can perform a next event in the state to which E leads. A sequence E is *maximal* if *enabled*$(E) = \emptyset$.

We use $u, v, w, \ldots$ to range over sequences of events. We introduce the following notation, where E is an execution sequence and w is a sequence of events.

- $\langle\rangle$ denotes the empty sequence.
- $E \vdash w$ denotes that $E.w$ is an execution sequence.
- $w \backslash p$ denotes the sequence w with its first occurrence of p (if any) removed.
- $dom(E)$ denotes the set of events $\langle p, i\rangle$ in E, that is, $\langle p, i\rangle \in dom(E)$ iff E contains at least i events of p. We also write $e \in E$ to denote $e \in dom(E)$.
- $next_{[E]}(p)$ denotes the next event to be performed by the message p after the execution E if $p \in enabled(E)$, otherwise $next_{[E]}(p)$ is undefined.
- $\widehat{e}$ denotes the message that performs e, i.e., e is of form $e = \langle \widehat{e}, i\rangle$ for some i.
- $E'E$ denotes that E' is a (not necessarily strict) prefix of E.

We say that p *starts after* E if p has been posted in E, but not yet performed any events in E. We say that p *is active after* E if p has been posted in E, but not finished its execution in E.

Definition 1 (Happens-before). *Given an execution sequence E, we define the* happens-before relation *on E, denoted $\xrightarrow{\texttt{hb}}_E$, as the smallest irreflexive partial order on $dom(E)$ such that $e \xrightarrow{\texttt{hb}}_E e'$ if e occurs before e' in E and either*

- *e and e' are performed by the same message p,*
- *e and e' access a common shared variable $\boldsymbol{x}$ and at least one writes to $\boldsymbol{x}$, or*
- *$\widehat{e'}$ is the message that is posted by e and e' is the first event of $\widehat{e'}$.* □

The hb-*trace* (or *trace* for short) of E is the directed graph $(dom(E), \xrightarrow{\texttt{hb}}_E)$.

Definition 2 (Equivalence). *Two execution sequences E and E' are* equivalent, *denoted $E \simeq E'$, if they have the same trace. We let $[E]_{\simeq}$ denote the equivalence class of E.* □

Note that for programs that do not post or process messages, $\simeq$ is the standard Mazurkiewicz trace equivalence for multi-threaded programs [1,13,14,32]. We say that two sequences of events, w and w', with $E \vdash w$ and $E \vdash w'$, are *equivalent after* E, denoted $w \simeq_{[E]} w'$ if $E.w \simeq E.w'$.

5 The Event-DPOR Algorithm

In this section, we present *Event-DPOR*, a DPOR algorithm for event-driven programs. Given a terminating program on given input, the algorithm explores different maximal executions resulting from different thread interleavings.

5.1 Central Concepts in Event-DPOR

Definition 3 (Happens-before Prefix). *Let E and E' be execution sequences. We say that E' is a* happens-before prefix *of E, denoted $E' \sqsubseteq E$, if (i) $dom(E') \subseteq dom(E)$, (ii) $\xrightarrow{\texttt{hb}}_{E'}$ is the restriction of $\xrightarrow{\texttt{hb}}_E$ to E', and (iii) whenever $e \xrightarrow{\texttt{hb}}_E e'$ for some $e' \in dom(E')$, then $e \in dom(E')$. We let $w' \sqsubseteq_{[E]} w$ denote that $E.w' \sqsubseteq E.w$.* □

Intuitively, $E' \sqsubseteq E$ denotes that the execution E' is "contained" in the execution E in such a way that it is not affected by the events in E that are not in E'.[3] To illustrate, for the top left program of Fig. 2, the execution E' consisting of t: post(p_2,h) h: p_2: y = 2 is a happens-before prefix of any maximal execution of the program, since the event of p_2 cannot happen-after any other event than the event that posts p_2, which is already in E'.

Definition 4 (Weak Initials). *Let E be an execution sequence, and w be a sequence with $E \vdash w$. The set $WI_{[E]}(w)$ of* weak initials of w after E *is the set of messages p such that $E \vdash p.w'$ for some w' with $w \sqsubseteq_{[E]} p.w'$.* □

Intuitively, p is in $WI_{[E]}(w)$ if p can execute the first event in a continuation of E which "contains" w, in the sense of $\sqsubseteq$. In Event-DPOR, the concept of weak initials is used to test whether a new sequence is redundant, i.e., is "contained in" an execution that have been explored or in a wakeup sequence that is scheduled for exploration. Note that in Definition 4, we can generally not choose w' as $w \backslash p$. This happens, e.g., if p does not occur in w but instead w contains another message p' which executes on the same handler as p and does not conflict with p; in this case w' must contain a completed execution of p inserted before p'.

Consider the program shown on the right. If we let E be the execution $s.t$ and w be the sequence p_1, we have $p_2 \in WI_{[E]}(w)$, since $w \sqsubseteq_{[E]} p_2.p_2.p_1$. This illustration shows that in order to determine whether $p \in WI_{[E]}(w)$ for a message p, one must know which shared-variable access will be performed by $next_{[E]}(p)$, and, in case p starts after E but will execute after some other message on its handler, also the sequences of shared-variable accesses that p will perform when executing to completion (Fig. 5).

s	t	h's messages
post(p_1, h)	post(p_2, h)	p_1: [x = 1]
		p_2: [y = 2; z = 2]

Fig. 5. Program illustrating weak initials.

The weak initial check problem consists in checking whether $p \in WI_{[E]}(w)$.

Theorem 1. *The weak initial check problem is NP-hard.*

The proof of the above theorem can be found in the longer version of this paper [4]. There we also propose a sequence of inexpensive rendundancy checks, which have shown to be sufficient for all our benchmarks.

Definition 5 (Races). *Let E be a maximal execution sequence. Two events e and e' in different messages are in a* race, *denoted $e \lesssim_E e'$, if $e \xrightarrow{\text{hb}}_E e'$ and*

(i) e and e' access a common shared variable and at least one is a write, and
(ii) there is no event e'' with $e \xrightarrow{\text{hb}}_E e''$ and $e'' \xrightarrow{\text{hb}}_E e'$. □

[3] The relation $w' \sqsubseteq_{[E]} w$ is also introduced in [28], as "w is a dependence-covering sequence of w'.".

Intuitively, a race arises between conflicting accesses to a shared variable, by events which are in different messages but adjacent in the $\xrightarrow{\text{hb}}_E$ order.

5.2 The Event-DPOR Algorithm

The Event-DPOR algorithm, shown as pseudocode in Algorithm 1, performs a depth-first exploration of executions using the recursive procedure $Explore(E)$, where E is the currently explored execution, which also serves as the stack of the exploration. In addition the algorithm maintains three mappings from prefixes of E, named *done*, *wut*, and *parkedWuS*. For each prefix E' of E,

- $done(E')$ is a mapping whose domain is the set of messages p for which the call $Explore(E'.p)$ has returned. If p does not start after E', then $done(E')(p)$ is the shared variable-access performed by $next_{[E']}(p)$. If p starts after E', then $done(E')(p)$ is the set of sequences of shared variable-accesses that can be performed in a completed execution of p after E'. The information in $done(E')(p)$ is collected by Algorithm 1 during the call $Explore(E'.p)$ (Lines 22 to 31).
- $wut(E')$ is a *wakeup tree*, i.e., an ordered tree $\langle B, \prec\rangle$ where B is a prefix-closed set of sequences, whose leaves are wakeup sequences. For each sequence $u \in B$, the order $\prec$ orders its children (of form $u.p$) by the order in which they were added to $wut(E')$. The order $\prec$ between children of a node is extended to a total order $\prec$ on B by letting $\prec$ be the induced post-order relation between the nodes in B (i.e., if the children $u.p_1$ and $u.p_2$ are ordered as $u.p_1 \prec u.p_2$, then $u.p_1 \prec u.p_2 \prec u$ in the induced post-order). The leaves of $wut(E')$ will subsequently be extended to maximal execution by the recursive exploration, in order of increasing $\prec$.
- $parkedWuS(E')$ is a set of wakeup sequences v that were previously being inserted into some wakeup tree $wut(E'')$ with $E'' \leq E'$, but were "parked" at the sequence E' because at that time there was not enough information to determine where in $wut(E'')$ to place v. Later, when a branch of $wut(E'')$ has been extended to a maximal execution, it should be possible to determine where to insert v.

Each call to $Explore(E)$ first initializes $done(E)$ and $parkedWuS(E)$ ($wut(E)$ was initialized before the call), and thereafter enters one of two phases: *race detection* (Lines 4 to 11) or *exploration* (Lines 13 to 31). The race detection phase is invoked when E is a maximal execution sequence. First, for each wakeup sequence v parked at a prefix E' of E it invokes $InsertParkedWuS(v, E')$ to insert v into the appropriate wakeup tree (Lines 5 to 7). Thereafter, each race (of form $e \lesssim_E e'$) in E is analyzed by $ReverseRace(E, e, e')$, which returns a set of executions that reverse the race. Each such execution $E'.v$ is returned as a pair $\langle E', v\rangle$, where v is a wakeup sequence that should be considered for insertion in the wakeup tree at E'. Each wakeup sequence v is checked for redundancy (Line 10), using the information in *done*. If v is not redundant, it is inserted into the wakeup tree at E' for future exploration (Line 11).

Algorithm 1: Event-DPOR

```
   Initial call: Explore(⟨⟩) with wut(⟨⟩) = ⟨{⟨⟩}, ∅⟩
1  Explore(E)// Returns set of sequences of shared-variable access of messages active after E
2      done(E) := ∅;
3      parkedWuS(E) := ∅;
4      if enabled(E) = ∅ then                      // When E is maximal, enter race detection
5          foreach E' ≤ E do
6              foreach v ∈ parkedWuS(E') do            // Parked wakeup sequences
7                  InsertParkedWuS(v, E');        // are inserted at the appropriate place
8          foreach e, e' such that e ≲_E e' do                     // For each race in E
9              foreach ⟨E', v⟩ ∈ ReverseRace(E, e, e') do      // For each race reversal
10                 if ¬∃E'', w, p  s.t.  E''.w = E' ∧ p ∈ dom(done(E'')) ∧ p ∈
                    WI_[E''](w.v) then                      // If v is not redundant
11                     Insert(v, E', ⟨⟩);           // insert v into the wakeup tree at E'
12     else                               // If not at a maximal execution sequence, explore.
13         if wut(E) = ⟨{⟨⟩}, ∅⟩ then            // If tree of wakeup sequences is empty ...
14             choose p ∈ enabled(E);                       // ... select an arbitrary p.
15             wut(E) := ⟨{⟨⟩, p}, {(p, ⟨⟩)}⟩;             // Adapt wakeup tree accordingly
16         foreach message q that is active after E do
17             msgAccesses(q) := ∅;   // Initialize the sequences of accesses for messages
18         while ∃q ∈ wut(E) do                      // While the wakeup tree is not empty...
19             let p = min_≺{q ∈ wut(E)};                        // ... pick next branch, ...
20             wut(E.p) := subtree(wut(E), p);           // ... extract next wakeup tree, ...
21             let tmpAccesses = Explore(E.p);            // ... and make a recursive call
22             if next_[E](p) is the last event of message p then
23                 add p to dom(tmpAccesses) with tmpAccesses(p) = {⟨⟩}
24             if next_[E](p) performs a global access then
25                 prepend next_[E](p)'s access to each sequence in tmpAccesses(p)
26             foreach message q that is active after E do
27                 msgAccesses(q) ∪= tmpAccesses(q)
28             add p to the domain of done(E);                       // Mark p as explored
29             if If p starts after E then                // If p starts a message after E, ...
30                 done(E)(p) := msgAccesses(p);    // ... store p's sequences of accesses
31             else done(E)(p) := next_[E](p)'s access;   // else, store next_[E](p)'s access
32             remove all sequences of form p.w from wut(E);             // At end, cleanup
33         return msgAccesses
```

The exploration phase (Lines 13 to 33) is entered if exploration has not reached the end of a maximal execution sequence. First, if $wut(E)$ only contains the empty sequence, then an arbitrary enabled message is entered into $wut(E)$ (Lines 14 and 15). Thereafter, each sequence in $wut(E)$ is subject to recursive exploration. We find the $\prec$-minimal child p of the root of $wut(E)$ (Line 19), and make the recursive call $Explore(E.p)$ (Line 21). Before the call, $wut(E.p)$ is initialized (Line 20) to the subtree rooted at p in $wut(E)$. During the call $Explore(E)$, information is also collected about the sequences of shared-variable accesses that can be performed by each message that is active after E, and subsequently stored in the mapping *done*. The information is collected in the variable *msgAccesses*, which is initialized at Line 17. Each recursive call $Explore(E.p)$ returns the sets of access sequences performed by messages that are active after $E.p$ (Line 21). After prepending the access performed by $next_{[E]}(p)$ to the sets of access sequences performed by p (Line 25), the sets returned by $Explore(E.p)$ are added to the corresponding sets in *msgAccesses* (Line 27). Finally, p is added to the domain of $done(E)$ (Line 28). If p starts a message after E, then $done(E)(p)$ is assigned the set of access sequences performed by p (Line 30), otherwise only the access of $next_{[E]}(p)$. Thereafter, the subtree rooted at p is removed from $wut(E)$ (Line 32). When all recursive calls of form $Explore(E.p)$ have returned, the accumulated sets of access sequences are returned (Line 33).

Event-DPOR calls functions that are briefly described in the following paragraphs. More elaborate descriptions (with pseudocode) are in the longer version of this paper [4].

$ReverseRace(E, e, e')$ is given a race $e \lesssim_E e'$ in the execution E (Line 8), and returns a set of executions that reverse the race in the sense that they perform the second event e' of the race without performing the first one, and (except for e') only contain events that are not affected by the race. More precisely, it returns a set of pairs of form $\langle E', u.e' \rangle$, such that (i) $E'.u$ is a maximal happens-before prefix of E such that $E'.u.e'$ is an execution, and (ii) $dom(E')$ is a maximal subset of $dom(E'.u)$ such that $E' \leq E$. An illustration of the *ReverseRace* function was given for the race on x in the program of Fig. 4.

$Insert(v, E', \langle\rangle)$, called at Line 11, inserts the wakeup sequence v into the wakeup tree $wut(E')$. If there is already some leaf u of $wut(E')$ such that $u \sqsubseteq_{[E']} v$ or $v \sqsubseteq_{[E']} u$, then the insertion leaves $wut(E')$ unaffected. Otherwise $Insert(v, E', \langle\rangle)$ attempts to find the $\prec$-minimal non-leaf sequence u in $wut(E')$ with $u \sqsubseteq_{[E']} v$, and insert a new leaf of form $u.v'$ into $wut(E')$, such that $v \sqsubseteq_{[E']} u.v'$, which is ordered after all existing descendants of u in $wut(E')$. The function finds such a u by descending into $wut(E')$ one event at a time; from each node u' it searches a next node $u'.p$ as the $\prec$-minimal child with $u'.p \sqsubseteq_{[E']} v$. If, during this search, a message p starts after $E'.u'$ it may happen that the wakeup tree does not contain enough subsequent events to determine whether $u'.p \sqsubseteq_{[E']} v$; in this case the sequence v is "parked" at the node $u'.p$: the insertion of v will be resumed when $E'.u'.p$ is extended to a maximal execution (at Line 7 with E' being $E'.u'$).

$InsertParkedWuS(v, E')$ inserts a wakeup sequence v, which is parked after a prefix E' of the execution E, into an appropriate wakeup tree. The function first decomposes E' as $E''.p$, and checks whether $p \in WI_{[E'']}(v)$, using information about the accesses of p that can be found in E. If the check succeeds, then insertion proceeds recursively one step further in the execution E, otherwise v conflicts with p and should be inserted into the wakeup tree after E''.

Checking for Redundancy. Tests of form $p \in WI_{[E]}(w)$ for a message p and an execution $E.w$ appear at Line 10 and in the functions *InsertWuS* and

InsertParkedWuS. If p does not start after E, then the check can be straightforwardly performed using sleep sets [14]. If p starts after E, then checking whether $p \in WI_{[E]}(w)$ is NP-hard in the general case (see Theorem 1). To avoid expensive calls to a decision procedure, Event-DPOR employs a sequence of incomplete checks, starting with simple ones, and proceeding with a next test only if the preceding was not conclusive. These tests are in order: 1) If p is the first message (if any) on its handler in w, then $p \in WI_{[E]}(w)$ is trivially true. 2) If the happens-before relation precludes p from executing first on its handler, then $p \in WI_{[E]}(w)$ is false; checking this may require w to be extended so that p (and possibly other messages) are executed to completion. 3) An attempt is made to construct an actual execution in which p is the first message on its handler, which respects the happens-before ordering. 4) If all previous tests were inconclusive, a decision procedure is invoked as a final step.

6 Correctness and Optimality

A program is defined to be *non-branching* if each message, which executes on the same handler as some other message, performs the same sequence of accesses (reads or writes) to shared variables during its execution, regardless of how its execution is interleaved with other threads and messages. Note that the non-branching restriction does not apply to non-handler threads nor to messages that are the only ones executing on their handler. For illustration, all the programs in Sect. 3, except the one in Fig. 3, are non-branching.

The following theorems state that Event-DPOR is *correct* (explores at least one execution in each equivalence class) for *all* event-driven programs and *optimal* (explores exactly one execution in each equivalence class) for non-branching programs. Proofs can be found in the longer version of this paper [4].

Theorem 2 (Correctness). *Whenever the call to Explore*($\langle\rangle$) *returns during Algorithm 1, then for all maximal execution sequences E, the algorithm has explored some execution sequence in* $[E]_{\simeq}$.

Theorem 3 (Optimality). *When applied to a non-branching program, Algorithm 1 never explores two maximal execution sequences which are equivalent.*

7 Implementation

Event-DPOR was implemented in a prototype on top of Nidhugg. Nidhugg [2] is a state-of-the-art stateless model checker for C/C++ programs with Pthreads, which works at the level of the LLVM Intermediate Representation. Nidhugg comes with a selection of DPOR algorithms. One of them is Optimal-DPOR, which we have used as a basis for Event-DPOR's implementation.

For our prototype, we have extended the data structures of Nidhugg with the information needed by Event-DPOR. For instance, nodes in wakeup trees contain new information, such as the set of parked wakeup sequences, and events in executions include the information in *tmpAccesses*, used to compute the *done* set as shown in Lines 23 to 30 of Algorithm 1. The relation $\xrightarrow{\texttt{hb}}_E$ is represented by a vector clock per event, containing the set of preceding events. When reversing races (in *ReverseRace*) and checking for redundancy (Line 10 of Algorithm 1), the relation $\xrightarrow{\texttt{hb}}_E$ is extended by a saturation operation that captures ordering constraints induced by serialized message execution.

Concerning race reversal, instead of reversing multiple races between messages executed on the same handler, our implementation detects and reverses only the race induced by the first conflict, since other races cannot be reversed, as explained using the example in Fig. 2. Moreover, in cases where *ReverseRace* would return several maximal executions that reverse a race, our implementation instead returns their union, even though it may not form an execution (e.g., since it may contain several incomplete executed messages on a handler). From this union, events will be removed adaptively during wakeup tree insertion to extract only those maximal executions that generate new leaves in a wakeup tree.

8 Evaluation

In this section, we evaluate the performance of our prototype implementation and put it into context. Since currently there is no other SMC tool for event-driven programs to compare against,[4] we have created an API, in the form of a C header file, that implements event handlers as pthread mutexes (locks) and simulates messages as threads that wait for their event handler to be free. This API allows us to use plain C/pthread programs to compare Event-DPOR with the Optimal-DPOR algorithm implemented in Nidhugg as baseline, but also with the *Lock-Aware Partial Order Reduction* (*LAPOR*) algorithm [24], implemented in GenMC. The LAPOR algorithm is often analogous to Event-DPOR w.r.t. the amount of reduction that it can achieve when event handlers are modeled as global locks. We also include in our comparison the baseline DPOR algorithm of GenMC that tracks the modification order (`-mo`) of shared variables. For Nidhugg, we used its `master` branch at the end of 2022; for GenMC, we used version 0.6.1.[5] We have run all benchmarks on a Ryzen 5950X desktop running Arch Linux and used a timeout of ten hours. All the benchmark programs we use are parametric, typically on the number of threads used (and thus messages posted); their parameters are shown inside parentheses.

We will compare implementations of different DPOR algorithms based on the number of executions that they explore, as well as the time that this takes. For some programs, LAPOR also examines a fair amount of *blocked* executions (i.e., executions that cannot be serialized and need to be aborted), which naturally affects its time performance. In Table 1, we show the number of executions

[4] All our attempts to use R4 failed miserably; the tool has not been updated since 2016.

[5] GenMC v0.6.1 (released July 2021) warns that LAPOR usage with `-mo` is experimental; in fact, LAPOR support has been dropped in more recent GenMC versions.

Table 1. Performance of different DPOR algorithm implementations.

	Executions (Traces+Blocked)				Time (secs)			
	GenMC		Nidhugg		GenMC		Nidhugg	
Benchmark	`-mo`	`-lapor`	`-optimal`	`-event`	`-mo`	`-lapor`	`-optimal`	`-event`
posters(3)	90	90	90	90	0.02	0.03	0.09	0.09
posters(4)	2520	2520	2520	2520	0.18	0.81	0.94	1.42
posters(5)	113400	113400	113400	113400	9.43	47.11	50.87	84.64
buyers(6)	720	720+2383	720	720	0.08	2.51	0.36	0.51
buyers(7)	5040	5040+20301	5040	5040	0.56	25.80	2.53	3.96
buyers(8)	40320	40320+191369	40320	40320	5.03	306.95	23.59	37.70
ping-pong(6)	3276	3276+8271	3276	3276	0.23	3.99	1.45	2.61
ping-pong(7)	27252	27252+79435	27252	27252	2.01	44.51	13.78	26.42
ping-pong(8)	253296	253296+835509	253296	253296	20.63	572.07	149.26	299.12
consensus(2)	4	4+4	4	4	0.01	0.01	0.06	0.06
consensus(3)	216	125+347	216	125	0.04	0.29	0.20	0.20
consensus(4)	331776	50625+242828	331776	50625	75.43	293.91	419.90	177.63
prolific(5)	120	30+26	120	30	0.17	5.34	0.21	0.18
prolific(7)	5040	126+120	5040	126	16.12	98.14	11.79	2.12
prolific(9)	362880	510+502	362880	510	2462.83	1132.65	1363.31	26.28
sparse-mat(4,3)	204	34	204	34	0.16	0.06	0.16	0.09
sparse-mat(4,5)	185520	1546	185520	1546	212.51	3.56	126.06	1.66
sparse-mat(4,7)	⏲	130922	⏲	130922	⏲	603.31	⏲	234.27
plb(4)	105	1	105	1	0.02	0.01	0.10	0.06
plb(6)	10395	1	10395	1	1.99	0.02	6.61	0.06
plb(8)	2027025	1	2027025	1	556.46	0.02	1808.24	0.06

explored by an entry of the form $T{+}B$, where T is the number of complete traces and B is the number of blocked executions. (We omit the B part when it is zero.)

In the first benchmark program (posters), each thread posts to a single event handler two messages containing stores to some atomic global variable, and then the value of this variable is checked by an assertion. This simple program allows us to establish the baseline speed of all implementations. We can see that GenMC `-mo` is the fastest implementation. The reason is that by default it does not perform any checks whether the explored executions are sequentially consistent, which allows it to be five times faster than LAPOR, and seven to nine times faster than Nidhugg's algorithm implementations. We can also observe that Event-DPOR incurs a small but noticeable overhead over Optimal-DPOR for the extra machinery that its implementation requires.

The next two benchmark programs were taken from a paper by Kragl et al. [27]. In buyers, n "buyer" threads coordinate the purchase of an item from a "seller" as follows: one buyer requests a quote for the item from the seller, then the buyers coordinate their individual contribution, and finally if the contributions are enough to buy the item, the order is placed. In ping-pong, the "pong" handler thread receives messages with increasing numbers from the "ping" thread, which are then acknowledged back to the "ping" event handler.

Looking at Table 1, we notice that, in both buyers and ping-pong, all algorithms explore the same number of traces, but LAPOR also explores a significant number of executions that cannot be serialized and need to be aborted. In fact, for both benchmarks, the aborted executions significantly outnumber the traces explored. This affects negatively the time that LAPOR takes, and GenMC -lapor becomes the slowest implementation. In contrast, Event-DPOR does not suffer from this problem and shows similar scalability as baseline GenMC and Optimal-DPOR.

With the four remaining benchmarks, we evaluate all implementations in programs where algorithms tailored to event-driven programming, either natively (Event-DPOR) or which are lock-aware (when handlers are implemented as locks), have an advantage. The first program (consensus), again from the paper by Kragl et al. [27], is a simple *broadcast consensus* protocol for n nodes to agree on a common value. For each node i, two threads are created: one thread executes a `broadcast` method that sends the value of node i to every other node, and the other thread is an event handler that executes a `collect` method which receives n values and stores the maximum as its decision. Since every node receives the values of all other nodes, after the protocol finishes, all nodes have decided on the same value. The next program (prolific) is synthetic: n threads send n messages with an increasing number of stores to and loads from an atomic global variable to one event handler. The sparse-mat program computes the number of non-zero elements of a sparse matrix of dimension $m \times n$, by dividing the work into n tasks sent as messages to different handlers, which compute and join their results. The last benchmark (plb) is taken from a paper by Jhala and Majumdar [21]. A fixed sequence of task requests is received by the main thread. Upon receiving a task, the main thread allocates a space in memory and posts a message with the pointer to the allocated memory that will be served by a thread in the future.

Refer again to Table 1. In consensus, all algorithms start with the same number of traces, but LAPOR and Event-DPOR need to explore fewer and fewer traces than the other two algorithms, as the number of nodes (and threads) increases. Here too, LAPOR explores a significant number of executions that need to be aborted, which hurts its time performance. On the other hand, Event-DPOR's handling of events is optimal here. The prolific program shows a case where algorithms not tailored to events (or locks) explore $(n-1)!$ traces, while LAPOR and Event-DPOR explore only $2^n - 2$ consistent executions, when running the benchmark with parameter n. It can also be noted that Event-DPOR scales *much* better than LAPOR here in terms of time, due to the extra work that LAPOR needs to perform in order to check consistency of executions (and abort some of them). The sparse-mat program shows another case where algorithms that are not tailored to events explore a large number of executions unnecessarily (⊙ denotes timeout). This program also shows that Event-DPOR beats LAPOR time-wise even when LAPOR does not explore executions that need to be aborted. Finally, plb shows a case on which Event-DPOR and LAPOR really shine. These algorithms need to explore only one trace, independently of the size of the matrices and messages exchanged, while DPOR algorithms not tailored to event-driven programs explore a number of executions which increases exponentially and fast.

We remark that, in all benchmarks, the inexpensive checks for redundancy were sufficient. Moreover, in all benchmarks, also those that are not non-branching (such as the one in Fig. 3), Event-DPOR explored the optimal number of traces. Results from an extended set of benchmarks appear in the longer version of this paper [4].

9 Concluding Remarks

In this paper, we presented a novel SMC algorithm, Event-DPOR, tailored to the characteristics of event-driven multi-threaded programs running under the SC semantics. The algorithm was proven correct and optimal for event-driven programs in which the variable accesses of events do not depend on how their execution is interleaved with other threads.

We have implemented Event-DPOR in a publicly available prototype based on the Nidhugg tool. With a wide range of event-driven programs, we have shown that Event-DPOR incurs only a moderate constant overhead over its baseline implementation (Optimal-DPOR), it is exponentially faster than existing state-of-the-art SMC algorithms in time and number of traces examined on programs where events' actions do not conflict, and does not suffer from performance degradation caused by having to examine non-serializable executions.

Event-DPOR assumes that handlers can process their events in arbitrary order. Directions for future work include to retarget Event-DPOR for event-driven programs with other policies (e.g., FIFO), and for specific event-driven execution models.

Artifact. An artifact containing the benchmarks and all the tools used in the evaluation, including the version of Nidhugg with Event-DPOR support, is available at https://doi.org/10.5281/zenodo.7929004.

Acknowledgements. This work was partially supported by the Swedish Research Council through grants #621-2017-04812 and 2019-05466, and by the Swedish Foundation for Strategic Research through project aSSIsT. We thank the anonymous reviewers for comments and suggestions which have improved the presentation.

References

1. Abdulla, P., Aronis, S., Jonsson, B., Sagonas, K.: Optimal dynamic partial order reduction. In: Symposium on Principles of Programming Languages, POPL 2014, pp. 373–384. ACM, New York (2014). https://doi.org/10.1145/2535838.2535845. http://doi.acm.org/10.1145/2535838.2535845
2. Abdulla, P.A., Aronis, S., Atig, M.F., Jonsson, B., Leonardsson, C., Sagonas, K.: Stateless model checking for TSO and PSO. In: Baier, C., Tinelli, C. (eds.) TACAS 2015. LNCS, vol. 9035, pp. 353–367. Springer, Heidelberg (2015). https://doi.org/10.1007/978-3-662-46681-0_28

3. Abdulla, P.A., Aronis, S., Jonsson, B., Sagonas, K.: Source sets: a foundation for optimal dynamic partial order reduction. J. ACM **64**(4), 25:1–25:49 (2017). https://doi.org/10.1145/3073408. http://doi.acm.org/10.1145/3073408
4. Abdulla, P.A., et al.: Tailoring stateless model checking for event-driven multi-threaded programs. arXiv CoRR (2023). https://doi.org/10.48550/arXiv.2307.15930. Extended Version with Proofs
5. Abdulla, P.A., Atig, M.F., Jonsson, B., Lång, M., Ngo, T.P., Sagonas, K.: Optimal stateless model checking for reads-from equivalence under sequential consistency. Proc. ACM Program. Lang. **3**(OOPSLA), 150:1–150:29 (2019). https://doi.org/10.1145/3360576
6. Albert, E., Arenas, P., de la Banda, M.G., Gómez-Zamalloa, M., Stuckey, P.J.: Context-sensitive dynamic partial order reduction. In: Majumdar, R., Kunčak, V. (eds.) CAV 2017. LNCS, vol. 10426, pp. 526–543. Springer, Cham (2017). https://doi.org/10.1007/978-3-319-63387-9_26
7. Aronis, S., Jonsson, B., Lång, M., Sagonas, K.: Optimal dynamic partial order reduction with observers. In: Beyer, D., Huisman, M. (eds.) TACAS 2018. LNCS, vol. 10806, pp. 229–248. Springer, Cham (2018). https://doi.org/10.1007/978-3-319-89963-3_14
8. Bielik, P., Raychev, V., Vechev, M.T.: Scalable race detection for android applications. In: Aldrich, J., Eugster, P. (eds.) Proceedings of the 2015 ACM SIGPLAN International Conference on Object-Oriented Programming, Systems, Languages, and Applications, OOPSLA 2015, pp. 332–348. ACM (2015). https://doi.org/10.1145/2814270.2814303
9. Chalupa, M., Chatterjee, K., Pavlogiannis, A., Sinha, N., Vaidya, K.: Data-centric dynamic partial order reduction. Proc. ACM Program. Lang. **2**(POPL), 31:1–31:30 (2018). https://doi.org/10.1145/3158119. http://doi.acm.org/10.1145/3158119
10. Christakis, M., Gotovos, A., Sagonas, K.: Systematic testing for detecting concurrency errors in Erlang programs. In: Sixth IEEE International Conference on Software Testing, Verification and Validation, ICST 2013, Los Alamitos, CA, USA, pp. 154–163. IEEE (2013). https://doi.org/10.1109/ICST.2013.50
11. Dabek, F., Zeldovich, N., Kaashoek, M.F., Mazières, D., Morris, R.T.: Event-driven programming for robust software. In: Muller, G., Jul, E. (eds.) Proceedings of the 10th ACM SIGOPS European Workshop, pp. 186–189. ACM (2002). https://doi.org/10.1145/1133373.1133410
12. Desai, A., Gupta, V., Jackson, E.K., Qadeer, S., Rajamani, S.K., Zufferey, D.: P: safe asynchronous event-driven programming. In: Boehm, H., Flanagan, C. (eds.) ACM SIGPLAN Conference on Programming Language Design and Implementation, PLDI 2013, pp. 321–332. ACM (2013). https://doi.org/10.1145/2491956.2462184
13. Flanagan, C., Godefroid, P.: Dynamic partial-order reduction for model checking software. In: Principles of Programming Languages, (POPL), pp. 110–121. ACM, New York (2005). https://doi.org/10.1145/1040305.1040315. http://doi.acm.org/10.1145/1040305.1040315
14. Godefroid, P.: Partial-order methods for the verification of concurrent systems: an approach to the state-explosion problem. Ph.D. thesis, University of Liège (1996). https://doi.org/10.1007/3-540-60761-7. http://www.springer.com/gp/book/9783540607618, also, volume 1032 of LNCS, Springer
15. Godefroid, P.: Model checking for programming languages using VeriSoft. In: Principles of Programming Languages, (POPL), New York, NY, USA, pp. 174–186. ACM Press (1997). https://doi.org/10.1145/263699.263717. http://doi.acm.org/10.1145/263699.263717

16. Godefroid, P.: Software model checking: the VeriSoft approach. Form. Methods Syst. Des. **26**(2), 77–101 (2005). https://doi.org/10.1007/s10703-005-1489-x
17. Godefroid, P., Hanmer, R.S., Jagadeesan, L.: Model checking without a model: an analysis of the heart-beat monitor of a telephone switch using VeriSoft. In: Proceedings of the ACM SIGSOFT International Symposium on Software Testing and Analysis, ISSTA, pp. 124–133. ACM, New York (1998). https://doi.org/10.1145/271771.271800
18. Hsiao, C., et al.: Race detection for event-driven mobile applications. In: O'Boyle, M.F.P., Pingali, K. (eds.) ACM SIGPLAN Conference on Programming Language Design and Implementation, PLDI 2014, pp. 326–336. ACM (2014). https://doi.org/10.1145/2594291.2594330
19. Hu, Y., Neamtiu, I., Alavi, A.: Automatically verifying and reproducing event-based races in android apps. In: Zeller, A., Roychoudhury, A. (eds.) Proceedings of the 25th International Symposium on Software Testing and Analysis, ISSTA 2016, pp. 377–388. ACM (2016). https://doi.org/10.1145/2931037.2931069
20. Jensen, C.S., Møller, A., Raychev, V., Dimitrov, D., Vechev, M.T.: Stateless model checking of event-driven applications. In: Proceedings of the 2015 ACM SIGPLAN International Conference on Object-Oriented Programming, Systems, Languages, and Applications, OOPSLA 2015, pp. 57–73. ACM, New York (2015). https://doi.org/10.1145/2814270.2814282
21. Jhala, R., Majumdar, R.: Interprocedural analysis of asynchronous programs. In: Hofmann, M., Felleisen, M. (eds.) Proceedings of the 34th ACM SIGPLAN-SIGACT Symposium on Principles of Programming Languages, POPL 2007, Nice, France, 17–19 January 2007, pp. 339–350. ACM (2007). https://doi.org/10.1145/1190216.1190266
22. Kokologiannakis, M., Lahav, O., Sagonas, K., Vafeiadis, V.: Effective stateless model checking for C/C++ concurrency. Proc. ACM Program. Lang. **2**(POPL), 17:1–17:32 (2018). https://doi.org/10.1145/3158105
23. Kokologiannakis, M., Marmanis, I., Gladstein, V., Vafeiadis, V.: Truly stateless, optimal dynamic partial order reduction. Proc. ACM Program. Lang. **6**(POPL), 1–28 (2022). https://doi.org/10.1145/3498711
24. Kokologiannakis, M., Raad, A., Vafeiadis, V.: Effective lock handling in stateless model checking. Proc. ACM Program. Lang. **3**(OOPSLA), 173:1–173:26 (2019). https://doi.org/10.1145/3360599
25. Kokologiannakis, M., Sagonas, K.: Stateless model checking of the Linux kernel's hierarchical read-copy-update (tree RCU). In: Proceedings of International SPIN Symposium on Model Checking of Software, SPIN 2017, pp. 172–181. ACM, New York (2017). https://doi.org/10.1145/3092282.3092287
26. Kokologiannakis, M., Vafeiadis, V.: GenMC: a model checker for weak memory models. In: Silva, A., Leino, K.R.M. (eds.) CAV 2021. LNCS, vol. 12759, pp. 427–440. Springer, Cham (2021). https://doi.org/10.1007/978-3-030-81685-8_20
27. Kragl, B., Enea, C., Henzinger, T.A., Mutluergil, S.O., Qadeer, S.: Inductive sequentialization of asynchronous programs. In: Donaldson, A.F., Torlak, E. (eds.) Proceedings of the 41st ACM SIGPLAN International Conference on Programming Language Design and Implementation, PLDI 2020, pp. 227–242. ACM (2020). https://doi.org/10.1145/3385412.3385980
28. Maiya, P., Gupta, R., Kanade, A., Majumdar, R.: Partial order reduction for event-driven multi-threaded programs. In: Chechik, M., Raskin, J.-F. (eds.) TACAS 2016. LNCS, vol. 9636, pp. 680–697. Springer, Heidelberg (2016). https://doi.org/10.1007/978-3-662-49674-9_44

29. Maiya, P., Kanade, A.: Efficient computation of happens-before relation for event-driven programs. In: Bultan, T., Sen, K. (eds.) Proceedings of the 26th International Symposium on Software Testing and Analysis, ISSTA 2017, pp. 102–112. ACM, New York (2017). https://doi.org/10.1145/3092703.3092733
30. Maiya, P., Kanade, A., Majumdar, R.: Race detection for android applications. In: O'Boyle, M.F.P., Pingali, K. (eds.) ACM SIGPLAN Conference on Programming Language Design and Implementation, PLDI 2014, Edinburgh, United Kingdom, 09–11 June 2014, pp. 316–325. ACM (2014). https://doi.org/10.1145/2594291.2594311
31. Mazières, D.: A toolkit for user-level file systems. In: Park, Y. (ed.) Proceedings of the General Track: 2001 USENIX Annual Technical Conference, pp. 261–274. USENIX (2001). http://www.usenix.org/publications/library/proceedings/usenix01/mazieres.html
32. Mazurkiewicz, A.: Trace theory. In: Brauer, W., Reisig, W., Rozenberg, G. (eds.) ACPN 1986. LNCS, vol. 255, pp. 278–324. Springer, Heidelberg (1987). https://doi.org/10.1007/3-540-17906-2_30
33. Mednieks, Z., Dornin, L., Meike, G.B., Nakamura, M.: Programming Android. O'Reilly Media, Inc. (2012)
34. Musuvathi, M., Qadeer, S., Ball, T., Basler, G., Nainar, P.A., Neamtiu, I.: Finding and reproducing heisenbugs in concurrent programs. In: Proceedings of the 8th USENIX Symposium on Operating Systems Design and Implementation, OSDI 2008, pp. 267–280. USENIX Association, Berkeley (2008). https://dl.acm.org/citation.cfm?id=1855741.1855760
35. Norris, B., Demsky, B.: A practical approach for model checking C/C++11 code. ACM Trans. Program. Lang. Syst. **38**(3), 10:1–10:51 (2016). https://doi.org/10.1145/2806886. http://doi.acm.org/10.1145/2806886
36. Petrov, B., Vechev, M.T., Sridharan, M., Dolby, J.: Race detection for web applications. In: Vitek, J., Lin, H., Tip, F. (eds.) ACM SIGPLAN Conference on Programming Language Design and Implementation, PLDI 2012, Beijing, China, 11–16 June 2012, pp. 251–262. ACM (2012). https://doi.org/10.1145/2254064.2254095
37. Raychev, V., Vechev, M.T., Sridharan, M.: Effective race detection for event-driven programs. In: Hosking, A.L., Eugster, P.T., Lopes, C.V. (eds.) Proceedings of the 2013 ACM SIGPLAN International Conference on Object Oriented Programming Systems Languages & Applications, OOPSLA 2013, part of SPLASH 2013, Indianapolis, IN, USA, 26–31 October 2013, pp. 151–166. ACM (2013). https://doi.org/10.1145/2509136.2509538
38. Santhiar, A., Kaleeswaran, S., Kanade, A.: Efficient race detection in the presence of programmatic event loops. In: Zeller, A., Roychoudhury, A. (eds.) Proceedings of the 25th International Symposium on Software Testing and Analysis, ISSTA 2016, Saarbrücken, Germany, 18–20 July 2016, pp. 366–376. ACM (2016). https://doi.org/10.1145/2931037.2931068
39. Trimananda, R., Luo, W., Demsky, B., Xu, G.H.: Stateful dynamic partial order reduction for model checking event-driven applications that do not terminate. In: Finkbeiner, B., Wies, T. (eds.) VMCAI 2022. LNCS, vol. 13182, pp. 400–424. Springer, Cham (2022). https://doi.org/10.1007/978-3-030-94583-1_20
40. Yang, Yu., Chen, X., Gopalakrishnan, G., Kirby, R.M.: Efficient stateful dynamic partial order reduction. In: Havelund, K., Majumdar, R., Palsberg, J. (eds.) SPIN 2008. LNCS, vol. 5156, pp. 288–305. Springer, Heidelberg (2008). https://doi.org/10.1007/978-3-540-85114-1_20

41. Yi, X., Wang, J., Yang, X.: Stateful dynamic partial-order reduction. In: Liu, Z., He, J. (eds.) ICFEM 2006. LNCS, vol. 4260, pp. 149–167. Springer, Heidelberg (2006). https://doi.org/10.1007/11901433_9
42. Zhang, N., Kusano, M., Wang, C.: Dynamic partial order reduction for relaxed memory models. In: Programming Language Design and Implementation (PLDI), pp. 250–259. ACM, New York (2015). https://doi.org/10.1145/2737924.2737956. http://doi.acm.org/10.1145/2737924.2737956

Fast Equivalence Checking of Quantum Circuits of Clifford Gates

Dimitrios Thanos(✉), Tim Coopmans(✉), and Alfons Laarman(✉)

Leiden Institute of Advanced Computer Science (LIACS), Leiden University, 2333 CA Leiden, The Netherlands
{d.thanos,t.j.coopmans,a.w.laarman}@liacs.leidenuniv.nl

Abstract. Checking whether two quantum circuits are equivalent is important for the design and optimization of quantum-computer applications with real-world devices. We consider quantum circuits consisting of Clifford gates, a practically-relevant subset of all quantum operations which is large enough to exhibit quantum features such as entanglement and forms the basis of, for example, quantum-error correction and many quantum-network applications. We present a deterministic algorithm that is based on a folklore mathematical result and demonstrate that it is capable of outperforming previously considered state-of-the-art method. In particular, given two Clifford circuits as sequences of single- and two-qubit Clifford gates, the algorithm checks their equivalence in $O(n \cdot m)$ time in the number of qubits n and number of elementary Clifford gates m. Using the performant Stim simulator as backend, our implementation checks equivalence of quantum circuits with 1000 qubits (and a circuit depth of 10.000 gates) in ∼22 s and circuits with 100.000 qubits (depth 10) in ∼15 min, outperforming the existing SAT-based and path-integral based approaches by orders of magnitude. This approach shows that the correctness of application-relevant subsets of quantum operations can be verified up to large circuits in practice.

1 Introduction

Quantum computing promises to perform classically intractable tasks for a wide range of applications [38,40]. While we are entering the era of Noisy Intermediate-Scale Quantum computing [43], the high noise levels necessitate precise compilation of textbook quantum circuits onto real-world devices, which can only handle shallow-depth circuits and have various constraints (connectivity, topology, native gate sets, etc.) [20,23]. A crucial part of the design and optimization over quantum circuits is *verifying* whether two quantum circuits, each presented by a classical description, implement the same quantum operation, i.e. checking equivalence of quantum circuits.

Correctness verification is a well-studied field in the classical domain [26,34, 35] but unfortunately not all methods directly carry over to quantum computing because the state of n quantum bits is generally represented as 2^n complex values [40]. Due to the reversibility of quantum circuits, verifying equivalence of circuits C_1, C_2 is reducible to checking if the circuit $C_1 \cdot C_2^{-1}$, i.e., C_1 followed by the

É. André and J. Sun (Eds.): ATVA 2023, LNCS 14216, pp. 199–216, 2023.
https://doi.org/10.1007/978-3-031-45332-8_10

inverse of C_2, is equivalent to the identity circuit, i.e., a circuit that implements an operator that does not modify the inputs. Exact and approximate identity checking, i.e., determining whether the circuit is close to the identity circuit, fall in quantum complexity classes which are analogs of NP [2,11] (NQP [44] and QMA [31,32], respectively). Thus we should not hope for efficient algorithms in general.

Existing deterministic methods analyzing circuits consisting of only quantum gates as quantum operations (no quantum measurements) are based on encoding as Boolean satisfiability instances [10] (also [52,53] for restricted circuits), satisfiability modulo theories [9], path-sums [4,5], rewrite rules [22,42,51], and on various flavors of decision diagrams, including QMDD [17,18,41,46], LIMDD [47,48], Tensor-DD [30], BDD [19,50] and others [49,54]. In addition, some probabilistic methods are known [16,36].

In this paper, we focus on exact equivalence checking of two (classical descriptions of) circuits with Clifford gates only, a subset of all quantum gates which is ubiquitous to quantum computing and is highly relevant for quantum error correction [27,45] and quantum networking applications [29]. For exact identity checking of Clifford circuits, a reduction to satisfiability was presented by [10], in a tool called QuSAT, and an approach based on path-sums in the Feynman tool [4]. For approximate identity check, a polynomial-time algorithm exists [7] whose runtime scales with the accuracy of the approximation (a polynomial in the number of qubits).

We demonstrate that a folklore characterization of equivalence of general circuits translates into an $O(m \cdot n)$-time deterministic algorithm for exact equivalence checking of Clifford circuits, with n the number of qubits and m the total number of elementary Clifford gates in the two circuits. The algorithm (many-one) reduces the equivalence check to circuit simulation which can be done efficiently [1,28], in the particular case of equivalence checking of Clifford circuits.

We empirically evaluate the algorithm by using the performant Clifford-circuit simulator Stim [25], reaching circuit depths of 1000 qubits and 10.000 elementary Clifford gates in less than a minute, and 100.000 qubits for depth-10 circuits in approximately 15 min, outperforming the state-of-the-art SAT-based and path-sum approaches by orders of magnitude. Our open-source implementation can be found on [21].

We emphasize that the task in this work is equivalence checking given a white-box *classical* descriptions of the quantum circuit, as opposed to the different task where one is given access to a *quantum* computer which performs the quantum circuit as black box [39]. For Clifford circuits, specifically see [12] and [36].

In Sect. 2, we provide the necessary background to quantum computing and a simple example of applying the algorithm for comparing two equivalent circuits. We state the theorem explicitly and give the resulting algorithm in Sect. 3. In Sect. 4, we empirically evaluate our implementation, using the Stim simulator as a backend. We conclude in Sect. 5.

2 Preliminaries

We briefly introduce relevant quantum computing concepts and refer to [40] for a more elaborate introduction.

2.1 Quantum Circuits and Fundamental Concepts

Classical circuits are limited to bits, which take values 0 and 1. In contrast, the state of a quantum bit or qubit can be expressed as a complex-valued 2-vector of unit norm. Examples of single-qubit states are $\begin{bmatrix}\frac{1}{\sqrt{2}}\\ \frac{1}{\sqrt{2}}\end{bmatrix}$ and $\begin{bmatrix}\frac{1}{\sqrt{5}}\\ \frac{2i}{\sqrt{5}}\end{bmatrix}$ where i is the imaginary unit ($i^2 = -1$). Two possible quantum states are the computational-basis states $\begin{bmatrix}1\\0\end{bmatrix}$ and $\begin{bmatrix}0\\1\end{bmatrix}$, usually denoted in Dirac notation as $|0\rangle$ and $|1\rangle$. Thus, we can rewrite the two examples from before as $\frac{1}{\sqrt{2}}(|0\rangle + |1\rangle) = \begin{bmatrix}\frac{1}{\sqrt{2}}\\ \frac{1}{\sqrt{2}}\end{bmatrix}$ and $\frac{1}{\sqrt{5}}(|0\rangle + 2i\,|1\rangle) = \begin{bmatrix}\frac{1}{\sqrt{5}}\\ \frac{2i}{\sqrt{5}}\end{bmatrix}$. More generally, we can write an arbitrary single-qubit state $|\phi\rangle = \begin{bmatrix}\alpha_0\\ \alpha_1\end{bmatrix} = \alpha_0\,|0\rangle + \alpha_1\,|1\rangle$ where the complex numbers α_i satisfy $|\alpha_0|^2 + |\alpha_1|^2 = 1$. Here, $|z|$ denotes the modulus of the complex number z: when writing $z = a + b \cdot i$ for real numbers a, b, the modulus equals $|z| = \sqrt{a^2 + b^2}$ and can also be defined through the complex conjugate $z^* = a - b \cdot i$ as $|z| = \sqrt{z \cdot z^*}$.

Two single-qubit quantum states $|\phi\rangle, |\psi\rangle$ are combined into a two-qubit state $|\phi\rangle \otimes |\psi\rangle$, where $\otimes$ denotes the tensor product (Kronecker product) from linear algebra. In general, an n-qubit state is a complex vector of 2^n entries and can be written in Dirac notation as $\sum_{x\in\{0,1\}^n} \alpha_x\,|x\rangle$, where $|x\rangle$ are defined as e.g. $|0010\rangle = |0\rangle \otimes |0\rangle \otimes |1\rangle \otimes |0\rangle$. Here, the complex values α_x should satisfy $\sum_{x\in\{0,1\}^n} |\alpha_x|^2 = 1$, i.e. the norm of the vector representing the quantum state equals 1. Examples of two-qubit states are $|00\rangle$ and $\frac{1}{\sqrt{6}}(|00\rangle + i\,|01\rangle - 2\,|11\rangle)$. Any $(n_A + n_B)$-qubit quantum state $|\phi\rangle$ that cannot be written as a product state $|\phi_A\rangle \otimes |\phi_B\rangle$, with $|\phi_A\rangle$ ($|\phi_B\rangle$) a state of n_A (n_B) qubits, is called entangled, e.g. $\frac{1}{\sqrt{2}}(|00\rangle + |11\rangle)$.

There are two main operations on quantum states in the usual circuit model: quantum gates and quantum measurements. We will only use gates here. A quantum gate on n qubits is a unitary operator that is represented by a 2^n by 2^n unitary matrix U. (Unitarity, defined below, ensures that the operator is reversible and norm-preserving.) A quantum state $|\phi\rangle$ is updated by a unitary matrix as $U \cdot |\phi\rangle$ where $\cdot$ denotes matrix-vector multiplication. As example, consider the following single-qubit gates:

$$\text{Hadamard: } H = \frac{1}{\sqrt{2}}\begin{bmatrix}1 & 1\\ 1 & -1\end{bmatrix} \qquad \text{Phase gate: } S = \begin{bmatrix}1 & 0\\ 0 & i\end{bmatrix}.$$

Applying the Hadamard gate to the state $|0\rangle$ for example, we obtain

$$H \cdot |0\rangle = \frac{1}{\sqrt{2}} \begin{bmatrix} 1 & 1 \\ 1 & -1 \end{bmatrix} \cdot \begin{bmatrix} 1 \\ 0 \end{bmatrix} = \frac{1}{\sqrt{2}} \begin{bmatrix} 1 \\ 1 \end{bmatrix} = \frac{|0\rangle + |1\rangle}{\sqrt{2}}$$

and similarly one can compute $S\,|1\rangle = i\,|1\rangle$.

A quantum gate U is a unitary matrix, which means $U \cdot U^\dagger = U^\dagger \cdot U = \mathbb{1}_{2^n}$, where $\mathbb{1}_{2^n}$ is the identity matrix on vectors of 2^n entries (i.e. the matrix that has the property $\mathbb{1}_{2^n} \cdot \boldsymbol{v} = \boldsymbol{v}$ for each vector $\boldsymbol{v}$ of 2^n complex numbers) and the adjoint operator $(.)^\dagger$ means transposing the matrix and replacing each matrix entry by its complex conjugate. For example, the Hadamard gate and phase gate have adjoint operators

$$H^\dagger = \frac{1}{\sqrt{2}} \begin{bmatrix} 1 & 1 \\ 1 & -1 \end{bmatrix} = H \qquad S^\dagger = \begin{bmatrix} 1 & 0 \\ 0 & -i \end{bmatrix}.$$

It is not hard to check that indeed $H^\dagger \cdot H = S^\dagger \cdot S = \mathbb{1}_2 = \begin{bmatrix} 1 & 0 \\ 0 & 1 \end{bmatrix}$. Applying an n-qubit gate A to the first part of an $(n+m)$-qubit quantum state $|\phi\rangle$ is done by tensoring with the identity, i.e. $A \otimes \mathbb{1}_{2^m}$ is applied to the entire state $|\phi\rangle$.

Another notion which we will use later is the bra $\langle\phi| = (|\phi\rangle)^\dagger$ and the inner product $\langle\phi| \cdot |\psi\rangle = \langle\phi|\psi\rangle = \sum_{x\in\{0,1\}^n} a_x^* \cdot b_x$ for $|\phi\rangle = \sum_{x\in\{0,1\}^n} a_x\,|x\rangle$ and $|\psi\rangle = \sum_{x\in\{0,1\}^n} b_x\,|x\rangle$. Observe that state normalization implies that $\langle\phi|\phi\rangle = 1$.

A quantum circuit is composed of qubits represented by horizontal lines (wires) and quantum gates represented by boxes, with each gate acting on one or more qubits. The input state is represented to the left of the wires of the circuit (typically $|0\rangle^{\otimes n}$), and the output state is obtained after the sequential application of the circuit's gates. These gates, which are typically unitary operators of small size, can be combined with matrix multiplication into a single unitary operator describing the entire circuit as a single operator. See Example 1 for an explicit calculation of a quantum circuit's output state. A quantum algorithm is a uniform family of quantum circuits (like in circuit complexity [6]).

A special but important class of quantum circuits are the Clifford circuits. Any Clifford gate can be written as a Clifford circuit[1] consisting only of three elementary Clifford gates: H, S and $CNOT$. The controlled not ($CNOT$) gate acts on two qubits: The first is called the "control" and the second one the "target" qubit. It is symbolized by a vertical line connecting the two qubits, with a dot representing the control qubit and $\oplus$ representing the target (see Example 1). The $CNOT$ gate and its inverted counterpart $NOTC$ (see circuit B in Example 1) are defined as the following two-qubit operators:

$$CNOT = \begin{bmatrix} 1&0&0&0 \\ 0&1&0&0 \\ 0&0&0&1 \\ 0&0&1&0 \end{bmatrix}, \qquad NOTC = \begin{bmatrix} 1&0&0&0 \\ 0&0&0&1 \\ 0&0&1&0 \\ 0&1&0&0 \end{bmatrix}.$$

[1] When we say 'circuit', we mean the sequence of quantum gates, i.e. without the input state, e.g., $|0\rangle^{\otimes n}$.

One of the significant features of Clifford circuits is that they can be simulated in polynomial time in the number of qubits and number of elementary Clifford gates by classical computers, as shown by the Gottesman-Knill theorem [28] (see also Sect. 2.2). In addition, with the usual input $|0\rangle^{\otimes n}$, Clifford circuits can generate various entangled states, and become universal—meaning they can approximate any quantum circuit—if non-Clifford gates are added to the gate set [14].

Example 1. *We provide an example for calculating the output states of the two circuits A and B below. This example uses Hadamard gates and CNOT gates.*

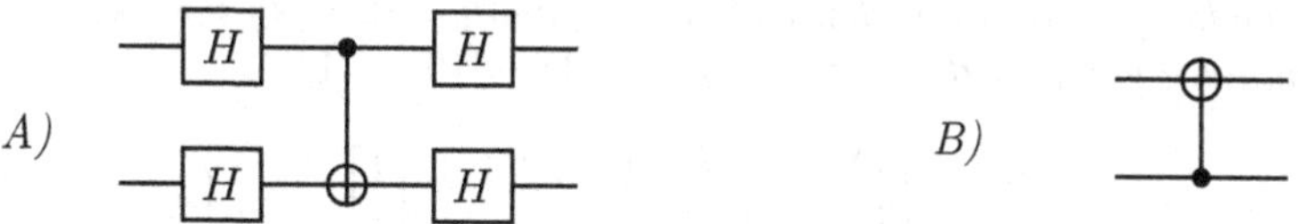

In this example, we assume here that the initial state on each qubit is $|0\rangle$.

A) We start by making the calculations for circuit A. For a Hadamard gate applied on the first qubit we get:

$$H|0\rangle = \frac{1}{\sqrt{2}}\begin{bmatrix}1 & 1\\1 & -1\end{bmatrix}\begin{bmatrix}1\\0\end{bmatrix} = \frac{1}{\sqrt{2}}\begin{bmatrix}1\cdot 1 + 1\cdot 0\\1\cdot 1 + (-1)\cdot 0\end{bmatrix} = \frac{1}{\sqrt{2}}\begin{bmatrix}1\\1\end{bmatrix} = \frac{1}{\sqrt{2}}(|0\rangle + |1\rangle)$$

The result of applying a Hadamard gate on the second qubit will be the same. Since the two qubits are independent we can calculate the state of this system by tensoring the two states:

$$\begin{aligned}
&\left(\frac{1}{\sqrt{2}}(|0\rangle + |1\rangle)\right) \otimes \left(\frac{1}{\sqrt{2}}(|0\rangle + |1\rangle)\right)\\
&= \frac{1}{\sqrt{2}}\frac{1}{\sqrt{2}}(|0\rangle + |1\rangle) \otimes (|0\rangle + |1\rangle)\\
&= \frac{1}{2}(|0\rangle \otimes |0\rangle + |0\rangle \otimes |1\rangle + |1\rangle \otimes |0\rangle + |1\rangle \otimes |1\rangle).\\
&= \frac{1}{2}(|00\rangle + |01\rangle + |10\rangle + |11\rangle).
\end{aligned}$$

In matrix notation this would be:

$$\frac{1}{2}\begin{bmatrix}1\\0\\0\\0\end{bmatrix} + \frac{1}{2}\begin{bmatrix}0\\1\\0\\0\end{bmatrix} + \frac{1}{2}\begin{bmatrix}0\\0\\1\\0\end{bmatrix} + \frac{1}{2}\begin{bmatrix}0\\0\\0\\1\end{bmatrix} = \frac{1}{2}\begin{bmatrix}1\\1\\1\\1\end{bmatrix}.$$

Now we will calculate how this state is transformed when we apply a CNOT gate where the first qubit is the control qubit and the second one is the target qubit:

$$CNOT \cdot \frac{1}{2}\begin{bmatrix}1\\1\\1\\1\end{bmatrix} = \begin{bmatrix}1\,0\,0\,0\\0\,1\,0\,0\\0\,0\,0\,1\\0\,0\,1\,0\end{bmatrix} \cdot \frac{1}{2}\begin{bmatrix}1\\1\\1\\1\end{bmatrix} = \frac{1}{2}\begin{bmatrix}1\\1\\1\\1\end{bmatrix}$$

So the state remains the same. The CNOT is interpreted as follows: whenever $b_1 = 1$ *flip the second input of* $|b_1 b_2\rangle$. *So we can directly calculate* $\frac{1}{2}(|00\rangle + |01\rangle + |10\rangle + |11\rangle)$ *which becomes* $\frac{1}{2}(|00\rangle + |01\rangle + |11\rangle + |10\rangle)$ *without explicitly performing the matrix multiplication. We observe that, as expected, this method returns an identical state. Finally, we apply the two remaining Hadamard gates to the state* $\frac{1}{2}(|00\rangle + |01\rangle + |10\rangle + |11\rangle)$.

$$(H \otimes H)\left(\frac{1}{2}\begin{bmatrix}1\\1\\1\\1\end{bmatrix}\right) = \frac{1}{4}\begin{bmatrix}1 & 1 & 1 & 1\\1 & -1 & 1 & -1\\1 & 1 & -1 & -1\\1 & -1 & -1 & 1\end{bmatrix}\begin{bmatrix}1\\1\\1\\1\end{bmatrix} = \begin{bmatrix}1\\0\\0\\0\end{bmatrix} = |00\rangle$$

Therefore, applying Hadamard gates to each qubit of the circuit starting with the initial state $\frac{1}{2}(|00\rangle + |01\rangle + |10\rangle + |11\rangle)$ *results to the state* $|00\rangle$.

B) Now for the much simpler circuit B, we start again by both qubits in the state $|0\rangle$. *Following the same rules that we applied for the CNOT of circuit B, the resulting state will also be* $|00\rangle$.

Note that in the examples above, we have applied the gates in steps. Generally, this in not necessary, as one can combine the small unitary transformations (the gates) into a single unitary transformation. This, typically large, unitary operator will have the same effect as applying the gates in steps. For instance, for circuit A, we obtain the following operator U_A, *which is equal to the* U_B *unitary (NOTC) for circuit B:*

$$U_A = (H \otimes H) \cdot CNOT \cdot (H \otimes H) = \begin{bmatrix}1\,0\,0\,0\\0\,0\,0\,1\\0\,0\,1\,0\\0\,1\,0\,0\end{bmatrix} = NOTC = U_B.$$

2.2 Stabilizer States

The Pauli gates are defined as follows:

$$I = \mathbb{1}_2 = \begin{bmatrix}1\,0\\0\,1\end{bmatrix}, \quad X = \begin{bmatrix}0\,1\\1\,0\end{bmatrix}, \quad Y = \begin{bmatrix}0 & -i\\i & 0\end{bmatrix}, \quad Z = \begin{bmatrix}1 & 0\\0 & -1\end{bmatrix}.$$

The n-qubit Pauli group $\mathcal{P}_n$ is the set $\{\alpha P \mid \alpha \in \{\pm 1, \pm i\}, P \in \textsc{Pauli}_n\}$ where $\textsc{Pauli}_n$ is the tensor product of n Pauli operators (a "Pauli string"). For example, we have $X \otimes Z \otimes Y \otimes Y \in \textsc{Pauli}_4$ and $-iX \otimes Z \otimes Y \otimes Y \in \mathcal{P}_4$. The Pauli group forms a group under matrix multiplication. Any two elements $P_k, P_l \in \mathcal{P}_n$ either commute or anti-commute: either $P_k \cdot P_l = P_l \cdot P_k$ or $P_k \cdot P_l = -P_l \cdot P_k$. Finally, we can give an alternative, equivalent definition of the Clifford group in terms of Pauli matrices: the Clifford group is the set of unitary operators that leave the Pauli group fixed when acting on it by conjugation, i.e. all the $2^n \times 2^n$ unitary matrices V such that $VPV^\dagger \in \mathcal{P}_n$ for all $P \in \mathcal{P}_n$.

We will now lay out the stabilizer formalism for efficient classical simulation of Clifford circuits [1,28]. A unitary operator U *stabilizes* a quantum state if $U|\phi\rangle = |\phi\rangle$. The so-called stabilizer states form a strict subset of all quantum states which can be described as stabilized by maximal commutative subgroups of the Pauli group using n elements of $\mathcal{P}_n$. For example, the state $|0\rangle$ is stabilized by the group $\{I, Z\}$ because $I|0\rangle = |0\rangle$ and $Z|0\rangle = |0\rangle$. Another example is the state $|+\rangle = \frac{1}{\sqrt{2}}(|0\rangle + |1\rangle)$, which is stabilized by $\{I, X\}$. If $|\phi\rangle$ and $|\psi\rangle$ are stabilizer states with stabilizer groups G, H, respectively, then $|\phi\rangle \otimes |\psi\rangle$ is also a stabilizer state with stabilizer group $\{g \otimes h \mid g \in G, h \in H\}$. For example, the state $|11\rangle = |1\rangle \otimes |1\rangle$ is stabilized by the group $\{I \otimes I, -I \otimes Z, -Z \otimes I, Z \otimes Z\}$. Some stabilizer states are entangled, such as $\frac{1}{\sqrt{2}}(|00\rangle + |11\rangle)$, which is stabilized by $\{I \otimes I, X \otimes X, -Y \otimes Y, Z \otimes Z\}$.

Maximal commutative subgroups of the Pauli group only have a single quantum state they stabilize [40]; thus, we can *represent* any stabilizer state by its stabilizer group, instead of by providing its description as a vector of 2^n complex numbers. The stabilizer group of an n-qubit stabilizer state has 2^n elements, so storing all of those would not yield a succinct description of the state. However, the stabilizer group can be succinctly represented by the generator set of the stabilizer group, which only has n elements $\in \mathcal{P}_n$. For example, the set $E = \{-Z \otimes I, -I \otimes Z\}$ is a set of generators for the stabilizer group $G = \{I \otimes I, -I \otimes Z, -Z \otimes I, Z \otimes Z\}$ of the state $|11\rangle$ because each element of G can be written as a product of elements of E. Since there are four Pauli gates, we can represent Pauli gate using $\log_2(4) = 2$ bits. Furthermore, one can show that each element of a stabilizer group is of the form $\pm P_1 \otimes \cdots \otimes P_n$ with P_j a Pauli gate; thus, $2n+1$ bits are needed to represent an element of an n-qubit stabilizer group [1,24] ($2n$ for the Pauli gates in the Pauli string and the 1 bit for the prefactor $\pm$). Therefore, by this method, only $n \cdot (2n+1) = 2n^2 + n$ bits are required for the description of a quantum state that can be generated by Clifford circuits while a naive description would require 2^n complex numbers. To emphasize the quadratic structure of the generator set, we will write the generators in the so-called *tableau form*, e.g. for the stabilizer generators of $|11\rangle$:

$$E = \begin{Bmatrix} -Z \otimes I \\ -I \otimes Z \end{Bmatrix} \cong \begin{Bmatrix} Z \otimes Z \\ -I \otimes Z \end{Bmatrix}$$

Here, the tableau after the "$\cong$" symbol, consists of a different set of generators for the same stabilizer group, i.e. representing the same stabilizer state. Such alternate generators can be obtained by swapping and multiplying tableau rows (elements from the stabilizer generator), in a process similar to Gaussian elimination [8].

Updating the generators of a stabilizer state after an elementary Clifford gate is applied to the corresponding stabilizer state can be done in time $O(n)$, as

Table 1. Lookup table for the action of conjugating Pauli gates by Clifford gates. The subscripts "c" and "t" stand for "control" and "target".

Gate	Input	Output	Gate	Input	Output
H	X	Z	CNOT	I_cX_t	I_cX_t
	Y	$-Y$		X_cI_t	X_cX_t
	Z	X		I_cY_t	Z_cY_t
S	X	Y		Y_cI_t	Y_cX_t
	Y	$-X$		I_cZ_t	Z_cZ_t
	Z	Z		Z_cI_t	Z_cI_t

follows. Suppose that $P = \pm P_1 \otimes \cdots \otimes P_n$ stabilizes an n-qubit state $|\phi\rangle$. Then given an n-qubit gate U, $UPU^\dagger$ stabilizes $U|\phi\rangle$. This is because $UPU^\dagger U|\phi\rangle = UP|\phi\rangle = U|\phi\rangle$, because $U^\dagger U = \mathbb{1}_{2^n}$ (as U is unitary). Now if U is a single-qubit operation, we can write $U_j = I \otimes I \otimes \cdots \otimes I \otimes U \otimes I \otimes \cdots \otimes I$ with U at the j-th position in the tensor product. Therefore, the application of U to the j-th qubit of $|\phi\rangle$ updates each element of the stabilizer group to $U_jPU_j^\dagger = \pm IP_1I \otimes \cdots \otimes UP_jU^\dagger \otimes \cdots \otimes IP_nI = \pm P_1 \otimes \cdots \otimes UP_jU^\dagger \otimes \cdots \otimes P_n$. Since Clifford gates map elements of the Pauli group to elements of the Pauli group, $UP_jU^\dagger$ is of the form αP for P a Pauli gate and some $\alpha \in \{\pm 1\}$.[2] Thus, only the $\pm$ factor in front and j-th entry in the tensor product of P should be updated. This can be done in constant time by a lookup table for each of H, S and each Pauli gate (see Table 1). Computing the state after applying H or S takes $O(n)$ time in the tableau representation, since we only need to update the n generators of its stabilizer group (a column in the tableau and possibly the column with $\pm$ factors). A similar procedure works for the two-qubit gate CNOT, also requiring $O(n)$ time to update the stabilizer generators, in this case by modifying two columns of the table and the $\pm$ factors.

Example 2. *To illustrate the use of the tableau form, we will update the generators $\{Z_1, Z_2\}$ of the $|00\rangle$ state, according to the gates in circuit A of Example 1. The "$\rightarrow$" symbol will indicate applying one or more gates to the tableau.*

$$\{Z_1, Z_2\} = \begin{Bmatrix} Z \otimes I \\ I \otimes Z \end{Bmatrix} \xrightarrow{H_1, H_2} \begin{Bmatrix} HZH^\dagger \otimes HIH^\dagger \\ HIH^\dagger \otimes HZH^\dagger \end{Bmatrix} = \begin{Bmatrix} X \otimes I \\ I \otimes X \end{Bmatrix}$$

$$\xrightarrow{CNOT} \begin{Bmatrix} CNOT\ (X \otimes I)\ CNOT^\dagger \\ CNOT\ (I \otimes X)\ CNOT^\dagger \end{Bmatrix} = \begin{Bmatrix} X \otimes X \\ I \otimes X \end{Bmatrix}$$

$$\xrightarrow{H_1, H_2} \begin{Bmatrix} HXH^\dagger \otimes HXH^\dagger \\ HIH^\dagger \otimes HXH^\dagger \end{Bmatrix} = \begin{Bmatrix} Z \otimes Z \\ I \otimes Z \end{Bmatrix}$$

[2] α cannot be $\pm i$ because $|\alpha|^2 = 1$, which follows from $|\alpha|^2 I = (\alpha P) \cdot (\alpha P)^\dagger = (UP_jU^\dagger)(UP_jU^\dagger)^\dagger = UP_jU^\dagger UP_j^\dagger U^\dagger = UP_jP_j^\dagger U^\dagger = UIU^\dagger = I$.

2.3 Circuit Equivalence-Check Problem

We proceed to formally state the main problem. We are presented with two n-qubit Clifford quantum circuits U and V, each represented by (a classical description of) a circuit of only elementary Clifford gates (e.g., H, S and CNOT). The aim of the method is to determine whether or not U and V are equivalent.

Definition 1. *Fix the number of qubits $n \geq 1$. Given two n-qubit unitaries U, V, we say that U is* equivalent *to V, denoted $U \simeq V$, if $U = cV$ for some complex number c.*

The factor c is often called 'global phase' and is irrelevant to any observable properties of the two unitaries (for details, see [40]). We remark that if $U = cV$, then c satisfies $|c|^2 = 1$. This follows from the fact that U and V are unitaries: $\mathbb{1} = UU^\dagger = (cV) \cdot (cV)^\dagger = cV \cdot c^* V^\dagger = |c|^2 \cdot VV^\dagger = |c|^2 \cdot \mathbb{1}$, hence $|c|^2 = 1$.

3 Reducing Circuit Equivalence to Classical Simulation

We explicitly formulate the folkore result (e.g. the two-qubit case is mentioned in [40, §10.5.2]) that gives the necessary and sufficient conditions for two unitaries to be equivalent. We give a self-contained proof which requires minimal prior knowledge.

Theorem 1. *Let U, V be two unitaries on $n \geq 1$ qubits. Then U is equivalent to V if and only if the following conditions hold:*

1. *for all $j \in \{1, 2, \ldots, n\}$, we have $UZ_jU^\dagger = VZ_jV^\dagger$; and*
2. *for all $j \in \{1, 2, \ldots, n\}$, we have $UX_jU^\dagger = VX_jV^\dagger$.*

Here, as before, we have denoted $Z_j = I \otimes \cdots \otimes I \otimes Z \otimes I \otimes \cdots \otimes I$, i.e. an n-fold tensor product of identity gates I with the Pauli Z gate at the j-th position. Analogously, $X_j = I \otimes \cdots \otimes I \otimes X \otimes I \otimes \cdots \otimes I$ where X is the Pauli X gate.

Proof. If $U \simeq V$, then $U = cV$ for some $c \in \mathbb{C}, |c| = 1$, so $UZ_jU^\dagger = cVZ_j(cV)^\dagger = cVZ_j(V)^\dagger \cdot c^* = |c|^2 VZ_jV^\dagger = VZ_jV^\dagger$ and similarly for X_j where c^* is the complex conjugate of c.

For the converse direction, we first note that if U and V coincide on X_j and Z_j by conjugation, then they must coincide by conjugation on *all Pauli strings*. The reason for this is that any Pauli string can be written as a product of $\{X_j, Z_j\}_{j=1}^n$ modulo a complex number from $\{\pm 1, \pm i\}$. Given such a product $P = \prod_{k=1}^n X_k^{x_k} Z_k^{z_k}$ where $x_k, z_k \in \{0, 1\}$ determine if X_k or Z_k is included in the product, we see that $UPU^\dagger = U\left(\prod_{k=1}^n X_k^{x_k} Z_k^{z_k}\right)U^\dagger = \prod_{k=1}^n UX_k^{x_k}U^\dagger UZ_k^{z_k}U^\dagger$. This shows that $UPU^\dagger = VPV^\dagger$ if $UX_kU^\dagger = VX_kV^\dagger$ and $UZ_kU^\dagger = VZ_kV^\dagger$ for all $k = 1, 2, \ldots, n$.

Given an n-qubit quantum state $|\phi\rangle$, we can write

$$|\phi\rangle\langle\phi| = \sum_P \alpha_P P \tag{1}$$

where the summation runs over all Pauli strings of length n, i.e. $P \in \text{PAULI}_n = \{I, X, Y, Z\}^{\otimes n}$, and the weights $\alpha_P \in \mathbb{C}$ are unique, i.e. each PAULI_n string P is associated with a weight α_P. The reason this can be done is that any $2^n \times 2^n$ matrix with complex entries can be written as linear combination of n-qubit Pauli strings [33,40] (the 'Pauli basis') and $|\phi\rangle\langle\phi|$ indeed is an $2^n \times 2^n$ matrix. Now by conjugating both sides of Eq. 1, we obtain

$$U |\phi\rangle\langle\phi| U^\dagger = \sum_P \alpha_P U P U^\dagger \tag{2}$$

which by the observation above (that U and V coincide on all Pauli strings by conjugation) equals

$$V |\phi\rangle\langle\phi| V^\dagger = \sum_P \alpha_P V P V^\dagger \tag{3}$$

hence

$$A |\phi\rangle\langle\phi| A^\dagger = |\phi\rangle\langle\phi| \tag{4}$$

where $A = V^\dagger U$. This arises from the fact that $A^\dagger = (V^\dagger U)^\dagger = U^\dagger V$ and, since U and V coincide on all Pauli strings by conjugation,

$$\begin{aligned} A |\phi\rangle\langle\phi| A^\dagger &= V^\dagger U |\phi\rangle\langle\phi| U^\dagger V = V^\dagger \Big(\sum_P \alpha_P U P U^\dagger\Big) V^\dagger \\ &= V^\dagger \Big(\sum_P \alpha_P V P V^\dagger\Big) V = |\phi\rangle\langle\phi| \end{aligned} \tag{5}$$

since $V^\dagger$ cancels out with V.

By applying $\langle\phi|$ from the left and $|\phi\rangle$ to the right on both sides of Eq. 4, we obtain $| \langle\phi|A|\phi\rangle |^2 = |\langle\phi|\phi\rangle|^2 = 1$. Thus, the modulus of the inner product between $A|\phi\rangle$ and $|\phi\rangle$ equals the product of their norms (which both equal 1), hence the tightness condition of the Cauchy-Schwarz inequality implies that $A|\phi\rangle$ and $|\phi\rangle$ are linearly dependent. That is, $|\phi\rangle$ is an eigenvector of A.

Since this holds for arbitrary n-qubit states $|\phi\rangle$, each vector is an eigenvector of A. By standard linear algebra, we know that this implies that A is a multiple of the identity operator. Thus $A = c\mathbb{1}_{2^n}$ for some complex number c, hence $V^\dagger U = c\mathbb{1}_{2^n}$ by definition of A. Applying V to the left of both sides of $V^\dagger U = c\mathbb{1}_{2^n}$ yields $U = cV$. □

The above theorem is applicable to general quantum circuits. However, for the purposes of this study, we will concentrate on Clifford circuits. In that case, the theorem induces an algorithm which reduces the equivalence checks in Part 1 and 2 of the theorem to simulating the circuits U and V, which for the case of Clifford circuits, is well known to be efficient [1,28].

The Algorithm. From Sect. 2, we know that $S_0 = \{Z_j \mid j = 1, 2, \ldots, n\}$ generate the stabilizer group of the state $|0\rangle^{\otimes n}$, and thus S_0 "represents" $|0\rangle^{\otimes n}$ in the stabilizer formalism. The same holds for $\{X_j \mid j = 1, 2, \ldots, n\}$ and the state $|+\rangle^{\otimes n}$, where $|+\rangle = \frac{1}{\sqrt{2}}(|0\rangle + |1\rangle)$. Furthermore, updating a stabilizer state representation $\{g_1, g_2, \ldots, g_n\}$ (i.e. the g_j are generators of the state's stabilizer group), after a Clifford gate U is found as $\{Ug_1U^\dagger, \ldots, Ug_nU^\dagger\}$. So computing $UZ_jU^\dagger$ for all $j = 1, 2, \ldots, n$ is the same as computing the classical simulation of $U|0\rangle^{\otimes n}$ in the stabilizer formalism and computing $UX_jU^\dagger$ for all $j = 1, 2, \ldots, n$ is the same as classical simulation of $U|+\rangle^{\otimes n}$. Combining these facts with Theorem 1, we obtain the following algorithm for equivalence checking of Clifford circuits which is essentially a (many-one) reduction to Clifford circuit simulation.

To be explicit, given Clifford circuits U, V, we determine whether they are equivalent as follows:

1. Simulate U gate-by-gate in the stabilizer formalism, where the stabilizer group generators of the input state are $\{Z_1, Z_2, \ldots, Z_n\}$, i.e. the input state is $|0\rangle^{\otimes n}$. This yields the output generator set $\{UZ_1U^\dagger, UZ_2U^\dagger, \ldots, UZ_nU^\dagger\}$.
2. Do the same for V, yielding $\{VZ_1V^\dagger, VZ_2V^\dagger, \ldots, VZ_nV^\dagger\}$.
3. Check for each $j = 1, 2, \ldots, n$, whether the Pauli elements $UZ_jU^\dagger$ and $VZ_jV^\dagger$ are equal. If there is some j for which they are non-equal, return "Non-equivalent."
4. Repeat steps (1–3) for the input stabilizer generator set $\{X_1, X_2, \ldots, X_n\}$, which is produced by starting with the generator set of $|0\rangle^{\otimes n}$, followed by applying the Hadamard gate H on each qubit (since $HZH^\dagger = X$).
5. If the algorithm reaches this point, U and V agree by conjugation on all X_j and Z_j. Return "Equivalent."

Example 3 shows an example execution of the algorithm on the two-qubit circuits we saw before.

Example 3. *We aim to determine whether circuits A and B from Example 1 are equivalent. Following the algorithm above, we need to compute the output, under conjugation, of the two circuits for each of the inputs Z_1, Z_2, X_1, X_2.*

a) Circuit A on $\{Z_1, Z_2\}$:

Example 2 shows that the resulting tableau is $\begin{Bmatrix} Z \otimes Z \\ I \otimes Z \end{Bmatrix}$

b) Circuit B on $\{Z_1, Z_2\}$:

$$\begin{Bmatrix} Z \otimes I \\ I \otimes Z \end{Bmatrix} \xrightarrow{NOTC} \begin{Bmatrix} NOTC\ (Z \otimes I)\ NOTC^\dagger \\ NOTC\ (I \otimes Z)\ NOTC^\dagger \end{Bmatrix} = \begin{Bmatrix} Z \otimes Z \\ I \otimes Z \end{Bmatrix}$$

c) Circuit A on $\{X_1, X_2\}$:

$$\begin{Bmatrix} X \otimes I \\ I \otimes X \end{Bmatrix} \xrightarrow{H_1, H_2} \begin{Bmatrix} HXH^\dagger \otimes HIH^\dagger \\ HIH^\dagger \otimes HXH^\dagger \end{Bmatrix} = \begin{Bmatrix} Z \otimes I \\ I \otimes Z \end{Bmatrix}$$

$$\xrightarrow{CNOT} \begin{Bmatrix} CNOT\ (Z \otimes I)\ CNOT^\dagger \\ CNOT\ (I \otimes Z)\ CNOT^\dagger \end{Bmatrix} = \begin{Bmatrix} Z \otimes I \\ Z \otimes Z \end{Bmatrix}$$

$$\xrightarrow{H_1, H_2} \begin{Bmatrix} HZH^\dagger \otimes HIH^\dagger \\ HZH^\dagger \otimes HZH^\dagger \end{Bmatrix} = \begin{Bmatrix} X \otimes I \\ X \otimes X \end{Bmatrix}$$

d) Circuit B on $\{X_1, X_2\}$*:*

$$\begin{Bmatrix} X \otimes I \\ I \otimes X \end{Bmatrix} \xrightarrow{NOTC} \begin{Bmatrix} NOTC\ (X \otimes I)\ NOTC^\dagger \\ NOTC\ (I \otimes X)\ NOTC^\dagger \end{Bmatrix} = \begin{Bmatrix} X \otimes I \\ X \otimes X \end{Bmatrix}$$

We observe that the two circuits output, under conjugation, the same elements of the Pauli group, for each of Z_1*,* Z_2*,* X_1 *and* X_2*. Therefore, we can conclude that circuits* A *and* B *are equivalent.*

We note that requiring that U and V agree on all X_j and Z_j by conjugation (step 3 of the Algorithm) is a stronger statement than requiring that U and V output the same state on input $|0\rangle^{\otimes n}$ and $|+\rangle^{\otimes n}$. As counterexample for $n = 2$, consider the identity circuit $\mathbb{1}_4$. We have $\mathbb{1}_4 |00\rangle = |00\rangle = U_A |00\rangle = U_B |00\rangle$ and $\mathbb{1}_4 |{++}\rangle = |{++}\rangle = U_A |{++}\rangle = U_B |{++}\rangle$, where U_A and U_B are the unitaries for circuits A and B from Example 1, respectively. This calculation can also be done in terms of stabilizer tableaux using the $\cong$ relation to check if the tableaux generate the same stabilizer group:

$$\underbrace{\begin{Bmatrix} Z \otimes I \\ I \otimes Z \end{Bmatrix}}_{\text{for } \mathbb{1}_4|00\rangle} \cong \underbrace{\begin{Bmatrix} I \otimes Z \\ Z \otimes Z \end{Bmatrix}}_{\text{for } U_A|00\rangle = U_B|00\rangle} \quad \text{and} \quad \underbrace{\begin{Bmatrix} X \otimes I \\ I \otimes X \end{Bmatrix}}_{\text{for } \mathbb{1}_4|{++}\rangle} \cong \underbrace{\begin{Bmatrix} X \otimes I \\ X \otimes X \end{Bmatrix}}_{\text{for } U_A|{++}\rangle = U_B|{++}\rangle}$$

That is, the list of generators of the stabilizer groups of $\mathbb{1}_4 |00\rangle$ ($\mathbb{1}_4 |{++}\rangle$) and $U_A |00\rangle = U_B |00\rangle$ ($U_A |{++}\rangle = U_B |{++}\rangle$) are *equivalent* in the sense that they give rise to the same stabilizer group (and hence represent the same quantum state) but they are not *equal*. Unitaries are only equivalent if they output equal Pauli group elements under conjugation. Indeed, $\mathbb{1}_4$ is not equivalent to U_A or U_B: a witness to their non-equivalence is the state $|01\rangle$, since $\mathbb{1}_4 |01\rangle = |01\rangle \neq |11\rangle = U_A |01\rangle = U_B |01\rangle$.

Since storing the n stabilizer generators for an n-qubit state requires $O(n^2)$ space, naively initializing the tableaux $\{Z_1, \ldots, Z_n\}$ and $\{X_1, \ldots, X_n\}$ takes $O(n^2)$ time. Next, updating a tableau for a single-qubit gate or two-qubit gate takes time $O(n)$. Hence the runtime of the algorithm is $O(n^2 + m \cdot n)$ with m the sum of the number of elementary Clifford gates in U and V. However, we can avoid the $O(n^2)$ initialization time, by amortizing the creation of the stabilizer generator set over the update operations using a lazy initialization approach. To be precise, let us keep track of the stabilizer generators by listing them in an $n \times (n + 1)$ matrix where the $(n + 1)$-th column consists of factors ± 1 and the entries of the first n columns are Pauli gates [24]. Instead of initializing this matrix, we only mark all columns as uninitialized. The uninitialized entries in column k of the matrix are filled when a gate is applied to the k-th qubit for the first time, in which case the algorithm runs over all elements of column k anyway (and the column of $\pm$ factors). This lazy initialization brings the total runtime of the algorithm down to $O(m \cdot n)$.

4 Experiments

We implemented the algorithm from Sect. 3 in Python using the open-source Stim Clifford-circuit simulator [25] as a backend. See [21] for our open-source implementation.

We empirically evaluated the implementation and compared the runtime to QuSAT [10,37], a recent SAT-based Clifford equivalence checker and the Feynman tool [4]. We used a laptop with a 3.2 GHz M1 processor with 8Gb RAM.

To make a fair comparison, we adopt the experimental setting of [10] and generate random circuits using QuSAT, which consists of generating random sequences of elementary Clifford gates $H, S,$ CNOT. QuSAT generates circuits which are completely "filled" in the sense that if the depth is d, the number of gates applied to each qubit is also d; thus, since only $H, S,$ CNOT are used, the number of gates in a depth-d circuit is between $d \cdot \frac{n}{2}$ (only two-qubit gates) and $d \cdot n$ (only single-qubit gates). We emphasize that the runtime of this work's method is deterministic and a function of the number of qubits and the number of gates only, and is hence independent of the gates that the two input circuits consist of, or the ordering of the gates.

We validated the correctness of our implementation by comparing its results with QuSAT. Across all circuit pairs in which QuSAT terminated, we found a consistent classification as either equivalent or non-equivalent by both approaches.

First, we ran both QuSAT and our implementation on both equivalent and non-equivalent random Clifford circuits which were thus produced by QuSAT. The results are shown in Fig. 1, for varying number of qubits (Fig. 1a, Fig. 1b and Fig. 1c) and varying quantum-circuit depth (Fig. 1d). We performed an equal amount of experiments with non-equivalent circuit pairs, again drawing them from the experimental setting of QuSAT [10]. The resulting plots appear indistinguishable from the ones for equivalent circuit pairs, and for that reason we omit them here.

We observe that the implementation is very fast and can handle large circuits: up to 1000 qubits with a depth of 10.000 gates in ~22 s, and 100.000 qubits with 10 gates in ~15 min (Fig. 1b). The tested regime of the method consistently outperforms QuSAT by one to two orders of magnitude (10× to 100×) or even more. We also see that the runtime of QuSAT, whose runtime is heuristic, seems to scale exponentially in the number of qubits whereas the runtime of our approach is deterministic and scales polynomially in both number of qubits and number of gates (Sect. 3).

Next, we also compare with the Feynver submodule for circuit-equivalence checking of the Feynman tool [4]. Feynver is based on Feynman path-integrals and it can verify the equivalence of general quantum circuits. For Clifford circuits specifically, its runtime scales polynomially in the number of elementary gates for Clifford circuits, just like the method presented in this work. To compare to Feynver, we again let QuSAT generate random circuits and input them to both Feynver and our implementation. We found that Feynver terminated on all equivalent circuit pairs, but for non-equivalent pairs it often aborted. This behavior is known [3]. Our experiments showed that Feynver is outperformed by

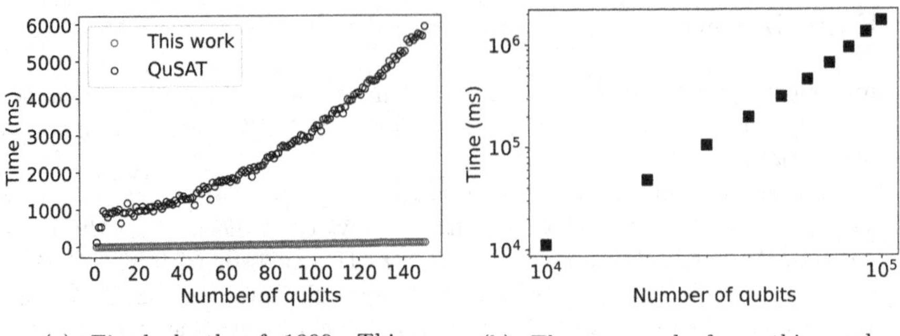

(a) Fixed depth of 1000. This data-set reappears in Figure 1c.

(b) The approach from this work, reaching beyond what was previously feasible: Fixed depth 10 and the number of qubits up to 100.000. Both axes are in logarithmic scale, so that a polynomial scaling shows up as a straight line.

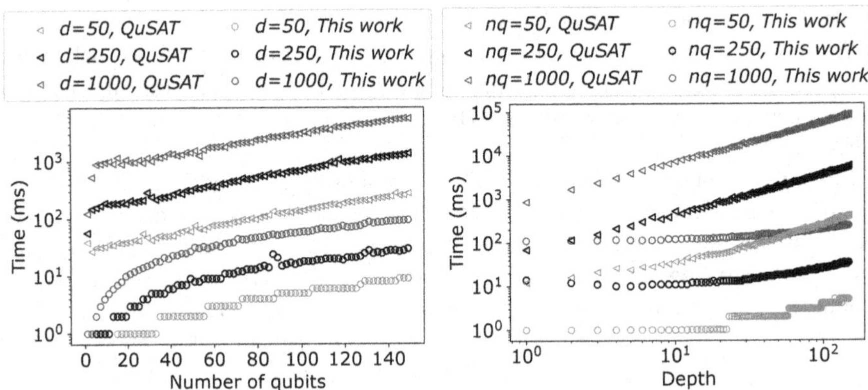

(c) Fixed depths ("d") and increasing number of qubits. The vertical axis is on logarithmic scale.

(d) Fixed number of qubits ("nq") and increasing depth. Both axes are on logarithmic scale, so that a polynomial scaling shows up as a straight line.

Fig. 1. Runtime comparison of circuit-equivalence checking between equivalent randomly-generated Clifford circuits, for both the method from this work and QuSAT. The step pattern observed for lower values is a result of the limitations of the time-measuring function which operates in milliseconds. The runtimes for non-equivalent circuits (not displayed) have an indistinguishable appearance.

both QuSAT and our implementation. For equivalent circuit pairs, the runtimes of Feynver and our implementation are shown in Fig. 2 for a varying number of qubits (Fig. 2a) and a varying quantum-circuit depth (Fig. 2b). The running times for the non-equivalent pairs for which Feynver terminated successfully were similar.

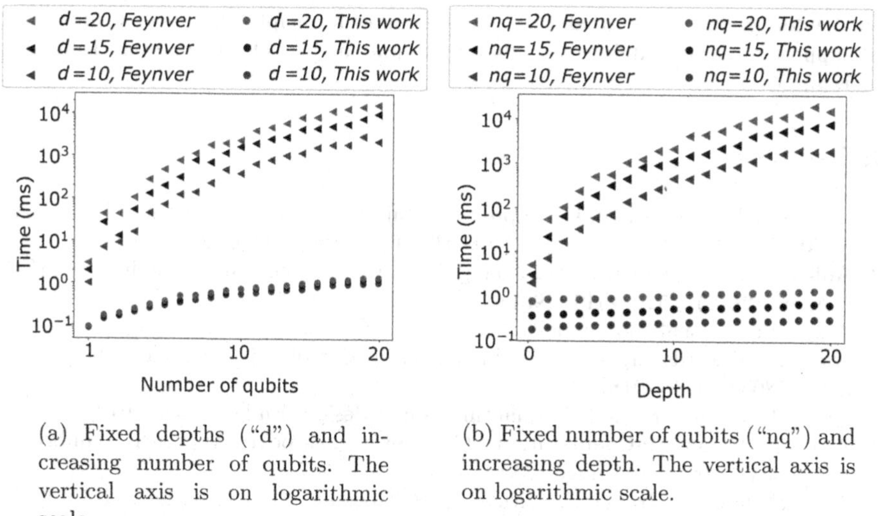

(a) Fixed depths ("d") and increasing number of qubits. The vertical axis is on logarithmic scale.

(b) Fixed number of qubits ("nq") and increasing depth. The vertical axis is on logarithmic scale.

Fig. 2. Runtime of circuit-equivalence checking between equivalent randomly-generated Clifford circuits for various circuit depths and the number of qubits.

5 Conclusions

In this paper, we demonstrate that a deterministic algorithm, which is based on a folklore mathematical result, can surpass the efficiency of current methods for exact equivalence checking of quantum circuits consisting of Clifford gates. The algorithm reduces equivalence checking to classical simulation of Clifford circuits and runs in time $O(n \cdot m)$, with n the number of qubits and m the total number of elementary Clifford gates of the two input circuits. This scaling implies efficient equivalence checking for various application-relevant circuits, for example the circuits for producing the two-dimensional cluster states (resource states for universal quantum computing [15]), GHZ states (resource states for various quantum communication protocols [29]) or performing error detection (excluding the measurement) in quantum error correction [45].

We have implemented the algorithm using the Stim simulator and tested it on a variety of benchmark circuits with different sizes and depths, and compared it to two existing state-of-the-art methods, QuSAT and Feynver. Our results, reaching 1000 qubits (with depth 10.000) in less than a minute and 100.000 qubits (depth 10) in ~15 min, demonstrate that this approach consistently outperforms both. Furthermore, since the method is deterministic, its scaling behavior is known.

Possible future work includes extending this method to arbitrary circuits using non-Clifford gates [4,7], following existing classical simulation formalisms of such circuits [13]. Our preliminary results towards this direction appear promising.

Acknowledgments. We thank Prof. M. Bonsangue for helpful discussions. This work was supported by the Dutch National Growth Fund, as part of the Quantum Delta NL program.

References

1. Aaronson, S., Gottesman, D.: Improved simulation of stabilizer circuits. Phys. Rev. A **70**(5) (2004). https://doi.org/10.1103%2Fphysreva.70.052328
2. Adleman, L.M., Demarrais, J., Huang, M.D.A.: Quantum computability. SIAM J. Comput. **26**(5), 1524–1540 (1997)
3. Amy, M.: Personal communication (2023)
4. Amy, M.: Towards large-scale functional verification of universal quantum circuits. arXiv:1805.06908 (2018)
5. Amy, M.: Formal methods in quantum circuit design. Ph.D. thesis (2019)
6. Arora, S., Barak, B.: Computational Complexity: A Modern Approach. Cambridge University Press, Cambridge (2009)
7. Arunachalam, S., Bravyi, S., Nirkhe, C., O'Gorman, B.: The parameterized complexity of quantum verification. arXiv:2202.08119 (2022)
8. Audenaert, K.M.R., Plenio, M.B.: Entanglement on mixed stabilizer states: normal forms and reduction procedures. New J. Phys. **7**(1), 170 (2005)
9. Bauer-Marquart, F., Leue, S., Schilling, C.: symQV: automated symbolic verification of quantum programs. In: Chechik, M., Katoen, J.P., Leucker, M. (eds.) FM 2023. LNCS, vol. 14000, pp. 181–198. Springer, Cham (2023). https://doi.org/10.1007/978-3-031-27481-7_12
10. Berent, L., Burgholzer, L., Wille, R.: Towards a SAT encoding for quantum circuits: a journey from classical circuits to Clifford circuits and beyond. arXiv:2203.00698 (2022)
11. Bookatz, A.D.: QMA-complete problems. arXiv:1212.6312 (2012)
12. Brakerski, Z., Sharma, D., Weissenberg, G.: Unitary subgroup testing. arXiv:2104.03591 (2021)
13. Bravyi, S., Browne, D., Calpin, P., Campbell, E., Gosset, D., Howard, M.: Simulation of quantum circuits by low-rank stabilizer decompositions. Quantum **3**, 181 (2019). https://doi.org/10.22331/q-2019-09-02-181
14. Bravyi, S., Kitaev, A.: Universal quantum computation with ideal Clifford gates and noisy ancillas. Phys. Rev. A **71**, 022316 (2005). https://link.aps.org/doi/10.1103/PhysRevA.71.022316
15. Briegel, H.J., Browne, D.E., Dür, W., Raussendorf, R., Van den Nest, M.: Measurement-based quantum computation. Nat. Phys. **5**(1), 19–26 (2009). https://doi.org/10.1038/nphys1157
16. Burgholzer, L., Kueng, R., Wille, R.: Random stimuli generation for the verification of quantum circuits. In: Proceedings of the 26th Asia and South Pacific Design Automation Conference, pp. 767–772 (2021)
17. Burgholzer, L., Wille, R.: Advanced equivalence checking for quantum circuits. IEEE Trans. Comput. Aided Des. Integr. Circuits Syst. **40**(9), 1810–1824 (2020)
18. Burgholzer, L., Wille, R.: Improved DD-based equivalence checking of quantum circuits. In: 2020 25th Asia and South Pacific Design Automation Conference (ASP-DAC), pp. 127–132 (2020)
19. Chen, T.F., Jiang, J.H.R., Hsieh, M.H.: Partial equivalence checking of quantum circuits. In: 2022 IEEE International Conference on Quantum Computing and Engineering (QCE), pp. 594–604. IEEE (2022)

20. Córcoles, A.D., et al.: Challenges and opportunities of near-term quantum computing systems. arXiv:1910.02894 (2019)
21. Dimitrios Thanos, T.C., Laarman, A.: CCEC (Clifford-circuit equivalence checking) (2023). https://github.com/System-Verification-Lab/CCEC
22. Duncan, R., Kissinger, A., Perdrix, S., van de Wetering, J.: Graph-theoretic simplification of quantum circuits with the ZX-calculus. Quantum **4**, 279 (2020). https://doi.org/10.22331/q-2020-06-04-279
23. Finigan, W., Cubeddu, M., Lively, T., Flick, J., Narang, P.: Qubit allocation for noisy intermediate-scale quantum computers. arXiv:1810.08291 (2018)
24. García, H.J., Markov, I.L., Cross, A.W.: On the geometry of stabilizer states. Quantum Inf. Comput. **14**, 683–720 (2014)
25. Gidney, C.: Stim: a fast stabilizer circuit simulator. Quantum **5**, 497 (2021). https://doi.org/10.22331/q-2021-07-06-497
26. Goldberg, E., Novikov, Y.: How good can a resolution based SAT-solver be? In: Giunchiglia, E., Tacchella, A. (eds.) SAT 2003. LNCS, vol. 2919, pp. 37–52. Springer, Heidelberg (2004). https://doi.org/10.1007/978-3-540-24605-3_4
27. Gottesman, D.: Stabilizer codes and quantum error correction. arXiv:quant-ph/9705052 (1997)
28. Gottesman, D.: The Heisenberg representation of quantum computers. arXiv:quant-ph/9807006v1 (1998)
29. Hein, M., Dür, W., Eisert, J., Raussendorf, R., Nest, M., Briegel, H.J.: Entanglement in graph states and its applications. arXiv:0602096 (2006)
30. Hong, X., Ying, M., Feng, Y., Zhou, X., Li, S.: Approximate equivalence checking of noisy quantum circuits. In: 2021 58th ACM/IEEE Design Automation Conference (DAC), pp. 637–642 (2021)
31. Janzing, D., Wocjan, P., Beth, T.: "non-identity-check" is QMA-complete. Int. J. Quantum Inf. **3**(03), 463–473 (2005)
32. Ji, Z., Wu, X.: Non-identity check remains QMA-complete for short circuits. arXiv:0906.5416 (2009)
33. Kimura, G.: The bloch vector for n-level systems. Phys. Lett. A **314**(5), 339–349 (2003)
34. Kuehlmann, A.: Dynamic transition relation simplification for bounded property checking. In: IEEE/ACM International Conference on Computer Aided Design, ICCAD-2004, pp. 50–57 (2004)
35. Kuehlmann, A., Paruthi, V., Krohm, F., Ganai, M.: Robust boolean reasoning for equivalence checking and functional property verification. IEEE Trans. Comput. Aided Des. Integr. Circuits Syst. **21**(12), 1377–1394 (2002)
36. Linden, N., de Wolf, R.: Lightweight detection of a small number of large errors in a quantum circuit. Quantum **5**, 436 (2021)
37. Lucas Berent, L.B., Wille, R.: MQT QuSAT - a tool for utilizing sat in quantum computing (2022). https://github.com/cda-tum/qusat
38. Montanaro, A.: Quantum algorithms: an overview. NPJ Quantum Inf. **2**(1), 15023 (2016). https://doi.org/10.1038/npjqi.2015.23
39. Montanaro, A., de Wolf, R.: A survey of quantum property testing. arXiv:1310.2035 (2013)
40. Nielsen, M.A., Chuang, I.L.: Quantum Information and Quantum Computation, vol. 2, no. 8, p. 23. Cambridge University Press, Cambridge (2000)
41. Niemann, P., Wille, R., Drechsler, R.: Equivalence checking in multi-level quantum systems. In: Yamashita, S., Minato, S. (eds.) RC 2014. LNCS, vol. 8507, pp. 201–215. Springer, Cham (2014). https://doi.org/10.1007/978-3-319-08494-7_16

42. Peham, T., Burgholzer, L., Wille, R.: Equivalence checking of quantum circuits with the ZX-calculus. IEEE J. Emerg. Sel. Top. Circuits Syst. **12**(3), 662–675 (2022)
43. Preskill, J.: Quantum Computing in the NISQ era and beyond. Quantum **2**, 79 (2018). https://doi.org/10.22331/q-2018-08-06-79
44. Tanaka, Y.: Exact non-identity check is NQP-complete. Int. J. Quantum Inf. **8**(05), 807–819 (2010)
45. Terhal, B.M.: Quantum error correction for quantum memories. Rev. Mod. Phys. **87**, 307–346 (2015). https://doi.org/10.1103/RevModPhys.87.307
46. Viamontes, G.F., Markov, I.L., Hayes, J.P.: Checking equivalence of quantum circuits and states. In: 2007 IEEE/ACM International Conference on Computer-Aided Design, pp. 69–74 (2007)
47. Vinkhuijzen, L., Coopmans, T., Elkouss, D., Dunjko, V., Laarman, A.: LIMDD a decision diagram for simulation of quantum computing including stabilizer states. Quantum (2023, accepted for publication). https://arxiv.org/abs/2108.00931
48. Vinkhuijzen, L., Grurl, T., Hillmich, S., Brand, S., Wille, R., Laarman, A.: Efficient implementation of LIMDDs for quantum circuit simulation. In: Caltais, G., Schilling, C. (eds.) SPIN 2023. LNCS, vol. 13872, pp. 3–21. Springer, Cham (2023). https://doi.org/10.1007/978-3-031-32157-3_1
49. Wang, S.A., Lu, C.Y., Tsai, I.M., Kuo, S.Y.: An XQDD-based verification method for quantum circuits. IEICE Trans. Fundam. Electron. Commun. Comput. Sci. **91**(2), 584–594 (2008)
50. Wei, C.Y., Tsai, Y.H., Jhang, C.S., Jiang, J.H.R.: Accurate BDD-based unitary operator manipulation for scalable and robust quantum circuit verification. In: Proceedings of the 59th ACM/IEEE Design Automation Conference, pp. 523–528 (2022)
51. van de Wetering, J.: ZX-calculus for the working quantum computer scientist. arxiv (2020). https://arxiv.org/abs/2012.13966
52. Wille, R., Przigoda, N., Drechsler, R.: A compact and efficient sat encoding for quantum circuits. In: 2013 Africon, pp. 1–6. IEEE (2013)
53. Yamashita, S., Markov, I.L.: Fast equivalence-checking for quantum circuits. In: 2010 IEEE/ACM International Symposium on Nanoscale Architectures, pp. 23–28. IEEE (2010)
54. Yamashita, S., Minato, S.I., Miller, D.M.: DDMF: an efficient decision diagram structure for design verification of quantum circuits under a practical restriction. IEICE Trans. Fundam. Electron. Commun. Comput. Sci. **91**(12), 3793–3802 (2008)

Automatic Verification of High-Level Executable Models Running on FPGAs

Morgan McColl(✉), Callum McColl, and René Hexel

Griffith University, Brisbane, Australia
morgan.mccoll@griffithuni.edu.au, {c.mccoll,r.hexel}@griffith.edu.au

Abstract. The increasing complexity of Field-Programmable Gate Array (FPGA) applications necessitates high-level design and formal verification. Traditional approaches often fall short, prompting a shift towards Model-Driven Development (MDD) strategies utilising executable models. Executable models simplify the design process by directly translating high-level, human-readable models into executable code, eliminating manual transcoding errors. However, the challenge of verifying these models in an automated manner remains largely unsolved. The contribution of this paper is a model-driven software engineering methodology utilising logic-labelled finite-state machines (LLFSMs) that enable the automated generation of executable FPGA code from high-level, human-readable models as well as associated Kripke structures for the verification (through model-checking) of high-level executable models running on FPGA platforms. We present a method that utilises the semantics of logic-labelled finite state machines on an FPGA to significantly reduce the size of the created Kripke structures compared with existing LLFSM approaches.

Keywords: Automatic Verification · Model-Driven Software Engineering · Logic-Labelled Finite State Machines · FPGAs

1 Introduction

The evolution of technology has brought about increasing reliance on Field-Programmable Gate Arrays (FPGAs) for their versatility, speed, and real-time performance capabilities. These unique properties have made them instrumental in the design and development of real-time systems, telecommunication networks, computer vision, and embedded systems. However, as FPGA applications grow more complex, their design and verification become increasingly challenging. This necessitates a shift from traditional design methods towards Model-Driven Development (MDD) approaches, where high-level, human-readable models are employed to design, verify, and implement these systems.

Model-Driven Development provides an abstraction layer that enables designers to focus on the functionality of the system while abstracting away lower-level hardware details. This high-level approach simplifies the development process

É. André and J. Sun (Eds.): ATVA 2023, LNCS 14216, pp. 217–234, 2023.
https://doi.org/10.1007/978-3-031-45332-8_11

and reduces the likelihood of errors that arise from manual translation into code. However, the verification of these high-level models in an automated manner is a challenge that remains to be addressed.

The primary contribution of this paper is an MDD design that allows the automated generation of Kripke structures that allow verification of high-level executable models running on FPGA platforms. We discuss the issues and limitations of existing methods and how to overcome them to handle the complexity of models that utilise FPGA designs while maintaining the advantages of high-level model abstraction.

The rest of this paper is structured as follows. Section 2 explores the background of verifiable MDD utilising high-level, human-readable models. This is followed in Sect. 3 by our detailed design of executable models of logic-labelled finite-state machines running on an FPGA. We then demonstrate how we can create Kripke structures for automated model-checking (Sect. 4). Finally, we summarise our findings in Sect. 5.

2 Background

The Unified Modelling Language (UML) has unified the various disparate notational systems for software design and modelling and has become the de-facto standard for model-driven software engineering (MDSE). There has been remarkable progress in MDSE [1–3] in creating verifiable executable models that define behaviour at a high level. However, the automatic verification of deployable systems remains a challenge. By far, the biggest challenge with common modelling systems are semantic variations. In other words, while the UML has unified notation, formal correctness of resulting execution semantics only holds in some scenarios [4], even in current versions of executable UML (fUML) [5]. Moreover, concurrency and parallelism are severely hampered by the fact that execution paths may diverge due to race conditions or other sensitivities towards instruction execution order. This is the case, even if the same sources and systems are utilised in building and executing the model, as ambiguities remain when it comes to the semantics of these systems [6]. In essence, this violates the promise that executable models allow us to create a fully automated one-to-one mapping between design and implementation so that we can perform formal verification on the real software that executes on the target system. These ambiguities in UML semantics have repeatedly been identified as causing confusion in the industry and leading to inconsistencies and suboptimal results [7,8]. This is not helped by the fact that almost from the beginning, inconsistencies have been created in different UML implementations with different semantics [9] that frustrate the reproducibility of model checking.

It is, therefore, unsurprising that the predominant focus has been on testing approaches, such as test-driven development [10] and continuous integration [11]. However, we argue that, while pragmatic, this is a flawed approach, as testing is, by definition, incomplete. In particular, testing can only prove the existence of defects, not their absence. We will therefore focus on formal methods for verifying the correctness of executable models. We have already demonstrated earlier [3] that we can achieve consistent and faithful execution semantics of executable models of real-time systems that allow verification in both the time and value domains. Without going into detail here, suffice it to say that while event-driven modelling has been the predominant paradigm that has been productive for traditional systems such as desktop computers or cloud architectures, it has long been recognised that such systems fundamentally follow a best-effort approach that cannot guarantee bounded execution and completion times sufficient to meet hard deadlines [12]. By contrast, time-triggered systems guarantee consistency in both the value and time domains, making formal verification feasible for a much larger class of systems [13].

A key challenge that remains is the creation and verification of graphs used for model-checking. While some systems create a combinatorial state explosion when deriving their Kripke structures, making them too complex to formally verify as-is, we have already shown that we can utilise dependency analysis to isolate modules and verify them independently without jeopardising the verifiability of the composite system as a whole [14]. Moreover, we have shown that we can utilise the same MDSE approach that has traditionally been used on computer systems, but achieve orders of magnitude higher execution speeds when utilising FPGAs [15]. This is essential as embedded architectures often exhibit semantic differences between the original UML design and the compiled software executing on the embedded device [4]. This phenomenon has been especially pronounced when examining UML translations into FPGAs [16–18]. Common translation differences in FPGAs include implicit priorities on transitions, distributed event queues and semantic differences between formal event processing and the limitations of the underlying hardware.

While we have been able to overcome these inconsistencies and are now able to create consistent, high-level executable models that run on FPGAs [15], formal verification has, thus far, eluded us. Before we detail the design that allows us to now create Kripke structures of an executable model on an FPGA, we need to recall the principles of logic-labelled finite-state machines that make these executable models possible.

2.1 Logic-Labelled Finite-State Machines

Logic-labelled finite-state machines (LLFSMs) are an approach to modelling that follows the ubiquitous footsteps of modelling with finite-state machines (FSMs). However, in contrast to the event-driven nature of UML statecharts, LLFSMs utilise expressions in a decidable logic to decorate transitions [19]. In other words, they follow the principles of UML state diagrams where only guards, but not events are used, effectively capturing the fact that an event has occurred into a Boolean expression that reflects this. This avoids the impossibility of translating mathematically perfect events, i.e. a semantics of zero duration with perfect order, into a feasible implementation that has to work with event queues and other approximations. With the departure from the notion that reactiveness needs to be driven by events, we can achieve real-time object-oriented modelling [20].

LLFSMs utilise the notion that execution is subdivided into atomic ringlets. Each ringlet execution is an activity that comprises a sequence of actions:

1. A snapshot of external input variables is taken.
2. Where a state ringlet is executed for the first time (e.g. a different state was executed previously), an *OnEntry* action is run.
3. All transitions are evaluated in a pre-defined order of priority.
4. If a transition fires, an *OnExit* action gets run.
5. Otherwise, an *Internal* action gets executed.
6. A snapshot of resulting output variables is written.

We will now detail our design that, for the first time, enables us to run an executable LLFSM model on an FPGA while creating the corresponding Kripke structure on-device to enable formal verification.

3 Design

We begin this section by presenting our design for creating executable models in FPGAs. We then discuss the methods used to reduce the Kripke structure by using the semantics of our models. We have previously used LLFSMs on FPGAs by segregating each ringlet into a periodic process that maps to clock edges [15], as shown in Fig. 1. This mapping creates a synchronous execution between parallel FSMs that allows for the separation of *read* and *write* actions between shared variables. This structure is fundamental to LLFSMs on FPGAs, allowing more complex forms of behaviour by composing and ordering different ringlets. Importantly, this overcomes any race conditions that might otherwise occur between finite-state machines running in parallel and facilitates atomic execution. In other words, the ringlet process is never executed partially but instead presents an indivisible structure that always completes once started [15].

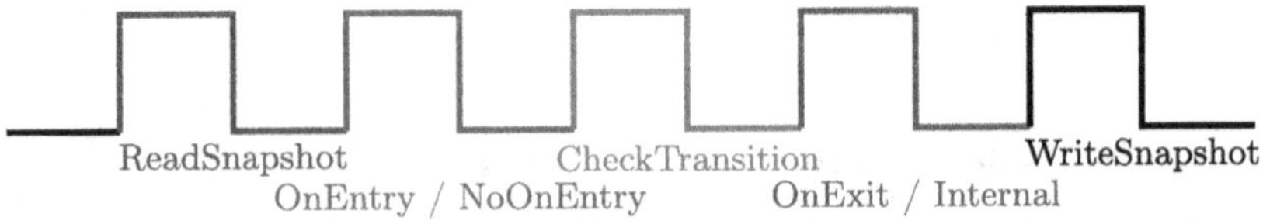

Fig. 1. The Ringlet Execution Cycle [15]

Our FPGA models are executable in the complete sense, as we define state actions and variables in VHDL, a hardware description language used to describe hardware constructs in the FPGA. We perform code generation to translate the graphical depiction of our LLFSM into the executable code that the FPGA enacts. This automatic translation removes semantic differences between design and implementation as the translation software moves the user's code within the machine into the correct sections within a VHDL template. We have constructed our LLFSM template to enforce the formal semantics of LLFSMs without incurring semantic differences or gaps.

Our main contribution here is that we can now generate corresponding VHDL that performs automatic and optimised Kripke structure construction for our executable models on-device. Generating Kripke structures in this way creates a graph directly derived from the behaviour of the software on the target hardware as it executes. This graph is in a format that can be used to run automated proofs using a model checker such as nuXmv [21]. The Kripke structure reflects precisely what is executed on the FPGA, ensuring there is no semantic gap between the high-level model and the executable. This process is well aligned with formally verifying safety-critical and dependable systems, as formal verification takes place on structures derived directly from the physical hardware.

Since we will be examining the Kripke structure of our LLFSMs, it is important to be aware of some key variables used in the VHDL template to enforce the LLFSM semantics. We will use three variables in our Kripke structures that are generated in the VHDL template, namely *internalState*, *previousRinglet* and *targetState*. The *internalState* variable is used to track which step in the ringlet the LLFSM is currently in (see Sect. 2.1) and reflects the values within the timing diagram of Fig. 1. The *previousRinglet* variable captures the state the machine executed immediately before the current ringlet the machine is executing. This variable allows us to determine whether or not *OnEntry* should be executed in the current ringlet. The final variable, *targetState*, is used to determine if the LLFSM is about to transition to a new state. This variable then contains the state the LLFSM will transition to in the next ringlet.

Another key contribution is the reduction of the Kripke structure size by taking advantage of the LLFSM semantics. We can leverage a ringlet's execution cycle (see Fig. 1) to minimise the Kripke structure size while supporting parallel execution. Let us examine how these Kripke structure optimisations work by examining a simple LLFSM. Consider the LLFSM depicted in Fig. 2 containing the variables within Table 1. This LLFSM starts in an empty initial state that performs no functions and then transitions to state S_0. Within state S_0, the machine sets the value of external variable y to the value of external variable x. The external variables x and y are examples of variables that map to inputs

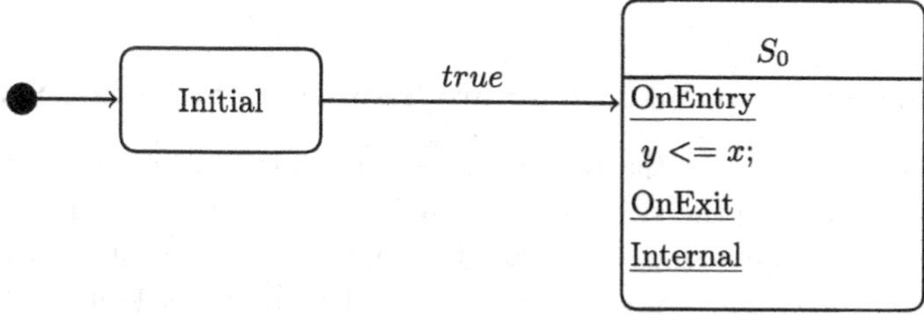

Fig. 2. LLFSM *I*, depicting an initial state and a state S_0 executing a simple VHDL value assignment.

Table 1. The variables within LLFSM *I*.

Name	Type	Scope	Mode
x	*std_logic*	*External*	*input*
y	*std_logic*	*External*	*output*

and outputs respectively, as associated, for example, with sensors and actuators. This variable assignment only occurs once during the first ringlet of the S_0 state (*OnEntry*). All subsequent ringlets will perform no function as the *Internal* action of state S_0 is empty.

We can now derive a partial Kripke structure for the first ringlet of state S_0 (Fig. 3). This Kripke structure assumes that the variable x has the value of *'0'* (logic low) at the beginning of the ringlet. We have also removed the snapshot semantics to demonstrate the state explosion without our optimisations. This is very close to typical UML translations into FPGAs. The Kripke structure in Fig. 3 shows the Kripke states between the *OnEntry* action and the *CheckTransition* phase of state S_0's first ringlet. Notice that several Kripke states are describing the *CheckTransition* phase of this ringlet due to the different values that are possible for the variable x. This Kripke structure represents the actual code that is executed on an FPGA and must account for each value of x (a *std_logic* variable in VHDL). There are 9 possible values that a *std_logic* variable can be in, however, these values will generally resolve to a combination of logic low and logic high bit values when executed on the actual hardware. This resolution is dictated by the synthesiser and FPGA fabric [22], so we cannot ignore this for the general case.

Since x is an external variable representing a sensor reading, this value can change at any point in time and must be accounted for in the Kripke structure in these circumstances. For each *CheckTransition* Kripke state in this figure, we will also have the same edges for the next Kripke state (*Internal* in this case) where the same sensor may change its value. The total number of Kripke states for this ringlet is 171 (for each *OnEntry* state, we have 9 *CheckTransition* states and 9 *Internal* states). There are 9 *OnEntry* states in total, therefore the total Kripke structure for the first ringlet is $9 \cdot 19 = 171$. This combinatorial state space represents an example of the state explosion problem for our LLFSM.

3.1 Reducing the Kripke Structure Size Using Snapshot Semantics

We now demonstrate how the Kripke structure is altered by introducing snapshot semantics. Before the start of each ringlet, a snapshot of all input external variables is taken. This snapshot takes the input (sensor) value at the start of the ringlet and writes it into a local copy that the LLFSM acts upon during the ringlet's execution. The LLFSM acts upon local copies of the output external variables during the ringlet's execution as well. At the end of the ringlet, the output local variables are written back to the external variables of the LLFSM.

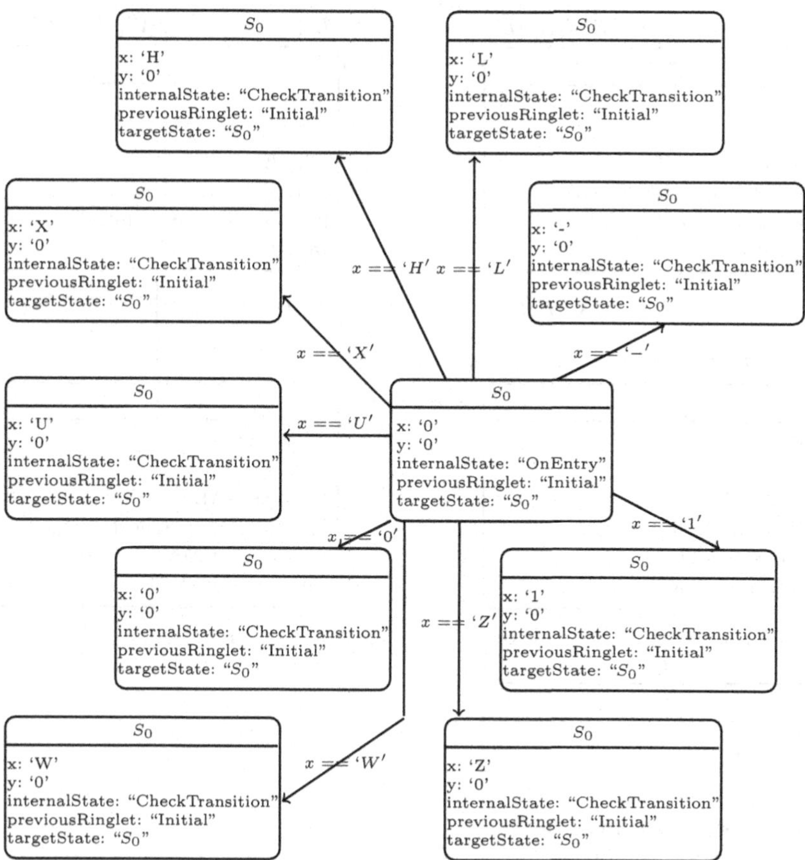

Fig. 3. The Kripke Structure of the First Ringlet in State S_0 without Snapshot Semantics.

These *read* and *write* sections of an LLFSMs execution are depicted as *ReadSnapshot* and *WriteSnapshot* in Fig. 1 respectively.

The advantage of this semantics is that the local snapshot variable representing x in our example is not modified after the *ReadSnapshot* phase of the ringlets execution. The result of this semantics drastically reduces the number of Kripke states in our ringlet. We have updated the Kripke structure for this example in Fig. 4. Please note that x now represents the snapshot variable x while *EXTERNAL*_x represents the corresponding sensor variable x. We again assume that the first sensor reading is $x =$ '0'. For brevity, we have reduced the number of edges in this figure into a set of values. The actual Kripke structure would represent each value in the sets labelling the edges as a separate edge. In the Kripke structure in Fig. 4, we have omitted the external variable *EXTERNAL*_x as the number of states to depict would be too large to show here. The main trend that is observable from this Kripke structure is that the x snapshot

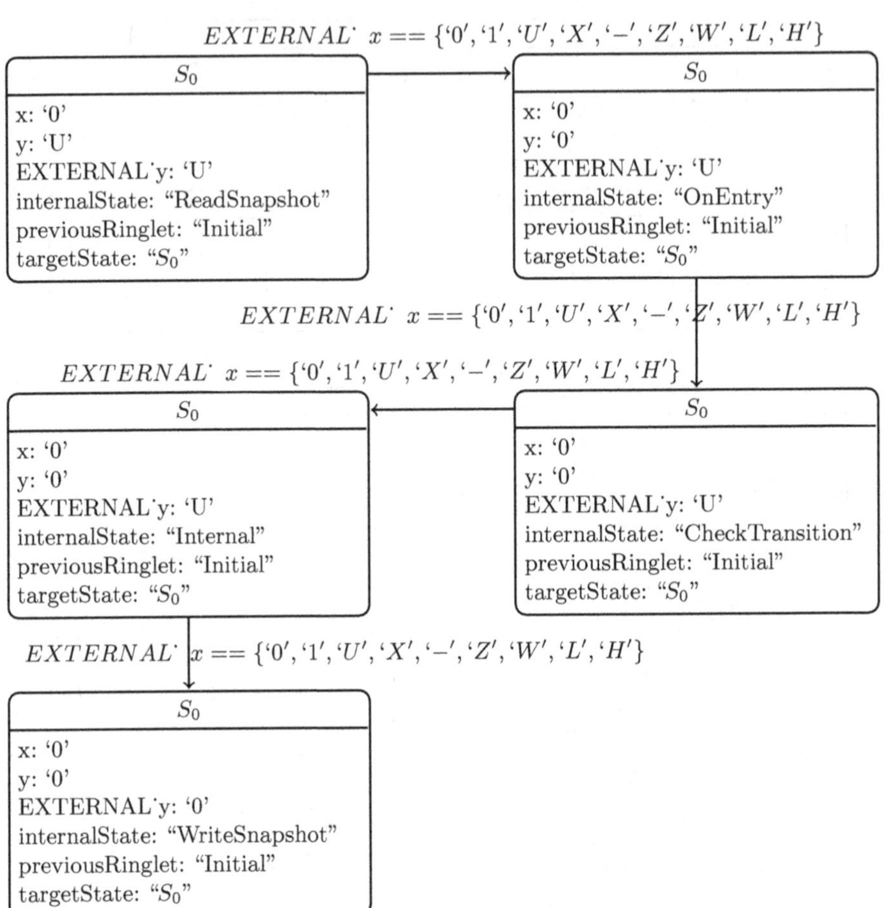

Fig. 4. The Kripke Structure of the First Ringlet in State S_0 with Snapshot Semantics.

variable no longer needs to be mutated during every phase of the ringlet. To illustrate this, assume that *EXTERNAL_x* represents a sensor measuring some property in the environment. Even though the corresponding sensor values may continuously change, we are only interested in the value that is present when we take a snapshot. Therefore, the sensor reading has no further influence over the LLFSM until the next ringlet's *ReadSnapshot* phase. We can also observe that the *EXTERNAL_y* variable is not assigned the value of snapshot variable y until the *WriteSnapshot* Kripke state. We can use these properties to further reduce the complexity and size of the Kripke structure.

Consider the new Kripke structure in Fig. 5. In this Kripke structure, we have two Kripke states designated S_{0Read} and S_{0Write}. These states represent the state of the LLFSM immediately before *ReadSnapshot* and immediately after *WriteSnapshot* respectively. Due to the snapshot semantics, our external vari-

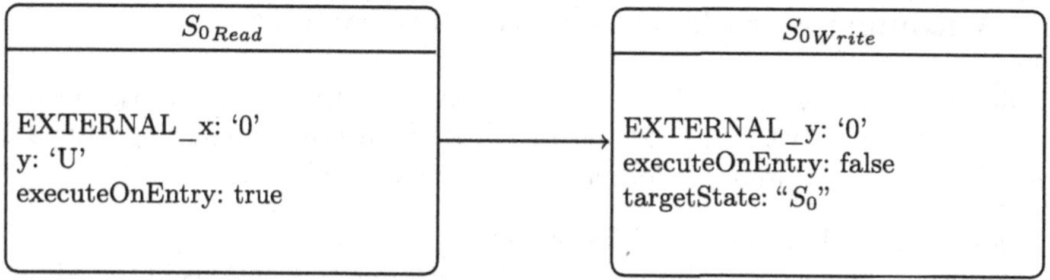

Fig. 5. The Optimized First Ringlet of State S_0 when $EXTERNAL\_x$ = '0'.

ables (which map to sensors and actuators) only affect (or are affected by) the execution of our machine during these points in time. Therefore, since these values do not impact the machine's runtime during the ringlet execution, we can treat the ringlet as a black box removing the intermediate states from the Kripke structure entirely.

We can also remove unnecessary variables from the Kripke structure that are used to track and execute the LLFSM semantics. For example, we can remove *previousRinglet* since the only influence this variable has is to decide whether to execute *OnEntry* or not. Since this condition is a boolean, we can replace the *previousRinglet* variable with a simple *executeOnEntry* variable. This optimisation removes the possibility of state explosions from additional state transitions in the LLFSM. We also remove *internalState* since this variable is used to track the ringlets execution. Since we are treating the ringlet as a black box, we do not need to include this variable in the Kripke structure.

In $S_{0\,Read}$, we can also remove *targetState* since this variable has no influence over how the ringlet is executed and the x snapshot since it is the same as $EXTERNAL\_x$. In $S_{0\,Write}$, we can remove the y snapshot since it is equal to $EXTERNAL\_y$ and the $EXTERNAL\_x$ variable and x snapshot since their values will be modified in the next *Read* state. The x variables in the $Write$ state do not influence the next *Read* state.

The new Kripke structure contains 2 states per value of $EXTERNAL\_x$ (*Read* and $Write$). Since there are 9 values of x in this ringlet, we have a total of $9 \cdot 2 = 18$ Kripke states for this ringlet. This number presents an 89% reduction in the size of the Kripke structure for this ringlet.

There is one further optimisation that we have included in the LLFSM semantics. During the *ReadSnapshot* phase of the ringlets execution, we read all input external variables into local copies. We have modified this semantics slightly to only read the input variables that a state is using in one of its ringlets. This further optimisation removes additional external variables from a *Read* Kripke state if those variables were not used in that Kripke states ringlet. This approach allows us to use many different variables in different states without creating a combinatorial state explosion.

4 Automatic Kripke Structure Generation

To evaluate our design, we have implemented several tools to perform Kripke structure generation for LLFSMs on FPGAs. The process of creating LLFSMs for FPGAs and performing a formal verification is as follows.

1. Design the LLFSM in an LLFSM editor.
2. Perform code generation using the built-in compilation options in the editor. The generated code will contain the VHDL code for the LLFSM and the Kripke structure generator.
3. Synthesis, place and route.
4. Generate the bitstream and load onto the FPGA.
5. Use external interfaces such as Ethernet, or UART to retrieve the generated Kripke structure.

Our Kripke structure generator takes advantage of the parallel architecture of the FPGA to generate the correct Kripke structure. To parallelise our generation, we have decomposed the LLFSM into ringlets that need to be executed and evaluated. The generator begins in the initial state of the LLFSM and executes the first ringlet to determine the next reachable state to execute. The generator then follows a specific procedure until it has executed all reachable states. The procedure of the generator is composed of the following steps.

1. Choose the next state to execute. This will include the state to execute, the value of its output external variables, the machine variables, the state variables, and whether the LLFSM needs to execute *OnEntry*.
2. Choose all possible combinations of input external variables that this state uses and execute them on the LLFSM in parallel for each combination. In the example shown in Fig. 2, this would be 1 LLFSM for the *Initial* state and 9 LLFSMs for the S_0 state.
3. Execute the LLFSMs starting in *ReadSnapshot* and wait until they reach *WriteSnapshot*.
4. Stop the LLFSMs and save the *Read* and *Write* states, removing all duplicates.
5. Determine the next set of states to execute by observing the *Write* states and the previous states that were executed.
6. If there are no more states to execute, stop generating, otherwise go to Step 1.

Following this procedure, the LLFSM dictates the states to explore in the Kripke structure generation. Each new Kripke state that is *discovered* is recorded by the generator and used to explore the state-space of the LLFSM further. If the Kripke state is *new*, then the generator will place it onto a queue of states to explore further (i.e. subsequent *Read* states resulting from the new *Write* state). Following this process, the generator will continue to discover new Kripke states until it has explored the entire reachable state space of the LLFSM. Throughout the Kripke structure generation, the generator tracks previously explored Kripke states to remove duplicate pathways. If a *Read* state has been explored previously, then the Kripke structure generator will not execute that ringlet again. The generator finishes when there are no more Kripke states left to explore.

The accuracy and completeness of the Kripke structure generation is guaranteed since the execution of the LLFSM drives the entire process. The Kripke structure generator is simply *observing* and *recording* the Kripke states as the LLFSM encounters them. When the generator *observes* all reachable Kripke states (i.e. there are no more *Read* states queued), the generation is *finished* and the Kripke structure is complete. Moreover, the structure is completely representative of the behaviour of the LLFSM as the structure is directly generated from the LLFSM execution.

The Kripke structure generator is generated for each machine from the states and variables contained within the LLFSM. The entire Kripke Structure generator exists within a small number of VHDL source files, including the generated code for the LLFSMs. These files may be included in existing HDL projects to facilitate interoperability between other components within the project. No additional tooling is required to facilitate the new VHDL source files in these projects.

4.1 Furnace Relay Case Study

We now demonstrate our approach with an example taken from the literature. Consider the UML state machine shown in Fig. 6. This FSM is taken directly from McUmber and Cheng's paper [17]. McUmber and Cheng's FSM is converted to VHDL using their code generator. Due to the embedded hardware in FPGAs, this translation is not exact and incurs semantic differences between model definition and execution. The authors use a process block to represent each state within the *FurnaceRelay* FSM. This process block does not contain any signals in its sensitivity list, nor does it incorporate any clock sources. This code is not synthesisable as signals within this FSM are latched with flip-flops during the rising edge of a clock signal. The authors of this paper have ignored this and tried to create a purely event-triggered semantics consistent with UML by setting event signals high within extremely small durations (1 fs in this example) before exiting. This behaviour tries to emulate the instantaneous nature of

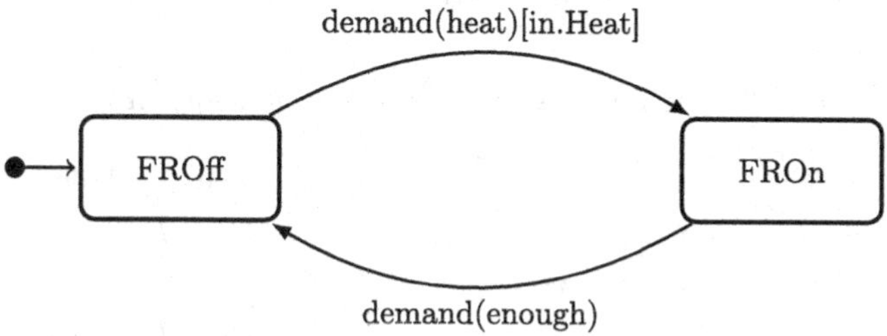

Fig. 6. The FurnaceRelay UML State Machine

formal events but incurs a small, but finite amount of time as a result of executing on real hardware. Physics dictates that instantaneous events are not possible within digital circuits, as it takes time to latch and propagate signals within the FPGAs fabric. The delays are considerable (when compared to the 1 fs specification) using the limited clock frequencies of FPGAs. More importantly, they can create an inconsistent behaviour due to the partial ordering of events [23,24] creating divergence points in the UML semantics.

4.2 Utilising LLFSM Semantics

Even though the authors reference event-driven UML semantics [17], the actual semantics of their FSM is more akin to that of an LLFSM, but hiding the crucial fact that a latched logic value is what is being evaluated. An LLFSM polls its variables and assigns new values at specific points in time [19]. This process translates well into FPGAs as they latch signals based on clock edges [15]. We may thus translate LLFSM models into FPGAs without incurring semantic differences [15]. Therefore, to formally verify the FSM in Fig. 6, it is preferable to perform a mapping into an LLFSM first.

To perform an accurate formal verification, we first convert the UML FSM into an LLFSM. We have attempted to match the UML FSM with variables of the same size and type. However, some of the code is missing from the publication and conservative assumptions were made to create a synthesisable LLFSM. Specifically, the *demand* variable needed to support at least 4 different values, so we have chosen a 2-bit *std_logic_vector* instead of the enumeration in the original publication. We have also replaced the *instate* signal that was indicating the state of the relay with a *std_logic* signal called *relayOn*. The *instate* signal definition was not shown in the original publication. The resulting LLFSM is depicted in Fig. 7 with the variables in Table 2. The resulting VHDL code for this LLFSM and its Kripke structure generator is available on *GitHub* [25] and consists of 729 *FurnaceRelay* LLFSMs executing in parallel. The Kripke structure size of this LLFSM is 4543 Kripke states and it took 740 ns to generate the entire graph on the FPGA at 125 MHz. The Kripke structure size of the corresponding UML FSM is estimated to be greater than 4,782,969 Kripke states. The LLFSM-equivalent Kripke structure is thus reduced by more than 99.9%. To highlight the Kripke structure generation, we have provided screenshots of simulation results for some of these ringlets.

Table 2. The variables within the *FurnaceRelay* LLFSM.

Name	Type	Scope	Mode
heat	*std_logic*	*External*	*input*
demand	*std_logic_vector(1 downto 0)*	*External*	*input*
relayOn	*std_logic*	*External*	*output*

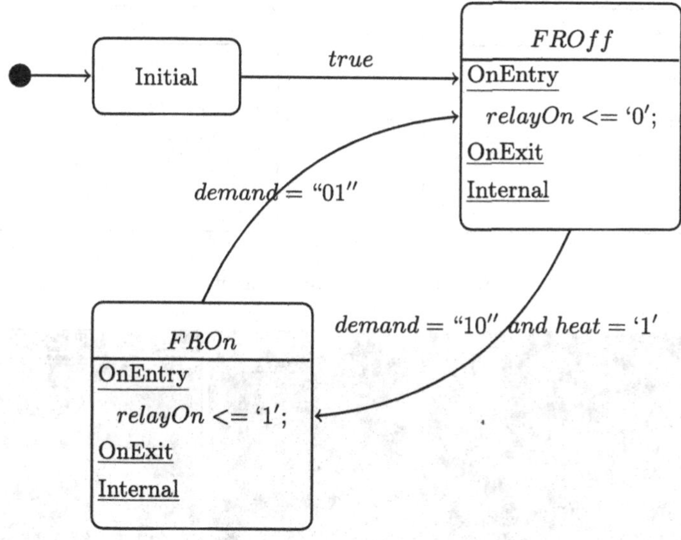

Fig. 7. The FurnaceRelay LLFSM.

We begin in the *Initial* state by executing the initial ringlet of the LLFSM (Figs. 8 and 9).

[0]	(U,TRUE),(U,1,TRUE),TRUE	(U,TRUE),(U,1,TRUE),TRUE
readSnapshot	U,TRUE	U,TRUE
.fr_relayOn	U	
.executeOnEntry	TRUE	TRUE
writeSnapshot	U,1,TRUE	U,1,TRUE
.fr_relayOn	U	
nextState[1:0]	1	1
.executeOnEntry	TRUE	TRUE
.observed	TRUE	TRUE

Fig. 8. The *Initial* Ringlet Waveforms.

This ringlet transitions the LLFSM into the *FROff* state. Once in that state, the LLFSM will either transition to *FROn* if *demand* is "10" and *heat* is '1' (Figs. 10 and 11) or otherwise remain in *FROff* (Figs. 12 and 13). Please note that the figures for the *FROff* ringlets represent the ringlet where the previous state was *FROn*. This is why *relayOn* is logic high during the *Read* phase of this Kripke structure. When the LLFSM is in *FROn*, it will either transition back to *FROff* when *demand* is "01" (Figs. 14 and 15) or otherwise remain in *FROn* (Figs. 16 and 17).

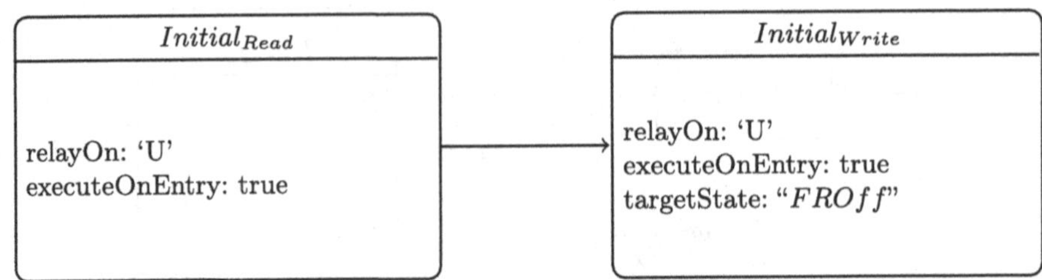

Fig. 9. The *Initial* Ringlet.

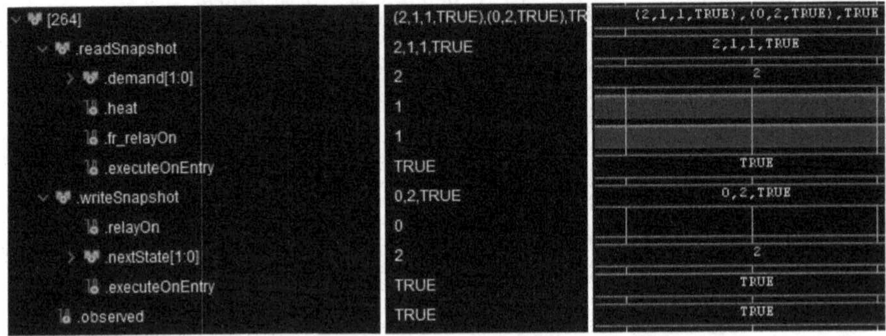

Fig. 10. Waveforms of an *FROff* Ringlet that Transitions to *FROn*.

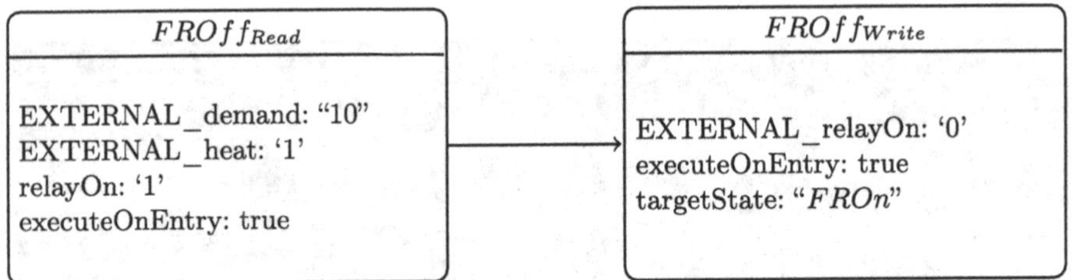

Fig. 11. An *FROff* Ringlet that Transitions to *FROn*.

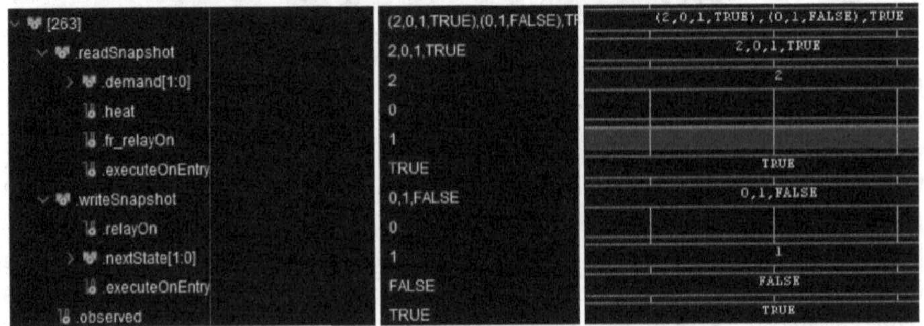

Fig. 12. Waveforms of an *FROff* Ringlet that doesn't Transition.

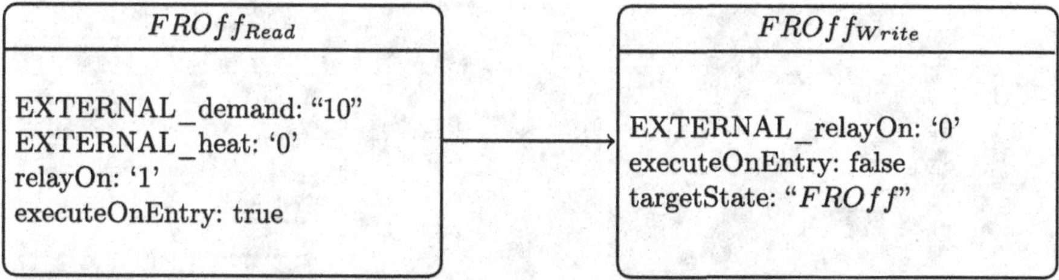

Fig. 13. An *FROff* Ringlet that doesn't Transition.

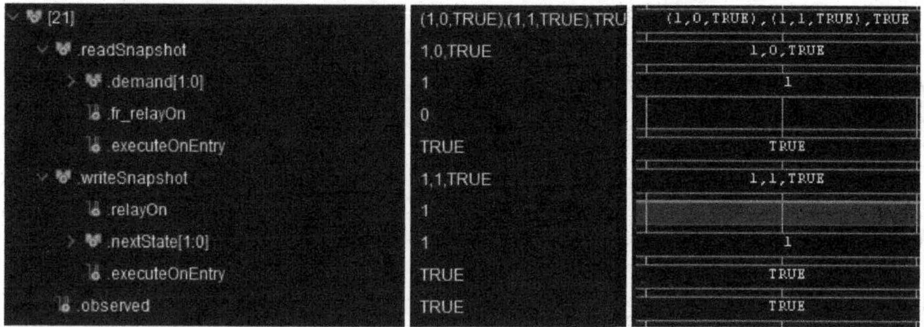

Fig. 14. Waveforms of an *FROn* Ringlet that Transitions to *FROff*.

The previous description provided an overview of the behaviour of our LLFSM by examining the ringlets executed in the Kripke structure. Covering these cases, the Kripke structure generator executes these ringlets until all reachable ringlets have been executed. Once this has been achieved, the generator stops and the Kripke structure is complete.

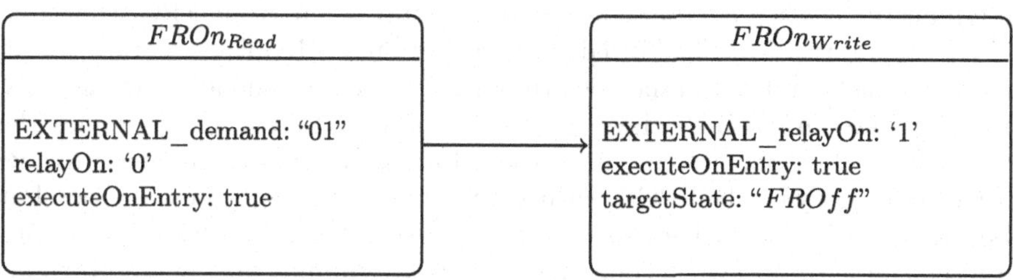

Fig. 15. An *FROn* Ringlet that Transitions to *FROff*.

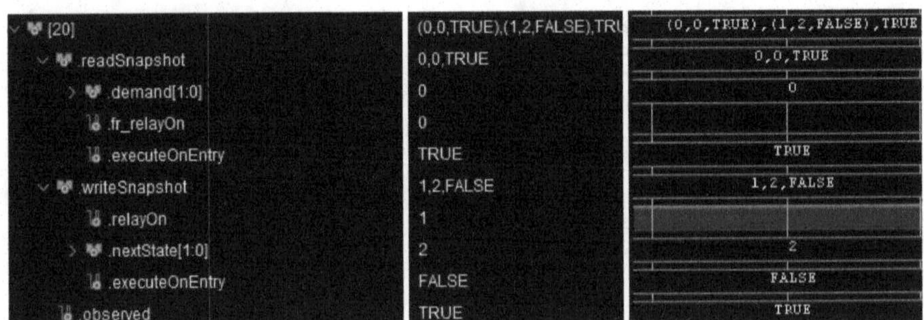

Fig. 16. Waveforms of an *FROn* Ringlet that doesn't Transition.

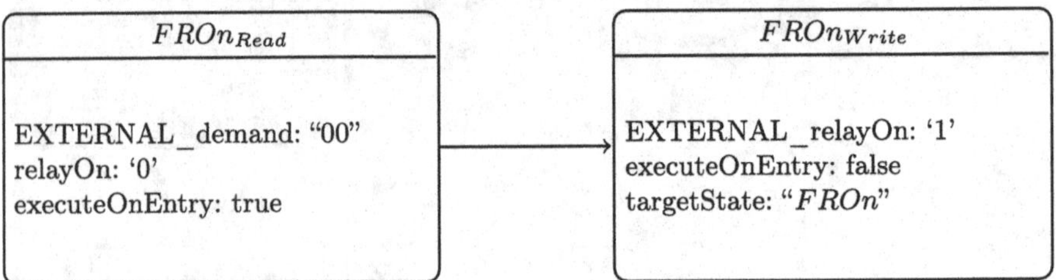

Fig. 17. An *FROn* Ringlet that doesn't Transition.

5 Conclusion

In this paper, we have demonstrated the feasibility of automatic verification of high-level executable models running on FPGAs. We have shown how we can model system behaviour using logic-labelled finite-state machines. Importantly, we can utilise the parallelism that FPGAs provide without jeopardising the atomicity of executing ringlets, implementing snapshot behaviour utilising deterministic, clock-synchronised execution of states across the FPGA fabric.

We have further demonstrated how we can create Kripke structures in an automated fashion that can then be utilised using standard model-checking tools. Moreover, we can optimise these Kripke structures to significantly reduce the state-space needed for system verification. Finally, we can create these Kripke structures directly on the FPGA, ensuring not only consistency in semantics, but also dramatically increasing the speed with which we can create these Kripke structures in hardware when compared to software running on a microprocessor.

References

1. Bucchiarone, A., Cabot, J., Paige, R.F., Pierantonio, A.: Grand challenges in model-driven engineering: an analysis of the state of the research. Softw. Syst. Model. **19**(1), 5–13 (2020). https://doi.org/10.1007/s10270-019-00773-6
2. Bucchiarone, A., et al.: What is the future of modeling? IEEE Softw. **38**(02), 119–127 (2021)

3. McColl, C., Estivill-Castro, V., McColl, M., Hexel, R.: Verifiable executable models for decomposable real-time systems. In: MODELSWARD, pp. 182–193 (2022)
4. Besnard, V., Brun, M., Jouault, F., Teodorov, C., Dhaussy, P.: Unified LTL verification and embedded execution of UML models. In: Proceedings of the 21th ACM/IEEE International Conference on Model Driven Engineering Languages and Systems, MODELS 2018, pp. 112–122. Association for Computing Machinery, New York (2018)
5. Guermazi, S., Tatibouet, J., Cuccuru, A., Seidewitz, E., Dhouib, S., Gérard, S.: Executable modeling with fUML and Alf in Papyrus: tooling and experiments. In: Mayerhofer, T., Langer, P., Seidewitz, E., Gray, J. (eds.) Proceedings of the 1st International Workshop on Executable Modeling Co-Located with ACM/IEEE 18th International Conference on Model Driven Engineering Languages and Systems (MODELS 2015), Volume 1560 of CEUR Workshop Proceedings, pp. 3–8. CEUR-WS.org (2015)
6. Pham, V.C., Radermacher, A., Gérard, S., Li, S.: Complete code generation from UML state machine. In: Ferreira Pires, L., Hammoudi, S., Selic, B. (eds.) Proceedings of the 5th International Conference on Model-Driven Engineering and Software Development, MODELSWARD 2017, Porto, Portugal, 19–21 February 2017, pp. 208–219. SciTePress (2017)
7. Iqbal, M., Ali, S., Yue, T., Briand, L.: Applying UML/MARTE on industrial projects: challenges, experiences, and guidelines. Softw. Syst. Model. **14**(4), 1367–1385 (2015). https://doi.org/10.1007/s10270-014-0405-5
8. Petre, M.: UML in practice. In: 2013 35th International Conference on Software Engineering (ICSE), pp. 722–731 (2013)
9. Beeck, M.: A comparison of Statecharts variants. In: Langmaack, H., de Roever, W.-P., Vytopil, J. (eds.) FTRTFT 1994. LNCS, vol. 863, pp. 128–148. Springer, Heidelberg (1994). https://doi.org/10.1007/3-540-58468-4_163
10. Mäkinen, S., Münch, J.: Effects of test-driven development: a comparative analysis of empirical studies. In: Winkler, D., Biffl, S., Bergsmann, J. (eds.) SWQD 2014. LNBIP, vol. 166, pp. 155–169. Springer, Cham (2014). https://doi.org/10.1007/978-3-319-03602-1_10
11. Hilton, M., Tunnell, T., Huang, K., Marinov, D., Dig, D.: Usage, costs, and benefits of continuous integration in open-source projects. In: Proceedings of the 31st IEEE/ACM International Conference on Automated Software Engineering, ASE 2016, pp. 426–437. Association for Computing Machinery, New York (2016)
12. Lamport, L.: Using time instead of timeout for fault-tolerant distributed systems. ACM Trans. Program. Lang. Syst. **6**, 254–280 (1984)
13. Furrer, F.J.: Future-Proof Software-Systems: A Sustainable Evolution Strategy. Springer, Berlin (2019). https://doi.org/10.1007/978-3-658-19938-8
14. Estivill-Castro, V., Hexel, R.: Module isolation for efficient model checking and its application to FMEA in model-driven engineering. In: Proceedings of the 8th International Conference on Evaluation of Novel Approaches to Software Engineering, pp. 218–225 (2013)
15. Estivill-Castro, V., Hexel, R., McColl, M.: High-level executable models of reactive real-time systems with logic-labelled finite-state machines and FPGAs. In: 2018 International Conference on ReConFigurable Computing and FPGAs (ReConFig), pp. 1–8 (2018)
16. Wood, S.K., Akehurst, D.H., Uzenkov, O., Howells, W.G.J., McDonald-Maier, K.D.: A model-driven development approach to mapping UML state diagrams to synthesizable VHDL. IEEE Trans. Comput. **57**(10), 1357–1371 (2008)

17. McUmber, W.E., Cheng, B.H.C.: UML-based analysis of embedded systems using a mapping to VHDL. In: Proceedings of the 4th IEEE International Symposium on High-Assurance Systems Engineering, pp. 56–63 (1999)
18. Labiak, G., Borowik, G.: Statechart-based controllers synthesis in FPGA structures with embedded array blocks. Int. J. Electron. Telecommun. **56**(1), 13–24 (2010)
19. Estivill-Castro, V., Hexel, R.: Arrangements of finite-state machines - semantics, simulation, and model checking. In: Proceedings of the 1st International Conference on Model-Driven Engineering and Software Development, MODELSWARD, vol. 1, pp. 182–189. INSTICC, SciTePress (2013)
20. Selic, B., Gullekson, G., Ward, P.T.: Real-Time Object-Oriented Modeling. Wiley, Hoboken (1994)
21. Cavada, R., et al.: The nuXmv symbolic model checker. In: Biere, A., Bloem, R. (eds.) CAV 2014. LNCS, vol. 8559, pp. 334–342. Springer, Cham (2014). https://doi.org/10.1007/978-3-319-08867-9_22
22. Vivado Design Suite User Guide: Synthesis (UG901)
23. Lamport, L.: Time, clocks, and the ordering of events in a distributed system, pp. 179–196. Association for Computing Machinery, New York (2019)
24. Kopetz, H.: Sparse time versus dense time in distributed real-time systems. In: 1992 Proceedings of the 12th International Conference on Distributed Computing Systems, pp. 460–467 (1992)
25. McColl, M.: FurnaceRelay LLFSM, version 1.0.0 (2023). https://github.com/Morgan2010/FurnaceRelay

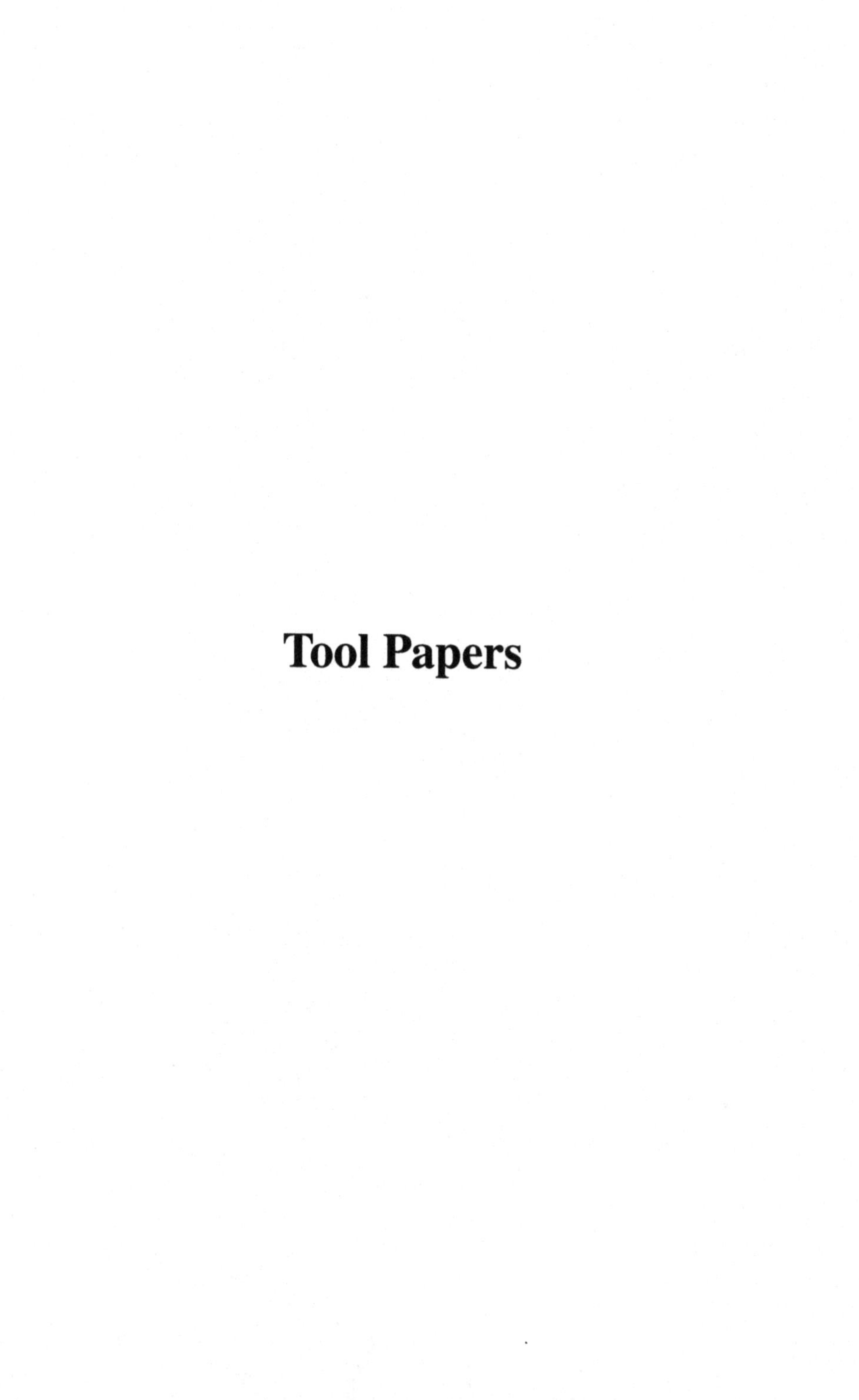

Tool Papers

AutoKoopman: A Toolbox for Automated System Identification via Koopman Operator Linearization

Ethan Lew[1(✉)], Abdelrahman Hekal[2], Kostiantyn Potomkin[2], Niklas Kochdumper[3], Brandon Hencey[4], Stanley Bak[3], and Sergiy Bogomolov[2]

[1] Galois Inc., Portland, OR, USA
elew@galois.com
[2] School of Computing, Newcastle University, Newcastle Upon Tyne, UK
[3] Department of Computer Science, Stony Brook University, New York, NY, USA
[4] Air Force Research Laboratory, Wright-Patterson Air Force Base, Dayton, OH, USA

Abstract. While Koopman operator linearization has brought many advances for prediction, control, and verification of dynamical systems, its main disadvantage is that the quality of the resulting model heavily depends on the correct tuning of hyper-parameters such as the number of observables. Our `AutoKoopman` toolbox is a Python package that automates learning accurate models in a Koopman linearized representation with low effort, offering several tuning strategies to optimize the hyper-parameters associated with the Koopman operator techniques automatically. `AutoKoopman` supports discrete as well as continuous-time models and implements all major types of observables, which are polynomials, random Fourier features, and neural networks. As we demonstrate on several benchmarks, our toolbox is able to automatically identify very accurate dynamic models for symbolic, black-box, as well as real systems. AutoKoopman is available at https://github.com/EthanJamesLew/AutoKoopman and on PyPI as `autokoopman`.

Keywords: Koopman operator linearization · system identification · random Fourier features · deep Koopman

1 Introduction

Identifying models that represent the dynamic behavior of systems is a central challenge in science and engineering. Koopman operator theory has emerged as a useful perspective of these systems because it equivalently represents nonlinear systems by higher-dimensional linear systems [17], allowing one to leverage a robust body of linear system analysis methods. In particular, Koopman operator linearization transforms the states of the original system into a new space of observables where the dynamics are linear. Obtaining the nonlinear mapping from states to observables is a prime challenge and often inhibits practical

É. André and J. Sun (Eds.): ATVA 2023, LNCS 14216, pp. 237–250, 2023.
https://doi.org/10.1007/978-3-031-45332-8_12

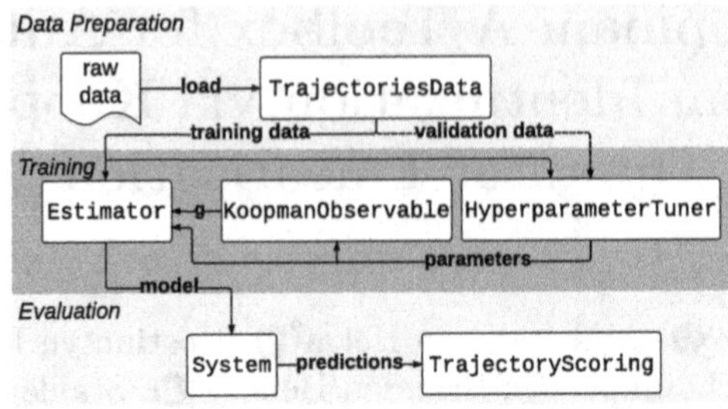

Fig. 1. High-level structure of the `AutoKoopman` toolbox

application. Our `AutoKoopman` toolbox addresses this issue by automating this process, which also enables non-experts to efficiently use the Koopman framework.

Let us first summarize the state of the art for Koopman operator linearization. Koopman theory has long been used for analysis [5,26], control [18,31], and verification [2,3] of dynamical systems, and also several theoretical contributions motivate it as a well-suited representation for data-driven models [25,27]. For identifying linear systems, dynamic mode decomposition (DMD) is the ubiquitous method for learning the system matrices from data trajectories [35,37]. While DMD produces a best-fit linear model, advances have been made to extend it to highly nonlinear systems by fixing the observables in the Koopman framework to a specified function [43,44]. In addition, variants for DMD have been developed for many adjacent problems, such as control [33], noisy models [41], and multi-resolution components [19]. More recently, techniques leverage deep learning to discover arbitrary Koopman representations. These techniques often use autoencoders to learn an observables mapping [1,42,46]. A notable variation to the autoencoder architecture aims to reduce the dimensionality of the observable space by adding an auxiliary network that parameterizes continuous spectra of a system [22]. Finally, Koopman linearization is related to the more general problem of coordinate discovery. While Koopman linearization embeds states in a space where their dynamics become linear, coordinate discovery embeds in them a space where the dynamics become simpler but can remain weakly nonlinear. Recent work combines sparse symbolic regression and deep learning approaches to identify such spaces [8,28].

Some libraries exist for identifying dynamics: pySINDy [39] uses sparse regression to learn system equations. The packages pyDMD [11] and pyKoopman [32] implement system identification algorithms via variants of DMD, though they do not provide deep learning-based approaches. Moreover, the estimators in these packages depend on numerous hyper-parameters that need to be tuned either manually or with another framework. To the best of our knowledge, there do not exist any libraries that provide general implementations of Koopman approaches with neural network observables.

2 Problem Statement

We aim to identify the dynamics of a continuous-time system $\dot{\mathbf{x}}(t) = \mathbf{f}(\mathbf{x}(t), \mathbf{u}(t))$ with state $\mathbf{x}(t) \in \mathcal{X} \subseteq \mathbb{R}^n$ and input $\mathbf{u}(t) \in \mathcal{U} \subseteq \mathbb{R}^m$ from a set of o trajectories

$$\mathcal{T} = \left\{ [(\mathbf{x}_i(t_0), \mathbf{u}_i(t_0)), \ldots, (\mathbf{x}_i(t_{s_i - 1}), \mathbf{u}_i(t_{s_i - 1}))] \right\}_{i=1}^{o},$$

where the i-th trajectory has s_i snapshots. For the ease of presentation we assume that the observations are sampled with time step $\Delta t = t_{k+1} - t_k$, though `AutoKoopman` does not require this. Since we only require the states at specific time points, we from now on consider the equivalent discrete-time system

$$\mathbf{x}_{k+1} = \mathbf{F}_{\Delta t}(\mathbf{x}_k, \mathbf{u}_k), \tag{1}$$

where the flow function $\mathbf{F}_t : \mathbb{R}^n \times \mathbb{R}^m \to \mathbb{R}^n$ is defined as

$$\mathbf{F}_t\left(\mathbf{x}_0, \mathbf{u}(t)\right) = \mathbf{x}_0 + \int_0^t \mathbf{f}(\mathbf{x}(\tau), \mathbf{u}(\tau)) d\tau, \tag{2}$$

and we use the shorthand notation $\mathbf{x}_k = \mathbf{x}(t_k)$. The only requirement we have on the system in (1) is that it is possible to generate system trajectories from it. Consequently, the system dynamics can be described by an arbitrary black-box function $\mathbf{f}(\mathbf{x}(t), \mathbf{u}(t))$, which includes hybrid systems, discrete-time systems, and even real systems.

Rather than learning $\mathbf{f}$ generically, we use Koopman operator linearization, which results in a globally linear representation of the system. Koopman linearization utilizes a new space $\mathcal{H}$, which is defined by the image of the states and inputs through an observables function $\mathbf{g} : \mathcal{X} \times \mathcal{U} \to \mathcal{H}$. The dynamics of the system are then governed by a linear operator $\mathcal{K}_t : \mathcal{H} \to \mathcal{H}$,

$$\mathcal{K}_t\big(\mathbf{g}(\mathbf{x}_0, \mathbf{u}_0)\big) = \mathbf{g}\big(\mathbf{F}_t(\mathbf{x}_0, \mathbf{u}_0), \mathbf{u}(t)\big), \tag{3}$$

which is the so-called Koopman operator. Note that since it is linear, the Koopman operator $\mathcal{K}_t(\mathbf{x}) = K_t\mathbf{x}$ can be represented by a matrix $K_t \in \mathbb{R}^{p \times p}$. While for each nonlinear system there exists a space $\mathcal{H}$ that enables the exact Koopman linearization in (3), this space is infinite dimensional in general. While techniques exist which can learn an infinite dimensional linear operator implicitly—e.g. kernel methods [44]—we utilize ones that learn the operator explicitly. Therefore, our goal is to find a finite space $\mathcal{H}$ where the dynamics can be approximated well by a linear operator. This corresponds to the following optimization problem for finding the observables $\mathbf{g}$ and the Koopman operator $K_{\Delta t}$ via minimization of the mean square error over the set of trajectories $\mathcal{T}$:

$$\operatorname{argmin}_{\mathbf{g},\, K_{\Delta t}} \sum_{(\mathbf{x}_k, \mathbf{u}_k) \in \mathcal{T}} \left\| \mathbf{g}\left(\mathbf{x}_{k+1}, \mathbf{u}_{k+1}\right) - K_{\Delta t}\mathbf{g}\left(\mathbf{x}_k, \mathbf{u}_k\right) \right\|_{\mathrm{MSE}}. \tag{4}$$

While (4) considers the error for the prediction over one time step, it is also possible to minimize the aggregated error for the prediction over multiple time steps. Since finding the optimal solution for the optimization problem (4) is infeasible in general, one instead aims to compute a close-to-optimal solution in a heuristic way, often by fixing the observables $\mathbf{g}$ and then learning $K_{\Delta t}$. Moreover, it is common practice to consider an observable mapping $\mathbf{g}(\mathbf{x}_k, \mathbf{u}_k) = [\mathbf{g}_x(\mathbf{x}_k), \mathbf{u}_k]$ with an observable function $\mathbf{g}_x$ that acts only on the states. In this case the dynamics of the Koopman linearized system (3) can be formulated as

$$\mathbf{g}_x(\mathbf{x}_{k+1}) = A\,\mathbf{g}_x(\mathbf{x}_k) + B\,\mathbf{u}_k, \quad A \in \mathbb{R}^{p\times p},\ B \in \mathbb{R}^{p\times m}, \tag{5}$$

where $K_{\Delta t} = [A, B]$. Note that it is also possible to directly identify a continuous-time instead of a discrete-time model, which we describe in detail in Sect. 3.3.

3 Toolbox Features

We now present the features and implementation details of the `AutoKoopman` package. `AutoKoopman` is written in Python 3.9 and uses the third-party packages Pytorch for deep learning, pySindy for system identification, and pyDMD for dynamic mode composition. Figure 1 outlines the package architecture. The toolbox uses a modular design, making it very easy to exchange single modules by custom implementations and to add new functionality. For example, one can easily add different optimization algorithms for performing the hyper-parameter tuning. Moreover, the toolbox provides a convenience function `auto_koopman` that allows the user to access the whole functionality of the toolbox with a single function call and without requiring any knowledge about the underlying class structure. Let us demonstrate this convenience function with the following code example:

```
from autokoopman import auto_koopman

experiment_results = auto_koopman(
    training_data,      # list of trajectories
    obs_type="rff",     # random Fourier feature observables
    opt="bopt")         # auto-tuning via bayesian optimization
```

The results returned by this code example contain the identified Koopman model as well as the optimal parameter values determined by hyper-parameter optimization. The convenience function provides many settings to refine the training and optimization process, but they all have reasonable defaults to learn accurate models even if the user does not specify any settings.

3.1 Trajectories Data Preparation

The input to `AutoKoopman` is a set of trajectories $\mathcal{T}$, which is represented as an object of class `TrajectoriesData` class. This class provides many data preparation methods so that `AutoKoopman` can automatically pre-process the data before training. For example, if a discrete-time model should be identified and the provided data is not uniformly sampled, interpolation methods are used to convert the data to a uniform time series. Moreover, numerical differentiation methods for approximating the time-derivative are available, which is required for identifying continuous-time models. Overall, `AutoKoopman` therefore has no special requirements on the format of the data, making it very convenient to use the toolbox.

3.2 Types of Observables

The observable mapping is represented by the `KoopmanObservable` class. The main method of that class accepts a state and input and returns an element in the observables space $\mathbf{g} : \mathcal{X} \times \mathcal{U} \to \mathcal{H}$. One convenient feature is that the observable functions are composable: Any two observables functions $\mathbf{g}_1, \mathbf{g}_2$ can be augmented together to create larger sets of observables $\mathbf{g}(\mathbf{x}, \mathbf{u}) = [\mathbf{g}_1(\mathbf{x}, \mathbf{u}), \mathbf{g}_2(\mathbf{x}, \mathbf{u})]$. An exemplary use-case for this are applications where it is required to recover the original system state from the observable space, which can be achieved by adding identity observables $\mathbf{g}_1(\mathbf{x}, \mathbf{u}) = \mathbf{x}$.

Random Fourier Features. Random Fourier features [34] are used to approximate kernel DMD using extended DMD [10]. Kernel DMD is part of a class of algorithms that employ kernel functions, a symmetric, positive definite function $k : \mathcal{X} \times \mathcal{X} \to \mathbb{R}$ that encodes the similarity of two observations. Kernels are especially advantageous for high-dimensional feature spaces, where instead of explicitly computing elements of that space, one can instead efficiently compute the similarity between data pairs via the kernel function. Commonly used kernel functions are radial basis functions, polynomials, and spline kernels. In our case we cannot use the kernel function directly since we require an explicit representation of the observable mapping $\mathbf{g}$. We therefore need a method to exploit the advantageous properties of kernels, without sacrificing the explicit observable mapping. Random Fourier features achieve this for stationary kernels by utilizing a connection of a kernel to its Fourier transform [34]. The function $\mathbf{g}_x(\mathbf{x}) = [g_1(\mathbf{x}), \dots, g_p(\mathbf{x})]$ approximately preserves the kernel function $k(\mathbf{x}, \mathbf{x}') \approx \mathbf{g}_x(\mathbf{x})^T \mathbf{g}_x(\mathbf{x}')$ within some error bound, where the scalar observables take the form

$$g_i(\mathbf{x}) = \sqrt{2} \cos\left(\omega_i^T \mathbf{x} + b_i\right), \quad i = 1, \dots, p.$$

Here, $b_i \in \mathbb{R}$ is selected uniformly from the interval $[0, 2\pi]$ and $\omega_i \in \mathbb{R}^n$ is drawn from a probability distribution $\mu(\omega)$ corresponding to the kernel function used. A normal distribution, for example, is used for the radial basis function kernel [34, Fig. 1].

Polynomials. Carleman linearization equivalently represents the dynamic behavior of a polynomial system by an infinite dimensional linear system [7]. This linearization can be viewed as Koopman linearization using a polynomial basis to span the function space. So, a natural choice for observables is a set of multi-variate monomials. For a specific polynomial system only a finite number of monomial terms are required if the vector space spanned by the observables is closed under the operation of Lie-derivatives [36]. However, the number of monomials that exist grows significantly with the dimensions and maximum order of the polynomial. For high polynomial orders, it is therefore often advantageous to represent the polynomial observables implicitly using kernel DMD.

Neural Network Observables. Since neural networks can be trained to represent arbitrary functions, a natural idea is to use them as observables. This approach has been shown to perform very well in many applications such as fluid control [29], object-centric physics [20], and autonomous driving [45]. To find both the mapping and linear dynamics simultaneously, deep learning has been applied successfully. For this, an autoencoder architecture consisting of a encoder/decoder pair $\mathbf{g}_x$, $\mathbf{g}_x^{-1}$ is used, where the encoder $\mathbf{g}_x : \mathcal{X} \rightarrow \mathcal{H}$ maps from the original state space to the observable space and the decoder $\mathbf{g}_x^{-1} : \mathcal{H} \rightarrow \mathcal{X}$ maps from the observable space back to the original space. Both, the encoder as well as the decoder are represented by neural networks. These networks depend on several hyper-parameters—e.g., the number of hidden layers, the dimensions of the hidden layers, and the type of activation function—which can either be set by the user or tuned automatically by `AutoKoopman`. Finally, the loss function for neural network training consists of several loss terms:

(1) Reconstruction loss: $\left\| \mathbf{x}_k - \mathbf{g}_x^{-1}\left(\mathbf{g}_x\left(\mathbf{x}_k\right)\right) \right\|_{\text{MSE}}$

(2) Prediction loss: $\left\| \mathbf{x}_{k+1} - \mathbf{g}_x^{-1}\left(K_{\Delta t}\, \mathbf{g}\left(\mathbf{x}_0, \mathbf{u}_0\right)\right) \right\|_{\text{MSE}}$

(3) Linearity loss: $\left\| \mathbf{g}\left(\mathbf{x}_{k+1}, \mathbf{u}_{k+1}\right) - K_{\Delta t}\, \mathbf{g}\left(\mathbf{x}_k, \mathbf{u}_k\right) \right\|_{\text{MSE}}$

(4) Metric loss: $\sum_{i,j} \left| \|\mathbf{g}_x(\mathbf{x}_i) - \mathbf{g}_x(\mathbf{x}_j)\| - \|\mathbf{x}_i - \mathbf{x}_j\| \right|$

Here, the reconstruction loss captures the reconstruction accuracy of the autoencoder, the prediction loss quantifies how well the network predicts future states, the linearity loss, which is identical to the general cost function in (4), evaluates how well the network predicts future states in the observable space, and the metric loss encourages that distances between states in the original and in the observable space are preserved, which aims to prevent obtaining observables with very large values. Note that the prediction and linearity loss can also be computed over multiple time steps, which often improves the results.

3.3 Regression Estimators

The algorithms represented by the `Estimator` class implement different methods for solving the optimization problem (4).

Dynamic Mode Decomposition. While for neural network observables the Koopman operator is determined together with the observables via deep learning, the common practice for polynomial and random Fourier feature observables is to first determine suitable observables, and then find the Koopman operator that yields the best-fit linear model for these observables. In this case the optimal solution for the optimization problem (4) can be determined via extended dynamic mode decomposition (eDMD) which performs DMD in the observables space [43]. For eDMD one first constructs the matrices $X = [\mathbf{g}_x(\mathbf{x}_0), \dots, \mathbf{g}_x(\mathbf{x}_{s-1})]$, $X' = [\mathbf{g}_x(\mathbf{x}_1), \dots, \mathbf{g}_x(\mathbf{x}_s)]$ and $U = [\mathbf{u}_0, \dots, \mathbf{u}_{s-1}]$ from the set of trajectories $\mathcal{T}$. The dynamics of the Koopman linearized system (5) can then be expressed as $X' = A\,X + B\,U = K_{\Delta t}[X, U]$, so that the optimization problem (4) becomes

$$\text{argmin}_{K_{\Delta t}} \|X' - K_{\Delta t}[X, U]\|_{MSE}.$$

It is well known that the solution that minimizes the mean square error is given as $K_{\Delta t} = X'[X, U]^{+}$, where $[X, U]^{+}$ denotes the Moore-Penrose inverse. Since we usually have a lot of data, the matrix $[X, U]$ is very large. For computational efficiently, the Moore-Penrose inverse is therefore estimated by a low-rank matrix approximation using singular value decomposition (SVD). The rank for SVD is a hyper-parameter, which if tuned properly helps to avoid over-fitting the model to high-frequency noise in the data. If the goal is to identify a continuous-time instead of a discrete-time linear system, we simply have to exchange the matrix X' by the corresponding time-derivatives $X' = [\partial\, \mathbf{g}_x(\mathbf{x}_0)/\partial t, \dots, \partial\, \mathbf{g}_x(\mathbf{x}_{s-1})/\partial t]$, which can be estimated using numerical differentiation

Sparse Regression. Though Koopman theory treats the dynamics in the observables space as linear, techniques exist that relax the observables to a change of coordinates yielding simpler but still nonlinear dynamics [8]. In particular, the goal is to obtain dynamics with only few nonlinear terms, where the nonlinear dynamics is represented as a symbolic closed-form expression. This method is called sparse identification of nonlinear dynamics (SINDy). SINDy treats system identification as a sparse regression problem, attempting to determine terms in the dynamics that are similar to terms in a provided library [6]. This approach comes with a collection of hyper-parameters, which are the library of terms to consider during regression as well as additional sparsity optimization parameters.

3.4 Hyper-parameter Tuning

As shown in the previous section, the overall Koopman linearization process introduces several hyper-parameters. The accuracy of an identified model is typically very sensitive to the choice of these parameters, making adequate manual tuning challenging. `AutoKoopman` therefore provides several strategies for tuning these hyper-parameters automatically, which are presented in this section. All of these strategies apply cross-validation, where the dataset $\mathcal{T}$ is split into a training set $\mathcal{T}_{train}$ and a validation set $\mathcal{T}_{val}$. `AutoKoopman` also supports k-folds cross-validation, which trains the model k times over disjoint validation datasets. This usually results in a better model, but also prolongs the computation time. As a metric for the accuracy of the identified model the loss function for the optimization problem in (4) is used.

Grid Search. Grid search exhaustively samples values for hyper-parameters by generating candidates from a grid. While suitable default values for the search ranges for all hyper-parameters are provided, `AutoKoopman` also allows the user to manually specify ranges for the hyper-parameters that should be optimized. This range is then discretized automatically for the grid search. Grid search is reliable but suffers from the curse of dimensionality; it works well in low-dimensional spaces, but the number of candidates grows exponentially as the hyper-parameter space dimension increases. Grid search is therefore well-suited for polynomial and random Fourier feature observables which only depend on few hyper-parameters, but computationally demanding for neural network observables that come with many parameters.

Random Search. For random search all hyper-parameters are treated as independent random variables with either uniform or log-uniform distribution. The optimization algorithm then samples a fixed number of times or until a given compute budget is exceeded to determine good hyper-parameters. While by default `AutoKoopman` automatically decides for which parameters to use a uniform and for which a log-uniform distribution, this can also be explicitly specified by the user if desired. Random search has many practical advantages compared to grid search—simplicity and parallelism—and performs better in high-dimensional spaces [4].

Bayesian Optimization. Bayesian optimization can quickly find the global minimum of a multi-dimensional function by incorporating information learned from previous hyper-parameter evaluations [38]. This is achieved by constructing the posterior predictive distribution for the loss function. While Bayesian optimization is known for being a more efficient hyper-parameter tuning method than random or grid search, it comes with its own set of hyper-parameters: a covariance function to model the posterior distribution and an acquisition function to select the next batch of points. For the Bayesian optimizer implemented in `AutoKoopman` we choose the commonly used Matern52 covariance function and use a heuristic to determine its lengthscale.

Table 1. Comparison of the constructed Koopman linearized models.

	System		Baseline		Polynomial		Fourier		Neural Net.	
		dims	error	time	error	time	error	time	error	time
symbolic	Pendulum	2	21.4%	0.30	1.37%	14.8	**1.62%**	16.4	43.2%	114
	FitzHugh-Nagumo	2	49.6%	0.18	35.6%	6.23	**0.55%**	15.2	67.8%	147
	Robertson	2	**6.43%**	0.19	**6.43%**	2.79	26.0%	15.0	19.23%	173
	Production-Destruction	2	26.5%	0.19	26.5%	2.77	**2.07%**	15.31	59.3%	323
	Spring Pendulum	4	89.7%	0.19	89.7%	3.73	**0.03%**	15.6	8.6%	98.2
	Laub-Loomis	7	5.47%	0.26	0.21%	9.82	**0.04%**	16.0	22.25%	92.4
	Biological Model	9	0.06%	0.35	0.06%	4.81	**0.01%**	15.7	22.3%	178
	Trans. Regulator Network	48	27.5%	0.53	27.5%	4.57	4.60%	18.4	**3.11%**	165
sim	Engine Control	2	13.5%	3.25	13.5%	40.2	**2.54%**	119	22.9%	429
	Longitudinal Control	7	3.24%	0.32	3.24%	2.09	**0.00%**	35.9	3.13%	164
	Collision Avoidance	16	2.61%	13.1	2.61%	236	**2.39%**	600	95.1%	849
real	Electric Circuit	3	**14.4%**	25.1	**14.4%**	2217	**14.4%**	1609	14.9%	1240
	F1tenth Racecar	4	64.1%	1.88	64.1%	53.9	60.1%	41.7	**50.7%**	177
	Robot Arm	12	66.4%	11.1	66.4%	163	33.0%	517	**23.9%**	360

4 Numerical Experiments

In this section we evaluate the performance of `AutoKoopman` on several benchmark systems. These benchmarks can be categorised into three groups: symbolic models, black-box models, and real data. The results for different types of observables are summarized in Table 1. For comparison, we also added the results for baseline linearization, which identifies a linear model without using the Koopman framework. As a metric for the accuracy of the identified models we use the relative error based on the Euclidean norm, which is defined as

$$\epsilon = \frac{1}{s} \sum_{i=1}^{s} \frac{\| \mathbf{x}(t_i) - \mathbf{x}_{pred}(t_i) \|_2}{\| \mathbf{x}(t_i) \|_2},$$

where $\mathbf{x}(t)$ is the ground truth data and $\mathbf{x}_{pred}(t)$ is the prediction of the identified model. The error is computed on a validation dataset that is different from the training dataset. For a fair comparison, we use 200 observables for all experiments. Moreover, we apply grid search as the auto-tuning method for baseline linearization, polynomial, random Fourier feature observables and Bayesian optimization for neural network observables. This choice is motivated by the observation that Bayesian optimization usually performs much better than grid search if many hyper-parameters have to be tuned, as it the case for neural network observables. All computations are carried out on a 4-core machine with 60 GB of memory and an NVIDIA K80 GPU.

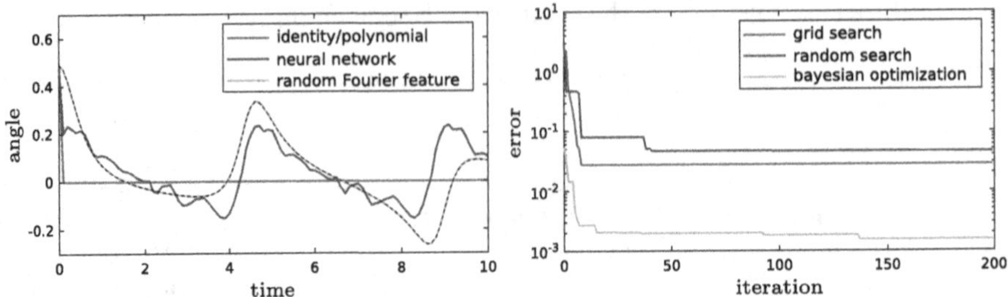

Fig. 2. Left: Predictions for the spring pendulum using different types of observables, where the ground truth is shown by the dashed black line. Right: Hyper-parameter optimization strategies for identifying a Koopman linearized model with random Fourier feature observables for the Laub-Loomis benchmark.

Symbolic Models. First, we examine models for which the dynamics is given by a symbolic nonlinear first-order differential equation. In particular, we consider a pendulum (see [40, Fig. 8.11]), a spring pendulum (see [24, Fig. 1.4]), the FitzHugh-Nagumo model [12], the Robertson chemical reaction system [14, Sect. 3.1], the production destruction and Laub-Loomis benchmarks from [13], the biological model in [9, Example 5.2.4], and a transcriptional regulator network from [23, Sect. VIII.D]. We use a randomly generated training and validation dataset consisting of 10 trajectories each as well as a sampling period of 0.1 s and a final time of 10 s for all models. The results in Table 1 demonstrate that the Koopman linearized models computed with `AutoKoopman` are on average much more accurate compared to identifying a linear model, where random Fourier feature observables achieve especially good results. This can also be seen in Fig. 2 (left), where the predicted trajectories for different types of observables are exemplary visualized for the spring pendulum system. Moreover, training neural network observables via deep learning takes significantly longer than DMD used for the other observables. Finally, the comparison of the different hyper-parameter optimization strategies shown in Fig. 2 (right) demonstrates that more sophisticated optimization strategies such as Bayesian optimization often perform better than simple strategies such as random search.

Black-Box Systems. To evaluate the performance of `AutoKoopman` for black-box systems, we consider the model of a F-16 fighter jet ground collision avoidance system [15]. In particular, we examine the following three scenarios: 2-dimensional engine control, 7-dimensional longitude control, and the full 16-dimensional model. We use 400 trajectories for training the 16-dimensional system, and 20 trajectories for the lower-dimensional cases. Moreover, the final time is 50 s for the 2-dimensional model and 15 s for the two other systems. All other settings are identical to the ones for the symbolic models. The results in Table 1 demonstrate that even for very complex black-box systems `AutoKoopman` is able to identify very accurate models in reasonable time. Note that the computation time for the 16-dimensional model is higher since we used a larger training set.

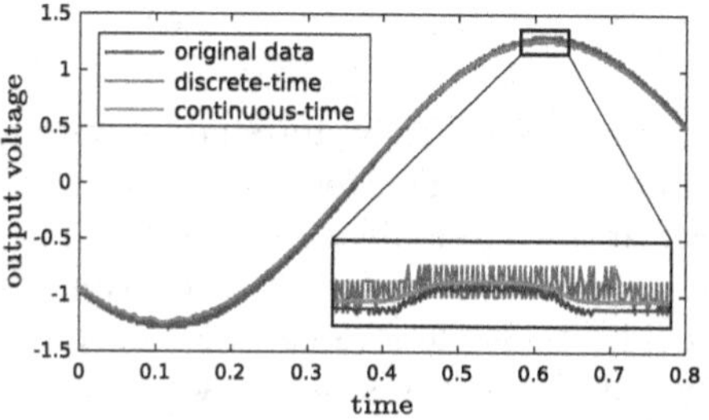

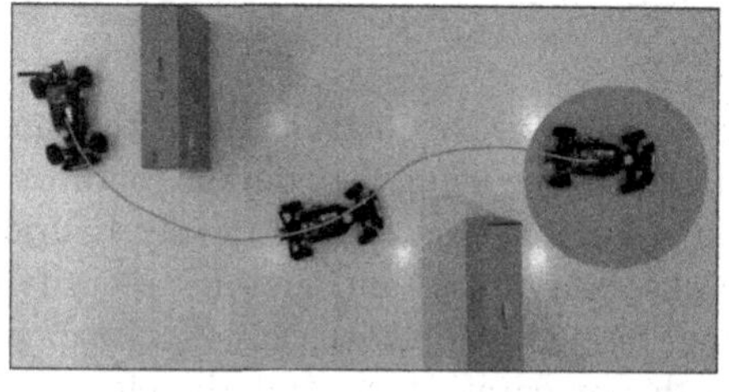

Fig. 3. Left: Predictions from a discrete-time and a continuous-time model identified with `AutoKoopman` on noisy data measured from an electric circuit. Right: Trajectory driven by the F1tenth car during application of model predictive control, where the goal set is shown in green.

Real Measurements. Finally, we can also apply `AutoKoopman` directly to data measured from the real system, which completely eliminates the requirement for a system model. For this we consider a dataset from an electric circuit that represents a LMC6484 lowpass filter [16] consisting of 7 trajectories, a dataset from a 6 degree-of-freedom Schunk LWA 4P robot arm [21] consisting of 100 trajectories, and a dataset from a F1tenth racecar [30] consisting of 41 trajectories. The randomly generated validation dataset consists of 2 trajectories for the electric circuit and 10 trajectories for the two other benchmarks, and we train on all remaining trajectories. The results in Table 1 demonstrate that `AutoKoopman` robustly generates accurate models, even though the measured data traces are perturbed by high-frequent measurement errors. Moreover, as shown in Fig. 3 (left), identifying a continuous-time instead of a discrete-time model can often further improve the results since it might prevent over-fitting to noisy data.

Application to System Control. One of the main advantages of the Koopman framework is that the dynamics of the resulting models is linear, which makes them easier to analyse, verify, and control. We demonstrate this on the example of the F1tenth car, for which we design a model predictive controller that solves a reach-avoid task. In particular, we use the Koopman model that we obtained by applying `AutoKoopman` together with random Fourier feature observables to traces measured from the F1tenth car. Since the dynamics of the system is linear, the optimization problem for model predictive control can be solved very efficiently, which enables us to perform the computations online on the real F1tenth car with a control frequency of 10 Hz. Moreover, the results of the experiments visualized in Fig. 3 (right) demonstrate that the model obtained with `AutoKoopman` is accurate enough to steer the car to the desired goal set while avoiding obstacles.

5 Conclusion

In this paper, we present `AutoKoopman`, a toolbox for fully automated system identification using Koopman operator linearization. The toolbox implements polynomial observables, random Fourier feature observables, and neural network observables, and enables identifying discrete-time as well as continuous time models. Moreover, `AutoKoopman` provides multiple strategies for optimizing hyper-parameters, and therefore fully automates the system identification process. The numerical results demonstrate that `AutoKoopman` is able to identify accurate Koopman linearized models for symbolic system models, black-box systems as well as data measured from real systems. Moreover, the obtained models are well suited for system control, as shown in the example of a F1tenth car.

Acknowledgements. This material is based upon work supported by the Air Force Office of Scientific Research and the Office of Naval Research under award numbers FA9550-19-1-0288, FA9550-21-1-0121, FA9550-23-1-0066 and N00014-22-1-2156. The material of Galois, Inc. is based upon work supported by the Air Force Research Laboratory (AFRL) and DARPA under Contract No. FA8750-20-C-0534. Any opinions, findings, and conclusions or recommendations expressed in this material are those of the authors and do not necessarily reflect the views of the United States Air Force, DARPA, or the United States Navy.

References

1. Alford-Lago, D.J., Curtis, C.W., Ihler, A.T., Issan, O.: Deep learning enhanced dynamic mode decomposition. Chaos: Interdisc. J. Nonlinear Sci. **32**(3), 033116 (2022)
2. Bak, S., et al.: Reachability of black-box nonlinear systems after Koopman operator linearization. In: Proceedings of the International Conference on Analysis and Design of Hybrid Systems, pp. 253–258 (2021)
3. Bak, S., et al.: Reachability of Koopman linearized systems using random Fourier feature observables and polynomial zonotope refinement. In: Shoham, S., Vizel, Y. (eds.) CAV 2022. LNCS, vol. 13371, pp. 490–510. Springer, Cham (2022). https://doi.org/10.1007/978-3-031-13185-1_24
4. Bergstra, J., Bengio, Y.: Random search for hyper-parameter optimization. J. Mach. Learn. Res. **13**(2), 281–305 (2012)
5. Bevanda, P., Sosnowski, S., Hirche, S.: Koopman operator dynamical models: learning, analysis and control. Annu. Rev. Control. **52**, 197–212 (2021)
6. Brunton, S.L., Proctor, J.L., Kutz, J.N.: Discovering governing equations from data by sparse identification of nonlinear dynamical systems. Proc. Natl. Acad. Sci. **113**(15), 3932–3937 (2016)
7. Carleman, T.: Application de la théorie des équations intégrales linéaires aux systèmes d'équations différentielles non linéaires. Acta Math. **59**, 63–87 (1932)
8. Champion, K., Lusch, B., Kutz, J.N., Brunton, S.L.: Data-driven discovery of coordinates and governing equations. Proc. Natl. Acad. Sci. **116**(45), 22445–22451 (2019)
9. Chen, X.: Reachability Analysis of Non-Linear Hybrid Systems Using Taylor Models. Ph.D. thesis, RWTH Aachen University (2015)

10. DeGennaro, A.M., Urban, N.M.: Scalable extended dynamic mode decomposition using random kernel approximation. SIAM J. Sci. Comput. **41**(3), 1482–1499 (2019)
11. Demo, N., Tezzele, M., Rozza, G.: PyDMD: python dynamic mode decomposition. J. Open Source Softw. **3**(22), 530 (2018)
12. FitzHugh, R.: Impulses and physiological states in theoretical models of nerve membrane. Biophys. J . **1**(6), 445–466 (1961)
13. Geretti, L., et al.: ARCH-COMP20 category report: continuous and hybrid systems with nonlinear dynamics. In: Proceedings of the International Workshop on Applied Verification of Continuous and Hybrid Systems, pp. 49–75 (2020)
14. Geretti, L., et al.: ARCH-COMP21 category report: continuous and hybrid systems with nonlinear dynamics. In: Proceedings of the International Workshop on Applied Verification of Continuous and Hybrid Systems, pp. 32–54 (2021)
15. Heidlauf, P., Collins, A., Bolender, M., Bak, S.: Verification challenges in F-16 ground collision avoidance and other automated maneuvers. In: Proceedings of the International Workshop on Applied Verification of Continuous and Hybrid Systems, pp. 208–217 (2018)
16. Kochdumper, N., et al.: Establishing reachset conformance for the formal analysis of analog circuits. In: Proceedings of the Asia and South Pacific Design Automation Conference, pp. 199–204 (2020)
17. Koopman, B.O.: Hamiltonian systems and transformation in Hilbert space. Proc. Natl. Acad. Sci. **17**(5), 315–318 (1931)
18. Korda, M., Mezić, I.: Linear predictors for nonlinear dynamical systems: Koopman operator meets model predictive control. Automatica **93**, 149–160 (2018)
19. Kutz, J.N., Fu, X., Brunton, S.L.: Multiresolution dynamic mode decomposition. SIAM J. Appl. Dyn. Syst. **15**(2), 713–735 (2016)
20. Li, Y., et al.: Learning compositional Koopman operators for model-based control. In: Proceedings of the International Conference on Learning Representations (2020)
21. Liu, S.B., Althoff, M.: Reachset conformance of forward dynamic models for the formal analysis of robots. In: Proceedings of the International Conference on Intelligent Robots and Systems, pp. 370–376 (2018)
22. Lusch, B., Kutz, J.N., Brunton, S.L.: Deep learning for universal linear embeddings of nonlinear dynamics. Nat. Commun. **9**, 4950 (2018)
23. Maïga, M., Ramdani, N., Travé-Massuyè, L., Combastel, C.: A comprehensive method for reachability analysis of uncertain nonlinear hybrid systems. Trans. Autom. Control **61**(9), 2341–2356 (2015)
24. Meiss, J.D.: Differential Dynamical Systems. SIAM (2007)
25. Mezić, I.: Spectral properties of dynamical systems, model reduction and decompositions. Nonlinear Dyn. **41**(1), 309–325 (2005)
26. Mezić, I.: Analysis of fluid flows via spectral properties of the Koopman operator. Annu. Rev. Fluid Mech. **45**, 357–378 (2013)
27. Mezić, I., Banaszuk, A.: Comparison of systems with complex behavior. Physica D **197**(1–2), 101–133 (2004)
28. Michoski, C., Milosavljević, M., Oliver, T., Hatch, D.R.: Solving differential equations using deep neural networks. Neurocomputing **399**, 193–212 (2020)
29. Morton, J., Jameson, A., Kochenderfer, M.J., Witherden, F.: Deep dynamical modeling and control of unsteady fluid flows. In: Advances in Neural Information Processing Systems, vol. 31 (2018)

30. O'Kelly, M., Zheng, H., Karthik, D., Mangharam, R.: F1tenth: an open-source evaluation environment for continuous control and reinforcement learning. Proc. Mach. Learn. Res. **123**, 77–89 (2020)
31. Otto, S.E., Rowley, C.W.: Koopman operators for estimation and control of dynamical systems. Ann. Rev. Control, Robot. Auton. Syst. **4**, 59–87 (2021)
32. Pan, S., Kaiser, E., Kutz, N., Brunton, S.: PyKoopman: a python package for data-driven approximation of the Koopman operator. Bull. Am. Phys. Soc. (2022)
33. Proctor, J.L., Brunton, S.L., Kutz, J.N.: Dynamic mode decomposition with control. SIAM J. Appl. Dyn. Syst. **15**(1), 142–161 (2016)
34. Rahimi, A., Recht, B.: Random features for large-scale kernel machines. In: Proceedings of the International Conference on Neural Information Processing Systems, pp. 1177–1184 (2007)
35. Rowley, C.W., et al.: Spectral analysis of nonlinear flows. J. Fluid Mech. **641**, 115–127 (2009)
36. Sankaranarayanan, S.: Automatic abstraction of non-linear systems using change of bases transformations. In: Proceedings of the International Conference on Hybrid Systems: Computation and Control, pp. 143–152 (2011)
37. Schmid, M.R., Maehlisch, M., Dickmann, J., Wuensche, H.J.: Dynamic level of detail 3D occupancy grids for automotive use. In: Proceedings of the IEEE Intelligent Vehicles Symposium, pp. 269–274 (2010)
38. Shahriari, B., et al.: Taking the human out of the loop: a review of Bayesian optimization. Proc. IEEE **104**(1), 148–175 (2015)
39. de Silva, B., et al.: PySINDy: a python package for the sparse identification of nonlinear dynamical systems from data. J. Open Source Softw. **5**(49), 2014 (2020)
40. Stanford, A.L., Tanner, J.M.: Physics for Students of Science and Engineering. Academic Press, Cambridge (2014)
41. Takeishi, N., Kawahara, Y., Tabei, Y., Yairi, T.: Bayesian dynamic mode decomposition. In: Proceedings of the AAAI Conference on Artificial Intelligence, pp. 2814–2821 (2017)
42. Takeishi, N., Kawahara, Y., Yairi, T.: Learning Koopman invariant subspaces for dynamic mode decomposition (2017)
43. Williams, M.O., Kevrekidis, I.G., Rowley, C.W.: A data-driven approximation of the Koopman operator: extending dynamic mode decomposition. J. Nonlinear Sci. **25**(6), 1307–1346 (2015)
44. Williams, M.O., Rowley, C.W., Kevrekidis, I.G.: A kernel-based approach to data-driven Koopman spectral analysis. J. Comput. Dyn. **2**(2), 247–265 (2014)
45. Xiao, Y., et al.: Deep neural networks with Koopman operators for modeling and control of autonomous vehicles. Trans. Intelli. Veh. **8**, 135–146 (2022). IEEE Early Access
46. Yeung, E., Kundu, S., Hodas, N.: Learning deep neural network representations for Koopman operators of nonlinear dynamical systems. In: Proceedings of the American Control Conference, pp. 4832–4839 (2019)

Leveraging Static Analysis: An IDE for RTLola

Bernd Finkbeiner, Florian Kohn, and Malte Schledjewski(✉)

CISPA Helmholtz Center for Information Security, 66123 Saarbrücken, Germany
{finkbeiner,florian.kohn,malte.schledjewski}@cispa.de

Abstract. Runtime monitoring is an essential part of guaranteeing the safety of cyber-physical systems. Recently, runtime monitoring frameworks based on formal specification languages gained momentum. These languages provide valuable abstractions for specifying the behavior of a system. Yet, writing specifications remains challenging as, among other things, the specifier has to keep track of the timing behavior of streams. This paper presents the RTLola Playground, a browser-based development environment for the stream-based runtime monitoring framework RTLola. It features new methods to explore the static analysis results of RTLola, leveraging the advantages of such a formal language to support the developer in writing and understanding specifications. Specifications are executed locally in the browser, plotting the resulting stream values, allowing for intuitive testing. Step-wise execution based on user-provided system traces enables the debugging of identified errors.

Keywords: Integrated Development Environment · Runtime Monitoring · Static Analysis · Visualization

1 Introduction

Cyber-physical systems have become an essential part of our everyday lives. Being safety-critical, their failure threatens humans and the environment. Consequently, new methods are needed to ensure their correct and safe behavior. While synthesizing or verifying such systems based on logics is an active field of research, applying these approaches to more extensive systems is computationally infeasible. Runtime verification techniques provide scalability by monitoring the system's behavior at runtime. This methodology has proven to be applicable in many real-world scenarios [14,18]. In Runtime Verification, a monitoring component is deployed alongside the system, observing it and producing verdicts about its health and conformity. Such monitors can be realized through conventional programming or generated automatically from a specification given in a formal specification language. One class of formal specification languages adequate for such a task are stream-based specification languages. Pioneered by Lola [15], they process incoming data as streams from which new streams can be computed. Trigger conditions can be defined to assess the system's state and

É. André and J. Sun (Eds.): ATVA 2023, LNCS 14216, pp. 251–262, 2023.
https://doi.org/10.1007/978-3-031-45332-8_13

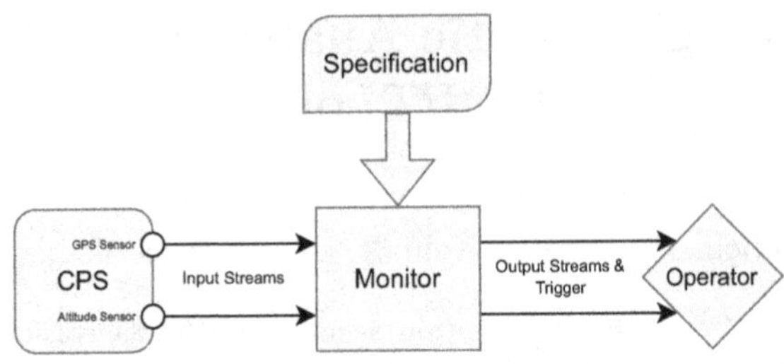

Fig. 1. The stream-based Monitoring Approach

notify an operator in case of a violation. This stream-based monitoring approach is summarized in Fig. 1. One stream-based specification language is RTLola [17]. It features real-time capabilities paired with a strong type system. Other such languages are, for example, TeSSLa [21], and Striver [19].

While stream-based specification languages provide useful abstractions to model the behavior of cyber-physical systems, writing correct specifications and reasoning about them is equally crucial as it is challenging [16]. Especially concerning autonomous aircraft, understanding the specification is essential with regard to certification and regulation conformity [23].

This paper presents the RTLola Playground[1]. A new web-based integrated development environment for RTLola. It eases the process from adopting runtime verification techniques to writing and testing specifications. It is based on the RTLola Framework extended with new static analyses that are then visualized by the tool. For example, directed graph-based analysis results can be explored interactively, similar to Evonne [13], a tool for visualizing proof trees generated by automated reasoning methods. Taking inspiration from other "playground"-style web-based IDEs for programming languages [4,20], the RTLola Playground executes specifications directly in the browser based on user-provided system traces. Monitor verdicts and intermediate values are plotted in graphs to assess the specification's correctness visually. To ease the debugging of specifications, a method for their step-wise execution is included. Other web-based tools for formal methods take a similar approach. The stream-based specification language TeSSLa also features a playground [21] where users can quickly test specifications. Yet, it does not aid the specifier in understanding static analysis results.

The rest of this paper is organized as follows: Section 2 presents motivating examples highlighting the benefits of the RTLola Playground. Following, Sect. 3 presents an overview of the RTLola specification language. Section 4 gives the main points of the existing RTLola toolchain and its library structure. In Sect. 5, we present the web-based IDE for RTLola and briefly overview the tool's architecture. Section 6 reviews the RTLola Playground from a users perspective before Sect. 7 concludes the paper.

[1] RTLola Playground: https://rtlola.org/playground.

2 Writing Specifications is Hard

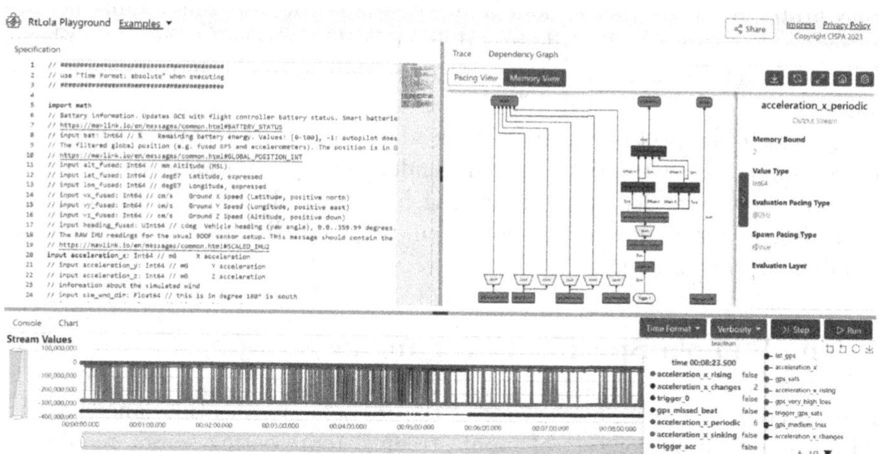

Fig. 2. Screenshot of the RTLola playground. The left panel contains the specification editor, the right panel the dependency graph and the trace editor, and the bottom panel contains the output of the interpreter as the CLI output and a plot.

Writing specifications poses similar challenges as programming in general. Large specifications do not fit into the human working memory and small errors such as simple typos or copy&paste errors can creep in. The RTLola Playground tackles these problems on several fronts.

As depicted in the screenshot of the user interface in Fig. 2 it is divided into three sections. The left panel features a rich text editor for specifications. The right panel contains the editor for traces and the dependency graph, a static analysis result of the RTLola framework. The visualization of static analysis results is complemented by the integration of an interactive execution of the monitor on a user-provided trace. The bottom panel features either a plot or a textual representation of the resulting stream values allowing for a quick exploration of the specification's behavior. Just like the dependency graph, the plot also allows zooming and hiding uninteresting streams.

RTLola is a language with a rich type system that is already used to check the specification prior to execution but showing the inferred types directly in line with the specification further improves the feedback loop. Some of the simple copy&paste errors such as forgetting to change the accessed stream can already have an influence on the inferred pacing type and therefore more easily spotted as seen in Fig. 3a. The RTLola framework already uses another static analysis artifact: the dependency graph. It consists of all streams, sliding windows, and accesses. A more complete definition of the dependency graph is given in Definition 1. The same error as described above would lead to a different edge in the graph which can break the symmetry between copied parts as seen in Fig. 3b.

Other simple errors such as accessing a stream with a wrong offset cannot be spotted by checking the inferred types. A wrong offset does not change the inferred type but it changes the thickness of the edge when viewing the dependency graph in *memory view* mode and potentially the buffering requirement of the accessed stream which leads to a different color as seen in Fig. 4. Similarly, a mismatch in a periodic pacing type leads to different color in the *pacing view* mode.

To tackle the aspect of cognitive overload, the RTLOLA PLAYGROUND allows for merging connected nodes in the dependency graph to hide currently uninteresting parts as is demonstrated in Fig. 5. This could be augmented on the language level by adding a module system. Some preliminary exploration has been done in this direction.

3 The RTLola Specification Language

In this section, we give an overview of the RTLola specification language. An RTLola specification consists of input streams, representing sensor reading of the system, output streams, representing internal computations and trigger conditions, constituting an assessment of the system's health. Furthermore, RTLola distinguishes streams by their timing behavior. This timing behavior is part of RTLola's type system and is called the pacing type of a stream. There are two disjunct timing variants: Event-based streams are evaluated in an ad-hock manner whenever the streams they depend on produce a new value. Periodic streams produce values at a fixed frequency. The specification in Listing 1.1 is used as a running example throughout this section and monitors abrupt altitude changes of an autonomous aircraft.

```
1 input altitude : Float
2
3 output avg_altitude @1Hz :=
4         altitude.aggregate(over: 1min, using: avg)
5
6 output altitude_diff :=
7         abs(altitude - avg_altitude.hold(or: altitude))
8
9 trigger altitude_diff > 10.0 "Altitude changed too quickly"
```

Listing 1.1. RTLola: A running Example.

In this specification's first line, the input stream `altitude` is declared. As for all input streams, only its value type, `Float` in this case, is known. Distinctly, RTLola does not pose any assumptions on the timing behavior of input streams, i.e. the time when a new sensor reading arrives at the monitor remains unknown till runtime.

As the name suggests, the output stream `avg_altitude` declared in line 3 computes the average as a sliding window over the `altitude` input stream. A sliding window accumulates all values of the target stream in the given time frame. In

```
import math
input lat: Float64
input lon: Float64
output check_lat:Bool @lat  := lat < lat.offset(by: -1).defaults(to: lat)
// copy&paste error: should default to lon
output check_lon:Bool @(lat ∧ lon)  := lon < lon.offset(by: -1).defaults(to: lat)
```

(a) Specification containing an erroneous access from *check_lon* to *lat*.

(b) Dependency graph with the additional edge.

Fig. 3. A specification with a typical copy&paste error in the form of an access from *check_lon* to *lat* instead of *lon*. This error can be spotted in the editor due to a change in the inferred pacing type of the accessing stream. Likewise, the dependency graph shows an additional edge width breaks the symmetry and therefore can also be spotted easily.

```
import math
input lat: Float64
input lon: Float64
output check_lat:Bool @lat  := lat < lat.offset(by: -1).defaults(to: lat)
// typo in offset
output check_lon:Bool @lon  := lon < lon.offset(by: -11).defaults(to: lon)
```

(a) Specification containing an error in the offset of the access from *check_lon* to *lat*.

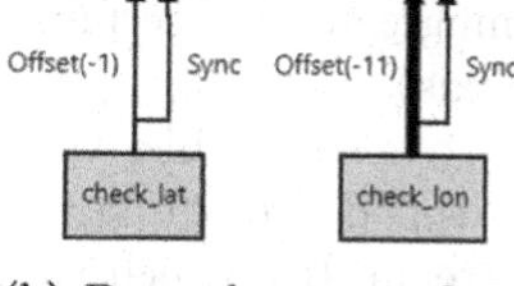

(b) Dependency graph in *memory view* mode.

Fig. 4. A specification with a typical typo in the offset of a stream access. This error does not change the inferred pacing type but the different offset changes the required memory of the accessed stream and therefore its color in the *memory view* mode. In addition, the corresponding edge in the dependency graph is thicker.

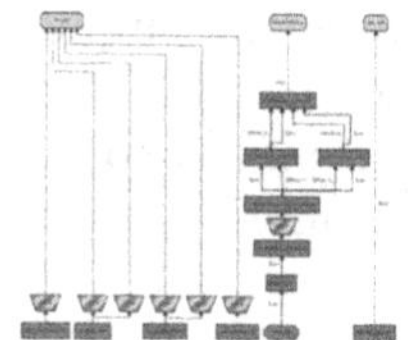

(a) Fully expanded dependency graph.

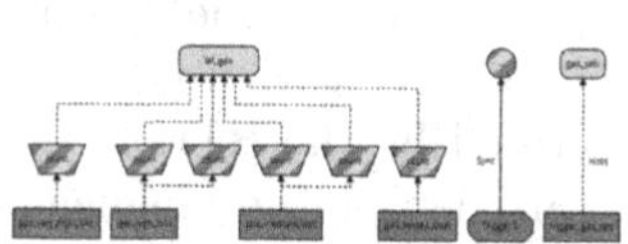

(b) Dependency graph with the parts relevant only for Trigger 0 merged.

Fig. 5. The dependency graph of the same specification. Once fully expanded and once a large part of it merged to better focus on the rest.

the example above, this time frame is one minute. Because sliding windows do not imply any timing for their evaluation, the stream has to be annotated with an explicit frequency of `1 Hz`, inducing that a new stream value, and therefore for the window, is computed every second. Note that sliding windows must have a periodic timing to have bounded memory. We refer the interested reader to [17] for more details on sliding windows.

The following output stream in line 6 computes the difference between the average altitude and the currently measured one. It highlights an essential part of the RTLola type system: Periodic and event-based streams must not be accessed synchronously in the same expression. The `altitude` access in the stream's expressions constitutes a synchronous access. A synchronous access reads the target stream's current value and additionally binds the accessing stream's timing to the accessed stream's timing. This guarantees that the accessing stream is only evaluated if the accessed value exists. As events can never be assumed to happen with a fixed frequency the type-checking procedure fails if a stream accesses both a periodic and an event-based stream synchronously, as no common timing can be determined in which both accessed values are always guaranteed to exist.

To resolve this, the stream in line 6 of Listing 1.1 uses a `hold` access to the timed average stream. A `hold` access refers to the last computed value of a stream. If no such value exists, a provided default value is substituted. Last, a `trigger` is defined to alert the operator if the current altitude deviates more than ten units from its average.

4 The RTLola Framework

The RTLola framework is split into two purviews. The RTLola Frontend is responsible for parsing and analyzing specifications. A Backend handles the event input, executes the specification, and forwards the output to the user. Executing a specification can follow different paradigms. The specification can be interpreted by the RTLola Interpreter or cross-compiled to a programming or hardware description language by the RTLola Compiler.

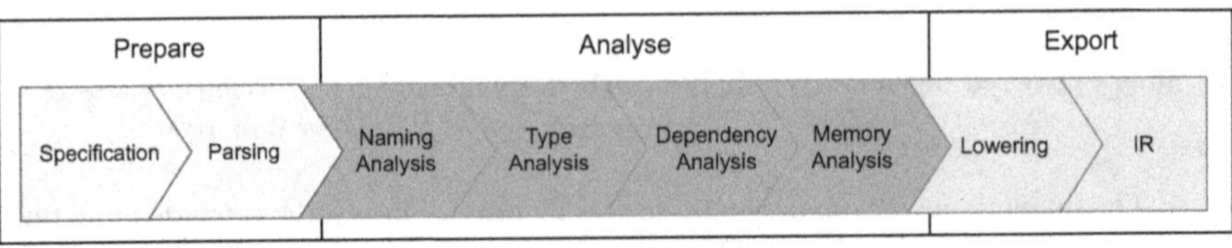

Fig. 6. An overview of the RTLola Frontend

4.1 The RTLola Frontend

The RTLola Frontend[2] is divided into multiple phases consisting of multiple stages. Figure 6 depicts an overview of these stages. In the first phase, the specification is parsed into an abstract syntax tree. The AST is then transformed into its de-sugarized form by representing all syntactic sugar constructs by basic RTLola expressions.

Next, the **naming analysis** checks the AST for duplicated or undefined stream names. For example, this stage rejects all specifications in which the same stream is defined multiple times. Afterward, the AST is transformed into a high-level intermediate representation by replacing stream name occurrences with numerical ids based on the previous analysis.

The **type analysis** infers a value and a pacing type for every stream. The value type of a stream determines the semantics of produced values. The value type system is similar to the one of programming languages. Consequently, RTLola also supports the usual value types, such as signed and unsigned integers, floats, strings, and booleans, including combinations of those types through tuples.

The pacing type of a stream determines the temporal behavior of a stream, i.e., when a new stream value is computed. As described in Sect. 3, there are two classes of pacing types. An event-based type (e.g. `@(lat ∧ lon)` in Fig. 3a) signals that the stream is computed whenever an event occurs. An event is a combination of input streams receiving a new value synchronously. Such a combination is described through a positive boolean formula over input streams. A synchronous access from one event-based stream to another is allowed iff the accessing stream's pacing type implies the pacing of the accessed stream.

A periodic type (`@1 Hz`) indicates that a stream is computed at a fixed frequency. A synchronous access from one periodic stream to another is allowed iff the accessing stream's frequency divides the frequency of the accessed stream. A synchronous access from an event-based stream to a periodic stream or vice versa is not allowed.

The **dependency analysis** computes the dependency graph of the specification and checks its well-formedness as presented in [15]. The dependency graph of a specification is defined as follows:

Definition 1. *The dependency graph of a specification with inputs $i_1, ..., i_m$ and outputs $o_1, .., o_n$ is a directed weighted multi-graph $G = \langle V, E\rangle$ with $V = \{i_1, ..., i_m, o_1, ..., o_n\}$. An edge $e = \langle o_i, o_k, w\rangle$ is in E iff the expression of o_i contains o_k.offset(by: w, or: c) as a sub-expression or $e = \langle o_i, i_k, w\rangle$ if i_k.offset(by: w, or: c) is a sub-expression. Synchronous accesses are reflected as offsets by 0.*

To recap, the dependency graph of a not well-formed specification contains a cycle with an accumulated weight of 0. As a result, specifications such as:

```
output a:= b
output b:= a
```

[2] RTLola Frontend: https://crates.io/crates/rtlola-frontend.

are rejected.

The **memory analysis** computes a per stream upper bound for the number of values that must be stored as defined in [17]. Intuitively, if the maximal offset a stream is accessed with is 2, then three values must be stored for that stream, including the current value.

After the high-level intermediate representation is validated through the static analyses, it is lowered into the final intermediate representation, dropping information irrelevant to backends.

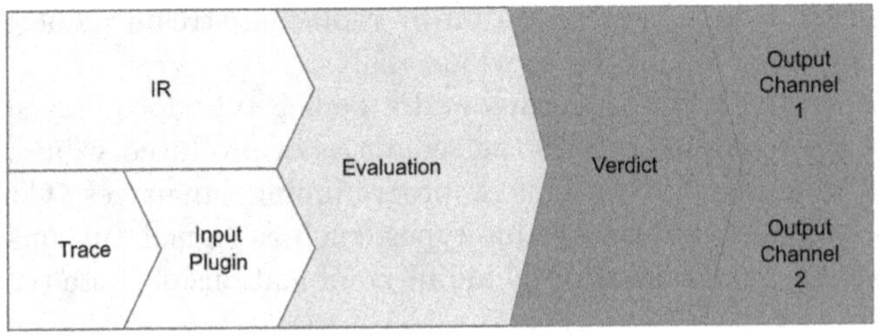

Fig. 7. An overview of the RTLola Interpreter

4.2 The RTLola Interpreter

The RTLola Interpreter[3] is an interpreter for RTLola specifications. Developed for the rapid prototyping of specifications, it forms the basis for evaluating specifications in the RTLOLA PLAYGROUND. Figure 7 shows an overview of the interpreter architecture. The specification can be processed directly in the form of its intermediate representation. To handle a variety of trace formats, the interpreter adds a layer of indirection through input plugins that translate events from their trace representation to an internal representation. This way, the interpreter can accept events in various formats like CSV, network packet capture (PCAP), or serialized as bytes.

Each event starts a new evaluation cycle in which all periodic streams up to the current point are evaluated before all event-based streams are evaluated that were activated by the event. Which information the produced verdict contains is up to configuration and ranges from trigger messages to the current state of all streams. The verdict is forwarded to one or multiple output channels responsible for displaying or forwarding that information.

5 Tool Overview

The RTLOLA PLAYGROUND is a progressive web application based on the *Vue* [11] framework and in general written in *TypeScript* [9]. An overview of

[3] RTLola Interpreter: https://crates.io/crates/rtlola-interpreter.

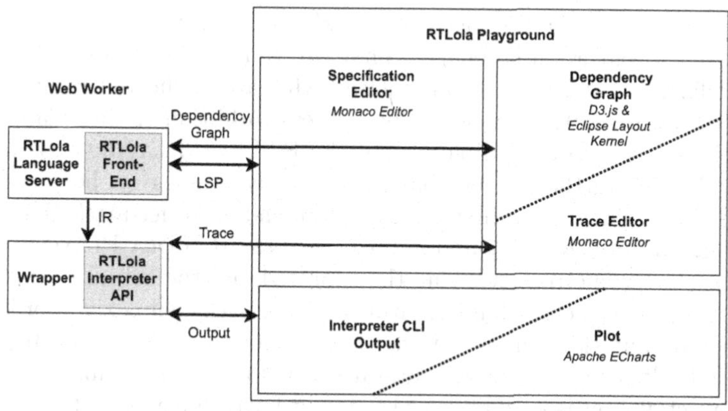

Fig. 8. Simplified overview of the main software components and their interaction. The blue boxes are deployed as WebAssembly compiled from Rust code. The other parts are implemented in TypeScript. Web workers from third-party libraries are not shown. (Color figure online)

the main components and their interaction is shown in Fig. 8. The components communicate mostly via shared *Pinia* [7] stores.

The RTLola framework is implemented in the *Rust* [8] language. This allows for easy compilation to *WebAssembly* [12] which means, that the code running in the browser matches the code powering the RTLola Interpreter executable.

The text editing is provided by the *Monaco Editor* [5] which is extracted from *Visual Studio Code* [10]. For the specification editor, we also provide a language server for RTLola which is mostly a wrapper written in TypeScript and Rust around the RTLola Frontend. This ensures that the user gets the same errors as if they were using the RTLola interpreter executable. The language server mostly communicates with the specification editor via the *Language Server Protocol* [6] to enable inline hints and diagnostics but it also provides additional artifacts such as the dependency graph and the intermediate representation of the specification.

The dependency graph is mostly based on the *D3.js* [2] library while the layout is handled by the *Eclipse Layout Kernel (elkjs)* [3] guided by information from the static analysis. A thin wrapper written in TypeScript and Rust around the RTLola interpreter API allows for executing monitors directly in the browser. One can inspect the CLI output as if one were to use RTLola interpreter executable but in addition the playground also contains a plot of all scalar numerical and boolean stream values. The plot is based on *Apache ECharts* [1] which provides the typical interactions such as hover, filtering, and zooming.

6 Application Scenarios

This section reviews the benefits of the RTLola Playground by considering two usage scenarios.

Firstly, new users of RTLola can quickly test their mental model about stream-based specification languages. They can run specifications and try them against different traces without interacting with a complicated command line interface or dealing with an installation process. Additionally, we plan to integrate an interactive tutorial directly into the RTLola Playground to lower the entry barrier further. There have been many studies on how and when to give feedback during learning [22,24]. More elaborate feedback than simple right/wrong improves learning and in the case of the RTLola Playground we believe that for type errors, showing the expected and the actual type strikes a good balance between enough information and feedback complexity. For learning basic programming skills immediate feedback seems to work best for beginners. Immediate feedback can be detrimental if it leads to simply gaming the system until a correct answer is found but as we do not have a given task this is not the case for the RTLola Playground.

Secondly, expert users of RTLola can use the RTLola Playground to get better insights into the specification's memory consumption, timing behavior, or locality. Exemplary, expert users can use the dependency graph to identify possible optimizations. In Fig. 5, one can see that the `count` aggregation is repeated five times with an identical duration. This can be optimized by outsourcing this aggregation into a separate stream.

These application scenarios show, that the RTLola Playground is not only suitable for users of different knowledge backgrounds but can also be a step towards a wide adoption of runtime verification techniques.

7 Conclusion

This paper presented the RTLola Playground, a web-based integrated development environment for the stream-based specification language RTLola. Built with cutting-edge web technologies like WebAssembly and web workers, it features a rich text editor for specifications, integrated testing and debugging capabilities, and interactive visualizations for static analysis results. We have demonstrated how specific specification errors can be identified using either the editor's feedback or the static analysis results. We elaborated on how different user groups can use the playground to their advantage and hence conclude that the RTLola Playground helps specifiers to write correct specifications faster while keeping the entry barrier for new users low.

In the future, we plan to reuse most of the components of the tool in an extension for the Visual Studio Code editor and integrate an interactive tutorial into the playground.

Lastly, we encourage other community members to port their research tools to the browser. Many modern compiler toolchains support a compilation to WebAssembly, which keeps the overhead feasible. A web-based tool enables easy adoption and makes research easier to reproduce and transfer.

Acknowledgements. This work was supported by the European Research Council (ERC) Grant HYPER (No. 101055412), by DFG grant 389792660 as part of TRR 248, and by the Aviation Research Programm LuFo of the German Federal Ministry for Economic Affairs and Energy as part of "Volocopter Sicherheits-Technologie zur robusten eVTOL Flugzustands- Absicherung durch formales Monitoring" (No. 20Q1963C).

References

1. Apache echarts. https://echarts.apache.org/en/index.html. Accessed 08 May 2023
2. D3.js - data-driven documents. https://d3js.org/. Accessed 08 May 2023
3. Github - kieler/elkjs: Elk's layout algorithms for javascript. https://github.com/kieler/elkjs. Accessed 08 May 2023
4. The go playground. https://go.dev/play/. Accessed 08 May 2023
5. Monaco editor. https://microsoft.github.io/monaco-editor/. Accessed 08 May 2023
6. Official page for language server protocol. https://microsoft.github.io/language-server-protocol/. Accessed 08 May 2023
7. Pinia – the intuitive store for vue.js. https://pinia.vuejs.org/. Accessed 08 May 2023
8. Rust programming language. https://www.rust-lang.org/. Accessed 08 May 2023
9. Typescript: Javascript fith syntax for types. https://www.typescriptlang.org/. Accessed 08 May 2023
10. Visual studio code - code editing. redefined. https://code.visualstudio.com/. Accessed 08 May 2023
11. Vue.js the progressive javascript framework. https://vuejs.org/. Accessed 08 May 2023
12. Webassembly. https://webassembly.org/. Accessed 08 May 2023
13. Alrabbaa, C., Baader, F., Borgwardt, S., Dachselt, R., Koopmann, P., Méndez, J.: Evonne: Interactive proof visualization for description logics (system description). In: Blanchette, J., Kovács, L., Pattinson, D. (eds.) IJCAR 2022. LNCS, pp. 271–280. Springer, Cham (2022)
14. Baumeister, J., Finkbeiner, B., Schirmer, S., Schwenger, M., Torens, C.: RTLola cleared for take-off: monitoring autonomous aircraft. In: Lahiri, S.K., Wang, C. (eds.) CAV 2020. LNCS, vol. 12225, pp. 28–39. Springer, Cham (2020). https://doi.org/10.1007/978-3-030-53291-8_3
15. d'Angelo, B., et al.: Lola: runtime monitoring of synchronous systems. In: 12th International Symposium on Temporal Representation and Reasoning (TIME 2005), pp. 166–174. IEEE (2005)
16. Dauer, J.C., Finkbeiner, B., Schirmer, S.: Monitoring with verified guarantees. In: Feng, L., Fisman, D. (eds.) RV 2021. LNCS, vol. 12974, pp. 62–80. Springer, Cham (2021). https://doi.org/10.1007/978-3-030-88494-9_4
17. Faymonville, P., et al.: StreamLAB: stream-based monitoring of cyber-physical systems. In: Dillig, I., Tasiran, S. (eds.) CAV 2019. LNCS, vol. 11561, pp. 421–431. Springer, Cham (2019). https://doi.org/10.1007/978-3-030-25540-4_24
18. Friese, M.J., Kallwies, H., Leucker, M., Sachenbacher, M., Streichhahn, H., Thoma, D.: Runtime verification of autosar timing extensions. In: Proceedings of the 30th International Conference on Real-Time Networks and Systems, pp. 173–183. RTNS 2022, Association for Computing Machinery, New York, NY, USA (2022). https://doi.org/10.1145/3534879.3534898
19. Gorostiaga, F., Sánchez, C.: Striver: stream runtime verification for real-time event-streams. In: Colombo, C., Leucker, M. (eds.) RV 2018. LNCS, pp. 282–298. Springer, Cham (2018)

20. Goulding, J.: The rust playground. https://play.rust-lang.org. Accessed 08 May 2023
21. Kallwies, H., Leucker, M., Schmitz, M., Schulz, A., Thoma, D., Weiss, A.: Tessla-an ecosystem for runtime verification. In: Dang, T., Stolz, V. (eds.) RV 2022. LNCS, vol. 13498, pp. 314–324. Springer, Cham (2022). https://doi.org/10.1007/978-3-031-17196-3_20
22. der Kleij, F.M.V., Feskens, R.C.W., Eggen, T.J.H.M.: Effects of feedback in a computer-based learning environment on students' learning outcomes: a meta-analysis. Rev. Educ. Res. **85**(4), 475–511 (2015). https://doi.org/10.3102/0034654314564881
23. Schirmer, S., Torens, C.: Safe operation monitoring for specific category unmanned aircraft. In: Dauer, J.C. (ed.) Automated Low-Altitude Air Delivery. RTA, pp. 393–419. Springer, Cham (2022). https://doi.org/10.1007/978-3-030-83144-8_16
24. Shute, V.J.: Focus on formative feedback. Rev. Educ. Res **78**(1), 153–189 (2008). https://doi.org/10.3102/0034654307313795

pymwp: A Static Analyzer Determining Polynomial Growth Bounds

Clément Aubert[1(✉)], Thomas Rubiano[2], Neea Rusch[1], and Thomas Seiller[2,3]

[1] School of Computer and Cyber Sciences, Augusta University, Augusta, USA
{caubert,nrusch}@augusta.edu

[2] LIPN – UMR 7030 Université Sorbonne Paris Nord, Villetaneuse, France

[3] CNRS, Paris, France

Abstract. We present pymwp, a static analyzer that automatically computes, if they exist, polynomial bounds relating input and output sizes. In case of exponential growth, our tool detects precisely which dependencies between variables induced it. Based on the sound mwp-flow calculus, the analysis captures bounds on large classes of programs by being non-deterministic and not requiring termination. For this reason, implementing this calculus required solving several non-trivial implementation problems, to handle its complexity and non-determinism, but also to provide meaningful feedback to the programmer. The duality of the analysis result and compositionality of the calculus make our approach original in the landscape of complexity analyzers. We conclude by demonstrating experimentally how pymwp is a practical and performant static analyzer to automatically evaluate variable growth bounds of C programs.

Keywords: Static Program Analysis · Automatic Complexity Analysis · Program Verification · Bound Inference · Flow Analysis

1 Introduction – Making Use of Implicit Complexity

Certification of any program is incomplete if it ignores resource considerations, as runtime failure will occur if usage exceeds available capacity. To address this deficiency, automatic complexity analysis produced many different implementations [9,13–15] with varying features. This paper presents the development and specificities of our automatic static complexity analyzer, pymwp.

The first original dimension of our tool is its inspiration, coming from Implicit Computational Complexity (ICC) [10]. This field designs systems guaranteeing

This research is supported by the Transatlantic Research Partnership of the Embassy of France in the United States and the FACE Foundation, and has benefited from the research meeting 21453 "Static Analyses of Program Flows: Types and Certificate for Complexity" in Schloss Dagstuhl. Th. Rubiano and Th. Seiller are supported by the Île-de-France region through the DIM RFSI project "CoHOp".

É. André and J. Sun (Eds.): ATVA 2023, LNCS 14216, pp. 263–275, 2023.
https://doi.org/10.1007/978-3-031-45332-8_14

program's runtime resource usage that tend to possess practically useful properties. For this reason, it is conjectured that ICC systems could be used to achieve realistic complexity analysis [18, p. 16]. Our series of work [5,6] is testing this hypothesis, and resulted in the tool we present in this paper: pymwp is one of the first ICC-inspired applications, and the first mechanization of the specific technique it implements. Let us first exemplify what pymwp calculates.

Example 1. Consider an imperative program with a fixed number of parameters:

```
void increasing(int X1, int X2, int X3) {
    while (X2 < X1) { X2 = X1 + X1; }
    while (X3 < X2) { X3 = X2 + X2; }
}
```

Independently of the arguments passed (henceforth called initial values), once computation concludes, X1 will hold the same value, but the values held by X2 and X3 may have changed. By manual analysis, we can deduce that the variable values "growth bound" between the *initial values* X1, X2 and X3 (overloading initial values and parameter names) and their *final values* (denoted X1', X2' and X3'), omitting constants, is X1' = X1, X2' $\leq$ max(X1, X2) and X3' $\leq$ max(X3, X2 + X1)[1]. Therefore, for all initial values, the value growth of the variable's value is bounded by a polynomial w.r.t. its initial values. Our analysis is designed to either produce such bounds, or to pinpoint variables that grow exponentially.

Introducing more variables, or potentially non-terminating iteration, or complicating the logic would make manual analysis difficult. However, our static analyzer handles all those cases automatically. It determines if a program accepts at least one polynomial bounding the final value of its variables in terms of their initial values—what we call its *growth bound.* If a bound cannot be established, it provides feedback on sources of failure, identifying variable pairs that have "too strong" dependencies. The technique is sound [16, p. 11], meaning a positive result guarantees program has satisfactory value growth behavior at runtime.

The mwp-flow analysis [16], that powers this tool, is of interest for its flexibility, originality, and uncommon features [9] such as being compositional and not requiring termination. However, using it to implement an automatic analyzer required important theoretical adjustments, and to sidestep or solve computationally expensive steps in the derivation of the bounds. For example, approaches to determine bounds were motivated by the need to compute them rapidly and present them in a concise human-interpretable manner, which is problematic for potentially exponential number of outputs. The theoretical improvements were presented previously [5] and serve as basis for pymwp. In this paper, we focus on the tool and its recent advancements, with following contributions.

1. We present the static analyzer pymwp in Sect. 3. It evaluates automatically if an input program has a polynomial growth bound and provides actionable

[1] Observe that the bound for X3' involves X1 *and* X2: the presence of X1 in the bound of X2' transitively impacts the bound for X3', because the analysis is compositional.

feedback on failure. Our tool is easy to use and install; open-source, well-documented, and persistently available for future reuse.
2. Implementing the theoretical mwp-calculus required to solve several non-trivial implementation problems. Specifically, how to obtain fast and concise results was solved by recent tool developments, and discussed in Sect. 4.
3. Sect. 5 demonstrates that pymwp is a practical and performant static analyzer by experimentally analyzing a set of canonical `C` programs. The evaluation also includes every example presented in this paper.

2 Calculating Bounds with mwp-Analysis

Given a deterministic imperative program over integers constructed using `while`, `if` and assignments, the mwp-analysis aims at discovering the polynomials bounding the variables final values `X1'`, ..., `Xn'` in terms of their initial values `X1`, ..., `Xn` [16, p. 5]. This section gives insight on how to interpret the results of pymwp, exemplifies those bounds in more detail, and identifies its distinctive features in the landscape of automatic complexity analysis.

2.1 Interpreting Analysis Results: mwp-Bounds and ∞

The mwp-flow analysis internally captures dependencies between program's variables to determine existence of growth bounds and locates problematic data flow relations. A flow can be 0, meaning no dependency; *m*aximal of linear, *w*eak polynomial, *p*olynomial or ∞, in increasing order of dependency. When the value of *every variable* in a program is bounded by at most a polynomial in initial values, the flow calculus assigns each variable an *mwp-bound*. It is a number-theoretic expression of form $\max(\boldsymbol{x}, \text{poly}_1(\boldsymbol{y})) + \text{poly}_2(\boldsymbol{z})$, where variables characterized by m-flow are listed in $\boldsymbol{x}$; w-flows in $\boldsymbol{y}$, and p-flows in $\boldsymbol{z}$. Honest polynomials poly_1 and poly_2 are build up from constants and variables by applying $+$ and $\times$. Any of the three variable lists might be empty and poly_1 and poly_2 may not be present. A bound of a program is conjunction ($\wedge$) of mwp-bounds. Variables that depend "too strongly" are assigned ∞-flow, to indicate exponential growth.

Expression	reads as "The growth of `X'` is bounded by ..."
$\texttt{X'} \leq 0$	"... a constant."
$\texttt{X'} \leq \texttt{X}$	"... a polynomial in `X`." (its initial value)
$\texttt{X}' \leq \max(\texttt{X}, \texttt{X1}) + \texttt{X2} \times \texttt{X3}$	"... a polynomial in `X` or `X1`, `X2` and `X3`."

Determining program bounds is complicated because the flow calculus is non-deterministic. This enables to analyze a larger class of programs, but also means that one program may be assigned multiple bounds. If a program is assigned a bound, it is derivable in the calculus. An impossibility result occurs when all derivation "paths" yields an ∞-result.

2.2 Additional Foundational Examples

One important and original aspect is that the mwp-flow analysis ignores Boolean conditions, assuming that both `if`-branches evaluate, and that loops executes an arbitrary number of cycles. This lets pymwp analyze non-terminating programs without complications, and justifies why all conditions will be abstracted as `b`.

Letting `C1` $\equiv$ `X2 = X1 + X1` and `C2` $\equiv$ `X3 = X2 + X2`, Example 1 established that the iterative composition `while b C1; while b C2` has a polynomial growth bound, i.e., the property of interest[2]. We now elaborate on mwp-flow analysis behavior by inspecting two more expository programs, letting `C3` $\equiv$ `X3 = X3 * X3`.

Example 2. Consider program `while b C3`. Even if `C3` in itself admits the bound `X3'` $\leq$ `X3`, the value stored in variable `X3` will grow exponentially on each iteration. Therefore, the program cannot get a growth bound, due to the ∞ flow between `X3` and itself introduced by the `while` statement.

Example 3. Combining elements from the previous two examples, we construct `while b C1; while b C2; C3`. Variables `X1` and `X2` are unaffected by `C3`, but `X3` changes. We over-approximate the final value of `X3` to obtain the program's growth bound $\texttt{X1'} \leq \texttt{X1} \wedge \texttt{X2'} \leq \max(\texttt{X2}, \texttt{X1}) \wedge \texttt{X3'} \leq \texttt{X1} + \texttt{X2} + \texttt{X3}$. This example shows how partial results ($\texttt{X3'} \leq \max(\texttt{X3}, \texttt{X1}+\texttt{X2})$ and $\texttt{X3'} \leq \texttt{X3}$) can be combined to obtain new bounds ($\texttt{X3'} \leq \texttt{X1} + \texttt{X2} + \texttt{X3}$) by compositionality.

In the tool user guide, we present even more examples with in-depth discussion, to elaborate on the behavior and results of mwp-analysis.

2.3 Originalities of mwp-flow Analysis

The mwp technique offers many properties that make it unique and practically useful. It is a syntactic analysis, not based on general purpose reasoners e.g., abstract interpreters or model checkers. It requires little structure, and no manual annotation from the analyzed program. This enables its implementation on any imperative programming language, and potentially at different stages of compilation. Compositionality is another significant feature. Non-compositional techniques require inlining programs and are common among automated complexity analyses [9]. With compositionality, analysis can be performed on parts of whole-programs, and after refactoring, repeated only on those parts that changed.

Several tools that evaluate resource bounds already exist [1,2,8,12–15,17]; including LOOPUS [25] and C4B [9], that specialize in `C` language inputs. Comprehensive evaluations of these tools have also been performed recently [9,11,25]. The main distinguishing factor between these tools and pymwp is the program's complexity property of interest: pymwp evaluates the existence of polynomial growth bounds w.r.t. initial values. We illustrate the difference in obtained bounds in Table 1. It is not an extensive comparison but suffices to show that pymwp differs in its aims from the other related techniques.

[2] pymwp actually outputs $\texttt{X1'} \leq \texttt{X1} \wedge \texttt{X2'} \leq \max(\texttt{X2}, \texttt{X1}) \wedge \texttt{X3'} \leq \max(\texttt{X3}, \texttt{X1} + \texttt{X2})$.

Table 1. Comparison of obtained resource bounds for various C language analyzers, on examples from Carbonneaux et al. [9, p. 26]. LOOPUS and C4B find asymptotically tight bounds based on amortization. LOOPUS calculates bounds on loop iterations, C4B derives global whole-program bounds, and pymwp analyzes variables growths. The inputs are part of Sect. 5 benchmark suite, and available in the pymwp repository [24].

Input	LOOPUS	C4B	pymwp
`t19.c`	$\max(0, i - 10^2) + \max(0, k + i + 51)$	$50 + \|[-1, i]\| + \|[0, k]\|$	$\texttt{i'} \leq \texttt{i} + \texttt{k} \wedge \texttt{k'} \leq \texttt{k}$
`t20.c`	$2 \cdot \max(0, y - x) + \max(0, x - y)$	$\|[x, y]\| + \|[y, x]\|$	$\texttt{X'} \leq \texttt{X} \wedge \texttt{y'} \leq \texttt{y}$
`t47.c`	$1 + \max(n, 0)$	$1 + \|[0, n]\|$	$\texttt{n'} \leq \texttt{n} \wedge \texttt{flag'} \leq 0$

3 Technical Overview of pymwp

In this section we present the main contribution of the paper: the pymwp static analyzer. It is a command-line tool that analyzes programs written in subset of C programming language presented in Sect. 3.3. The name alludes to its implementation language, Python, which we selected for its flexibility and use in previous related works [4,19,20]. Our tool takes as input a path to a C program, and returns for each function it contains a growth bound—if at least one can be established—or a list of variable dependencies that may cause the exponential growth.[3] The pymwp development is open source [24] with releases published at Python Package Index (PyPI) [22], GitHub [24] and Zenodo [7]. A tool user guide is available at https://statycc.github.io/.github/pymwp/.

3.1 Program Analysis in Action

The default procedure for performing mwp-analysis is as follows:

1. Parse input file to obtain an abstract syntax tree (AST).
2. Initialize a `Result` object T.
3. For each function (or "program", interchangeably) in the AST:
   (a) Create an initial `Relation` R—briefly, this complex structure represents variables and their dependencies, at a program point (Sect. 4.1).
   (b) Sequentially for each statement in function body:
      i Recursively apply inference rules to obtain R_i.
      ii Compose R_i with previous relation: $R = R \circ R_i$.
      iii If no bound exists, terminate analysis of function body.
   (c) If bounds exist, evaluate R to determine the bounds (Sect. 4.3)
   (d) Append function analysis result to T.
4. Return T.

3.2 Usage

There are multiple ways to use pymwp. It has a text-based application interface, and can be run from terminal, or it can be imported as a Python module into

[3] Obtaining this feedback requires to specify the `--fin` argument.

larger software engineering developments. The analysis is automatic and read-only, therefore it is possible to pair pymwp with other tools and integrate it into compilation or verification toolchains. The online demo provides one example use case. It is a web server application with pymwp as a package dependency. Other derived uses can be developed similarly. The easiest way to install pymwp is from PyPI, using command `pip install pymwp`. The default interaction command is

```
pymwp path/to/file.c [args]
```

where the first positional argument is required. By default, pymwp displays the analysis result with logging information, and writes the result to a file. This behavior is customizable by specifying arguments. For a list of currently supported arguments run `pymwp --help`.

3.3 Scope of Analyzable Programs

The programs analyzable with pymwp are determined by its supported syntax. pymwp delegates the task of parsing `C` files to its dependency, pycparser [21], which aims to support the full `C99` specification. Programs that cannot be parsed will expectedly throw an error. Otherwise, analysis proceeds on the generated AST, and pymwp handles nodes that are syntactically supported by its calculus[4]. It skips unsupported nodes with a warning. We decided on this permissive approach, because it allows to obtain partial results and manually inspect unsupported operations. However, to establish a guaranteed bound, the input program must fully conform to the supported syntax of the calculus. Currently the syntax has limitations, e.g., arrays and pointer operations are unsupported. Extending the analysis to richer syntax is a direction for future work.

4 Implementation Advancements

Notable technical progress has occurred since the initial mention of pymwp in the literature [5][5]. We will discuss those solutions in this section.

4.1 Motivations for Refining Analysis Results

Understanding pymwp's advances requires to briefly reflect on its past. The mwp-flow, as originally designed [16], is an inference system that has an unbearable computational cost, as it manipulates non-deterministically an exponential number of sizable matrices [5, Sect. 2.3] to try to establish a bound. Our enhanced mwp-technique [5] resolved this challenge by internalizing the non-determinism in a single matrix, containing coefficients and functions from choices

[4] List of supported features: https://statycc.github.io/pymwp/features.

[5] Full comparison: https://github.com/statycc/pymwp/compare/FSCD22...0.4.2.

into coefficients. This way, all derivations—including the ones that will fail—are constructed at the same time, moving the problem from "Is there a derivation?" to "Among all the derivations you constructed, is there one without ∞ coefficient?"—an equivalent question that however complicates the production of the actual bound.

While answering the first question is too computationally expensive, pymwp's FSCD 2022 version can answer the second, and it can further, if all derivations contain ∞ coefficients, terminate early for faster result [5, Sect. 4.4]. This was achieved thanks to a complex `Relation` data structure[6], but extracting finer information from that data structure remained an outstanding problem. In particular, we wanted to provide the following feedback to the programmer: (i) If no bound exists, the location of the exponential growth. (ii) If bounds exist, the value of at least one of them. The current version of pymwp can now provide this feedback, thanks to a long maturation that we now detail.

4.2 Exposing Sources of Failure

Since pymwp identifies polynomial bounds, it reports failure on programs containing at least one variable whose value grows exponentially w.r.t. at least one of its initial value. Earlier tool versions would indicate that failure was detected without reporting the involved variables. Determining this information is complicated because of our treatment of non-determinism, but it is valuable, as addressing one of those points of failure would suffice to obtain a polynomial growth bound. Even if the program cannot be refactored satisfactorily, then analyzing the exponential growth allows to assess potential impact on the parent software application.

Our solution is to record additional information about ∞-coefficient in the `Relation` data structure, and to list all variable pairs on which failure may occur. Since detailed failure information may not be relevant in some use-cases, and is costly to compute, it was added as an optional `-fin` argument.

Example 4. From our tool user guide (output abridged for clarity):

```
int foo(int X1, int X2, int X3){
  if (X1 == 1){
    X1 = X2+X1;
    X2 = X3+X2;
  }
  while(X1 < 10){
    X1 = X2+X1;
  }
}
```

```
$ pymwp infinite/infinite_3.c --fin
foo is infinite
Possibly problematic flows:
X1 → X1 || X2 → X1 || X3 → X1
```

Reads as "`X1` depends too strongly on all variables."

[6] A complex data structure sounds daunting, but it is in fact one of the highlights of the system, and enables to solve a difficult derivation problem efficiently. For details, see the documentation at https://statycc.github.io/pymwp/relation.

4.3 Efficiently Determining Bounds

In the alternative case, where bounds are determined to exist, the next step is to evaluate the bounds—step 3(c) in the pymwp workflow (Sect. 3.1). This is problematic because the calculus can yield an exponential number of bounds w.r.t. the program size, as illustrated in Table 3 with e.g., benchmark 32. long. As a result, the evaluation phase—e.g., extracting the bounds from this conglomerate of derivations—is increasingly costly. Handling this task efficiently required us to discover a computational solution, and finding a compact format to represent the results in interpretable and memory-efficient manner. For simplicity we describe this process only at high-level, but refer to the implementation for complete details.

Determining mwp-bounds requires two separate steps, starting with the `Relation` data structure generated during analysis phase. The first challenge is to determine which paths in our conglomerate of derivations produce bounds (i.e., does not contain ∞). A naïve brute force solution would iterate over all paths, but this is too slow for practical use. Instead, we developed a set-theoretic approach, that determines first all derivation paths that lead to ∞ and then negates those paths. We capture this process in a structure called `Choice`, and the result of this computation is called a choice vector. A choice vector contains all derivation paths yielding a bound in a compact, regular expression-like representation. Once those paths are known, it is possible to extract from a `Relation` an mwp-bound (represented as a `Bound` object), by applying a selected path. Currently, we take the first choice from the choice vector, and display it as a result. Leveraging this set of bounds and its utilities is discussed in conclusion and left for future work.

5 Experimental Evaluation

To establish that pymwp is a practical and performant static analyzer, we evaluated it on a benchmark suite of canonical `C` programs. We ran the analyzer on the benchmarks and measured the results, thus conducting an evaluation of performance and behavioral correctness. We did not perform tool comparison or use a standard suite for two reasons: absence of a representative comparison target (cf. Sect. 2.3) and syntactic restrictions that limit the scope of analyzable programs (cf. Sect. 3.3). However, the choice methodology judiciously evaluates pymwp, and facilitates transparency and reproduction of experiments. We actively put heavy emphasis to ensure—with software engineering best practices e.g., tests, documentation [23], and long-term archival deposits [7]—that pymwp, and the evaluation presented here, are available and reusable for future comparisons.

5.1 Methodology

Benchmarks Description. The suite contains 50 `C` programs, written in the subset of `C99` syntax supported by pymwp. The benchmarks are designed purposely to exercise various data flows that pose challenges to the analyzer, e.g., increasing parameters, binary operations, loops and decisions, and various combinations of those operations. The benchmarks are organized into seven categories based on their expected result (∞ vs. non-∞); origin in related publications [5,16], and in this tool paper; and interest (basic examples, others). We omit these categories here, but they are apparent in the benchmarks distribution. The suite is available from pymwp repository [24], as a release asset on GitHub, and Zenodo [7].

Metrics. For each benchmark, we record 1. Benchmark name, corresponding to `C` file name, followed by "*: program name*" if a file contains multiple programs. 2. The lines of code (loc) in the benchmark. Observe this number ranges between 4 and 45: this is reasonable and representative, because the analysis is compositional. Analysis of even a large `C` file reduces to analysis of its functions, that would be expectedly similar in size to these benchmarks. 3. The time (ms) required to complete program analysis. We use milliseconds for precision since all analyses conclude within seconds. For ∞-programs, the time is for performing full evaluation with feedback, although a result of existential failure could be obtained faster. 4. Number of program initial values (vars), which internally impacts complexity of the analysis. 5. Number of polynomial bounds discovered by the analyzer. The number of bounds is 0 if the result is ∞. 6. If a program is derivable, we capture one of its bounds.

Experimental Setup. The measurements were performed on a Linux x86_64, kernel v.5.4.0-1096-gcp, Ubuntu 18.04, with 8 cores and 32 GB virtual memory. The machine impacts only observed execution time; other metrics are deterministic. The software environment was Python runtime 3.8.0, gcc 7.5.0, GNU Make 4.1, and the dev dependencies of pymwp. Because the measurement utilities of pymwp are not distributed with its release, the experiments must be run from source. We used source code version 0.4.2. The command to repeat experiments is `make bench`. It runs analysis on benchmarks and generates two tables of results.

5.2 Results

The evaluation results are presented in Table 2. We emphasize in these results the obtained bounds and their correctness, while the obtained execution times provide referential information of performance. The analyzer correctly finds a polynomial bound for noninfinite benchmarks, and rejects exponential and infinite benchmarks. The analyzer is also able to derive bounds for potentially nonterminating `while` benchmarks. Observe that the analysis concludes rapidly even for a long example with 45 loc, and for explosion, that has initial values count 18. The number of bounds for long is high, because it is a complicated derivation with high degree of internalized non-determinism.

For programs that have polynomial growth bounds, we give a simplified example bound in Table 3. We omit in this representation variables whose only

Table 2. Benchmark results for a canonical test suite of C programs. Benchmark that have 0 bounds represents case where analyzer reports an ∞-result.

#	Benchmark	loc	ms	vars	bounds	#	Benchmark	loc	ms	vars	bounds
1.	assign_expression	8	0	2	3	26.	infinite_4	9	2189	5	0
2.	assign_variable	9	0	2	3	27.	infinite_5	11	518	5	0
3.	dense	16	15	3	81	28.	infinite_6	14	1031	4	0
4.	dense_loop	17	66	3	81	29.	infinite_7	15	298	5	0
5.	example14: *f*	4	2	2	1	30.	infinite_8	23	722	6	0
6.	example14: *foo*	11	0	2	3	31.	inline_variable	9	0	2	3
7.	example16	15	7	4	27	32.	long	45	2875	5	177147
8.	example3_1_a	10	1	3	9	33.	notinfinite_2	4	1	2	9
9.	example3_1_b	10	2	3	9	34.	notinfinite_3	9	7	4	9
10.	example3_1_c	11	3	3	1	35.	notinfinite_4	11	30	5	3
11.	example3_1_d	12	1	2	0	36.	notinfinite_5	11	29	4	9
12.	example3_2	12	2	3	0	37.	notinfinite_6	16	34	4	81
13.	example3_4	22	14	5	0	38.	notinfinite_7	15	283	5	9
14.	example5_1	10	0	2	1	39.	notinfinite_8	22	856	6	27
15.	example7_10	10	1	3	9	40.	simplified_dense	9	1	2	9
16.	example7_11	11	9	4	27	41.	t19_c4b	9	2	2	81
17.	example8	8	1	3	9	42.	t20_c4b	7	1	2	9
18.	explosion	23	405	18	729	43.	t47_c4b	12	1	2	3
19.	exponent_1	16	7	4	0	44.	tool_ex_1	7	5	3	1
20.	exponent_2	13	4	4	0	45.	tool_ex_2	7	0	2	0
21.	gcd	12	10	2	0	46.	tool_ex_3	9	8	3	3
22.	if	7	0	2	3	47.	while_1	7	1	2	3
23.	if_else	7	0	2	9	48.	while_2	7	1	2	1
24.	infinite_2	6	16	2	0	49.	while_if	9	3	3	9
25.	infinite_3	9	7	3	0	50.	xnu	26	17	5	6561

Table 3. Examples of obtained bounds for corresponding benchmarks. For compactness, the bounds are simplified to exclude variables that have dependency only on self.

#	Benchmark bound
1.	$\mathtt{y2}' \leq \mathtt{y1}$
2.	$\mathtt{x}' \leq \mathtt{y}$
3.	$\mathtt{X0}' \leq \max(\mathtt{X0}, \mathtt{X2}) + \mathtt{X1} \land \mathtt{X1}' \leq \mathtt{X0} \times \mathtt{X1} \times \mathtt{X2}$ $\land\, \mathtt{X2}' \leq \max(\mathtt{X0}, \mathtt{X2}) + \mathtt{X1}$
4.	$\mathtt{X0}' \leq \max(\mathtt{X0}, \mathtt{X2}) + \mathtt{X1} \land \mathtt{X1}' \leq \mathtt{X0} \times \mathtt{X1} \times \mathtt{X2}$ $\land\, \mathtt{X2}' \leq \max(\mathtt{X0}, \mathtt{X2}) + \mathtt{X1}$
5.	$\mathtt{X2}' \leq \max(\mathtt{X2}, \mathtt{X1})$
6.	$\mathtt{X2}' \leq \mathtt{X1}$
7.	$\mathtt{X1}' \leq \mathtt{R} + \mathtt{X1} \land \mathtt{X2}' \leq \mathtt{X1} \land \mathtt{X\_1}' \leq \mathtt{X1} \land \mathtt{R}' \leq \mathtt{R} + \mathtt{X1}$
8.	$\mathtt{X1}' \leq \mathtt{X2} + \mathtt{X3}$
9.	$\mathtt{X1}' \leq \mathtt{X2} \times \mathtt{X3}$
10.	$\mathtt{X1}' \leq \max(\mathtt{X1}, \mathtt{X2} + \mathtt{X3})$
15.	$\mathtt{X3}' \leq \mathtt{X3} + \mathtt{X1} \times \mathtt{X2}$
16.	$\mathtt{X1}' \leq \mathtt{X1} + \mathtt{X2} \times \mathtt{X3} \times \mathtt{X4} \land \mathtt{X2}' \leq \mathtt{X2} + \mathtt{X3} \times \mathtt{X4}$ $\land\, \mathtt{X3}' \leq \mathtt{X3} + \mathtt{X4}$
17.	$\mathtt{X1}' \leq \mathtt{X1} + \mathtt{X2} \times \mathtt{X3}$
18.	$\mathtt{x0}' \leq \mathtt{x1} + \mathtt{x2} \land \mathtt{x3}' \leq \mathtt{x4} + \mathtt{x5} \land \mathtt{x6}' \leq \mathtt{x7} + \mathtt{x8}$ $\land\, \mathtt{x9}' \leq \mathtt{x10} + \mathtt{x11} \land \mathtt{x12}' \leq \mathtt{x13} + \mathtt{x14}$ $\land\, \mathtt{x15}' \leq \mathtt{x16} + \mathtt{x17}$
22.	$\mathtt{y}' \leq \max(\mathtt{x}, \mathtt{y})$
23.	$\mathtt{x}' \leq \max(\mathtt{x}, \mathtt{y}) \land \mathtt{y}' \leq \max(\mathtt{x}, \mathtt{y})$
31.	$\mathtt{y2}' \leq \mathtt{y1}$
32.	$\mathtt{X0}' \leq \mathtt{X2} + \mathtt{X1} \times \mathtt{X4} \land \mathtt{X1}' \leq \max(\mathtt{X2}, \mathtt{X3}, \mathtt{X4}) + \mathtt{X1}$ $\land\, \mathtt{X2}' \leq \max(\mathtt{X2}, \mathtt{X3}) + \mathtt{X1} \times \mathtt{X4}$ $\land\, \mathtt{X3}' \leq \max(\mathtt{X2}, \mathtt{X3}) + \mathtt{X1}$ $\land\, \mathtt{X4}' \leq \mathtt{X1} \times \mathtt{X2} \times \mathtt{X3} \times \mathtt{X4}$
33.	$\mathtt{X0}' \leq \mathtt{X0} + \mathtt{X1} \land \mathtt{X1}' \leq \mathtt{X0} \times \mathtt{X1}$
34.	$\mathtt{X0}' \leq \max(\mathtt{X0}, \mathtt{X1}) + \mathtt{X2} \times \mathtt{X3}$ $\land\, \mathtt{X1}' \leq \mathtt{X1} + \mathtt{X2} \land \mathtt{X2}' \leq \mathtt{X2} + \mathtt{X3}$
35.	$\mathtt{X1}' \leq \max(\mathtt{X1}, \mathtt{X2} + \mathtt{X3}) \land \mathtt{X2}' \leq \max(\mathtt{X2}, \mathtt{X3})$ $\land\, \mathtt{X4}' \leq \max(\mathtt{X4}, \mathtt{X5})$
36.	$\mathtt{X1}' \leq \max(\mathtt{X1}, \mathtt{X4}) + \mathtt{X2} \times \mathtt{X3}$ $\land\, \mathtt{X2}' \leq \max(\mathtt{X2}, \mathtt{X4}) + \mathtt{X3}$ $\land\, \mathtt{X3}' \leq \max(\mathtt{X3}, \mathtt{X4})$
37.	$\mathtt{X1}' \leq \max(\mathtt{X1}, \mathtt{X4}) + \mathtt{X2} \times \mathtt{X3}$ $\land\, \mathtt{X2}' \leq \max(\mathtt{X2}, \mathtt{X4}) + \mathtt{X3}$
38.	$\mathtt{X1}' \leq \max(\mathtt{X1}, \mathtt{X2} + \mathtt{X3} + \mathtt{X4} + \mathtt{X5})$ $\land\, \mathtt{X2}' \leq \max(\mathtt{X2}, \mathtt{X3} + \mathtt{X4} + \mathtt{X5})$ $\land\, \mathtt{X3}' \leq \max(\mathtt{X3}, \mathtt{X4} + \mathtt{X5})$ $\land\, \mathtt{X4}' \leq \max(\mathtt{X4}, \mathtt{X5})$
39.	$\mathtt{X1}' \leq \mathtt{X1} + \mathtt{X2} \times \mathtt{X3} \times \mathtt{X4} \times \mathtt{X5}$ $\land\, \mathtt{X2}' \leq \max(\mathtt{X2}, \mathtt{X1} + \mathtt{X3} + \mathtt{X4} + \mathtt{X5})$ $\land\, \mathtt{X3}' \leq \max(\mathtt{X3}, \mathtt{X1} + \mathtt{X4} + \mathtt{X5}) + \mathtt{X2}$ $\land\, \mathtt{X4}' \leq \max(\mathtt{X4}, \mathtt{X1} + \mathtt{X5}) + \mathtt{X2}$ $\land\, \mathtt{X6}' \leq \max(\mathtt{X6}, \mathtt{X1} + \mathtt{X3} + \mathtt{X4} + \mathtt{X5}) + \mathtt{X2}$
40.	$\mathtt{X0}' \leq \mathtt{X0} + \mathtt{X1} \land \mathtt{X1}' \leq \mathtt{X1} + \mathtt{X0}$
41.	$\mathtt{i}' \leq \mathtt{i} + \mathtt{k}$
43.	$\mathtt{flag}' \leq 0$
44.	$\mathtt{X2}' \leq \max(\mathtt{X2}, \mathtt{X1}) \land \mathtt{X3}' \leq \max(\mathtt{X3}, \mathtt{X1} + \mathtt{X2})$
46.	$\mathtt{X2}' \leq \max(\mathtt{X2}, \mathtt{X1}) \land \mathtt{X3}' \leq \mathtt{X1} + \mathtt{X2} + \mathtt{X3}$
47.	$\mathtt{y}' \leq \max(\mathtt{x}, \mathtt{y})$
48.	$\mathtt{x}' \leq \max(\mathtt{x}, \mathtt{y})$
49.	$\mathtt{y2}' \leq \max(\mathtt{y2}, \mathtt{y1}) \land \mathtt{r}' \leq \max(\mathtt{y2}, \mathtt{y1})$
50.	$\mathtt{beg}' \leq 0 \land \mathtt{end}' \leq 0 \land \mathtt{i}' \leq 0$

dependency is on self, e.g.,`X'` $\leq$ `X`.[7] The table serves to demonstrate that pymwp can derive complex multivariate bounds automatically, and to present the result of a non-deterministic computation in a digestible form. It also clarifies what the analyzer computes and that those results are original in form.

6 Conclusion

This paper presented pymwp, its recent technical advancements, and evaluated its performance. Our tool reasons efficiently about existence of the variables' growth bounds w.r.t. its initial value, and can be paired with other tools for extended verification and compound analyses. Possible enhancements of the tool involve extending it to support richer syntax, and exploring the space of discovered bounds. For example, we could investigate whether constraints such as "Is there a bound where this particular variable growth linearly?" can be satisfied. Another open question is to identify *distinct* bounds.

Beyond enhancements of pymwp, several future directions and extended applications can follow. Perhaps the most interesting of those is to formally verify the analysis technique, and work is already underway in that direction [3]. Since the analysis does not require much structure from an input program, it could be useful for analyzing intermediate representations during compilation. It could also find use cases in restricted domain-specific languages, and resource-restricted hardware, to establish guarantees of their runtime behavior. Long term, the fast compositional analysis could also be useful to construct IDE plug-ins to provide low-latency feedback to programmers.

Acknowledgments. The authors wish to express their gratitude to the reviewers for their thoughtful comments, and to Antonio Flores Montoya, for the preparation and public sharing of his PhD thesis experimental evaluation resources [11].

References

1. Albert, E., Arenas, P., Genaim, S., Puebla, G., Zanardini, D.: Cost analysis of object-oriented bytecode programs. Theor. Comput. Sci. **413**(1), 142–159 (2012). https://doi.org/10.1016/j.tcs.2011.07.009
2. Alias, C., Darte, A., Feautrier, P., Gonnord, L.: Multi-dimensional rankings, program termination, and complexity bounds of flowchart programs. In: Cousot, R., Martel, M. (eds.) SAS 2010. LNCS, vol. 6337, pp. 117–133. Springer, Heidelberg (2010). https://doi.org/10.1007/978-3-642-15769-1_8
3. Aubert, C., Rubiano, T., Rusch, N., Seiller, T.: Certifying complexity analysis (2023). https://hal.science/hal-04083105v1/file/main.pdf. Presented at the Ninth International Workshop on Coq for Programming Languages (CoqPL)
4. Aubert, C., Rubiano, T., Rusch, N., Seiller, T.: LQICM On C Toy Parser (2021). https://github.com/statycc/LQICM_On_C_Toy_Parser

[7] Bound of example5_1 does not appear in Table 3 because of this simplification.

5. Aubert, C., Rubiano, T., Rusch, N., Seiller, T.: mwp-analysis improvement and implementation: realizing implicit computational complexity. In: Felty, A.P. (ed.) 7th International Conference on Formal Structures for Computation and Deduction (FSCD 2022). Leibniz International Proceedings in Informatics, vol. 228, pp. 26:1–26:23. Schloss Dagstuhl-Leibniz-Zentrum für Informatik (2022). https://doi.org/10.4230/LIPIcs.FSCD.2022.26
6. Aubert, C., Rubiano, T., Rusch, N., Seiller, T.: Realizing Implicit Computational Complexity (2022). https://hal.archives-ouvertes.fr/hal-03603510. Presented at the 28th International Conference on Types for Proofs and Programs (TYPES 2022) (Recording)
7. Aubert, C., Rubiano, T., Rusch, N., Seiller, T.: pymwp: MWP analysis on C code in Python (2023). https://doi.org/10.5281/zenodo.7908484
8. Brockschmidt, M., Emmes, F., Falke, S., Fuhs, C., Giesl, J.: Analyzing runtime and size complexity of integer programs. ACM Trans. Programm. Lang. Syst. (TOPLAS) **38**(4), 1–50 (2016). https://doi.org/10.1145/2866575
9. Carbonneaux, Q., Hoffmann, J., Shao, Z.: Compositional certified resource bounds. In: Grove, D., Blackburn, S.M. (eds.) Proceedings of the 36th ACM SIGPLAN Conference on Programming Language Design and Implementation, Portland, OR, USA, 15–17 June 2015, pp. 467–478. Association for Computing Machinery (2015). https://doi.org/10.1145/2737924.2737955
10. Dal Lago, U.: A short introduction to implicit computational complexity. In: Bezhanishvili, N., Goranko, V. (eds.) ESSLLI 2010-2011. LNCS, vol. 7388, pp. 89–109. Springer, Heidelberg (2012). https://doi.org/10.1007/978-3-642-31485-8_3
11. Flores Montoya, A.: Cost Analysis of Programs Based on the Refinement of Cost Relations. Ph.D. thesis, Technische Universität, Darmstadt (2017). http://tuprints.ulb.tu-darmstadt.de/6746/
12. Flores-Montoya, A., Hähnle, R.: Resource analysis of complex programs with cost equations. In: Garrigue, J. (ed.) APLAS 2014. LNCS, vol. 8858, pp. 275–295. Springer, Cham (2014). https://doi.org/10.1007/978-3-319-12736-1_15
13. Giesl, J., et al.: Resource analysis of complex programs with cost equations. J. Autom. Reasoning **58**(1), 3–31 (2016). https://doi.org/10.1007/s10817-016-9388-y
14. Hainry, E., Jeandel, E., Péchoux, R., Zeyen, O.: ComplexityParser: an automatic tool for certifying poly-time complexity of Java programs. In: Cerone, A., Ölveczky, P.C. (eds.) ICTAC 2021. LNCS, vol. 12819, pp. 357–365. Springer, Cham (2021). https://doi.org/10.1007/978-3-030-85315-0_20
15. Hoffmann, J., Aehlig, K., Hofmann, M.: Resource aware ML. In: Madhusudan, P., Seshia, S.A. (eds.) CAV 2012. LNCS, vol. 7358, pp. 781–786. Springer, Heidelberg (2012). https://doi.org/10.1007/978-3-642-31424-7_64
16. Jones, N.D., Kristiansen, L.: A flow calculus of mwp-bounds for complexity analysis. ACM Trans. Comput. Logic **10**(4), 28:1-28:41 (2009). https://doi.org/10.1145/1555746.1555752
17. Moser, G., Schneckenreither, M.: Automated amortised resource analysis for term rewrite systems. In: Gallagher, J.P., Sulzmann, M. (eds.) FLOPS 2018. LNCS, vol. 10818, pp. 214–229. Springer, Cham (2018). https://doi.org/10.1007/978-3-319-90686-7_14
18. Moyen, J.: Implicit Complexity in Theory and Practice. Habilitation thesis, University of Copenhagen (2017). https://lipn.univ-paris13.fr/moyen/papiers/Habilitation_JY_Moyen.pdf

19. Moyen, J.-Y., Rubiano, T., Seiller, T.: Loop quasi-invariant chunk detection. In: D'Souza, D., Narayan Kumar, K. (eds.) ATVA 2017. LNCS, vol. 10482, pp. 91–108. Springer, Cham (2017). https://doi.org/10.1007/978-3-319-68167-2_7
20. Moyen, J., Rubiano, T., Seiller, T.: Loop quasi-invariant chunk motion by peeling with statement composition. In: Bonfante, G., Moser, G. (eds.) Proceedings 8th Workshop on Developments in Implicit Computational Complexity and 5th Workshop on Foundational and Practical Aspects of Resource Analysis, DICE-FOPARA@ETAPS 2017, Uppsala, Sweden, 22–23 April 2017. Electronic Proceedings in Theoretical Computer Science, 248, pp. 47–59, 2017. https://doi.org/10.4204/EPTCS.248.9, http://arxiv.org/abs/1704.05169
21. pycparser - Complete C99 parser in pure Python. https://github.com/eliben/pycparser
22. pymwp at Python Package Index (2023). https://pypi.org/project/pymwp/
23. pymwp documentation (2023). https://statycc.github.io/pymwp/
24. pymwp source code repository (2023). https://github.com/statycc/pymwp
25. Sinn, M., Zuleger, F., Veith, H.: Complexity and resource bound analysis of imperative programs using difference constraints. J. Autom. Reasoning **59**(1), 3–45 (2017). https://doi.org/10.1007/s10817-016-9402-4

ppLTLTT: Temporal Testing for Pure-Past Linear Temporal Logic Formulae

Shaun Azzopardi(✉), David Lidell, Nir Piterman, and Gerardo Schneider

University of Gothenburg, Gothenburg, Sweden
shaun.azzopardi@gmail.com

Abstract. This paper presents ppLTLTT, a tool for translating pure-past linear temporal logic formulae into temporal testers in the form of automata. We show how ppLTLTT can be used to easily extend existing LTL-based tools, such as LTL-to-automata translators and reactive synthesis tools, to support a richer input language. Namely, with ppLTLTT, tools that accept LTL input are also made to handle pure-past LTL as atomic formulae. While the addition of past operators does not increase the expressive power of LTL, it opens up the possibility of writing more intuitive and succinct specifications. We illustrate this intended use of ppLTLTT for Slugs, Strix, and Spot's command line tool LTL2TGBA by describing three corresponding wrapper tools pSlugs, pStrix, and pLTL2TGBA, that all leverage ppLTLTT. All three wrapper tools are designed to seamlessly fit this paradigm, by staying as close to the respective syntax of each underlying tool as possible.

Keywords: Past Linear Temporal Logic · Temporal Testers · Omega-Automata · Reactive Synthesis

1 Introduction

Linear temporal logic (LTL) is a popular choice of specification language for both the formal verification and the synthesis of programs. It has been established that LTL with past (pLTL) can be exponentially more succinct than LTL [13], and perhaps more importantly, it allows for arguably more natural specifications of real-world properties, reducing the risk of incorrectly formulating them. As a fictional but plausible example, consider a program that may flag for two different errors, represented by the variables err_1 and err_2. We may wish to express that a termination signal, represented by the variable *end*, should be triggered as soon as both errors have occurred, and only then. This can be done in pLTL with the formula,

$$\mathbf{G}\,((\mathbf{O}\,err_1 \wedge \mathbf{O}\,err_2 \wedge \widetilde{\mathbf{Y}}\,\mathbf{H}\,\neg end) \Leftrightarrow end). \quad (1)$$

This research is supported by the Swedish research council (VR) project (No. 2020-04963) and the ERC Consolidator grant DSynMA (No. 772459).

É. André and J. Sun (Eds.): ATVA 2023, LNCS 14216, pp. 276–287, 2023.
https://doi.org/10.1007/978-3-031-45332-8_15

An equivalent LTL formula is,

$$\mathbf{G}\,(end \Rightarrow \mathbf{X}\,\mathbf{G}\,\neg end) \wedge$$
$$((\neg err_1 \wedge \neg err_2 \wedge \neg end)\,\mathbf{W}\,((err_1 \wedge ((\neg err_2 \wedge \neg end)\,\mathbf{W}\,(err_2 \wedge end))) \vee$$
$$(\neg err_1 \wedge \neg err_2 \wedge \neg end)\,\mathbf{W}\,((err_2 \wedge ((\neg err_1 \wedge \neg end)\,\mathbf{W}\,(err_1 \wedge end)))))).$$

The above formula becomes significantly more complex when we add more errors that should trigger termination (in fact, it is factorial in the number of errors [9]). Doing the same for its pLTL counterpart only requires adding conjuncts of the form $\mathbf{O}\,(err_i)$. The past has been also suggested as a way to increase the expressiveness of fragments of LTL that can be handled more efficiently for synthesis, such as GR(1) [4].

Despite the above considerations, there is a lack of general-purpose tool support for pLTL. For example, LamaConv only allows for the translation of pLTL to two-way Büchi (or parity(3)) automata [1], which limits opportunities for further processing. FRET supports a limited notion of past in its specification language [10], and SpeAR provides a natural language interface for writing pure-past LTL requirements and checking them for logical consistency [8]. But neither FRET nor SpeAR enable the usage of pure-past LTL beyond their workflows. GOAL, with its capability to translate full pLTL to different types of ω-automata, comes close to providing general support [17]. However, while feature-rich, GOAL was designed to be used for educational purposes [18], and these translations are not implemented with performance in mind. The lack of support for past is particularly glaring for reactive synthesis tools, where it is vital to express specifications as concisely as possible, due to the high computational complexity of synthesis.

An interesting fragment of pLTL is LTL augmented atomically with pure-past LTL (ppLTL) formulae, which we call *LTL+pp*. The property of exponential succinctness of pLTL w.r.t. LTL is maintained by this fragment (the example formula that proves it for pLTL is also in LTL+pp [13], as is the example above). This fragment is arguably more intuitive than full pLTL, since it does not require reasoning that in a complex manner mixes different time directions, by disallowing the occurrence of future temporal operators under past temporal operators in the syntax tree. Moreover, as we briefly describe in Sect. 4, LTL+pp allows for a straightforward compositional approach to constructing corresponding automata.

In the next section, we describe the syntax and semantics of pLTL and of the fragments LTL+pp and ppLTL, and define temporal testers [15]. Following that, we describe `ppLTLTT`, a tool for generating temporal testers from ppLTL formulae, and then propose this tool as the basis for a toolchain to allow the input of existing tools for LTL-based tasks (e.g., for automata generators and reactive synthesis) to be expanded from LTL to LTL+pp. We further describe the application of our approach to `Slugs` [7], `Strix` [12,14], and `Spot`'s command line tool `LTL2TGBA` [5], and describe three corresponding wrapper tools `pSlugs`, `pStrix` and `pLTL2TGBA`, that all leverage `ppLTLTT`. We describe some experiments performed to investigate the viability of this approach. ppLTLTT and the three wrapper tools are available at GitHub[1].

2 Linear Temporal Logic with Past and Temporal Testers

Formulae of pLTL are constructed from a set of propositional variables, Boolean values and operators, and the temporal operators **X**, **U**, **Y**, and **S**.

Definition 1 (Syntax of pLTL). *Given a set of propositional variables AP, the well-formed formulae of pLTL are generated by the following grammar:*

$$\varphi ::= \top \mid p \mid \neg\varphi \mid \varphi \wedge \varphi \mid \mathbf{X}\,\varphi \mid \varphi\,\mathbf{U}\,\varphi \mid \mathbf{Y}\,\varphi \mid \varphi\,\mathbf{S}\,\varphi,$$

where $p \in AP$.

Formulae of pLTL are evaluated over infinite words, which are sequences of truth assignments to the variables in AP. We call such a truth assignment a *valuation*. We write $(\sigma, t) \models \varphi$ to denote that the infinite word σ models φ at time t.

Definition 2 (Semantics of pLTL). *Let $\sigma = \sigma_0\sigma_1 \cdots \in (2^{AP})^\omega$ be an infinite word over a set of propositional variables AP, φ a pLTL formula, and $t \in \mathbb{N}$. The semantic entailment relation $\models$ is defined by,*

$$\begin{array}{lcl}
(\sigma,t) \models \top & & \\
(\sigma,t) \models p & \Leftrightarrow & p \in \sigma_t \\
(\sigma,t) \models \neg\varphi & \Leftrightarrow & (\sigma,t) \not\models \varphi \\
(\sigma,t) \models \varphi_1 \wedge \varphi_2 & \Leftrightarrow & (\sigma,t) \models \varphi_1 \textit{ and } (\sigma,t) \models \varphi_2 \\
(\sigma,t) \models \mathbf{X}\,\varphi & \Leftrightarrow & (\sigma,t+1) \models \varphi \\
(\sigma,t) \models \varphi_1\,\mathbf{U}\,\varphi_2 & \Leftrightarrow & \exists k \geq t\,.\,((\sigma,k) \models \varphi_2 \wedge \forall j \in [t,k)\,.\,(\sigma,j) \models \varphi_1) \\
(\sigma,t) \models \mathbf{Y}\,\varphi & \Leftrightarrow & t > 0 \textit{ and } (\sigma,t-1) \models \varphi \\
(\sigma,t) \models \varphi_1\,\mathbf{S}\,\varphi_2 & \Leftrightarrow & \exists k \leq t\,.\,((\sigma,k) \models \varphi_2 \wedge \forall j \in (k,t]\,.\,(\sigma,j) \models \varphi_1)
\end{array}$$

The rest of the standard Boolean and temporal operators can be formulated in this language in the usual manner. We assume the reader is familiar with the derivation of other Boolean operators, and only present the following derived temporal operators:

$$\begin{array}{rlrl}
\mathbf{F}\,\varphi := \top\,\mathbf{U}\,\varphi & & \mathbf{O}\,\varphi := \top\,\mathbf{S}\,\varphi \\
\mathbf{G}\,\varphi := \neg\mathbf{F}\,\neg\varphi & & \mathbf{H}\,\varphi := \neg\mathbf{O}\,\neg\varphi \\
\varphi_1\,\mathbf{W}\,\varphi_2 := \varphi_1\,\mathbf{U}\,\varphi_2 \vee \mathbf{G}\,\varphi_1 & & \varphi_1\,\widetilde{\mathbf{S}}\,\varphi_2 := \varphi_1\,\mathbf{S}\,\varphi_2 \vee \mathbf{H}\,\varphi_1 \\
\varphi_1\,\mathbf{R}\,\varphi_2 := \varphi_2\,\mathbf{W}\,(\varphi_1 \wedge \varphi_2) & & \widetilde{\mathbf{Y}}\,\varphi := \mathbf{Y}\,\varphi \vee \neg\mathbf{Y}\,\top
\end{array}$$

We define the fragments of *pure-past LTL* (ppLTL) and *LTL with pure-past* subformulae as atoms (LTL+pp).

[1] https://github.com/DoppeD/ppLTLTT.

Definition 3 (ppLTL and LTL+pp). *Given a set of propositional variables AP, the well-formed formulae of ppLTL (ψ) and LTL+pp (φ) are generated by the following grammar:*

$$\psi ::= \top \mid p \mid \neg\psi \mid \psi \wedge \psi \mid \mathbf{Y}\,\psi \mid \psi\,\mathbf{S}\,\psi$$
$$\varphi ::= \psi \mid \neg\varphi \mid \varphi \wedge \varphi \mid \mathbf{X}\,\varphi \mid \varphi\,\mathbf{U}\,\varphi.$$

The semantics is the same as that of pLTL.

Definition 4 (Temporal testers). *Let φ be a ppLTL formula and z a propositional variable that does not appear in φ. A temporal tester $T_z(\varphi) = (S, s_0, \delta)$ for φ is a deterministic Büchi automaton with alphabet $2^{Var(\varphi)\cup\{z\}}$, that recognizes exactly the formula $\mathbf{G}\,(z \Leftrightarrow \varphi)$, where S is its set of states, of which all are accepting, s_0 is its initial state and δ its transition relation.*

Since temporal testers contain no sink states, the variable z acts as a monitor for the truth value of φ for every prefix of an input word. In the sequel, we will refer to z in the above definition as the *monitor variable* of the temporal tester.

We refer the reader to [15] for a more in-depth presentation of temporal testers, and of pLTL and its properties.

3 ppLTLTT

We present ppLTLTT, a tool that translates ppLTL formulae into temporal testers, which are output in Hanoi Omega-Automata format [3]. For example, a temporal tester for the simple formula $\varphi := \mathbf{Y}\,p$ generated by ppLTLTT is represented in Fig. 1.

In addition to the Boolean operators $\wedge, \vee, \neg, \Rightarrow, \Leftrightarrow$, and $\oplus$ (exclusive or), ppLTLTT supports both the primitive and the derived past operators described in Sect. 2.

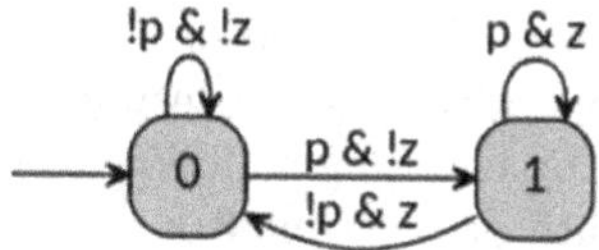

Fig. 1. Temporal tester for the formula $\varphi = \mathbf{Y}\,\psi$, generated by ppLTLTT.

3.1 ppLTL to Temporal Testers

The tool takes a pure-past LTL formula φ and constructs a temporal tester for it. Each state of the temporal tester corresponds to the subset of subformulae of φ that are true when a run reaches that state. Accordingly, every transition, updates the set of true subformulae after reading one more input letter. The

Algorithm 1: The ppLTLTT algorithm

1 **Function** BuildTT(φ, z):
2 $AP \leftarrow \mathrm{Var}(\varphi)$
3 $Q, q_0, \delta \leftarrow \emptyset$
4 $P_\varphi \leftarrow \{\psi \mid \mathbf{Y}\,\psi \in \mathrm{Sub}(\varphi) \vee \exists \psi_1, \psi_2 \,.\, \psi \in \{\mathbf{O}\,\psi_1, \psi_1\,\mathbf{S}\,\psi_2\} \cap \mathrm{Sub}(\varphi)\}$
5 $P_\varphi \leftarrow P_\varphi \cup \{\neg\psi \mid \widetilde{\mathbf{Y}}\,\psi \in \mathrm{Sub}(\varphi) \vee \exists \psi_1, \psi_2 \,.\, \psi \in \{\mathbf{H}\,\psi_1, \psi_1\,\widetilde{\mathbf{S}}\,\psi_2\} \cap \mathrm{Sub}(\varphi)\}$
6 $S \leftarrow S.\mathrm{push}(q_0)$
7 **while** $\neg(S.empty)$ **do**
8 $s \leftarrow S.\mathrm{pop}$
9 **if** $s \notin Q$ **then**
10 $Q \leftarrow Q \cup \{s\}$
11 **forall** $v \in 2^{AP}$ **do**
12 $s' \leftarrow \{\psi \in P_\varphi \mid [\![\psi, s, v]\!] = \top\}$
13 $S \leftarrow S.\mathrm{push}(s')$
14 **if** $[\![\varphi, s, v]\!] = \top$ **then**
15 $\delta \leftarrow \delta \cup \{(s, v \cup \{z\}, s')\}$
16 **else**
17 $\delta \leftarrow \delta \cup \{(s, v, s')\}$
18 **return** (Q, q_0, δ)

construction is detailed in Algorithm 1, which uses the evaluation function in Algorithm 2. Given a ppLTL formula φ, Algorithm 1 first collects all subformulae that appear immediately under a $\mathbf{Y}$ and all subformulae that appear in $\mathbf{O}$ and $\mathbf{S}$ subformulae (line 4). Moreover, it collects the negation of subformulae that appear immediately under a $\widetilde{\mathbf{Y}}$ and all subformulae that appear in $\mathbf{H}$ and $\widetilde{\mathbf{S}}$ subformulae (line 5). States of the constructed temporal tester will then be subsets of these collected formulae (P_φ), where a subformula $\psi \in P_\varphi$ is in a given state s iff all prefixes that reach s satisfy, at their final position, $\mathbf{Y}\,\psi$. For each subformula we choose the polarity that is suitable for our choice of identifying the initial state q_0 as the empty set of formulae. At the beginning of a trace before having read even the first letter, every formula of the form $\mathbf{Y}\,\psi$, $\mathbf{O}\,\psi$, or $\psi_1\,\mathbf{S}\,\psi_2$ does not hold. Conversely, every formula of the form $\widetilde{\mathbf{Y}}\,\psi$, $\mathbf{H}\,\psi$, or $\psi_1\,\widetilde{\mathbf{S}}\,\psi_2$ does hold. Thus, by choosing to follow the negations of the latter we can start with the initial state $q_0 = \emptyset$ (line 3).

The algorithm then proceeds to construct a temporal tester for φ incrementally, starting from a stack of states consisting of only the initial state. At each step, all possible transitions are considered (line 11), and for each such transition the set of formulae of P_φ that are true after the transition are collected (line 12), capturing the next state s'. This state is added to the state stack, and z added to the transition label only if the full formula φ is true at that time point (lines 14-17).

The evaluation function from Algorithm 2 is used to determine when a formula is true on a transition from a state s (see lines 12 and 14), by using the knowledge of what happened now (the transition label v) and what held

Algorithm 2: The evaluation function

1 **Function** $[\![\psi, s, v]\!]$:
2   **switch** ψ **do**
    `/* We omit the cases for Boolean connectives */`
3   **case** p **do**
4   **return** $(p \in v)$
5   **case** $\mathbf{Y}\,\psi_1$ **do**
6   **return** $(\psi_1 \in s)$
7   **case** $\widetilde{\mathbf{Y}}\,\psi_1$ **do**
8   **return** $(\neg\psi_1 \notin s)$
9   **case** $\mathbf{O}\,\psi_1$ **do**
10   **return** $([\![\psi_1, s, v]\!] \vee (\mathbf{O}\,\psi_1 \in s))$
11   **case** $\mathbf{H}\,\psi_1$ **do**
12   **return** $([\![\psi_1, s, v]\!] \wedge (\neg\mathbf{H}\,\psi_1 \notin s))$
13   **case** $\psi_1\,\mathbf{S}\,\psi_2$ **do**
14   **return** $(([\![\psi_1, s, v]\!] \wedge (\psi_1\,\mathbf{S}\,\psi_2 \in s)) \vee [\![\psi_2, s, v]\!])$
15   **case** $\psi_1\,\widetilde{\mathbf{S}}\,\psi_2$ **do**
16   **return** $(([\![\psi_1, s, v]\!] \wedge (\neg(\psi_1\,\widetilde{\mathbf{S}}\,\psi_2) \notin s)) \vee [\![\psi_2, s, v]\!])$

true before (the formulae from P_φ in s). This algorithm exploits the expansion law for the temporal operators, which implies that the truth value of each (pure-past) temporal subformula at each time step is completely determined by its truth value in the previous state, together with the current valuation. For example, the expansion of the Since operator (lines 13-14 in Algorithm 2) is $\varphi_1\,\mathbf{S}\,\varphi_2 \equiv \varphi_2 \vee (\varphi_1 \wedge \mathbf{Y}\,(\varphi_1\,\mathbf{S}\,\varphi_2))$. We omit the cases for the Boolean connectives in the algorithm; these are as expected.

As states are represented by subsets of subformulae of φ, the algorithm returns an automaton with at most 2^n states, where n is the size of the formula. Moreover, since the transitions from a state correspond in a one-to-one manner to valuations of the propositional variables in φ, the automaton is deterministic.

3.2 Implementation Notes

The tool is implemented in Haskell. Subformulae are collected by traversing the abstract syntax tree of the input formula. Each unique subformula with a top-level past operator is annotated with an index, as is every propositional variable. Each state (set of subformulae) is internally represented as an `Integer`[2], where bit i represents the truth value of the subformula with index i.

[2] Note that Haskell `Integers` are of arbitrary precision; the input formula's size is only limited by the computer's memory.

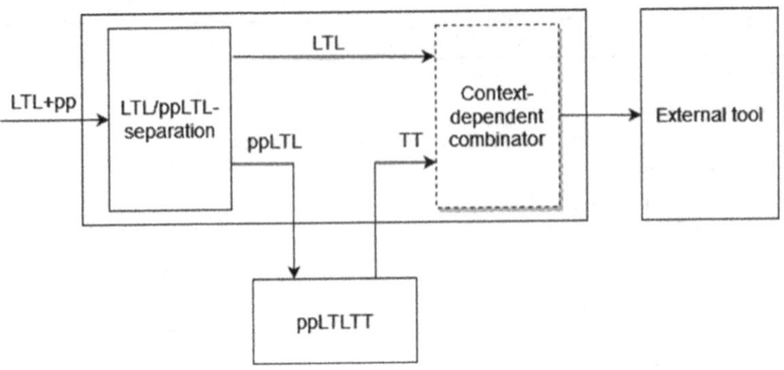

Fig. 2. The proposed toolchain.

4 Adding Past to Existing Tools

ppLTLTT is intended to be used as part of a toolchain to extend existing LTL-based tools to LTL+pp, as illustrated in Fig. 2. A given LTL+pp specification is first separated into an LTL and a ppLTL part by replacing each pure-past subformula with a fresh variable. Each such subformula and its corresponding monitor variable are then translated into a temporal tester by ppLTLTT. The resulting temporal tester is combined with the LTL specification in a way that is dependent on the target tool, to which the result is then passed on. By using ppLTLTT in this way, it is possible to extend existing tools that interact with LTL specifications to support a larger fragment of pLTL, namely LTL+pp, in a straightforward manner.

As a proof of concept, we implemented this toolchain for three existing tools: Slugs, Strix, and Spot's command-line tool LTL2TGBA, which we describe below. These are (if not the best then among the best) state-of-the-art tools for different usage of LTL: Slugs handles GR(1) synthesis, Strix handles general LTL synthesis, and Spot converts LTL to automata and implements many automata transformations. We begin by explaining the encoding of the *characteristic LTL formula* of a given temporal tester.

4.1 Encoding Temporal Testers in LTL

Let $T_z(\varphi) = (S, s_0, \delta)$ be a temporal tester generated for the ppLTL formula φ, with monitor variable $z \notin \text{Var}(\varphi)$ and alphabet $AP = \text{Var}(\varphi) \cup \{z\}$. For every state s, let $\beta(s)$ denote its encoding as a Boolean formula[3]. We encode $T_z(\varphi)$ as the following LTL formula:

[3] The auxiliary tools described in Sect. 4 default to a binary encoding, but users can opt for a one-hot encoding instead.

$$\beta(s_0) \wedge \bigwedge_{s \in S} \bigwedge_{v \in 2^{AP}} \mathbf{G}\left(\beta(s) \wedge \bigwedge_{p \in v \cap \mathrm{Var}(\varphi)} p \wedge \bigwedge_{q \in \mathrm{Var}(\varphi) \setminus v} \neg q \Rightarrow [\![z]\!] \wedge \mathbf{X}\left(\beta(\delta(s, v))\right)\right) \quad (2)$$

$$\text{where } [\![z]\!] = z \text{ if } z \in v \text{ and } [\![z]\!] = \neg z \text{ otherwise}$$

Note that we here treat δ as a function, to simplify the presentation.

In practice, instead of generating complete temporal testers, we do not generate and encode transitions in which the truth value of the monitor variable z does not match the current truth value of the formula φ, which is entirely determined by the valuation $v \cap \mathrm{Var}(\varphi)$ together with the current state.

Consider the temporal tester in Fig. 1. It consists of two states s_0 and s_1 (0 and 1 in the figure). Using a binary encoding, these are represented by a single propositional variable s. With the state encoding $\beta(s_0) = \neg s, \beta(s_1) = s$, the tester is encoded as,

$$\neg s \wedge \mathbf{G}(\neg s \wedge p \Rightarrow \neg z \wedge \mathbf{X}\, s) \wedge \mathbf{G}(\neg s \wedge \neg p \Rightarrow \neg z \wedge \mathbf{X} \neg s)$$
$$\wedge \mathbf{G}(s \wedge p \Rightarrow z \wedge \mathbf{X}\, s) \wedge \mathbf{G}(s \wedge \neg p \Rightarrow z \wedge \mathbf{X} \neg s).$$

4.2 Adding Past to `Slugs`: `pSlugs`

`Slugs` [7] is a tool for GR(1) synthesis [16]. It requires input GR(1) specifications written in the `slugsin` format, using prefix notation. A more syntactically expressive structured format is also available; specifications written in this format must be converted into `slugsin` before being passed to `Slugs`.

Given a `slugsin` specification, `pSlugs` converts the pure-past subformulae into temporal testers as described at the start of Sect. 4, and encodes each into the specification in the manner described in Sect. 4.1. To encode the temporal tester in `slugsin`, we allocate the required number of Boolean variables to encode the states (in binary or unary as explained). These new variables are added as output variables, while the initialization and transition invariants mentioned in Sect. 4.1 are added to the system's initialization and transition invariants, respectively. As `Slugs` treats specifications as well-separated [11], there is no problem with the controller breaking safety.

4.3 Adding Past to `Strix`: `pStrix`

`Strix` [12,14] is a reactive synthesis tool for full LTL. It takes as input an LTL formula and a designation of input and output variables. The corresponding wrapper tool `pStrix` is broadly identical to `pSlugs` in function and interface, but the temporal testers generated from its input are encoded directly as conjuncts in the form of Eq. 2. To avoid issues with well-separation of the resulting specification, the final format of the formula given to `Strix` is the conjunction of the formulae relating to the newly allocated output variables with the LTL formula resulting from the removal of pure-past. That is, if φ is an LTL+pp formula with non-overlapping pure-past subformulae $\psi_1, \ldots, \psi_n$, then the final specification for `Strix` is $\varphi[z_1/\psi_1, ..., z_n/\psi_n] \wedge \bigwedge_{i \in [1..n]} T_{z_i}(\psi_i)$.

4.4 Adding Past to LTL2TGBA: pLTL2TGBA

LTL2TGBA [5] is a component of Spot [6]. It is a command-line tool that translates LTL formulae into various kinds of automata. Although the wrapper tool pLTL2TGBA follows the same initial steps of formula separation and conversion into temporal testers as pSlugs and pStrix, it combines the results differently. While pSlugs and pStrix syntactically manipulate the input, pLTL2TGBA works directly with the automata by making use of autfilt (another Spot command-line tool). Once the input has been separated, the LTL part is translated by LTL2TGBA into the desired automaton type. This *LTL-automaton* is then composed with the temporal testers by taking their product using autfilt. Finally, monitor variables become redundant and we instruct autfilt to remove them.

To exemplify the process, let φ be the pLTL formula presented in the introduction (1). The pure-past subformula will be replaced with a fresh variable z by pLTL2TGBA, resulting in the two formulae,

$$\varphi_f = \mathbf{G}\,(z \Leftrightarrow end)$$
$$\varphi_p = z \Leftrightarrow \mathbf{O}\,err_1 \wedge \mathbf{O}\,err_2 \wedge \widetilde{\mathbf{Y}}\,\mathbf{H}\,\neg end.$$

The formula φ_f is translated into an automaton $A(\varphi_f)$ by LTL2TGBA, while φ_p is translated into a temporal tester $T_z(\varphi_p)$ by ppLTLTT. The two are then combined by autfilt to obtain an automaton whose language is exactly the models of φ_f,

$$\mathbf{G}\,(z \Leftrightarrow end) \wedge \mathbf{G}\,(z \Leftrightarrow \mathbf{O}\,err_1 \wedge \mathbf{O}\,err_2 \wedge \widetilde{\mathbf{Y}}\,\mathbf{H}\,\neg end),$$

which is clearly equivalent to φ.

5 Experimental Evaluation

All experiments in this section were performed on a Dell Latitude 5420, with an Intel Core i7-1185G7 clocked at 3 GHz, and 32 GB of DDR4 RAM clocked at 3200 MHz, running 64-bit Ubuntu 22.04.1 LTS. For comparisons with other tools we use the latest versions at time of writing. For Goal we use the version dated 2020-05-06, for Strix v.21.0.0, for Spot v.2.11.5, and for Slugs we use the code in commit dc2b1e0 from [2].

For pStrix and pSlugs we use arbiter specifications as test cases, a commonly used example for synthesis. An arbiter is conceived of as a controller granting access to resources as they are requested by clients. For n clients, there are request variables $r_1, r_2, \ldots, r_n$ and grant variables $g_1, g_2, \ldots, g_n$. The requirements of the controller are that a) only one grant is given at a time, b) it is strongly fair, and c) it will not grant access to a resource if there is no open request for it. We can express these conditions as follows:

$$\bigwedge_{i \neq j} \mathbf{G}(\neg g_i \vee \neg g_j) \wedge \bigwedge_i (\mathbf{GF} r_i \Rightarrow \mathbf{GF} g_i) \wedge \bigwedge_i \mathbf{G}(g_i \Rightarrow \mathbf{Y}(\neg g_i\, \mathbf{S}\, r_i)).$$

Table 1. Results of synthesizing arbiters with `pStrix` and `pSlugs`.

No. of Clients	# of Added Variables	Synthesis (s)	No. of States
Arbiter with Strong Fairness, `pStrix`			
1	2	0.03 s	2
2	4	0.04 s	8
3	6	0.6 s	48
4	8	1.04 s	384
5	10	16.37 s	3840
6	12	`OOM`	N/A
Arbiter, `pSlugs`			
1	4	0.02 s	6
2	8	0.03 s	72
3	12	0.10 s	552
4	16	1.46 s	3904
5	20	34.30 s	26720
6	24	714.43 s	180096

Table 2. Timings of translating arbiters to NBA with `pLTL2TGBA` and different algorithms of Goal.

Arbiter with Strong Fairness, `pLTL2TGBA` and Goal timings						
No. of Clients	`pLTL2TGBA`	`ltl2aut`	`ltl2aut+`	`couvreur`	`ltl2buchi`	`modella`
1	0.058 s	0.646 s	0.587 s	0.622 s	0.629 s	0.651 s
2	0.071 s	5.108 s	2.956 s	9.864 s	5.690 s	11.779 s
3	15.143 s	`TO`	`TO`	`TO`	`TO`	`TO`

The multi-variable strong fairness condition cannot be expressed in GR(1), however. In `pSlugs`, we replace it with $\mathbf{GF}(\neg r_i \widetilde{\mathbf{S}}\, g_i)$, which is equivalent to the requirement $\mathbf{G}(r_i \Rightarrow \mathbf{F} g_i)$. That is, every request should eventually be followed by a grant. It is well known how to encode future-time formulae of the latter form in GR(1) by adding an additional variable [4]. In our case, however, we use the LTL+pp equivalent, which is automatically handled by `ppLTLTT`:

$$\bigwedge_{i \neq j} \mathbf{G}(\neg g_i \vee \neg g_j) \wedge \bigwedge_{i} \mathbf{GF}(r_i \,\widetilde{\mathbf{S}}\, g_i) \wedge \bigwedge_{i} \mathbf{G}(g_i \Rightarrow \mathbf{Y}(\neg g_i \,\mathbf{S}\, r_i)).$$

Table 1 shows the result of synthesizing arbiters with a varying number of clients using `pStrix` and `pSlugs`. It shows how many variables were added to each specification, the time it took to synthesize the translated specification, and the number of controller states. `OOM` indicates that the program ran out of memory. For general reactive synthesis with `pStrix` (or Strix) `OOM` is to be expected with larger formulae, given the 2EXPTIME-complete complexity of reactive synthesis.

As Goal is the only tool that we are aware of able to translate pLTL to Büchi automata, we compare the performance of pLTL2TGBA to Goal in translating arbiters to nondeterministic Büchi automata, using the same specifications as for pStrix. Because Goal offers a choice of several translation algorithms, we only include the five most performant. We set a timeout of ten minutes; TO indicates that the process did not finish within this time limit. The results are shown in Table 2.

6 Conclusion

We have presented ppLTLTT, a tool for translating pure-past linear temporal logic formulae into temporal testers in the form of automata. We have integrated ppLTLTT with three existing LTL-based tools, namely Slugs, Strix and Spot's command-line tool LTL2TGBA, with the aim, among other things, of making controller synthesis more scalable. As future work we intend to optimize the encoding of temporal testers in LTL, and add features such as allowing the user to have fine grained control over how pure-past subformulae are abstracted.

References

1. Lamaconv-logics and automata converter library. https://www.isp.uni-luebeck.de/lamaconv. Institute for Software Engineering and Programming Languages, University of Lübeck. Accessed 14 Oct 2022
2. Slugs. https://github.com/VerifiableRobotics/slugs. Verifiable Robotics Research Group, Cornell University. Accessed 14 Oct 2022
3. Babiak, T., et al.: The Hanoi Omega-automata format. In: Kroening, D., Păsăreanu, C.S. (eds.) CAV 2015. LNCS, vol. 9206, pp. 479–486. Springer, Cham (2015). https://doi.org/10.1007/978-3-319-21690-4_31
4. Bloem, R., Jobstmann, B., Piterman, N., Pnueli, A., Sa'ar, Y.: Synthesis of reactive(1) designs. J. Comput. Syst. Sci. **78**(3), 911–938 (2012)
5. Duret-Lutz, A.: LTL translation improvements in Spot 1.0. Int. J. Crit. Comput. Based Syst. **5**(1/2), 31–54 (2014)
6. Duret-Lutz, A., et al.: From spot 2.0 to spot 2.10: what's new? In: Shoham, S., Vizel, Y. (eds.) CAV 2022. LNCS, vol. 13372, pp. 174–187. Springer, Cham (2022). https://doi.org/10.1007/978-3-031-13188-2_9
7. Ehlers, R., Raman, V.: Slugs: extensible GR(1) synthesis. In: Chaudhuri, S., Farzan, A. (eds.) CAV 2016. LNCS, vol. 9780, pp. 333–339. Springer, Cham (2016). https://doi.org/10.1007/978-3-319-41540-6_18
8. Fifarek, A.W., Wagner, L.G., Hoffman, J.A., Rodes, B.D., Aiello, M.A., Davis, J.A.: SpeAR v2.0: formalized past LTL specification and analysis of requirements. In: Barrett, C., Davies, M., Kahsai, T. (eds.) NFM 2017. LNCS, vol. 10227, pp. 420–426. Springer, Cham (2017). https://doi.org/10.1007/978-3-319-57288-8_30
9. Grekula, O.: SeqLTL and ωLTL – tight witnesses for composing LTL formulas. Master's thesis, Chalmers University of Technology and University of Gothenburg, Gothenburg, Sweden (2023)

10. Katis, A., Mavridou, A., Giannakopoulou, D., Pressburger, T., Schumann, J.: Capture, analyze, diagnose: Realizability checking of requirements in fret. In: Shoham, S., Vizel, Y. (eds.) CAV 2022. LNCS, vol. 13372, pp. 490–504. Springer, Cham (2022). https://doi.org/10.1007/978-3-031-13188-2_24
11. Klein, U., Pnueli, A.: Revisiting synthesis of GR(1) specifications. In: Barner, S., Harris, I., Kroening, D., Raz, O. (eds.) HVC 2010. LNCS, vol. 6504, pp. 161–181. Springer, Heidelberg (2011). https://doi.org/10.1007/978-3-642-19583-9_16
12. Luttenberger, M., Meyer, P.J., Sickert, S.: Practical synthesis of reactive systems from LTL specifications via parity games. Acta Informatica **57**(1–2), 3–36 (2020)
13. Markey, N.: Temporal logic with past is exponentially more succinct. Bull. Eur. Assoc. Theor. Comput. Sci. **79**, 122–128 (2003)
14. Meyer, P.J., Sickert, S., Luttenberger, M.: Strix: explicit reactive synthesis strikes back! In: Chockler, H., Weissenbacher, G. (eds.) CAV 2018. LNCS, vol. 10981, pp. 578–586. Springer, Cham (2018). https://doi.org/10.1007/978-3-319-96145-3_31
15. Piterman, N., Pnueli, A.: Temporal logic and fair discrete systems. In: Handbook of Model Checking, pp. 27–73. Springer, Cham (2018). https://doi.org/10.1007/978-3-319-10575-8_2
16. Piterman, N., Pnueli, A., Sa'ar, Y.: Synthesis of reactive(1) designs. In: Emerson, E.A., Namjoshi, K.S. (eds.) VMCAI 2006. LNCS, vol. 3855, pp. 364–380. Springer, Heidelberg (2005). https://doi.org/10.1007/11609773_24
17. Tsai, M.-H., Tsay, Y.-K., Hwang, Y.-S.: GOAL for games, omega-automata, and logics. In: Sharygina, N., Veith, H. (eds.) CAV 2013. LNCS, vol. 8044, pp. 883–889. Springer, Heidelberg (2013). https://doi.org/10.1007/978-3-642-39799-8_62
18. Tsay, Y.-K., Chen, Y.-F., Tsai, M.-H., Wu, K.-N., Chan, W.-C.: GOAL: a graphical tool for manipulating Büchi automata and temporal formulae. In: Grumberg, O., Huth, M. (eds.) TACAS 2007. LNCS, vol. 4424, pp. 466–471. Springer, Heidelberg (2007). https://doi.org/10.1007/978-3-540-71209-1_35

AquaSense: Automated Sensitivity Analysis of Probabilistic Programs via Quantized Inference

Zitong Zhou(✉), Zixin Huang(✉), and Sasa Misailovic(✉)

University of Illinois Urbana-Champaign, Urbana, IL, USA
{zitongz4,zixinh2,misailo}@illinois.edu

Abstract. We propose a novel tool, AquaSense, to automatically reason about the sensitivity analysis of probabilistic programs. In the context of probabilistic programs, sensitivity analysis investigates how the perturbation in the parameters of prior distributions affects the program's result, i.e., the program's posterior distribution. AquaSense leverages quantized inference, an efficient and accurate approximate inference algorithm that represents distributions of random variables with quantized intervals. AquaSense is the first tool to support sensitivity analysis of probabilistic programs that is at the same time symbolic, differentiable, and practical.

Our evaluation compares AquaSense with an existing system PSense (a system that relies on fully symbolic inference). AquaSense can compute the sensitivity of all 45 parameters from 12 programs, compared to 11/45 that PSense computes. AquaSense is particularly effective on programs with continuous distributions: it achieves an average speedup of 18.10× over PSense (which, in contrast, can solve only a handful of problems). Our evaluation shows that AquaSense computes exact results on discrete programs. On 91% of evaluated continuous parameters, AquaSense computed the sensitivity results within 40 s with high accuracy (below 5% error). The paper also discusses AquaSense's performance-accuracy trade-offs, which can enable different operational points for programs with different input data sizes.

Keywords: Probabilistic Programming · Sensitivity Analysis · Quantized Inference

1 Introduction

Probabilistic programming (PP) provides an intuitive way to encode statistical models in the form of programs. It is a quickly rising discipline that has seen applications in areas like computer vision [22], robotics [25], scientific simulation [4], and data science [28]. Probabilistic programming allows a developer to encode uncertainty in the program as random variables. When declaring random variables, the developer specifies the *prior* beliefs of the random variables using probability distributions and encodes the model in the program by relating the random variables to data observations. The developer then makes queries

É. André and J. Sun (Eds.): ATVA 2023, LNCS 14216, pp. 288–301, 2023.
https://doi.org/10.1007/978-3-031-45332-8_16

about the *posterior* distribution of these random variables after execution of the program.

When developing a probabilistic program, developers need to make assumptions regarding the model and the data on which the inference is performed (e.g., a common assumption is Gaussian distributions with a fixed variance). However, it is unknown how reliable these assumptions are. Many studies have reported that a wrong prior could lead to incorrect results [5,21,27]. Testing the sensitivity of the parameters of prior distributions is a way to identify such incorrectly-chosen priors and improve the underlying statistical model.

In this work, we focus on the sensitivity analysis of probabilistic programs, which addresses the question: *if we change the prior distribution, how will the posterior distribution of random variables change?*

AquaSense. We present AquaSense, an automated tool for efficient and accurate sensitivity analysis of probabilistic programs. AquaSense takes a probabilistic program as input, injects a symbolic perturbation ϵ for each prior parameter in the program, then simulates the change in the posterior distribution due to the ϵ values.

At its core, AquaSense leverages *quantized inference* of probabilistic programs. Quantized inference splits the values of continuous random variables into finite intervals and thus works around intractable integrals [17]. Our quantization-based sensitivity analysis can solve a significantly broader range of probabilistic programs than existing tools, while guaranteeing the point-wise convergence of the result sensitivity for continuous programs and small error in practice.

Results. We compare our approach to PSense [19], a system for exact sensitivity analysis, which uses PSI [14], an exact symbolic inference engine, together with a computer algebra system to computes a symbolic and exact sensitivity function.

We evaluated AquaSense on 12 probabilistic programs and analyzed the sensitivity of 45 prior parameters. Results show that AquaSense computes the sensitivity of all 45 parameters, compared to 11 by the baseline PSense. On all 11 discrete parameters, AquaSense produces exact results with comparable performance with PSense. On 34 continuous parameters, AquaSense achieves an average speedup of 18.10$\times$ over PSense. On 31 (91%) continuous parameters, AquaSense produces results within 5% of relative error in 40 s, averaging 5.89s. We also show that the time-accuracy trade-off of AquaSense is reasonable.

Contributions. We summarize our contributions as follows:

1. We design and build a quantization-based sensitivity analyzer AquaSense for real-world probabilistic programs. AquaSense supports multiple front-end languages and leverages quantized inference to analyze models that are out of reach of existing tools.
2. We formally prove the point-wise convergence of AquaSense analysis to the exact analysis results on continuous programs with bounded support. We present empirical evidence that AquaSense is exact on discrete programs.

Listing 1.1. Example Prob. Program

```
1  # Data observations
2  vector x[N] = [3.0,...]
3  vector y[N] = [0.6094,...]
4
5  # Model
6  b0 ~ uniform(-1, 1)
7  b1 ~ uniform(-1, 1)
8  sigma ~ uniform(0, 2)
9  for (i in 1:N)
10     y[i] ~ normal(b0+x[i]*b1, sigma)
```

3. We experimentally show AquaSense supports a broader set of continuous programs and achieves orders-of-magnitude speedup than the existing tool PSense, while having comparable capability and speed on discrete programs.

Availability. Latest source code and artifact is available at https://github.com/uiuc-arc/aquasense.

2 Example: Sensitivity-Driven Development

Probabilistic programming is an intuitive way to express a statistical model as a computer program. Listing 1.1 shows such a simple probabilistic program representing a regression model. Suppose we observed a dataset with pairs of `x` and `y`, and we want to fit a line `y = b0 + x * b1` to the dataset, where `b0` (the slope) and `b1` (the intercept) are unknowns. We write such a probabilistic program to solve the distributions of `b0` and `b1` in the program.

In the program, we first specify the prior distributions of intercept `b0`, slope `b1`, and standard deviation `sigma` as uniform distributions, indicating they are equally likely everywhere on their support `[-1,1]` and `[0,2]` (Lines 6–8). Next, we specify that each datum `y[i]` is drawn from a normal distribution with mean `b0 + x[i] * b1` and standard deviation `sigma` (Lines 9–10). In Bayesian terms, in each iteration, we update our belief (prior) about the slope, intercept, and error, upon learning that the datum `y[i]` follows the specified distribution. In the end, the program is represented by a joint posterior probability density f(`b0, b1, sigma`). Given a probabilistic program, probabilistic systems can automatically compute the joint probability density defined by the program.

Choosing Prior Parameters. In this program, the developer chose a uniform prior to reflect the lack of a prior knowledge of `b1`. However, when choosing the parameters of the uniform prior - the lower and upper bounds (marked in **brown** in Listing 1.1) - the developers are unaware of how such ad-hoc decisions would affect the final result. Given the program as input, AquaSense can automatically

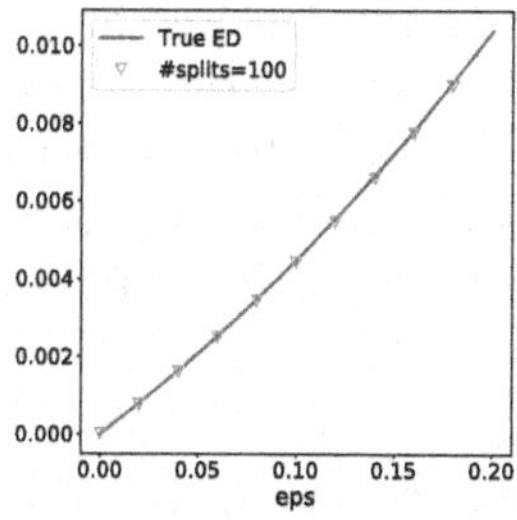

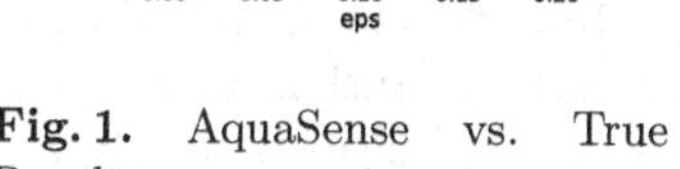

Fig. 1. AquaSense vs. True Results

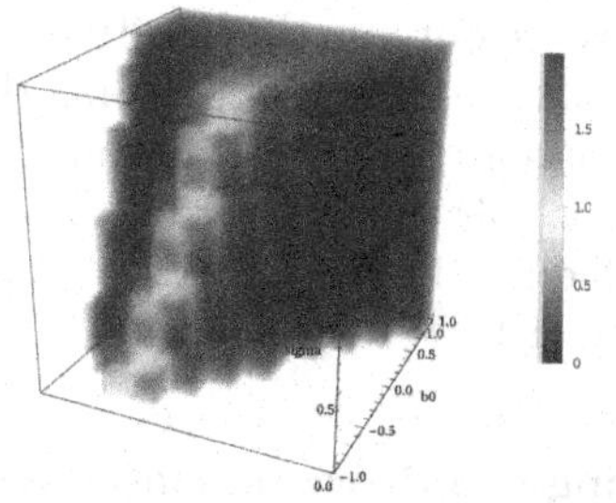

Fig. 2. Density Cube Visualization

test the sensitivity of these parameters, which guide developers to adjust the prior distributions/parameters so that the model's sensitivity is fitting. We detail the example at the end of this section.

Sensitivity Analysis with AquaSense. Given the program (Listing 1.1), AquaSense first performs a pre-analysis to identify the three random variables and their six prior parameters. AquaSense injects noise to test each parameter's sensitivity. For example, to test how the posterior of `b1` changes if its upper bound parameter of the prior `1` is perturbed, AquaSense injects a perturbation parameter ϵ and updates the prior to `b1~uniform(-1, 1+`ϵ`)`.

AquaSense measures sensitivity as the distance between the posteriors with and without perturbation, as in previous works [19]. For simplicity, we use the Expectation Distance (*ED*) that measures the absolute difference between the expectations of posteriors; AquaSense also supports standards such as Total Variation Distance, Kolmogorov-Smirnov distance [24], and user-defined metrics. The sensitivity of a random variable X measured in Expectation Distance is

$$ED_X(\epsilon) = |\mathbb{E}_{X\sim P(0)}[X] - \mathbb{E}_{X\sim P(\epsilon)}[X]|,$$

where $\mathbb{E}_{X\sim P(\epsilon)}[X]$ and $\mathbb{E}_{X\sim P(0)}[X]$ are the expectations of the posterior distribution of X with and without ϵ added to its prior parameters, respectively.

In the example above, AquaSense would sample evenly-distributed ϵs, whose range can be supplied by the user or inferred by AquaSense using heuristics. It calls AQUA [17], the quantized inference algorithm, to run the programs with and without noise (i.e., $\epsilon = 0$). AQUA would return the approximated posterior distribution density functions, $\hat{p}_{X\sim P(\epsilon)}(x)$ and $\hat{p}_{X\sim P(0)}(x)$, for the programs with and without noise. Next, AquaSense integrates the approximated density functions to get the approximated posterior expectation as $\hat{\mathbb{E}}_{X\sim P(\epsilon)}[X]$ and $\hat{\mathbb{E}}_{X\sim P(0)}[X]$. Because AQUA outputs the posterior densities $\hat{p}_{\cdot}(\cdot)$ as piecewise constant functions, AquaSense can get around integration with summation. In the end, AquaSense computes the approximated $\hat{ED}_X(\epsilon)$. We can show that $\hat{ED}_X(\epsilon)$ could converge pointwisely to the exact $ED_X(\epsilon)$ with more quantization splits (see Sect. 4).

AquaSense outputs the sensitivity of the program as an interpolated function of ϵ. AquaSense can also visualize the distance function by plotting distance against the noise like the yellow markers in Fig. 1. To demonstrate AquaSense's accuracy, we also show the true expectation distance computed manually with a solid blue line in Fig. 1. For this simple example, PSense fails to compute the sensitivity of `b1` (See Sect. 5).

Improving the Program Based on Sensitivity Results. As the function of difference between posterior expectations with respect to perturbation, a steep *ED* indicates the prior chosen is sensitive to perturbation. In the example above, as the developer supplies an upper bound parameter (`1`) to the uniform distribution, the probability will be truncated to zero when `b1` is larger than `1`. If the incoming data exhibit a probability distribution that is "substantial" on $[1, \infty]$, e.g., the part $[1, \infty]$ has more likelihood than the prior support [`-1`,`1`], then the computed posterior will "miss" this part of the likelihood due to the prior. In Fig. 1, AquaSense helps detect that the *ED* is 0.01 when ϵ is 0.2. This means if the developer has chosen a different prior `b1 ~ uniform(-1, 1.2)`, the result expectation of `b1` would change by 0.01, which is negligible for `uniform(-1, 1)`. This result indicates the chosen prior parameter is relatively insensitive to perturbation. In contrast, suppose the sensitivity at $\epsilon = 0.2$ is high, e.g. $ED = 1$, which means changing the prior from `b1 ~ uniform(-1, 1)` to `uniform(-1, 1.2)` would increase the expectation of the posterior of `b1` by 1, so the developer is advised to modify the prior to `b1 ~ uniform(-1, 1.2)` in order to capture the "missing" posterior density of `b1` on $[1, 1.2]$. Sensitivity analysis and prior updates can be applied iteratively this way until sensitivity is deemed suitable.

In conclusion, sensitivity analysis can help a) expose such misses of density outside of the prior support and, b) quantitatively measure its severity. Analogously, sensitivity analysis can also be used to identify other types of poorly-chosen prior parameters, e.g., mean, standard deviation, and degrees of freedom.

3 Background: Automated Inference Algorithms

The goal of probabilistic programming is to compute the joint probability density f. To this end, probabilistic programming languages (e.g., AQUA [17], PSI [15], Stan [6]) are coupled with automated inference algorithms that compute the density f either exactly or approximately. For example, PSI implements exact inference using computer algebra, computes the posterior symbolically via $p(\texttt{b0}, \texttt{b1}, \texttt{sigma}) = \frac{f(\texttt{b0,b1,sigma})}{\int f(\texttt{b0,b1,sigma}) d\texttt{b0,b1,sigma}}$, which requires integration that is often intractable. The prior work PSense uses PSI to compute posterior distributions of probabilistic programs, and thus also suffers from intractable integrals.

AquaSense implements sensitivity analysis on top of AQUA's quantized inference. AQUA approximates the symbolic joint probability density $f(\texttt{b0}, \texttt{b1}, \texttt{sigma})$ with quantized samples, by storing the quantization of f's domain and co-domain in multidimensional arrays. In the example above, AQUA quantizes `b0`, `b1`, `sigma` into evenly spaced values, e.g., $[-1, -0.8, ..., 0.8, 1]$, when using 10 splits. Then AQUA computes $f(\texttt{b0}, \texttt{b1}, \texttt{sigma})$ at all combinations of the variable values, to obtain a three-dimensional array, called Density Cube. Figure 2 shows a visualization of the Density Cube, with each dimension representing a random variable. Among the 10^3 mini-cubes, a warmer color means higher probability. In AQUA, normalization is reduced to summation over the Density Cube. AQUA outputs the approximated joint posterior density function, denoted $\hat{p}(\texttt{b0}, \texttt{b1}, \texttt{sigma})$.

Alternatives to AQUA include computer-algebra-based exact inference like PSI and sampling-based inference like Stan. Intractability severely limits exact inference to simple models with few continuous distributions (see Sect. 5). Sampling-based inference are not accurate enough for sensitivity analysis, as studies have shown [19] [17]. For the particular task of sensitivity analysis, quantized inference is an ideal candidate as it can get around the intractability problem while being more accurate than sampling-based inference.

4 AquaSense Workflow

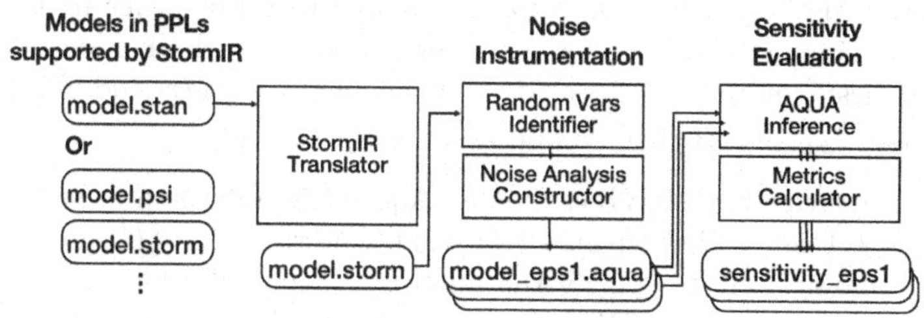

Fig. 3. AquaSense Workflow

Input: A Probabilistic Program. AquaSense takes a probabilistic program in any probabilistic programming language (PPL) supported by StormIR [13] (which is an intermediate probabilistic programming language), including Stan [16], PSI [15], Pyro [26], or StormIR itself. See Fig. 4 for its syntax.

Noise Instrumentation. Given a program P, AquaSense applies a pre-analysis to find the random variables and their prior parameters. The bound of noise of each parameter is user-supplied or computed using a heuristic. For each prior parameter, it generates a new program, as $P(\epsilon)$, by injecting a symbolic noise variable ϵ at the parameter. AquaSense evenly samples a set of values of ϵ from its bounds as $\mathcal{B}$.

$x \in$ Vars
$c \in$ Consts
$op \in \{+, -, *, >, \ldots\}$
$d \in$ {**Normal**, **Uniform**, ...}

```
E := c | x | E[E*] | E op E |d(E*).pdf(E*) |f(E*)
S := x = E |x ~ d(E*)|factor(E) |observe(d(E*),x)
     | if (E) S* else S* | for x ∈ 1..N; {S*}
P := S+; return x+
```

Fig. 4. Syntax of StormIR

AQUA Inference. AquaSense employs AQUA [17], the quantized inference engine, to solve a probabilistic program. AQUA takes a probabilistic program P and outputs the approximated posterior of a random variable x as a piece-wise constant function, denoted as $\hat{p}_{X\sim P}(x)$.

Figure 5 illustrates an example of AQUA analysis results. The red line represents the true density that PSI would calculate, and the gray bars represent AQUA's approximation. With AquaSense noise instrumentation, AquaSense runs AQUA on the program $P(\epsilon)$ with quantized values of ϵ, to simulate the program results due to different ϵ, as $\{\hat{p}_{X\sim P(\epsilon_i)}(x)|\epsilon_i \in \mathcal{B}\}$.

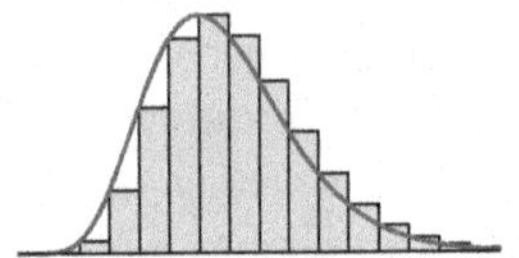

Fig. 5. AQUA Inference Example

Metrics Calculator. Next, AquaSense computes the sensitivity metrics based on inference results, e.g., the Expectation Distance (ED) [19], Kolmogorov-Smirnov statistic [24], Total Variation Distance (TVD) or other user-provided metrics. For simplicity, we use ED throughout this work. For each $\epsilon_i \in \mathcal{B}$, AquaSense first computes $\hat{\mathbb{E}}_{X\sim P(0)} = \int_x x \cdot \hat{p}_{X\sim P(0)}(x)dx$ and $\hat{\mathbb{E}}_{X\sim P(\epsilon_i)} = \int_x x \cdot \hat{p}_{X\sim P(\epsilon_i)}(x)dx$, and then computes $\hat{ED}_X(\epsilon_i) = |\hat{\mathbb{E}}_{X\sim P(0)} - \hat{\mathbb{E}}_{X\sim P(\epsilon_i)}|$.

Output: Program Sensitivity. Finally, AquaSense interpolates sensitivity as a function of ϵ. Using ED, it outputs $ED_X(\epsilon)$ by interpolating $\{\hat{ED}_X(\epsilon_i)|\epsilon_i \in \mathcal{B}\}$. AquaSense allows users to specify the number of ϵ samples and the number of quantization splits used in AQUA to control the analysis' time-accuracy trade-off. This design allows AquaSense to produce accurate sensitivity estimates on a much wider range of probabilistic programs than existing tools.

Formal Guarantee of AquaSense Accuracy. For continuous PPs with bounded support, we formally state the convergence of AquaSense's quantized sensitivity at any concrete $\epsilon \in \mathcal{B}$. For discrete PPs, we show in Sect. 5 with empirical experiments that AquaSense is exact up to machine imprecision. Without loss of generality, we assume AquaSense uses the ED metric; and one can show the convergence for other metrics (e.g. KS and TVD) analogously.

Theorem 1. *Given any $\epsilon \in \mathcal{B}$, denote AquaSense output as $\hat{ED}_X^{N,\mathbf{C}}(\epsilon)$, where N is number of quantization splits of each random variable and $\mathbf{C}$ is the bounded domain of all the random variables required by AQUA. Let $ED_X(\epsilon)$ be the exact sensitivity at ϵ. If the support of all the random variables is a subset of $\mathbf{C}$, then*

$$\lim_{N\to\infty} \hat{ED}_X^{N,\mathbf{C}}(\epsilon) = ED_X(\epsilon).$$

We can prove the theorem using the following lemma from [17].

Lemma 1. *Let the posterior density function of the program P computed by AQUA be $\hat{p}^{N,\mathbf{C}}_{X\sim P}(x)$, which defines the cumulative density function (CDF), $\hat{F}^{N,\mathbf{C}}_{X\sim P}(x) = \int \hat{p}^{N,\mathbf{C}}_{X\sim P}(x)dx$. Let the exact CDF of the program be $F_{X\sim P}(x)$. Then by Theorem 1 of AQUA algorithm [17], one can guarantee the convergence in distribution:*

$$\lim_{N\to\infty} \hat{F}^{N,\mathbf{C}}_{X\sim P}(x) = F_{X\sim P}(x).$$

Corollary 1. *Given that* $\mathbf{C}$ *is a* bounded *domain containing all the support of random variables in the program, we can apply the Portmanteau lemma [20] to get the convergence of approximated expectation to the exact one:*

$$\lim_{N\to\infty} \hat{\mathbb{E}}^{N,\mathbf{C}}_{X\sim P}[X] = \mathbb{E}_{X\sim P}[X].$$

Here, $\hat{\mathbb{E}}^{N,\mathbf{C}}_{X\sim P}[X] = \int_{x\in \mathbf{C}_X} x \cdot \hat{p}^{N,\mathbf{C}}_{X\sim P}(x)dx$ will be computed by AquaSense without additional approximation; $\hat{p}^{N,\mathbf{C}}_{X\sim P}(x)$ is a piecewise constant function (output of AQUA), and AquaSense can evaluate the integral with summation. The corollary also holds for $\hat{\mathbb{E}}^{N,\mathbf{C}}_{X\sim P(\epsilon)}[X]$ when we inject a constant value ϵ in the program.

Proof of Theorem 1. AquaSense employs AQUA to compute the posteriors and it sets a hyper-parameter N to be the quantization splits for each random variable. Given that the support of all the random variables is a subset of $\mathbf{C}$, by Corollary 1 and the definition of limits (i.e. the subtraction and absolute rules of limits),

$$\lim_{N\to\infty} |\hat{\mathbb{E}}^{N,\mathbf{C}}_{X\sim P(0)}[X] - \hat{\mathbb{E}}^{N,\mathbf{C}}_{X\sim P(\epsilon)}[X]| = |\mathbb{E}_{X\sim P(0)}[X] - \mathbb{E}_{X\sim P(\epsilon)}[X]|.$$

By definition of *ED*, we prove Theorem 1.

5 Evaluation

Benchmarks. We evaluate AquaSense on a benchmark suite consisted of 12 probabilistic programs: 7 from PSense [19] benchmarks, 3 from AQUA [17], and 2 new programs; they have a total of 11 discrete and 34 continuous parameters. We performed the experiments on AMD Ryzen 7 5800X 8-Core CPU @ 3.00 GHz with 32 GM RAM and one Nvidia Geforce RTX 3090 with 24 GB memory (running Ubuntu 20.04). AquaSense's tensor computation is performed on the GPU.

Accuracy Metrics. For each parameter, we evaluated two metrics: the average absolute error $|\text{Err}| = \frac{1}{|\mathcal{B}|}\sum_{\epsilon\in\mathcal{B}} |ED_X(\epsilon) - ED_{truth}(\epsilon)|$, and average relative error $\text{Err}\% = \sum_{\epsilon\in\mathcal{B}} \frac{|ED_X(\epsilon)-ED_{truth}(\epsilon)|}{|\mathcal{B}|\, ED_{truth}(\epsilon)}$, i.e., the average distance (and its ratio) between AquaSense interpolated *ED* and true *ED*. We consider $\mathcal{B}$ to be a valid set of noises with moderate sensitivity to evaluate both tools. The ground truth of sensitivity ED_{truth} is computed using two methods: a) PSense, b) manually computed with the assistance of Mathematica when PSense fails. Computing the true sensitivity may take hours or days, which adds to the necessity of an automated tool like AquaSense. We discard the sensitivity below the threshold 1e-6 when computing the errors to tolerate machine imprecision.

5.1 Performance and Accuracy of AquaSense

Table 1 presents AquaSense's accuracy and performance compared to PSense. Each row represents a parameter of which AquaSense evaluates the sensitivity. The first three columns shows the **Parameter Properties**: "Prog." shows the name of the program; "Dist." shows the distributions in the program, where prior distributions are underlined; "D/C" shows whether the program is discrete (D) or continuous (C); "Param" shows the parameter to analyze. For example, the program "expl_away" contains four discrete, Uniform Integer distributions ($\mathcal{U}_I$), where two of them are priors ($\underline{\mathcal{U}_I}$). Each Discrete Uniform Integer distribution has two parameters, i.e. the lower and upper bound (*lb*, *ub*), so AquaSense analyzed four parameters for this program.

We run AquaSense doubling #splits from 100 until Err% is below 5% or |Err| is below 1e-6 (colored in green), or AquaSense runs out of memory (in red). "#spl" (Column 5) shows the largest #splits that produces the corresponding Err% (Column 7) and |Err| (Column 8). On discrete programs with finite support, AquaSense uses the cardinality of the distribution support as #spl, denoted by *Sup*. The column "Acc." shows if AquaSense is accurate enough (Err% is below 5% or |Err| is below 1e-6). Column "**PSense Time(s)**" shows PSense execution time in seconds. We report a timeout (T.O.) if it exceeds 10 min, and an error (Err.) if the result finished but not solved to closed form. Column "**AquaSense Time(s)**" shows the total time, minus the time to initialize the GPU. Total time include the noise instrumentation time ("NI(s)") and sensitivity evaluation time ("SE(s)"). "**Speedup**" is AquaSense's speedup over PSense.

Capability. Our results show that AquaSense successfully computes the sensitivity of all parameters. In comparison, PSense is only able to solve the sensitivity of 8 out of 11 discrete parameters and 3 out of 34 continuous parameters. We observe that for most continuous program, PSense failed to solve integrals to the closed form, which is the fundamental problem of exact inference, meaning PSense's capability cannot be improved much by simply allocating more time.

Execution Time and Accuracy. Compared to PSense, AquaSense is on average faster by 18.10× on continuous models, and for discrete models has similar execution time (slower by 11%). The maximum speedup is 35.16× (for the "gamma" model). For all the discrete models, AquaSense results are exact (with error smaller than machine imprecision). For 31/34 (91%) continuous parameters, AquaSense has an average relative error less than 5% or an average absolute error less than 1e-6. Two parameters in "tug" show higher relative error as the sensitivities are close to zero (<1e–4), but the absolute error is already at around 1e−3. One parameter in "sgl_reg" has higher (6%) relative error for the same reason. *Overall, AquaSense works on many real-world models out of reach of PSense, and offers orders-of-magnitude speedup at a reasonable cost of accuracy.*

Table 1. Performance of AquaSense vs. PSense

Parameter Properties				**AquaSense Accuracy**				**PSense**	**AquaSense Performance**			
Prog.	Dist.	D/C	Param	#spl	Acc.	Err%	|Err|	Time(s)	Time(s)	NI(s)	SE(s)	Speedup
coins	$\mathcal{B}^2$	D	$\mathcal{B}, p$	*Sup*	T	0.00	0.00	1.24	1.38	0.28	1.11	0.90
			$\mathcal{B}, p$	*Sup*	T	0.00	0.00	1.26	1.42	0.28	1.14	0.89
murder	$\mathcal{B}^3{\times}\mathcal{B}^1$	D	$\mathcal{B}, p$	*Sup*	T	0.00	0.00	1.26	1.26	0.19	1.06	1.00
			$\mathcal{B}, p$	*Sup*	T	0.00	0.00	1.07	1.23	0.19	1.04	0.87
			$\mathcal{B}, p$	*Sup*	T	0.00	0.00	1.01	1.33	0.19	1.13	0.76
binomial	$\mathcal{B}_m^1$	D	$\mathcal{B}_m, n$	*Sup*	T	0.00	0.00	T.O.	1.81	0.36	1.45	∞
			$\mathcal{B}_m, p$	*Sup*	T	0.00	0.00	1.76	1.81	0.36	1.45	0.97
expl_away	$\mathcal{U}_I^2{\times}\mathcal{U}_I^2$	D	$\mathcal{U}_I, ub$	*Sup*	T	0.00	0.00	Err.	1.34	0.26	1.08	∞
			$\mathcal{U}_I, lb$	*Sup*	T	0.00	0.00	2.27	1.36	0.26	1.11	1.67
			$\mathcal{U}_I, lb$	*Sup*	T	0.00	0.00	2.46	1.35	0.26	1.10	1.82
			$\mathcal{U}_I, ub$	*Sup*	T	0.00	0.00	Err.	1.34	0.26	1.08	∞
gamma	Γ^1	C	Γ, α	12800	T	3.62	0.01	158.63	8.64	0.09	8.55	18.36
			Γ, β	100	T	2.68	0.01	39.29	1.12	0.09	1.03	35.16
true_obs	$\mathcal{N}^2{\times}\mathcal{N}^1$	C	$\mathcal{N}, \sigma$	200	T	2.81	0.00	T.O.	2.08	0.04	2.04	∞
			$\mathcal{N}, \mu$	200	T	0.07	0.00	1.72	2.17	0.04	2.12	0.79
rect_game	$\mathcal{U}^4{\times}\mathcal{U}^{16}$	C	$\mathcal{U}, lb$	200	T	1.88	0.00	T.O.	38.84	0.02	38.81	∞
			$\mathcal{U}, ub$	100	T	3.06	0.01	T.O.	2.66	0.02	2.63	∞
			$\mathcal{U}, lb$	100	T	2.61	0.00	T.O.	2.64	0.02	2.62	∞
			$\mathcal{U}, ub$	200	T	4.20	0.00	T.O.	38.62	0.02	38.60	∞
			$\mathcal{U}, ub$	100	T	4.14	0.00	T.O.	2.63	0.02	2.61	∞
			$\mathcal{U}, lb$	200	T	1.88	0.00	T.O.	38.72	0.02	38.69	∞
			$\mathcal{U}, lb$	100	T	4.98	0.00	T.O.	2.67	0.02	2.64	∞
			$\mathcal{U}, ub$	100	T	4.14	0.00	T.O.	2.63	0.02	2.61	∞
sgl_reg	$\mathcal{U}^3{\times}\mathcal{N}^1$	C	$\mathcal{U}, lb$	100	T	2.38	0.00	T.O.	1.21	0.03	1.18	∞
			$\mathcal{U}, lb$	800	F	6.21	0.01	T.O.	10.56	0.03	10.53	∞
			$\mathcal{U}, ub$	100	T	3.17	0.00	T.O.	1.14	0.03	1.11	∞
			$\mathcal{U}, ub$	100	T	2.20	0.00	T.O.	1.18	0.03	1.15	∞
			$\mathcal{U}, lb$	100	T	2.60	0.00	T.O.	1.12	0.03	1.09	∞
			$\mathcal{U}, ub$	100	T	2.84	0.00	T.O.	1.17	0.03	1.14	∞
post_pred	$\mathcal{U}^1{\times}\mathcal{B}_m^2$	C	$\mathcal{U}, ub$	400	T	4.48	0.00	T.O.	3.24	0.09	3.15	∞
			$\mathcal{U}, lb$	200	T	4.03	0.00	T.O.	2.21	0.09	2.12	∞
altermu	$\mathcal{N}^3{\times}\mathcal{N}^{40}$	C	$\mathcal{N}, \mu$	100	T	2.58	0.00	T.O.	1.55	0.17	1.38	∞
			$\mathcal{N}, \sigma$	100	T	N/A	0.00	T.O.	1.55	0.17	1.37	∞
			$\mathcal{N}, \mu$	100	T	2.66	0.00	T.O.	1.54	0.17	1.36	∞
			$\mathcal{N}, \sigma$	100	T	3.32	0.00	T.O.	1.55	0.17	1.38	∞
			$\mathcal{N}, \sigma$	100	T	N/A	0.00	T.O.	1.56	0.17	1.39	∞
			$\mathcal{N}, \mu$	100	T	2.58	0.00	T.O.	1.58	0.17	1.41	∞
tug	$\mathcal{U}^2{\times}\mathcal{N}^4{\times}\mathcal{B}^{40}$	C	$\mathcal{U}, ub$	1600	T	3.80	0.00	T.O.	6.28	0.35	5.92	∞
			$\mathcal{U}, lb$	1600	T	4.74	0.00	T.O.	6.33	0.35	5.98	∞
			$\mathcal{U}, ub$	25600	F	77.08	0.00	T.O.	76.65	0.35	76.30	∞
			$\mathcal{U}, lb$	25600	F	11.27	0.00	T.O.	76.70	0.35	76.35	∞
neural	$\mathcal{U}^2{\times}\mathcal{B}_{\log}^{39}$	C	$\mathcal{U}, lb$	100	T	2.79	0.00	T.O.	1.51	0.34	1.16	∞
			$\mathcal{U}, lb$	100	T	3.47	0.00	T.O.	1.50	0.34	1.16	∞
			$\mathcal{U}, ub$	100	T	2.51	0.00	T.O.	1.44	0.34	1.09	∞
			$\mathcal{U}, ub$	100	T	4.50	0.00	T.O.	1.46	0.34	1.11	∞

- Dist.: $\mathcal{B}$: Bernoulli, $B_{\log}$: Bernoulli-Logit, $\mathcal{B}_m$: Binomial, $\mathcal{U}$: Continuous Uniform, $\mathcal{U}_I$: Discrete Uniform (Integer), $\mathcal{N}$: Normal, β: Beta, Γ: Gamma
- Param: p: flip chance, n: No. of flips, lb/ub: lower/upper bound of Uniform, μ: mean, σ: standard deviation, α, β: shape parameters.

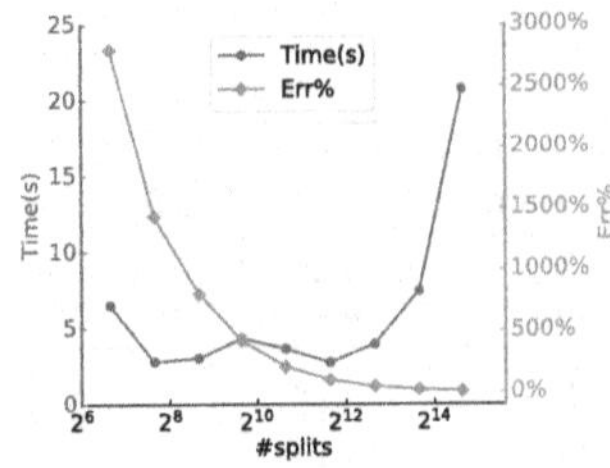

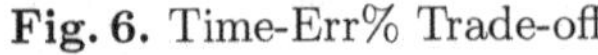

Fig. 6. Time-Err% Trade-off

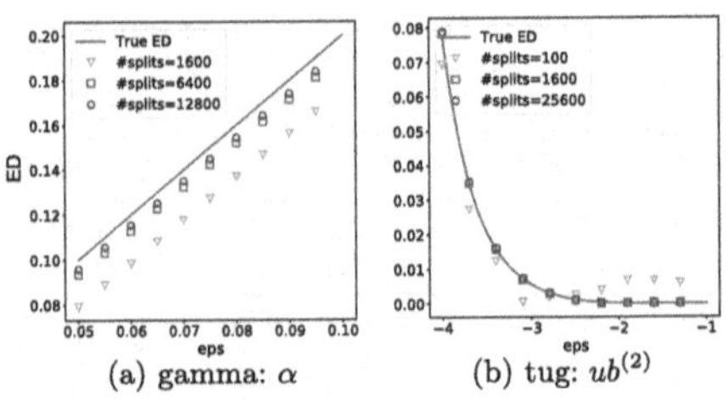

(a) gamma: α (b) tug: $ub^{(2)}$

Fig. 7. Examples of AquaSense results

5.2 Trade-Off Between Accuracy and Performance

The number of quantization splits (#splits) controls the trade-off between performance and accuracy of AquaSense. Figure 6 shows AquaSense's relative error and execution time w.r.t. #splits. Error and time are averaged over all 34 continuous benchmarks. Execution time fluctuates when #splits is less than 12800 due to overhead, but grows exponentially afterward as expected. Relative error decreases exponentially as #splits increase. *Our key observation: on average, the relative error is already small when execution time starts growing exponentially.*

To illustrate the trade-off, we pick the two parameters that used the most #splits in Table 1, i.e. on which AquaSense performed the worst. We plot their True *ED* against AquaSense's interpolations with different #splits. In Fig. 7, the x-axis shows the values of ϵ and the y-axis shows *ED*. The True *ED* is shown in a blue line, and AquaSense results are shown in markers of different styles/colors. These plots demonstrate that AquaSense converges as #splits increases.

6 Related Work

Existing sensitivity analysis techniques suffer from scalability and/or precision problems. PSense [19] is the state-of-the-art sensitivity analysis tool for probabilistic programs. PSense symbolically evaluates integrals that represent the program's posterior distribution. This approach works only for small programs, and becomes intractable when the program has multiple continuous distributions (See Table 1). Sound logic frameworks for bounding the sensitivity of probabilistic programs [1–3,30] often yield a coarse over-approximation of sensitivity for soundness. Also, they are not fully automated and require developers' effort to implement the proof for general probabilistic programs. Chan and Darwiche [7] implemented the tool SamIam to compute the sensitivity of belief networks. However, it only supports discrete distributions.

Sensitivity analysis, as illustrated in our example (Sect. 2), can help developers debug anomalies in the model through an iterative process. The previous methods for debugging probabilistic programs targeted different challenges: [23] focuses on debugging probabilistic assertion failures, while [8] concentrates on addressing convergence issues of MCMC. Other approaches [9–12] focus on debugging the implementation of the probabilistic programming systems or machine learning applications. Furthermore, through the lens of statistical modeling, researchers in statistics have proposed various strategies [5,29,31] to improve the model robustness. According to a recent study [18] that systematically evaluated these strategies, sensitivity analysis can aid developers select the most appropriate among these strategies.

7 Conclusion

We propose a new system, AquaSense, for sensitivity analysis on real-world probabilistic programs. AquaSense leverages quantized inference to interpolate parameter sensitivity. Our evaluation on 12 programs with 45 parameters shows that AquaSense achieved better efficiency and scalability than the baseline. AquaSense empowers software engineers and data scientists with the ability to understand and improve the reliability of their probabilistic programs.

Acknowledgements. This research was supported in part by NSF Grants No. CCF-1846354, CCF-1956374, CCF-200888, and CCF-2217144, and C3.ai DTI research award.

References

1. Aguirre, A., Barthe, G., Hsu, J., Kaminski, B.L., Katoen, J.P., Matheja, C.: Kantorovich continuity of probabilistic programs. arXiv preprint arXiv:1901.06540 (2019)
2. Aguirre, A., Barthe, G., Hsu, J., Kaminski, B.L., Katoen, J.P., Matheja, C.: A pre-expectation calculus for probabilistic sensitivity. Proc. ACM Program. Lang. **5**(POPL), 1–28 (2021)
3. Barthe, G., Espitau, T., Grégoire, B., Hsu, J., Strub, P.Y.: Proving expected sensitivity of probabilistic programs, vol. 2 (2017)
4. Baydin, A.G., et al.: Etalumis: bringing probabilistic programming to scientific simulators at scale. In: Proceedings of the International Conference for High Performance Computing, Networking, Storage and Analysis. SC '19, Association for Computing Machinery, New York, NY, USA (2019). https://doi.org/10.1145/3295500.3356180
5. Berger, J.O., et al.: An overview of robust Bayesian analysis. TEST **3**(1), 5–124 (1994)
6. Blei, D., Lafferty, J.: Topic models. In: Text Mining: Classification, Clustering, and Applications (2009)
7. Chan, H., Darwiche, A.: Sensitivity analysis in Bayesian networks: from single to multiple parameters. In: Proceedings of the 20th Conference on Uncertainty in Artificial Intelligence, pp. 67–75. UAI '04, AUAI Press (2004)
8. Dutta, S., Huang, Z., Misailovic, S.: SixthSense: debugging convergence problems in probabilistic programs via program representation learning. In: FASE 2022. LNCS, vol. 13241, pp. 123–144. Springer, Cham (2022). https://doi.org/10.1007/978-3-030-99429-7_7
9. Dutta, S., Legunsen, O., Huang, Z., Misailovic, S.: Testing probabilistic programming systems. In: FSE (2018)

10. Dutta, S., Selvam, J., Jain, A., Misailovic, S.: Tera: optimizing stochastic regression tests in machine learning projects. In: ISSTA (2021)
11. Dutta, S., Shi, A., Choudhary, R., Zhang, Z., Jain, A., Misailovic, S.: Detecting flaky tests in probabilistic and machine learning applications. In: ISSTA (2020)
12. Dutta, S., Shi, A., Misailovic, S.: Flex: fixing flaky tests in machine learning projects by updating assertion bounds. In: FSE (2021)
13. Dutta, S., Zhang, W., Huang, Z., Misailovic, S.: Storm: program reduction for testing and debugging probabilistic programming systems. In: Proceedings of the 2019 27th ACM Joint Meeting on European Software Engineering Conference and Symposium on the Foundations of Software Engineering, pp. 729–739. ACM (2019)
14. Gehr, T., Misailovic, S., Vechev, M.: PSI: exact symbolic inference for probabilistic programs. In: Chaudhuri, S., Farzan, A. (eds.) CAV 2016. LNCS, vol. 9779, pp. 62–83. Springer, Cham (2016). https://doi.org/10.1007/978-3-319-41528-4_4
15. Gehr, T., Misailovic, S., Vechev, M.: PSI: exact symbolic inference for probabilistic programs. In: Computer Aided Verification, pp. 62–83 (2016)
16. Gelman, A., Lee, D., Guo, J.: Stan: A probabilistic programming language for Bayesian inference and optimization. J. Educ. Behav. Stat. **40**(5), 530–543 (2015)
17. Huang, Z., Dutta, S., Misailovic, S.: AQUA: automated quantized inference for probabilistic programs. In: Hou, Z., Ganesh, V. (eds.) ATVA 2021. LNCS, vol. 12971, pp. 229–246. Springer, Cham (2021). https://doi.org/10.1007/978-3-030-88885-5_16
18. Huang, Z., Dutta, S., Misailovic, S.: Astra: understanding the practical impact of robustness for probabilistic programs. In: Uncertainty in Artificial Intelligence, pp. 900–910. PMLR (2023)
19. Huang, Z., Wang, Z., Misailovic, S.: PSense: automatic sensitivity analysis for probabilistic programs. In: 16th International Symposium on Automated Technology for Verification and Analysis. ATVA (2018)
20. Klenke, A.: Probability Theory, January 2008. https://doi.org/10.1007/3-540-33414-9
21. Lavine, M.: Sensitivity in Bayesian statistics: the prior and the likelihood. J. Am. Stat. Assoc. **86**(414), 396–399 (1991)
22. Mansinghka, V.K., Kulkarni, T.D., Perov, Y.N., Tenenbaum, J.: Approximate Bayesian image interpretation using generative probabilistic graphics programs. In: Burges, C., Bottou, L., Welling, M., Ghahramani, Z., Weinberger, K. (eds.) Advances in Neural Information Processing Systems, vol. 26. Curran Associates, Inc. (2013), https://proceedings.neurips.cc/paper/2013/file/fa14d4fe2f19414de3ebd9f63d5c0169-Paper.pdf
23. Nandi, C., Grossman, D., Sampson, A., Mytkowicz, T., McKinley, K.S.: Debugging probabilistic programs. In: Proceedings of the 1st ACM SIGPLAN International Workshop on Machine Learning and Programming Languages, pp. 18–26. ACM (2017)
24. Nikulin, M.: Kolmogorov-Smirnov test (2011). https://encyclopediaofmath.org/wiki/Kolmogorov-Smirnov_test
25. Potapov, A., Rodionov, S., Potapova, V.: Real-time GA-based probabilistic programming in application to robot control. In: Steunebrink, B., Wang, P., Goertzel, B. (eds.) AGI -2016. LNCS (LNAI), vol. 9782, pp. 95–105. Springer, Cham (2016). https://doi.org/10.1007/978-3-319-41649-6_10
26. Pyro (2018). http://pyro.ai
27. Roos, M., Martins, T.G., Held, L., Rue, H.: Sensitivity analysis for Bayesian hierarchical models. Bayesian Anal. **10**(2), 321–349 (2015)

28. Saad, F., Mansinghka, V.K.: A probabilistic programming approach to probabilistic data analysis. In: Lee, D., Sugiyama, M., Luxburg, U., Guyon, I., Garnett, R. (eds.) Advances in Neural Information Processing Systems, vol. 29. Curran Associates, Inc. (2016). https://proceedings.neurips.cc/paper/2016/file/46072631582fc240dd2674a7d063b040-Paper.pdf
29. Wang, C., Blei, D.M.: A general method for robust Bayesian modeling. Bayesian Anal. **13**(4), 1159–1187 (2018)
30. Wang, P., Fu, H., Chatterjee, K., Deng, Y., Xu, M.: Proving expected sensitivity of probabilistic programs with randomized variable-dependent termination time. arXiv preprint arXiv:1902.04744 (2019)
31. Wang, Y., Kucukelbir, A., Blei, D.M.: Robust probabilistic modeling with Bayesian data reweighting. In: Proceedings of the 34th International Conference on Machine Learning, vol. 70, pp. 3646–3655. ICML'17, JMLR.org (2017). http://dl.acm.org/citation.cfm?id=3305890.3306058

RTAEval: A Framework for Evaluating Runtime Assurance Logic

Kristina Miller[1(✉)], Christopher K. Zeitler[2], William Shen[1], Mahesh Viswanathan[1], and Sayan Mitra[1]

[1] University of Illinois Urbana Champaign, Champaign, IL 61820, USA
kmmille2@illinois.edu

[2] Rational CyPhy, Inc., Urbana, IL 62802, USA

Abstract. Runtime assurance (RTA) addresses the problem of keeping an autonomous system safe while using an untrusted (or experimental) controller. This can be done via logic that explicitly switches between the untrusted controller and a safety controller, or logic that filters the input provided by the untrusted controller. While several tools implement specific instances of RTAs, there is currently no framework for evaluating different approaches. Given the importance of the RTA problem in building safe autonomous systems, an evalutation tool is needed. In this paper, we present the RTAEval framework as a low code framework that can be used to quickly evaluate different RTA logics for different types of agents in a variety of scenarios. RTAEval is designed to quickly create scenarios, run different RTA logics, and collect data that can be used to evaluate and visualize performance. In this paper, we describe different components of RTAEval and show how it can be used to create and evaluate scenarios involving multiple aircraft models.

Keywords: Runtime assurance · Autonomous systems

1 Introduction

Safe operation of autonomous systems is critical as their real world deployment becomes more common place in domains such as aerospace, manufacturing and transportation. However, the need for safety is often at odds with the need to experiment with, and therefore deploy, new untrusted technologies in the public sphere. For example, experimental controllers created using reinforcement learning can provide better performance in simulations and controlled environments, but assuring safety in real world circumstances is currently beyond our capabilities for such controllers. *Runtime assurance (RTA)* [3,15–17] addresses this tension. The idea is to introduce a *decision module* that somehow chooses between a well-tested *Safety controller* and the experimental, *Untrusted controller*, assuring safety of the overall system while also allowing experimentation with the new untrusted technology where and when possible. Specific RTA technologies are being researched and tested for aircraft engine control [1], air-traffic management [4], and satellite rendezvous and proximity operations [9].

É. André and J. Sun (Eds.): ATVA 2023, LNCS 14216, pp. 302–313, 2023.
https://doi.org/10.1007/978-3-031-45332-8_17

The Simplex architecture [16,17] first proposed this idea in a form that is recognizable as RTA. Since then, the central problem of designing a *decision module* that chooses between the different controllers has been addressed in a number of works such as SimplexGen [3], Black-Box Simplex [13], and SOTER [5]. The two main approaches for building the decision module are based on (a) an RTASwitch which chooses one of the controllers using the current state or (b) an RTAFilter which blends the outputs from the two controllers to create the final output. In creating an RTASwitch, the decision can be based on forward-simulation of the current state [19], model-based [3] and model-free forward reachability [13], or model-based backward reachability [3]. The most common filtering method is Active Set Invariance Filtering (ASIF) [2], wherein a control barrier function is used to blend the control inputs from the safety and untrusted controllers such that the system remains safe with respect to the control barrier functions [7,12,14].

While these design methods for the decision module have evolved quickly, a software framework for evaluating the different techniques has been missing. In this paper, we propose such a flexible, low-code framework called RTAEval (Fig. 1). A *low-code* framework is one which simplifies the development of applications by providing a library of tools which reduces the amount of code required to be written by the user. Low-code frameworks are becoming more commonplace as the need to quickly experiment, deploy, and test new technologies becomes more urgent. One example of a low-code framework is the Scenic Library [11] which can be used to quickly and easily spin up new test environments for testing perception and control algorithms. In this work, we introduce a framework in a similar vein which can be used to test new runtime assurance technologies. This framework consists of a module for defining scenarios, possibly involving multiple agents; a module for executing the defined scenario with suitable RTASwitches and RTAFilters; and a module for collecting and visualizing execution data. RTAEval allows different agent dynamics, decision modules, and metrics to be plugged-in with a few lines of code. In creating RTAEval, we have defined standardized interfaces between the agent simulator, the decision module (RTA), and data collection.

In Sect. 2, we give an overview of RTAEval. In Sect. 2.1, we discuss how scenarios are defined, and, in Sect. 2.2, we discuss how the user should provide decision modules (also called the RTALogic). In Sect. 2.3, we discuss data collection, evaluation, and visualization. Finally, in Sect. 3, we show a variety of examples implemented in RTAEval. A tool suite for this framework can be found at https://github.com/RationalCyPhy/RTAEval.

2 Overview of the RTAEval Framework

The three main components of RTAEval are (a) the scenario definition, (b) the scenario execution, and (c) the data collection, evaluation, and visualization module (See Fig. 1). A scenario is defined by the agent and its low-level controller, the unsafe sets, the untrusted and safety controllers, the time horizon for analysis, and the initial conditions. Given this scenario definition, the scenario is executed iteratively over the specified time horizon.

During each iteration of the closed-loop execution of the RTA-enabled autonomous system, the current state of the agent and the sets of unsafe states are collected. This observed state information is given to both the untrusted and safety controller, which each compute control commands. Both of these commands are evaluated by the user-provided decision module (i.e., RTA logic), which computes and returns the actual command to be used by the agent. The agent then updates its state, and the computation moves to the next iteration. While the execution proceeds, data – such as the RTA computational performance, controller commands, agent states, and observed state information of the unsafe sets – is collected via the data collection module. At the end of an execution, this data is evaluated to summarize the overall performance of the RTA. This summary includes computation time of the RTA logic, untrusted versus safety controller usage, and the agent's distance from the unsafe set. We also provide a visualization of this data.

A low-code tool suite of the RTAEval framework is written in Python, which was chosen for its ease of implementation and interpretibility. The tool is flexible in that it allows for a wide variety of simulators and coding languages and can be generalized to scenarios where multiple agents are running a variety of different RTA modules. Simple Python implementations of vehicle models (some of which we provide in simpleSim) can be incorporated directly. However, users can incorporate new agent models within simpleSim as long as the agent has a function `step` that defines the dynamics and low-level controller of the agent and returns the state of the agent at the next time step. An example of this is provided in Example 1 and Fig. 4. The safety and untrusted controllers should also be encoded in `step`, which simply takes in the command (or mode) to be used over the next time step. Higher fidelity simulators such as CARLA [6] and AirSim [18] can also be used in place of simpleSim for the execution block. The observed state information would need to be provided to our data collection, evaluation, and visualization tool in the format seen in Fig. 2.

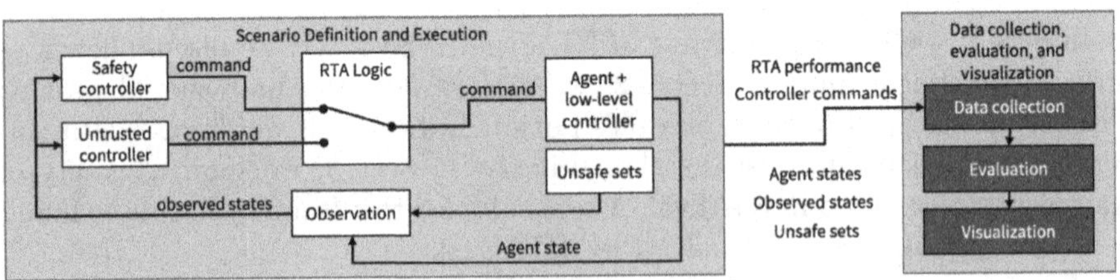

Fig. 1. RTAEval framework. (Scenario Definition and Execution) Some user-defined scenario is executed. The scenario is defined by the safety controller, untrusted controller, plant and low level controllers, unsafe sets, and sensor. (Data collection, evaluation, and visualization) The execution data is collected, evaluated, and visualized using our provided suite of tools.

2.1 Scenario Definition and Execution

A *scenario* is defined by the *agent*, *unsafe sets*, *safety* and *untrusted controllers*, *initial conditions*, and *time horizon* $T > 0$. The *simulation state at time* $t \in [0, T]$ consists of the *agent state*, the *unsafe set definition*, and the *control command* at time t. The agent has an identifier, a state, and some function `step` that takes in some control command at time t and outputs the system state at time $t+1$. The *unsafe sets* are the set of states that the system must avoid over the execution of the scenario. We say that the agent is *safe* if it is outside the unsafe set. The safety and untrusted controllers compute control commands for the system, which are then filtered through the RTA logic, as discussed further in Sect. 2.2. The initial conditions define the simulation state at time 0. Then, given a scenario with some time horizon T and an RTA logic, an *execution* of the scenario is a sequence of time-stamped simulation states over $[0, T]$. Note that, while we define an execution as a discrete time sequence of simulation states, the actual or real-world execution of the scenario may be in continuous time; thus, we simply sample the simulation states at a predefined interval. We call the part of the execution that contains only the sequence of agent states the *agent state trace.* Similarly, we call the part of the execution that only contains the sequence control commands the *mode trace* and the part that only contains the sequence of unsafe set states the *unsafe set state trace.*

In order for our evaluation and visualization to work, the execution must be given to the data collection as a dictionary, the structure of which is shown in Fig. 2. Here, there are three levels of dictionaries. The highest level dictionary has the keys `'agents'` and `'unsafe'`, which point to dictionaries containing the state and mode traces of the agents and state traces of the unsafe sets respectively. The second level of dictionaries has keys that correspond to different agents and unsafe sets. We call these keys the agent and unsafe set IDs. Each agent ID points to a dictionary containing the state and mode traces of that agent. The state trace is a list of time-stamped agent states, and the mode trace is a sequential list of control commands. Each unsafe set ID points to a dictionary containing the set type and state trace of that unsafe set. The set type is a string that tells RTAEval what type of set that particular unsafe set is. Currently, RTAEval supports the following set types: *point*, *ball*, *hyperrectangle*, and *polytope*. Each set has a *definition* that, together with the type, defines the set of states contained within the unsafe set. Then, the state trace for an unsafe set is a sequence of time stamped definitions of the set.

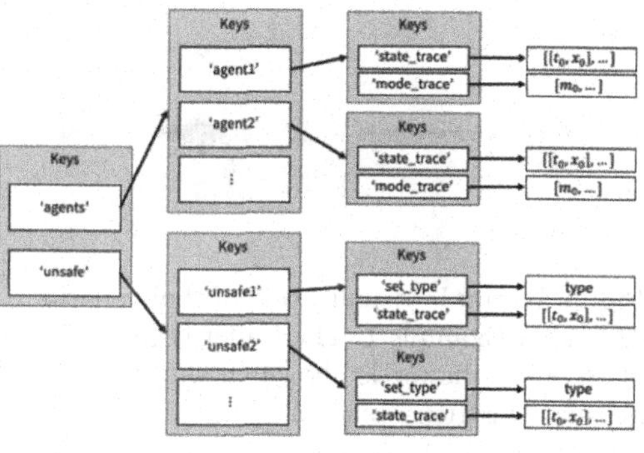

Fig. 2. Execution structure required by the RTAEval evaluation and visualization

Example 1. Consider the following adaptive cruise control (ACC) scenario shown in Fig. 3 as a running example. An agent with state $x = [p, v]^\top$ has dynamics given by

$$f(x, m) = \begin{bmatrix} 0 & 1 \\ 0 & 0 \end{bmatrix} x + \begin{bmatrix} 0 \\ 1 \end{bmatrix} a(x, m),$$

where $a(x, m) = g_{\mathtt{S}}(x)$ if $m = \mathtt{S}$ and $a(x, m) = g_{\mathtt{U}}(x)$ if $m = \mathtt{U}$. The agent tries to follow at distance $d > 0$ behind a leader moving at constant speed $\bar{v}$. The position of the leader at time t is given by $p_L(t)$. Then, the untrusted controller $g_{\mathtt{U}}$ and safety controller $g_{\mathtt{S}}$ are given by

$$g_{\mathtt{S}}(x) = k_1((p_L(t) - d) - p) + k_2(\bar{v} - v) \text{ and } g_{\mathtt{U}}(x) = \begin{cases} a_{\max} & (p_L(t) - p) > d \\ -a_{\max} & \text{else} \end{cases},$$

where $k_1 > 0$ and $k_2 > 0$. The function `step` is a composition of the untrusted controller, the safety controller, and the dynamics function of the system.

A collision between the agent and leader occurs if $\|p_L(t) - p(t)\| \leq c$, $c < d$. There is then an unsafe set centered on the leader agent, and it is defined by $\mathcal{O} = \{[p, v, t]^\top \in \mathcal{X} \times \mathbb{R}_{\geq 0} \mid \|p_L(t) - p\| \leq c\}$. The function `updateDef` then takes in the current state of the simulator and creates the unsafe set centered on the leader. The initial conditions for this scenario are then the initial agent state x_0, the initial leader state x_{L0}, and the time horizon $T > 0$.

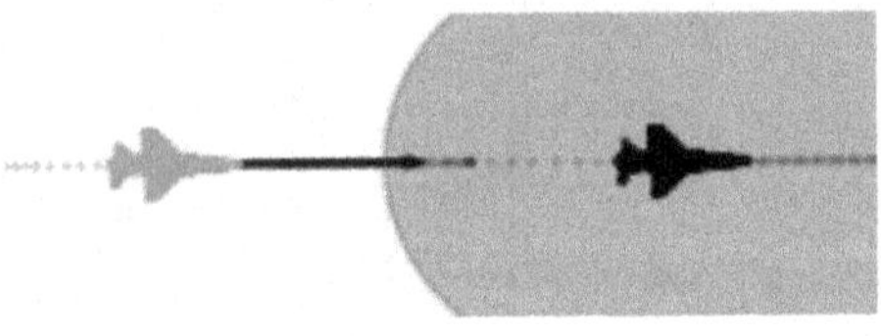

Fig. 3. Example visualization of the scenario defined in Example 1. The leader is shown in black, the follower is shown in orange, and the unsafe region is shown in red.

This scenario is shown in our low code framework in Figs. 4 and 5. The dynamics of the agent are defined in `step` in lines 11–26 of Fig. 4. The proportional controller is defined in lines 1–4 and the bang-bang controller is defined in lines 6–9. This is all contained within a class `AccAgent`. In Fig. 5, we set up the scenario. In lines 2–5, we define the goal point for the agent. In lines 7–15, we create the agent, the leader, and the unsafe set. Finally, in line 18, we initialize the scenario to be executed; in lines 21–26, we add the agents and unsafe sets to the scenario; and in lines 29–30, we set up the scenario parameters.

2.2 RTA Logics

We provide an RTA base class that can be used in RTAEval. The user must provide the RTA logic to be evaluated. This logic takes in an observed state and outputs the control command to be used by the plant. This observed state information has to be provided in the format shown in Fig. 2 for data collection, evaluation, and visualization to work. The RTA base class is shown in Fig. 6. We provide the functions `RTASwitch` and `setupEval`. Users must provide the switching logic as `RTALogic`. When creating RTA, the user can decide to use

```
1 def P(self, time_step): #Proportional controller
2     xrel = self.goal_state[0] - self.state_hist[-1][0]
3     vrel = self.goal_state[1] - self.state_hist[-1][1]
4     return self.Kp[0]*xrel + self.Kp[1]*vrel
5
6 def BangBang1D(self, time_step): # Bang-bang controller
7     x_err_curr = self.goal_state[0] - self.state_hist[-1][0]
8     v_err_curr = self.goal_state[1] - self.state_hist[-1][1]
9     return np.sign(x_err_curr)*self.a_max
10
11 def step(self, mode, initialCondition, time_step, simulatorState):
12         self.goal_state = self.desired_traj(simulatorState)
13         if mode == 'SAFETY':
14             self.control = self.P
15         elif mode == 'UNTRUSTED':
16             self.control = self.BangBang1D
17         else:
18             self.control = self.no_control()
19         a_curr = self.control(time_step)
20         if abs(a_curr) > self.a_max:
21             a_curr = np.sign(a_curr)*self.a_max
22         x_next = initialCondition[0] + initialCondition[1]*time_step
23         v_next = initialCondition[1] + a_curr*time_step
24         if abs(v_next) >= self.v_max:
25             v_next = np.sign(v_next)*self.v_max
26         return [x_next, v_next]
```

Fig. 4. Controller and step functions for the agent in Example 1. The first function defined is the proportional controller (Safety) and the second function is the Bang-bang controller (Untrusted). The step function (lines 11–26) takes in the current mode and state of the agent, as well as the time stpe and current suimulator state. In lines 13–18 it decides which controller to use, and in lines 19–26, it updates the staet of the agent.

our data collection by running `setupEval` in `__init__`. This will create a data collection object called `eval`, which saves the data used for our evaluation (see Sect. 2.3). The switch is performed in `RTASwitch`, which also stores the current perceived state of the simulator from the point of view of the agent, as well as the time to compute the switch. The user provided switching logic `RTALogic` takes in the current state of the simulator and returns the mode that the agent should operate in. To create different logics, the user must create an RTA class derived from the RTA base class, which implements the function `RTALogic`. An example of this is given in Example 2.

Example 2. An example of a simple RTA switching logic can be seen in Fig. 7. This is a simulation-based switching logic that was designed for the adaptive cruise control introduced in Example 1. Here, the future states of the simulator are predicted over some time horizon T and saved as `predictedTraj` in line 2. We then check over this predicted trajectory to see if the agent ever enters the unsafe set in lines 3–11. If it does, then the safety controller is used, and if it does not, then the untrusted controller is used. Once `RTALogic` is created, we add it to a new class called `accSimRTA` and use it to create an RTA object called `egoRTA` for `egoAgent1`. We can then change line 22 in Fig. 5 to `RTAs = [egoRTA, None]`. This will associate `egoRTA` with `egoAgent1` and run the RTA switching logic every time the state of `egoAgent1` is updated.

```
1  # Define desired goal point for the follower agent (ego):
2  def agent1_desiredTraj(simulationTrace):
3      lead_state = simulationTrace['agents']['leader']['state_trace'][-1][1:]
4      return [lead_state[0] - 10, lead_state[1]]
5
6  # Create the ego agent:
7  agent1 = AccAgent("follower",file_name=controllerFile)
8  agent1.follower = True
9  agent1.desired_traj = agent1_desiredTraj
10
11 # Create the leader agent:
12 leader = AccAgent("leader",file_name=controllerFile)
13
14 # Create the unsafe set centered on leader agent:
15 unsafe1 = relativeUnsafeBall("unsafe1", [5], 7, "leader")
16
17 # Initialize the ACC scenario:
18 accSim = simpleSim()
19
20 # Initialize agents and unsafe sets in the scenario:
21 agents = [agent1, leader]
22 RTAs = [None, None]
23 modes = [ccMode.UNTRUSTED, ccMode.NORMAL]
24 inits = [[0,1], [5,1]]
25 accSim.addAgents(agents=agents, modes=modes, RTAs=RTAs, initStates=inits)
26 accSim.addUnsafeSets(unsafe_sets = [unsafe1])
27
28 # Set simulation parameters
29 accSim.setSimType(vis=False, plotType="2D", simType="1D")
30 accSim.setTimeParams(dt=0.1, T=5)
```

Fig. 5. Python code snippet defining the scenario in our low-code RTAEval framework. The untrusted and safety controllers are contained within the dynamics of the `AccAgent`, which is defined in a separate file. The scenario is executed in a simply python simulator, which is initiated on line 18. Initially, the agents are not assigned RTAs, but this will be done in Sect. 2.2. The agents and unsafe sets are added to the scenario, and the simulation parameter are set in lines 29 and 30.

2.3 Data Collection, Evaluation, and Visualization

We now discuss the data collection, evaluation, and visualization tool which is provided as a part of RTAEval. This tool is a class that has some collection functions and post-processing functions. To use the data collection and evaluation functionalities provided, the user must add the line `self.setupEval()` when creating the RTA object. Data collection occurs via the functions `collect_trace` and `collect_computation_times`. Here, `collect_trace` collects the simulation traces, and `collect_computation_times` collects the time it takes for the RTA module to compute a switch. An example of how the data collection can be incorporated in the RTA module is shown in Fig. 7. The traces are collected and stored as a dictionary of the form shown in Fig. 2. Once the data has been collected over a scenario, we can use them to evaluate the performance of the RTA over a scenario. Examples of the data evaluation, as well as screenshots from our simulator are shown in Sect. 3. A summary of the RTA's performance in the scenario can be quickly given by running `eval.summary()`. The main metrics that we study are the following: **Computation time** gives the running time of `RTASwitch` each time it is invoked. We provide the average, minimum, and maximum times to compute the switch. **Distance from unsafe set** is the distance

```
class baseRTA(abc.ABC):
    def __init__(self):
        self.do_eval = False # Don't automatically set up RTAEval
        pass

    @abc.abstractmethod
    def RTALogic(self, simulationTrace: dict) -> Enum:
        # User provided logic for switching RTA
        pass

    def RTASwitch(self, simulationTrace: dict) -> Enum:
        start_time = time.time()
        rtaMode = self.RTALogic(simulationTrace)
        running_time = time.time() - start_time

        if self.do_eval:
            self.eval.collect_computation_time(running_time)
            self.eval.collect_trace(simulationTrace)
        return rtaMode

    def setupEval(self):
        # Add this to init when inheriting baseRTA to inclde evaluation
        self.do_eval = True
        self.eval = RTAEval()
```

Fig. 6. Base RTA class used in the low-code RTAEval framework. Users need only provide the decision logic, which we call `RTALogic`.

```
def RTALogic(simulationTrace):
    predictedTraj = simulate_forward(simulationTrace)
    egoTrace = predictedTraj['agents'][egoAgent.id]['state_trace']
    for unsafeSet in self.unsafeSets:
        unsafeSetTrace = predictedTraj['unsafe'][unsafeSet.id]['state_trace']
        for i in range(len(unsafeSetTrace)):
            egoPos = egoTrace[i][1]
            unsafeSetDef = unsafeSetTrace[i][1]
            pos_max = unsafeSetDef[0][0] - unsafeSetDef[1]
            if egoPos > pos_max:
                return egoModes.SAFETY
    return egoModes.UNTRUSTED
```

Fig. 7. Example RTA switching logic for Example 2. Here, the trajectory of the follower agent is simulated forward, and if it ever comes within collision distance of the leader, then the safety controller is used.

between the ego agent and the unsafe sets. We also allow the user to find the distance from other agents in the scenario. **Time to collision (TTC)** is the time until collision between the ego agent and the other agents if none of them change their current trajectories. Finally, we also provide information on the **percent controller usage**, which is the proportion of time each controller is used over the course of the scenario. We also provide information on the number of times a switch occurs in a scenario. Example results are shown in Sect. 3.

3 RTAEval Examples

In this section, we present some examples using our provided suite of tools for RTAEval. We evaluate two different decision module logics: SimRTA and

ReachRTA. SimRTA is the simulation based switching logic introduced in Example 2. ReachRTA is similar to SimRTA but uses reachable sets that contain all possible trajectories of the agent as the basis of the switching logic. We evaluate these RTAs in 1-, 2-, and 3-dimensional scenarios with varying numbers of agents. These scenarios are described in more detail in Table 1. Here, the workspace denotes the dimensions of the physical space that the systems live in. Note that, while all the examples presented have some physical representation, this is not a necessary requirement of the tool. We also provide pointers to where the dynamics of the agents can be found, as well as the untrusted and safety controllers used. Visualizations of the scenarios can be seen in Figs. 3 and 8.

Table 1. Brief description of evaluated scenarios.

	ACC	Dubins	GCAS
Workspace	1	2	3
Dynamics Untrusted	Example 1 Bang-bang controller (Example 1)	Dubin's car [8] PID with accleration [10]	Dubin's plane [8] PID with acceleration [10]
Safety	PID (Example 1)	PID with deceleration [10]	PID with deceleration and pitching up [10]
Unsafe	Leader (ball)	Leader (ball) and building (rectangle)	Leader (ball) and ground (polytope)
Visualization	Fig. 3	Fig. 8	Fig. 8
Scenario length	10 s	20 s	40 s

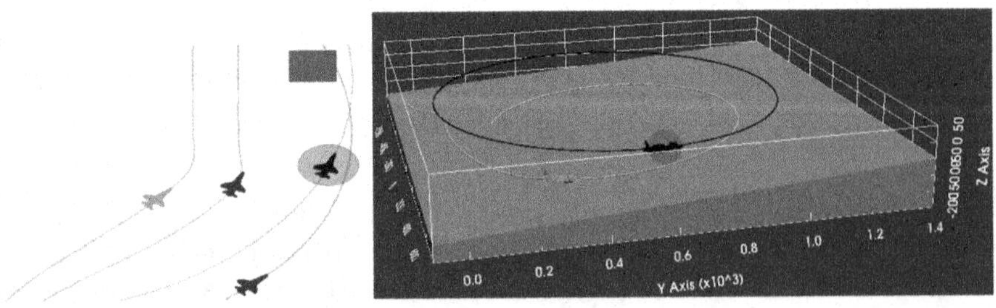

Fig. 8. Example scenarios in Table 1. Left: 2-dimensional dubins aircraft with building collision avoidance. The leader is shown in black, and the followers are shown in orange and blue. The desired trajectories are shown in gray. Right: Ground collision avoidance. The leader is shown in black and the follower is shown in orange. The desired trajectory is shown in white.

Each of these scenarios is executed using simpleSim, and the two RTA logics are created for them. Data is collected over the scenario lengths in Table 1. Note that the scenario length is the simulation time for the scenario and not the real time needed to run the scenario. We run these scenarios with varying numbers of agents and present the running time of the scenario execution and evaluations in Table 2. The simulation time step is set to 0.05 for all scenarios. Here, exec time is the time it takes to run the scenario, RTA comp time is the average time it takes to run the user-provided RTA logic per iteration, and % RTA comp is the percentage of the exec time that is taken by the RTA decision module. That is, % RTA computation is roughly the number of time steps in a scenario multiplied by the the average RTA comp time and divided by the execution time. Finally, eval time is the time it takes to get a full summary of how the RTA performs for each agent. The evaluation summary includes the average decision module computation time, controller usage, distance from the unsafe sets and other agents, and time to collision with the unsafe sets and other agents. We note that a majority of the run time for the scenario execution is due to the RTA logic computation time and not our tool. Additionally, while the run time of the evaluation is affected by the number of agents in the scenario, it is mostly affected by the set type of the unsafe set, where the polytope in the GCAS scenario causes the biggest slow down in evaluation time.

Table 2. Running time for execution and evaluation of RTAs with the tool suite provided for RTAEval.

		SimRTA				ReachRTA			
Scenario	Num agents	Exec time (s)	RTA comp time (ms)	% RTA Comp	Eval time (s)	Exec time (s)	RTA comp time (ms)	% RTA Comp	Eval time (s)
ACC	1	18.49e-3	0.07	76.63	7.27e-3	0.35	1.71	97.89	8.22e-3
	2	50.08e-3	0.10	84.12	18.16e-3	1.12	2.76	98.66	17.96e-3
	5	0.18	0.16	90.47	87.96e-3	6.01	5.96	99.10	0.10
Dubins	1	2.32	4.99	86.06	32.88e-3	15.18	37.10	97.76	34.15e-3
	3	15.30	11.84	92.89	0.18	71.60	58.83	98.60	0.11
	10	203.87	49.77	97.65	0.70	461.71	114.08	98.83	0.76
GCAS	1	5.85	6.08	83.12	30.62	39.28	47.65	97.02	31.423
	1	45.27	17.84	94.60	83.61	174.00	71.11	98.07	98.10

The summary of an RTA performance is given out in a text file from which visualizations like the one in Fig. 9 can be easily created. In addition to the computation time, distance from the unsafe sets, distance from the other agents, and controller usage, the minimum times to collision (TTC) for the unsafe sets and other agents are also reported. The summary information is saved in such a way that users can pull up snapshots of the scenario at any point in time. This means that the user can examine the state of the scenario that caused an unwanted result. Such functionality aids in the rapid prototyping of RTA technologies and logics.

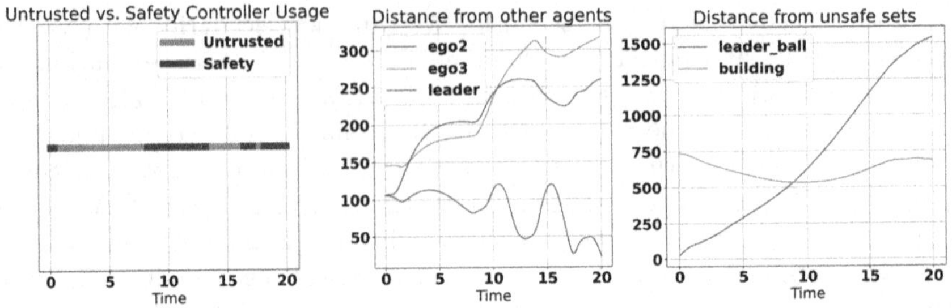

Fig. 9. Example visualization from three agent dubins scenario. From left to right: Controller usage plot, distance from other agents, and distance from unsafe sets. **ego2** and **ego3** denote the other aircraft.

4 Conclusion

We presented the RTAEval suite of Python-based tools for evaluating different runtime assurance (RTA) logics. Different RTA switching logics can be quickly coded in RTAEval, and we demonstrate its functionality in rapid prototyping of RTA logics on a variety of examples. RTAEval can be used in multi-agent scenarios and scenarios with perception models. Interesting next steps might include extending the functionality of RTAEval to filtering methods such as ASIF and scenarios that involve effects of proximity-based communication.

References

1. Aiello, A., Berryman, J., Grohs, J., Schierman, J.: Run-time assurance for advanced flight-critical control systems. In: Proceedings of AIAA Guidance, Navigation, and Control Conference, AIAA 2010–8041, Toronto, Ontario Canada, Aug., 2010 (2010)
2. Ames, A.D., Coogan, S., Egerstedt, M., Notomista, G., Sreenath, K., Tabuada, P.: Control barrier functions: theory and applications. In: 2019 18th European control conference (ECC), pp. 3420–3431. IEEE (2019)
3. Bak, S., Manamcheri, K., Mitra, S., Caccamo, M.: Sandboxing controllers for cyber-physical systems. In: 2011 IEEE/ACM Second International Conference on Cyber-Physical Systems, pp. 3–12. IEEE (2011)
4. Cofer, D., et al.: Flight test of a collision avoidance neural network with run-time assurance. In: Digital Avionics Systems Conference (2022)
5. Desai, A., Ghosh, S., Seshia, S.A., Shankar, N., Tiwari, A.: Soter: a run-time assurance framework for programming safe robotics systems. In: 2019 49th Annual IEEE/IFIP International Conference on Dependable Systems and Networks (DSN), pp. 138–150. IEEE (2019)
6. Dosovitskiy, A., Ros, G., Codevilla, F., Lopez, A., Koltun, V.: Carla: an open urban driving simulator. In: Conference on robot learning, pp. 1–16. PMLR (2017)
7. Dunlap, K.: Run Time Assurance for Intelligent Aerospace Control Systems. Ph.D. thesis, University of Cincinnati (2022)
8. Dunlap, K., Hibbard, M., Mote, M., Hobbs, K.: Comparing run time assurance approaches for safe spacecraft docking. IEEE Control Syst. Lett. **6**, 1849–1854 (2021)

9. Dunlap, K., Mote, M., Delsing, K., Hobbs, K.L.: Run time assured reinforcement learning for safe satellite docking. J. Aerosp. Inf. Syst. **20**(1), 25–36 (2023)
10. Fan, C., Miller, K., Mitra, S.: Fast and guaranteed safe controller synthesis for nonlinear vehicle models. In: Lahiri, S.K., Wang, C. (eds.) CAV 2020. LNCS, vol. 12224, pp. 629–652. Springer, Cham (2020). https://doi.org/10.1007/978-3-030-53288-8_31
11. Fremont, D.J., Dreossi, T., Ghosh, S., Yue, X., Sangiovanni-Vincentelli, A.L., Seshia, S.A.: Scenic: a language for scenario specification and scene generation. In: Proceedings of the 40th ACM SIGPLAN Conference on Programming Language Design and Implementation, pp. 63–78 (2019)
12. Hibbard, M., Topcu, U., Hobbs, K.: Guaranteeing safety via active-set invariance filters for multi-agent space systems with coupled dynamics. In: 2022 American Control Conference (ACC), pp. 430–436. IEEE (2022)
13. Mehmood, U., Sheikhi, S., Bak, S., Smolka, S.A., Stoller, S.D.: The black-box simplex architecture for runtime assurance of autonomous cps. In: Deshmukh, J.V., Havelund, K., Perez, I. (eds.) NFM 2022. LNCS, vol. 13260, pp. 231–250. Springer, Cham (2022). https://doi.org/10.1007/978-3-031-06773-0_12
14. Mote, M.L., Hays, C.W., Collins, A., Feron, E., Hobbs, K.L.: Natural motion-based trajectories for automatic spacecraft collision avoidance during proximity operations. In: 2021 IEEE Aerospace Conference (50100), pp. 1–12. IEEE (2021)
15. Schierman, J., Ward, D., Dutoi, B., et al.: Run-time verification and validation for safety-critical flight control systems. In: AIAA Paper 2008–6338, Proceedings of the AIAA Guidance, Navigation, and Control Conference, Honolulu, Hawaii, Aug., 2008 (2008)
16. Seto, D., Krogh, B., Sha, L., Chutinan, A.: The simplex architecture for safe online control system upgrades. In: American Control Conference (ACC) (1998)
17. Sha, L., et al.: Using simplicity to control complexity. IEEE Softw. **18**(4), 20–28 (2001)
18. Shah, S., Dey, D., Lovett, C., Kapoor, A.: AirSim: high-fidelity visual and physical simulation for autonomous vehicles. In: Hutter, M., Siegwart, R. (eds.) Field and Service Robotics. SPAR, vol. 5, pp. 621–635. Springer, Cham (2018). https://doi.org/10.1007/978-3-319-67361-5_40
19. Wadley, J., et al.: Development of an automatic aircraft collision avoidance system for fighter aircraft. In: AIAA Infotech@ Aerospace (I@ A) Conference, p. 4727 (2013)

Checking and Sketching Causes on Temporal Sequences

Raven Beutner(✉), Bernd Finkbeiner, Hadar Frenkel, and Julian Siber

CISPA Helmholtz Center for Information Security, Saarbrücken, Germany
{raven.beutner,finkbeiner,hadar.frenkel,julian.siber}@cispa.de

Abstract. Temporal causality describes what concrete input behavior is responsible for some observed output behavior on a trace of a reactive system, and can be used to, e.g., generate explanations for counterexamples uncovered by a model checker. In this paper, we present CATS, the first tool that can automatically verify whether a given temporal property (specified in QPTL) is a cause for some observed ω-regular effect. In addition to *checking* whether a given property is a cause, CATS can *search* for potential causes by exhaustively exploring a cause sketch, i.e., a temporal formula in which some parts are left unspecified. Our experiments show that CATS can effectively check causes and search for causes in small reactive systems.

1 Introduction

Causality analysis plays an increasingly important role in computer science and has practical applications such as explaining the behavior of systems [3,5,15,17], establishing accountability in multi-agent systems [19], and as a reasoning tool for verification [35,36] and synthesis [2]. These approaches rely on the philosophical foundations of Lewis and Hume [33,39] that suggest *counterfactual reasoning* as a method of establishing a causal relationship between events. Following this reasoning, a property (or, in previous works, an event) is only a cause if, in case the cause does not occur, the effect is absent as well. Halpern and Pearl [29,30] formalized these notions into a rigorous system of structural equations over *finite* sets of events (variables). However, when naïvely applying it to reactive systems, i.e., systems that continuously interact with their environment, Halpern and Pearl's original definition fails as the behavior is characterized by *infinitely* many variables. Recently, Coenen et al. [18] lifted the ideas of Halpern and Pearl to the temporal domain and presented a framework in which (symbolic) temporal properties, expressed in temporal logic such as LTL or QPTL, constitute causes and effects.

Example 1. Consider the system of Fig. 1 over inputs i_1, i_2 and output $\lightning$, which marks a failure. When checking whether the system satisfies $\Box\neg\lightning$, a model checker might return $\pi = \{i_1, i_2\}\{i_1, i_2\}\{i_1\}(\{i_1, \lightning\})^\omega$ as a concrete counterexample. We are interested in explaining the effect $\varphi_E = \Diamond\lightning$ on the given (actual)

É. André and J. Sun (Eds.): ATVA 2023, LNCS 14216, pp. 314–327, 2023.
https://doi.org/10.1007/978-3-031-45332-8_18

error trace. Using the theory presented in [18] we can formally show that $\varphi_C = i_1 \wedge \bigcirc\bigcirc\big((\neg i_2)\,\mathcal{U}(i_1 \wedge \neg i_2)\big)$ constitutes an actual cause for φ_E. Such a cause provides important information for debugging: It pinpoints that, in the first position, only i_1 is relevant; it does not refer to the second position on the trace as those inputs are irrelevant; and it precisely captures the information that, in order to reach the error state, i_1 must occur *strictly before* i_2. △

Coenen et al. [18] showed that checking if an ω-regular property constitutes an actual cause on a lasso-shaped trace is decidable. However, as their theory was not implemented, reasoning about causal relationships required manual computation. Given the intricate nature of causality (which encompasses complex features such as contingencies and interventions [18,29,30]), this manual reasoning is both time-consuming and error-prone.

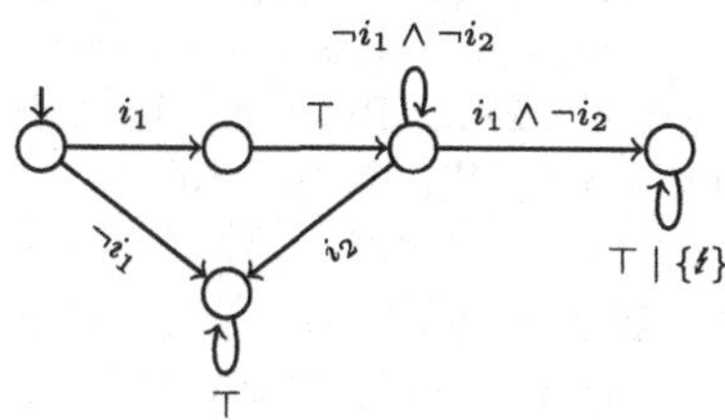

Fig. 1. An example system. Each edge has the form $\phi \mid o$ where ϕ is a Boolean formula over the inputs and $o \in 2^{\{\lightning\}}$ is a set of outputs. We write ϕ instead of $\phi \mid \emptyset$.

CATS. In this paper, we present CATS [11], short for *Causal Analysis on Temporal Sequences*, a fully-automatic implementation of the theory of [18]. CATS can check if a given temporal property (specified in QPTL [42]) qualifies as a cause on an actual lasso trace. Internally, our tool relies on encoding the cause-checking problem into the model-checking problem for *hyperproperties* [16,21], i.e., properties that relate multiple traces in a system.

Our tool serves two purposes: First and foremost, CATS allows for the automatic checking of symbolic causes (temporal formulas). This is a useful feature in many settings, perhaps most prominently in counterexample debugging, where we are interested in getting succinct yet informative summaries of what temporal input behavior triggered the violation of a property.

Secondly, CATS serves as a playground to experiment with temporal cause definitions. Causality definitions are inherently linked to human intuition, and coming up with a useful one is difficult (as, e.g., witnessed by the multiple updates of Halpern and Pearl's definitions [28–30]). A fully-automatic tool for cause checking allows us to experiment with more evolved causality definitions and see (within a few seconds; and with no manual computation) how small changes in the definition transfer to actual examples. This is particularly important in a temporal setting, where many parameters need to be fixed (e.g., what constitutes a "closer" trace as defined by Lewis [18,22,39]).

Cause Sketching. The main purpose of CATS is to check if a given temporal property qualifies as a cause. However, often it is also useful to *infer* a cause automatically. While general synthesis of temporal causes is not possible yet (cause synthesis corresponds to the search for an appropriate *set of traces*, a problem that is notoriously difficult [10]), we propose a very useful approximation in the form of cause sketching. Inspired by program sketching [43] and query checking [12], CATS supports cause *sketches* – temporal properties in which some propositional holes are left unspecified. CATS then attempts to find an appropriate instantiation for all holes to generate an actual cause. On the theoretical side, we show that for time-bounded effects (i.e., properties whose satisfaction or violation can be determined by only looking at the first n steps), any potential cause only needs to refer to the first n steps. On the practical side, this implies that for time-bounded effects (which naturally occur in counterexample analysis where an error occurs after a fixed number of steps), there exists a cause sketch that encompasses all potential causes.

Related Work. We base our causality analysis on the theoretical foundations for temporal causality by Coenen et al. [18] (recapped in Sect. 3). For a comprehensive survey on applications of causality in formal methods and for providing explanations, see [3]. Leue et al. [13,37] propose a symbolic description of counterfactual causes in *Event Order Logic* (implemented into the tool SpinCause [38]), which can reason about the *ordering* of LTL-definable events. In particular, the logic cannot reason about the *absolute* timing as is, e.g., needed to specify that the input at the second position is part of the cause (cf. Example 1). Gössler and Métayer [23] define causality for component-based systems, and Gössler and Stefani [24] study theoretical foundations of causality based on counterfactual builders. Both works differ from our approach as we consider *actual* causality on the property level.[1]

Many existing works focus on explaining *finite* counterexamples [4,25,26,44]. Beer et al. [5] present a tool for causal analysis of finite traces with respect to LTL specifications by highlighting events that led to the violation. HyperVis [31] provides visualization of counterexamples for hyperproperties through highlighting. Coenen et al. [17] infer a cause for a hyperproperty violation, defined as a finite set of events (i.e., time points) on the trace. In contrast to all of the above, CATS provides *symbolic* causes (defined in QPTL) that can refer to infinitely many time points and – given their logical nature – are easier to understand. At the same time, the underlying theory provides strong guarantees for time-bounded effects as, e.g., encountered in error analysis (cf. Proposition 1).

Structure. In the next section, we provide preliminaries and recap the theory presented in [18]. Section 4 gives an overview of CATS. In Sect. 5, we evaluate the cause-checking ability of CATS on both hand-crafted examples and systems drawn from the SYNTCOMP competition [34]. In Sect. 6, we study CATS's cause-sketching functionality.

[1] The term "actual causality" was coined by Halpern and Pearl [29] and describes causes in a concrete (actual) instance (e.g., a trace) of a system. In contrast, *global* causality describes all of the system behavior that can cause an effect.

2 Preliminaries

Systems and Traces. We model a reactive system as a finite state transition system $\mathcal{T}$ over a set of atomic propositions $\text{AP} = I \uplus O$, which is partitioned into inputs I and outputs O. A system then generates a set of traces $\mathit{Traces}(\mathcal{T}) \subseteq (2^{\text{AP}})^\omega$. For more details, see [18, § 5.1].

QPTL and HyperQPTL. HyperQPTL [9,41] extends linear-time temporal logic (LTL) [40] by adding quantification over atomic propositions, as well as explicit quantification over traces in a system. Given a set of trace variables $\mathcal{V}$, HyperQPTL formulas are defined by the following grammar

$$\varphi ::= \forall \pi.\, \varphi \mid \exists \pi.\, \varphi \mid \forall q.\, \varphi \mid \exists q.\, \varphi \mid \psi$$
$$\psi ::= a_\pi \mid q \mid \neg\psi \mid \psi \wedge \psi \mid \bigcirc \psi \mid \psi\, \mathcal{U}\, \psi$$

where $\pi \in \mathcal{V}$ is a trace variable, $a \in \text{AP}$ is an atomic proposition, and $q \notin \text{AP}$ is a fresh quantified proposition. We also consider the usual derived Boolean constants $(\top, \bot)$, Boolean connectives $(\vee, \rightarrow, \leftrightarrow, \not\leftrightarrow)$, and temporal operators *eventually* $(\Diamond \psi := \top\, \mathcal{U}\, \psi)$ and *globally* $(\square \psi := \neg(\Diamond \neg\psi))$.

In a HyperQPTL formula, atomic propositions are indexed by trace variables. For example, $\psi := \square(a_\pi \leftrightarrow b_\sigma)$ states that, on the trace that is bound to trace variable π, a holds iff b holds on the trace bound to trace variable σ. This allows us to compare multiple traces within a temporal formula which we use, e.g., to define a distance metric on traces. The trace variables in the formula are (existentially or universally) quantified at the top level. For example $\forall\pi.\exists\sigma.\, \psi$ states that for every trace π in the system, there exists a trace σ such that ψ holds on those two traces. In addition to trace quantification, HyperQPTL features propositional quantification (as found in QPTL [42]). This allows us to capture all ω-regular causes and effects, even those that are not LTL-definable. For more details on HyperQPTL and the full semantics, see [9] or [41].

3 Temporal Causality

Our tool is based on the theory of temporal causality as defined by Coenen et al. [18], extending Halpern and Pearl's foundational definition of actual causality to the setting of temporal causes and effects in reactive systems. In this section, we recall the key aspects from [18].

Interventions. Interventions define the counterfactual scenarios where the cause does not appear. Counterfactuals are the *closest* worlds in which the cause does not appear [39].

Example 2. Consider, for example, the LTL property $\varphi = \square a$ and the actual trace $\pi = \{a\}^\omega$. To have a meaningful definition of counterfactuals, that is, closest worlds in which the cause φ does not appear, it is not enough to negate the formula φ, as this would result in a set of traces that are not necessarily close enough to the original trace π. $\triangle$

Instead, Coenen et al. [18] adopt the idea of distance metrics known from Lewis [39]. Given a trace π, a *distance metric* $<_\pi$ is a *strict* partial order such that $\sigma <_\pi \sigma'$ if trace σ is closer to π than trace σ'. The *intervention set* $V(\varphi, <_\pi)$ then consists of the *closest* traces σ that do not satisfy φ:

$$V(\varphi, <_\pi) = \{\sigma \in \mathit{Traces}(\mathcal{T}) \mid \sigma \models \neg\varphi \wedge \neg\exists \sigma' \in \mathit{Traces}(\mathcal{T}).\, \sigma' \models \neg\varphi \wedge \sigma' <_\pi \sigma\}.$$

Distance Metrics in HyperQPTL. To handle distance metrics algorithmically, we consider them as being defined by a HyperQPTL formula. For example

$$\sigma <_\pi^{min} \sigma' \iff \square\Big(\bigwedge_{i \in I}(i_\pi \not\leftrightarrow i_\sigma) \rightarrow (i_\pi \not\leftrightarrow i_{\sigma'})\Big) \wedge \diamond \bigvee_{i \in I}(i_\sigma \not\leftrightarrow i_{\sigma'}) \qquad (1)$$

specifies that σ is closer to π than σ' iff whenever σ and π differ on some input, so should σ' and π, *and* σ' and σ differ at least in one position.

Example 3. In Example 2, $\{\}(\{a\})^\omega$ is closer (w.r.t. $<_\pi^{min}$) to π than $\{\}\{\}(\{a\})^\omega$. The intervention set $V(\varphi, <_\pi^{min})$ thus contains all traces in which a does not appear at *exactly* one position, i.e., traces of the form $(\{a\})^*\{\}(\{a\})^\omega$. △

Causality on Temporal Sequences. We are now ready to recall Coenen et al.'s [18] definition of temporal causality. Following Halpern and Pearl, Coenen et al. [18] use *contingencies* to deal with cases of preemption, i.e., scenarios where a possible cause gets nullified by another earlier cause for the same effect. Formally, they define the *counterfactual automaton* $\mathcal{C}_\pi^{\mathcal{T}}$ to account for the contingencies of a lasso trace π. See [18, § 5.2] for details.

Definition 1 ([18]). *Let $\mathcal{T}$ be a system over $AP = I \uplus O$, $\pi \in \mathit{Traces}(\mathcal{T})$ a trace, $<_\pi$ a distance metric, and φ_C, φ_E two QPTL formulas over I and O, respectively. We say that φ_C is a* cause *of φ_E on π in $\mathcal{T}$ if the following three conditions hold:*

PC1: $\pi \models \varphi_C$ *and* $\pi \models \varphi_E$.
PC2: *For every counterfactual input sequence $\sigma \in V(\varphi_C, <_\pi)$, there is some trace $\pi' \in \mathcal{C}_\pi^{\mathcal{T}}$ s.t. $\pi' \models \neg\varphi_E$ and $\bigwedge_{i \in I} \square(i_\pi \leftrightarrow i_{\pi'})$.*
PC3: *There is no φ'_C s.t. $\varphi'_C \rightarrow \varphi_C$ is valid and φ'_C satisfies PC1 and PC2.*

The *counterfactual* condition (PC2) requires that for every closest input sequences in which the cause does *not* hold, we can use contingencies to avoid the effect. PC1 requires that cause and effect are satisfied by the *actual* trace at hand, and PC3 poses that the cause is *semantically minimal.*

Infinite Chains and Vacuity Condition. The above $<_\pi^{min}$ metric may admit infinite chains of ever smaller interventions, resulting in an empty intervention set $V(\varphi, <_\pi)$, which renders PC2 vacuously valid.

Example 4 ([18]). Let us consider the cause candidate $\varphi := \square\diamond a$ and the trace $\pi = \{a\}^\omega$. Under the distance metric $<_\pi^{min}$ (1), there exists no closest traces that negate φ. For example, $\{\}^\omega >_\pi^{min} \{a\}(\{\})^\omega >_\pi^{min} \{a\}\{a\}(\{\})^\omega >_\pi^{min} \cdots$ forms an infinite chain with no minimal element. Formula φ thus qualifies as a cause for all effects that hold on π. △

To catch such situations, we add an additional *vacuity condition*, which, e.g., ensures that $\Box\Diamond a$ (cf. Example 4) never constitutes a non-vacuous cause.

Definition 2 (Vacuity Condition). *Under the conditions of Definition 1, φ_C is a* non-vacuous *cause, if, in addition to PC1-PC3, the following holds:*

PC4: *The intervention set $V_\pi(\varphi_C, <_\pi)$ is non-empty.*

Some distance metrics are strong enough to always satisfy PC4. For example, Coenen et al. [18] propose an extension of $<_\pi^{min}$ which only orders traces that have the same *rejection structure*, that is, traces that falsify the cause formula at the same positions of the trace (see [18]). An alternative extension of $<_\pi^{min}$ we have discovered when experimenting with CATS is the following:

$$\sigma <_\pi^{full} \sigma' \iff (\sigma <_\pi^{min} \sigma') \wedge \bigwedge_{i \in I} \left(\Box\Diamond(i_\pi \not\leftrightarrow i_\sigma)\right) \rightarrow \left(\Box(i_\sigma \leftrightarrow i_{\sigma'})\right)$$

The metric $<_\pi^{full}$ only orders traces that have the same infinite interventions (with respect to individual atomic propositions).

Example 5. Recall Example 4. The traces $\sigma = \{\}^\omega$ and $\sigma' = \{a\}(\{\})^\omega$ are not ordered by $<_\pi^{full}$, as σ already intervenes on infinitely many positions against a in $\pi = \{a\}^\omega$ and σ' does not equal σ when both are projected to a. The infinite chain w.r.t. $<_\pi^{min}$ from Example 4 thus does not exist; all elements in the chain are minimal w.r.t. $<_\pi^{full}$. △

The modular design of CATS encourages experiments with *different* distance metrics. By default, CATS uses $<_\pi^{min}$ (1) ([18]) together with the vacuity condition PC4, as our experiments show that this performs best in practice.

4 CATS: Tool Overview

In this section, we discuss the input of CATS (Sect. 4.1) and provide a basic overview of the internal working (Sect. 4.2). All experiments in this paper were conducted on a Macbook Pro with an M1 Pro CPU and 32 GB of memory.

4.1 Input Specification

CATS supports arbitrary ω-regular properties specified in QPTL [42], an extension of LTL with explicit quantification over propositions. A *cause-checking* instance specifies the following: **(1)** The system – given as an arbitrary automaton in the HANOI-automaton format [1]; **(2)** a partition of the atomic propositions into inputs and outputs; **(3)** the cause and effect as QPTL formulas; and **(4)** a lasso-shaped trace. When given a cause-*checking* instance, CATS determines if the given cause candidate qualifies as an actual cause.

CATS can also be used in cause-*sketching* mode. In this mode, the cause is a QPTL formula that includes holes, and CATS tries to find a formula within this sketch (i.e., a formula where all holes in the sketch are instantiated with propositional – non-temporal – formulas) that qualifies as a cause. In sketching mode, CATS either provides an actual cause or determines that no formula within the given sketch qualifies as a cause. See [12] for details on sketching in the context of *query checking*.

4.2 Algorithmic Core

Internally, CATS relies on a HyperQPTL-based encoding of the cause-checking problem. As observed in [18], the causality requirements PC1-PC3 can be expressed as a HyperQPTL model-checking problem. CATS decomposes this model checking problem as much as possible into 5 separate checks instead of one large one as used in [18]. Having multiple (but smaller) checks is crucial for the performance of CATS on larger cause formulas. By leveraging the HyperQPTL-encoding, CATS can discharge most of the heavy computation as HyperQPTL model-checking problems. For this, CATS relies on the automata-based model checker AutoHyper [8,9]; alternative hyperproperty verification approaches [6,7,32] can be substituted easily.

Handling Contingencies. If desired by the user, CATS adds the ability to reason about contingencies – a central feature of Halpern and Pearl's actual causality. For details on this so-called *contingency automaton*, see [18, Def. 8].[2]

Trace Checking for Cause Sketching. When invoked in sketching mode, most cause candidates within a sketch do not hold on the given trace and thus violate PC1. CATS can filter out these instances very effectively by employing an inexpensive trace-check of the candidate on the given lasso, which prunes the search space significantly. While there are exponentially many candidates within each cause sketch, in practice, only a few satisfy PC1 and thus progress to the algorithmically harder stages that require (proper) hyperproperty model checking.

5 Evaluation 1 - Cause Checking

To evaluate the cause-checking with CATS, we use both hand-crafted examples (Sect. 5.1) and instances from the annual SYNTCOMP competition (Sect. 5.2).

5.1 Hand-Crafted Examples

We collected a range of hand-crafted instances (consisting of system, lasso, cause, and effect). These systems are typically very small (so performance is not an issue) and serve as a test of the underlying causality definition. We depict the results in Table 1.

[2] Coenen et al. [18] use the assumption that every state of the transition system is labeled by a unique set of outputs. In practice, this assumption is unrealistic, so, in many cases, the contingency automaton leads to unintuitive results and prevents the discovery of causes. In CATS, we thus decided to allow the user to decide whether or not to use contingencies.

Table 1. Hand-crafted cause-checking instances. We display whether or not the cause candidate is a cause (✓ if it is a cause and ✗ if it is not) and the time taken by CATS in seconds. EXAMPLE 1, MOD changes the actual trace to $\pi = \{i_1, i_2\}\{i_1, i_2\}\{i_1\}(\{\not i\})^\omega$ such that φ_C is no longer a cause.

Instance	Res	t	Instance	Res	t
SPURIOUS ARBITER [18]	✗	0.6	EXAMPLE 6, GLOBALLY	✗	0.7
ARBITER SIMPLE [18]	✓	1.2	EXAMPLE 7	✓	2.1
ARBITER [18]	✓	9.7	EXAMPLE 8	✓	1.1
EXAMPLE 1	✓	0.9	EXAMPLE 8 mod	✗	1.2
EXAMPLE 1, MOD	✗	1.0	TP LEFT [18, Thm. 6]	✗	0.3
EXAMPLE 6, ODD	✓	1.4	TP RIGHT [18, Thm. 6]	✓	1.1

Example 6. Consider the system in Fig. 3a, which models a simple arbiter for two processes; each can issue a request ($I = \{r_0, r_1\}$) and might be answered by a grant ($O = \{g_0, g_1\}$). Importantly, the arbiter is biased towards process 0, i.e., prioritizes process 0 if both issue a request. Suppose we observe the trace $(\{r_0, r_1\}\{r_0, g_0\})^\omega$ and are interested in a cause for $\varphi_E = \Box\neg g_1$, i.e., process 1 never gets a grant. CATS can automatically verify the cause $\varphi_C = \exists q.q \wedge \Box(q \leftrightarrow \bigcirc\neg q) \wedge \Box(q \rightarrow r_0)$ (instance EXAMPLE 6, ODD), stating that the cause is that process 0 issues requests at all *odd* positions. In particular, CATS can also infer that $\Box r_0$ is *not* a cause (instance EXAMPLE 6, GLOBALLY); the requests at even positions are irrelevant for the effect. Such a precise cause cannot be expressed in LTL and requires the ω-regularity possible in QPTL. We stress that such an *automatic* analysis was not possible before, and each instance required manual (error-prone) checking. △

5.2 Syntcomp Evaluation

In the previous section, we considered hand-crafted examples that stress the underlying theory. In this section, we test the performance of CATS on a larger set of benchmarks. To obtain an interesting set of reactive systems, we use benchmarks from the reactive synthesis competition (SYNTCOMP) [34]. SYNTCOMP includes a collection of LTL formulas that specify requirements for a diverse collection of reactive systems. We use existing LTL synthesis tools (in our case `ltlsynt` [20]) to synthesize a strategy/system for each (realizable) LTL specification (within a timeout of 5 min). We obtain a collection of 204 systems of varying sizes. For each SYNTCOMP system, we randomly generate 10 different lasso traces and use `spot`'s `randltl` to generate random cause and effect formulas (over the inputs and outputs, respectively). This gives us a total of $204 * 10 = 2040$ cause-checking instances. In Fig. 2, we depict the running time of CATS against the size of the underlying system. We observe that the vast majority of instances can be solved in less than 10 s. We can also see how the running time of each

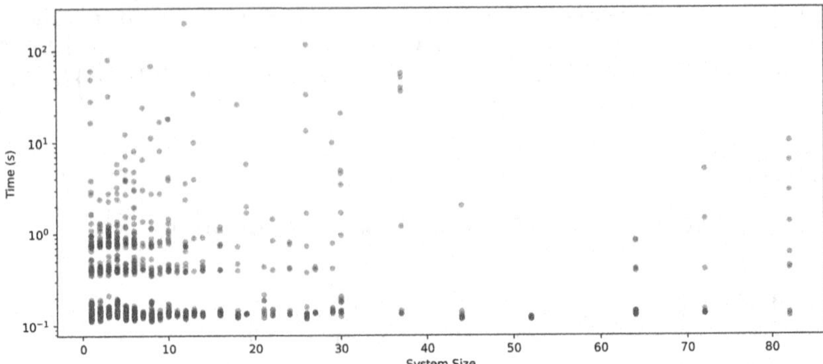

Fig. 2. We use CATS to check different cause-effect pairs in systems obtained from SYNTCOMP [34] benchmarks. Note that the time scale is logarithmic.

instance depends on the number of checks that are needed; due to the incremental checking by CATS (based on the decomposition of the cause-checking formula), instances that, e.g., already violate PC2 are not checked further. The overall running time thus depends on the number of stages that are passed.

6 Evaluation 2 - Cause Sketching

As already alluded to in the introduction, a typical use case of causal analysis is the analysis of a counterexample. The user can use such a cause to, e.g., extract a minimal error from the concrete error trace and effectively debug the system.

Example 7. Consider the simple system in Fig. 3b in which output $\lightning$ marks an error. A model checker might return the concrete path $\pi = \{i_1, i_2\}^4(\{\lightning\})^\omega$. While the concrete path reaches the error state, it provides very little information about which inputs actually caused the error. Instead, we can use CATS to find a cause for the effect $\varphi_E = \bigcirc\bigcirc\bigcirc\bigcirc\lightning$. When given to CATS with an appropriate sketch, it will compute the cause $\varphi_C = i_1 \wedge \bigcirc\bigcirc(i_1 \vee i_2)$, which characterizes exactly the events on π that are of relevance: i_1 must hold in the first step, and either i_1 or i_2 must hold in the third (to avoid the self-loop). Note that this cause is tightly coupled with the concrete trace π. In particular, the cause does not describe *all* input events that lead to the error state, but only the minimal changes needed to *avoid* the error on the concrete example. The time for *checking* this causal relationship is depicted in Table 1 (instance EXAMPLE 7). △

Example 8. As a second example, consider the system in Fig. 3c and the concrete path $\pi = \{i\}^2(\{\lightning\})^\omega$. CATS can automatically verify the cause $\varphi_C = i \vee \bigcirc i$ for the effect $\varphi_E = \bigcirc\bigcirc\lightning$. Note that this cause is disjunctive as we need to intervene on i in the first *and* second step to avoid the effect. Symbolic causes (as supported by CATS) can describe such effects very succinctly. In contrast, previous methods cannot handle such examples: they are either limited to a finite-variable setting

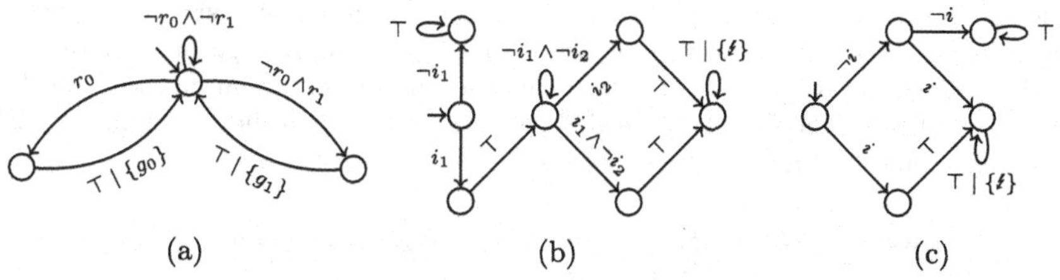

Fig. 3. Three example systems. Each edge has the form $\phi \mid o$ where ϕ is a boolean formula over I and $o \subseteq O$ a set of outputs. We write ϕ instead of $\phi \mid \emptyset$.

and *conjunctive* causes [29,30] or can only reason about the order of events but *not* about the concrete time using $\bigcirc$'s [37,38]. The time for *checking* this causal relationship is given in Table 1 (instance EXAMPLE 8). Table 1 also depicts a modified version using trace $\pi = \{i\}\{\}(\{\lightning\})^\omega$ (instance EXAMPLE 8,MOD). This results in $\varphi_C = i \vee \bigcirc i$ no longer being a cause. △

6.1 Causes for Time-Bounded Effects

When employing causality-based analysis on counterexamples, we often encounter effects of the form $\bigcirc^n \lightning$ for some $n \in \mathbb{N}$. We refer to such effects as *time-bounded effects.* We can formally prove that – within the causality framework of Coenen et al. [18] – an effect that is time-bounded by $n \in \mathbb{N}$ has a cause iff it has a time-bounded cause, i.e., a cause that only refers to the first n steps.

Proposition 1. *Let $\varphi_E = \bigcirc^n \psi$ be an effect, where ψ does not contain temporal operators, and let π be a trace. Then, there exists a cause for φ_E on π iff there exists a cause that uses at most n nested $\bigcirc$'s, and no other temporal operators.*

When looking for causes of the form $\bigcirc^n \lightning$ for some n, it thus suffices to check for causes that refer to the first n positions. It is easy to see that there exists a cause sketch that captures all such candidates (a simple DNF with atoms of the form $\bigcirc^j \psi$ with $j \leq n$).

6.2 Automatically Sketching Causes

To evaluate CATS's cause-sketching ability, we use spot's randaut [20] to generate 100 random systems of varying size (between 10 and 50 states) and randomly mark one state with a fresh $\lightning$ proposition. Using a model checker (in our case, a simple breath-first-search), we verify whether the error state is reachable, and if it is, compute a concrete (lasso) trace reaching the error in say n steps. We then use CATS to infer a cause for $\varphi_E = \bigcirc^n \lightning$, which, by Proposition 1, can be done by exploring an appropriate sketch.

Our results are displayed in Table 2. We find that although CATS explores many candidates, most of them can be pruned early using the inexpensive trace

Table 2. Evaluation of CATS's sketching for counterexample analysis. We depict the average length of the counterexample trace (avg. $|\pi|$), the average number of cause candidates checked (avg. $\#_{check}$), the average time (in seconds) spent on cause *checking* (avg. t_{check}), the average total time needed by CATS (avg. t), and the percentage of cases in which we could find a cause (avg. success).

avg. $\|\pi\|$	avg. $\#_{check}$	avg. t_{check}	avg. t	avg. success
6.28	169.1	2.08 s	2.19 s	86%

check for PC1 (cf. Section 4.2). The actual time t_{check} for checking (which takes up the vast majority of CATS's total computation time) is thus reasonable, as only a few of the (on average) 169.1 candidates progress to the expensive hyperproperty model-checking phase.

Limitations. We emphasize that CATS can, obviously, not compete with dedicated methods for counterexample analysis [5,14,27]. The big advantage of CATS stems from its reliance on an advanced theory that is *not limited* to counterexample analysis but applicable to arbitrary causal relationships. Despite the strong theoretical foundations (dating back to Halpern and Pearl's seminal definition [29,30]), CATS provides strong guarantees on the existence of causes (Proposition 1) and performs well in small systems.

7 Conclusion

Causal analysis has a long tradition in the analysis of systems. While most efforts on comprehensive causal definitions (mainly originating in philosophy) focused on finite settings, recent work discussed causality in reactive systems, where cause and effect reason about the infinite behavior of a system [18]. In this paper, we have presented CATS, the first tool that pushes causality in reactive systems towards automation. With CATS, causality definitions are no longer condemned to be purely theoretical endeavors but can be applied and tested fully automatically in actual systems. This allows for discovery and verification of causal relationships and serves as a playground to experiment with more advanced causality definitions.

With CATS, we have shown that verifying causes based on an advanced causality theory is possible in practice and that sketching is a viable method to infer causes. For future work, it is interesting to attempt to synthesize a (ω-regular) cause directly. In such developments, CATS can serve as a useful baseline and debugger.

Acknowledgments. This work was supported by the European Research Council (ERC) Grant HYPER (No. 101055412) and by DFG grant 389792660 as part of TRR 248 - CPEC.

References

1. Babiak, T., et al.: The Hanoi omega-automata format. In: Kroening, D., Păsăreanu, C.S. (eds.) CAV 2015. LNCS, vol. 9206, pp. 479–486. Springer, Cham (2015). https://doi.org/10.1007/978-3-319-21690-4_31
2. Baier, C., Coenen, N., Finkbeiner, B., Funke, F., Jantsch, S., Siber, J.: Causality-based game solving. In: Silva, A., Leino, K.R.M. (eds.) CAV 2021. LNCS, vol. 12759, pp. 894–917. Springer, Cham (2021). https://doi.org/10.1007/978-3-030-81685-8_42
3. Baier, C., et al.: From verification to causality-based explications. In: International Colloquium on Automata, Languages, and Programming, ICALP 2021. LIPIcs, vol. 198. Dagstuhl (2021). https://doi.org/10.4230/LIPIcs.ICALP.2021.1
4. Ball, T., Naik, M., Rajamani, S.K.: From symptom to cause: localizing errors in counterexample traces. In: Symposium on Principles of Programming Languages, POPL 2003. ACM (2003). https://doi.org/10.1145/604131.604140
5. Beer, I., Ben-David, S., Chockler, H., Orni, A., Trefler, R.J.: Explaining counterexamples using causality. Formal Meth. Syst. Des. **40**(1), 20–40 (2012). https://doi.org/10.1007/s10703-011-0132-2
6. Beutner, R., Finkbeiner, B.: Prophecy variables for hyperproperty verification. In: Computer Security Foundations Symposium, CSF 2022. pp. 471–485. IEEE (2022). https://doi.org/10.1109/CSF54842.2022.9919658
7. Beutner, R., Finkbeiner, B.: Software verification of hyperproperties beyond k-safety. In: Shoham, S., Vizel, Y. (eds.) CAV 2022. LNCS, vol. 13371, pp. 341–362. Springer, Cham (2022). https://doi.org/10.1007/978-3-031-13185-1_17
8. Beutner, R., Finkbeiner, B.: AutoHyper: explicit-state model checking for HyperLTL. In: Sankaranarayanan, S., Sharygina, N. (eds.) TACAS 2023. LNCS, vol. 13993, pp. 145–163. Springer, Cham (2023). https://doi.org/10.1007/978-3-031-30823-9_8
9. Beutner, R., Finkbeiner, B.: Model checking omega-regular hyperproperties with AutoHyperQ. In: International Conference on Logic for Programming, Artificial Intelligence and Reasoning, LPAR 2023. EPiC Series in Computing, vol. 94, pp. 23–35. EasyChair (2023). https://doi.org/10.29007/1xjt
10. Beutner, R., Finkbeiner, B., Frenkel, H., Metzger, N.: Second-order hyperproperties. In: Enea, C., Lal, A. (eds.) CAV 2023. LNCS, vol. 13965, pp. 309–332. Springer, Cham (2023). https://doi.org/10.1007/978-3-031-37703-7_15
11. Beutner, R., Siber, J.: CATS - causal analysis on temporal sequences. Zenodo (2023). https://doi.org/10.5281/zenodo.8192053
12. Bruns, G., Godefroid, P.: Temporal logic query checking. In: IEEE Symposium on Logic in Computer Science, LICS 2001. IEEE (2001). https://doi.org/10.1109/LICS.2001.932516
13. Caltais, G., Guetlein, S.L., Leue, S.: Causality for general LTL-definable properties. In: Workshop on Formal Reasoning About Causation, Responsibility, and Explanations in Science and Technology, CREST 2018. EPTCS, vol. 286 (2018). https://doi.org/10.4204/EPTCS.286.1
14. Chaki, S., Groce, A., Strichman, O.: Explaining abstract counterexamples. In: International Symposium on Foundations of Software Engineering, FSE 2004. ACM (2004). https://doi.org/10.1145/1029894.1029908
15. Chockler, H., Halpern, J.Y., Kupferman, O.: What causes a system to satisfy a specification? ACM Trans. Comput. Log. **9**(3), 1–26 (2008). https://doi.org/10.1145/1352582.1352588

16. Clarkson, M.R., Schneider, F.B.: Hyperproperties. J. Comput. Secur. **18**(6), 1157–1210 (2010). https://doi.org/10.3233/JCS-2009-0393
17. Coenen, N., et al.: Explaining hyperproperty violations. In: Shoham, S., Vizel, Y. (eds.) CAV 2022. LNCS, vol. 13371, pp. 407–429. Springer, Cham (2022). https://doi.org/10.1007/978-3-031-13185-1_20
18. Coenen, N., Finkbeiner, B., Frenkel, H., Hahn, C., Metzger, N., Siber, J.: Temporal causality in reactive systems. In: Bouajjani, A., Holík, L., Wu, Z. (eds.) ATVA 2022. Lecture Notes in Computer Science, vol. 13505, pp. 208–224. Springer, Cham (2022). https://doi.org/10.1007/978-3-031-19992-9_13
19. Datta, A., Garg, D., Kaynar, D.K., Sharma, D., Sinha, A.: Program actions as actual causes: A building block for accountability. In: Computer Security Foundations Symposium, CSF 2015. IEEE (2015). https://doi.org/10.1109/CSF.2015.25
20. Duret-Lutz, A., et al.: From spot 20 to spot 210: what's new? In: Shoham, S., Vizel, Y. (eds.) CAV 2022. LNCS, vol. 13372, pp. 174–187. Springer, Cham (2022). https://doi.org/10.1007/978-3-031-13188-2_9
21. Finkbeiner, B.: Logics and algorithms for hyperproperties. ACM SIGLOG News **10**(2), 4–23 (2023). https://doi.org/10.1145/3610392.3610394
22. Finkbeiner, B., Siber, J.: Counterfactuals modulo temporal logics. In: International Conference on Logic for Programming, Artificial Intelligence and Reasoning, LPAR 2023. EPiC Series in Computing, vol. 94, pp. 181–204. EasyChair (2023). https://doi.org/10.29007/qtw7
23. Gössler, G., Le Métayer, D.: A general trace-based framework of logical causality. In: Fiadeiro, J.L., Liu, Z., Xue, J. (eds.) FACS 2013. LNCS, vol. 8348, pp. 157–173. Springer, Cham (2014). https://doi.org/10.1007/978-3-319-07602-7_11
24. Gössler, G., Stefani, J.: Causality analysis and fault ascription in component-based systems. Theor. Comput. Sci. **837**, 158–180 (2020). https://doi.org/10.1016/j.tcs.2020.06.010
25. Groce, A., Chaki, S., Kroening, D., Strichman, O.: Error explanation with distance metrics. Int. J. Softw. Tools Technol. Transf. **8**(3), 229–247 (2006). https://doi.org/10.1007/s10009-005-0202-0
26. Groce, A., Kroening, D., Lerda, F.: Understanding Counterexamples with Explain. In: Alur, R., Peled, D.A. (eds.) CAV 2004. LNCS, vol. 3114, pp. 453–456. Springer, Heidelberg (2004). https://doi.org/10.1007/978-3-540-27813-9_35
27. Groce, A., Visser, W.: What went wrong: explaining counterexamples. In: Ball, T., Rajamani, S.K. (eds.) SPIN 2003. LNCS, vol. 2648, pp. 121–136. Springer, Heidelberg (2003). https://doi.org/10.1007/3-540-44829-2_8
28. Halpern, J.Y.: A modification of the Halpern-pearl definition of causality. In: International Joint Conference on Artificial Intelligence, IJCAI 2015. AAAI Press (2015)
29. Halpern, J.Y., Pearl, J.: Causes and explanations: a structural-model approach. Part I: causes. Brit. J. Philos. Sci. **56**(4) (2005)
30. Halpern, J.Y., Pearl, J.: Causes and explanations: a structural-model approach. Part II: explanations. Brit. J. Philos. Sci. **56**(4) (2005)
31. Horak, T., et al.: Visual analysis of hyperproperties for understanding model checking results. IEEE Trans. Vis. Comput. Graph. **28**(1), 357–367 (2022). https://doi.org/10.1109/TVCG.2021.3114866
32. Hsu, T.-H., Sánchez, C., Bonakdarpour, B.: Bounded model checking for hyperproperties. In: TACAS 2021. LNCS, vol. 12651, pp. 94–112. Springer, Cham (2021). https://doi.org/10.1007/978-3-030-72016-2_6
33. Hume, D.: An Enquiry Concerning Human Understanding. London (1748)

34. Jacobs, S., et al.: The reactive synthesis competition (SYNTCOMP): 2018–2021. CoRR abs/2206.00251 (2022). https://doi.org/10.48550/arXiv.2206.00251
35. Kupriyanov, A., Finkbeiner, B.: Causality-based verification of multi-threaded programs. In: D'Argenio, P.R., Melgratti, H. (eds.) CONCUR 2013. LNCS, vol. 8052, pp. 257–272. Springer, Heidelberg (2013). https://doi.org/10.1007/978-3-642-40184-8_19
36. Kupriyanov, A., Finkbeiner, B.: Causal termination of multi-threaded programs. In: Biere, A., Bloem, R. (eds.) CAV 2014. LNCS, vol. 8559, pp. 814–830. Springer, Cham (2014). https://doi.org/10.1007/978-3-319-08867-9_54
37. Leitner-Fischer, F., Leue, S.: Causality checking for complex system models. In: Giacobazzi, R., Berdine, J., Mastroeni, I. (eds.) VMCAI 2013. LNCS, vol. 7737, pp. 248–267. Springer, Heidelberg (2013). https://doi.org/10.1007/978-3-642-35873-9_16
38. Leitner-Fischer, F., Leue, S.: SpinCause: a tool for causality checking. In: International Symposium on Model Checking of Software, SPIN 2014. ACM (2014). https://doi.org/10.1145/2632362.2632371
39. Lewis, D.K.: Counterfactuals. Blackwell, Cambridge (1973)
40. Pnueli, A.: The temporal logic of programs. In: Annual Symposium on Foundations of Computer Science, FOCS 1977. IEEE (1977). https://doi.org/10.1109/SFCS.1977.32
41. Rabe, M.N.: A temporal logic approach to information-flow control. Ph.D. thesis, Saarland University (2016)
42. Sistla, A.P.: Theoretical issues in the design and verification of distributed systems. Ph.D. thesis, Harvard University (1983)
43. Solar-Lezama, A.: Program sketching. Int. J. Softw. Tools Technol. Transf. **15**(5–6), 475–495 (2013). https://doi.org/10.1007/s10009-012-0249-7
44. Wang, C., Yang, Z., Ivančić, F., Gupta, A.: Whodunit? Causal analysis for counterexamples. In: Graf, S., Zhang, W. (eds.) ATVA 2006. LNCS, vol. 4218, pp. 82–95. Springer, Heidelberg (2006). https://doi.org/10.1007/11901914_9

Author Index

É. André and J. Sun (Eds.): ATVA 2023, LNCS 14216, pp. 329–330, 2023.
https://doi.org/10.1007/978-3-031-45332-8

Printed in the United States
by Baker & Taylor Publisher Services